Legal Reasoning Across Commercial Disputes

Legal Reasoning Across Commercial Disputes

Comparing Judicial and Arbitral Analyses

SI STRONG
DPhil (Oxon), PhD (Cantab)
JD (Duke), MPW (Southern California), BA (California, Davis)
Attorney (New York, Illinois), Solicitor (England and Wales), Solicitor (Ireland)
Associate Professor, University of Sydney Law School

OXFORD
UNIVERSITY PRESS

OXFORD
UNIVERSITY PRESS

Great Clarendon Street, Oxford, OX2 6DP,
United Kingdom

Oxford University Press is a department of the University of Oxford.
It furthers the University's objective of excellence in research, scholarship,
and education by publishing worldwide. Oxford is a registered trade mark of
Oxford University Press in the UK and in certain other countries

First Edition published in 2020

Published in the United States of America by Oxford University Press
198 Madison Avenue, New York, NY 10016, United States of America

British Library Cataloguing in Publication Data
Data available

Library of Congress Control Number: 2020942775

ISBN 978–0–19–884284–2

Dedicated to the judges and arbitrators around the world who work to establish, maintain, and protect the rule of law

Foreword

Reliable, neutral, and effective dispute resolution in a globalized economy in an era of rising nationalism is more important than ever.

Adjudication is fundamental to dispute settlement. Whether the forum is court litigation or arbitration, these venues offer a space for neutral decision making, using the rule of law to apply the applicable law to the facts of specific disputes. Without such an adjudicative backstop, it is impossible for parties to exercise the autonomy and judgment necessary to 'bargain in the shadow of the law' or explore the net utility of other dispute resolution mechanisms. Put differently, adjudication provides a core baseline for binding decision making, is preferable to the exercise of power politics, and promotes effective dispute resolution choices.

Having an empirical appreciation of how various adjudicative forums may resolve disputes is critical, particularly as stakeholders—including parties, counsel, and arbitrators—may have different experiential baselines. Understanding the contexts underpinning legal reasoning therefore aids the management of expectations about both likely results and the predictability of ultimate outcomes. These factors make Professor Strong's book, which explores that legal reasoning, a vital academic contribution with real practical value.

This book's methodological approach is particularly inventive. Rather than relying on urban legends or crowdsourcing from social media, Professor Strong offers a vigorous mixed-methods technique that permits her to explore legal reasoning through three different lenses, each of which aids the assessment of the relative value and quality of dispute settlement.

One of the most critical distinctions that Professor Strong explores is the domestic and international divide. As I wrote in the *Oxford Research Encyclopedia of Economics and Finance*, particularly in the context of arbitration, the distinction between national and international norms is vital. Arbitration can be applied in many contexts, yet the policy and legal considerations applicable in domestic arbitration (in one of the over 190 different countries on the planet) reflect unique local politics and can be radically different than the concerns dominant in international arbitration. This book's recognition of the national–international divide and its evidence-based exploration offer a valuable lens for understanding adjudication options.

Particularly in a globalized world, understanding variation as a result of historical legal family also aids assessments of the relative value and likely outcomes in adjudication. Much like Erin Meyer's classic book, *The Culture Map: Breaking Through the Invisible Boundaries of Global Business*, Professor Strong's analysis aids our understanding of adjudicative variation and distinctions amongst different historical legal traditions, with a focus on common and civil law. Better yet, she does this by focusing upon data.

Ultimately, this book is a fundamental contribution to the field both of legal reasoning and dispute settlement, as it allows us to reality test our perceptions and gain a more nuanced understanding about what we can and should expect from adjudication performed by human beings in the modern era.

Professor Susan D Franck
American University, Washington College of Law
Charlottesville, Virginia, USA
July 2020

Acknowledgements

Although only one individual is named on the title page of this book, the text is actually the culmination of many years of work by many people. The design and analysis of the project was greatly assisted by the insights of colleagues from around the world, including Lisa Bernstein, Bob Bone, Petra Butler, Gilles Cuniberti, Maksymilian del Mar, Rafael Gely, Brook Gotberg, Mark Kantor, John Lande, Ethan Lieb, Margaret Moses, Chad Oldfather, Rodrigo Polanco, Dennis Solomon, Edna Sussman, Shauhin Talesh, and Catharine Titi. I also must acknowledge the invaluable contributions of research assistants Niyati Ahuja, Ibrahim Amir, Jarred Boyer, Brian Chihera, Sisonke Dyonta, Elizabeth Kaganda, Shajiah Jaffri, Elywill Paja, David Robinson, Jane Rose, Samantha Sweet, Shefali Tanna, and Jennifer Ware, without whom the coding exercise could not have been completed. I am also deeply appreciative of Resa Kerns, whose technical expertise greatly facilitated creation of the electronic survey. I thank all of these individuals for their help in making this project a reality. I really could not have done it without you.

I also owe a debt of gratitude to the judges, arbitrators, and judge–arbitrators who agreed to be interviewed for this book, including Rebecca A Bowman, PE, Independent Arbitrator; The Honourable Stephen R Bough, Judge, United States District Court for the Western District of Missouri; The Honourable Charles N Brower, Judge, Iran-United States Claims Tribunal, Judge *ad hoc*, International Court of Justice, Formerly Judge *ad hoc*, Inter-American Court of Human Rights, 20 Essex Street Chambers; Bernard Hanotiau, Independent Arbitrator; Jean Kalicki, Independent Arbitrator; Mark Kantor, Independent Arbitrator; Prof Gabrielle Kaufmann-Kohler, Lévy Kaufmann-Kohler; Joseph M Matthews, Independent Arbitrator; The Honourable Connie L Peterson, Independent Arbitrator; Prof WW Park, Boston University; John R Phillips, Independent Arbitrator; Francis Raucci, Independent Arbitrator; Lucy Reed, Independent Arbitrator; The Honourable Shira A Scheindlin, Stroock & Stroock & Lavan LLP and Independent Arbitrator and Mediator; John A Sherrill, American Arbitration Association; Nicolas C Ulmer, Budin Associés; Prof dr Hans van Houtte, Independent Arbitrator, former President, Iran-United States Claims Tribunal; Eduardo Zuleta, Independent Arbitrator; Michael Hwang, Independent Arbitrator; and an additional individual who asked to remain anonymous.

I also wish to thank the University of Missouri School of Law, where the underlying research was conducted during my tenure as the Manley O Hudson Professor of Law, and the University of Sydney Law School, where I completed the writing-up and production phase of the project, for their forbearance while I focused on this book. I also wish to acknowledge both the University of Missouri Law School Foundation and the American Arbitration Association-International Centre for Dispute Resolution

(AAA-ICDR) Foundation for financial assistance associated with researching and writing this book. Although the AAA-ICDR Foundation (a 501(c)(3) not-for-profit organization that is separate from both the AAA and the ICDR) provided funding for certain aspects of this research, neither the AAA-ICDR Foundation nor the AAA/ICDR was in any way involved in the design, content, or analysis of the study.

Finally, I would like to acknowledge the tradition of custodianship and law of the Country on which the University of Sydney campuses stand and to pay my respects to those who have cared and continue to care for Country, including Elders past, present, and emerging.

SI Strong
April 2020
Sydney, Australia

Contents

1
Introduction

I. Introduction

Legal reasoning is central to the resolution of legal disputes, and, as such, has been subjected to a wide range of scholarly studies. Theorists have debated the essential nature and purpose of legal reasoning,[1] while behavioural scientists have considered how informational deficiencies and unconscious biases affect rational decision-making.[2] Other strands of commentary focus on the practical nature of legal reasoning to promote best practices in the field.[3]

[1] E.g. Jan H Dalhuisen, *Dalhuisen on Transnational Comparative, Commercial, Financial and Trade Law* (Hart Publishing 2019) pt. IV (discussing legal reasoning of international arbitrators); James Gordley, 'Legal Reasoning: An Introduction', (1984) 72 Cal L Rev 138 (discussing historical, philosophical, and judicial perspectives on legal reasoning); HLA Hart, 'Discretion', (2013) 127 Harv L Rev 652 (consisting of a newly discovered article by HLA Hart on legal reasoning); William NR Lucy, 'Criticizing and Constructing Accounts of Legal Reasoning', (1994) 14 OJLS 303; Richard A Posner, 'Judicial Behavior and Performance: An Economic Analysis', (2005) 32 Florida St U L Rev 1259 (proposing an economic analysis of the performance of both judges and arbitrators). Scholarship on legal reasoning is often related to but not always synonymous with scholarship on legal theory. E.g. Fernando Atria, 'Legal Reasoning and Legal Theory Revisited', (1999) 18 L & Phil 537; Ronald Dworkin, *Law's Empire* (Harvard University Press 1986); John Gardner, *Law as a Leap of Faith: Essays on Law in General* (Oxford University Press 2012); HLA Hart, *The Concept of Law* (Oxford University Press 1961) 112; Neil MacCormick, *Legal Reasoning and Legal Theory* (Clarendon Press 1994); Joseph Raz, *Ethics in the Public Domain* (rev edn, Clarendon Press 1999) 326–40 (distinguishing between reasoning *about* the law and reasoning *according* to the law); Fábio P Shecaira, 'Gardner on Legal Reasoning', (2014) 33 L & Phil 747. Legal philosophers often rely on principles of rhetoric for their analyses. E.g. Leonard G Boonin, 'The Logic of Legal Decisions', (1965) 75 Ethics 179; Neil MacCormick, *Rhetoric and the Rule of Law: A Theory of Legal Reasoning* (Oxford University Press 2009).

[2] Robert Counson, 'The Decisionmaking Process in Arbitration', (1990) 45 Arb J 37; Richard A Posner, *Economic Analysis of Law* (4th edn, Aspen 1992) 429–38; Susan D Franck and others, 'Inside the Arbitrator's Mind', (2017) 66 Emory LJ 1115, 1135 (Franck and others, Arbitrator's Mind); Christopher R Drahozal, 'Empirical Findings on International Arbitration: An Overview', in Thomas Schultz and Federico Ortino (eds), *Oxford Handbook on International Arbitration* (Oxford University Press forthcoming 2020) (Drahozal, Overview); Chris Guthrie, Jeffrey J Rachlinski, and Andrew J Wistrich, 'Blinking on the Bench: How Judges Decide Cases', (2007) 93 Cornell L Rev 1; Chris Guthrie, Jeffrey J Rachlinski, and Andrew J Wistrich, 'Judging by Heuristic Cognitive Illusions in Judicial Decision Making', (2002) 86 Judicature 44; Edward L Rubin, 'Rational Choice and Rat Choice: Some Thoughts on the Relationship Among Rationality, Market, and Human Beings', (2005) 80 Chi-Kent L Rev 1091, 1094; Edna Sussman, 'Biases and Heuristics in Arbitrator Decision-Making: Reflections on How to Counteract or Play to Them', in Tony Cole (ed), *The Roles of Psychology in International Arbitration* (Wolters Kluwer 2017) 45; Robert B Wilson, 'Strategic and Informational Barriers to Negotiation', in Kenneth J Arrow and others (eds), *Barriers to Conflict Resolution* (WW Norton and Co 1995) 108, 108–19 (discussing economic and game theory).

[3] Charles L Barzun, 'The Forgotten Foundations of Hart and Sacks', (2013) 99 Va L Rev 1, 6 (noting US jurisprudence has characterized legal reasoning as both theoretical and practical); Leonard G Boonin, 'The Theoretical and Practical Approaches to Legal Reasoning', (1963) 49 Archiv für Rechts- und Sozialphilosophie 433, 433 (Boonin, Theoretical and Practical); see also *Judicial Writing Manual: A Pocket Guide for Judges* (2d edn, Federal Judicial Center 2013) <https://www.fjc.gov/publications> accessed 11 April 2020; International Bar Association, Toolkit for Award Writing (September 2016), <https://www.ibanet.org> accessed 11 April 2020; ICC Award Checklist 1998, 2012, and 2017 Rules, International Chamber of Commerce, <https://iccwbo.org/publication/icc-award-checklist-1998-2012-icc-arbitration-rules/> accessed 11 April 2020.

As useful as these works may be, some gaps remain. In particular, it appears that many of the fundamental principles on which scholarship regarding legal reasoning is based have not been empirically tested.[4]

While studies in this field can be challenging,[5] this book undertakes the first-ever multi-faceted empirical study on legal reasoning in commercial disputes. The project not only provides novel insights into general practices, it also analyses potential differences along the judicial-arbitral divide, the domestic-international divide, and the common law-civil law divide.

The study is also distinct in that it focuses on first-instance rather than appellate decision makers.[6] This particular methodology was adopted in order to delve more deeply into the important but often overlooked role that factual determinations play in legal reasoning[7] and to create more suitable comparisons across the judicial-arbitral divide.[8] In so doing, the discussion not only provides scholars with a new understanding of the reasoning process but also provides practitioners and policy makers with rigorous, fact-based analyses that can improve how justice is delivered on a systemic and individual level.[9]

[4] Jack Knight, 'Are Empiricists Asking the Right Questions About Judicial Decisionmaking?', (2009) 58 Duke LJ 1531, 1545 (noting gap between theoretical and empirical research on legal reasoning and the lack of integration between the two approaches).

[5] Ibid; Lucy (n 1) 310–11.

[6] Much of the existing empirical research on legal reasoning focuses primarily on theoretical concerns raised by the Legal Realism movement, even though most legal realists were concerned with appellate rather than first-instance litigation. Brian Leitner, 'Legal Realism', in Dennis Patterson (ed), *A Companion to Philosophy of Law and Legal Theory* (Wiley-Blackwell 1999) 261, 267; Karl Lewellyn, 'Some Realism About Realism', (1931) 44 Harv L Rev 1222; William Twining, *Karl Llewellyn and the Legal Realist Movement* (2d edn, Cambridge University Press 2014).

[7] Richard Michael Fischl, 'It's Conflict All the Way Down', (2001) 22 Cardozo L Rev 773, 786 (suggesting rule application is understudied); Michael S Pardo, 'Juridical Proof, Evidence, and Pragmatic Meaning: Toward Evidentiary Holism', (2000) 95 Northwest. U L Rev 399, 401 (noting that the role of facts and evidence in legal determination is 'undertheorized'). In the United States, this lacuna may arise because fact-finding is generally associated with juries rather than judges, although that hypothesis does not explain why analysis of the role that facts play in legal reasoning is largely unstudied in other jurisdictions. Michael J Saks, 'What Do Jury Experiments Tell Us About How Juries (Should) Make Decisions?', (1997) 6 So Cal Interdisciplinary LJ 1, 42. In the United Kingdom and Commonwealth, this gap may be due to the contention 'that decisions on questions of law are generally required to be supported by public justifications, whereas there is no such general requirement for determinations of fact'. William Twining and David Miers, *How to Do Things with Rules* (5th edn, Cambridge University Press 2010) 126; Robin Creyke and others, *Laying Down the Law* (10th edn, LexisNexis Butterworths 2018) 249. In any case, the scholarly emphasis on the finding of facts, as opposed to the use of facts in the determination of the legal dispute, creates a false dichotomy between law and facts in judicial and arbitral reasoning. Boonin, Theoretical and Practical (n 3) 436–37.

[8] As a theoretical matter, authorities are unclear as to whether arbitration constitutes a substitute for, an alternative to, or a supplement to litigation. Larry E Edmonson, *Domke on Commercial Arbitration* s 1:1, at 1–3 (3d edn, Thomson Reuters 2010) (noting arbitration coexists with litigation as 'part of the American system of administering justice'); Pierre Mayer, 'Comparative Analysis of Power of Arbitrators to Determine Procedures in Civil and Common Law Systems', (1996) 7 ICCA Congress Series 24, 25 (noting arbitration is sometimes considered 'a substitute for State justice, albeit of a private nature, but nevertheless pursuing the same ends'); Jeffrey W Stempel, 'Keeping Arbitrations from Becoming Kangaroo Courts', (2007) 8 Nevada LJ 251, 260 (noting 'arbitration is a substitute for adjudication by litigation'). Some variation may also exist according to the type of arbitration in question. Edmonson (n 8) s 1:3, at 1–8 to 1–9 (noting that early precedent distinguished between commercial arbitration as a substitute for litigation and labour arbitration as a substitute for avoiding industrial strife, but suggesting that these distinctions may no longer apply). In any event, regardless of how arbitration is characterized, arbitral awards are more properly considered the functional equivalents of decisions from first-instance courts than of appellate opinions, since appellate judges focus primarily on questions of law rather than questions of law and fact.

[9] Michael Heise, 'The Past, Present and Future of Empirical Legal Scholarship: Judicial Decision Making and the New Empiricism', 2002 U Ill L Rev 819, 839 (noting a call for 'a revival of interest in the actual judgment process' as opposed to behavioural and attitudinal models of judicial decision making).

Because decision makers may approach legal reasoning differently depending on the subject matter at issue, this project focused exclusively on commercial disputes, defined throughout the study as business-to-business or commercial state entity-to-business disputes. To avoid confusion, research subjects were explicitly advised that the definition of commercial disputes did not include investor-state arbitration, since that procedure is considered quasi-public in nature.[10] This is not to say that some of the information gleaned from this study may not be applicable to investment arbitration or indeed to other fields of law, but more research would be needed before any firm conclusions could be drawn.[11]

Empirical studies are only as good as the research questions they seek to answer,[12] and this project focuses on three interrelated issues. The first involves the longstanding assumption that legal reasoning in judicial settings is not only different than that used in arbitral settings but is somehow superior to arbitral reasoning.[13] However, some forms of arbitration are extremely sophisticated, suggesting that conventional wisdom about the 'second-class' nature of arbitral justice may be the result of error or unconscious cognitive distortions.[14] For example, one non-governmental organization that recently filed an *amicus curiae* brief in the United States Supreme Court case of *GE Energy Power Conversion France SAS Corp v Outokumpo Stainless USA LLC* claimed that it was acting to 'defend[] access to justice for workers, consumers, and others harmed by corporate wrongdoing' pursuant to its mission to 'fight[] abuse of mandatory arbitration', even though the dispute did not involve these categories of individuals but instead reflected a relatively standard dispute between international commercial actors.[15]

Although a handful of empiricists have conducted independent analyses of judicial or arbitral decision making, relatively few scholars have sought to compare legal reasoning across the judicial-arbitral divide, and those studies that do exist are not in the

[10] Public and private law disputes have traditionally been said to generate very different concerns with respect to legal reasoning, although there are those who dispute the continued relevance of this distinction. Guillermo Alvarez and W Michael Reisman, *The Reasons Requirement in International Investment Arbitration* (Brill 2008); Lukas van den Berge, 'Rethinking the Public-Private Divide in the Age of Governmentality and Network Governance', (2018) 5 Eur J Comp L & Gov 119. The public nature of court proceedings has often been lauded as one of the reasons why litigation is superior to arbitration. Hazel Genn, 'Why the Privatisation of Civil Justice is a Rule of Law Issue, 36th FA Mann Lecture, Lincoln's Inn (19 November 2012) 17–18; Judith Resnik, 'Diffusing Disputes: The Public in the Private of Arbitration, the Private in Courts, and the Erasure of Rights', (2015) 124 Yale LJ 2804, 2806–07; William Twining, 'Alternative to What? Theories of Litigation, Procedure and Dispute Settlement in Anglo-American Jurisprudence: Some Neglected Classics', (1993) 56 MLR 380, 383 (discussing the views of Jeremy Bentham).

[11] Those who are interested in pursuing similar lines of inquiry might want to consider adopting the methodology used herein so as to allow cross-study comparisons. Chs. 2.II, 3.II, 4.II; Appx. I, II, III.

[12] Anselm Strauss and Juliet Corbin, *Basics of Qualitative Research: Techniques and Procedures for Developing Grounded Theory* (Sage Publishing 1998) 41 (discussing the need for precisely formulated research questions).

[13] Ch 1.III.A.

[14] Gary B Born, *International Commercial Arbitration* (Wolters Kluwer 2014) 2129–30; SI Strong, 'Truth in a Post-Truth Society: How Sticky Defaults, Status Quo Bias and the Sovereign Prerogative Influence the Perceived Legitimacy of International Arbitration', 2018 U Ill L Rev 533, 535, 549 (Strong, Status Quo Bias).

[15] Brief of *Amicus Curiae* Public Justice in Support of Neither Party, *GE Energy Power Conversion France SAS Corp v Outokumpo Stainless USA LLC* at 1, Docket No 18-1048 (United States Supreme Court 24 September 2019) <https://www.supremecourt.gov/DocketPDF/18/18-1048/116894/20190924171950842_18-1048%20Amicus%20Brief.pdf> accessed 11 April 2020.

commercial realm.[16] Therefore, the first research question, presented as a null hypothesis to be disproven, is that no differences exist between legal reasoning in commercial litigation and legal reasoning in commercial arbitration.[17]

As important and innovative as that issue is, the study does not stop there. The second line of inquiry focuses on actual or purported differences across the domestic-international divide.[18]

Recent research in the area of international commercial arbitration suggests that the procedure is becoming increasingly legalistic, which affects the way in which arbitral awards are reasoned and written.[19] Questions therefore arise as to whether domestic forms of commercial arbitration can or should be distinguished from international commercial arbitration.

Similar inquiries arise in judicial settings, although the analysis is slightly different. At this point, there is no truly international court, similar to the International Court of Justice, that addresses cross-border commercial disputes.[20] While several countries have developed so-called international commercial courts within their own national legal systems, it is too early to analyse decisions arising out of those tribunals.[21] Instead, international commercial litigation is best understood in its traditional sense as involving cross-border disputes seated in national courts that are not entirely dedicated to international commercial matters.

As a result, the second research question in this study, presented as a null hypothesis to be disproven, is that no difference exists between legal reasoning in domestic and international commercial matters, including disputes that arise in both litigation and arbitration. For purposes of this research, an international dispute is defined as a matter where at least two parties came from different countries; where the property at issue was located in a country different than that of the disputants; or

[16] E.g. Pat K Chew, 'Arbitral and Judicial Proceedings: Indistinguishable Justice or Justice Denied?' (2011) 46 Wake Forest L Rev 185 (considering civil rights disputes); David Horton, 'Clause Construction: A Glimpse Into Judicial and Arbitral Decision-Making', (2019) 68 Duke LJ 1323 (comparing class actions and class arbitrations). Some theorists have discussed the relative merits of judicial and arbitral decision making, although theoretical studies are not the same as empirical studies. Chris Guthrie, 'Misjudging', (2007) 7 Nevada LJ 420, 452–55.

[17] Robert W Frick, 'The Appropriate Use of Null Hypothesis Testing', (1996) 1 Psych Methods 379–90 (discussing the appropriate use and function of null hypothesis testing); Mike Townsend and Thomas Richardson, 'Probability and Statistics in the Legal Curriculum: A Case Study in Disciplinary Aspects of Interdisciplinarity', (2002) 40 Duquesne L Rev 447, 460.

[18] Ch. 1.III.B.

[19] SI Strong, 'Increasing Legalism in International Commercial Arbitration: A New Theory of Causes, A New Approach to Cures', (2013) 7 World Arb & Med Rev 117, 117 (noting increasing legalism (also referred to as increasing formalism) is considered a negative by many in the arbitral community); SI Strong, 'Reasoned Awards in International Commercial Arbitration: Embracing and Exceeding the Common Law-Civil Law Dichotomy', (2015) 37 Mich J Intl L 1, 40 (Strong, Reasoned Awards).

[20] Calls have been made for the development of an international court of civil justice that would have jurisdiction over certain commercial matters. Maya Steinitz, *The Case for an International Court of Civil Justice* (Cambridge University Press 2018).

[21] These courts can vary significantly in how they are structured. Xandra E Kramer and John Sorabji (eds), *International Business Courts: A European and Global Perspective* (Eleven International Publishing 2019).

where performance or enforcement was anticipated in a country different than that of the disputants.[22]

The third and final issue considered in this book involves longstanding assumptions about the nature of legal reasoning in the common law and civil law legal traditions.[23] The conventional view is that the common law relies primarily on case law and uses an inductive approach to legal reasoning while the civil law emphasizes the primacy of statutory law and adopts a deductive approach to legal reasoning.[24] However, recent scholarship has begun to challenge this dichotomy, suggesting that the two legal traditions are becoming more similar.[25] Therefore, the third research question, presented as a null hypothesis to be disproven, is that no difference exists between legal reasoning in common law and civil law legal systems, at least in the commercial context.[26]

The three research questions are analysed through a multi-faceted empirical study that triangulates individual results across different research components so as to confirm the validity of the results.[27] Detailed discussions of the individual methodologies are provided elsewhere,[28] but it is useful to describe how the various pieces fit together within the overall research strategy.

The first element of the study, which is discussed in Chapter 2, involved a large-scale international survey addressed exclusively to judges and arbitrators with experience in commercial dispute resolution. The survey generated responses from 465 individuals from 41 different countries and included 73 different questions regarding the use of legal authorities, the use of factual authorities (evidence), the reasoning process, the drafting process, and judicial and arbitration education regarding these concerns. The survey was designed not only to test the validity of longstanding theoretical assumptions about

[22] While the definition of an international commercial arbitration is relatively clear, the same level of detail does not exist with respect to international commercial litigation. United Nations Commission on International Trade Law (UNCITRAL), UNCITRAL Model Law on International Commercial Arbitration, art 1, 18th Session, Annex 1, UN Document A/40/17 (21 June 1985), revised by UNCITRAL, Revised Articles of the UNCITRAL Model Law on International Commercial Arbitration, 39th Session, Annex, UN Document A/61/17 (7 July 2006); American Law Institute, *Restatement (Third) US Law of International Commercial and Investor-State Arbitration*, Proposed Final Draft s 1.1 (24 April 2019); Born (n 14) 70; Emmanuel Gaillard and John Savage (eds), *Fouchard Gaillard Goldman on International Commercial Arbitration* (Wolters Kluwer 1999) 12. The definition used herein is based on criteria found in the US Federal Arbitration Act. 9 USC s 202.

[23] Ch 1.III.C.

[24] H Patrick Glenn, *Legal Traditions of the World: Sustainable Diversity in Law* (5th edn, Oxford University Press 2014) chs. 5, 7; Roscoe Pound, 'What Is the Common Law' in *The Future of the Common Law* (Harvard University Press 1937) 3, 18; SI Strong, Katia Fach Gómez, and Laura Carballo Piñeiro, *Comparative Law for Spanish-English Speaking Lawyers: Legal Cultures, Legal Terms and Legal Practices / Derecho comparado para abogados anglo- e hispanoparlantes: Culturas jurídicas, términos jurídicos y prácticas jurídicas* (Edward Elgar Publishing 2016) ch. 3.III.A-B; K Zweigert and H Kötz, *An Introduction to Comparative Law* (Tony Weir tr, 3rd edn, Oxford University Press 1998) chs. 7, 14, 18.

[25] Ch 1.III.C.

[26] The study also included data from jurisdictions outside the common law and civil law legal traditions, although those jurisdictions were not subjected to individual analysis.

[27] Rob Timans, Paul Wouters, and Johan Heilbron, 'Mixed Methods Research: What It Is and What It Could Be', (2019) 48 Theory & Soc'y 193–216 (discussing methods and benefits of triangulation and mixed methods research in social sciences).

[28] Chs. 1.II (concerning overarching methodological concerns), 2.II (concerning survey), 3.II (concerning semi-structured interviews), 4.II (concerning coding of decisions and awards).

legal reasoning across the judicial-arbitral, domestic-international, and common law-civil law divides but also to generate new insights into the reasoning process in those contexts. Survey responses were subjected to statistical analysis to determine whether any relevant differences arose across the three axes of comparison.

The second element of the study, which is discussed in Chapter 3, involved a series of hour-long, semi-structured interviews of 20 judges and arbitrators from around the world. The interview protocol consisted of 27 different questions (not including sub-parts) covering the same issues addressed by the survey (i.e. the use of legal authorities, the use of factual authorities (evidence), the reasoning process, the drafting process, and judicial and arbitration education regarding these concerns). Interviewees were chosen to represent a wide variety of demographic attributes, including those that are central to the current study (e.g. those relating to potential differences across the judicial-arbitral, domestic-international, and common law-civil law divides) as well as those that reflect best practices in representative sampling (i.e. age, gender, seniority, etc.).[29]

The interview protocol was purposely designed to use questions that were the same or similar to those used in the survey so as to allow comparisons between interview and survey responses and overcome limitations inherent in each of the different methodologies.[30] For example, the survey was able to collect data from a larger and more diverse group of individuals than was possible with the interviews, although the interviews allowed participants to go into more depth in their responses and answer questions in their own words. This latter feature was particularly useful in minimizing any unconscious biases that might have been incorporated into the design of the survey and interview instruments.

The third and final element of the study, which is discussed in Chapter 4, involved a quantitative analysis of original judicial decisions and arbitral awards. These materials were coded across 76 different data points and subjected to several statistical analyses. The coding exercise not only compiled demographic information about the parties and neutrals hearing the dispute, it also generated information about the types of disputes heard in different fora and the nature of legal and factual reasoning used in the various matters. While it was impossible to duplicate all of the questions reflected in the survey and interviews in the coding exercise, the coding analysis nevertheless tested the validity of some of the results generated by the other two studies as well as certain theoretical assumptions regarding legal reasoning across the judicial-arbitral, domestic-international and common law-civil law divides.

Although it would have been interesting to link coded material to individual survey respondents or interviewees, that approach was considered undesirable, both because it might have reduced the candour of survey or interview responses and because it

[29] Lee Epstein and Gary King, 'The Rules of Inference', (2002) 69 U Chi L Rev 1, 113 (2002) (Epstein and King, Rules) (discussing how to generate representative samples in small-n studies).

[30] Saks (n 7) 5 (noting every empirical technique has its own distinct advantages and disadvantages).

would have severely limited the scope of the study.[31] The project therefore focused on a wider range of decisions and awards.[32]

The coding analysis experienced a number of unanticipated difficulties associated with obtaining commercial decisions and awards suitable for the current study,[33] but the exercise nevertheless considered 28 decisions from first-instance courts in Quebec, Canada;[34] 92 decisions from the English Commercial Court; 7 trial-level decisions from US state and federal courts; 22 reasoned awards rendered in domestic commercial arbitrations seated in the United States; 32 reasoned arbitration awards rendered in international commercial arbitrations seated in 8 different countries; 12 unreasoned (standard) awards rendered in domestic commercial arbitrations seated in the United States; and 4 unreasoned (standard) awards rendered in international commercial arbitrations seated in the United States.

Together, the three strands of inquiry, combined with the three methodological approaches, create an extremely wide-ranging research project. Various cross-references between the different segments of the study are found in the substantive chapters (i.e. Chapters 2, 3, and 4, discussing the survey, the interviews, and the coding exercise, respectively). However, a number of overarching considerations can be found in Chapter 5, which also pulls together the various strands of research and offers a number of proposals on how to move forward in this area of law.

As broad as this study may be, some limitations do apply. Most notably, this study does not seek to determine whether litigation or arbitration is somehow better than the other, either in domestic or international disputes or in common law or civil law traditions. Instead, the discussion simply seeks to identify primarily whether and to what extent any differences in legal reasoning arise across the three comparative axes and, secondarily, whether and to what extent actual practice reflects theoretical models and assumptions involving legal reasoning.

In order to achieve that second goal, it is necessary to appreciate current theoretical views on legal reasoning across the judicial-arbitral, domestic-international and common law-civil law divides. Although considerations of space make it impossible to engage fully with the debates reflected in each of these areas of study, this chapter provides an overview of the basic principles as well as extensive references to resource material to assist individuals who are interested in learning more about the various concerns.[35]

[31] The survey was intentionally made anonymous to increase the candour of the responses.

[32] Ch. 4.II.A (discussing how decisions and awards were selected).

[33] Ch. 4.II.A.

[34] Quebec is often characterized as a civil law system with respect to private law concerns despite being considered a mixed legal system as a general matter. William Tetley, 'Mixed Jurisdictions: Common Law v Civil Law (Codified and Uncodified)', (2000) 60 Louisiana L Rev 677, 684, 695 (discussing how principles of English and commercial law were combined with principles of French law in the Civil Code of Lower Canada of 1866, which was in place when Quebec became part of the Dominion of Canada). However, some scholars question whether legal reasoning in Quebec is as civil law-oriented in practice as it is said to be as a formal matter. Catherine Valcke, 'Quebec Civil Law and Canadian Federalism', (1996) 21 Yale J Intl L 67, 114

[35] Ch. 1.III.

Before undertaking that discussion, it is necessary to consider whether and to what extent the overarching methodology adopted in this book conforms to best practices in social science research. The following section therefore describes empirical issues taken into consideration during the design of this project. Specific matters relating to individual empirical elements are considered in the relevant chapter.[36]

II. Best Practices in Empirical Legal Studies

The standard means of evaluating the validity of social science research is by considering the propriety of the study's methodology.[37] This is particularly true when the project seeks to break new empirical ground, since the findings have not yet been replicated by other scholars.[38]

The first step in designing a new empirical study involves determining whether and to what extent the research questions are amenable to empirical analysis.[39] In this case, the current topic appeared eminently suitable. Not only has legal reasoning itself been subjected to numerous empirical studies over the years in both the judicial and arbitral contexts,[40] but so, too, have dispute resolution processes themselves, including

[36] Chs. 2.II (concerning the survey), 3.II (concerning the semi-structured interviews), 4.II (concerning the coding exercise).

[37] Daniel R Cahoy, 'Considerations in the Rise of Empirical Legal Scholarship', (2010) 47 Am Bus LJ v, vii–viii; Susan D Franck, 'Empiricism and International Law: Insights From Investment Treaty Dispute Resolution', (2008) 48 Va J Intl 767, 784–95 (Franck, Empiricism). Rigorous methodology is particularly important in the context of empirical legal research, given the general lack of familiarity among legal audiences regarding the merits of empirical work. Lee Epstein and Gary King, 'Building An Infrastructure for Empirical Research in the Law', (2003) 53 J L Ed 311, 316–17; Gregory Mitchell, 'Empirical Legal Scholarship as Scientific Dialogue', (2014) 83 N Carolina L Rev 167, 185.

[38] Replicability is another major means of validating social science research. Saks (n 7) 5.

[39] Epstein and King, Rules (n 29) 54; Franck, Empiricism (n 37) 790 (noting 'not all research questions are well-suited to empirical methodologies'); Matthias Schonlau, Ronald D Fricker and Marc N Elliott, *Conducting Research Surveys via E-Mail and the Web* (RAND Corporation 2002) 5–18 (discussing studies on research methodology conducted by the RAND Corporation).

[40] Jeremy A Blumental, 'Does Mood Influence Moral Judgment? An Empirical Test With Legal and Policy Implications', (2005) 29 L & Psych Rev 1; Tony Cole (ed), *The Roles of Psychology in International Arbitration* (Wolters Kluwer 2017); Stefan H Krieger and Katrina Fischer Kuh, 'Accessing Law: An Empirical Study Exploring the Influence of Legal Research Medium', 2014 (16) Vanderbilt J Ent & Tech L 757; Richard Posner, *How Judges Think* (Harvard University Press 2008) (Posner, *Think*); Dan Simon, 'A Third View of the Black Box: Cognitive Coherence in Legal Decision Making', (2004) 71 U Chi L Rev 511; Gregory C Sisk, 'The Quantitative Moment and the Qualitative Opportunity: Legal Studies of Judicial Decision Making', (2008) 93 Cornell L Rev 873 (discussing sources and trends in empirical research involving legal reasoning); Gregory C Sisk and Michael Heise, 'Judges and Ideology: Public and Academic Debates About Statistical Measures', (2005) 99 Northwest. U L Rev 743 (conducting empirical analyses and surveying recent analyses); Gregory C Sisk, Michael Heise, and Andrew P Morriss, 'Charting the Influences on the Judicial Mind: An Empirical Study of Judicial Reasoning', (1998) 73 NYU L Rev 1377; Anne van Aaken and Tomer Broude, 'Arbitration From a Law and Economics Perspective', in Thomas Schultz and Federico Ortino (eds), *The Oxford Handbook of International Arbitration* (Oxford University Press forthcoming); Vern R Walker, 'A Default-Logic Paradigm for Legal Fact-Finding', (2007) 47 Jurimetrics J 193 (Walker, Default-Logic) (reflecting one of the few studies considering factual or evidentiary issues in legal reasoning); Vern R Walker, 'Discovering the Logic of Legal Reasoning', (2007) 35 Hofstra L Rev 1687; W Mark C Weidemaier, 'Judging-Lite: How Arbitrators Use and Create Precedent', (2012) 90 N Carolina L Rev 1091 (Weidemaier, Judging-Lite); W Mark C Weidemaier, 'Toward a Theory of Precedent in Arbitration', (2010) 51 Wm & Mary L Rev 1895. One recent study involved simulated decision-making scenarios testing cognitive biases found no difference between judges and arbitrators. Rebecca K Helm, Andrew J Wistrich, and Jeffrey J Rachlinski, 'Are Arbitrators Human?' (2016) 13 J Empirical LS 666, 692.

adjudicative mechanisms such as litigation[41] and arbitration[42] as well as consensual mechanisms such as mediation.[43]

As important as it is to gauge the amenability of a particular subject matter to empirical research, scholars need not be tied to the same methodology used in the past. In fact, developing new methodological approaches is critical to generating new data, since different research techniques test different assumptions and practices.[44] However, it is also important not to stray too far from the established research norms, lest the findings be considered unreliable.

The current study sought to chart a middle path between novelty and orthodoxy.[45] For example, numerous studies of judicial and arbitral decision making seek to gain insight through detailed outcome analyses that consider whether legal reasoning is

[41] E.g. Jason A Cantone, *Report on Federal-State Court Cooperation: A Survey of Federal Chief District Judges* (Federal Judicial Center 2017) <https://www.fjc.gov/publications> accessed 11 April 2020; Tom Ginsburg and Glenn Hoetker, 'The Unreluctant Litigant? An Empirical Analysis of Japan's Turn to Litigation', (2006) 35 JLS 31; Diana Richards, 'Learning to Sentence: An Empirical Study of Judicial Attitudes Towards Judicial Training in Romania', (2015) 7 Intl J Court Administration 68; Virginia Rosales and Dolores Jiménez-Rubio, 'Empirical Analysis of Civil Litigation Determinants: The Case of Spain', (2017) 44 Eur J L Econ 321; SI Strong, 'International Litigation – Arbitration', in Jürgen Georg Backhaus (ed), *Encyclopedia of Law and Economics* (2d ed 2020) (listing authorities).

[42] E.g. Tony Cole and others, Arbitration in the Americas: Report on a Survey of Arbitration Practitioners, <https://www2.le.ac.uk/departments/law/research/arbitration> accessed 11 April 2020; Tony Cole, Pietro Ortolani, and Barbara Warwas, 'Arbitration in Southern Europe: Insights From a Large-Scale Empirical Study', (2015) 26 Am Rev Intl Arb 187; Yves Dezalay and Bryant G Garth, *Dealing in Virtue: International Commercial Arbitration and the Constructions of a Transnational Legal Order* (University of Chicago Press 1996) 298; Christopher R Drahozal, 'Contracting Out of National Law: An Empirical Look at the New Law Merchant', (2005) 80 Notre Dame L Rev 523; Christopher R Drahozal, 'Arbitration by the Numbers: The State of Empirical Research on International Commercial Arbitration', (2006) 22 Arb Intl 291; Drahozal, Overview (n 2); Christopher R Drahozal and Richard W Naimark (eds), *Towards A Science of International Arbitration: Collected Empirical Research* (Wolters Kluwer 2005); Christopher R Drahozal and Samantha Zyontz, 'An Empirical Study of AAA Consumer Arbitration', (2010) 25 Ohio State J Disp Res 843; Susan D Franck, 'Empirically Evaluating Claims About Investment Treaty Arbitration', (2007) 86 N Carolina L Rev 1 (Franck, Empirically Evaluating); Franck, Empiricism (n 37) 792; Gus Van Harten, 'Arbitrator Behaviour in Asymmetrical Adjudication: An Empirical Study of Investment Treaty Arbitration', (2012) 50 Osgoode Hall LJ 211; Tom Ginsburg and Gregory Shaffer, 'How Does International Law Work?: What Empirical Research Shows', in Peter Cane and Herbert Kritzer (eds), *Oxford Handbook of Empirical Legal Studies* (Oxford University Press 2010) 753, 754; William H Knull, III, and Noah D Rubins, 'Betting the Farm on International Arbitration: Is It Time to Offer an Appeal Option?,' (2000) 11 Am Rev Intl Arb 531, 533–34; Loukas Mistelis, 'International Arbitration—Corporate Attitudes and Practices – 12 Perceptions Tested: Myths, Data and Analysis Research Report', (2004) 15 Am Rev Intl Arb 525; Christopher A Whytock, 'The Arbitration-Litigation Relationship in Transnational Dispute Resolution: Empirical Results from the Federal Courts', (2009) 2 World Arb & Med Rev 39. The School of International Arbitration at Queen Mary, University of London, has been particularly active in the area of international commercial arbitration and has conducted a number of studies that have adopted a research methodology that is somewhat similar to that which is used in the current project. Queen Mary, University of London, Research at the School of International Arbitration, <http://www.arbitration.qmul.ac.uk/research/index.html> accessed 11 April 2020 (containing details regarding nine different empirical studies concerning international arbitration).

[43] Penny Brooker and Anthony Lavers, 'Mediation Outcomes: Lawyers' Experience with Commercial and Construction Mediation in the United Kingdom', (2005) 5 Pepperdine Disp Res LJ 161; Ewald Filler, *ommercial Mediation in Europe: An Empirical Study of the User Experience* (Wolters Kluwer 2012); Thomas J Stipanowich and J Ryan Lamare, 'Living With ADR: Evolving Perceptions and Use of Mediation, Arbitration, and Conflict Management in Fortune 1000 Corporations', (2014) 19 Harv Negotiation L Rev 1; SI Strong, 'Realizing Rationality: An Empirical Assessment of International Commercial Mediation', (2016) 73 Wash & Lee L Rev 1973 (2016).

[44] Donna Shestowsky, 'The Psychology of Preference: How Litigants Evaluate Legal Procedures *Ex Ante*', (2014) 99 Iowa L Rev 637, 641; see also Michael Heise, 'The Importance of Being Empirical', (1999) 26 Pepperdine L Rev 807, 834 (discussing the need for and types of empirical legal research); Richard K Neumann, Jr and Stefan H Krieger, 'Empirical Inquiry Twenty-Five Years After the Lawyering Process', (2003) 10 Clinical L Rev 349, 353 (outlining various types of empirical research in law).

[45] One methodology that was not adopted here involves simulated decision making, which has been used in both judicial and arbitral contexts. Franck and others, Arbitrator's Mind (n 2) 1115; Helm, Wistrich, and Rachlinski (n 40) 666; Kristina Kylkova, 'Bias in Arbitral-Decision-Making: Rescuing the Mentschikoff Archives

affected by extra-legal considerations.[46] This strand of scholarship typically adopts the perspective of the Legal Realists[47] and considers whether and to what extent the presumed ideology of the decision maker, as determined by the political affiliation of the entity that appointed a judge[48] or arbitrator,[49] and can be used to predict the outcome or the dispute. As useful as these types of studies may be, they would be largely if not wholly inappropriate in the current context, both because the judicial decisions discussed herein come from a range of jurisdictions, thereby making it difficult or impossible to devise reliable methods of identifying ideological patterns of judicial appointment across jurisdictional lines, and because the commercial nature of the arbitral awards makes it difficult or impossible to attribute any ideological perspectives to the parties appointing the arbitrators.[50]

Another type of quantitative empirical study involves citation counts of legal authorities found in publicly available decisions and awards.[51] This particular methodology is not only suitable in the current study but also extremely useful, since it promotes a certain amount of comparative analysis by building upon earlier, analogous research. However, the research conducted herein introduces several innovative elements, including the expansion of citation count studies from legal authorities to factual (evidentiary) authorities and the creation of a new paragraph-by-paragraph analysis that calculates the amount of time decisions and awards spend on legal, factual, and other issues.[52]

From a Half Century of Oblivion', (2014) 31 J Intl Arb 289; Soia Mentschikoff, 'Commercial Arbitration', (1961) 61 Colum L Rev 846.

[46] Outcome studies often involve reversal rates. Knight (n 4) 1552. Some empirical studies have shown no discernible difference in outcome between judicial decisions and arbitral awards. Chew (n 16) 185 (considering civil rights disputes).

[47] Jerome Frank, *Law and the Modern Mind* (Brentano's 1930).

[48] Numerous studies consider whether outcomes can be anticipated on the basis of the political affiliation of the individual who appointed the judge in question. E.g. CK Rowland and Robert A Carp, *Politics and Judgment in Federal District Courts* (University Press of Kansas 1996) 24–57; Sisk and Heise (n 40) 743.

[49] Andrea Cann Chandrasekher and David Horton, 'Arbitration Nation: Data From Four Providers', (2019) 107 Cal L Rev 1, 7–8 (citing studies of domestic arbitration). Numerous studies consider whether outcome can be anticipated on the basis of whether an arbitrator is appointed by a state or by an investor in treaty-based arbitration. E.g. Susan D Franck, 'Conflating Politics and Development? Examining Investment Treaty Arbitration Outcomes', (2014) 55 Va J Intl L 13; Susan D Franck, 'The ICSID Effect? Considering Potential Variations in Arbitration Awards', (2011) 51 Va J Intl L 825; Susan D Franck and Lindsey E Wylie, 'Predicting Outcomes in Investment Treaty Arbitration', (2015) 65 Duke LJ 459.

[50] However, some scholars have suggested empirical research based on systemic considerations in international commercial arbitration. Stavros Brekoulakis, 'Systemic Bias and the Institution of International Arbitration: A New Approach to Arbitral Decision-Making', (2013) 4 J Intl Disp Settlement 553. Theorists have argued that arbitrators may be prone to bias because of reputational or financial benefits associated with serving as an arbitrator, but empirical research suggests that concern is unfounded. Susan D Franck and others, 'International Arbitration: Demographics, Precision and Justice', in Albert Jan van den Berg (ed), *International Council of Commercial Arbitrators Series Number 18: Legitimacy: Myths, Realities, Challenges* (ICCA 2015) 33, 85–91 (Franck and others, Demographics).

[51] Stephen J Choi and G Mitu Gulati, 'Bias in Judicial Citations: A Window Into the Behavior of Judges?' (2008) 37 JLS 87 (Choi and Gulati, Bias); Stephen J Choi and G Mitu Gulati, 'Trading Votes for Reasoning: Covering in Judicial Opinions', (2008) 81 So Cal L Rev 735 (Choi and Gulati, Trading Votes); Jeffrey P Commission, 'Precedent in Investment Treaty Arbitration: A Citation Analysis of a Developing Jurisprudence', (2007) 24 J Intl Arb 129; Joshua B Fischman and David S Law, 'What is Judicial Ideology, and How Should We Measure It?' (2009) 29 Wash U J L & Pol'y 133, 167; Weidemaier, Judging-Lite (n 40) 1105–06.

[52] Sisk (n 40) 885 (noting the need to 'examin[e] and classify[] the content of judicial opinions rather than merely counting outcomes in cases').

Existing empirical studies also make frequent use of surveys and semi-structured interviews, particularly in research involving alternative dispute resolution.[53] Although similar investigations would be equally useful in the judicial context, it has traditionally been difficult to obtain unfiltered access to judges.[54] However, the ever-increasing number of judges who have retired and taken up work as arbitrators has not only helped scholars understand the judicial mindset but has also facilitated comparisons of judicial and arbitral reasoning, since judge-arbitrators can be asked directly whether they change their approach to legal reasoning depending on the context in which they are working.

Another reason why surveys and interviews are seldom used in judicial settings involves concerns about whether judges can or will be fully candid about their actions and motivations, an issue that has as much to do with standard issues regarding self-awareness (i.e. whether the subject of a research study can or will ever be truly honest about his/her beliefs and behaviours) as it does with the judicial desire to protect the sanctity of the deliberation process.[55] However, scholars have successfully conducted surveys and interviews of neutrals in arbitration and mediation, suggesting that there is nothing inherently problematic with these particular methodologies so long as the researcher incorporates sufficient safeguards into the process.[56] Therefore, this study uses surveys as well as semi-structured interviews to investigate the beliefs and behaviours of judges, arbitrators, and judge-arbitrators.[57]

The next step in designing an empirical research study involves ensuring that the chosen methodology is appropriately tied to the underlying research question(s).[58] This project uses a mixed qualitative-quantitative approach to investigate legal reasoning in commercial disputes, focusing on potential differences across the judicial-arbitral, domestic-international, and common law-civil law divides. The mixed approach is both necessary and appropriate, not only because the study seeks to determine what judges and arbitrators do and why they do it,[59] but also because a mixed approach allows the 'triangulation' of individual research streams within the study, thereby creating an internal confirmation mechanism to test the validity of the results.[60]

[53] E.g. Dezalay and Garth (n 42) *passim*; Dieter Flader and Charles W Anderson III, 'Some Psychological Preconditions for the Process of International Arbitration: Preliminary Findings of a Research Project with a Qualitative Approach', in Tony Cole (ed), *The Roles of Psychology in International Arbitration* (Wolters Kluwer 2017) 267.

[54] Many studies of judicial conduct are conducted by 'insiders', meaning those who work at judicial research centres and who thus are unlikely to publish anything that might prove embarrassing to the judges in question. E.g. Cantone (n 41) (conducting a survey for the US Federal Judicial Center); James B Eaglin and Matthew Alex Ward, 'Enhancing the Administration of Justice and Strengthening Judicial Independence Through Independent, Judicial-Based Applied Research Centers', (2014) 7 J L Tech Risk Mgmt 77. One judge who has sought to pull back the veil on judicial reasoning is Judge Richard Posner, formerly of the US Federal Court of Appeals for the Seventh Circuit. E.g. Posner, *Think* (n 40).

[55] Frank B Cross, 'Decisionmaking in the US Circuit Courts of Appeals', (2003) 91 Cal L Rev 1451, 1446–47, 1466; Milton Heumann, 'Interviewing Trial Judges', (1989–1990) 73 Judicature 200.

[56] E.g. Dezalay and Garth (n 42) *passim*; John Lande and Peter W Benner, 'Why and How Businesses Use Planned Early Dispute Resolution', (2017) 13 U St Thomas LJ 248.

[57] Chs. 4, 5.

[58] Strauss and Corbin (n 12) 41.

[59] The motivation assessed herein focuses more on justificatory practices rather than extra-legal influences, which are often found to have relatively little effect on legal reasoning. Knight (n 4) 1553; Sisk (n 40) 888.

[60] Saks (n 7) 5; Timans, Wouters, and Heilbron (n 27) 193.

Triangulation arose in two different ways. First, the project asked very similar questions in the survey and the semi-structured interviews, thereby providing an immediate check for information discrepancies, including those that might have arisen as a result of interviewees' desire to 'look good' to the interviewer.[61] Second, the project correlated data generated by the survey and interviews against information produced from the coding exercise.[62] While these techniques were not entirely aligned—for example, there was no way to check whether an interviewee who had completed the survey had answered both sets of questions similarly, since the survey was entirely anonymous, and no efforts were made to conduct a coding analysis of particular decisions or awards written by interviewees—the cross-referencing of data nevertheless allowed comparisons to be conducted on a general basis.

Innovation was not limited to methodological considerations. The research also broke new ground with respect to substantive concerns, particularly with respect to the understanding of the concept of 'legal reasoning'. Traditionally, scholarship on legal reasoning has focused nearly exclusively on judicial and arbitral treatment of legal authorities and argumentation, using citation counts[63] or computer-assisted linguistic analyses[64] to measure the frequency with which certain legal materials or words were used.[65] However, similar studies have not been conducted with respect to factual authorities (evidence),[66] even though a growing amount of research suggests that

[61] Anonymous online surveys, such as the one conducted here, are often considered more accurate than interviews because respondents typically feel free to be entirely candid. Interviewees, on the other hand, can consciously or unconsciously seek to please the interviewee by providing what is perceived as the 'right' answer or can avoid divulging information that the interviewee perceives as shameful or embarrassing. Olena Kaminska and Tom Foulsham, *Understanding Sources of Social Desirability Bias in Different Modes: Evidence from Eye-Tracking* (Institute for Social and Economic Research 2013) 1.

[62] One problem of non-directed interviews is that the results can devolve into mere anecdotal evidence if the study is not properly constructed. Neumann and Krieger (n 44) 380; see also Deborah L Rhode, 'Legal Scholarship', (2002) 115 Harv L Rev 1327, 1343. Those issues can be resolved by testing the results of the semi-structured interviews against survey data.

[63] Choi and Gulati, Bias (n 51) 87; Choi and Gulati, Trading Votes (n 51) 735; Commission (n 51) 129; Fischman and Law (n 51) 167; Weidemaier, Judging-Lite (n 40) 1105–06.

[64] E.g. John S Ehrett, 'Against Corpus Linguistics', (2019) 108 Georgetown LJ Online 50 (discussing judicial use of corpus linguistics); Penn Lai 'Perry' Li, 'Natural Language Processing', (2016) 1 Georgetown L Tech Rev 98 (discussing the effect of natural language processing, an outgrowth of artificial intelligence and computational linguistics, on legal practice and research); Friedemann Vogel, Hanjo Hamann, and Isabelle Gauer, 'Computer-Assisted Legal Linguistics: Corpus Analysis as a New Tool for Legal Studies', (2018) 43 L & Soc Inquiry 1340 (discussing legal linguistic projects on British, German, and European law).

[65] Studies on legal reasoning have also adopted more holistic methodologies. E.g. James J Brudney and Corey Ditslear, 'Canons of Construction and the Elusive Question for Neutral Reasoning', (2005) 58 Vanderbilt L Rev 1; Mark A Hall and Ronald F Wright, 'Systematic Content Analysis of Judicial Opinions', (2008) 96 Cal L Rev 63; Daniel M Schneider, 'Empirical Research on Judicial Reasoning: Statutory Interpretation in Federal Tax Cases', (2001) 31 New Mexico L Rev 325. However, such projects can experience coder error and variation due to the subjectivity of the coding process. R Polk Wagner and Lee Petherbridge, 'Is the Federal Circuit Succeeding? An Empirical Assessment of Judicial Performance', (2004) 152 U Penn L Rev 1105, 1139.

[66] 'The Legal Concept of Evidence', *Stanford Encyclopedia of Philosophy* (2015) 3.1, <https://plato.stanford.edu/entries/evidence-legal/#StrEviProWei> accessed 11 April 2020; Jan BM Vranken, *Exploring the Jurist's Frame of Mind: Constraints and Preconceptions in Civil Law Argumentation* (Kluwer Law International 2006) 46–47 (calling for more empirical research on factual matters in civil law systems). A few exceptions exist. Catherine D Perry, 'What Works – Evidence From A Trial Judge's Perspective', (1999) 25 Litigation 3; Edna Sussman, 'The Arbitrator Survey – Practices, Preferences and Changes on the Horizon', (2015) 26 Am Rev Intl Arb 517, 519 (Sussman, Survey); see also Chester Brown, *A Common Law of International Adjudication* (Oxford University Press 2007) 83–118 (discussing evidentiary concerns in international courts); Jeffrey Waincymer, *Procedure and Evidence in International Arbitration* (Kluwer International 2012) chs. 10–13 (seeking to blend theoretical and practical analyses regarding factual authorities but without an empirical element); Walker, Default-Logic (n 40) 193. In

factual issues are more important than legal issues in many commercial disputes.[67] Furthermore, experts from both common law and civil law jurisdictions agree that finding 'the appropriate methodology for distinguishing questions of fact from questions of law [is], to say the least, elusive', and note that 'the practical truth [is] that the decision to label an issue a "question of law", a "question of fact", or a "mixed question of law and fact" is sometimes as much a matter of allocation as it is of analysis'.[68]

Heeding the concerns of scholars who believe that existing studies are too narrow,[69] this study therefore expanded the concept of 'legal reasoning' to include evidentiary authorities and arguments. In so doing, this research not only amplified the understanding of how commercial disputes are resolved but also addressed the longstanding assumption that arbitration focuses primarily on facts while litigation focuses primarily on law.[70]

Another substantive innovation involved the scope of analysis, which was both more detailed and more comparative than analogous studies. For example, rather than relying on generalized citation counts, this project distinguished between different categories of legal and factual authorities to determine which materials are most persuasive to judges and arbitrators.[71] The research also considered whether judges and arbitrators approach authorities differently depending on whether the issue was procedural or substantive in nature and investigated a number of related issues, such as the extent to which judges and arbitrators conducted independent legal and factual research.

Another substantive innovation involved attempts to identify the extent to which legal reasoning was affected by factors such as policy and equity.[72] The research was also unusual in that it distinguished between the reasoning process and the drafting process, and asked a separate series of questions about how judges and arbitrators

some countries, most notably the United States, analysis of the relative weight of different types of evidence may be curtailed by the ongoing belief that factual decision making in civil litigation is within the exclusive purview of the jury, not the judge, even though many commercial matters are actually heard as bench trials and even though the judge must be the one to write the reasoned decision that includes information about evidentiary concerns.

[67] Benjamin N Cardozo, *The Nature of the Judicial Process* (Yale University Press 1949) 164–65 (discussing three types of judicial writings); Knight (n 4) 1554. Those involved in legal education have also recognized the need to expand the conception of 'legal reasoning', as taught in law schools, to include factual considerations. American Bar Association Section of Legal Education and Admissions to the Bar, *Legal Education and Professional Development: An Education Continuum* (American Bar Association 1992) 40, 53, 138–39 151–57, 163–72 (MacCrate Report).

[68] *Miller v Fenton*, 474 US 104, 113–14 (1985) (citations omitted); see also *Collector of Customs v Agfa-Gevaert Ltd*, (1996) 186 CLR 389, 384 (Australia) ('The distinction between questions of fact and questions of law is a vital distinction in many fields of law. Notwithstanding attempts by many distinguished judges and juries to formulate tests for finding the line between the two questions, no satisfactory test of universal application has yet been formulated.'); *Ruddock v Taylor*, (2005) 222 CLR 612, 627 (Australia) (noting there are 'many cases ... in which a distinction between mistake of law and mistake of fact could not readily be drawn, if drawn at all'); Creyke and others (n 7) 250–51 (discussing the test in *Collector of Customs v Pozzolanic*, (1993) 43 FCR 280, for distinguishing facts and law and subsequent cases); SI Strong, 'Legal Reasoning in International Commercial Disputes: Empirically Testing the Common Law-Civil Law Divide', in Mélida N Hodgson and Antonio Crivellaro (eds), *Dossier XVII: Reasoning in Arbitration* (ICC Institute of World Business Law 2020) 41 (Strong, Legal Reasoning).

[69] Knight (n 4) 1539–40 (discussing criticisms of the inappropriate narrowness of previous studies on judicial decision making).

[70] Ch. 1.III.A.

[71] Previous studies often made no distinctions between the types of authorities cited. Weidemaier, Judging Lite (n 40) 1105–06.

[72] John Bell, *Policy Arguments in Judicial Decisions* (Clarendon Press 1983); Knight (n 4) 1539–40, 1547; James Plunkett, 'Principle and Policy in Private Law Reasoning', (2016) 75 CLJ 366.

approached the actual writing of decisions and awards. In so doing, the project tested the often-repeated notion that the mere act of writing a decision or award improves the reasoning process.[73]

The final major innovation involved the series of questions in both the survey and the interviews regarding judicial and arbitral education. While these inquires do not address legal reasoning per se, they can help educational providers develop courses on legal reasoning that more accurately reflect the needs of the participants.[74] At this point, there is a dearth of scholarship—particularly empirical scholarship—about judicial and arbitral education, largely as a result of the assumption in many jurisdictions that new judges and arbitrators simply step into their roles with a minimum of effort.[75] Other difficulties have stemmed from the outmoded belief that judicial and arbitral education focuses primarily if not exclusively on current developments in the law.[76] Problems have also arisen as a result of the 'bias blind spot', a type of unconscious cognitive distortion that leads individuals—including both judges and arbitrators—to fail to see shortcomings in themselves even while they identify similar shortcomings in others.[77] These factors strongly suggest the need to undertake additional research, including empirical research, into matters relating to judicial and arbitral education.

III. Existing Scholarship on Legal Reasoning

The best empirical studies do not exist in a vacuum but are instead appropriately situated within existing substantive scholarship. As a result, this project not only sought to take previous studies of legal reasoning into account during the design phase but also consciously aimed to test some of the theories reflected in the legal literature. While

[73] Strong, Reasoned Awards (n 19) 19–20; SI Strong, 'Writing Reasoned Decisions and Opinions: A Guide for Novice, Experienced and Foreign Judges', 2015 J Disp Res 93, 104 (Strong, Reasoned Decisions). Other rationales exist for reasoned decisions and awards. Strong, Reasoned Awards (n 19) 15–20 (identifying both structural and process-oriented rationales for such awards, such as making sure the parties feel heard and protecting the award from subsequent review or annulment); ibid at 31–33 (discussing the audience for reasoned awards); Strong, Reasoned Decisions (n 73) 101–05 (identifying both structural and process-oriented rationales for such decisions, such as making sure the parties feel heard); ibid 116–17 (discussing the audience for reasoned decisions).

[74] Recent years have seen a significant increase in interest in matters relating to judicial and arbitral education. Livingston Armytage, *Educating Judges: Towards Improving Justice* (Brill 2015); SI Strong, 'Judicial Education and Regulatory Capture: Does the Current System of Educating Judges Promote a Well-Functioning Judiciary and Adequately Serve the Public Interest?' 2015 J Disp Res 1, 1–18 (Strong, Judicial Education); Strong, Reasoned Awards (n 19) 5–8; Strong, Reasoned Decisions (n 73) 95–96; Chartered Institute of Arbitrators, Training at CIArb, <https://www.ciarb.org/training/> accessed 11 April 2020 (discussing pathway programme of advanced education); Professor Cheryl Thomas QC (Hon) Appointed the First Ever Dean of Education at Inner Temple, UCL Faculty of Laws, <https://www.ucl.ac.uk/laws/news/2019/jul/professor-cheryl-thomas-qc-hon-appointed-first-ever-dean-education-inner-temple> accessed 11 April 2020.

[75] Strong, Reasoned Awards (n 19) 5–8; Strong, Judicial Education (n 74) 1–18; see also Emily Kadens, 'The Puzzle of Judicial Education: The Case of Chief Justice William de Grey', (2009) 75 Brooklyn L Rev 143, 146–47 (noting that many believe judges learn their new roles 'by doing' or through socialization (acculturation)).

[76] In fact, leaders in judicial and arbitral education focus primarily on programming involving professional skills. Strong, Judicial Education (n 74) 20 (discussing courses on 'judge-craft'); Strong, Reasoned Awards (n 19) 43 (discussing courses on 'arbitrator-craft').

[77] Strong, Status Quo Bias (n 14) 553. Judges and arbitrators can also be prone to overconfidence. Franck and others, Arbitrator's Mind (n 2) 1163 (discussing empirical research on egocentrism, also known as self-serving bias, in both judges and arbitrators); Strong, Judicial Education (n 74) 14 (discussing judicial hubris).

space restrictions make it impossible to engage with the ongoing theoretical debates in detail, the relevant concepts are introduced in the following subsections along with extensive references to resource material for those who want to read more about the various ideas. The discussion is organized along the three comparative axes (judicial-arbitral, domestic-international and common law-civil law), although some issues are equally relevant to more than one line of inquiry.

A. Comparing Judicial and Arbitral Practice

The primary focus of this research project involved a desire to determine whether judges and arbitrators differed in their approaches to legal reasoning and legal process. Although relatively few studies specifically seek to compare the two processes directly,[78] a considerable body of empirical research strongly refutes longstanding assumptions about arbitral reasoning, including the notion that arbitrators simply 'split the baby'[79] or unfairly benefit 'repeat players' to an extent not seen in litigation.[80] Despite these findings, arbitration is nevertheless routinely considered 'lesser' than litigation, particularly in the domestic realm, where arbitration is frequently characterized as 'second class justice'.[81] While most of the concerns about the quality of arbitral justice refer to consumer or employment arbitration rather than commercial arbitration,[82] many

[78] One common method of comparing judicial and arbitral beliefs and behaviours involves taking a research technique that was previously used in the judicial realm, applying it to the arbitral realm, then analysing whether any differences arise. E.g. Franck and others, Arbitrator's Mind (n 2) 1166; Helm, Wistrich, and Rachlinski (n 40) 667 n 3.

[79] Christopher R Drahozal, 'A Behavioral Analysis of Private Judging', (2004) 67 L & Contemp Probs 105, 115–16 (Drahozal, Private Judging) (summarizing studies); Drahozal, Overview (n 2); Franck and others, Arbitrator's Mind (n 2) 1167; Carter Greenbaum, 'Putting the Baby to Rest: Dispelling a Common Arbitration Myth', (2015) 26 Am Rev Intl Arb 101.

[80] Chandrasekher and Horton (n 49) 1 (discussing the repeat player phenomenon in litigation); Lee Epstein, 'Some Thoughts on the Study of Judicial Behavior', (2016) 57 Wm & Mary L Rev 2017, 2066 (noting studies on litigation from around the world show that courts tend to favour repeat players). Most studies of the repeat player phenomenon appear in consumer, employment, and investment arbitration rather than commercial arbitration, which tends to reflect 'one shot' players and customized, rather than standardized, arbitration agreements. E.g. Sarah Rudolph Cole, 'The Lost Promise of Arbitration', (2017) 17 SMU L Rev 849, 858–61 (distinguishing commercial arbitration from other mechanisms); Drahozal, Private Judging (n 79) 127–28 (citing studies and noting evidence of a repeat player bias is 'inconclusive'); Franck, Empirically Evaluating (n 42) 80; Franck and Wylie (n 49) 501; Catherine A Rogers, 'The Arrival of the "Have Nots" in International Arbitration', (2007) 8 Nevada LJ 341, 343–44 (discussing traditional nature of international commercial arbitration).

[81] E.g. *Cellinfo, LLC v American Tower Corp*, 352 F Supp 3d 127, 135–38 (D Mass 2018) (providing empirically faulty data on arbitration and one-sided policy analyses); Strong, Status Quo Bias (n 14) 562. Notably, a number of former judges who subsequently became arbitrators have remarked on the quality of justice in arbitration, with one highly esteemed US magistrate judge—Wayne Brazil—going so far as to claim that arbitration was in many ways better than litigation. Wayne D Brazil, 'When "Getting it Right" is What Matters Most, Arbitrations are Better Than Trials', (2017) 18 Cardozo J Conflict Res 277, 277–78 ('[I]n many circumstances and for certain kinds of cases, arbitrations conducted by conscientious arbitrators are likely to yield higher quality decisions than trials conducted by conscientious judges.').

[82] In the United States, this criticism is most frequently aimed at consumer, employment, and labour arbitration, which are relatively informal processes. SI Strong, 'The Special Nature of International Insurance and Reinsurance Arbitration', 2015 J Disp Res 283, 287–89 (citing sources). International commercial arbitration, on the other hand, is frequently considered to reflect 'Rolls Royce justice' because of its complexity and sophistication. Russell J Weintraub, *International Litigation and Arbitration: Practice and Planning* (Carolina Academic Publishers 1994) 455; see also Born (n 14) 2129.

individuals within both the lay and legal communities fail to distinguish between the various processes, which can lead to commercial arbitration being damned simply by association.[83]

Although empirical scholarship is not always successful in overcoming pervasive misperceptions,[84] this study nevertheless seeks to put an end to some of the more enduring myths about legal reasoning in judicial and arbitral proceedings. For example, one issue that is tested herein involves conventional wisdom suggesting that arbitrators in commercial disputes rely on legal authority less frequently than judges and on facts and/or equitable arguments more frequently than judges.[85] Indeed, some people appear to believe that arbitrators are not bound by precedent and instead rely solely on equitable principles to decide dispute, even though most commercial arbitrations are governed by the law of a particular jurisdiction named by the parties, and the ability to rely on equitable principles (as when the arbitral tribunal decides *ex aequo et bono* or as an *amiable compositeur*) is only possible with the express consent of the parties.[86] This project tests that assumption by studying the frequency with which judges and arbitrators rely on both law and facts in resolving commercial disputes, an issue that has seldom been considered.[87] The study even goes a step further and considers whether any difference in practice exists across the substantive-procedural divide.[88]

As important as it is to understand the role that different types of legal and factual authorities play in judicial and arbitral proceedings, the process of legal reasoning involves much more than consideration of binding and persuasive authorities. For example, legal decision makers are often influenced by conscious and unconscious beliefs about what constitutes the proper role of a judge or arbitrator.[89] Views about what constitutes the 'ideal' judge or arbitrator can have ramifications on everything from the

[83] Jan Heiner Nedden and Aaron de Jong, 'Arbitration in a Post-Truth World: Perception v Reality', (2018) 12 Disp Res Intl 165, 170–72; Strong, Status Quo Bias (n 14) 535, 537 (listing authorities).

[84] SI Strong, 'Alternative Facts and the Post-Truth Society: Meeting the Challenge', (2017) 165 U Penn L Rev Online 137, 138; Strong, Status Quo Bias (n 14) 530.

[85] Some studies outside the commercial setting have addressed this issue. Chew (n 16) 205–06 (noting arbitrators in civil rights cases cited legal principles and interpreted legal principles in much the same manner as judges); Andrew J Wistrich, Jeffrey J Rachlinski, and Chris Guthrie, 'Heart Versus Head: Do Judges Follow the Law or Follow Their Feelings?', (2015) 93 Texas L Rev 855, 912 (noting that judges are affected by emotional or equitable concerns).

[86] SI Strong, 'Navigating the Borders Between International Commercial Arbitration and U.S. Federal Courts: A Jurisprudential GPS', 2012 J Disp Res 119, 132–33.

[87] Knight (n 4) 1555.

[88] Most research in this field focuses on how judges and arbitrators use legal authorities to determine substantive disputes. E.g. Klaus Peter Berger, *The Creeping Codification of the New* Lex Mercatoria (2d edn, Wolters Kluwer 2010); Orsolya Toth, *The* Lex Mercatoria *in Theory and Practice* (Oxford University Press 2017); Zweigert and Kötz (n 24) chs. 1, 2, 4. However, a few commentators have studied how judges and arbitrators use legal authorities in procedural disputes. Brown (n 66) 36–55 (discussing sources of procedural law in international courts); SI Strong, 'General Principles of Procedural Law and Procedural *Jus Cogens*,' (2018) 122 Penn State L Rev 347; SI Strong, *Research and Practice in International Commercial Arbitration: Sources and Strategies* (Oxford University Press 2009); SI Strong, 'Research in International Commercial Arbitration: Special Skills, Special Sources', (2009) 20 Am Rev Intl Arb 119.

[89] Paul F Kirgis, 'Judicial Review and the Limits of Arbitral Authority: Lessons From the Law of Contract', (2007) 81 St John's L Rev 99, 99 (discussing two ways of characterizing the role of the arbitrator); Chad M Oldfather, 'Writing, Cognition, and the Nature of the Judicial Function', (2008) 96 Georgetown LJ 1283; Rowland and Carp (n 48) 190 n 2 ('[M]any trial judges appear to be motivated primarily by their role orientation—that is, their "secondary" perceptions of what a judge should do—and not by their personal preferences.'); Strong, Judicial Education (n 74) 8–9.

use of law clerks or assistants to help research or draft decisions or awards[90] to whether a judge or arbitrator conducts independent legal[91] or factual[92] research.[93] Many of these ancillary beliefs and behaviours are understudied and undertheorized.[94] As a result, this project included a number of questions, both general and specific, about these additional practices and principles so as to gain a greater understanding of legal reasoning as a whole.

Another area that has proven problematic in the past involves the distinction between legal reasoning and legal drafting.[95] Although most commentators appear to conflate

[90] Letter from Alex Kozinski, US Circuit Judge, 9th Circuit, to Samuel A Alito, Jr, US Circuit Judge, 3rd Circuit (16 January 2004) 5, 9–10 (noting appellate judges in the United States spend 5–10 minutes reviewing unpublished opinions that have been drafted entirely by law clerks or staff attorneys, whereas judges spend weeks or even months crafting published opinions), <http://www.nonpublication.com/kozinskiletter.pdf> accessed 11 April 2020; see also Stephen J Choi and G Mitu Gulati, 'Which Judges Write Their Opinions (And Should We Care)?' (2005) 32 Florida St U L Rev 1077; *Law Clerk Handbook: A Handbook for Law Clerks to Federal Judges* (rev 3d edn, Federal Judicial Center 2017) 106–08 <https://www.fjc.gov/publications> accessed 11 April 2020 (discussing how to draft judicial opinions). Significant debate exists regarding the use, influence and billing of law clerks and tribunal secretaries. E.g. J Ole Jensen, *Tribunal Secretaries in International Arbitration* (Oxford University Press 2019); Todd C Peppers, Michael W Giles, and Bridget Tainer-Parkins, 'Inside Judicial Chambers: How Federal District Court Judges Use and Select Their Law Clerks', (2008) 71 Albany L Rev 623, 623.

[91] Most authorities suggest that judges can conduct such research, although judges vary considerably as to whether they do in fact undertake such efforts. Robert Barnes, 'Should Supreme Court Justices Google?' Wash Post (8 July 2012), <https://www.washingtonpost.com/politics/should-supreme-court-justices-google/2012/07/08/gJQAMC0kWW_story.html> accessed 11 April 2020; Robert Barnes, 'Supreme Court Rule: (Other) Justices Shouldn't Conduct Independent Research', Wash Post (25 March 2018), <https://www.washingtonpost.com/politics/courts_law/supreme-court-rule-other-justices-shouldnt-conduct-independent-research/2018/03/25/7a4f790a-2ebd-11e8-b0b0-f706877db618_story.html> accessed 11 April 2020; Strong, Reasoned Decisions (n 73) 126–27 (citing authorities); SI Strong, 'Richard A. Posner, *Divergent Paths: The Academy and the Judiciary* – How Legal Academics Can Participate in Judicial Education: A How-To Guide by Richard Posner', (2017) 66 J L Ed 421, 430 (suggesting judges should conduct independent legal and factual research). However, the same degree of consensus does not appear to exist with respect to independent legal research by arbitrators, since the process is private, rather than public, and awards do not carry the same type of precedential value as judicial decisions. Jennifer Kirby, 'How Far Should an Arbitrator Go to Get it Right?', in Patricia Shaughnessy and Sherlin Tung (eds), *The Powers and Duties of an Arbitrator:* Liber Amicorum *Pierre A Karrer* (Wolters Kluwer 2017) 193; Strong, Reasoned Awards (n 19) 25–27 (citing authorities).

[92] Significant doubts exist about whether judges and arbitrators should engage in independent factual research. Strong, Reasoned Awards (n 19) 25–27 (citing authorities); Strong, Reasoned Decisions (n 73) 126–27 (citing authorities); see also American Bar Association, Formal Opinion 478, Independent Factual Research by Judges Via the Internet (8 December 2017), <https://www.americanbar.org/content/dam/aba/administrative/professional_responsibility/aba_formal_opinion_478.pdf> accessed 11 April 2020.

[93] For example, one issue of interest involved whether and to what extent judges and arbitrators provide parties with feedback about the parties' arguments or provide insight into any legal or factual research conducted by the decision maker. Sussman, Survey (n 66) 524. Not only was it important to consider whether such discussions took place, it was also important to appreciate why, when, and how those conversations took place. Geoffrey M Beresford Hartwell, 'Assessing Evidence, Constructive Mistrust and the Loneliness of Decision-Making: "There's Not Art to Find the Mind's Construction in the Face"', in Tony Cole (ed), *The Roles of Psychology in International Arbitration* (Wolters Kluwer 2017) 299, 311.

[94] Stavros L Brekoulakis, 'International Arbitration Scholarship and the Concept of Arbitration Law,' (2013) 36 Fordham Intl LJ 745, 746–47; Strong, Judicial Education (n 74) 8–9.

[95] Numerous theoretical works exist with respect to the goals associated with drafting reasoned decisions and awards, along with a handful of empirical or first-hand accounts of the drafting process. Cardozo (n 67) 164–65 (discussing three types of judicial writings); Teresa Giovannini, 'Philosophy Can Help Tribunals Draft Awards That Parties Will Accept as Legitimate', (May–July 2011) 66 Disp Res J 78; Knight (n 4) 1542–43, 1545–46; Giacomo Marchisio, 'The Notion of Award in International Commercial Arbitration – The Case of English and French Law', (2016) 6 Revue d'Arbitrage et de Médiation 53; Richard A Posner, 'Judges' Writing Styles (And Do They Matter?)', (1994) 62 U Chi L Rev 1421, 1447–48; Posner, *Think* (n 40) 110–11; Alan Redfern, 'Opinions in International Commercial Arbitration: The Good, the Bad and the Ugly', (2004) 20 Arb Intl 223; Strong, Reasoned Awards (n 19) 1; Strong, Reasoned Decisions (n 73) 93; Sussman, Survey (n 66) 531. However, relatively few studies integrate theoretical and empirical analysis, which underscores the usefulness of the current research. Knight (n 4) 1546; Sisk (n 40) 897. For example, questions exist as to whether arbitrators write awards for the review of third parties

the two processes, reasoning is in fact quite different from drafting, which is why this study separates the two elements.[96] Thus, questions on the reasoning side break down the constituent elements of judicial and arbitral decision making, such as the interaction between facts, law, equity, and policy,[97] while drafting-oriented inquiries focus on how and why judges and arbitrators reflect their reasoning in written decision and awards. This latter category of questions provides insights into a number of previously unstudied issues, such as the scope and nature of legal and factual materials considered by judges and arbitrators and the extent to which those items are ultimately reflected in the final decision or award.[98]

Analysis of drafting considerations necessarily implicates the concept of what constitutes a reasoned decision or award. Questions about the nature of reasoned rulings have been discussed to a limited degree in the arbitral context by commentators[99] and judges[100] considering the difference between reasoned awards and unreasoned

interested in the outcome of the dispute and whether arbitrators write reasoned awards, at least in part, for their own edification. Sussman, Survey (n 66) 534.

[96] A few exceptions exist. Knight (n 4) 1542–43; Posner, *Think* (n 40) 110–11; Strong, Reasoned Awards (n 19) 21–54; Strong, Reasoned Decisions (n 73) 106–27.

[97] Sussman, Survey (n 66) 519, 531.

[98] Knight (n 4) 1542 (discussing factual determinations); ibid 1548–49 (discussing legal determinations); Sussman, Survey (n 66) 528.

[99] Peter Gillies and Niloufer Selvadurai, 'Reasoned Awards: How Extensive Must the Reasoning Be?' (2008) 74 Arb 125; John Burritt McArthur, 'The Tom Brady Award and the Merit of Reasoned Awards', (2017) 8 J Sports & Ent L 147; Strong, Reasoned Awards (n 19) 10–13; Strong, Reasoned Decisions (n 73) 100–01; Strong, Legal Reasoning 41 (n 68).

[100] Thomas Bingham, 'Reasons and Reasons and Reasons: Differences Between a Court Judgment and an Arbitral Award', (1988) 4 Arb Intl 1 (presenting the views of a former Lord Chief Justice of England). For example, the English Court of Appeal (Civil Division) described the duty to give reasons in a judicial decision as follows:

> (1) The duty is a function of due process, and therefore of justice. Its rationale has two principal aspects. The first is that fairness surely requires that the parties—especially the losing party—should be left in no doubt why they have won or lost. This is especially so since without reasons the losing party will not know ... whether the court has misdirected itself, and thus whether he may have an available appeal on the substance of the case. The second is that a requirement to give reasons concentrates the mind; if it is fulfilled, the resulting decision is much more likely to be soundly based on the evidence than if it is not.
>
> (2) The first of these aspects implies that want of reasons may be a good self-standing ground of appeal. Where because no reasons are given it is impossible to tell whether the judge has gone wrong on the law or the facts, the losing party would be altogether deprived of his chance of an appeal unless the court entertains an appeal based on the lack of reasons itself.
>
> (3) The extent of the duty, or rather the reach of what is required to fulfil it, depends on the subject-matter. Where there is a straightforward factual dispute whose resolution depends simply on which witness is telling the truth about events which he claims to recall, it is likely to be enough for the judge (having, no doubt, summarised the evidence) to indicate simply that he believes X rather than Y; indeed there may be nothing else to say. But where the dispute involves something in the nature of an intellectual exchange, with reasons and analysis advanced on either side, the judge must enter into the issues canvassed before him and explain why he prefers one case over the other. This is likely to apply particularly in litigation whereas here there is disputed expert evidence; but it is not necessarily limited to such cases.
>
> (4) This is not to suggest that there is one rule for cases concerning the witnesses' truthfulness or recall of events, and another for cases where the issue depends on reasoning or analysis (with experts or otherwise). The rule is the same: the judge must explain why he has reached his decision. The question is always, what is required of the judge to do so; and that will differ from case to case. Transparency should be the watchword.

Flannery v Halifax Estate Agencies Ltd [2000] 1 WLR 377, 381 (England); cf *Schwebel v Schwebel* [2011] 2 AER (Comm) 1048 at [23] (England) (holding a reasoned award does not have to list all the argument or pieces of

(standard) awards. However, such matters are not frequently discussed with respect to judicial decisions themselves, since the standard mechanism for addressing problematic decisions (i.e. an appeal) typically focuses on the correctness of the reasoning and the outcome rather than the nature of the reasoning itself.[101] However, Gary Born has noted that being correct as a matter of law is 'not a requirement for a well-reasoned award: bad or unpersuasive reasons are still reasons, and satisfy statutory requirements for reasoned awards'.[102] This suggests that judges and arbitrators would both benefit from a better understanding of what constitutes a well-reasoned ruling as opposed to a ruling that is legally correct.[103]

evidence that are accepted or rejected but should typically identify the primary evidence which is found compelling, if the case depends upon factual findings, since that will be part of the reasoning). Other countries have formulated similar but jurisdictionally unique standards for both judicial decisions and arbitral awards. E.g. *Westport Insurance Corporation v Gordian Runoff Ltd* [2011] HCA 37 (Australia) (concerning the Australian Commercial Arbitration Act 1984); Court of Appeal Brussels, 6 December 2011, *Management Service bvba v Vlaamse Media Maatschappij* (Belgium), published in (2014) 1 *b-Arbitra*, pp 215–219 (suggesting that an award will be considered reasoned if the arbitrator has addressed all the arguments raised, even if s/he does not go into the details of each argument); Court of First Instance of Liege, 6 March 1984, *Q v C*, published in *Jurisprudence de Liege, 1984*, pp 197–200 (Belgium) (holding that the reasoning in an arbitral award shall meet the same quality standards as those required for judicial decisions); Federal Supreme Court, 14.05.1992, File Number III ZR 169/90 (Germany), published in 1992 *Neue Juristische Wochenschrift* (NJW), p 2299 (holding an arbitral tribunal is not obligated to address every assertion of the parties in an award, but only to consider those assertions); Higher Regional Court Munich, 29.10.2009, File Number 34 Sch 15/09 (Germany), published in *BeckRS 2009*, p 86918 (noting that parties in arbitration must be able to comment on all the facts and evidence on which the award was based but noting that principle did not impose a general duty on the arbitral tribunal to clarify or ask questions or the parties nor a general right of the parties to a legal discussion); Svea Court of Appeal, 20 June 2013, Case No T 10913-11 (Sweden) (noting a tribunal's lack of reasoning can be a ground for setting aside an award only if there is essentially a complete lack of reasoning, which is a very high standard); Svea Court of Appeal, 7 December 2006, Case No T 5044 (Sweden) (noting the Swedish Arbitration Act does not require reasoned awards); Svea Court of Appeal, 29 March 2001, Case No T 5781-00 (Sweden) (denying the party's claim that award lacked reasoning and that the arbitral tribunal had not addressed each argument raised); Swiss Federal Tribunal, First Civil Law Court, 29 January 2010, *A GmbH v B SA*, No 4A_550/2009, para 5 (Switzerland) (noting the right to be heard does not include the right to a reasoned decision, and that although arbitral tribunals have an obligation to hear and consider those allegations that are legally relevant, this does not require tribunals to expressly address every argument advanced by the parties in the award); Swiss Federal Tribunal, First Civil Law Court, 30 September 2003, *A v B Ltd, C GmbH, D Ltd and E Ltd*, No 4P.100/2003, paras 5–6 (*Tvornica* decision) (Switzerland) (annulling an award that relied on a provision that neither of the parties had considered to be central to the matter and that had generated legal reasoning that was very different from the positions advanced by the parties); High Court of the Basque Country 14/2015, 2 December (Spain), published in *Id Cendoj* 48020310012015100030 (noting a failure to address all the claims submitted to arbitration implied a lack of defence of the counterclaimants and a violation of the procedural public policy (*orden público procesal*), which requires awards to be logical, well-reasoned and consistent with the parties' petitions); *Cat Charter LLC v Schurtenberger*, 646 F 3d 836, 844 (11th Cir 2011) (US); *Rain CII Carbon, LLC v ConocoPhillips Co.*, 674 F 3d 469, 473–74 (5th Cir 2012) (US) (distinguishing a reasoned award from an award with findings of fact and conclusions of law); *Leeward Construction Co v American University of Antigua-College of Medicine*, 826 F 3d, 634, 640 (2d Cir 2016) (US); *Hart v Massanari*, 266 F 3d 1155, 1176–77 (9th Cir 2001) (US) (discussing and reflecting on the qualities of a reasoned judicial ruling); *Smarter Tools Inc v Chongqing Senci Import & Export Trade Co*, Civ 18-cv-2714 (AJN), 2019 WL 1349527 at 6 (SDNY 26 March 2019) (US); see also *Exemplary Legal Writing*, The Green Bag Almanac and Reader, <http://www.greenbag.org/green_bag_press/almanacs/almanacs.html> accessed 11 April 2020 (listing well-written judicial rulings on an annual basis); International Bar Association, Annulment of Arbitral Awards by State Court: Review of National Case Law With Respect to the Conduct of the Arbitral Process (October 2018), <https://www.ibanet.org/Document/Default.aspx?DocumentUid=b4b532bb-90e1-40ab-ab3d-f730c19984fb> accessed 11 April 2020.

[101] Jeffrey J Rachlinski and Andrew J Wistrich, 'Judging the Judiciary by the Numbers: Empirical Research on Judges', (2017) 13 Ann Rev L & Soc Sci 203, 223. Some exceptions do exist. E.g. *Hart v Massanari*, 266 F3d 1155, 1170–71 (9th Cir 2001); *Flannery v Halifax Estate Agencies Ltd* [2000] 1 WLR 377, 381 (England).

[102] Born (n 14) 3044.

[103] Indeed, commentators have specifically indicated that judges need to receive more feedback on their reasoning skills. Rachlinski and Wistrich (n 103) 223 (noting that appeals are not an appropriate means of providing useful feedback).

Interestingly, the connection between law and fact is often made obvious in definitions of reasoned rulings, thus justifying the inclusion of inquiries relating to the consideration of factual authorities (evidence) in the current study. For example, one definition of a reasoned ruling states:

> [A]ll findings of fact shall be based upon sufficient competent evidence to justify same. All parties to an adjudicatory proceeding are entitled to a reasoned decision containing findings of fact and conclusions of law based upon the evidence as a whole which clearly and concisely states and explains the rationale for the decisions so that all can determine why and how a particular result was reached. The ... judge shall specify the evidence upon which the ... judge relies and state the reasons for accepting it in conformity with this section. When faced with conflicting evidence, the ... judge must adequately explain the reasons for rejecting or discrediting competent evidence. Uncontroverted evidence may not be rejected for no reason or for an irrational reason; the ... judge must identify that evidence and explain adequately the reasons for its rejection.[104]

This study sought to increase the understanding of these issues by asking judges and arbitrators to identify the hallmarks of reasoned decision or award.[105] Answers to these and other questions may help providers of judicial and arbitral education develop curricula that more closely meets the needs of the target populations.[106]

B. Comparing Domestic and International Practice

The majority of issues discussed in the preceding subsection are equally applicable to questions involving domestic and international practice. However, comparisons across the domestic-international divide raise a number of additional and unique concerns.

Perhaps the most notable of these involves the way in which many members of the lay and legal communities routinely conflate domestic and international forms of arbitration, often to the detriment of international arbitration.[107] While it can be difficult to compare 'domestic' arbitral practices in various jurisdictions to 'international' arbitral

[104] 77 Pennsylvania Statutes Annotated s 834. Although this definition arises in the context of the statutory duties of a workers' compensation board, the principles appear to apply equally in other situations, including arbitration. Jennifer Kirby, 'What Is An Award, Anyway?', (2014) 31 J Intl Arb 475, 476; see also Born (n 14) 3040–41, 3043–44.

[105] Views on this issue can vary considerably between different individuals. Cross (n 55) 1465–66; SI Strong and Jeremy Fogel, 'Judicial Education, Dispute Resolution and the Life of a Judge: A Conversation with Judge Jeremy Fogel, Director of the Federal Judicial Center', 2016 J Disp Res 259, 276(noting that individuals' 'judicial philosophy is very important, and it affects every facet of the litigation process' and recognizing that judicial philosophy varies significantly between individuals as a matter of institutional design and judicial independence); Sussman, Survey (n 66) 519 (discussing the 'applied legal storytelling movement').

[106] For example, significant debate exists regarding whether and to what extent programming regarding unconscious bias should be mandated within the judicial community. E.g. Kathleen Mahoney, 'Judicial Bias: The Ongoing Challenge', 2015 J Disp Res 43, 43; Elizabeth Thornberg, '(Un)Conscious Judging', (2019) 76 Wash & Lee L Rev 1567, 1569–70 (noting how unconscious biases affect factual inferences); ibid at 1644–46 (noting need for training on unconscious bias).

[107] Strong, Status Quo Bias (n 14) 538.

practices, empiricists have begun to study those differences, and this project seeks to contribute to the continuing developments in this field.[108]

While it would be useful to compare domestic and international judicial practices, there were no true 'international commercial courts' at the time the study was conducted, although recent developments in this regard would support future analyses of this type.[109] However, many judges who hear commercial disputes in existing national courts currently handle both domestic and international disputes, and this study sought to determine whether and to what extent judges adapted their approaches depending on the nature of the dispute.

C. Comparing Common Law and Civil Law Practice

The third major area of inquiry in this study involved purported differences between legal reasoning in common law and civil law countries. Again, many of the issues raised across the judicial-arbitral and domestic-international divides applied to the comparison of common law and civil law jurisdictions in equal measure. However, the common law-civil law dichotomy gave rise to a number of unique considerations that were important not only from a scholarly perspective but also from a practical one, since one of the primary means of resolving international commercial disputes—i.e. international commercial arbitration—consciously blends elements of the common and civil law.[110] International commercial arbitration's unique combination of common law and civil law elements is evident both in its approach to both reasoning[111] and drafting.[112]

[108] E.g. Epstein (n 80) 2029–35 (discussing empirical studies on domestic judges outside the United States and on international judges); Pietro Ortolani and Donna Shestowsky, 'Disputant Psychology in International Arbitration: What Can a Comparison with Domestic Arbitration Teach Us?' in Tony Cole (ed), *The Roles of Psychology in International Arbitration* (Wolters Kluwer 2017) 113.

[109] *International Business Courts: A European and Global Perspective* (n 21) (discussing developments in various jurisdictions).

[110] Born (n 14) 61–63, 68, 78, 99; Otto Sandrock, 'The Choice Between Forum Selection, Mediation and Arbitration Clauses: European Perspectives', (2009) 20 Am Rev Intl Arb 8, 37 (suggesting up to 90 per cent of international commercial contracts include an arbitration provision); SI Strong, *International Commercial Arbitration: A Guide for US Judges* (Federal Judicial Center 2012) 1, <https://www.fjc.gov/publications> accessed 11 April 2020.

[111] Some questions exist as to how the two traditions are balanced as a matter of arbitral procedure and reasoning. For example, the French approach to legal reasoning does not appear to be widely adopted in international commercial arbitration, despite the esteem with which France is held in the field. Marcel Fontaine, 'Drafting the Award: A Perspective From a Civil Law Jurist', (1994) 5 ICC Court Bulletin 30, 36; James M Gaitis, 'International and Domestic Arbitration Procedure: The Need for a Rule Providing a Limited Opportunity for Arbitral Reconsideration of Reasoned Awards', (2004) 15 Am Rev Intl Arb 9, 17. Instead, reasoned awards in international commercial arbitration have more frequently resembled judicial decisions generated by courts in common law countries and in civil law jurisdictions like Germany, although a shift toward civil law techniques may currently be underway, given increasing concerns within the international arbitral community about excess cost and formality of procedures. Klaus Peter Berger, 'Common Law vs. Civil Law in International Arbitration: The Beginning or the End?' 36 J Intl Arb 296, 299–300 (2019) (questioning whether the adoption of the Rules on the Efficient Conduct of Proceedings in International Arbitration (Prague Rules) reflected a movement away from the traditional view of international arbitration proceedings as a blend of common law and civil law procedures); Fontaine (n 111) 36 (noting that French-style 'whereas' clauses (*attendus*) are generally not used in international awards, even in those countries where that style of writing is common in the judicial context). But see Interim Award in ICC Case No 4131, IX *Yearbook Commercial Arbitration* 131, 135 (1984) (using *attendu* clauses, although the decision was translated from French and comes from an earlier era in international commercial arbitration).

[112] For example, most awards in international commercial arbitration run dozens of pages in length. E.g. *Contractor* (Zambia) *v Producer* (Zambia), Final Award, ICC Case No 16484, 2011, XXXIX YB Comm Arb 216

The legal literature has identified numerous differences been legal reasoning in common law and civil law jurisdictions. For example, the common law has traditionally been said to rely on inductive, analogical reasoning, whereas the civil law is considered to be more deductive and rules-based.[113] Similarly, the common law tradition has long been considered to rely heavily on oral testimony as an evidentiary matter, whereas the civil law tradition relies more on documentary evidence.[114] Furthermore, civil law jurisdictions tend to prohibit or severely discredit testimony from party witnesses, whereas common law jurisdictions routinely hear such evidence.[115] These and other differences are believed to affect not only the nature of legal reasoning but also the conduct of judicial and arbitral proceedings[116] as well as the manner in which reasoned decisions and awards are drafted.[117]

The situation is further exacerbated by suggestions that longstanding differences are no longer as pronounced, signalling a possible convergence between the two systems.[118] Indeed, while reasoned rulings may at one time have been said to be associated

(2014); Fontaine (n 111) 36; see also XXXIX YB Comm Arb 30-305 (2014) (publishing a variety of recent awards); Kai Schadbach, 'The Benefits of Comparative Law: A Continental European View', (1998) 16 Boston U Intl LJ 331, 343 n 63 (comparing German and Dutch legal decisions); Queen Mary, University of London, International Arbitral Award Writing, <https://www.qmul.ac.uk/law/postgraduate/courses/short/arbitration-award-writing/> accessed 11 April 2019 (offering a course in award writing and indicating that the mock award produced by students must exceed 5,000 words). A somewhat shorter example can be found at *Consortium member* (Italy) *v Consortium leader* (Netherlands), Final Award, ICC Case No 14630, XXXVII *Yearbook Commercial Arbitration* 90 (2012). Notably, some commentators have suggested that 'in some instances, longer is not better' when it comes to drafting arbitral awards. Born (n 14) 3041–42.

[113] Joseph Dainow (ed), *The Role of Judicial Decisions and Doctrine in Civil Law and in Mixed Jurisdictions* (Louisiana State University Press 1974); Phoebe C Ellsworth, 'Legal Reasoning', in Keith J Holyoak and Robert G Morrison (eds), *The Cambridge Handbook of Thinking and Reasoning* (Cambridge University Press 2005) 685; Strong, Fach, and Carballo (n 24) ch. 3.III.A-B; Vranken (66) *passim*; Zweigert and Kötz (n 24) chs. 7, 14, 18.

[114] Australian Law Reform Commission, Review of the Adversarial System of Litigation: Rethinking the Federal Civil Litigation System, Issues Paper (1997) 20; Javier H Rubinstein, 'International Commercial Arbitration: Reflections at the Crossroads of the Common Law and Civil Law Traditions', (2004) 5 Chi J Intl L 303, 308.

[115] Caslav Pejovic, 'Civil Law and Common Law: Two Different Paths Leading to the Same Goal', (2001) 32 Victoria U Wellington L Rev 817, 833.

[116] E.g. Marcello Gaboardi, 'How Judges Can Think: The Use of Expert's Knowledge as Proof in Civil Proceedings', (2018) 18 Global Jurist 1 (discussing fact-finding processes for common and civil law judges); Pejovic (n 115) 834–35 (discussing, for example, the common law's use of party-appointed experts versus the civil law's use of court-appointed experts as well as the single hearing in common law courts as opposed to multiple hearings in civil law courts). Some scholars have discussed 'the litigant-driven theory of decisionmaking', which posits that 'actual decisions produced by courts will be controlled largely by the strategic litigation decisions made by the parties to the action'. Cross (n 55) 1491; see also ibid 1494; Flader and Anderson (n 53) 285. This issue is particularly relevant to the extent that common law lawyers are said to favour 'adversarial' proceedings while civil law lawyers prefer 'inquisitorial' proceedings. Zweigert and Kötz (n 24) chs 7, 14, 18.

[117] For example, it is often said that civil lawyers rely more on scholarly commentary than common law lawyers, whereas common law lawyers rely more on judicial precedent. Jan K Schäfer, 'Focusing a Dispute on the Dispositive Legal and Factual Issues, or How German Arbitrators Think: An Introduction to a Traditional German Method', (2013) 2 *b-Arbitra* 333; SI Strong, *How to Write Law Essays and Exams* (5th edn, Oxford University Press 2018) chs 3–6 (discussing reasoning and drafting in England); SI Strong, *How to Write Law Exams: IRAC Perfected* (2d edn, West Academic Publishing forthcoming 2020) chs. 3–6 (discussing reasoning and drafting in the United States); Strong, Reasoned Awards (n 19) 21–54; Strong, Reasoned Decisions (n 73) 107–27; Vranken (n 66) 57–58.

[118] Guido Calabresi, *A Common Law for the Age of Statutes* (Harvard University Press 1982) 5–7; Peter de Cruz, *Comparative Law in a Changing World* (3d edn, Routledge-Cavendish 2007) 70; Neal Devins and David Klein, 'The Vanishing Common Law Judge?' (2017) 165 U Penn L Rev 595, 597; Strong, Legal Reasoning (n 68) 48–53.

primarily with the common law legal tradition, civil law jurisdictions also consider fully reasoned legal decisions to be essential to procedural justice.[119]

Interestingly, a reasoned decision from a civil law nation can not only look very different from a reasoned decision from a common law country, it can also vary significantly in comparison to other civil law decisions.[120] At one end of the spectrum lie French judgments, which are usually 'formulated in a single sentence, including several "whereas-es" (*attendus*)'.[121] Although some common law commentators appear to believe that 'French practice belies the notion that well-reasoned [apparently meaning fully reasoned] opinions are in some sense necessary',[122] French decisions have been described as being 'consistent with—and probably produced by—the primacy of text, conceptualism, and deduction, as well as the post-revolutionary caution on the part of judges not to exceed their limited powers'.[123]

As well-known as the French style may be, it is by no means standard within the civil law legal tradition. For example, it has been said that

> [w]hoever compares the arguments of a decision of a German Landgericht with those of a Dutch rechtbank will be impressed by the length and thoroughness of the German argument on the one hand, the straightforward, paper-saving decision of the Dutch court on the other. In appeal courts and before the highest courts the differences in elaborateness are even more apparent. German legal style is much more differentiated, scholarly worded; the style of Dutch courts is pragmatic . . . .[124]

Similar distinctions also appear to exist within the common law world.[125] While there is no known commentary comparing legal reasoning within the common law tradition, scholarship on comparative common law procedures identifies a number of clear differences between leading jurisdictions, particularly with respect to the taking of evidence during the pre-trial period.[126] While procedures relating to the taking of evidence are not directly related to legal reasoning, there is an indirect connection in that the amount and type of evidence that can be collected will affect the amount and type of evidence that is subsequently introduced at trial and considered by the judge.

[119] Mathilde Cohen, 'When Judges Have Reasons Not to Give Reasons: A Comparative Law Approach', (2015) 72 Wash & Lee L Rev 483, 533; Michael L Wells, '"Sociological Legitimacy" in Supreme Court Opinion', (2007) 64 Wash & Lee L Rev 1011, 1029.

[120] Fontaine (n 111) 33; Allen Shoenberger, 'Change in the European Civil Law Systems: Infiltration of the Anglo-American Case Law System of Precedent Into the Civil Law System', (2009) 55 Loyola Law Review 5, 5.

[121] Jeffrey L Friesen, 'When Common Law Courts Interpret Civil Codes', (1996) 15 Wisconsin Intl LJ 1, 8; see also Louis Goutal, 'Characteristics of Judicial Style in France, Britain and the USA', (1976) 24 Am J Comp L 43, 45.

[122] Wells (n 119) 1029.

[123] Friesen (n 121) 8.

[124] Schadbach (n 112) 343 n 63 (citing Erhard Blankenburg, 'Patterns of Legal Culture: The Netherlands Compared to Neighboring Germany', (1998) 46 Am J Comp L 1, 40, and Arthur Taylor von Mehren and James Russell Gordley, *The Civil Law System, An Introduction to the Comparative Study of Law* (2d edn, Little, Brown and Co 1977) 1140); Goutal (n 23) 45).

[125] Strong, Fach, and Carballo (n 24) chs. 3–6 (comparing various common law countries, including Australia, Canada, England, and the United States).

[126] These procedures are referred to as 'discovery' in the United States and 'disclosure' in most other common law jurisdictions. SI Strong, 'Jurisdictional Discovery in United States Federal Courts', (2010) 67 Wash & Lee L Rev 489, 501–02, 510–11.

The variations within both the common law and civil law traditions suggest that it may be difficult or even impossible to identify differences based solely on legal families. Instead, it may be that it is only possible to discuss the extent to which a particular jurisdiction reflects standard assumptions about common law and civil law techniques. Nevertheless, this project tests both the standard understanding of common law and civil law attributes as well as allegations about a potential convergence between the two legal traditions.

D. Background and Demographic Considerations

Traditional analyses of legal reasoning assume that the reasoning process is relatively standard within a particular country or legal community. However, experts in feminist and critical race theory have challenged the concept of a unitary norm involving legal reasoning,[127] raising questions as to whether legal reasoning in commercial disputes varies as a result of demographic considerations involving gender, age, seniority, or race.[128]

Empirical studies relating to judicial and arbitral appointment rates suggest that bias relating to certain demographic attributes does in fact exist. For example, numerous studies have shown that women have been appointed as judges and arbitrators far less frequently than men,[129] which suggests a conscious or unconscious assumption that women approach legal reasoning differently than men.[130] Other studies have suggested that parties prefer to appoint older and/or more 'experienced' arbitrators or former judges to arbitral tribunals,[131] presumably based on the belief that older individuals

[127] E.g. Bridget J Crawford and Anthony C Infanti (eds), *Feminist Judgments: Rewritten Tax Opinions* (Cambridge University Press 2017); Kimberlé Williams Crenshaw, 'Twenty Years of Critical Race Theory: Looking Back to Move Forward', (2011) 43 Connecticut L Rev 1253, 1253–54, 1260; Richard Delgado and Jean Stefancic, *Critical Race Theory: An Introduction* (3d edn, NYU Press 2017) 3; Rosemary Hunter, Clare McGlynn, and Erika Rackley (eds), *Feminist Judgments: From Theory to Practice* (Hart Publishing 2010); Kathryn M Stanchi, Linda L Berger, and Bridget J Crawford (eds), *Feminist Judgments: Rewritten Opinions of the United States Supreme Court* (Cambridge University Press 2016).

[128] Some studies do exist, but they often focus on outcome rather than on the constituent elements of legal reasoning and thus could be affected by a variety of influences. Rachlinski and Wistrich (n 103) 205–08.

[129] Franck and others, Demographics (n 50) 95–115; Susan D Franck and others, 'The Diversity Challenge: Exploring the "Invisible College" of International Arbitration', (2015) 53 Colum J Transnatl L 429 (Franck and others, Diversity); Malia Reddick, Michael J Nelson, and Rachel Payne Caufield, 'Racial and Gender Diversity on State Courts', (2009) 48 Judges' J 28; Organisation for Economic Co-operation and Development (OECD), Women in the Judiciary: Working Towards a Legal System Reflective of Society (March 2019), <https://www.oecd.org/gender/data/women-in-the-judiciary-working-towards-a-legal-system-reflective-of-society.htm> accessed 11 April 2020.

[130] Some academics have studied whether and to what extent gender-based differences arise in legal reasoning. E.g. Rosemary Hunter, 'More Than Just a Different Face? Judicial Diversity and Decision-Making', (2015) 68 Current L Probs 119.

[131] Stephen J Choi, Jill E Frisch, and AC Pritchard, 'The Influence of Arbitrator Background and Representation on Arbitration Outcomes', (2014) 9 Va L & Bus Rev 43, 76 (considering age among domestic arbitrators); Franck and others, Diversity (n 129) 454 (considering age among international arbitrators); Stipanowich and Lamare (n 43) 64 (discussing the appointment of experienced lawyers and former judges as 'the prevailing norm' in commercial arbitration); Thomas J Stipanowich and Zachary P Ulrich, 'Commercial Arbitration and Settlement: Empirical Insights Into the Roles Arbitrators Play', (2014) 6 YB Arb & Med 1, 2 n10; E Norman Veasey and Grover C Brown, 'An Overview of the General Counsel's Decision Making on Dispute Resolution Strategies in Complex Business

and former judges have superior legal reasoning skills. However, there is no known research indicating that judges and arbitrators change their approach to legal reasoning, for better or worse, as a result of the passage of time or that former judges provide a different or better quality of justice than arbitrators. Indeed, many judges appear unaware of arbitral norms before entering the field, suggesting that they may not function as well as individuals who have specialized in arbitration throughout their careers.[132]

While this project did not consider these types of issues in detail, some of the material collected in this project will be used to support future studies involving the role that demographic considerations such as gender, age, and level of experience play on legal reasoning.[133] Some of the background and demographic information reported here may also prove useful to other scholars working in this area of law, both as theoreticians and empiricists.

Having established the scholarly foundations for the current project, it is time to move to a detailed analysis of the international survey, which was the first element of the empirical study. That discussion is found in the next chapter.

Transactions', (2015) 7 Bus Lawyer 407, 413, 416. Some studies consider whether any difference in outcomes arises depending on whether the arbitrator is a former or retired judge. Chandrasekher and Horton (n 49) 103.

[132] For example, Lord Neuberger, former President of the Supreme Court of the United Kingdom, stated in a public address that he believed that judges who became arbitrators might be inclined not to follow the law, as they did on the bench, which suggested a lack of familiarity with the requirement, in virtually all commercial arbitrations, that arbitrators follow the law. 'Lord Neuberger on Judge-Arbitrators, and on Brexit', CIArb News (26 April 2019) <https://www.ciarb.org/news/london-branch-keynote-speech-lord-neuberger-on-judge-arbitrators-and-on-brexit/> accessed 11 April 2020.

[133] SI Strong, 'Does Gender Affect Legal Reasoning in Commercial Dispute Resolution? An Empirical Analysis' (forthcoming); SI Strong, 'Does Experience Matter? An Empirical Analysis of Seniority and Number of Disputes Heard on Legal Reasoning in Commercial Dispute Resolution' (forthcoming).

2

International Survey on Legal Reasoning

I. Introduction

The first of the three empirical elements to consider involves a large-scale, international survey of judges' and arbitrators' views of legal reasoning in commercial dispute resolution. This portion of the research project sought to identify general practices and motivations regarding legal reasoning to determine whether and to what extent the theoretical assumptions and conventional wisdom reflected in the legal literature were correct.[1] Many of the questions in the survey mirrored those asked in the semi-structured interviews, which allowed a certain amount of validity testing across the two studies. The survey also addressed issues considered in the quantitative (coding) exercise, thereby facilitating further triangulation of results. A copy of the survey instrument is provided in Appendix I.[2]

The survey was designed to be both broad and deep so as to generate a significant amount of novel information. The diversity of qualitative and quantitative (statistical) information produced by the survey provides rich fodder for comparative analysis, so much so that it is impossible to discuss all possible permutations in exhaustive detail in this text. While the author will use the underlying data to conduct analyses on a number of related topics in the future,[3] it is hoped that other scholars will use the material contained in this chapter as the basis for their own analyses. In order to facilitate that task, the text not only presents the underlying data and statistical analyses in 41 detailed tables, it also provides additional comments generated by respondents through open text boxes offered throughout the survey. The chapter also offers an extensive discussion of the underlying methodology and demographic make-up of the survey population to assist with evaluation of the material presented herein.

[1] Ch. 1.I.

[2] Providing copies of research instruments is considered a best practice in empirical research. Susan D Franck, 'Empiricism and International Law: Insights for Investment Treaty Dispute Resolution', (2008) 48 Va J Intl L 767, 787–88.

[3] E.g. SI Strong, 'Does Experience Matter? An Empirical Analysis of Seniority and Number of Disputes Heard on Legal Reasoning in Commercial Dispute Resolution' (forthcoming) (Strong, Experience); SI Strong, 'Does Gender Affect Legal Reasoning in Commercial Dispute Resolution? An Empirical Analysis' (forthcoming) (Strong, Gender); SI Strong, 'The Effect of Motion Practice on the Nature of Dispute Resolution and the Creation of Precedent: An Empirical Analysis' (forthcoming); SI Strong, 'The Fallacy of Transparency: How to Address Arbitral and Judicial (Non)Cooperation With Independent Scholarship' (forthcoming) (Strong, Transparency). Some such works are already available. E.g. SI Strong, 'Legal Authorities and Comparative Law in International Commercial Arbitration: Best Practices Versus Empirically Determined Actual Practices', (2020 forthcoming) 1 Ius Comparatum; SI Strong, 'Legal Reasoning in International Commercial Disputes: Empirically Testing the Common Law-Civil Law Divide', in Mélida Hodgson and Antonio Crivellaro (eds), *Dossier XVII: Legal Reasoning in International Commercial Arbitration* (ICC Institute of World Business Law 2020) 41 (Strong, Legal Reasoning).

The chapter is organized as follows. The discussion begins by discussing methodological and demographic information before moving on to the substantive findings of the study. The presentation of the survey findings includes subsections concerning the use of legal authorities, the use of factual authorities (evidence), the reasoning process and the drafting process before concluding with several questions on judicial and arbitration education. Interim conclusions are offered at the end of each section, with a more general conclusion at the end of the chapter. The discussion contains a variety of cross-references to the semi-structured interviews and coding exercise, with additional overarching conclusions appearing in Chapter 5.

II. Methodology

As a general rule, the credibility of any empirical research study turns on the quality of the methodology and how well the study addresses the underlying research question.[4] In this case, the research question considered how judges and arbitrators conduct legal reasoning in complex commercial disputes in both national and international settings.[5] The data generated from the study is expected not only to help scholars, judges, arbitrators, and parties understand common practices in the field (which may not be the same as best practices), but also to help providers of judicial and arbitral education determine the type of programming that is most needed by judges and arbitrators.

When considering empirical methodology, it is useful to differentiate between general concerns and practices, on the one hand, and special issues related to the filtering of data to generate comparisons between relevant groups (in this case, judges and arbitrators; domestic disputes and international disputes; and common law and civil law respondents), on the other. These two matters are considered separately in the following subsections.

A. General Methodological Concerns

The survey addressed the core research interests through a series of questions focusing on the use of legal authorities, factual and evidentiary issues, the legal reasoning process, drafting reasoned decisions or awards; and judicial and arbitral education involving legal reasoning. The content and structure of the survey questions were very similar to those asked as part of the semi-structured interviews so as to allow triangulation of research findings.[6]

Prior to beginning the survey, respondents were advised that the study focused exclusively on commercial disputes, which was defined as business-to-business or

[4] Ch. 1.II.

[5] Anselm Strauss and Juliet Corbin, *Basics of Qualitative Research: Techniques and Procedures for Developing Grounded Theory* (Sage Publishing 1998) 41 (discussing the need for precisely formulated research questions).

[6] Ch. 1.II; cf Appx. I–Appx. II.

commercial state entity-to-business disputes. The survey instructions also defined a reasoned decision or award as including but not limited to decisions or awards with findings of fact and conclusions of law and defined an international dispute as a matter where at least two parties came from different countries; where the property in dispute was located in a country different than that of the disputants; or where performance or enforcement was anticipated in a country different than that of the disputants.[7] These definitions were identical to those used in the semi-structured interviews and coding exercise.

The survey instructions indicated that all responses to survey questions should focus solely on the individual's experience as a judge or arbitrator of commercial disputes, even if the respondent also acted as a judge or arbitrator in other types of matters. In particular, respondents were told not to discuss their experience with investor-state arbitration or consumer arbitration in their answers.

The survey was conducted online and was made available to judges and arbitrators from around the world, including individuals from both the common law and civil law traditions. Although the survey was entirely anonymous, it did ask for certain general, non-identifying information about respondents to allow for analysis across certain demographic lines.

Anonymity was considered the best methodological choice for several reasons. First and foremost, judges and arbitrators are often bound by an ongoing duty of confidentiality with respect to disputes, parties, and/or deliberation processes, and requiring respondents to identify themselves might have been seen as a breach of that particular duty. Furthermore, judges and arbitrators both monitor their public statements carefully so as to avoid saying anything that might preclude them from hearing a future dispute, and, in the case of arbitrators who also work as advocates, from representing a future client. As a result, allowing anonymous responses was believed to increase sample size and allow a higher degree of candour from participants while also diminishing the likelihood of certain types of measurement errors.[8]

The survey was aimed at judges and arbitrators from all over the world and allowed participation from those who specialized in domestic disputes as well as those who specialized in international (cross-border) disputes.[9] This approach was appropriate given the goal of comparing practices across both the domestic–international and common law–civil law divides.[10]

The survey consisted of 73 questions in total, although the use of conditional branching (skip logic) meant that not every respondent was provided with an opportunity to answer every question.[11] The survey was entirely voluntary, and participants

[7] This definition was based on section 202 of the US Federal Arbitration Act. 9 USC s 202.

[8] Matthias Schonlau, Ronald D Fricker, and Marc N Elliott, *Conducting Research Surveys via E-Mail and the Web* (RAND Corporation 2002) 16.

[9] Individuals who indicated that they had worked solely as investment arbitrators were excluded from the survey, since investment matters did not fall within the definition of a commercial dispute.

[10] While it might be useful in future to study judicial and arbitral practices in jurisdictions that do not fall within the common law–civil law dichotomy, those distinctions were beyond the scope of the current survey.

[11] Conditional branching, also known as skip logic, automatically directs survey participants to different series of questions, depending on how participants respond to certain preliminary questions.

were allowed to bypass individual questions or abandon the survey at any time. While surveys that allow participants to skip individual questions can experience certain types of non-response errors, this technique is believed to increase the likelihood that respondents will continue with the survey after facing a difficult question and avoids skewing the data by forcing participants to select a response with which they are uncomfortable.[12] Allowing participants to abandon the survey is also consistent with the need to respect participants' personal autonomy, a key ethical principle in human subject research. Statistical analyses took the varying response rates into account by conducting calculations on a question-by-question basis.

Of the 73 questions, 67 required participants to choose among various pre-existing answers, with 20 of those questions allowing participants to explain their answer in a written text box. Six questions did not provide any pre-existing alternatives but instead asked participants to respond in their own words.

Questions with pre-existing answers followed several different patterns. Some questions required participants to choose one alternative among several (as in cases where participants were asked to choose their primary form of employment or identify their home jurisdiction). Other questions used a Likert scale, which required respondents to select an answer from a range of alternatives of varying intensity, or asked participants to rank some or all of several possible alternatives.

Questions were designed to test conventional wisdom about legal reasoning in commercial disputes and thus offered pre-existing alternatives that have been frequently discussed in the legal literature.[13] However, in many cases respondents were also allowed to expand upon the pre-existing options by checking 'other' and providing additional information in their own words.

The results are reported in the following narrative and in 41 different tables interspersed throughout this chapter. Most of the data is presented in terms of weighted averages[14] or percentage of population.[15] In most cases, responses were subsequently analysed across three separate criteria: (1) the relative standing of individual options within individual cohorts (i.e. judges only; arbitrators only; domestic disputes only; international disputes only; common law respondents only; and civil law respondents only); (2) the relative standing of individual options between comparative cohorts (i.e. judges versus arbitrators; domestic disputes versus international disputes; and common law respondents versus civil law respondents); and (3) the statistical significance of the difference between intensity markings of comparative cohorts.

Cross-group intensity comparisons appear in separate columns in the various tables and were evaluated under either a t-statistical test, which compares the averages

[12] Schonlau, Fricker, and Elliott (n 8) 16–18.

[13] Ch. 1.III.

[14] Weighted averages were obtained by multiplying the number of individuals who selected a particular option by the corresponding rating value (1 to 5), adding the results of those calculations and dividing that result by the total number of responses to the question.

[15] Percentages were obtained by dividing the number of respondents who chose a particular option by the total population answering that question. Ranked responses are presented based on percentage of population of that particular question.

(means) of two independent populations (μ_1 and μ_2) along a single variable to determine whether any difference exists other than that attributable to chance,[16] or a two-tailed z-statistical test, which compares the proportional responses of two independent populations (μ_1 and μ_2) along a single variable to determine whether any difference exists other than that attributable to chance.[17] In both cases, the null hypothesis (H_0) anticipated that the comparative cohorts were the same (H_0: $\mu_1 - \mu_2 = 0$ or, equivalently, $\mu_1 = \mu_2$), while the alternate hypothesis (H_1) was that the comparative cohorts were not the same (H_1: $\mu_1 \neq \mu_2$). Statistical significance was deemed to exist in cases with an alpha (*a1*) level of $p<.05$ or lower.[18] The study reports *a1* levels of $p<.05$ (designated in tables by a single asterisk), $p<.01$ (designated by two asterisks) and $p<.001$ (designated by three asterisks).[19] A similar approach was adopted in the analysis of coded decisions and awards to facilitate cross-study comparisons.[20]

The methodology adopted herein complied with best practices in a number of ways. For example, the survey, which remained open for responses from 19 January 2018 through 1 May 2018,[21] was made available to potential respondents through a website whose address was distributed to judges and arbitrators with the assistance of hundreds of judicial and arbitral organizations from around the world.[22] Although electronic surveys can be problematic in situations where potential participants find it difficult to access the website in question,[23] those types of concerns did not exist in the current study because the target population was extremely likely to have easy access to both computers and the internet. In fact, experts consider internet surveys to be particularly useful in cases where participants have adequate access to computers, since the accuracy associated with electronic means of data collection can minimize concerns regarding data validation, skip pattern errors and transcription.[24] Website distribution methods have been considered particularly appropriate in cases where,

[16] Eighteen questions used a t-test analysis. Tables 2.5–3.9, 3.12, 3.14–3.19, 3.22, 3.24, 3.28, 3.35, and 3.41. T-statistics were calculated via Medcalc. Medcalc <https://www.medcalc.org/calc/comparison_of_means.php> accessed 11 April 2020. Because Medcalc would not allow calculations where the standard deviation was zero (as it was in a few circumstances due to small sample size), those t-statistics involving a standard deviation of zero were calculated with a standard deviation of .0001.

[17] Nineteen questions used a two-tailed z-test analysis. Tables 2.10, 3.11, 3.13, 3.20, 3.21, 3.23, 3.25, 3.26, 3.29–3.34, 3.36–3.40. The two-tailed test is appropriate in situations, as here, where there is no pre-established norm against which subsequent data can be tested. Z-test statistics were calculated via Social Science Statistics. Social Science Statistics <https://www.socscistatistics.com/tests/ztest/default2.aspx> accessed 11 April 2020.

[18] Statistical significance refers to 'the likelihood, or probability, that a statistic derived from a sample represents some genuine phenomenon in the population'. Timothy C Urdan, *Statistics in Plain English* (Routledge 2005) 50 (discussing statistical analysis in empirical legal research); see also Lee Epstein and Gary King, 'The Rules of Inference', (2002) 51 U Chi L Rev 1, 60; W Mark C Weidemaier, 'Judging-Lite: How Arbitrators Use and Create Precedent', (2012) 90 N Carolina L Rev 1091, 1091.

[19] A *p* value of .05 or less means there is a 5 per cent likelihood (or less) that the difference between the two populations is attributable to chance, while a *p* level of .01 means there is a 1 per cent likelihood that the difference between the two populations is attributable to chance. *P* levels of .001 are even more robust, meaning that there is a .1 per cent likelihood that the difference between the two populations is random. Robert W Frick, 'The Appropriate Use of Null Hypothesis Testing', (1996) 1 Psych Methods 379–90 (discussing the appropriate *p* value associated with null hypothesis testing).

[20] Ch. 4.II.B.

[21] This period exceeded the ten-day response period that experts in internet and web-based survey design believe is necessary to produce adequate data. Schonlau, Fricker, and Elliott (n 8) 28.

[22] Appx. I (containing the instrument used in the survey).

[23] Schonlau, Fricker, and Elliott (n 8) 14–15, 29.

[24] Ibid 30.

as here, the population in question is electronically connected and is otherwise hard to reach.[25] Indeed, the large-scale, international nature of this study would have made individualized contact impossible.

Concerns about the validity of the research could arise as a result of the fact that the participants were self-selected. However, several studies have concluded that 'self-selected respondents give higher-quality responses than randomly selected respondents',[26] which supports the methodology adopted in the current survey.

Finally, potential problems might have arisen with respect to the lack of control over the ultimate distribution of the survey. For example, issues with uncontrolled distribution methods can arise because there is no way to verify that all respondents come from the target population.[27] Errors can also be generated as a result of malicious or repeat responders. However, in this case, the survey software precluded the possibility of repeat takers from the same computer, and the subject matter of the survey was not one that would likely attract persons intent on skewing the results.[28]

Although the survey methodology complied with best practices in social sciences, some concerns did arise. The first issue involves language. The survey was conducted in English, which was considered appropriate given the widespread use of English in the field of international commercial dispute resolution.[29] However, this approach created a potential bias toward the common law, since most common law jurisdictions are also English-speaking jurisdictions, and toward internationally oriented civil law lawyers, who would be more likely to speak English.[30] This distinction could result in sampling errors, since it is not currently known whether and to what extent the opinions of non-English-speaking judges and arbitrators differ from the opinions of English-speaking judges and arbitrators with respect to the matters addressed in the survey instrument.[31]

The second issue involves problems gaining access to potential participants. Although the survey was distributed to hundreds of judicial and arbitral organizations in order to generate a robust and diverse respondent base, numerous organizations declined to forward information about the survey to their members or only agreed to forward that information if the organization was able to exercise a certain degree of control over the content and/or publication of the subsequent analysis.[32] These requests

[25] Ibid 34 (discussing the usefulness of convenience surveys).

[26] Ibid 32; see also ibid 17 (suggesting that the difference in the levels of candour may be particularly marked for 'surveys on sensitive topics or for surveys that contain sensitive questions', as is arguably the case here, where confidentiality is a concern).

[27] Schonlau, Fricker, and Elliott (n 8) 35.

[28] But see ibid (suggesting that sophisticated users can overcome survey software intended to block repeat responses).

[29] Ignacio Gómez-Palacio and Garrett Epps, 'International Commercial Arbitration: Two Cultures in a State of Courtship and Potential Marriage of Convenience', (2009) 20 Am Rev Intl Arb 235, 244–45 (noting that English is the predominant language in the field of international commercial arbitration). English has also become increasingly popular in international commercial litigation, with several national courts adopting English-language procedures. Xandra E Kramer and John Sorabji (eds), *International Business Courts: A European and Global Perspective* (Eleven International Publishing 2019).

[30] Schonlau, Fricker, and Elliott (n 8) 13 (discussing problems when the population of inference (in this case, both common law and civil law judges and arbitrators) is not the same as the target population (in this case, both common law and civil law judges and arbitrators who speak English)).

[31] Ibid 15.

[32] Similar problems occurred with respect to access to arbitral awards. Ch. 4.II.A.

were rejected, and the study went forward without the participation of those organizations. While this approach protected the independence of the study, the obstacles to survey distribution resulted in some unevenness in the number of responses from certain groups and regions.[33] Nevertheless, the size of the study was large enough to produce reliable information across the desired data points.

The difficulties experienced during this study generated some interesting questions for future researchers about whether and to what extent judicial and arbitral institutions can and should assist with independent scholarly research.[34] As empirical research becomes more prevalent, these organizations will doubtless receive an increasing number of requests from scholars studying different aspects of the civil justice system. While no one suggests that judges and arbitrators can or should agree to participate in every survey or interview opportunity that comes their way, formal or informal policies that either prohibit scholars from gaining access to these individuals or interfere with the analysis and dissemination of research results are extremely problematic. While it is beyond the scope of the current research to provide precise recommendations on what practices should be adopted, it would be beneficial if judicial and arbitral organizations reconsidered their existing approach to research requests so as to allow a reasonable number of legitimate, independent studies to be conducted each year.[35]

B. Comparative Methodology

Although this chapter includes data based on the survey population as a whole, most of the analysis involves comparisons across three different axes that are of particular interest to this study: the judicial–arbitral divide (abbreviated in individual tables below as J–A); the domestic–international divide (abbreviated as D–I); and the common law–civil law divide (abbreviated as C–C). The relevant sub-populations were generated by filtering the data on specific questions. For example, judicial and arbitral cohorts were created by filtering answers on question one, which asked whether the respondent was currently acting as an arbitrator, and question two, which asked whether the respondent was currently acting as a judge. Although this approach eliminated answers

[33] For example, more arbitrators than judges participated in the survey because several leading judicial organizations declined to forward solicitation information to their members. Among arbitrators, the highest response rate came from those based in the United States, since the American Arbitration Association and the International Centre for Dispute Resolution were the only arbitral institutions that agreed to forward information about the survey to their entire rosters without asking to exert control over the analysis or dissemination of the survey results.

[34] Some of these issues will be discussed in future articles. E.g. Strong, Transparency (n 3).

[35] While some within the judicial education community have advocated independent judicial research, many of those organizations are closely aligned with the judiciary and therefore cannot be considered entirely independent. James B Eaglin and Matthew Alex Ward, 'Enhancing the Administration of Justice and Strengthening Judicial Independence Through Independent, Judicial-Based Research Centers', (2014) 7 J L Tech Risk Mgmt 77, 92–93; SI Strong, 'Judicial Education and Regulatory Capture: Does the Current System of Educating Judges Promote a Well-Functioning Judiciary and Adequately Serve the Public Interest?' 2015 J Disp Res 1, 4–6 (Strong, Judicial Education).

from respondents who were not currently acting as judges or arbitrators but who had experience in one or both capacities, it was considered the best way to compare judicial and arbitral practices. Notably, even though the two cohorts are independent (in that no one in the judges-only population is also in the arbitrators-only population), some individuals were expected to have had experience as both judges and arbitrators, either sequentially or simultaneously.[36] That phenomenon was not considered problematic, since it reflects the reality of contemporary commercial practice.

The domestic and international cohorts were derived by filtering the responses on question 24, which asked respondents to identify whether they would be discussing domestic disputes or international disputes.[37] While some individuals with experience in both international and domestic disputes likely adopt behaviours that are reflective of both specialties, that phenomenon was again anticipated and accepted as a routine feature of commercial dispute resolution. Furthermore, detailed analysis of the two cohorts demonstrated that the respondents' experience was primarily in the area they chose to address. For example, more than half of the respondents who chose to focus on domestic disputes had no recent experience in international matters, with the remaining individuals indicating relatively small international caseloads.[38] A similar phenomenon was seen in the international cohort, with half of the respondents indicating that they handled international matters between 81 and 100 per cent of the time (the highest possible category), with the remaining individuals indicating relatively robust international caseloads.[39]

Although international commercial arbitrators often work simultaneously as investment arbitrators, the two processes differ in several key regards.[40] The survey excluded any individual who worked exclusively as an investment arbitrator, although it allowed those who worked in both investment and commercial matters to participate, so long as the respondent focused exclusively on commercial disputes when completing the survey.[41] While arbitrators who work in both investment and commercial could be affected by behavioural norms developed in investment proceedings, those influences

[36] Further analysis of the data discovered that only one individual who was currently acting as a judge had also acted as an arbitrator. Conversely, 10 per cent of those currently working as arbitrators had also worked as judges.

[37] The proportion of respondents who indicated that they would be discussing domestic commercial disputes was 66 per cent, as compared to 34 per cent who indicated that they would be discussing international commercial disputes.

[38] When asked to identify the percentage of disputes handled over the last three years that were international in scope, 52 per cent of the respondents who chose to focus on domestic disputes indicated that they had handled no international matters. Of the remaining respondents, 35 per cent handled international matters between 1 and 20 per cent of the time, 8 per cent handled international matters between 21 and 40 per cent of the time and 4 per cent handled international matters between 41 and 60 per cent of the time.

[39] When asked to identify the percentage of disputes handled over the last three years that were international in scope, 50 per cent of the respondents who chose to focus on international disputes indicated that they had handled international matters between 81 and 100 per cent of the time. Of the remaining respondents, 23 per cent handled international matters between 61 and 80 per cent of the time, 12 per cent handled international matters between 41 and 60 per cent of the time, 8 per cent handled international matters between 21 and 40 per cent of the time and 6 per cent handled international matters between 1 and 20 per cent of the time.

[40] SI Strong, *International Commercial Arbitration: A Guide for U.S. Judges* (Federal Judicial Center 2012) 3, <https://www.fjc.gov/publications> accessed 11 April 2020.

[41] The data indicated that 36 per cent of the respondents who chose to focus on international commercial disputes had experience as an arbitrator in both investment and commercial disputes.

are a standard part of international commercial arbitration, thereby justifying the inclusion of individuals with both types of experience.

Although this study compares domestic disputes to international disputes in very general terms, domestic dispute resolution can differ significantly from country to country. While it is beyond the scope of the current study to distinguish between domestic practice in individual jurisdictions, the survey nevertheless asked those who chose to discuss domestic disputes (N=284) to identify the jurisdictions that they would address in order to identify any relevant trends. Of these individuals, 91 per cent discussed proceedings in common law countries (primarily the United States), 7 per cent discussed proceedings in civil law countries and 2 per cent discussed proceedings in countries other than those falling within the common law/civil law dichotomy.[42] Although the emphasis on the United States was unfortunate in some ways, the result was likely due to the fact that the American Arbitration Association was the only domestic institution among the hundreds of judicial and arbitral organizations that were approached that agreed to circulate solicitation information to its roster of arbitrators.

Notably, the majority of those who chose to discuss domestic disputes (83 per cent) were not currently acting as judges. Of those who were discussing domestic disputes and who were currently acting as arbitrators, 56 per cent indicated that they handled only domestic matters and 43 per cent handled both domestic and international matters, even though they focused on domestic disputes in the survey.

The third axis of comparison involved the comparison of respondents from common law and civil law traditions.[43] The data was filtered on the basis of responses regarding the primary jurisdiction in which the respondent was qualified as a judge or lawyer. Although this approach led to the exclusion of individuals who were not qualified as a judge or lawyer, this approach was considered appropriate because those neutrals who are not qualified as judges or lawyers are not typically engaging in legal reasoning that reflects a common law or civil law bias.[44] Furthermore, filtering on the basis of the place of the respondents' legal qualification was considered better than filtering on the basis of the place where the respondent was primarily based, since some individuals work in a place different than that where they are qualified.

[42] Once the filter was applied, the common law countries represented, calculated to the hundredth of a percentage point based on the total number of respondents to illuminate the appropriate detail, included Australia (0.35%), Canada (2.12% (all discussing provinces and territories other than Quebec)), Hong Kong (0.35%), India (0.35%), Singapore (0.35%), Trinidad and Tobago (0.35%), the United Kingdom (2.47% (all discussing England and Wales)), and the United States (85.10%). The civil law countries represented included Belgium (0.71%), Brazil (2.47%), Colombia (0.35%), Germany (0.35%), Italy (0.35%), Mexico (0.71%), Netherlands (0.35%), Poland (0.35%), Spain (1.06%), and Venezuela (0.35%). The countries represented outside the common law/civil law dichotomy included Lebanon (0.35%), Mauritius (0.35%), and the United Arab Emirates (1.41%).

[43] While this comparison does exclude respondents from countries other than those falling within the common law–civil law paradigm, those responses are captured elsewhere.

[44] Many of these individuals are likely engineers, surveyors or business people working as arbitrators. Thomas J Stipanowich and Zachary P Ulrich, 'Arbitration in Evolution: Current Practices and Perspectives of Experienced Commercial Arbitrators', (2014) 25 Am Rev Intl Arb 395, 440–44 (noting use of non-lawyer arbitrators in international commercial disputes appears to be waning). However, the survey did not seek to identify the area of these individuals' substantive expertise.

The individual common law countries represented (N=322), calculated to the hundredth of a percentage point based on the total number of respondents indicating they were qualified in a common law jurisdiction, included Australia (0.62%), the Bahamas (0.31%), Canada (4.35%), Hong Kong (0.93%), India (0.62%), Singapore (0.31%), the United Kingdom (6.83%), and the United States (86.02%). Ninety-nine per cent of the common law respondents were currently acting as arbitrators (of which 45 per cent were exclusively dedicated to domestic matters, 6 per cent were exclusively dedicated to international commercial matters, and 48 per cent were dedicated to both international commercial and investment matters), and 19 per cent were currently acting as judges. Ten per cent indicated that they had worked as both a judge and an arbitrator, either simultaneously or at different points of their careers. Fifteen individuals had worked simultaneously as a judge and arbitrator.

The individual civil law countries represented (N=83), calculated to the hundredth of a percentage point based on the total number of respondents indicating they were qualified in a civil law jurisdiction, included Argentina (2.41%), Austria (2.41%), Belarus (2.41%), Belgium (7.23%), Bolivia (1.20%), Brazil (7.23%), Colombia (2.41%), Denmark (1.20%), Egypt (1.20%), Finland (1.20%), France (13.25%), Germany (9.64%), Greece (1.20%), Guatemala (1.20%), Italy (4.82%), Latvia (1.20%), Mexico (3.61%), the Netherlands (1.20%), Norway (1.20%), Paraguay (1.20%), Peru (1.20%), Spain (8.43%), Sweden (3.61%), Switzerland (14.46%), Turkey (1.20%), Uzbekistan (1.20%), and Venezuela (2.41%). Ninety-five per cent of the civil law respondents were currently acting as arbitrators (of which 4 per cent were exclusively dedicated to domestic matters, 27 per cent were exclusively dedicated to international commercial matters, and 65 per cent were dedicated to both international commercial and investment matters), and 18 per cent were also currently acting as judges. Eleven per cent indicated that they had worked as both a judge and an arbitrator, either simultaneously or at different points of their careers. Four individuals had worked simultaneously as a judge and arbitrator.

III. Demographics of Participants

Before discussing the substantive findings, it is helpful to describe the demographics of the survey participants, both to provide some independently relevant data and to set subsequent discussions in context.[45] In this section, as in others, percentages have been rounded up or down to the nearest percentage point, unless otherwise indicated. As a result, the reported data may not always add up to 100 per cent. Any deviations that occur are quite small (in the range of 1 to 2 per cent) and arise only rarely.

The survey generated responses from 465 participants with very diverse characteristics. The sample size is robust and well within the norms prescribed for best practices in

[45] Additional demographic information is found in the preceding section. Ch. 2.II.B. Although all of the demographic data was self-reported, there is no reason to believe that any of the participants falsified their responses, particularly since the study was entirely anonymous. Schonlau, Fricker, and Elliott (n 8) 17, 32.

the field. Indeed, other international surveys have generated fewer responses and have still been considered valid.[46]

A. Judicial and Arbitral Roles

Commercial dispute resolution is a relatively fluid field, with individuals moving between judicial and arbitral roles at different points in their careers. The following discussion sets forth the number of respondents who can be classified as judges, arbitrators or both and describes the nature of the work that respondents do so as to assist with the analysis of the survey findings. However, the information contained in this subsection also offers important insights into a number of independent issues relating to judicial and arbitral performance, including those relating to possible career paths within and between the various professions. For example, questions have arisen about whether the lucrative nature of commercial arbitration is jeopardizing the optional operation of the judiciary by luring away senior members of the bench.[47] Concerns have also been raised about whether and to what extent judges, particularly those sitting on international tribunals such as the International Court of Justice and the Iran-US Claims Tribunal, can or should be allowed to act simultaneously as arbitrators in private commercial matters.[48]

The first three questions on the survey asked about the respondents' role as a judge and/or arbitrator. According to the results, 12 per cent of the respondents had worked as both a judge and an arbitrator, either at the same time or at different points in their career. However, 80 per cent of the general population were not sitting as judges at the time they took the survey but were instead only acting as arbitrators. Of the 20 per cent of the general population who were sitting as judges at the time of the survey, 9 per cent were acting as international (supranational) judges, 7 per cent were acting as national (federal) judges, and 3 per cent were acting as local or state (sub-federal) judges.

Only 2 per cent of the general population were not currently acting as an arbitrator. Of the remaining 98 per cent of respondents who were currently acting as

[46] Ibid 36 (discussing one international electronic survey that only generated 80 responses from 14 countries on 4 continents, with 40 per cent of the respondents coming from one country); Loukas Mistelis, 'International Arbitration—Corporate Attitudes and Practices – 12 Perceptions Tested: Myths, Data and Analysis Research Report', (2004) 15 Am Rev Intl Arb 525, 534 (involving 103 participants for a study of international commercial arbitration); see also Schonlau, Fricker, and Elliott (n 8) 85–86.

[47] For example, increasing numbers of federal judges in the United States are now choosing to retire completely from the bench, sometimes at a relatively young age, so that they may take up lucrative work as an arbitrator rather than working as a senior judge, thereby depriving the US federal judiciary of important judicial resources. Reynolds Holding, 'Judges' Action Cast Shadow on Court's Integrity / Lure of High-Paying Jobs as Arbitrators May Compromise Impartiality', San Francisco Gate (9 October 2001), <https://www.sfgate.com/news/article/Judges-action-cast-shadow-on-court-s-integrity-2870890.php> accessed 11 April 2020; James Middlemiss, 'Life After the Bench: Retired Judges Embrace ADR', Fin Post (19 March 2014), <https://business.financialpost.com/legal-post/life-after-the-bench-retired-judges-embrace-adr> accessed 11 April 2020.

[48] The president of the International Court of Justice banned that practice in late 2018. 'Judges of the International Court of Justice Decide to No Longer Participate as Arbitrators in ISDS Cases', Investment Treaty News (21 December 2018), <https://www.iisd.org/itn/2018/12/21/judges-of-the-international-court-of-justice-decide-to-no-longer-participate-as-arbitrators-in-isds-cases/> accessed 11 April 2020.

arbitrators, either simultaneously with their duties as judges or solely as arbitrators, 35 per cent were acting only as domestic commercial arbitrators, 10 per cent were acting only as international commercial arbitrators, and 52 per cent were acting as both domestic and international commercial arbitrators. Of those who were acting as international arbitrators, either exclusively or in conjunction with duties as domestic arbitrators, only 25 per cent worked in both international commercial and investment disputes.

The survey also investigated how long individuals who had acted as both judges and arbitrators at some point in their career (N=53) spent in each position and whether they tended to start in one field or another. As Table 2.1 (N=35) and Table 2.2 (N=14) show, individuals appear somewhat more likely to begin work as a judge and then move to arbitration, although the reverse is not unheard of.

Table 2.1 Length of time in each position for judges becoming arbitrators (number of respondents followed by proportion in parenthesis)

	1–5 years	6–15 years	16–25 years	26–35 years	36–45 years	More than 46 years
I worked first as a judge for	9 (.26)	8 (.24)	8 (.24)	5 (.15)	4 (.12)	0 (.00)
and have now worked as an arbitrator for	4 (.11)	15 (.43)	8 (.23)	6 (.17)	2 (.06)	0 (.00)

Table 2.2 Length of time in each position for arbitrators becoming judges (number of respondents followed by proportion in parenthesis)

	1–5 years	6–15 years	16–25 years	26–35 years	36–45 years	More than 46 years
I worked first as an arbitrator for	1 (.08)	5 (.38)	2 (.15)	4 (.31)	1 (.08)	0 (.00)
and have now worked as a judge for	3 (.33)	4 (.44)	1 (.11)	1 (.11)	0 (.00)	0 (.00)

There is no correlation between the first and second rows in Tables 2.1 and 2.2, so it is impossible to determine how long individual respondents spent in one career versus another. However, the data allows for two interesting observations. First, it is more than twice as likely that an individual with both judicial and arbitral experience will begin as a judge rather than as an arbitrator. Second, respondents who were judges first became arbitrators at a relatively constant rate in the first 25 years of their career, whereas arbitrators who became judges did so most frequently after acting as an arbitrator for either 6 to 15 years or 26 to 35 years.

The survey also found that 22 members of the full population had acted simultaneously as both a judge and an arbitrator.[49] Of those 22 individuals, 27 per cent worked in both capacities for 1 to 5 years, 50 per cent worked in both capacities for 6 to 15 years, 9 per cent worked in both capacities for 16 to 25 years, and 14 per cent worked in both capacities for 26 to 35 years.

B. Levels of Experience

The next series of questions considered the experience level of the various respondents. This information was useful not only to provide context for later analyses but also to determine whether and to what extent concerns about the 'aging' of the arbitral profession (and to a lesser extent, the judicial profession) are borne out in reality.[50]

The first question asked respondents to indicate how long they had been qualified as a practising lawyer, or, if their jurisdiction contemplated judicial employment directly after the completion of legal education rather than after a period of legal practice, how long they had been qualified as a judge. Because some arbitrators are not qualified as lawyers,[51] the question also indicated that those who were not qualified as a lawyer or judge should indicate the number of years that had passed since they completed their first university degree. As Table 2.3 shows, the population (N=452) skewed toward the more senior end of the spectrum.[52]

Table 2.3 Years since qualifying as a professional (proportions of the full population, N=452) (number of respondents followed by proportion in parenthesis)

1–5 years since qualifying as a professional	9 (.02)
6–15 years since qualifying as a professional	22 (.05)
16–25 years since qualifying as a professional	52 (.12)
26–35 years since qualifying as a professional	96 (.21)
36–45 years since qualifying as a professional	179 (.40)
More than 46 years since qualifying as a professional	94 (.21)

[49] Of those 22, 14 discussed purely domestic disputes rather than international disputes.

[50] Susan D Franck and others, 'The Diversity Challenge: Exploring the "Invisible College" of International Arbitration', (2015) 53 Colum J Transnatl L 429, 452–53 (Franck and others, Diversity) (noting the average age of an arbitrator in a study by the International Council of Commercial Arbitrators was 54, with the average age of a judge in California coming in at 60); see also ibid 450 (creating a range of arbitrator experience from the 'super elite' with more than 40 cases to the occasional arbitrator with 2–3 cases).

[51] Stipanowich and Ulrich (n 44) 440–44.

[52] While this study did not seek to differentiate responses based on seniority or amount of experience, future research will do so. Strong, Experience (n 3).

The next question asked how many years the respondent had acted as a neutral (i.e. a judge and/or arbitrator), either full- or part-time. In this case, the population (N=452) was more evenly dispersed and exhibited a slightly flattened bell curve, as indicated in Table 2.4.

Table 2.4 Years of experience as a neutral (number of respondents followed by proportion in parenthesis)

1–5 years' experience as a neutral	49 (.11)
6–15 years' experience as a neutral	126 (.28)
16–25 years' experience as a neutral	118 (.26)
26–35 years' experience as a neutral	105 (.23)
36–45 years' experience as a neutral	48 (.11)
More than 46 years' experience as a neutral	6 (.01)

Because experience can be calculated not only in terms of years but also in terms of the number of proceedings heard,[53] participants were asked to identify the number of arbitrations and/or litigations in which they had acted as an arbitrator or judge in the last five years. Interestingly, the data skewed slightly toward the lower end of the scale, with 7 per cent of respondents indicating that they had acted in 1 to 5 matters in the last five years, 27 per cent indicating that they had acted in 6 to 15 matters, 25 per cent indicating that they had acted in 16 to 25 matters, 14 per cent indicating that they had acted in 26 to 35 matters, 8 per cent indicating that they had acted in 36 to 45 matters, 6 per cent indicating that they had acted in 46 to 55 matters, 4 per cent indicating that they had acted in 56 to 65 matters, 3 per cent indicating that they had acted in 66 to 75 matters, and 6 per cent indicating that they had acted in more than 76 matters. This data suggests that a majority of neutrals (52 per cent) handle a relatively small number of proceedings (approximately 1 to 5) per year.

Another important demographic to consider involves gender. Empirical studies suggest that parties select female arbitrators far less often than male arbitrators, and women are appointed as judges far less frequently than men in many jurisdictions.[54]

[53] Parties often consider experience (calculated either in terms of years or the number of proceedings heard) to be an important indicator of quality in an arbitrator. 'High Quality Results, High-Quality Processes: Top In-House Counsel Discuss the Continuing Challenges in Commercial Arbitration', (2006) 24 Alternatives to the High Cost of Litigation 182, 182. While this chapter does not analyse whether and to what extent any differences in legal reasoning exist based on the number of proceedings respondents have heard, future research will do so. Strong, Experience (n 3).

[54] Markus Altenkirch and Jan Fohloff, 'Gender Diversity in International Arbitration – Statistics', Global Arb News (3 July 2017), <https://globalarbitrationnews.com/gender-diversity-in-international-arbitration-some-statistics/> accessed 11 April 2020; Peter Bert, 'Women Arbitrators in German – DIS Publishes 2016 Gender Balance Statistics', Dispute Resolution Germany (14 July 2017), <http://www.disputeresolutiongermany.com/2017/07/women-arbitrators-in-germany-dis-publishes-2016-gender-balance-statistics/> accessed 11 April 2020;

This phenomenon presumably arises as a result of gender-based biases regarding the quality of legal decision making, an issue that is beyond the scope of the current analysis but that will be discussed in future works.[55] However, it is useful to note for purposes of the current study that 18 per cent of the respondents identified as female, 79 per cent identified as male and 3 per cent indicated that they preferred not to indicate their gender. The female–male ratio was the same for those respondents choosing to focus on domestic disputes, although the percentage of women was slightly higher among respondents choosing to focus on international disputes (29 per cent female to 71 per cent male). Among respondents from the common law tradition (N=243), 19 per cent identified as female, as compared to 79 per cent who identified as male (3 per cent of common law respondents chose not to indicate their gender). Interestingly, all of the respondents from civil law countries (N=83) chose to skip this question.

One of the key areas of comparison in this study is between domestic and international disputes. The survey therefore asked respondents to state how many commercial disputes that they handled in the last three years were international in scope. Interestingly, the data indicated an inverse bell, skewed slightly toward domestic specialists. Thus, 35 per cent of respondents in the general population (N=448) had handled no international disputes in the last three years, 25 per cent of respondents had a case load that was 1 to 20 per cent international, 8 per cent had a case load that was 21 to 40 per cent international, 8 per cent had a case load that was 41 to 60 per cent international, 8 per cent had a case load that was 61 to 80 per cent international, and 17 per cent had a case load that was 81 to 100 per cent international.

Those respondents who were primarily qualified in common law countries (N=322) also skewed toward domestic disputes, in that 43 per cent had handled no international disputes in the last three years, 28 per cent had a case load that was 1 to 20 per cent international, 7 per cent had a case load that was 21 to 40 per cent international, 8 per cent had a case load that was 41 to 60 per cent international, 6 per cent had a case load that was 61 to 80 per cent international, and 8 per cent had a case load that was 81 to 100 per cent international. However, respondents who were primarily qualified in civil law countries (N=83) skewed much more heavily toward international disputes, in that 46 per cent had handled caseloads that were 81 to 100 per cent international, 15 per cent had a case load that was 61 to 80 per cent international, 7 per cent had a case load that was 41 to 60 per cent international, 11 per cent had a case load that was 21 to 40 per cent international, 16 per cent had a case load that was 1 to 20 per cent international and 6 per cent had a case load that was entirely domestic. This divergence can be explained

Susan D Franck, 'Introductory Remarks', (2017) 111 Am Soc'y Intl L Proceedings 289, 290–92 (citing statistics on the number of women judges and arbitrators in various fora around the world); Judicial Diversity Statistics 2019, Courts and Tribunals Judiciary (UK), <https://www.judiciary.uk/about-the-judiciary/who-are-the-judiciary/diversity/judicial-diversity-statistics-2019/> accessed 11 April 2020; 2019 US State Court Women Judges, National Association of Women Lawyers, <https://www.nawj.org/statistics/2019-us-state-court-women-judges> accessed 11 April 2020.

[55] Strong, Gender (n 3); see also Joseph D Garrison, 'Perceived Differences in Male and Female Arbitrators and Mediators', (2012) 18 Disp Res Magazine 29, 30–31.

by the likelihood that the call for participation was more likely to have been seen by civil law judges and arbitrators who were internationally-minded. It is also true that internationally-oriented individuals were more likely to be comfortable responding to a survey in English.

Of the survey participants who were currently working as judges, only 12 per cent had a case load that was 81 to 100 per cent international in nature. The remaining judicial respondents focused primarily on domestic matters, with 38 per cent indicating that they handled international matters 0 per cent of the time, 38 per cent indicating that they handled international matters 1 to 20 per cent of the time, and 12 per cent indicating that they handled international matters 41 to 60 per cent of the time. Interestingly, the judges answering this question (8 of the 11 in the judicial cohort) reflected an even mix of common law and non-common law jurisdictions, with 43 per cent of the respondents coming from the United States and 14 per cent each coming from Belgium, Brazil, Guatemala, and Iran.[56]

Of those who were currently working as arbitrators (N=361), 35 per cent had handled no international matters at all during the preceding three years. Of the remaining respondents, 25 per cent handled international matters 1 to 20 per cent of the time, 9 per cent handled international matters 21 to 40 per cent of the time, 8 per cent handled international matters 41 to 60 per cent of the time, 7 per cent handled international matters 61 to 80 per cent of the time, and 16 per cent handled international matters 81 to 100 per cent of the time. Those who were currently working as arbitrators came from a wide range of jurisdictions, although a large proportion of individuals (67 per cent) came from the United States.

Another major area of comparison in this study involved issues that arise across the common law–civil law divide. As a result, the survey asked respondents to identify the jurisdiction in which they were primarily based as well as the jurisdiction in which they were qualified to practice law. According to the data, 76 per cent of the general population were based in common law countries[57] and 21 per cent were based in civil law

[56] Some judges skipped this question. However, the remaining judges hailed from Afghanistan and Norway. The US judges were based in the states of Illinois, Maryland, and Missouri.

[57] The individual common law countries represented, calculated to the hundredth of a percentage point based on the total number of respondents to illuminate the appropriate detail, included Australia (0.90%), Bangladesh (0.22%), Canada (3.37%), Hong Kong (1.12%), India (0.22%), Singapore (0.45%), Trinidad and Tobago (0.22%), United Kingdom (4.04%), and United States (65.17%).

Those who indicated that they were primarily based in Canada (N=15) were asked to identify whether they were based in Quebec, which is alternatively classified as a mixed or civil-law jurisdiction (20% of the Canadian respondents), or in another territory or province, which would be common law-based (80% of the Canadian respondents). The survey analysis did not distinguish between these categories.

Those who indicated that they were primarily based in the United Kingdom (N=18) were asked to identify whether they were based in England and Wales, a common law jurisdiction (100% of the UK respondents), Northern Ireland, a common law jurisdiction (0% of the UK respondents), or Scotland, a civil law jurisdiction (0% of the UK respondents).

Those who indicated they were primarily based in the United States (N=286) were asked to identify their state or territory. All sub-federal US jurisdictions are common law, with the exception of Louisiana and Puerto Rico, which are characterized as civil law jurisdictions. Participants from the United States came from the following jurisdictions: Alabama (1.05%), Arizona (2.10%), Arkansas (0.35%), California (12.24%), Colorado (4.20%), Connecticut (2.80%), District of Columbia (3.15%), Florida (6.64%), Georgia (2.45%), Hawai'i (0.35%), Illinois (2.45%), Indiana (0.70%), Kansas (0.35%), Louisiana (1.05%), Maryland (1.40%), Massachusetts (4.20%), Michigan (3.50%), Minnesota (1.40%), Mississippi (0.35%), Missouri (3.15%), Montana (0.70%), Nevada

countries.[58] Only 3 per cent of respondents came from jurisdictions that did not fall within the traditional common law–civil law dichotomy.[59]

Although the standard assumption is that judges and arbitrators are professionally qualified in a single jurisdiction, an ever-increasing number of individuals are legally qualified in more than one jurisdiction, as this study showed.[60] Furthermore, not all judges and arbitrators are legally qualified. Therefore, the survey included questions about where respondents were qualified to practice as a lawyer or judge, if at all. As it turned out, 73 per cent of the general population indicated they were qualified to practice law or act as a judge in a common law country[61] and 19 per cent indicated that they were qualified to practise law or act as a judge in a civil law county.[62] Only one per cent of the general population was qualified in jurisdictions other than those traditionally

(0.35%), New Hampshire (1.05%), New Jersey (4.20%), New Mexico (0.35%), New York (12.59%), North Carolina (0.35%), Ohio (4.90%), Oregon (0.70%), Pennsylvania (4.90%), Puerto Rico (0.35%), Tennessee (0.70%), Texas (10.14%), Utah (1.75%), Virginia (1.40%), Washington (1.40%), and Wisconsin (0.35%).

[58] The individual civil law countries represented, calculated to the hundredth of a percentage point based on the total number of respondents to illuminate the appropriate detail, included Argentina (0.22%), Austria (0.67%), Belarus (0.45%), Belgium (2.02%), Bolivia (0.22%), Brazil (1.57%), Colombia (0.67%), Denmark (0.22%), Dominican Republic (0.22%), Egypt (0.22%), Finland (0.22%), France (2.92%), Germany (1.57%), Guatemala (0.22%), Hungary (0.22%), Italy (1.12%), Mexico (0.67%), Netherlands (0.67%), Paraguay (0.22%), Peru (0.22%), Poland (0.45%), Spain (1.80%), Sweden (0.22%), Switzerland (3.60%), Turkey (0.22%), and Venezuela (0.22%).

[59] The non-common law/civil law countries represented, calculated to the hundredth of a percentage point based on the total number of respondents to illuminate the appropriate detail, included Indonesia (0.22%), Iran (0.22%), Lebanon (0.22%), Mauritius (0.22%), Nigeria (0.22%), and United Arab Emirates (2.02%).

[60] Compare nn 56–58 (regarding where respondents were based) with nn 60–62 (regarding jurisdictions where respondents had their primary legal qualifications) and nn 63–65 (regarding jurisdictions where respondents had their secondary legal qualifications).

[61] The individual common law countries represented, calculated to the hundredth of a percentage point based on the total number of respondents to illuminate the appropriate detail, included Australia (0.45%), Bahamas (0.23%), Canada (3.18%), Hong Kong(0.68%), India (0.45%), Singapore (0.23%), United Kingdom (5.00%), and United States (62.95%). Notably, these numbers were not identical to those reported above in n 56.

Those who chose Canada as the primary jurisdiction where they were qualified as a lawyer or judge (N=14) were asked to identify whether they were based in Quebec, which is alternatively classified as a mixed or civil-law jurisdiction (14% of the Canadian respondents), or in another territory or province, which would be common law-based (86% of the Canadian respondents). The survey analysis did not distinguish between these categories.

Those who chose the United Kingdom as the primary jurisdiction where they were qualified as a lawyer or judge (N=21) were asked to identify whether they were based in England and Wales, a common law jurisdiction (100% of the UK respondents), Northern Ireland, a common law jurisdiction (0% of the UK respondents), or Scotland, a civil law jurisdiction (0% of the UK respondents).

Those who chose the United States as the primary jurisdiction where they were qualified as a lawyer or judge (N=276) were asked to identify their state or territory. All sub-federal US jurisdictions are common law, with the exception of Louisiana and Puerto Rico, which are characterized as civil law jurisdictions. Participants from the United States came from the following jurisdictions: Alabama (0.36%), Arizona (2.18%), Arkansas (0.36%), California (12.73%), Colorado (4.00%), Connecticut (2.55%), District of Columbia (3.64%), Florida (4.36%), Georgia (2.55%), Hawai'i (0.36%), Illinois (2.55%), Indiana (0.73%), Louisiana (1.09%), Maryland (1.82%), Massachusetts (4.36%), Michigan (3.64%), Minnesota (1.45%), Mississippi (0.36%), Missouri (3.64%), Montana (0.73%), New Hampshire (0.36%), New Jersey (4.00%), New Mexico (0.36%), New York (15.27%), North Carolina (0.36%), Ohio (5.09%), Oregon (0.36%), Pennsylvania (5.09%), Puerto Rico (0.36%), Tennessee (0.73%), Texas (10.18%), Utah (1.82%), Virginia (1.09%), Washington (1.09%), and Wisconsin (0.36%).

[62] The individual civil law countries represented, calculated to the hundredth of a percentage point based on the total number of respondents to illuminate the appropriate detail, included Argentina (0.45%), Austria (0.45%), Belarus (0.45%), Belgium (1.36%), Bolivia (0.23%), Brazil (1.36%), Colombia (0.45%), Denmark (0.23%), Egypt (0.23%), Finland (0.23%), France (2.50%), Germany (1.82%), Greece (0.23%), Guatemala (0.23%), Italy (0.91%), Latvia (0.23%), Mexico (0.68%), Netherlands (0.23%), Norway (0.23%), Paraguay (0.23%), Peru (0.23%), Poland (0.45%), Spain (1.59%), Sweden (0.68%), Switzerland (2.73%), Turkey (0.23%), Uzbekistan (0.23%), and Venezuela (0.45%). Notably, these numbers were not identical to those reported above in n 57.

classified as falling within the common or civil law,[63] and 6 per cent were not qualified as a lawyer or a judge.

Respondents were also asked to indicate whether they were qualified as a lawyer or judge in a second jurisdiction. Although 72 per cent of respondents indicated they did not hold such additional qualifications, 20 per cent of respondents indicated that they held secondary qualifications in a common law jurisdiction, with the United States coming in as the most popular option.[64] Five per cent indicated that they held secondary qualifications in a civil law jurisdiction, with France coming in as the most popular option.[65] Three per cent indicated that they held secondary qualifications in a legal system falling outside the common law/civil law dichotomy, with the United Arab Emirates coming in as the most popular option.[66]

Interestingly, there seemed to be a trend toward secondary qualifications in a common law country regardless of where an individual had obtained his/her initial qualification. Thus, 20 per cent of those who indicated that they were primarily qualified in a common law country also held qualifications in another second common law country, while only 4 per cent of the same group had a secondary qualification in a civil law country and 2 per cent had a secondary qualification in a non-common law/civil law country.[67] Similarly, of those who indicated that their primary qualification

[63] The non-common law/civil law countries represented, calculated to the hundredth of a percentage point based on the total number of respondents to illuminate the appropriate detail, included Cambodia (0.23%), Lebanon (0.23%), Mauritius (0.23%), Nigeria (0.23%), and Sudan (0.23%). Notably, these numbers were not identical to those reported above in n 58.

[64] The individual common law countries represented, calculated to the hundredth of a percentage point based on the total number of respondents to illuminate the appropriate detail, included Australia (0.23%), Bahamas (0.23%), Canada (0.70%), Hong Kong (0.47%), Trinidad and Tobago (0.23%), United Kingdom (3.50%), and United States (14.72%).

Those who chose Canada as the second jurisdiction where they were qualified as a lawyer or judge (N=3) were asked to identify whether they were based in Quebec, which is alternatively classified as a mixed or civil-law jurisdiction (0% of the Canadian respondents), or in another territory or province, which would be common law-based (100% of the Canadian respondents).

Those who chose the United Kingdom as the second jurisdiction where they were qualified as a lawyer or judge (N=15) were asked to identify whether they were based in England and Wales, a common law jurisdiction (100% of the UK respondents), Northern Ireland, a common law jurisdiction (0% of the UK respondents), or Scotland, a civil law jurisdiction (0% of the UK respondents).

Those who chose the United States as the second jurisdiction where they were qualified as a lawyer or judge (N=64) were asked to identify their state or territory. All sub-federal US jurisdictions are common law, with the exception of Louisiana and Puerto Rico, which are characterized as civil law jurisdictions. Participants from the United States came from the following jurisdictions: California (7.81%), Colorado (1.56%), Connecticut (1.56%), District of Columbia (6.25%), Florida (6.25%), Georgia (1.56%), Hawai'i (1.56%), Idaho (1.56%), Illinois (4.69%), Kansas (3.13%), Kentucky (1.56%), Maine (1.56%), Maryland (3.13%), Nevada (1.56%), New Hampshire (1.56%), New Jersey (3.13%), New York (37.50%), Pennsylvania (3.13%), Texas (6.25%), Virginia (1.56%), and Wyoming (3.13%).

[65] The individual civil law countries represented, calculated to the hundredth of a percentage point based on the total number of respondents to illuminate the appropriate detail, included Argentina (0.70%), Belgium (0.47%), Brazil (0.23%), China (0.47%), Czechia (0.23%), France (1.87%), Germany (0.23%), Peru (0.23%), Portugal (0.47%), Spain (0.23%), and Switzerland (0.23%).

[66] The non-common law/civil law countries represented, calculated to the hundredth of a percentage point based on the total number of respondents to illuminate the appropriate detail, included Andorra (0.23%), Indonesia (0.23%), Israel (0.23%), Libya (0.23%), Mauritius (0.23%), Syria (0.23%), United Arab Emirates (1.17%), and Zimbabwe (0.23%).

[67] Of those initially qualified in a common law country, 72 per cent did not hold secondary qualifications. Common law respondents who were secondarily qualified in another common law country named the Bahamas (0.32%), Canada (0.96%), Hong Kong (0.64%), Trinidad and Tobago (0.32%), United Kingdom (3.19%), and the United States (17.24%) as their secondary jurisdictions. Of those who named the United States as their secondary jurisdiction, 31 per cent qualified in New York. Common law respondents secondarily qualified in civil law

was in a civil law country, 16 per cent held secondary qualifications in a common law country (most often the United States), compared to 14 per cent who held secondary qualifications in another civil law jurisdiction (most often France) and 4 per cent who held secondary qualifications in a country outside the common law/civil law tradition.[68] While this data may be affected by the fact that the survey was in English and widely circulated in English-language outlets, it is nevertheless useful in suggesting which jurisdictions (i.e. the United States and France) are most popular among those seeking additional qualifications.[69]

IV. Substantive Findings

As illuminating as the demographic information is about commercial dispute resolution, the major focus of this study is on legal reasoning in commercial disputes. The remaining sections of the survey therefore focused on various issues of substantive concern, including use of legal authorities, use of factual authorities (evidence), the reasoning process, drafting a reasoned decision or award, and judicial and arbitral education relating to legal reasoning. Each of these are discussed separately below.

A. Use of Legal Authorities

1. Relative importance of legal authorities in substantive and procedural disputes

Every legal system has its own understanding about the relative importance of different types of legal authorities in resolving legal disputes. While these hierarchies may vary from country to country, conventional wisdom suggests that the persuasive value of

jurisdictions named Argentina (0.96%), Belgium (0.32%), Brazil (0.32%), China (0.64%), and France (1.28%) as their jurisdictions. Common law respondents with secondary qualifications in non-common law/civil law countries named Indonesia (0.32%), Israel (0.32%), Mauritius (0.32%), United Arab Emirates (0.64%), and Zimbabwe (0.32%) as their jurisdictions.

[68] Of those initially qualified in a civil law country, 67 per cent did not hold secondary qualifications. Civil law respondents who were secondarily qualified in a common law jurisdiction named the United Kingdom (4.94%) and the United States (11.11%) as their secondary jurisdictions. Of those who named the United States as their secondary jurisdiction, 79 per cent qualified in New York. Respondents secondarily qualified in civil law jurisdictions named Belgium (1.23%), Czechia (1.23%), France (3.70%), Germany (1.23%), Peru (1.23%), Portugal (2.47%), Spain (1.23%), and Switzerland (1.23%) as their jurisdictions. Respondents secondarily qualified in countries outside the common law/civil law dichotomy named Libya (1.23%), Syria (1.23%), and United Arab Emirates (1.23%) as their jurisdictions.

[69] The data is also consistent, to some extent, with research relating to characteristics of the international arbitral community. According to that study,

> the common law was the dominant legal training, with 46% of the subjects exclusively trained in a common law jurisdiction. There was also a strong civil law component, with 30% of subjects trained exclusively as civil lawyers. There was also a hybrid as 24% of subjects had training in *both* common and civil law. The dominance of common law training was also present in the subset of arbitrators, but was not as facially prominent. Specifically, 38.5% of ICCA arbitrators had training exclusively in common law whereas 33.8% of ICCA arbitrators were exclusively trained as civil lawyers, and 27.7% of ICCA arbitrators had training both in common and civil law.

Franck and others, Diversity (n 50) 455.

individual authorities, which can include everything from treaties and statutes to judicial decisions and scholarly commentary, remain constant within a particular legal system, regardless of whether the dispute is substantive and procedural in nature. However, that presumption has never been empirically tested, nor have any studies been conducted about the comparative use of legal authorities in national versus international disputes.

One area of where considerable academic and practical debate exists involves the purported difference between the way that legal authorities are used and regarded in common law countries as compared to civil law countries.[70] While many people continue to rely on conventional wisdom in this regard, numerous questions have arisen in recent years about the relative weight of different legal authorities in common law and civil law legal systems. For example, not only have commentators suggested that statutes are now nearly as important in common law countries as they are in civil law countries, but some civil law jurisdictions are said to rely on judicial decisions in much the same way that common law jurisdictions do.[71] However, these hypotheses are again largely unsupported by rigorous empirical research.

Given these gaps in knowledge, the section on legal authorities began by investigating how judges and arbitrators use legal authorities not only across the standard lines of inquiry (i.e. judicial–arbitral, domestic–international, and common law–civil law), but also within and between substantive and procedural decision making. The study achieved this goal by asking respondents to state how important ten different types of authority were to their decision-making process, using a five-point scale where one was to be considered 'not important at all' and five was to be considered 'very important'. The ten types of authorities are routinely discussed in the legal literature as relevant to legal decision making and so were generally expected to reflect the panoply of relevant options.[72] However, the study allowed respondents to supplement their answers by marking 'other' and indicating additional authorities in a text box.

The first question focused exclusively on substantive (rather than procedural) aspects of commercial disputes and tested conventional wisdom about the relative importance of different types of authorities across the common law–civil law divide as well as the pervasive (mis)perception that arbitrators are less rigorous about relying and applying the law.[73] The data generated from this question is represented in Table 2.5 and both confirms and rejects a number of widely held assumptions.

First, when comparing judges and arbitrators, the data appears to reject the traditional assumption that the two groups differ in how they address questions of

[70] For more on standard assumptions, see Vivienne O'Connor, *Common Law and Civil Law Traditions: Practitioner's Guide* (International Network to Promote the Rule of Law 2015) 11–15, <https://www.fjc.gov/sites/default/files/2015/Common%20and%20Civil%20Law%20Traditions.pdf> accessed 11 April 2020; see also Ch. 1.III.C.

[71] Guido Calabresi, *A Common Law for the Age of Statutes* (Harvard University Press 1982) 5–7; Peter de Cruz, *Comparative Law in a Changing World* (3d edn, Routledge-Cavendish 2007) 70; Neal Devins and David Klein, 'The Vanishing Common Law Judge?' (2017) 165 U Penn L Rev 595, 597.

[72] Ch. 1.III.A.

[73] Ch. 1.I.

Table 2.5 Importance of different types of legal authorities when deciding substantive disputes (weighted averages followed by standard deviation in parenthesis, sample (N) size, and ranking within the cohort)

	Full pop.	Current judges	Current arbitrators	J-A t-stat	Domestic disputes	Int'l disputes	D–I t-stat	Comm. law	Civil law	C–C t-stat
Arbitral awards involving the parties to this dispute	2.82 (1.52) 333	3.00 (2.00) 3 Rank: 4 (tied)	2.84 (1.49) 274 Rank: 7	–.18	2.75 (1.53) 232 Rank: 6	2.97 (1.50) 100 Rank: 7	1.21	2.79 (1.54) 261 Rank: 6	2.98 (1.42) 52 Rank: 7	.82
Arbitral awards involving parties other than those involved in this dispute	1.90 (1.13) 336	2.00 (1.00) 3 Rank: 10 (tied)	1.89 (1.12) 277 Rank: 11	–.17	1.74 (1.06) 234 Rank: 11	2.29 (1.18) 101 Rank: 11	4.21***	1.75 (1.11) 262 Rank: 11	2.31 (.86) 54 Rank: 11	3.50***
Domestic regulations, statutes or administrative rules	4.39 (.94) 334	4.25 (.96) 4.00 Rank: 2	4.41 (.90) 275 Rank: 2	.35	4.52 (.82) 233 Rank: 2	4.09 (1.12) 100 Rank: 3	–3.91***	4.41 (.92) 261 Rank: 2	4.46 (.84) 54 Rank: 1	.37
International treaties	2.92 (1.64) 327	3.00 (2.00) 3 Rank: 4 (tied)	2.89 (1.63) 269 Rank: 6	–.12	2.35 (1.53) 226 Rank: 8	4.20 (.99) 100 Rank: 2	11.10***	2.62 (1.61) 255 Rank: 8	4.37 (.84) 52 Rank: 2	7.62***
Judicial decisions from the jurisdiction whose law controls the matter	4.67 (.64) 336	4.50 (1.00) 4 Rank: 1	4.67 (.64) 276 Rank: 1	.52	4.76 (.57) 233 Rank: 1	4.46 (.73) 102 Rank: 1	–4.06***	4.76 (.52) 262 Rank: 1	4.35 (.78) 54 Rank: 3	–4.79***
Judicial decisions from jurisdictions other than the jurisdiction whose law controls the matter	3.04 (.94) 338	2.50 (1.00) 4 Rank: 9	2.99 (.92) 277 Rank: 3 (tied)	1.06	3.16 (.91) 235 Rank: 3	2.78 (.97) 102 Rank: 9	–3.45***	3.19 (.89) 263 Rank: 3	2.39 (.83) 54 Rank: 9	–6.08***

Legislative history of domestic regulations, statutes or administrative rules	2.96 (1.08) 334	4.00 (1.15) 4 Rank: 3	2.96 (1 04) 274 Rank: 5	−1.98*	3.06 (1.07) 233 Rank: 4	2.73 (1.05) 100 Rank: 10	−2.59**	2.96 (1.07) 261 Rank: 4	2.96 (1.01) 54 Rank: 8	.00
Legislative history of int'l treaties (travaux préparatoires)	2.17 (1.18) 328	3.00 (1.63) 4 Rank: 4 (tied)	2.16 (1.15) 269 Rank: 10	−1.44	1.80 (1.03) 225 Rank: 10	2.98 (1.06) 102 Rank: 6	9.51***	2.00 (1.15) 254 Rank: 10	3.00 (.89) 54 Rank: 6	6.02***
Scholarly works (articles, books, treatises)	3.01 (1.00) 334	2.00 (.82) 4 Rank: 10 (tied)	2.99 (1.00) 274 Rank: 3 (tied)	1.97*	2.85 (1.04) 232 Rank: 5	3.40 (.85) 101 Rank: 4	4.67***	2.91 (.98) 261 Rank: 5	3.54 (.75) 54 Rank: 4	4.46***
Soft law (i.e. non-binding but persuasive guidelines, declarations or codes of conduct)	2.77 (.91) 334	2.75 (.96) 4 Rank: 7	2.74 (.89) 274 Rank: 8	−.02	2.65 (.87) 232 Rank: 7	3.06 (.92) 101 Rank: 5	3.88***	2.70 (.86) 260 Rank: 7	3.09 (.96) 54 Rank: 5	2.97**
Other (please describe below)	2.36 (1.58) 103	2.67 (1.53) 3 Rank: 8	2.27 (1.55) 84 Rank: 9	−.44	2.22 (1.59) 81 Rank: 9	2.86 (1.46) 22 Rank: 8	1.70	2.33 (1.57) 87 Rank: 9	2.33 (1.61) 12 Rank: 10	.00

substantive law. Not only do the hierarchical arrangements of legal authorities come out very similarly between the two groups with respect to core authorities (such as judicial decisions from the jurisdiction whose law controls the matter and domestic regulations, statutes or administrative rules), but only two entries—legislative history of domestic regulations, statutes, or administrative rules and scholarly works—showed any statistically significant difference in terms of intensity marks. The judicial and arbitral hierarchies did produce some surprises—for example, judges ranked arbitral awards involving the parties to the instant dispute more highly than arbitrators did, while arbitrators ranked scholarly works more highly than judges did—which suggests some areas for future research.

The situation was very different with respect to the second set of comparators, i.e. domestic and international disputes. Here, nine of the 11 categories showed statistically significant differences in intensity, with eight types of authority demonstrating the highest level of significance ($p<.001$) and one type of authority demonstrating the second highest level of significance ($p<.01$). Differences were also found with respect to the hierarchical rankings within each cohort. Some of these disparities were foreseeable (for example, international treaties were understandably more important in international disputes, ranking second in importance as compared to eighth in importance for domestic disputes), while others were not. Thus, for example, judicial decisions from the jurisdiction whose law controls the matter was considered the most important authority in both domestic and international disputes, yet the intensity marks varied considerably (4.76 out of 5.00 for domestic disputes and 4.46 for international disputes). Several other categories showed statistically significant differences in intensity even though the ranking of the authority was similar or the same.

Since this is the first time this phenomenon has been identified, there is no theoretical explanation for the difference in intensity markings. In some cases, the domestic dispute markings were more intense, while in other cases, it was the international dispute markings. Furthermore, some but not all differences between the two cohorts' hierarchical rankings are explicable by reference to existing theoretical work.

The third area of comparison involves respondents from common law and civil law countries. Again, the data identified numerous authorities with a statistically significant difference in intensity markings, with six authorities demonstrating differences at the highest degree of confidence ($p<.001$) and one authority demonstrating differences at an intermediate level of confidence ($p<.01$). No overall pattern appeared to exist with respect to whether common law respondents or civil law respondents gave a higher intensity rating.

Interestingly, the data reflected in Table 2.5 confirmed standard assumptions about how legal authorities are considered in common law and civil law jurisdictions. For example, the five most important authorities for common law judges and arbitrators were, in decreasing order of importance: (1) judicial decisions from the jurisdiction whose law controls the issue; (2) domestic regulations, statutes or administrative rules; (3) judicial decisions from jurisdictions other than the jurisdiction whose law controls the matter; (4) legislative histories of domestic regulations, statutes or administrative rules; and (5) scholarly works. However, judges and arbitrators from the civil law tradition indicated that the five most important authorities for determining substantive disputes were, in decreasing order of importance: (1) domestic regulations, statutes, or administrative rules; (2) international treaties; (3) judicial decisions from the jurisdiction whose law controls the matter; (4) scholarly works; and (5) soft law. While the relatively high status of international treaties could be attributed to the fact that a considerable proportion of civil law respondents indicated that they were focusing on international rather than domestic disputes,[74] it is also consistent with the fact that most civil law nations adopt a monist perspective to international law.[75]

As useful as the hierarchical data is in comparing how common law and civil law lawyers conduct legal reasoning in substantive disputes, the intensity marks are equally illuminating. Seven of the ten types of legal authority showed a statistically significant difference between the two cohorts. Six items reflected differences at the highest level of statistical significance ($p<.001$): arbitral awards involving parties other than those involved in the instant dispute, which featured an intensity mark of 1.75 out of 5.00 from common law respondents and an intensity mark of 2.31 from civil law respondents; international treaties, which featured intensity marks of 2.62 from common law respondents and 4.37 from civil law respondents; judicial decisions from the jurisdiction whose law controls the matter, which featured intensity marks of 4.76 from common law respondents and 4.35 from civil law respondents; judicial decisions from jurisdictions other than the jurisdiction whose law controls the matter, which were given intensity marks of 3.19 by common law respondents and 2.39 by civil law respondents; legislative history of international treaties (*travaux préparatoires*), which earned intensity marks of 2.00 from common law respondents and 3.00 from civil law respondents; and scholarly works, which won intensity marks of 2.91 from common law respondents and 3.54 from civil law respondents. One type of authority—soft law—reflected a statistically significant degree of difference between common law and civil law respondents at an intermediate level of confidence ($p<.01$).[76] These results, like those generated from the hierarchical rankings, confirm the standard understanding of how common law and civil law training affects legal reasoning in substantive disputes.

The question was structured so that respondents could supplement the predetermined list of authorities by choosing 'other' and listing in a text box additional types of substantive authority that they believed were relevant to determining substantive aspects of commercial legal disputes. The 'other' option was not a popular choice

[74] Ibid.

[75] O'Connor (n 70) 11–15; SI Strong, 'Monism and Dualism in International Commercial Arbitration: Overcoming Barriers to Consistent Application of Principles of Public International Law', in Marko Novaković (ed), *Basic Concepts of Public International Law: Monism and Dualism* (University of Belgrade 2013) 547, 549–50.

[76] Notably, some confusion may have existed in the survey about the concept of soft law, which was intended to include arbitral rules. However, the survey question allowed participants to supplement their responses with additional written information in a text box, and a number of individuals indicated that they believed arbitral rules to be of central importance if the parties had adopted those rules. This suggests that some participants may have distinguished between different types of soft law in their responses. As a result, it may be helpful for researchers to develop targeted empirical studies that differentiate between various types of soft law in both substantive and procedural disputes.

for any of the various cohorts, ranking near the bottom of all six lists as a hierarchical matter. The importance of the 'other' option was further diminished by the fact that many of the responses essentially duplicated pre-existing options (for example, one respondent wrote in 'bar journal articles', which is within the survey's definition of scholarly work, while another listed 'international instruments and treaties and public policy' which would fall within the category of international treaties). Similarly, a number of entries focused on matters of procedure (e.g. burdens of proof) or on matters involving mixed questions of law and fact (e.g. 'expert testimony on industry standards in the dispute procedure' or 'pleadings by the attorneys'). Several respondents mentioned the importance of language contained in the governing contract, which can be considered more of an evidentiary concern.

Nine respondents mentioned custom and usage/customary industry practice as a relevant legal standard, which suggests the need to include such a category in future research.[77] Interestingly, only one respondent mentioned 'general principles of equity' and only one mentioned 'common sense', suggesting that most judges and arbitrators focus on legal rather than non-legal standards.[78]

The next question in this series asked judges and arbitrators to identify the importance of different types of legal authorities when deciding procedural disputes, offering the same list of 11 authorities (including 'other') that were discussed with respect to substantive disputes. The question provides useful independent data about the relative importance of different types of authorities in procedural disputes (an issue that has only really been discussed in international commercial arbitration)[79] while also providing an opportunity to determine the extent to which judges and arbitrators (who are both said to have broad discretion in procedural matters) rely on formal authority when deciding procedural disputes.[80] Again, respondents were instructed to consider one as 'not important at all' and five as 'very important'.

Interestingly, survey respondents did not place the authorities in the same hierarchical order that was seen with substantive disputes, nor did the respondents give the individual alternatives the same intensity ratings, as demonstrated in Table 2.6. Furthermore, a number of statistically significant differences arose between comparative cohorts when considering procedural authorities alone.

The analysis begins by comparing judicial and arbitral responses. As Table 2.6 shows, the data appears to reject the traditional assumption that the two groups differ in how

[77] This term may or may not refer to the *lex mercatoria*, which is often discussed in the arbitral literature. E.g. Klaus Peter Berger, *The Creeping Codification of the New* Lex Mercatoria (2d edn, Wolters Kluwer 2010); Christopher R Drahozal, 'Empirical Findings on International Arbitration: An Overview', in Thomas Schultz and Federico Ortino (eds), *Oxford Handbook on International Arbitration* (Oxford University Press forthcoming 2020).

[78] Cf Ch. 3.III.B.1, 3.III.D.3.

[79] SI Strong, *Research and Practice in International Commercial Arbitration: Sources and Strategies* (Oxford University Press 2009); SI Strong, 'Research in International Commercial Arbitration: Special Skills, Special Sources', (2009) 20 Am Rev Intl Arb 119.

[80] Gary B Born, *International Commercial Arbitration* (2d edn, Wolters Kluwer 2014) 2026, 2122–23 (noting arbitrators are often granted broad discretion, bounded by applicable rules and precedent). While much has been said about arbitral discretion, judges are also granted a significant amount of discretion in how they conduct proceedings, a phenomenon that some scholars have criticized. E.g. Robert G Bone, 'Who Decides? A Critical Look at Procedural Discretion', (2007) 28 Cardozo L Rev 1961, 1975.

Table 2.6 Importance of different types of legal authorities when deciding procedural disputes (weighted averages followed by standard deviation in parenthesis, sample (N) size, and ranking within the cohort)

	Full pop.	Current judges	Current arbitrators	J-A t-stat	Domestic disputes	Int'l disputes	D-I t-stat	Comm. law	Civil law	C-C t-stat
Arbitral awards involving the parties to this dispute	2.74 (1.51) 332	2.67 (1.53) 3 Rank: 8 (tied)	2.76 (1.51) 275 Rank: 4	.10	2.72 (1.54) 230 Rank: 3 (tied)	2.79 (1.47) 101 Rank: 6	.39	2.73 (1.53) 259 Rank: 3 (tied)	2.91 (1.43) 53 Rank: 6	.79
Arbitral awards involving parties other than those involved in this dispute	1.93 (1.11) 333	1.67 (1.15) 3 Rank: 11	1.94 (1.11) 276 Rank: 10	.42	1.77 (1.06) 231 Rank: 10	2.29 (1.17) 101 Rank: 11	3.98***	1.83 (1.09) 260 Rank: 10	2.26 (1.08) 53 Rank: 10	2.62**
Domestic regulations, statutes or administrative rules	3.81 (1.29) 334	4.25 (.96) 4 Rank: 2	3.77 (1.29) 276 Rank: 2	−.74	3.96 (1.22) 232 Rank: 2	3.45 (1.38) 101 Rank: 3	−3.37***	3.78 (1.28) 261 Rank: 2	3.89 (1.34) 53 Rank: 2	.57
International treaties	2.43 (1.47) 325	2.67 (1.53) 4 Rank: 8 (tied)	2.43 (1.44) 269 Rank: 9	−.33	1.92 (1.31) 224 Rank: 9	3.55 (1.14) 100 Rank: 2	10.76***	2.17 (1.37) 252 Rank: 9	3.57 (1.31) 53 Rank: 3	6.81***
Judicial decisions from the jurisdiction whose law controls the matter	4.13 (1.15) 334	4.50 (1.00) 4 Rank: 1	4.09 (1.16) 276 Rank: 1	−.70	4.25 (1.08) 231 Rank: 1	3.86 (1.27) 102 Rank: 1	−2.87**	4.17 (1.13) 261 Rank: 1	3.94 (1.29) 53 Rank: 1	−1.32
Judicial decisions from jurisdictions other than the jurisdiction whose law controls the matter	2.63 (1.10) 334	3.00 (.00) 4 Rank: 4 (tied)	2.59 (1.07) 276 Rank: 7	−.76	2.72 (1.10) 232 Rank: 3 (tied)	2.44 (1.06) 101 Rank: 10	−2.16*	2.68 (1.11) 260 Rank: 6	2.21 (.93) 53 Rank: 11	−2.88**

(continued)

Table 2.6 Continued

	Full pop.	Current judges	Current arbitrators	J-A t-stat	Domestic disputes	Int'l disputes	D-I t-stat	Comm. law	Civil law	C-C t-stat
Legislative history of domestic regulations, statutes or administrative rules	2.56 (1.17) 331	4.00 (1.54) 4 Rank: 3	2.50 (1.13) 273 Rank: 8	−2.62**	2.56 (1.18) 229 Rank: 7	2.53 (1.14) 101 Rank: 9	−.22	2.53 (1.16) 258 Rank: 8	2.60 (1.13) 53 Rank: 7	.40
Legislative history of int'l treaties (travaux préparatoires)	1.90 (1.08) 325	3.00 (2.00) 3 Rank: 4 (tied)	1.89 (1.03) 270 Rank: 11	−1.84	1.61 (.95) 223 Rank: 11	2.55 (1.05) 101 Rank: 8	7.98***	1.75 (1.02) 252 Rank: 11	2.49 (.97) 53 Rank: 8	4.84***
Scholarly works (articles, books, treatises)	2.86 (1.06) 329	2.25 (.96) 4 Rank: 10	2.86 (1.05) 270 Rank: 3	1.15	2.61 (1.02) 228 Rank: 6	3.43 (.93) 100 Rank: 4	6.88***	2.73 (1.02) 257 Rank: 3 (tied)	3.46 (.94) 52 Rank: 4	4.77***
Soft law (i.e. non-binding but persuasive guidelines, declarations or codes of conduct)	2.75 (1.06) 331	2.75 (.96) 4 Rank: 7	2.75 (1.05) 272 Rank: 5	.00	2.52 (.97) 229 Rank: 8	3.29 (1.07) 101 Rank: 5	6.42***	2.64 (1.01) 259 Rank: 7	3.23 (1.00) 52 Rank: 5	3.85***
Other (please describe below)	2.70 (1.74) 103	3.00 (2.00) 3 Rank: 4 (tied)	2.62 (1.74) 82 Rank: 6	−.37	2.69 (1.80) 84 Rank: 5	2.74 (1.48) 19 Rank: 7	.11	2.71 (1.78) 87 Rank: 5	2.46 (1.61) 13 Rank: 9	−.48

they address questions of procedural law.[81] Not only do the hierarchical arrangements of core authorities (such as judicial decisions from the jurisdiction whose law controls the matter and domestic regulations, statutes, or administrative rules) come out very similarly between the two groups, but only one entry—legislative history of domestic regulations, statutes or administrative rules—showed any statistically significant difference in terms of intensity marks. Thus, the fact that the two groups diverged with respect to how they rated authorities beyond the top two does not appear problematic, given that the disparity in intensity was not statistically significant in the vast majority of cases.

The situation was very different with respect to the second set of comparators, i.e. domestic and international disputes. Here, eight of the 11 categories—the highest proportion of the three comparative pairings—showed statistically significant differences in intensity, with six types of authority demonstrating the highest level of significance ($p<.001$) and the remaining two authorities each reflecting a different level of significance ($p<.01$ and $p<.05$). Disparities also arose with respect to hierarchical rankings. Most of these differences were predictable (for example, international treaties were more important in international disputes, ranking second in importance as compared to ninth in importance for domestic disputes), but what was not expected was the speed with which the two hierarchies diverged. Indeed, the only item that the two cohorts agreed on was the first-place ranking of judicial decisions from the jurisdiction whose law controls the matter. While domestic regulations, statutes, or administrative rules were ranked relatively similarly (second place for domestic disputes and third place for international disputes), procedural authorities appear to be used very differently in domestic and international disputes.

The third area of comparison involved respondents from common law and civil law countries. The data identified six authorities with a statistically significant difference in intensity markings, with four authorities demonstrating differences at the highest degree of confidence ($p<.001$) and two authorities demonstrating differences at an intermediate level of confidence ($p<.01$). While the number of differences were higher and at a higher level of confidence than was the case with the comparison of judges and arbitrators, the differences were less extensive and at a lower (but still statistically significant) level of confidence than was the case with differences between domestic and international disputes. No overall pattern appeared to exist with respect to whether common law respondents or civil law respondents gave higher intensity ratings.

Interestingly, common law and civil law respondents showed a much higher level of convergence with respect to the relative importance of procedural authorities as compared to substantive authorities. First, the two cohorts agreed on the two most important types of procedural authority: (1) judicial decisions from the jurisdiction whose law controls the matter and (2) domestic regulations, statutes, or administrative

[81] Bone (n 80) 1979 (assuming judicial discretion is different than arbitral discretion). But see SI Strong, 'General Principles of Procedural Law and Procedural *Jus Cogens*', (2018) 122 Penn St L Rev 347, 363–64 (arguing that general principles of procedural law can be derived, in part, from principles of arbitral procedure).

rules, which, in the procedural context, would mean rules of civil procedure (in litigation) and national laws on arbitration (in arbitration). Notably, these two categories of legal authorities did not differ to a statistically significant degree. Second, the two groups came to very similar conclusions about the importance of scholarly works, with common law respondents putting that particular authority in a tie for third place along with arbitral awards involving the parties to the instant dispute and civil law respondents placing scholarly works in fourth position.

As useful as it is to analyse Table 2.5 and Table 2.6 independently, comparing the two tables yields a number of unique insights not reflected in any other known studies. First, none of the comparative cohorts ranked legal authorities identically across the substantive–procedural divide, although the level of variation depended on the group in question. For example, judges followed the same approach only with respect to the first two forms of authority, whereas arbitrators followed the same approach for the first three authorities. As between domestic and international disputes, domestic disputes followed the same pattern across the first three authorities, whereas international disputes followed the same pattern across the first five authorities, the highest in the study. Common law lawyers showed divergence across the substantive–procedural divide after the first two authorities, whereas civil law lawyers diverged from the very first entry. Indeed, the data suggests that traditional views about how common law- and civil law-trained lawyers view legal authorities are incorrect when it comes to procedural authorities. Not only did respondents from the civil law rate judicial decisions more highly in procedural disputes than in substantive disputes, a phenomenon that is more typical of common law lawyers, but respondents from the common law rated scholarly works more highly in procedural disputes than in substantive disputes, a feature that is more frequently found among civil law lawyers. While the reasons for the different approaches to substantive and procedural disputes are unclear, these findings provide a useful starting point for additional research.[82]

As was the case with the previous question, the survey structured this inquiry so that respondents could supplement the pre-determined list of procedural authorities by choosing 'other' and identifying additional sources of procedural law in a text box. As a comparison of Tables 2.5 and 2.6 shows, the 'other' option was slightly more popular in cases of procedural law than substantive law. Rather than ranking near the bottom of all six lists as a hierarchical matter, respondents placed other types of procedural law in the middle of their lists, ranging from a tie for fourth position to ninth position.

One reason why the 'other' option may have ranked so highly is because of the approximately 30 respondents who referred to applicable arbitration rules in one way or another in the comment box. While the soft law option was intended to cover that

[82] E.g. Strong, Legal Reasoning (n 3) 48–53 (offering additional analyses across the common law–civil law divide). It is possible that the fact that the survey was conducted in English increased the likelihood that civil law respondents had been influenced by common law thinking and/or by the unique norms that were applicable in international commercial arbitration. However, a not insignificant number of civil law respondents (21 per cent) indicated that they were focusing exclusively on domestic disputes, which suggests that the results cannot be attributed solely to the influence of common law methods. Ibid.

option, the number of references to arbitral rules does raise the issue of interpretation. However, it is at least equally possible that some or all of these individuals did in fact interpret the question as intended and simply wanted to emphasize the importance of applicable arbitral rules in procedural matters, since this question, like the one reported by Table 2.5, saw comments echoing available options. For example, one respondent to this question specifically referred to 'secondary sources (e.g. IBA Rules) and protocols' while another referred to 'industry codes', which both would fall under the soft law option. Another respondent referred to 'bar journal articles', which fall squarely within the question's definition of scholarly work.

The comments also included references to authorities generally considered to be more substantive in nature (e.g. 'EU Regulations', 'custom and usage') or evidentiary in nature (e.g. the contract between the parties or attorney pleadings) as well as non-legal concepts such as 'general principles of equity' and 'common sense'. However, one respondent referred to 'general procedural principles (e.g. right to be heard, etc.)', which might be included in future analyses of procedural hierarchies.[83]

2. Independent legal research

The next series of questions focused on respondents' research methodology regarding legal issues. Individual inquires focused on a variety of issues, including the type and frequency of additional legal research that the respondents conducted, either themselves or with the help of legal clerks or assistants; the motivation for such research; and whether and to what extent parties or their counsel were allowed to respond to materials discovered through that research.

The first item in this series asked what type(s) of additional legal research respondents or their legal clerks/assistants conducted, apart from reading the submissions of the parties, and how often such research was conducted, if at all. As noted in Table 2.7, the question identified 16 specific types of legal research based on standard methodologies discussed in the legal literature and provided respondents with the opportunity to discuss additional research techniques by offering a seventeenth option entitled 'other' and allowing respondents to describe that additional technique in an open text box. Respondents were asked to indicate for each of the 17 options whether, on average, they engaged in that particular behaviour 0 per cent of the time (assigned the number '1' for purposes of calculating weighted averages), 1 to 29 per cent of the time ('2' for weighted averages), 30 to 59 per cent of the time ('3' for weighted averages), 60 to 99 per cent of the time ('4' for weighted averages), or 100 per cent of the time ('5' for weighted averages).

The question generated a great deal of useful and novel data. For example, the findings suggest that judges and arbitrators adopt very similar approaches to additional legal research, given that only three types of activities showed statistically significant

[83] Some interesting work is being done with respect to general principles of procedural law. E.g. Charles T Kotuby Jr and Luke A Sobota, *General Principles of Law and International Due Process: Principles and Norms Applicable in Transnational Disputes* (Oxford University Press 2017); SI Strong, 'General Principles of Procedural Law and Procedural *Jus Cogens*', (2018) 122 Penn State L Rev 347.

Table 2.7 Additional legal research conducted by judges, arbitrators, and/or their legal clerks/assistants (weighted averages followed by standard deviation in parenthesis, sample (N) size, and ranking within the cohort)

	Full pop.	Current judges	Current arbitrators	J-T t-stat	Domestic disputes	Int'l disputes	D-I t-stat	Comm. law	Civil law	C-C t-stat
Check for subsequent negative treatment or overruling of an arbitral award cited by the parties	1.98 (1.30) 331	3.00 (2.83) 2 Rank: 9 (tied)	1.97 (1.30) 272 Rank: 15	−1.11	1.85 (1.29) 229 Rank: 15	2.29 (1.28) 101 Rank: 16	2.86**	1.85 (1.28) 260 Rank: 16	2.59 (1.27) 51 Rank: 16	3.78***
Check for subsequent negative treatment or overruling of a judicial decision cited by the parties	3.00 (1.46) 334	4.00 (1.73) 3 Rank: 2 (tied)	2.97 (1.48) 273 Rank: 8	−1.20	3.08 (1.46) 233 Rank: 7	2.84 (1.42) 100 Rank: 9	−1.39	3.00 (1.48) 262 Rank: 7	3.15 (1.39) 52 Rank: 13	.67
Check for subsequent negative treatment or overruling of regulations, statutes or treaties identified by the parties	2.81 (1.47) 331	4.00 (1.73) 3 Rank: 2 (tied)	2.77 (1.48) 272 Rank: 9	−1.43	2.82 (1.49) 233 Rank: 9	2.80 (1.44) 97 Rank: 11	−.11	2.73 (1.46) 260 Rank: 9	3.33 (1.47) 51 Rank: 9	2.68**
Check for subsequent negative treatment or overruling of scholarly commentary, soft law or persuasive authority identified by the parties	2.06 (1.89) 332	2.67 (1.15) 3 Rank: 11 (tied)	2.03 (1.18) 273 Rank: 14	−.93	1.91 (1.14) 233 Rank: 14	2.45 (1.21) 98 Rank: 14	3.86***	1.91 (1.13) 261 Rank: 14	2.82 (1.20) 51 Rank: 14	5.21***
Conduct independent research into arbitral awards	1.69 (1.06) 330	3.50 (.71) 2 Rank: 6 (tied)	1.65 (1.05) 271 Rank: 17	−2.48*	1.57 (1.04) 230 Rank: 17	1.98 (1.06) 99 Rank: 17	3.26**	1.47 (.91) 259 Rank: 17	2.76 (1.41) 51 Rank: 15	8.35***

Conduct independent research into judicial decisions	2.71 (1.26) 326	3.00 (1.41) 2 Rank: 9 (tied)	2.67 (1.27) 268 Rank: 11	−.37	2.71 (1.23) 229 Rank: 10	2.71 (1.34) 96 Rank: 12 (tied)	.00	2.62 (1.22) 256 Rank: 11	3.40 (1.36) 50 Rank: 6	4.06***
Conduct independent research into regulations, statutes or treaties	2.61 (1.24) 322	3.33 (1.15) 3 Rank: 8	2.56 (1.25) 265 Rank: 12	−1.06	2.57 (1.22) 225 Rank: 12	2.71 (1.30) 96 Rank: 12 (tied)	.92	2.45 (1.15) 253 Rank: 12	3.57 (1.38) 49 Rank: 3	6.03***
Conduct independent research into scholarly commentary, soft law or persuasive authorities	2.26 (1.13) 330	2.00 (.00) 3 Rank: 13 (tied)	2.25 (1.15) 270 Rank: 13	.38	2.03 (.99) 232 Rank: 13	2.82 (1.22) 97 Rank: 10	6.15***	2.05 (.99) 260 Rank: 13	3.50 (1.09) 50 Rank: 4	9.33***
Read, in full, arbitral awards identified by the parties	3.18 (1.48) 322	4.50 (.71) 3 Rank: 1	3.15 (1.47) 264 Rank: 5	−1.59	3.20 (1.56) 225 Rank: 5	3.15 (1.29) 96 Rank: 7	−.28	3.18 (1.53) 252 Rank: 5 (tied)	3.24 (1.23) 51 Rank: 10	.26
Read, in full, judicial decisions identified by the parties	3.87 (1.07) 315	3.67 (1.53) 3 Rank: 4 (tied)	3.86 (1.08) 259 Rank: 2	.30	3.99 (1.01) 221 Rank: 1 (tied)	3.57 (1.15) 93 Rank: 2	−3.23**	3.94 (1.01) 250 Rank: 2	3.58 (1.25) 48 Rank: 2	−2.17*
Read, in full, regulations, statutes or treaties identified by the parties	3.92 (1.09) 330	3.67 (1.53) 3 Rank: 4 (tied)	3.92 (1.12) 259 Rank: 1	.38	3.99 (1.05) 230 Rank: 1 (tied)	3.76 (1.17) 99 Rank: 1	−1.76	3.97 (1.04) 259 Rank: 1	3.88 (1.24) 51 Rank: 1	−.55
Read, in full, scholarly commentary, soft law or persuasive authorities identified by the parties	3.17 (1.18) 332	2.67 (1.15) 3 Rank: 11 (tied)	3.14 (1.17) 272 Rank: 6	.69	3.13 (1.23) 232 Rank: 6	3.25 (1.06) 99 Rank: 5 (tied)	.85	3.18 (1.20) 261 Rank: 5 (tied)	3.35 (1.07) 51 Rank: 7 (tied)	.94
Read, in part, arbitral awards identified by the parties	2.76 (1.49) 320	3.50 (2.12) 2 Rank: 6 (tied)	2.73 (1.47) 263 Rank: 10	−.74	2.63 (1.53) 224 Rank: 11	3.08 (1.36) 95 Rank: 8	2.48*	2.69 (1.52) 251 Rank: 10	3.22 (1.33) 49 Rank: 11 (tied)	2.28*

(continued)

Table 2.7 Continued

	Full pop.	Current judges	Current arbitrators	J-T t-stat	Domestic disputes	Int'l disputes	D-I t-stat	Comm. law	Civil law	C-C t-stat
Read, in part, judicial decisions identified by the parties	3.36 (1.39) 314	1.67 (.58) 3 Rank: 15 (tied)	3.37 (1.40) 256 Rank: 3	2.10*	3.36 (1.43) 218 Rank: 3	3.37 (1.31) 95 Rank: 3	.06	3.46 (1.37) 246 Rank: 3	3.22 (1.46) 50 Rank: 11 (tied)	−1.12
Read, in part, regulations, statutes or treaties identified by the parties	3.32 (1.42) 317	1.67 (.58) 3 Rank: 15 (tied)	3.32 (1.43) 258 Rank: 4	1.99*	3.33 (1.43) 219 Rank: 4	3.31 (1.39) 97 Rank: 4	−.12	3.37 (1.40) 249 Rank: 4	3.35 (1.48) 48 Rank: 7 (tied)	−.09
Read, in part, scholarly commentary, soft law or persuasive authorities identified by the parties	2.97 (1.27) 322	2.00 (.00) 2 Rank: 13 (tied)	2.98 (1.28) 263 Rank: 7	1.08	2.86 (1.30) 224 Rank: 8	3.25 (1.18) 97 Rank: 5 (tied)	2.54*	2.92 (1.26) 253 Rank: 8	3.49 (1.28) 49 Rank: 5	2.89**
Other (please describe below)	1.81 (1.43) 59	.00 NA 0 Rank: 17	1.80 (1.39) 50 Rank: 16	NA	1.69 (1.37) 48 Rank: 16	2.36 (1.63) 11 Rank: 15	1.41	1.88 (1.51) 51 Rank: 15	1.00 (.00) 5 Rank: 17	−1.29

differences ($p<.05$) between the two groups. Furthermore, two of those three entries—reading, in part, judicial decisions identified by the parties and reading, in part, regulations, statutes, or treaties identified by the parties—show arbitrators undertaking those activities more frequently than judges, thereby offsetting longstanding allegations that arbitration is a 'second class' form of justice.[84] The third of the statistically significant items—conducting independent research relating to arbitral awards—was also surprising in that judges undertook that activity more frequently than arbitrators.

Although the statistical analysis identified relatively few differences between judges and arbitrators, the internal hierarchies associated with each of the two cohorts were quite distinct. However, this information seems somewhat less relevant than the hierarchies described in Tables 2.5 and 2.6 with respect to the importance of legal authorities in substantive and procedural disputes, since the information in Table 2.7 goes to various practices, which may vary from case to case, as opposed to beliefs about the weight of legal authorities, which are central to the reasoning process and less likely to change depending on the circumstances of the dispute.

A comparison of domestic and international disputes reflects far more differences with respect to research techniques. As Table 2.7 shows, seven of the 17 options reflected a statistically significant difference, with two at the highest degree of confidence ($p<.001$), three at an intermediate degree of confidence ($p<.01$), and two at the lowest degree of confidence ($p<.05$). Most of these arose at the lower end of the hierarchy, which translates to practices that are undertaken relatively infrequently. The one exception involved reading, in full, judicial decisions identified by the parties, which was tied for the highest position in domestic disputes and was the second position in international disputes. In that case, respondents discussing domestic disputes reported an intensity marking of 3.99 out of 5.00 as compared to a mark of 3.15 in international disputes.

Interestingly, the internal hierarchies were much more consistent across the domestic–international divide than across the judicial–arbitral divide, with the first four entries being essentially the same. While this phenomenon is likely not as significant as similarities in views about the importance of legal authorities, as reflected in Tables 2.5 and 2.6, it is nevertheless intriguing.

The final set of comparisons involved common law and civil law respondents. Interestingly, this pair of comparators generated the highest number of statistically significant differences of the three types of inquiries. Ten of the 17 entries were different, six at the highest level of statistical confidence ($p<.001$), two at an intermediate level of confidence ($p<.01$), and two at the lowest level of confidence ($p<.05$). However, common law and civil law respondents both identified the same two practices—reading regulations, statutes, and treaties identified by the parties in full and reading judicial decisions identified by the parties in full—as the two most frequently practiced behaviours.

[84] Ch. 1.III.A.

Respondents were also given the opportunity to provide additional information about the types of legal research they or their law clerks/assistant conducted.[85] A number of responses simply repeated criteria contained in the original list (e.g. the statement 'independently verify status of citations, i.e. were they modified, affirmed[,] overruled' fell clearly within the pre-existing option to 'check for subsequent negative treatment or overruling of a judicial decision cited by the parties'), while others simply referred to specific types of authorities, which was more relevant to the preceding two questions regarding the importance of different legal authorities.

Despite these difficulties, a number of responses yielded novel and relevant information. For example, one individual indicated that s/he reviewed 'my own past awards', while another person indicated that s/he 'check[ed] the internet to get definition of terms'.

Several write-in responses anticipated later questions, such as those addressed in Table 2.8 relating to why respondents did or did not read particular authorities. For example, one comment in this category indicated that 'I read everything submitted by the parties', while another said 'FINRA Rules prohibit independent research by arbitrators'. An important subset of responses in this grouping involved comments relating to relevance. Thus, one individual indicated that 'I read 100 per cent of what is produced', but 'if authorities are cited but not produced, I look for them only if they seem relevant. I conduct independent research if, on a specific issue, the parties have not produced enough material.' Another respondent similarly stated:

> Generally, I rely on opposing counsel to tell me if a case has been overturned. No one has ever cited an arbitral award to me, but if they did, I would read it if it seemed to be pertinent. Many authorities do not matter because they are on issues that are either obvious or not pertinent to the real issue.

Other comments anticipated issues relating to whether respondents discussed their research methodology with the parties (e.g. 'I only conduct independent research with the parties' consent'). Those matters are addressed in Table 2.9.

The next question in this series asked about the factors that affected the respondent's decision whether to read a legal authority in full or in part. The question offered several pre-determined options derived in part from the legal literature[86] and asked respondents to indicate how often each factor affects the decision whether to read a legal authority in full or in part. research was conducted, if at all. The question identified 12 different criteria, including the option of marking 'other' and providing additional information in the respondent's own words, and asked participants to indicate whether they relied on that factor 0 per cent of the time (assigned the number '1' for purposes of calculating weighted averages), 1 to 29 per cent of the time ('2'

[85] Responses to other write-in questions also addressed these issues. E.g. Table 2.11.

[86] This is not an issue that is heavily discussed by theoreticians or practitioners, so a number of rationales were generated specifically for this study. Ch. 1.III.

for weighted averages), 30 to 59 per cent of the time ('3' for weighted averages), 60 to 99 per cent of the time ('4' for weighted averages), or 100 per cent of the time ('5' for weighted averages). The structure of the question was identical to a later question involving additional factual (evidentiary) research, which allowed for comparisons across the legal–evidentiary divide.[87]

As Table 2.8 shows, no statistically significant difference arose on this question between judges and arbitrators, again suggesting that judges and arbitrators operate in very similar manners. The hierarchical data was somewhat difficult to evaluate, given several ties in intensity marks within each cohort, but the relative ranking appears to be broadly similar with respect to the importance of the legal principle to the disposition of the controversy, whether the parties dispute the interpretation or application of the particular legal authority, whether the parties dispute the interpretation or application of the underlying rule or principle, and the novelty of the underlying legal principle.

A marked contrast appeared with respect to the comparison of domestic and international disputes. In this case, four of the 12 items showed a statistically significant difference in intensity rankings, although these arose primarily with respect to lower ranked options. Notably, no statistical difference arose with respect to the three factors that most frequently affected respondents' decision whether to read a legal authority in full or in part: the importance of the legal principle to the disposition of the controversy (which received the highest marks in both domestic and international disputes), whether the parties dispute the interpretation or application of the particular legal authority, and whether the parties dispute the interpretation or application of the underlying rule or principle. Thus, judges and arbitrators appear to operate somewhat differently in domestic and international disputes, but only at the margins.

The data involving common law and civil law respondents fell in between the two other groups. Only one practice—the perceived likelihood that the losing party will seek to challenge the decision or award—generated a statistically significant difference in intensity marks ($p<.01$), and the two groups generally agreed as to the top three factors affecting the decision to read legal authorities in full or in part (importance of the legal principle to the disposition of the controversy, whether the parties dispute the interpretation or application of the particular legal authority, and whether the parties dispute the interpretation or application of the underlying rule or principle).

The survey appeared to have properly identified all the relevant factors to this particular decision, since 'other' factors were given the lowest intensity marks in all six cohorts. Many of the write-in responses reiterated factors that fell within pre-existing options, such as the importance of the legal principle to the disposition of the controversy (e.g. 'whether ... relevant to the facts of the case'; 'the parties' evidence'; and 'contract language') and whether the parties disputed a particular legal authority or legal principle (e.g. 'usually focus on key disputed legal issues. Often the controlling law is pretty much agreed to'; 'intricacy of the authority; difficulty of the arguments'). Other

[87] Table 2.19.

Table 2.8 Factors affecting the decision whether to read a legal authority in full or in part (weighted averages followed by standard deviation in parenthesis, sample (N) size, and ranking within the cohort)

	Full pop.	Current judges	Current arbitrators	J-T t-stat	Domestic disputes	Int'l disputes	D-I t-stat	Comm. law	Civil law	C-C t-stat
Credibility of the parties or counsel	2.47 (1.27) 326	2.00 (1.00) 3 Rank: 10	2.43 (1.24) 268 Rank: 10	.60	2.43 (1.30) 229 Rank: 10	2.54 (1.18) 96 Rank: 11	.72	2.43 (1.30) 257 Rank: 10	2.57 (1.10) 49 Rank: 11	.71
Extent of your pre-existing knowledge of the legal rule or principle in question	3.49 (1.13) 328	3.00 (1.73) 3 Rank: 7 (tied)	3.48 (1.11) 269 Rank: 5	.74	3.52 (1.16) 230 Rank: 6	3.42 (1.05) 97 Rank: 5	–.73	3.55 (1.24) 259 Rank: 6	3.38 (1.10) 48 Rank: 6	–.89
Importance of the legal principle to disposition of the controversy	4.30 (.88) 328	4.00 (1.73) 3 Rank: 1 (tied)	4.33 (.85) 269 Rank: 1	.66	4.34 (.89) 229 Rank: 1	4.21 (.86) 98 Rank: 1	–1.22	4.36 (.88) 259 Rank: 1	4.08 (.86) 49 Rank: 1 (tied)	–2.05*
Novelty of the legal authority (i.e. how recently the authority was adopted or enacted)	3.54 (1.24) 326	4.00 (1.00) 3 Rank: 1 (tied)	3.57 (1.24) 267 Rank: 6	–.60	3.66 (1.24) 230 Rank: 4 (tied)	3.26 (1.19) 95 Rank: 6	–2.68**	3.64 (1.24) 258 Rank: 5	3.32 (1.16) 47 Rank: 7	–1.64
Novelty of the underlying legal principle (i.e. how frequently the issue has been addressed in practice)	3.59 (1.20) 327	4.00 (1.73) 3 Rank: 1 (tied)	3.62 (1.19) 268 Rank: 4	–.55	3.66 (1.22) 229 Rank: 4 (tied)	3.43 (1.13) 97 Rank: 4	–1.59	3.69 (1.18) 258 Rank: 4	3.40 (1.14) 48 Rank: 5	–1.57
Perceived likelihood that the losing party will seek to challenge the decision or award	2.31 (1.36) 324	2.50 (2.12) 2 Rank: 9	2.34 (1.37) 267 Rank: 11	–.16	2.14 (1.32) 225 Rank: 11	2.68 (1.38) 98 Rank: 9	3.33***	2.20 (1.33) 255 Rank: 11	2.80 (1.29) 49 Rank: 10	2.91**
Standard practice (i.e. you follow the same practice in all cases, regardless of other factors)	3.03 (1.45) 319	3.00 (2.83) 2 Rank: 7 (tied)	3.08 (1.46) 264 Rank: 8	.08	3.14 (1.46) 226 Rank: 8	2.76 (1.42) 92 Rank: 10	–2.12*	3.09 (1.47) 251 Rank: 8	3.11 (1.37) 47 Rank: 8	.09

Type of legal authority (treaty, statute, judicial decision, etc.)	3.40 (1.26) 323	3.50 (2.12) 2 Rank: 6	3.43 (1.27) 266 Rank: 7	−.08	3.48 (1.27) 227 Rank: 7	3.19 (1.23) 95 Rank: 7	−1.89	3.41 (1.29) 256 Rank: 7	3.50 (1.19) 48 Rank: 4	.45
Type of legal dispute (contractual, regulatory, etc.)	2.98 (1.43) 308	1.00 (.00) 2 Rank: 11	2.96 (1.44) 254 Rank: 9	1.92	3.11 (1.46) 217 Rank: 9	2.69 (1.34) 90 Rank: 8	−2.35*	2.98 (1.47) 243 Rank: 9	3.00 (1.33) 46 Rank: 9	.09
Whether the parties dispute the interpretation or application of the particular legal authority	4.12 (1.06) 324	3.67 (1.15) 3 Rank: 4 (tied)	4.16 (1.02) 266 Rank: 2 (tied)	.83	4.15 (1.07) 227 Rank: 3	4.04 (1.05) 96 Rank: 2	−.85	4.16 (1.06) 256 Rank: 3	4.08 (.96) 48 Rank: 1 (tied)	−.49
Whether the parties dispute the interpretation or application of the underlying rule or principle	4.11 (1.06) 325	3.67 (1.15) 3 Rank: 4 (tied)	4.15 (1.01) 269 Rank: 2 (tied)	.84	4.16 (1.08) 230 Rank: 2	3.99 (1.00) 94 Rank: 3	−1.31	4.17 (1.04) 258 Rank: 2	4.04 (1.01) 48 Rank: 3	−.80
Other (please describe below)	1.92 (1.54) 52	.00 NA 0 Rank: 12	1.83 (1.50) 42 Rank: 12	NA	1.85 (1.59) 41 Rank: 12	2.18 (1.40) 11 Rank: 12	.63	2.00 (1.61) 46 Rank: 12	1.00 (.00) 5 Rank: 12	−1.38

comments simply described the respondent's standard practice (e.g. 'I always read the cited legal authorities in their entirety'; 'I read, in full, all authorities cited by a party') or provided the motivation for the action in question (e.g. 'I always read irrespective of what the parties tell me. Only way to get it right.').

However, some answers identified novel points. For example, one respondent indicated that s/he considered the 'abilities of other panel members to read and analyse', while another individual referred to a 'court decision involving same parties in a related case', which could be interpreted as a type of legal authority or as a practice relating to the decision to read a particular legal authority. Several respondents seemed to suggest that they varied their practice depending on the quality of the legal submissions from the parties, although the language was occasionally cryptic (e.g. 'sometimes the parties do not fully identify or articulate what appears to be a determinative, or at least relevant, rule or principle'; 'guidance when parties do not cite significant legal authorities'; 'so long as parties submit the particular legal authority').

Although there is not a lot of commentary on independent legal research by judges and arbitrators, some scholars have addressed concerns about independent factual research by judges and arbitrators, arguing that any independent factual research should be discussed with the parties as a matter of procedural justice.[88] Since one of the purposes of this study is to consider whether and to what extent judicial and arbitral practice regarding legal authorities resembles judicial and arbitral practice regarding factual authorities, it seemed appropriate to ask respondents how often they discussed their legal research methodology with the parties so that the answers could be compared to judicial and arbitral practices relating to factual research. The question used the same frequency breakdowns adopted in earlier questions (0 per cent of the time (assigned the number '1' for purposes of calculating weighted averages), 1 to 29 per cent of the time ('2' for weighted averages), 30 to 59 per cent of the time ('3' for weighted averages), 60 to 99 per cent of the time ('4' for weighted averages), and 100 per cent of the time ('5' for weighted averages)) and adopted a structure identical to a later question involving factual (evidentiary) research, which allowed for comparisons across the legal–evidentiary divide.[89]

As Table 2.9 shows, no statistically significant difference in intensity arose across any of the three axes of comparison. Furthermore, such discussions were relatively infrequent, and primarily occurred between 0 to 30 per cent of the time. While this data is consistent with theoretical literature suggesting that such discussions seldom arise, it does not reach the larger question of whether this practice is appropriate as a matter of substantive and procedural justice.[90]

Although judges and arbitrators appear to discuss their legal research methodology with the parties relatively infrequently, it is still helpful to know when during the process such discussions take place. The next question therefore asked respondents to

[88] Ch. 1.III.A.
[89] Table 2.22.
[90] Ch. 1.III.A.

identify when discussions about legal research methodology occurred, offering five different time periods as well as the option to indicate that no such discussions were held. The structure of the question was the same as that adopted in a later question involving factual (evidentiary) research so as to allow for comparisons across the legal–evidentiary divide.[91]

Table 2.9 Frequency of discussions regarding legal research methodology with parties (weighted averages followed by standard deviation in parenthesis and sample (N) size)

	Full pop.	Current judges	Current arbitrators	J-A t-stat	Domestic disputes	Int'l disputes	D-I t-stat	Comm. law	Civil law	C-C t-stat
Frequency rate	1.76 (1.07) 336	2.00 (1.00) 3	1.76 (1.06) 276	–.39	1.71 (1.02) 235	1.87 (1.16) 100	1.26	1.75 (1.05) 264	1.76 (1.09) 51	.06

As Table 2.10 shows, the top-ranking alternative across all comparative cohorts was the option indicating that the respondent did not discuss their legal research methodology with the parties. Although the percentage of respondents in each cohort marking that option varied somewhat, those differences were not statistically significant. Indeed, only one of the cells in Table 2.10—the option 'during the drafting of the award or decision' involving domestic and international disputes—showed a statistically significant difference (p<.05).

Overall, the table suggests that, if a judge or arbitrator discusses legal methodology with the parties, that discussion is most likely to come about during the hearing, regardless of the setting (litigation or arbitration) or nature (domestic or international, common law or civil law) of the dispute. Such discussions are least likely to come about during the drafting of the award or decision, again regardless of the setting or nature of the dispute.

After ascertaining respondents' general practice with respect to legal research, the survey sought to determine why judges and arbitrators acted as they did. Therefore, the next question in this series asked respondents to identify the rationale(s) that best described their position regarding discussions concerning their legal research methodology. The survey design anticipated that some respondents would be in favour of discussing their legal research methodology with the parties and others would not. As a result, the pre-established prompts included three options that explained why respondents shared their methodology with the parties and three options that explained why respondents did not, as well as one option ('other') that allowed respondents to provide additional rationales in their own words. Respondents were asked to check all categories that applied, so percentages do not add up to 100. The question was identical in structure to a later question involving factual research methodology so as to allow comparisons across the legal–evidentiary divide.[92]

[91] Table 2.25.
[92] Table 2.26.

Table 2.10 Time when respondents discussed legal research methodology with the parties (number of respondents followed by proportion in parenthesis and ranking within the cohort)

	Full pop.	Current judges	Current arbitrators	J-A z-stat	Domestic disputes	Int'l disputes	D-I z-stat	Comm. law	Civil law	C-C- z-stat
At the first procedural meeting	35 (.11)	0 (.00) Rank: 3 (tied)	29 (.11) Rank: 3	−.51	20 (.09) Rank: 5	15 (.17) Rank: 2 (tied)	−2.08*	24 (.10) Rank: 5	8 (.19) Rank: 2 (tied)	−1.79
Prior to the hearing	30 (.10)	0 (.00) Rank: 3 (tied)	26 (.10) Rank: 4	−.48	23 (.10) Rank: 3 (tied)	6 (.07) Rank: 5	.92	27 (.11) Rank: 4	3 (.07) Rank: 4	.74
During the hearing	45 (.15)	1 (.50) Rank: 1 (tied)	39 (.15) Rank: 2	1.35	30 (.14) Rank: 2	15 (.17) Rank: 2 (tied)	−.86	34 (.14) Rank: 2	8 (.19) Rank: 2 (tied)	−.91
After the hearing but before the drafting of the award or decision	31 (.10)	0 (.00) Rank: 3 (tied)	24 (.09) Rank: 5	−.46	23 (.10) Rank: 3 (tied)	8 (.09) Rank: 4	.29	28 (.11) Rank: 3	1 (.02) Rank: 5 (tied)	1.78
During the drafting of the award or decision	4 (.01)	0 (.00) Rank: 3 (tied)	4 (.02) Rank: 6	−.18	1 (.01) Rank: 6	3 (.04) Rank: 6	−2.11*	3 (.01) Rank: 6	1 (.02) Rank: 5 (tied)	−.60
Not applicable – I do not discuss my legal research methodology with the parties	163 (.53)	1 (.50) Rank: 1 (tied)	133 (.52) Rank: 1	−.06	124 (.56) Rank: 1	39 (.45) Rank: 1	1.70	132 (.53) Rank: 1	21 (.50) Rank: 1	.39
Total	308	2	255		221	86		248	42	

As Table 2.11 shows, only one item—the decision to discuss legal research methodologies to ensure accuracy in that research—showed a statistically significant difference ($p<.05$) and only with respect to comparisons across the common law–civil law divide. Interestingly, however, that item appeared in the same position in the internal ranking of the two cohorts (third/tied for third), which suggests the difference may not be as remarkable as the statistics suggest.

Analysis of the hierarchical data suggested that judges are somewhat different than the other groups. For example, all groups except for judges were most likely to say that they did not discuss legal research methodology because that approach is implicit in the task of acting as a judge or arbitrator, an option that tied for last position among judges. Furthermore, the intensity of this choice was relatively high for the five groupings, attracting 45 to 60 per cent of the respondents.[93] Two-thirds of judges, on the other hand, indicated that they did discuss their research methodology with the parties and that they did so because parties need to be able to respond to anything that was discovered as a matter of procedural justice. Interestingly, this item was ranked second (or tied for second) by all of the other cohorts, albeit at a relatively low rate of intensity, attracting only 24 to 39 per cent of the respondents.

The survey also allowed respondents to describe why they adopted their legal research methodology in their own words, although only a small percentage (16 per cent of the full population) did so. Although a number of the comments were not technically responsive to the question, they still provided useful insights.

For example, rather than discussing why they adopted a particular practice, several individuals used the text box to describe what they did with respect to legal methodology, an issue that was more relevant to the type of issues addressed in Table 2.7. Comments ranged from statements like 'if my research reveals a legal authority or statutory provision that was not argued by counsel, I might contact counsel for the purpose of obtaining their submissions on the legal authority in question' to 'parties are given an opportunity to make submissions, if they wish, on my legal line of questioning or research methodology'. Other respondents indicated that 'I typically first ask the parties to brief an issue. I then look at what they have found and determine whether it is good law or is trending in a consistent manner.' Still others mentioned that they 'frequently ask for closing briefing on specific applicable statute or case law and how they perceive evidence related to same', while others stated that they 'engage in back and forth with counsel about legal issues to be decided, usually in oral argument' or 'sometimes discuss how certain decisions are required by the authorities and proof'.

Other comments anticipated later questions involving whether the judge or arbitrator allowed the parties to respond to additional legal research and in what way, issues that are covered in Tables 2.12 and 2.13. These types of statements ranged from 'generally, I don't conduct independent research. If I do, I let the parties know and invite their

[93] Notably, the number of judges participating in the survey as compared to arbitrators was relatively low. Because judges and arbitrators were both included in the domestic–international and common law–civil law groups, a more equal representation of judges might have affected the data relating to these four cohorts.

Table 2.11 Rationales for discussing legal research methodology with parties (number of respondents followed by proportion in parenthesis and ranking within the cohort)

	Full pop.	Current judges	Current arbitrators	J-A z-stat	Domestic disputes	Int'l disputes	D-I z-stat	Comm. law	Civil law	C-C z-stat
Pro-discussion rationales										
I discuss my legal research methodology with the parties because they need to be able to respond to anything I discover as a matter of procedural justice	92 (.28)	2 (.67) Rank: 1	75 (.28) Rank: 2	1.47	54 (.24) Rank: 2 (tied)	37 (.39) Rank: 2	−2.80**	72 (.28) Rank: 2	12 (.25) Rank: 2	.40
I discuss my legal research methodology with the parties to ensure that what I have found is accurate	71 (.22)	1 (.33) Rank: 2 (tied)	58 (.22) Rank: 4	.48	55 (.24) Rank: 2 (tied)	15 (.16) Rank: 4 (tied)	1.64	61 (.24) Rank: 3	5 (.10) Rank: 3 (tied)	2.03*
I discuss my legal research methodology with the parties to increase their confidence in the process	63 (.19)	1 (.33) Rank: 2 (tied)	55 (.21) Rank: 3	.54	46 (.20) Rank: 4	16 (.17) Rank: 3	.68	54 (.21) Rank: 4	5 (.10) Rank: 3 (tied)	1.68
Contra-discussion rationales										
I do not discuss my legal research methodology with the parties because I am confident that what I have found is accurate	9 (.03)	0 (.00) Rank: 6 (tied)	9 (.03) Rank: 7	−.32	8 (.03) Rank: 7	1 (.01) Rank: 7	1.22	9 (.03) Rank: 7	0 (.00) Rank: 7	1.31

I do not discuss my legal research methodology with the parties because my approach is implicit in the task of acting as a judge or arbitrator	157 (.48)	0 (.00) Rank: 6 (tied)	126 (.47) Rank: 1	−1.63	114 (.50) Rank: 1	43 (.45) Rank: 1	.74	121 (.47) Rank: 1	29 (.60) Rank: 1	−1.74
I do not discuss my legal research methodology with the parties because that would decrease their confidence in the process	25 (.08)	1 (.33) Rank: 2 (tied)	21 (.08) Rank: 6	1.60	18 (.08) Rank: 6	7 (.07) Rank: 6	.15	17 (.07) Rank: 6	4 (.08) Rank: 5 (tied)	−.45
Other (please describe)	51 (.16)	1 (.33) Rank: 2 (tied)	41 (.15) Rank: 5	.85	36 (.16) Rank: 5	15 (.16) Rank: 4 (tied)	−.02	46 (.18) Rank: 5	4 (.08) Rank: 5 (tied)	1.62
Total	325	3	267		229	95		259	48	

comments on what I've found' to 'I would want to get agreement that it is okay with the parties to engage in independent research', in addition to other variations on this same theme.[94] Other comments in this category indicated that 'parties are given an opportunity to make submissions if they wish, on my legal line of questioning or research methodology'; 'I occasionally tell the parties that I ordinarily do not conduct independent research, but will read the legal authorities cited by the parties'; 'I may not discuss it at all if there are no new or different results of my own research'.

Some comments raised novel points that were not fully contemplated by the pre-existing options. For example, one respondent noted that s/he did not engage in additional legal research, but might be aware of relevant law as a result of his/her expertise in the field.[95] Another individual indicated that 'I always elicit proposed awards from each party. This is an indication to the parties that the final award will have considered their legal position'. Another respondent adopted a somewhat similar practice, noting that 'I discuss [legal research methodology] if the parties raise the issue. Sometimes I have provided draft decisions to the parties'. Although some of the participants in the semi-structured interview discussed the role that pre-existing knowledge plays on the decision-making process and how proposed or draft decisions or awards can affect litigation and arbitration, more research on these points would be useful.[96]

One popular category of comments provided additional details about the rationales reflected in the predetermined options. Perhaps the most frequent of these responses involved individuals describing their beliefs about what is implicit in the task of acting as a judge or arbitrator.[97] However, some people focused on the need to respect procedural justice ('[I want to] ensure full transparency and an opportunity to comment') or the need to raise confidence in the process (as one judge said, 'I want them to understand my decision even if they disagree with it', and as one arbitrator said, '[I want to] to inform the parties that I am fully prepared to conduct the hearing and render a well-reasoned and law-based award').

[94] Numerous individuals noted that they would allow the parties to respond to material discovered through additional legal research. These types of statements included the following: 'If I find some authority through my own research, I will ask parties to brief a certain issue and address the authority. I discuss the result, not the methodology'; 'I do not discuss my legal research methodology with the parties, but I do share my findings and ask for their respective position;' 'If my research reveals a legal authority or statutory provision that was not argued by counsel, I might contact counsel for the purpose of obtaining their submissions on the legal authority in question'; 'I do not discuss my methodology, but, if my search results will adversely affect a position taken by a party, I do discuss those results and provide an opportunity to the parties to brief the point I researched and the application of the authorities I found'; 'I may discuss the results with the parties, for them to comment or brief if appropriate'; 'I discuss my research if I feel the information the parties provide is inadequate to make a decision'; 'I do not discuss my legal research methodology with the parties because, to the extent that it results in questions on matters that the parties have not already addressed, they will be given an additional opportunity to address them'.

[95] 'I do not engage in legal research separate from that offered by the parties. If there is precedent I am aware of that the parties have not raised, I will ask them to address that authority.'

[96] Ch. 3.III.C.2.b.

[97] For example, respondents indicated that they did not discuss their legal research methodology because 'I don't think it is necessary'; 'It is not the role of the decision maker to have any communication with the parties outside of the award'; 'I do not consider it to be appropriate for commercial business to business arbitrations'; and 'I think most commercial arbitrators would agree that we don't and should not research outside the positions presented by the parties'.

As useful as the preceding comments are in illuminating judicial and arbitral practices, they were not technically responsive to the question, which asked why respondents adopted a particular legal research methodology. Fortunately, numerous respondents focused on precisely that issue and identified novel rationales that were not reflected in the pre-existing alternatives.

Several respondents focused on how research methods can affect cost considerations. For example, one individual noted that 'I discuss my legal research because it affects cost and the parties have the right to object to that process', while another stated that 'if I am discussing the case with counsel, I may discuss my legal research methodology to give them additional insight for the purpose of a further cost-benefit analysis of settling the case'.

Other respondents focused on how research methodology interacts with legal doctrine. For example, one individual indicated that s/he would conduct legal research when 'I want to establish the parties' standing on the principle of iura novit curia'. Another person stated that s/he would 'discuss my legal research methodology to encourage the parties to identify and properly brief applicable legal issues'. Conversely, one respondent said that 'I do not discuss [these matters] because I regard my research methodology to be part of the deliberative process'.

Another category of comments focused on practical considerations. For example, one respondent indicated that 'I discuss my research practice to reduce or eliminate gamesmanship, such as citing dissents, overturned or modified jurisprudence', while another said that 'I let the parties know that I will do a modest amount of research if they do not supply me with what I need'. One individual indicated that s/he would discuss legal research methodology 'only in rare cases when an issue of methodology is raised by a party'.

An important subset of the 'practical considerations' category involved the perceived need for additional legal research. For example, one person stated that 'I follow the law that the parties have provided to me so I don't need to discuss with them legal research methodologies'. Another individual echoed a sentiment expressed by a number of interviewees by writing that 'I generally do not do independent legal research. Most issues—nearly all—turn on the facts and evidence or the contract. The law is usually not disputed.'[98]

The concept of 'need' can be considered from both an objective and a subjective perspective. Scholarship concerning judicial and arbitral decision making has discussed various concerns about overconfidence among neutrals,[99] and several respondents indicated that their approach to legal research was strongly affected by their perceived need for additional information, based on their pre-existing expertise. For example, one individual indicated that, 'with over 30 years as a practicing lawyer and litigator in

[98] Ch. 3.III.E.3.

[99] Susan D Franck and others, 'Inside the Arbitrator's Mind', (2017) 66 Emory LJ 1115, 1163 (discussing empirical research on egocentrism, also known as self-serving bias, in both judges and arbitrators); Strong, Judicial Education (n 35) 14 (discussing 'judicial hubris'); see also Ch. 1.II.

highly technical areas of law, I am confident in my ability to do legal research'. Another person said that his/her 'methodology is to serve me and is personal to me', while another claimed that 'what is important is that the parties have an opportunity to address an issue, not how I identified the statute, case or issue that they omitted'. While these statements do not necessarily suggest problems of overconfidence, they do raise some concerns with respect to procedural justice.

Another potentially problematic practice that arose from the comments section involves the way in which some judges and arbitrators put the onus on the parties for triggering discussions about research methodology, since some parties may not feel comfortable in raising such a sensitive issue. Indeed, several individuals indicated that methodology is discussed only 'if party has a question about it'.[100]

Other comments reflected the litigant-driven philosophy of dispute resolution that is particularly predominant in common law jurisdictions.[101] Several respondents indicated that it would be improper for them to engage in legal research, since that task lies with the parties alone. Thus, for example, one person indicated that 'I do not independently research law. If I am aware of a key authority not cited, I may ask them to address it. Presenting the law is their job not mine. Many arbitrators are not lawyers and have no way of knowing the law.' Another respondent stated that 'my methodology is to read what the parties submit. If I am not satisfied with their submissions, I discuss with them the additional research I want them to do. I do not conduct independent legal research'.

As the preceding paragraphs show, numerous respondents focused on the need to allow parties to respond to independent legal research undertaken by judges and arbitrators, a perspective that is also frequently discussed in the legal literature.[102] This outcome was anticipated during the survey design process, so the next question in the series on legal authorities focused on how often respondents gave the parties an opportunity to provide written or oral responses to any independent legal research that was conducted. The question used the same frequency breakdowns adopted in earlier questions: 0 per cent of the time (assigned the number '1' for purposes of calculating weighted averages), 1 to 29 per cent of the time ('2' for weighted averages), 30 to 59 per cent of the time ('3' for weighted averages), 60 to 99 per cent of the time ('4' for weighted averages), and 100 per cent of the time ('5' for weighted averages). The question was identical in structure to a later question involving factual research methodology so as to allow comparisons across the legal–evidentiary divide.[103]

As Table 2.12 shows, the frequency of invitations made by respondents to parties to allow them to respond to independent legal research ranged from a low of 2.67 out

[100] Another individual stated 'I do not do 'independent' research but would discuss that with the parties if the issue arises' while another said, 'I do not usually do independent (i.e. other than what the parties present) legal research. It is discussed at the preliminary hearing if and when parties ask about it.'

[101] Frank B Cross, 'Decisionmaking in the US Circuit Courts of Appeals', (2003) 91 Cal L Rev 1451, 1491, 1494; Dieter Flader and Charles W Anderson III, 'Some Psychological Preconditions for the Process of International Arbitration: Preliminary Findings of a Research Project with a Qualitative Approach', in Tony Cole (ed), *The Roles of Psychology in International Arbitration* (Wolters Kluwer 2017) 267, 285; Ch. 1.III.C.

[102] Ch. 1.III.A (discussing legal literature relating to independent legal research by judges and arbitrators).

[103] Table 2.24.

of 5.00 (for judges) to a high of 3.68 (for international disputes). The only statistically significant difference to arise along the three comparative axes involved domestic and international disputes, where the level of confidence was quite high (p<.001).

Table 2.12 Frequency of invitations to parties to respond to independent legal research (weighted averages followed by standard deviation in parenthesis and sample (N) size)

	Full pop.	Current judges	Current arbitrators	J-A t-stat	Domestic disputes	Int'l disputes	D-I t-stat	Comm. law	Civil law	C-C t-stat
Frequency rate	3.18 (1.57) 317	2.67 (2.08) 3	3.15 (1.58) 259	.52	2.96 (1.59) 220	3.68 (1.43) 96	3.81***	3.26 (1.56) 247	3.16 (1.56) 50	−.41

Although the data reflected in Table 2.12 is useful on its own, it reflects a very interesting phenomenon not seen in most other tables: a clear reverse bell curve, which suggests that neutrals tend to operate at the extreme ends of this particular spectrum.[104] While this type of all-or-nothing approach avoids the theoretical and practical problems associated with case-by-case determinations of whether to issue invitations to parties to respond to independent legal research, it could prove problematic to the extent that parties may not know which type of decision maker they have and thus how they should proceed. More research and debate are therefore warranted on this point.

The final question in this series sought to determine why judges and arbitrators discuss the results of independent legal research with the parties. The question provided six pre-determined alternatives that were both for and against discussions with parties, based on rationales identified in the legal literature.[105] The question also offered an option marked 'other' so that respondents could provide additional rationales in their own words. The question was identical in structure to that discussed in Table 2.11, thereby allowing comparisons of reasons why respondents discussed their legal research methodology with parties, and to later questions involving factual research methodology so as to allow comparisons across the legal–evidentiary divide.[106] Respondents were asked to check all categories that applied, so percentages do not add up to 100.

As Table 2.13 demonstrates, the three comparative axes reflect a certain amount of consistency, with all of the of the six cohorts indicating that that they discuss results from independent legal research with the parties as a matter of procedural justice. However, the intensity marks on that option show a statistically significant difference (p<.05) between domestic and international disputes, and the hierarchical rankings diverge slightly after that point for that particular pairing.

The comparative analysis involving judges and arbitrators show consistency with respect to the second ranked item (tied for judges), which indicated that the two groups

[104] But see Table 2.22. Responses from the full population fell into the following pattern: 22 per cent of respondents issued invitations 0 per cent of the time; 18 per cent of respondents issued invitations 1 to 29 per cent of the time; 2 per cent of respondents issued invitations 30 to 59 per cent of the time; 18 per cent of respondents issued invitations 69 to 99 per cent of the time; and 31 per cent of respondents issued invitations 100 per cent of the time.

[105] Ch. 1.III.A.

[106] Table 2.23; see also Table 2.26.

Table 2.13 Rationales for discussing results of independent legal research with parties (number of respondents followed by proportion in parenthesis and ranking within the cohort)

	Full pop.	Current judges	Current arbitrators	J-A z-test	Domestic disputes	Int'l disputes	D-I z-test	Comm. law	Civil law	C-C z-test
Pro-discussion rationales										
I discuss the results of my independent legal research with the parties because they need to be able to respond to anything I discover as a matter of procedural justice	164 (.51)	2 (.67) Rank: 1	134 (.51) Rank: 1	.55	102 (.46) Rank: 1	61 (.61) Rank: 1	−2.54*	135 (.53) Rank: 1	22 (.44) Rank: 1	1.21
I discuss the results of my independent legal research with the parties to ensure that what I have found is accurate	98 (.30)	1 (.33) Rank: 2 (tied)	82 (.31) Rank: 2	.08	73 (.33) Rank: 2	23 (.24) Rank: 3	1.77	86 (.34) Rank: 2	8 (.16) Rank: 4	2.51*
I discuss the results of my independent legal research with the parties to increase their confidence in the process	76 (.23)	1 (.33) Rank: 2 (tied)	62 (.23) Rank: 4	.40	49 (.22) Rank: 4	26 (.26) Rank: 2	−.79	62 (.25) Rank: 3	9 (.18) Rank: 3	.99
Contra-discussion rationales										
I do not discuss the results of my independent legal research with the parties because I am confident that what I have found is accurate	10 (.03)	0 (.00) Rank: 5 (tied)	8 (.03) Rank: 7	−.30	7 (.03) Rank: 7	3 (.03) Rank: 7	.07	4 (.02) Rank: 7	3 (.06) Rank: 7	−1.90
I do not discuss the results of my independent legal research with the parties because my approach is implicit in the task of acting as a judge or arbitrator	86 (.27)	0 (.00) Rank: 5 (tied)	69 (.26) Rank: 3	−1.03	66 (.30) Rank: 3	20 (.20) Rank: 4	1.80	59 (.23) Rank: 4	19 (.38) Rank: 2	−2.17*
I do not discuss the results of my independent legal research with the parties because that would decrease their confidence in the process	15 (.05)	1 (.33) Rank: 2 (tied)	12 (.05) Rank: 6	2.30*	11 (.05) Rank: 6	4 (.04) Rank: 6	.37	10 (.04) Rank: 6	3 (.06) Rank: 6 (tied)	−.65
Other (please describe)	47 (.15)	0 (.00) Rank: 5 (tied)	41 (.16) Rank: 5	−.74	29 (.13) Rank: 5	18 (.18) Rank: 5	−1.18	39 (.15) Rank: 5	6 (.12) Rank: 5	.62
Total	324	3	264		223	100		253	50	

both discuss results of independent legal research to ensure accuracy in the results. The only statistically significant difference between judges and arbitrators ($p<.05$) involved the decision not to discuss the result of independent legal research on the grounds that doing so would decrease the parties' confidence in the process. While arbitrators, with other cohorts, ranked this option very low (sixth out of seven), judges put it in a tie for second place.

Two statistically significant differences—both at the $p<.05$ level—appeared between common law and civil law respondents. The entries in question—one noting respondents discussed results of independent legal research in order to ensure accuracy and one noting respondents did not discuss results of independent legal research because those activities are implicit in the task of acting as a judge or arbitrator—not only demonstrated statistically significant differences in intensity markings but also reflected opposing rank marks within the internal hierarchies (second and fourth positions). This is intriguing, since common law and civil law respondents ranked all other items similarly.

As with other questions, respondents were given the opportunity to supplement the pre-established options by identifying, in their own words, other reasons why they adopted their particular methodology. Numerous comments reiterated items found in the pre-existing list of rationales, particularly the one focused on procedural justice. However, these comments can be broken into two categories: those suggesting that parties have the right to be faced with the results of legal research only when the material differs from what has been presented by the parties[107] and those suggesting that the parties have the right to be faced with the result of legal research whenever it has been conducted.[108] Some respondents went a bit further and indicated that the results would be discussed only if the material was to provide a basis for the final ruling.[109] While this latter approach appears neutral, it could create some difficulties as a matter of procedural justice, to the extent that the additional research could trigger additional ideas or lines of argument that would assist the non-prevailing party, if it were disclosed by the judge or arbitrator.

Other comments produced similar concerns about whether technical compliance with formal procedural norms could mask a breach of core principles of procedural law. For example, one respondent indicated that 'I do not discuss the results of my independent legal research with the parties because my independent legal research

[107] Comments in this category included the following: 'If the research reveals something new, the parties have the right to be heard'; 'I discuss my legal research where my research has uncovered additional material authority not cited by the parties or additional legal arguments not present in the submissions'; 'When I have found something different from what their research and arguments have offered'; 'I discuss the results if they contain novel elements not yet discussed by the parties in order to grant the right to be heard'; 'If I find something seemingly clearly inconsistent with a party's legal position, I want to give them a chance to respond to/clarify the seeming inconsistency'.

[108] Comments in this category included the following: 'If I do my own research, rarely done, I will give the parties an opportunity to present their own research and any contrary authorities'; 'I discuss [the results of my research] only when [the parties] will have an opportunity to address and respond to what I have found'.

[109] Comments in this category included the following: 'If I were to perform my own legal research and I was considering basing a ruling on that legal research instead of what the parties provided to me, then I would ask the parties to comment on the viability of the law I found'; 'only discuss if I intend to rely on the authority'.

invariably occurs after the hearings have been declared closed', seemingly suggesting that procedural rights of response end with the closing of the hearing. Other individuals indicated that they would only discuss legal research if it rose to a particular level of significance or materiality.[110] However, this approach again ignores the possibility that the parties could successfully demonstrate the importance of a particular line of legal analysis if they were offered the opportunity to do so.

Although most of the comments focused on issues of procedural justice, some answers that duplicated pre-existing options focused on the desire to increase parties' confidence in the process (e.g. the intent to promote 'full transparency of the process'). Others provided further details about respondents' beliefs about the task of acting as a judge or arbitrators (e.g. the person who indicated that s/he did 'not undertake independent legal research because that is contrary to the duty of commercial arbitrators').

Another category of comments focused less on why the respondent allowed parties to respond to independent legal research and more on how that invitation was issued. Though somewhat off-point, these statements were nevertheless illuminating. For example, one respondent said, 'I discuss the results of my independent legal research indirectly, through asking questions at the hearing, or if need be, in writing', while another noted that 'I will disclose independent findings, or request further briefing on an issue independently identified, at or near the close of the hearing or during pre-hearing proceedings to enhance quality of award and supporting reasoning'.[111] Several individuals indicated that their preferred form of asking for feedback on independent legal research involved distributing draft decisions or awards, stating either that 'I do it in the form of a draft opinion' or 'I sometimes give parties an interim award about which to comment'.

Another series of statements focused on the scope of and motivation for the independent research itself, issues that are somewhat analogous to those discussed in Tables 2.7 and 2.8. For example, one individual said, 'I do not do independent research for purposes of the award; I may do independent research to make sure I understand principles that will be applicable and to make sure that I receive the evidence that I need to decide the case', an approach that is akin to that identified by several individuals participating in the semi-structured interviews.[112] Another respondent similarly indicated that

> I don't do any 'legal research' in the usual sense. If I am already aware of a possibly relevant authority, I may well call it to the attention of the parties and ask them to comment

[110] Comments in this category included the following: 'Occasionally, I will check what the parties have provided to me, but feel there is no need to discuss that with the parties absent a specific need'; 'I would discuss with the parties only if I encounter a line of authority or a precedent that they have not discussed and which, in my opinion, could have a significant impact on the award'.

[111] Similar statements included the following: 'I may ask for additional argument on a particular point indicating the parties briefing or argument to that point leave open certain questions or issues'; 'If I discover something, I normally request an oral hearing to enable myself to ask questions'; 'Socratic method: I put questions to the parties'; 'I do not conduct independent research, but if I am aware of legal precedent that I believe is pertinent. I will ask the parties to address it'; 'Typically, I would simply provide a citation to them and ask if they have any further comments'; 'My independent legal research may raise additional questions for the parties to address'.

[112] Ch. 3.III.B.4.a.

on what bearing, if any, it has on the situation; or I may run across the 'subsequent treatment' of a case when I am accessing it online; or I may be interested in the meaning of some terms/concepts used in a case or statute and look that up as background information. That is the scope of my 'legal research.' More than that is rarely, if ever, appropriate.

Some individuals suggested that they varied their approach on a case-by-case basis, indicating that 'I would not do independent legal research unless the parties were inept or telling me something that made no sense. I do read the authorities the parties cite to further understand them. I would not discuss such research with the parties, because they already have given me their view in their briefs'. While this type of flexibility may appear beneficial, it creates problems of consistency and can be affected by unconscious (implicit) biases.[113] Significant debate exists within the judicial and arbitral education communities as to whether and to what extent to offer or mandate programs seeking to minimize or eliminate the effect of implicit bias on legal decision making.[114] These types of discussions are critical because they shape how neutrals view their duties as legal decision makers. Indeed, one respondent specifically noted that s/he followed a particular approach 'because there is a consensus that it is good practice'.

Some remarks were directly responsive to the issue of why parties are allowed to respond to independent legal research. For example, one individual noted that 'the significance of the results of my independent research generally controls my decision as to whether or not to contact counsel about the product of my research', while another indicated that 'I suppose that I could find something radical enough that it would make it appropriate to inform the parties and ask for their reaction by additional briefs. Hasn't happened yet.' Both of these comments are similar to those made in response to the question associated with Table 2.11.

Other respondents identified some of the tensions that can arise with respect to independent legal research, including conflicts between the need to allow a party to respond to independent legal research as a matter of procedural justice and the need to keep deliberations confidential.[115] Another problem involved situations where independent legal research might be seen as assisting one party over another.[116] However, one respondent suggested that independent legal research could resolve problems rather than creating them, noting that 'I find that the counsel knowing I will research matters myself "keeps everyone honest" and reduces temptations to mislead the tribunal'.

3. Incorporating legal authorities into reasoned decisions and awards

The next topic addressed by the survey focused on how judges and arbitrators incorporate legal research in written decisions and awards. This particular line of

[113] Judges and arbitrators are often blind to their own unconscious biases. Chs. 1.I, 1.II.

[114] Ch. 1.III.A.

[115] E.g. 'When it has been an issue, I have only rarely discussed because such a discussion would tend to signal my thinking'.

[116] E.g. 'I discuss the results only when they are used in my reasoning and impact the outcome, however I am careful to remain independent and do not advocate in lieu of counsel of either party'.

questioning began by asking respondents to indicate what percentage of the legal authorities that they had read or reviewed, either in whole or in part, were subsequently mentioned in written decisions or awards. The question used the same frequency breakdowns adopted in earlier questions—0 per cent of the legal authorities read or reviewed (assigned the number '1' for purposes of calculating weighted averages), 1 to 29 per cent of the legal authorities read or reviewed ('2' for weighted averages), 30 to 59 per cent of the legal authorities read or reviewed ('3' for weighted averages), 60 to 99 per cent of the legal authorities read or reviewed ('4' for weighted averages), and 100 per cent of the legal authorities read or reviewed ('5' for weighted averages)—and was structured in the same way as a later question involving the incorporation of factual authorities (evidence) so as to allow for comparisons across the legal–evidentiary divide.[117]

Table 2.14 Percentage of legal authorities that have been read or reviewed and that are reflected in the written decision or award (weighted averages followed by standard deviation in parenthesis and sample (N) size)

	Full pop.	Current judges	Current arbitrators	J-A t-stat	Domestic disputes	Int'l disputes	D-I t-stat	Comm. law	Civil law	C-C t-stat
Weighted average	2.80 (.96) 326	3.50 (.71) 2	2.79 (.92) 269	−1.09	2.77 (.96) 226	2.87 (.95) 99	.87	2.77 (.90) 257	2.98 (1.04) 50	1.47

As Table 2.14 shows, none of the comparative pairings indicated a statistically significant difference in weighted averages. These findings are, of course, useful to the extent they reject allegations that certain groups (such as judges or civil law lawyers) are more legally oriented than other groups (such as arbitrators or common law lawyers). The data is also helpful to the extent it suggests that neutrals do not mention all the legal authorities they review in their final decision or award. To the contrary, it appears that judges and arbitrators only cite to a portion of the authorities that they have read or reviewed in their written decisions and awards.[118]

The next question in this series asked respondents to describe the factors that they took into account when deciding whether to mention a legal authority in a written decision or award. Respondents were asked to indicate how often they took each of 14 features, including an option marked 'other', into account, using the standard frequency breakdowns: 0 per cent of the time (assigned the number '1' for purposes of calculating weighted averages), 1 to 29 per cent of the time ('2' for weighted averages), 30 to 59 per cent of the time ('3' for weighted averages), 60 to 99 per cent of the

[117] Table 2.27.

[118] Some care should be taken in interpreting data such as this. A mark of 2.50, for example, does not mean that judges read materials 30 per cent of the time, which would be halfway between the percentages indicated by the numbers 2 (in this case, 1 to 29 per cent of the time) and 3 (in this case, 30 to 59 per cent of the time). Respondents could have marked a 2 if they routinely cited materials 25 per cent of the time and marked a 3 if they routine cited materials 55 per cent of the time. In that case, a 2.50 mark would be equivalent to 40 per cent. Instead, the most that can be said is that a mark of 2.50 (like a mark of 2.25 or 2.75) means that most respondents mentioned legal materials somewhere between 1 to 29 per cent of the time and 30 to 59 per cent of the time.

time ('4' for weighted averages), and 100 per cent of the time ('5' for weighted averages). The structure of the question was identical to a later question involving factors considered when determining whether to include factual authorities in a written decision or award, thereby permitting comparisons across the legal–evidentiary divide.[119]

The data generated some very interesting results across the three comparative axes, as noted in Table 2.15. First, no statistically significant differences arose between judicial and arbitral practices. While a number of minor differences arose with respect to hierarchical rankings within each cohort, that result was affected by the fact that many options were tied for the same position. Notably, both groups placed the same two items—the importance of the legal authority to the resolution of the controversy and the importance of the underlying legal principle to resolution of the controversy—in the top two positions.

Second, the comparison between domestic and international disputes showed only two statistically significant differences in intensity markings ($p<.05$), although the items in question (the importance of the legal authority to the resolution of the controversy and the importance of the underlying legal principle to resolution of the controversy) were ranked identically within the two groups (first and second, respectively). This consistency between internal rankings extended another three positions, including whether the parties dispute the interpretation or application of the underlying rule or principle (jointly ranked third), whether the parties dispute the interpretation or application of the particular legal authority (jointly ranked fourth) and a desire to make sure the losing party feels heard (jointly ranked fifth).

Third, the comparison between common law and civil law respondents also showed only two statistically significant difference in intensity markings, but at a much higher degree of confidence ($p<.001$) than existed in cases involving domestic and international disputes. Interestingly, the differences appeared on the same items that showed a statistically significant difference in domestic and international disputes (the importance of the legal authority to the resolution of the controversy and the importance of the underlying legal principle to resolution of the controversy) and also involved identical hierarchical rankings (first and second, respectively). Common law and civil law respondents were also consistent in terms of their internal hierarchies, placing the same items in the third and fourth positions (whether the parties dispute the interpretation or application of the underlying rule or principle and whether the parties dispute the interpretation or application of the particular legal authority, respectively).

Although the difference in intensity markings is important to note with respect to comparisons across the domestic–international and common law–civil law divides, that information only goes to how often the neutrals in those categories consider those factors when deciding whether to include a legal authority in a written decision or award. In this case, the hierarchical rankings are at least as important (if not more so) in evaluating and anticipating judicial and arbitral behaviour.

119 Table 2.28.

Table 2.15 Factors considered when determining whether to include legal authorities in the written decision or award (weighted averages followed by standard deviation in parenthesis, sample (N) size, and ranking within the cohort)

	Full pop.	Current judges	Current arbitrators	J-A t-stat	Domestic disputes	Int'l disputes	D-I t-stat	Comm. law	Civil law	C-C t-stat
A desire to make sure the losing party feels heard	3.41 (1.28) 317	3.33 (.58) 3 Rank: 6 (tied)	3.40 (1.28) 257 Rank: 5	.09	3.39 (1.31) 221 Rank: 5	3.45 (1.22) 95 Rank: 5	.38	3.48 (1.25) 248 Rank: 5	3.20 (1.29) 50 Rank: 6	−1.44
A desire to make sure the winning party feels heard	2.80 (1.31) 310	2.33 (.58) 3 Rank: 11 (tied)	2.77 (1.31) 251 Rank: 10 (tied)	.58	2.86 (1.33) 218 Rank: 9	2.67 (1.29) 91 Rank: 12	−1.16	2.85 (1.32) 243 Rank: 9	2.55 (1.24) 49 Rank: 13	−1.47
Concern about subsequent procedural review of the decision or award	2.83 (1.42) 315	3.33 (.58) 3 Rank: 6 (tied)	2.82 (1.40) 255 Rank: 9	−.63	2.76 (1.41) 219 Rank: 11	2.98 (1.43) 95 Rank: 6	1.27	2.77 (1.43) 246 Rank: 11	3.08 (1.32) 51 Rank: 7	1.43
Concern about subsequent review of the decision or award on the merits	2.81 (1.43) 315	3.00 (1.73) 3 Rank: 8 (tied)	2.77 (1.43) 255 Rank: 10 (tied)	−.28	2.77 (1.42) 219 Rank: 10	2.88 (1.46) 95 Rank: 7	.63	2.81 (1.42) 248 Rank: 10	2.69 (1.42) 49 Rank: 11	−.54
Importance of the legal authority to resolution of the controversy	4.20 (.97) 319	4.33 (1.15) 3 Rank: 2	4.20 (.95) 260 Rank: 1	−.24	4.27 (.89) 222 Rank: 1	4.01 (1.13) 96 Rank: 1	−2.20*	4.32 (.85) 251 Rank: 1	3.82 (1.12) 50 Rank: 1	−3.59***
Importance of the underlying legal principle to resolution of the controversy	4.16 (.96) 319	4.66 (.58) 3 Rank: 1	4.14 (.97) 260 Rank: 2	−.93	4.24 (.90) 219 Rank: 2	3.97 (1.07) 99 Rank: 2	−2.33*	4.28 (.87) 250 Rank: 2	3.76 (1.03) 51 Rank: 2	−3.77***
Novelty of the legal authority (i.e. how recently the authority was adopted or enacted)	2.91 (1.30) 313	3.67 (1.53) 3 Rank: 4 (tied)	2.94 (1.30) 255 Rank: 7	−.97	2.96 (1.33) 218 Rank: 7	2.79 (1.23) 94 Rank: 9	−1.06	2.99 (1.30) 248 Rank: 7	2.74 (1.24) 47 Rank: 9 (tied)	−1.28

Novelty of the underlying legal principle (i.e. how frequently the issue has been addressed in practice)	2.93 (1.27) 311	4.00 (.00) 2 Rank: 3	2.95 (1.27) 253 Rank: 6	−1.17	2.95 (1.30) 217 Rank: 8	2.87 (1.22) 93 Rank: 8	−.51	3.01 (1.25) 246 Rank: 6	2.74 (1.28) 47 Rank: 9 (tied)	−1.35
Perceived likelihood that the losing party will seek to challenge the decision or award	2.53 (1.38) 316	2.33 (1.53) 3 Rank: 11 (tied)	2.57 (1.36) 256 Rank: 12	.30	2.45 (1.39) 220 Rank: 13	2.71 (1.34) 95 Rank: 11	1.54	2.46 (1.38) 252 Rank: 13	2.87 (1.22) 46 Rank: 8	1.89
Type of legal authority (treaty, statute, judicial decision, etc.)	2.95 (1.35) 316	3.00 (1.73) 3 Rank: 8 (tied)	2.93 (1.34) 256 Rank: 8	−.09	3.01 (1.33) 222 Rank: 6	2.78 (1.41) 93 Rank: 10	−1.38	2.93 (1.34) 251 Rank: 8	3.28 (1.36) 47 Rank: 5	1.64
Type of legal dispute (contractual, regulatory, etc.)	2.56 (1.38) 305	1.33 (.58) 3 Rank: 13	2.52 (1.37) 246 Rank: 13	1.50	2.62 (1.38) 213 Rank: 12	2.41 (1.37) 91 Rank: 13	−1.22	2.56 (1.39) 241 Rank: 12	2.65 (1.35) 46 Rank: 12	.40
Whether the parties dispute the interpretation or application of the particular legal authority	3.86 (1.15) 311	3.67 (.58) 3 Rank: 4 (tied)	3.90 (1.14) 251 Rank: 4	.35	3.83 (1.17) 217 Rank: 4	3.90 (1.10) 93 Rank: 4	.49	3.97 (1.09) 246 Rank: 3 (tied)	3.64 (1.21) 47 Rank: 4	−1.87
Whether the parties dispute the interpretation or application of the underlying rule or principle	3.88 (1.14) 313	3.00 (1.41) 2 Rank: 8 (tied)	3.91 (1.14) 253 Rank: 3	1.12	3.86 (1.17) 218 Rank: 3	3.91 (1.06) 94 Rank: 3	.36	3.97 (1.10) 248 Rank: 3 (tied)	3.74 (1.05) 47 Rank: 3	−1.32
Other (please describe below)	1.57 (1.26) 37	.00 NA 0 Rank: 14	1.57 (1.22) 30 Rank: 14	NA	1.52 (1.24) 29 Rank: 14	1.75 (1.39) 8 Rank: 14	.45	1.66 (1.33) 32 Rank: 14	1.00 (.00) 5 Rank: 14	−1.10

The primary inference that can be gleaned from this data is that neutrals are primarily motivated by practical considerations (such as those involving the importance of the legal authority or principle and whether the parties dispute the interpretation or application of that authority or principle) rather than by philosophical ones (such as those relating to a desire to make one or the other of the parties feel heard). However, not all practical considerations are weighted the same. For example, concerns about subsequent challenges from the parties and subsequent procedural review ranked relatively low among several cohorts and demonstrated no statistically significant differences in terms of intensity marks.

The question allowed respondents to supplement their answers through use of an open text box. Although this was the least chosen option among all the cohorts, the comments nevertheless provided useful insights into the arbitral decision-making process.[120]

As was the case with previous text box responses, not all of the statements were precisely on-point. For example, rather than focusing on the factors relevant to the decision whether to include legal authorities in the decision or award, several individuals discussed how they wrote reasoned decisions and awards as a general matter, thereby anticipating issues that were addressed later in the survey, as reflected in Tables 2.35, 2.36 and 2.37. Comments in this category included a statement by one individual who said that s/he 'simply tr[ied] to frame the award in the terms that the parties have brought to the panel, trying to make sure to address the parties' expressed concerns, in particular a point or authority that one or both insisted was determinative, if I or the panel are rejecting that argument'. Another individual similarly stated that s/he focused on 'what the parties or their agreement have asked for in terms of a reasoned or explained award'.

Some answers appeared to repeat options offered in the pre-established responses, particularly those that focused on the contentiousness of the legal authorities or legal principles in question. Comments in this category noted that 'obviously, if the parties agree on a legal principle, there is no need to spend their money on [discussing] the issue' in the decision or award. Other respondents similarly noted that their determination depended on 'the degree of division of the parties and whether [including the legal authority] will aid resolution that is lasting' and on 'whether the authority substantially differs from authorities submitted in briefing by the parties'.

Other respondents used the text box to describe their standard practice, indicating either what they did or did not do. For example, one individual said, 'I try to always mention a cited legal authority (case law, statute, etc.), and any authority that forms a basis for my decision'. However, another person stated that 'I do not mention legal authorities' and 'virtually all my decisions are awards only, without reasons given, and without any legal analysis stated'. Another respondent took something of a middle road by 'refrain[ing] from quoting authorities not relied upon by the parties'.

120 None of the comments came from those currently acting as judges.

The final group of responses provided new insights that might be used to enlarge the theoretical understanding of legal citation practices.[121] For example, one individual suggested that s/he would mention an authority in a written decision or award 'if neither party cited to an authority I find persuasive' and doing so would 'clarify the legal basis for the award'. Other respondents focused on more procedural concerns, with one stating s/he would include a reference 'when appropriate to show that I have done the thorough job expected by the parties', while other indicated a citation would be appropriate when it would 'help the parties understand my reasoning'.

4. Interim conclusions regarding the use of legal authorities

As the preceding pages show, inquiries into the use and nature of legal authorities in commercial disputes produced a number of novel insights and both confirmed and rejected conventional wisdom on a number of issues. For example, Tables 2.5 and 2.6 suggested that judges and arbitrators are relatively consistent when it comes to how they view the relative importance of various legal authorities in substantive and procedural disputes, offsetting long-held assumptions about differences between judicial and arbitral decision making. Legal authorities were viewed differently in all types of domestic and international disputes and across the common law–civil law divide, but only with respect to substantive disputes. In procedural matters, many of the core distinctions between the common law and civil law were eliminated or at least muted.

The series of questions and tables involving independent legal research (Tables 2.7 through 2.13) provided a number of useful and novel insights, both through statistical analyses and through detailed comments provided in respondents' own words. Not only does this data describe what types of legal research judges, arbitrators and their legal clerks/assistants conduct apart from reading the parties' submissions, it also addresses why judges and arbitrators decide to pursue such research, how frequently they conduct that research, when they conduct that research, how they justify that research as a matter of principle, whether they discuss the results from such research with the parties, and why those results might be discussed with the parties.

Although the material involving independent legal research is quite nuanced, the general conclusion appears to be that judges and arbitrators adopt a very similar approach to these issues. The story is slightly different when it comes to comparisons between domestic and international disputes and between common law and civil law respondents. While the two groups were similar in many regards, a higher number of statistically significant differences arose with respect to these two comparative cohorts than with respect to judges and arbitrators.

The third group of questions involving legal authorities focused on how judges and arbitrators incorporated legal materials into written decisions and awards. Although statistical analysis suggested few if any relevant differences between the various comparative

[121] Ch. 1.II. One key question involves why judges cite particular materials but not others, although scholars must be careful about the inferences that they draw. Stephen J Choi and G Mitu Gulati, 'Bias in Judicial Citations: A Window Into the Behavior of Judges?' (2008) 37 JLS 87, 91; Epstein and King (n 18) 9–10.

cohorts, the data is nevertheless illuminating to the extent it suggests that neutrals are primarily motivated by practical rather than philosophical considerations. These results should be quite interesting not only to practitioners who will now appreciate which of the various practical considerations carry the most weight with neutrals but also to scholars who may need to revisit their theoretical assumptions about legal reasoning.

B. Use of Factual Authorities (Evidence)

Most commentary on legal reasoning focuses on the use and analysis of legal authorities.[122] However, interviews of judges and arbitrators suggest that factual determinations are central to the resolution of commercial disputes.[123] This possibility was anticipated during the design of the survey and led to the creation of a separate section concerning the use and analysis of factual authorities (evidence) and how factual authorities factor into the legal reasoning process.

Questions fell into several broad categories, including the relative importance of different types of factual authorities in substantive and procedural disputes, independent factual research by judges and arbitrators, and incorporating factual authorities into written decisions and awards. These issues are analogous to those reflected in the discussion of legal authorities,[124] and the use of identical or nearly-identical language in individual questions allowed for detailed cross-analysis of behaviours involving legal authorities and factual authorities.

1. Relative importance of factual authorities in commercial disputes

The analysis of evidentiary issues began by considering the relative importance of different types of factual authorities in commercial disputes. This question was structured similarly to those discussed in Tables 2.5 and 2.6, although the individual entries were of course different.

The survey asked respondents to state how important ten different types of factual authority (evidence) were to the decision-making process, using a five-point scale where one was to be considered 'not important at all' and five was to be considered 'very important'. Since commentators have seldom considered the relative persuasiveness of different types of evidentiary materials,[125] the list of factual authorities was generated as an exhaustive compilation of all possible forms of evidence across various jurisdictional lines.[126] Because respondents might rely on other, unanticipated types

[122] Ch. 1.III.A. Some exceptions exist. Edna Sussman, 'The Arbitrator Survey – Practices, Preferences and Changes on the Horizon', (2015) 26 Am Rev Intl Arb 517, 519.

[123] Ch. 3.III.C.

[124] Ch. 2.IV.A.

[125] Analysis in this area tends to be anecdotal rather than empirical, both in domestic and cross-cultural contexts. Ch. 1.III.A.

[126] Thus, for example, the survey referred to pre-hearing testimony via a witness statement (common in arbitration and in some judicial settings) or deposition (common in litigation and, to a lesser extent, domestic arbitration in the United States).

of evidentiary materials, the survey allowed respondents to supplement their answers by marking 'other' and describing additional authorities in their own words in an open text box.

The first question in this series focused on the relative importance of different types of evidence, an issue that is said to be particularly important across the common law–civil law divide.[127] The data generated from this question is represented in Table 2.16 and both confirms and rejects a number of widely held assumptions about judicial and arbitral reasoning in commercial disputes.

Analysis across the three comparative axes (judicial–arbitral, domestic–international and common law–civil law) generated some interesting results. First, relatively few differences arose between judges and arbitrators. Only one entry—documents written by a third party—showed a statistically significant difference in intensity marks (p<.05), although that item was relatively unimportant to both cohorts and was given an identical rank by both groups (tenth out of 11). Comparison of the two hierarchies was somewhat difficult due to multiple ties, but the two groups usually agreed or gave marks that were only one place off.

Interestingly, the intensity markings (which were, as noted, reflective of how important the various authorities were to the respondents' decision-making process) were substantially higher for factual authorities (noted in Table 2.16) than for legal authorities (noted in Table 2.5). The average intensity mark for judges (calculated by adding all the intensity marks and dividing by 11) was 3.06 in legal disputes but 3.67 in factual disputes. Similarly, the average intensity mark for arbitrators was 2.98 in legal disputes but 3.84 in factual disputes. While the difference between each cohort's approach to legal and factual authorities cannot be statistically analysed on the data generated here, it is interesting to note that both judges and arbitrators indicated that factual authorities were more important to the determination of substantive disputes than legal authorities were. This finding, which is consistent with comments made during the semi-structured interviews,[128] suggests the need for both further research and potential reconsideration of the nature of legal decision making in commercial disputes.

The second comparison involved domestic and international disputes. In this case, four items showed a statistically significant difference in intensity markings, two (oral testimony of a party and non-party witness at the hearing) at the highest level of confidence (p<.001) and two (documents written by a third party and pre-hearing testimony of a party witness) at the lowest level of confidence (p<.05). All but one of these items (oral testimony of a non-party witness at the hearing) also showed a difference in internal rankings. Interestingly, the ranking of the various authorities only converged three times in the domestic–international comparison: relevant contract(s) or transactional documents (jointly marked first); oral testimony of a non-party witness at the hearing (jointly ranked third) and other (jointly ranked eleventh). Similar discrepancies

[127] Ch. 1.III.C.
[128] Ch. 3.III.C.

Table 2.16 Importance of different types of evidence when deciding factual issues (weighted averages followed by standard deviation in parenthesis, sample (N) size, and ranking within the cohort)

	Full pop.	Current judges	Current arbitrators	J-A t-stat	Domestic disputes	Int'l disputes	D-I t-stat	Comm. law	Civil law	C-C t-stat
Documents written by an expert witness	3.74 (.88) 301	4.00 (1.73) 3 Rank: 5 (tied)	3.68 (.87) 247 Rank: 6	−.63	3.68 (.92) 210 Rank: 7 (tied)	3.87 (.75) 90 Rank: 6	1.73	3.67 (.89) 239 Rank: 7	4.02 (.78) 45 Rank: 2	2.47*
Documents written by a party (other than any relevant contracts or transactional documents)	4.03 (.92) 300	4.00 (1.00) 3 Rank: 5 (tied)	4.05 (.89) 246 Rank: 4	.10	4.08 (.88) 209 Rank: 4	3.89 (1.00) 90 Rank: 5	−1.64	4.09 (.90) 238 Rank: 4	3.89 (.96) 45 Rank: 4	−1.35
Documents written by a third party	3.44 (.93) 300	2.33 (1.53) 3 Rank: 10	3.46 (.91) 247 Rank: 10	2.12*	3.37 (.93) 210 Rank: 10	3.61 (.91) 89 Rank: 7	2.05*	3.42 (.94) 239 Rank: 10	3.66 (.86) 44 Rank: 6	1.58
Oral testimony from an expert witness at the hearing	3.96 (.82) 300	4.33 (.58) 3 Rank: 4	3.91 (.83) 246 Rank: 5	−.87	3.96 (.84) 210 Rank: 5	3.96 (.78) 89 Rank: 2	.00	3.95 (.81) 238 Rank: 5	3.98 (.84) 45 Rank: 3	.23
Oral testimony from a party witness at the hearing	4.37 (.81) 299	4.67 (.58) 3 Rank: 3	4.35 (.83) 246 Rank: 2	−.67	4.56 (.69) 208 Rank: 2	3.93 (.91) 90 Rank: 4	6.55***	4.54 (.67) 237 Rank: 2	3.62 (1.01) 45 Rank: 7 (tied)	−7.71***
Oral testimony from a non-party witness at the hearing	4.30 (.83) 301	5.00 (.00) 3 Rank: 1 (tied)	4.30 (.79) 247 Rank: 3	−1.53	4.45 (.76) 210 Rank: 3	3.94 (.88) 90 Rank: 3	−5.07***	4.41 (.78) 237 Rank: 3	3.82 (.86) 45 Rank: 5	−4.58***
Pre-hearing testimony of an expert witness (written witness statement or deposition testimony)	3.57 (.90) 299	3.33 (1.15) 3 Rank: 9	3.51 (.89) 245 Rank: 9	.35	3.55 (.90) 208 Rank: 9	3.59 (.89) 90 Rank: 8	.35	3.53 (.88) 237 Rank: 9	3.62 (.96) 45 Rank: 7 (tied)	.62

Pre-hearing testimony of a party witness (written witness statement or deposition testimony)	3.71 (.93) 300	3.67 (.58) 3 Rank: 8	3.66 (.94) 246 Rank: 7	−.02	3.78 (.93) 209 Rank: 6	3.52 (.90) 90 Rank: 10	−2.24*	3.76 (.93) 238 Rank: 6	3.40 (.89) 45 Rank: 10	−2.40*
Pre-hearing testimony of a third-party witness (written witness statement or deposition testimony)	3.64 (.94) 301	4.00 (.00) 3 Rank: 5 (tied)	3.61 (.92) 247 Rank: 8	−.73	3.68 (.96) 210 Rank: 7 (tied)	3.54 (.89) 90 Rank: 9	−1.18	3.65 (.95) 239 Rank: 8	3.51 (.87) 45 Rank: 9	−.92
Relevant contract(s) or transactional documents	4.93 (.30) 301	5.00 (.00) 3 Rank: 1 (tied)	4.93 (.32) 248 Rank: 1	−.38	4.94 (.31) 209 Rank: 1	4.91 (.28) 91 Rank: 1	−.79	4.97 (.18) 238 Rank: 1	4.89 (.31) 46 Rank: 1	−2.41*
Other (please describe below)	2.79 (1.72) 39	.00 NA 0 Rank: 11	2.78 (1.72) 32 Rank: 11	NA	2.79 (1.81) 28 Rank: 11	2.82 (1.54) 11 Rank: 11	.05	2.83 (1.76) 30 Rank: 11	2.50 (1.64) 6 Rank: 11	−.42

in hierarchical rankings were also reflected with respect to legal authorities in domestic and international disputes in Table 2.5, suggesting that there is something about the nature of these disputes that results in a different approach to legal reasoning, depending on the setting.

When comparing average intensity markings across the legal–evidentiary divide, factual disputes were again rated more highly. For example, for domestic disputes, the average intensity mark in legal disputes was 2.90, while in factual disputes it was 3.89. For international disputes, the average intensity mark in legal disputes was 3.26, while in factual disputes it was 3.78. Again, this discrepancy cannot be statistically analysed with the existing data, but does suggest the need for further empirical and theoretical analysis.

The third comparative axis involved respondents from common law and civil law jurisdictions. In this case, five statistically significant differences arose with respect to intensity markings, two (oral testimony from and party and no-party witness at the hearing) at the highest level of confidence ($p<.001$) and three (documents written by an expert witness, pre-hearing testimony from a party witness and relevant contract(s) or transactional documents) at the lowest level of confidence ($p<.05$). Four items also showed a divergence in ranking, with only one type of factual authority—relevant contract(s) or transactional documents, jointly ranked first—reflecting a common placement in the two cohorts' hierarchies.

The divergence in ranking and intensity markings can be attributed to longstanding differences in how common law lawyers and civil law lawyers view evidence. For example, the findings are consistent not only with claims that common law lawyers place a high premium on oral testimony while civil law lawyers prefer documentary evidence but also with widely reported concerns by civil law lawyers about the veracity of party witnesses.[129] The difference in intensity regarding documents written by experts can likely be attributed to common law lawyers' use of party-appointed experts (who have the reputation of being 'hired guns') and civil law lawyers' use of court- or arbitrator-appointed experts (which are viewed as more objective and thus more persuasive than party-appointed experts).[130]

Comparisons of intensity markings across the legal–evidentiary divide show results similar to what was seen along the judicial–arbitral and domestic–international axes. For example, in legal disputes, common law lawyers generated intensity marks of 2.95, while factual disputes generated intensity marks of 3.89. Similarly, civil law lawyers generated intensity marks of 3.52 in legal disputes, while factual disputes generated intensity marks of 3.72. Although these findings cannot be statistically analysed in the current study, they appear to reject conventional wisdom that common law lawyers are more concerned about facts than civil law lawyers are.[131] However, that conclusion will ned to be further tested through additional empirical studies.

[129] Ch. 1.III.C.
[130] Ch. 1.III.C.
[131] The coding analysis that was conducted as part of this project was inconclusive on this point. Ch. 4.IV.

The scarcity of practical and theoretical research regarding the relative importance of different types of evidentiary materials[132] meant that there could be one or more types of factual authorities that were important to respondents but that were not offered among the pre-existing options, so the question allowed respondents to identify other types of evidence that they considered important to the determination of factual issues. However, the survey design appeared to be appropriate, given that 'other' was the least-chosen option for all comparative cohorts.

Of the written responses that were generated, several mentioned materials that were covered by the pre-established alternatives, although the respondents provided additional detail. Thus, for example, respondents focusing on documentary evidence indicated the importance of 'correspondence between the parties prior to the arbitration', 'interparty communications about the dispute', 'documents signed by the parties under oath and submitted to third party institutions or the government before a dispute arose—e.g. tax returns', and 'emails-texts-ESI [electronically stored information]'. Respondents emphasizing oral testimony focused on 'cross-examination and/or rebuttal testimony', 'deposition transcripts', and 'how deeply familiar the witness is with the subject matter, frankness of demeanour'.

Some comments focused on the nature of expert evidence. For example, one individual indicated that '[m]y judicial experience as well as arbitral experience leads me to consider most "experts" to be hired guns of questionable reliability', while another respondent mentioned the importance of an 'expert appointed by tribunal', thus appearing to distinguish between party-appointed experts and those appointed by a court or tribunal.

Other comments that expanded on pre-determined alternatives in the survey underscored the role that timing played in the decision maker's analysis, echoing sentiments generated during the semi-structured interviews.[133] For example, various respondents noted the importance of 'relevant correspondence before the dispute arose', 'pertinent contemporaneous documents construing the contract', 'contemporaneous party-written documents', and 'specific records directly applicable to the dispute'.

As expected with a question of this nature, some respondents were unable to provide an answer in the abstract, merely saying 'it depends', 'the importance of any of the [pre-determined options] can vary significantly depending on the nature of the dispute' or that such analyses were 'very subjective'. One person went slightly further, noting,

> All of the [pre-existing] answers depend on the nature of dispute, parties and experts. Many party-appointed experts are treated with some scepticism, as is self-supporting oral testimony of witnesses that conflicts with documents created at the time. Original records and documents prior to dispute often given more weight than those after dispute becomes obvious.

[132] Ch. 1.III.A.
[133] Ch. 3.III.C.1.

Some respondents focused on how they weighed evidence, anticipating issues discussed in Table 2.19. For example, one individual noted that s/he 'measure[d] veracity of testimony against an impartial witness's documents', while another indicated that the 'credibility of all of the above' was important.

Other responses were more innovative. For example, one individual noted s/he considered 'official government documents as they may be relevant'. However, a number of comments appeared to be somewhat off-point in that they did not address evidence per se. For example, references to 'applicable case law' and 'applicable industry codes' seem to be more relevant to issues covered by Tables 2.5 and 2.6. Other respondents noted the importance of 'argument', without distinguishing between legal and factual elements.

Although relatively little commentary exists regarding judicial and arbitral approaches to evidence in commercial disputes, one issue that has occasionally arisen involves the increasing complexity and scope of materials, particularly written materials, submitted for the consideration of the decision maker.[134] As interviewees for the current study noted, it is often impossible for judges and arbitrators to read all of the evidentiary submissions in their entirety, which raises concerns about the proportion of documents submitted to a court or arbitral tribunal that are read by the decision maker, either in full or in part.[135]

As a result, the next two questions asked respondents to indicate what percentage of documents submitted to them by the parties were read in full or in part. The questions specifically excluded documents read during the hearing itself and used the same frequency breakdowns adopted elsewhere in the study: 0 per cent of the documents submitted (assigned the number '1' for purposes of calculating weighted averages), 1 to 29 per cent of the documents submitted ('2' for weighted averages), 30 to 59 per cent of the documents submitted ('3' for weighted averages), 60 to 99 per cent of the documents submitted ('4' for weighted averages), and 100 per cent of the documents submitted ('5' for weighted averages).

Table 2.17 reports the percentage of evidentiary documents read in full and identifies no statistically significant differences between any of the comparative cohorts. The weighted average of the full population was 3.89 out of 5.00, which suggested that respondents read, in full, between 30 and 59 per cent of the documents submitted by the parties.[136] This is a relatively low number and may suggest the need for counsel to change their approach to the submission of evidence in litigation and arbitration.

Table 2.18 reports the percentage of evidentiary documents read in part and also identifies no statistically significant differences between any of the comparative cohorts. In this case, the weighted average of the full population was 3.45 out of 5.00, slightly below that reported in Table 2.17. However, this data suggests that judges and arbitrators read, in part, between 30 and 59 per cent of the documents submitted by the

[134] Ch. 1.III.A–B.
[135] Ch. 3.III.C.2.b.
[136] Notably, no respondent indicated that s/he read zero per cent of the documents in full.

Table 2.17 Percentage of evidentiary documents read in full (weighted averages followed by standard deviation in parenthesis and sample (N) size)

	Full pop.	Current judges	Current arbitrators	J-A t-stat	Domestic disputes	Int'l disputes	D-I t-stat	Comm. law	Civil law	C-C t-stat
Weighted average	3.90 (.88) 303	4.00 (.00) 3	3.86 (.88) 249	–.28	3.94 (.85) 210	3.79 (.96) 92	−1.36	3.90 (.88) 240	3.96 (.87) 46	.42

Table 2.18 Percentage of evidentiary documents read in part (weighted averages followed by standard deviation in parenthesis and sample (N) size)

	Full pop.	Current judges	Current arbitrators	J-A t-stat	Domestic disputes	Int'l disputes	D-I t-stat	Comm. law	Civil law	C-C t-stat
Weighted average	3.45 (1.43) 299	2.67 (.58) 3	3.47 (1.39) 246	.99	3.55 (1.45) 208	3.20 (1.36) 90	−1.95	3.50 (1.43) 237	3.20 (1.41) 45	−1.29

parties. Again, this number suggests that counsel may wish to change their approach to the submission of evidence in litigation and arbitration so as to save time and costs.

Although Tables 2.16 and 2.17 cannot be statistically compared, some interesting phenomena nevertheless arose. For example, judges reported the highest weighted average in Table 2.16 but the lowest weighted average in Table 2.17. Although this information could suggest a different in how judges and arbitrators approach evidentiary materials, it could also reflect a difference in the scope or type of materials submitted in litigation versus arbitration.[137] More research is needed before a firm conclusion can be drawn.

It is also impossible to draw strict comparisons between respondents' treatment of evidentiary documents, on the one hand, and legal authorities on the other, since questions relating to whether and to what extent respondents read legal authorities in full or in part were not structured in a similar manner. However, Table 2.7 did ask respondents to indicate, among other things, how often they read different types of legal authorities in full as opposed to in part. As a rule, the weighted averages for reading various items in full were higher than weighted averages for reading the same items in part, a phenomenon that also appeared in Tables 2.17 and 2.18 with respect to evidentiary materials.[138] Again, this information should be further investigated, both empirically and theoretically.

Some additional observations can be pulled from the raw data, which is not reproduced here. Those materials show that none of the respondents indicated that

[137] Participants in the semi-structured interviewees provided some insights into the quantity of written materials submitted in different proceedings. Ch. 3.III.C.2.b.

[138] Table 2.7 used the same percentages and numbers for weighing frequency of certain behaviours as Tables 2.17 and 3.18.

they read zero per cent of the evidentiary documents in full, which means that judges and arbitrators do read at least some percentage of the evidentiary materials in full. The raw data also shows that 26 per cent of the full population read all of the documents submitted to them in full. While these figures may vary greatly depending on the nature of the underlying disputes, with smaller or less complex matters involving smaller and more manageable evidentiary submissions, the information suggests a relatively broad disparity in practices.

The raw data also showed that 31 per cent of the entire survey population indicated that they read 100 per cent of the evidentiary submissions, suggesting that every document has received at least a cursory review from the decision maker, although some variation may again arise as a result of the type of dispute at issue. Unfortunately, the interpretation of this data is somewhat difficult, since certain comments generated in response to other survey questions, as well as various statements made during the semi-structured interviews, suggested that some respondents did not know whether reading an evidentiary document in full should also be counted as reading that same document in part.[139] Although no clear conclusions can be drawn from this latter figure, the data nevertheless suggests that more research would be worthwhile to confirm what percentage of evidentiary documents are read, in whole or in part, by judges and arbitrators.

The survey design anticipated the possibility that respondents would indicate that they read different percentages of evidentiary documents in full as opposed to those read in part. Therefore, the next question in the series asked respondents to identify how important 15 pre-identified factors were to the respondent's decision to read evidentiary documents submitted by the parties in full or in part and provided an opportunity for the respondents to provide additional factors in a text box marked 'other'. The question, which indicated that 1 should be considered 'not important at all' and 5 should be considered 'very important', was structured similarly but not identically to an analogous question discussed in Table 2.8 about factors affecting the decision to read a legal authority in full or in part.[140]

Findings from this question are reported in Table 2.19 and provide a number of interesting and novel data points. First, the comparison between judges and arbitrators showed no statistically significant differences in terms of intensity markings. While this initially suggested that there were no relevant differences in the way that judges and arbitrators approach the task of reviewing evidentiary documents, the internal rankings of different factors varied considerably. Furthermore, these variations occur at the highest levels of the hierarchy, which differs from results generated in other contexts, where consistency generally existed among the highest-ranked options before diverging.

The highest-ranked factor for judges was the extent of their recollection of the document from the hearing, which was ranked eighth by arbitrators. The second

[139] Ch. 3.III.C.2.b.

[140] Table 2.8 only offered 12 alternatives, including 'other'.

Table 2.19 Factors important to the decision to read documents submitted by the parties in whole or in part (weighted averages followed by standard deviation in parenthesis, sample (N) size, and ranking within the cohort)

	Full pop.	Current judges	Current arbitrators	J-A t-stat	Domestic disputes	Int'l disputes	D-I t-stat	Comm. law	Civil law	C-C t-stat
Credibility of counsel	2.72 (1.45) 293	3.67 (2.31) 3 Rank: 8 (tied)	2.70 (1.44) 239 Rank: 15	−1.15	2.78 (1.46) 207 Rank: 15	2.55 (1.43) 85 Rank: 15	−1.23	2.78 (1.47) 235 Rank: 15	2.30 (1.26) 43 Rank: 15	−2.01*
Credibility of parties	3.17 (1.55) 292	3.67 (2.31) 3 Rank: 8 (tied)	3.12 (1.51) 239 Rank: 13	−.62	3.23 (1.55) 206 Rank: 13	2.99 (1.52) 85 Rank: 12	−1.21	3.29 (1.54) 233 Rank: 12	2.51 (1.35) 43 Rank: 14	−3.11**
Credibility of the witnesses	3.40 (1.53) 291	3.67 (2.31) 3 Rank: 8 (tied)	3.34 (1.51) 237 Rank: 11	−.37	3.46 (1.54) 206 Rank: 11	3.24 (1.50) 84 Rank: 11	−1.11	3.49 (1.54) 233 Rank: 11	2.88 (1.40) 42 Rank: 12 (tied)	−2.39*
Extent of your understanding of the document during the hearing	4.01 (1.17) 293	4.33 (1.15) 3 Rank: 3 (tied)	4.01 (1.76) 239 Rank: 6	−.31	4.04 (1.17) 206 Rank: 6	3.91 (1.19) 86 Rank: 5	−.86	4.13 (1.12) 234 Rank: 5 (tied)	3.34 (1.29) 44 Rank: 8	−4.19***
Extent of your recollection of the document from the hearing	3.79 (1.23) 293	5.00 (.00) 2 Rank: 1	3.85 (1.23) 240 Rank: 8	−1.32	3.87 (1.20) 206 Rank: 8	3.59 (1.27) 86 Rank: 9 (tied)	−1.79	3.93 (1.18) 235 Rank: 8	3.07 (1.30) 44 Rank: 11	−4.37***
Extent of your understanding of the facts generally during the hearing	3.93 (1.21) 296	4.00 (1.00) 3 Rank: 5 (tied)	3.95 (1.21) 242 Rank: 7	−.07	4.01 (1.19) 208 Rank: 7	3.72 (1.25) 87 Rank: 7	−1.88	4.01 (1.18) 235 Rank: 7	3.44 (1.34) 45 Rank: 7	−2.90**

(continued)

Table 2.19 Continued

	Full pop.	Current judges	Current arbitrators	J-A t-stat	Domestic disputes	Int'l disputes	D-I t-stat	Comm. law	Civil law	C-C t-stat
Extent of your recollection of the facts generally from the hearing	3.78 (1.27) 292	4.00 (1.41) 2 Rank: 5 (tied)	3.82 (1.27) 239 Rank: 9	–.20	3.85 (1.27) 205 Rank: 9	3.59 (1.25) 86 Rank: 9 (tied)	–1.60	3.87 (1.24) 234 Rank: 9	3.23 (1.39) 43 Rank: 9	–3.05**
Importance of the document to the disposition of the controversy	4.74 (.73) 290	4.67 (.58) 3 Rank: 2	4.75 (.74) 238 Rank: 1	.19	4.76 (.76) 207 Rank: 1	4.70 (.66) 82 Rank: 1	–.63	4.78 (.73) 233 Rank: 1	4.59 (.81) 41 Rank: 1	–1.51
Standard practice (i.e. you follow the same practice in all cases, regardless of other factors)	3.19 (1.44) 293	3.00 (1.00) 3 Rank: 13 (tied)	3.18 (1.45) 239 Rank: 12	.21	3.29 (1.44) 206 Rank: 12	2.94 (1.43) 86 Rank: 13	–1.90	3.20 (1.44) 234 Rank: 13	3.16 (1.56) 43 Rank: 10	–.17
Type of document (party-drafted document, expert report, transactional document, etc.)	3.74 (1.22) 293	3.00 (1.00) 3 Rank: 13 (tied)	3.74 (1.21) 239 Rank: 10	1.05	3.75 (1.25) 206 Rank: 10	3.71 (1.15) 86 Rank: 8	–.26	3.70 (1.24) 234 Rank: 10	3.88 (1.16) 43 Rank: 5	.88
Type of legal dispute (contractual, regulatory, etc.)	3.07 (1.52) 290	2.00 (1.00) 3 Rank: 15	2.99 (1.52) 236 Rank: 14	1.12	3.14 (1.53) 205 Rank: 14	2.87 (1.48) 84 Rank: 14	–1.38	3.08 (1.52) 232 Rank: 14	2.88 (1.47) 42 Rank: 12 (tied)	–.79
Whether the parties dispute the credibility or content of the document in question	4.43 (1.03) 293	3.33 (1.53) 3 Rank: 11 (tied)	4.45 (1.05) 239 Rank: 2 (tied)	1.83	4.50 (1.01) 206 Rank: 2	4.28 (1.08) 86 Rank: 3	–1.66	4.50 (.97) 234 Rank: 3	4.16 (1.29) 43 Rank: 3	–2.00*
Whether the parties dispute the interpretation or application of the document in question	4.46 (1.01) 293	3.33 (1.53) 3 Rank: 11 (tied)	4.45 (1.04) 240 Rank: 2 (tied)	1.85	4.48 (1.02) 207 Rank: 3	4.40 (1.00) 85 Rank: 2	–.61	4.51 (.96) 234 Rank: 2	4.28 (1.24) 43 Rank: 2	–1.38

Whether the parties referred to the document during the hearing	4.09 (1.08) 294	4.33 (1.15) 3 Rank: 3 (tied)	4.09 (1.10) 240 Rank: 5	−.38	4.19 (1.06) 207 Rank: 4	3.84 (1.12) 86 Rank: 6	−2.53*	4.17 (1.03) 235 Rank: 4	3.77 (1.25) 43 Rank: 6	−2.26*
Whether the parties referred to the document in their written submissions	4.10 (1.03) 292	4.00 (1.00) 3 Rank: 5 (tied)	4.10 (1.05) 240 Rank: 4	.16	4.14 (1.06) 207 Rank: 5	4.01 (.96) 84 Rank: 4	−.97	4.13 (1.01) 235 Rank: 5 (tied)	3.95 (1.13) 43 Rank: 4	−1.05
Other (please describe below)	2.49 (1.80) 37	.00 NA 0 Rank: 16	2.53 (1.85) 30 Rank: 16	NA	2.50 (1.84) 28 Rank: 16	2.44 (1.81) 9 Rank: 16	−.09	2.60 (1.83) 30 Rank: 16	2.17 (1.83) 6 Rank: 16	−.53

highest-ranked factor for judges was the importance of the document to the disposition of the controversy, which was ranked first by arbitrators. However, the second highest ranked options for arbitrators were tied between whether the parties disputed the credibility or content of the document in question and the interpretation or application of the document in question, which were ranked by judges in the eleventh (tied) and third (tied) positions, respectively.

The absence of any statistically significant difference in the intensity marks between judges and arbitrators means that the null hypothesis (i.e. that there is no difference between the two groups) has not been disproved as to this element of decision making.[141] However, the difference in hierarchical rankings suggests more research is needed.

The second comparative pairing—domestic disputes and international disputes—showed only one statistically significant difference ($p<.05$) in terms of intensity marks. That factor—whether the parties referred to the document during the hearing—was considered more important in domestic disputes than in international disputes, both in terms of intensity (4.19 out of 5.00 for domestic disputes and 3.84 for international disputes) and hierarchy (fourth for domestic disputes, sixth for international disputes). However, this one difference is the exception to what appears to be relatively consistent ratings. Not only are the hierarchical rankings very close throughout, but the top three entries (importance of the document to the disposition of the controversy, jointly ranked first, and whether the parties dispute the credibility or content of the document in question and whether the parties dispute the interpretation or application of the document in question, ranked second or third in both groups) are the same for the two cohorts.

The third comparative pairing focused on common law and civil law respondents. Numerous statistically significant differences arose in this regarding, with two—extent of the respondent's understanding of the document during the hearing and extent of the respondent's recollection of the document from the hearing—reflecting differences at the highest level of confidence ($p<.001$); three—credibility of the parties, extent of your understanding of the facts generally during the hearing, and extent of your recollection of the facts generally from the hearing—reflecting differences at an intermediate level of confidence ($p<.01$); and three—credibility of counsel, credibility of the witness, and whether the parties referred to the document during the hearing—reflecting differences at the lowest level of confidence ($p<.05$).

The data reflected in Table 2.19 can be compared to the information found in Table 2.8, which focused on factors affecting the respondent's decision whether to read a legal authority in whole or in part. Both tables reflected no statistically significant differences when comparing responses from judges and arbitrators, suggesting not only that no differences in practice arose across the judicial–arbitral divide but also across the legal–evidentiary divide.

However, that phenomenon was not true in cases involving domestic and international disputes. In that case, Table 2.8 generated more statistically significant

[141] Frick (n 19) 379–90 (discussing null hypothesis testing); Ch. 1.I (discussing null hypotheses in this study).

differences than Table 2.19 (four and one, respectively), suggesting that domestic and international practice were more dissimilar with respect to the decision to read legal authorities in full or in part than with respect to the decision to read evidentiary materials in full or in part.

Even more interesting was the analysis involving common law and civil law respondents. When comparing Tables 2.8 and 2.16, it can be seen that Table 2.8 generated fewer statistically significant differences than Table 2.19 (two and nine, respectively), suggesting that common law and civil law respondents are more similar when it comes to the decision to read legal authorities in full or in part than they are when it comes to the decision to read evidentiary materials in full or in part. This is not an issue that has been discussed in the legal literature, and so is an important improvement in the general understanding of common law and civil law practices.

Another means of analysing the data involves comparing the average intensity marks for factors affecting the decision to read evidentiary materials in full or in part (as noted in Table 2.19) and average intensity marks for factors affecting the decision to read legal authorities in full or in part (as noted in Table 2.8). Data adduced in this study showed that intensity markings relating to the importance of various authorities to the respondents' decision-making process were substantially higher for factual authorities (noted in Table 2.16) than for legal authorities (noted in Table 2.5). The question therefore is whether the true is same with respect to factors affecting the decision to read legal or factual authorities in full or in part.

As it turns out, average intensity marks[142] were higher with respect to evidentiary matters as opposed to legal matters, which was also the case with respect to comparisons between Table 2.5 and Table 2.16. For example, when comparing judges and arbitrators, Table 2.8 generated average intensity marks of 2.86 and 3.28 out of 5.00, respectively, whereas Table 2.19 generated average intensity marks of 3.50 and 3.69. When comparing domestic and international disputes, the numbers for Table 2.8 were 3.30 and 3.20, respectively, while Table 2.19 generated averages of 3.75 and 3.55. The trend held true for common law and civil law disputes, with Table 2.8 producing averages of 3.31 and 3.19, respectively, and Table 2.19 generating averages of 3.76 and 3.35.

Again, it is impossible to conduct a statistical analysis of these results given the current structure of the study, but the trend toward stronger intensity markings in matters involving evidence is consistent not only with the comparisons involving Tables 2.5 and 2.16 but also with information gleaned from the semi-structured interviews.[143] While more research is needed to understand the interaction between legal and factual analyses in commercial dispute resolution, the data appears to be suggesting that factual issues and authorities are more important than legal issues and authorities in this field.

[142] These figures were calculated by adding all of the intensity marks in each cohort in the individual tables and dividing by the number of entries, which was 12 for Table 2.8 and 16 for Table 2.19

[143] Ch. 3.III.C.

As with other questions, respondents were allowed to supplement their answers by providing additional comments regarding factors that were important to the decision whether to read evidentiary documents in whole or in part. Several participants chose to repeat or emphasize options that were included within the pre-existing options, particularly with respect to the importance of the document to the disposition of the controversy. Thus, a number of comments focused on relevancy as a core consideration.[144]

Other respondents focused on whether the items had been referred to by the parties during the hearing or in written submissions, an issue that was also identified as important by participants in the semi-structured interviews.[145] Comments in this category ranged from 'I don't read documents not referenced' to 'often the entire document need not be read (like a long contract) since the attorneys will highlight the relevant portions which usually is also the disputed portion'.

One of the pre-established options mentioned the respondent's standard practice, and several individuals expanded on this concept. Some individuals described the limitations that they set upon themselves, noting 'I tend not to read documents which are produced only to prove that they exist but which do not contain materially important information' or '[I] read everything but focus on important documents'. Others described a more expansive standard practice, noting, for example, 'I read all documents irrespective of any of the factors above'; 'I invariably read whatever is submitted'; 'if it is submitted, I read it' and 'my practice is to read, in whole, all documents submitted by the parties'. One respondent appeared to distinguish between best practices and actual practices, stating that 'all arbitrators should read all documents in their entirety. I suppose occasionally one could be skipped over as irrelevant, but there are little—and sometimes big—gems in those documents'.

Several respondents noted the difficulty in responding to this question in the abstract, stating it was an 'impossible question to provide a general answer to'. Others provided stock answers that focused on the document's 'authenticity, probity, relevance, materiality'. However, a number of individuals were able to provide some illuminating comments that went beyond the pre-existing options. For example, one person focused on 'whether the document is a back-up to a summary document', while another noted the 'importance of understanding the chronology of the event, particularly in contractual disputes, and understanding the context in which documents were prepared'. A third cited the 'length of document' as relevant.

Sometimes respondents' review protocols depended on party behaviour. Timing was cited by several individuals as relevant. For example, one respondent stated, 'I always begin with review of documents, whenever possible', a sentiment echoed by the individual who noted that his/her standard practice depended on 'if I can get the documents prior to the hearing'. Another person noted that

[144] Comments falling into this category included 'relevancy'; 'relevance to the disputed issues'; 'where the entire document is relevant'; 'whether the entire document is relevant'; 'I read all relevant parts of every document'; 'apparent relevance to issues'; and 'whether I perceive it as relevant to disputed issues'.

[145] Ch. 3.III.C.2.b.

> in 'large document cases', parties often mark exhibits they never use. I establish rules up front that 'if you don't mention it in your evidence presentation, I won't read it unless you specifically ask me to do so.' Many irrelevant documents are marked as exhibits out of an abundance of caution.

This practice of over-submission of evidentiary materials was also mentioned in the semi-structured interviews.[146]

2. Independent factual research

Legal scholars have seldom discussed issues relating to independent research by judges and arbitrators into questions of fact.[147] The next series of questions therefore focused on respondents' research methodology regarding evidentiary issues and focused on a variety of issues, including the type and frequency of additional factual research respondents conducted, either themselves or with the help of legal clerks or assistants; the motivation for such research; and whether and to what extent parties or their counsel were allowed to respond to materials discovered through that research. As a matter of survey design, questions regarding factual research methodology were structured similarly to those involving legal research methodology so as to allow comparisons across the legal–evidentiary divide.

The first question in this series simply asked whether the respondent or respondent's law clerk/assistant conducted independent factual research so as to establish a baseline for further analysis. The question specifically excluded asking questions of a witness who was already present at a hearing, since that is something that is relatively common in litigation in civil law countries as well as in some forms of arbitration.

Table 2.20 Whether respondents or their law clerks/assistants conducted independent factual research (number of respondents followed by proportion in parenthesis)

	Full pop.	Current judges	Current arbitrators	J-A z-stat	Domestic disputes	Int'l disputes	D-I z-stat	Comm. law	Civil law	C-C z-stat
No	241 (.80)	3 (1.0)	201 (.81)	.83	178 (.86)	62 (.68)	3.49**	207 (.87)	21 (.47)	6.27***
Yes	59 (.20)	0 (.00)	46 (.19)	–.83	30 (.14)	29 (.32)	–3.49**	31 (.13)	24 (.53)	-6.27***
Total	300	3	247		208	91		238	45	

The data, which is presented in Table 2.20, provided some very intriguing information across the three comparative divides. First, judges and arbitrators were both overwhelmingly unlikely to engage in independent factual research, with none of the judges and only 19 per cent of the arbitrators indicating that they would undertake such efforts. Although the split appears considerable, the difference is not statistically significant.

[146] Ch. 3.III.C.2.b.
[147] Ch. 1.III.A.

Furthermore, these results were consistent with legal literature suggesting that judges and arbitrators should seldom, if ever, conduct independent factual research.[148]

Some distinctions arose when comparing practices in domestic and international disputes. Here, 14 per cent of respondents discussing domestic disputes indicated that they would undertake independent factual research while 32 per cent of respondents discussing international disputes would do the same, a difference that was statistically significant ($p<.01$).

The disparities were even more apparent across the common law–civil law divide. Not only did a statistically significant difference arise between these two comparative cohorts ($p<.001$), but the civil law lawyers were the only group in which a majority of the respondents indicated that they would undertake independent factual research, with 53 per cent of civil law respondents saying that they or their legal clerks/assistants did conduct such research as compared to only 13 per cent of common law respondents.

These results appear to confirm conventional wisdom indicating that decision makers in civil law countries work cooperatively with the parties to develop the factual materials relevant to a particular dispute.[149] Counsel in common law countries, on the other hand, operate much more independently, with relatively little input from judges or arbitrators regarding the development of the facts of the case, consistent with a more litigant-driven philosophy of dispute resolution.[150]

The survey design anticipated that at least some respondents would have engaged in independent factual research, so the next question in this series asked those who had replied 'yes' to the previous question to identify the type of practices in which they engaged. The question offered five pre-established options culled from the legal literature and allowed respondents to check as many of the items that applied, which meant that the percentages did not add up to 100. Because commentators have not discussed the issue of independent factual research at length, respondents who wanted to supplement the pre-existing answers were allowed to check 'other' and write in additional practices.

Table 2.21 reports percentages of individuals who indicated that they engaged in a particular type of independent factual research. None of the individuals who were currently sitting as judges answered this question, since none of them had indicated in the previous question that they engaged in independent factual research, which made statistical comparison of responses from judges and arbitrators impossible. However, data from the arbitrators was interesting, in that the second most frequently chosen option was 'other', which suggested that the pre-existing alternatives had missed potentially important practices.

A comparison of domestic and international disputes shown a number of interesting similarities. The most frequently chosen item by both groups, attracting 52 per cent of respondents discussing domestic disputes and 66 per cent of respondents discussing

[148] Ch. 1.III.A. The situation is slightly different with respect to independent legal research, which is more common, although no consensus exists with respect to the extent and type of 'independent' legal research that is considered appropriate. Ch. 1.III.A.

[149] Ch. 1.III.C.

[150] Cross (n 101) 285; Ch. 1.III.C.

Table 2.21 Types of independent factual research conducted by respondents and their law clerks/assistants (number of respondents followed by proportion in parenthesis and ranking within the cohort)

	Full pop.	Current judges	Current arbitrators	J-A z-stat	Domestic disputes	Int'l disputes	D-I z-stat	Comm. law	Civil law	C-C z-stat
Ask for appointment of an expert that the parties have not proposed, regardless of whether the expert will be appointed by the parties or the panel	17 (.18)	NA	14 (.19) Rank: 5 (tied)	–	8 (.14) Rank: 5	9 (.26) Rank: 4 (tied)	−1.36	6 (.10) Rank: 5	6 (.23) Rank: 5	−1.54
Ask for a particular document to be produced	52 (.57)	NA	37 (.51) Rank: 1	–	29 (.52) Rank: 1	23 (.66) Rank: 1	−1.31	29 (.50) Rank: 1	19 (.73) Rank: 1	−1.98*
Call a witness to testify at a hearing even though a party has not called that person	16 (.17)	NA	14 (.19) Rank: 5 (tied)	–	7 (.12) Rank: 6	9 (.26) Rank: 4 (tied)	−1.61	4 (.07) Rank: 6	11 (.42) Rank: 4	−3.92***
Conduct a site visit	32 (.35)	NA	25 (.35) Rank: 3	–	16 (.29) Rank: 3	15 (.43) Rank: 3	−1.40	17 (.29) Rank: 3	12 (.46) Rank: 3	−1.50
Conduct factual research on the internet	28 (.30)	NA	20 (.28) Rank: 4	–	12 (.21) Rank: 4	16 (.46) Rank: 2	−2.44*	11 (.19) Rank: 4	15 (.58) Rank: 2	−3.55***
Other (please explain)	29 (.32)	NA	26 (.36) Rank: 2	–	20 (.36) Rank: 2	9 (.26) Rank: 4 (tied)	1.00	22 (.38) Rank: 2	5 (.19) Rank: 6	1.70
Total	92		72		56	35		58	26	

international disputes, involved requests for a particular document to be produced. Notably, this was also the first choice for the other comparative cohorts as well, attracting 51 per cent of the arbitrators, 50 per cent of the common law respondents and 73 per cent of the civil law respondents.

Resulting involving domestic and international disputes immediately diverged after this point. For example, respondents discussing domestic disputes identified 'other' as the second most frequent response (36 per cent), which was tied for fourth among internationalists (26 per cent), while international experts identified internet research as the second most frequent response (46 per cent), which was ranked fourth by domestic specialists (21 per cent). Although discrepancies in the order of practices chosen are notable, the only item that showed a statistically significant difference in terms of intensity involved internet research ($p<.05$).

Comparisons between common law and civil law respondents also revealed a number of differences. For example, even though the two cohorts both indicated that their most frequent means of conducting independent research involved asking for a particular document to be produced, respondents from civil law jurisdictions were far more likely to do so, with 73 per cent of the respondents marking that option as opposed to only 50 per cent of common law respondents, a difference that was statistically significant ($p<.05$). Two other practices—calling a witness to testify at a hearing even though a party had not called that person and conducting internet research—also yielded statistically significant differences ($p<.001$), with civil law respondents far more likely to engage in that behaviour than common law respondents. These discrepancies not only confirm the longstanding belief that judges and arbitrators from civil law jurisdictions are far more involved with the development of the factual elements of a dispute,[151] they also demonstrate the type of activities that are likely to be undertaken. For example, according to this data, 73 per cent of respondents from civil law countries ask for particular documents to be produced, 58 per cent conduct factual research on the internet, 46 per cent conduct site visits, 42 per cent call witnesses to testify at the hearing even though those persons have not been called by a party, and 23 per cent ask for the appointment of an expert. Notably, respondents from civil law countries were the least likely to mark 'other' as an option, with only 19 per cent doing so.

Three of the comparative cohorts (arbitrators, domestic disputes and common law respondents) chose 'other' with sufficient frequency for it to be ranked in second position in their internal hierarchies, making the individual comments particularly noteworthy. Unfortunately, a number of comments were not particularly illuminating, since they simply repeated pre-existing options, as was the case with the individual who noted that independent factual research was, in his/her case, 'highly unusual, and only in rare cases by appointment of independent expert'.

Other comments appeared to focus more on independent legal research, which was addressed in Table 2.7, rather than factual research, which was at issue here. For

[151] Ch. 1.III.C.

example, one individual said, 'if a clerk is available, [I] seek additional research, ask for copies of cases, etc., referred to and/or relied upon by parties and self'. One person sought to create a link between legal and factual matters, noting that 'where it is argued that particular rules or regulations apply, [I] attempt to satisfy myself that they either do apply or do not'.

Several other respondents focused on whether and to what extent a judge or arbitrator should conduct independent factual research in the first place, perhaps hearkening back to the question associated with Table 2.20, which did not offer respondents the opportunity to explain their answers. For example, one respondent indicated that 'stuff comes up that you need to check out; not often, but it happens, led as much by intuition and feel as anything else. Sometimes it just doesn't feel right, so you dig deeper'. Another individual sought to distinguish between independent and cooperative factual research, indicating that 'I believe independent factual research is prohibited. The parties must participate equally in any factual development'.

Several respondents used the comment section not to indicate methods of independent factual research but to discuss the frequency of such research. For instance, one respondent said that 'it all depends on the kind of proceedings. For example, you must be much more active in default proceedings'. Another individual noted that such research was '[h]ighly unusual, and only in rare cases by appointment of independent expert'.

Some respondents sought to justify or explain why they undertook particular forms of independent factual research. Thus, one person said that s/he had 'not done the other examples, but believe with appropriate restraint that such actions could be undertaken if parties do not submit documents/experts/witnesses'. Another said that s/he conducted factual research 'only in some cases to better understand the general context of the case or some technical terms used by the parties which I do not fully understand'. This approach seemed relatively popular, with another individual similarly stating that s/he conducted 'internet research for context or terminology only; never with respect to disputed factual issues' and a third indicating that s/he had gone 'to the internet—but only if I don't understand the terms used by lawyers'. One person said that s/he did 'background internet research for conflict disclosures only'.

Although the comments entered in response to this question were useful and provided important insights into judicial and arbitral practices, it is important to recognize that they do not suggest that the pre-established options reflected in the survey missed any key practices. Instead, respondents seemed more interested in providing information on ancillary matters, such as how often and why they conducted independent factual research. This phenomenon suggests several fruitful lines of future research.

One issue that arises out of scholarly commentary regarding the propriety of independent legal research involves whether and to what extent parties should be provided with an opportunity to respond to any materials found by judges and arbitrators, which suggests that similar inquiries should be made with respect to independent factual research.[152] As a result, the next question in this series asked respondents to indicate how often they offered parties an opportunity to provide written or oral responses to the results of any independent factual research conducted by the respondent and his/her law clerk or assistant. The question used the standard breakdown for frequency—0 per cent of the time (assigned the number '1' for purposes of calculating weighted averages), 1 to 29 per cent of the time ('2' for weighted averages), 30 to 59 per cent of the time ('3' for weighted averages), 60 to 99 per cent of the time ('4' for weighted averages), and 100 per cent of the time ('5' for weighted averages)—and used a structure that was similar to an earlier question involving the frequency of invitations to respond to independent legal research so as to allow for comparisons across the legal–evidentiary divide.[153]

Table 2.22 Frequency of invitations to parties to respond to independent factual research (weighted averages followed by standard deviation in parenthesis and sample (N) size)

	Full pop.	Current judges	Current arbitrators	J-A t-stat	Domestic disputes	Int'l disputes	D-I t-stat	Comm. law	Civil law	C-C t-stat
Weighted average	3.08 (1.86) 119	NA	3.08 (1.85) 89	NA	2.63 (1.88) 75	3.84 (1.56) 43	3.57***	3.03 (1.90) 79	3.71 (1.54) 28	1.70

The results from this question are reported in Table 2.22. None of the respondents who were currently sitting as judges responded to this question because they had previously indicated that they did not engage in independent legal research.[154] As a result, it was impossible to conduct statistical studies comparing judicial and arbitral practices. However, a majority of arbitrators indicated that they sought responses from the parties between 30 and 59 per cent of the time.

The data in Table 2.22 can be compared to that in Table 2.12, which addressed frequency of invitations to the parties to respond to independent legal research. That table saw no statistically significant difference in invitation rates between judges and arbitrators. However, the weighted average for invitation rates generated by arbitrators in legal disputes was slightly above that generated by arbitrators in factual disputes (3.15 out of 5.00 as compared to 3.08, respectively).

Comparisons across the domestic–international divide showed a statistically significant difference ($p<.001$), with specialists in international disputes offering parties an opportunity to respond to factual research 30 to 59 per cent of the time, which is more frequent than the rate reported in domestic disputes, which was 1 to 29 per cent of the time. This difference was statistically significant at a high level of confidence ($p<.001$).

When comparing Table 2.22 to Table 2.12, it appeared that the weighted average was higher for invitation rates to legal research than for invitation rates to factual research in cases involving domestic disputes (2.96 compared to 2.63, respectively), although

[152] Ch. 1.II.A. More commentary exists with respect to independent legal research than independent factual research, likely because of the longstanding emphasis on questions of law, as opposed to questions of fact, in legal scholarship. Ch. 1.I.

[153] Table 2.12

[154] Table 2.20.

the reverse was true in cases involving international disputes, where the weighted averages were higher for invitation rates to factual research than for invitation rates to legal research (3.84 compared to 3.68, respectively). While it is impossible to conduct a statistical analysis comparing Table 2.12 and Table 2.22, this phenomenon does suggest an interesting avenue for future research.

The final analysis involves respondents from common law and civil law jurisdictions. Here, no statistically significant differences arose with respect to either independent factual research (Table 2.22) or independent legal research (Table 2.12). However, the weighted average for invitations to respond to independent research was higher in legal disputes than in factual disputes for common law lawyers (3.26 out of 5.00 as compared to 3.03), although it was higher in factual disputes than in legal disputes for civil law lawyers (3.71 as compared to 3.16). Again, there is no way to conduct a statistical analysis of this data, but future research into this matter may be warranted.

Although the data reflected in Table 2.22 is useful on its own, it is interesting to note that the raw data indicated a clear reverse bell curve, a phenomenon that was only really evident with respect to one other question, namely that involving the frequency of invitations to respond to independent legal research, as reported in Table 2.12. Notably, the bell is even more pronounced with respect to factual research, suggesting that neutrals fall even more firmly into one end or another of this particular spectrum.[155] While this phenomenon is encouraging to the extent it avoids the kind of theoretical and practical problems associated with case-by-case determinations of whether to issue invitations to parties to respond to independent factual research, it does create systemic concerns about predictability and equal treatment. It would therefore be useful to have more empirical information about why and when judges and arbitrators engage in independent factual research and whether such practices should be tolerated or curtailed.

The survey design anticipated that at least a certain number of respondents would extend invitations to the parties to respond to independent factual research, so the next question asked respondents to identify the rationale(s) that best described the respondent's position regarding invitations to respond to independent factual research. Because the survey design anticipated that some but not all respondents would be in favour of discussing their factual research methodology with the parties, the pre-established prompts included three options that explained why respondents shared their methodology with the parties and three options that explained why respondents did not share their methodology. The question also allowed respondents to provide additional rationales in their own words. Respondents were asked to check all categories that applied, which meant that percentages do not add up to 100. The question was identical in structure to an earlier question involving legal research methodology so as to allow comparisons across the legal–evidentiary divide.[156]

[155] Responses from the full population fell into the following pattern: 38 per cent of respondents issued invitations 0 per cent of the time; 1 per cent of respondents issued invitations 1 to 29 per cent of the time; 2 per cent of respondents issued invitations 30 to 59 per cent of the time; 7 per cent of respondents issued invitations 69 to 99 per cent of the time; and 44 per cent of respondents issued invitations 100 per cent of the time.

[156] Table 2.13.

Table 2.23 Rationales for discussing results of independent factual research with parties (number of respondents followed by proportion in parenthesis and ranking within the cohort)

	Full pop.	Current judges	Current arbitrators	J-A z-stat	Domestic disputes	Int'l Disputes	J-A z-stat	Comm. law	Civil law	J-A z-stat
Pro-discussion rationales										
I discuss the results of my factual research with the parties because they need to be able to respond to anything I discover as a matter of procedural justice	59 (.45)	NA	45 (.44) Rank: 1	–	26 (.31) Rank: 2	32 (.70) Rank: 1	−4.29***	36 (.39) Rank: 1	18 (.62) Rank: 1	−2.21*
I discuss the results of my factual research with the parties to ensure that what I have found is accurate	38 (.29)	NA	27 (.26) Rank: 3	–	21 (.25) Rank: 3	16 (.35) Rank: 2	−1.22	27 (.29) Rank: 3	8 (.28) Rank: 2	.15
I discuss the results of my factual research with the parties to increase their confidence in the process	28 (.21)	NA	21 (.20) Rank: 4	–	15 (.18) Rank: 5	12 (.26) Rank: 3	−1.14	22 (.24) Rank: 4	3 (.10) Rank: 5	1.55
Contra-discussion rationales										
I do not discuss the results of my factual research with the parties because I am confident that what I have found is accurate	4 (.03)	NA	2 (.02) Rank: 7	–	3 (.04) Rank: 7	1 (.02) Rank: 7	.43	2 (.02) Rank: 7	1 (.03) Rank: 7	−.39
I do not discuss the results of my factual research with the parties because my approach is implicit in the task of acting as a judge or arbitrator	21 (.16)	NA	15 (.15) Rank: 5	–	19 (.22) Rank: 4	2 (.04) Rank: 5 (tied)	2.68**	14 (.15) Rank: 5	4 (.14) Rank: 4	.17
I do not discuss the results of my factual research with the parties because that would decrease their confidence in the process	6 (.05)	NA	5 (.05) Rank: 6	–	4 (.05) Rank: 6	2 (.04) Rank: 5 (tied)	.09	4 (.04) Rank: 6	2 (.07) Rank: 6	−.56
Other (please describe)	40 (.30)	NA	35 (.34) Rank: 2	–	29 (.34) Rank: 1	11 (.24) Rank: 4	1.21	33 (.35) Rank: 2	6 (.21) Rank: 3	1.49
Total	132		103		85	46		93	29	

As Table 2.23 shows, those who were currently sitting as judges chose not to respond to this question, most likely because they indicated previously that they did not engage in independent factual research.[157] As a result, it was impossible to conduct a statistical analysis across the judicial–arbitral divide. However, the data involving arbitrators was illuminating. For example, the most popular choice indicated that a large number (44 per cent) of current arbitrators discussed the results of independent factual research with the parties because the parties need to be able to respond to those findings as a matter of procedural justice. The second most frequently chosen option, 'other' (34 per cent), suggested that there could be some rationales that were not reflected in the predetermined options, although, as the discussion below demonstrates, that does not appear to be the case. Interestingly, the third and fourth most frequently chosen options for arbitrators fell within the pro-discussion rationales, which suggests that arbitrators may be highly motivated to discuss the results of their independent factual research with the parties.

The second comparative pairing—domestic and international disputes—reflected two statistically significant differences in response rates. One such difference appeared at the highest level of confidence ($p<.001$) and involved the propensity to discuss the results of independent factual research as a result of concerns about procedural justice. A considerably higher proportion of respondents chose this option in international disputes (70 per cent) than in domestic disputes (31 per cent). This disparity was also reflected in the individual hierarchies, with this rationale coming in first among international specialists but only second among domestic specialists. Interestingly, respondents discussing domestic disputes marked 'other' more frequently than any other option.

The other statistically significant difference appearing across the domestic–international divide ($p<.01$) involved the decision not to discuss results from independent factual research because that approach was implicit in the task of acting as a judge or arbitrator. This option was chosen relatively infrequently (ranked fourth in domestic disputes and tied for fifth in international disputes), so is not particularly important in this discussion.

Comparing Table 2.23 to Table 2.13 (involving rationales for discussing the results of independent legal research with the parties) shows that the only item in Table 2.13 that demonstrated a statistically significant difference across the domestic–international divide involved the choice involving procedural justice, as was also the case in Table 2.23. Although more research is needed, the fact that this option generated a statistically significant difference in both tables suggests that two communities view the importance of the concept differently, with international specialists holding the principle in higher regard, as reflected in the higher proportion of individuals who indicated that they were motivated by notions of procedural justice.

[157] Table 2.20.

The third axis of comparison involves respondents from common law and civil law jurisdictions. As Table 2.23 shows, only one item—the decision to discuss results of independent factual research with the parties as a matter of procedural justice—showed a statistically significant difference ($p<.05$). However, both groups chose that item most frequently, which suggests the difference is one of degree rather than of kind.

When the common law–civil law results in Table 2.23 are compared to those in Table 2.13, several interesting observations can be made. First, the strong cross-discipline concern for procedural justice that was seen in matters involving domestic and international disputes also exists across the common law–civil law divide, since this entry was the most frequently invoked rationale by both common law and civil law respondents in both legal and factual matters. However, the proportion of respondents choosing that option was considerably higher in factual matters, suggesting a higher degree of intensity. While it is impossible to compare intensity markings between Tables 2.13 and 2.23 through statistical analysis, the discrepancy is intriguing.

As Table 2.23 shows, the open option ('other') received a relatively high proportion of responses from most of the cohorts. Although this alternative was designed to generate responses that would supplement the rationales reflected in the six pre-determined categories, the majority of the responses simply reiterated or expanded on those six offerings.

Many of these types of comments reflected concerns about procedural justice and provided insights into different aspects of procedural justice that respondents considered important. For example, one individual noted that 'if the research shows something new, the parties must be given the right to be heard', whereas another focused on the right of 'full transparency'. However, one individual highlighted principles relating to the implicit parameters of the judicial or arbitral role, stating that 'I consider my role to be that of an arbitrator not an investigator and feel factual investigation is improper'.

Some comments focused on how the invitation to the parties to respond to independent factual research was made rather than why the invitation was made. For example, one commentator stated, 'I generally do not conduct outside research without making the request through the parties', while another indicated that 'if there is need to clarify something, I request an oral hearing'. Other individuals focused on the role that questions play in obtaining additional factual information, with one person noting that 'I do not discuss results directly, but indirectly through questions at hearing or in writing', while another stated, 'Socratic method—ask questions'.

The open text box also inspired a number of respondents to identify the limits of their independent factual research. For example, one individual said that 'I rely only on the evidence and submissions in coming to a decision and consider it improper to independently research in relation to contested issues'. Another person indicated a similarly constrained methodology, stating that, 'other than asking for a document, I do not rely on independent factual research'.

Some comments suggested that judicial and arbitral practice might vary according to circumstance or subject matter. For example, with respect to the former, one respondent indicated that 'I discuss when it is applicable but have no set practice to do so', while another said that 'I discuss only if it reveals factual points that are not already debated'. With respect to the latter, one person indicated that 'in construction matters I always conduct a site visit with the parties and counsel present'.[158] Another individual suggested that geographical concerns might affect the decision to discuss independent factual research with the parties, stating, 'I avoid independent research on domestic arbitrations as the culture here is against that'.

While these comments are all quite useful, they do not focus specifically on the rationales affecting a judge or arbitrator's decision to discuss the result of independent factual research, which suggests that the six pre-determined rationales in the question were for the most part correct. However, future research in this field might benefit from expanding the range of possible rationales to include concerns about annulment and concerns about the adequacy of the factual case to address the legal claims at issue, based on the statement of one individual who wrote that 'all elements of facts must be discussed with the parties. If not, this entails a possible (almost certain) annulment of the award. I will also make sure during the phase of instruction of the case that I have all elements that are necessary for me to decide the issue at hand'. While this second element—the desire to ensure that the factual case is sufficient to decide the legal claims—could create difficulties in those jurisdictions (primarily those within the common law tradition) that reflect the view that the decision maker must be neutral as to questions of content and should not act to assist one party in establishing or negating a legal claim, various comments generated in response to previous questions in this section demonstrate that some judges and arbitrators (primarily those within the civil law tradition) believe in the importance of that endeavour.

Before moving on to the next question, it is necessary to discuss a comment that was likely intended to denigrate the question about rationales relating to independent factual research. That comment indicated that 'I don't do independent factual research at all, so I don't discuss what I don't do with the parties at all'. While this approach may seem logical on its face, the diversity of individual approaches to independent factual research suggests that the failure to raise the issue is highly problematic. While silence could suggest that the neutral does not conduct independent factual research, it could also be the case that the neutral does engage in that practice but simply does not discuss the parameters of that research with the parties. Unfortunately, the parties have no way of knowing which is the case.

The survey design phase anticipated that a certain percentage of respondents would engage in independent factual research, which led to the need to determine how often respondents discussed their factual research methodology with the parties. However, as noted in the preceding paragraph, this question is equally important in cases where the judge or arbitrator does not engage in independent factual research. The question adopted the same frequency breakdowns used in earlier questions—0 per cent of the

[158] Another respondent similarly believed that questions about discussions involving independent factual research were 'only applicable to site visits where parties are usually given opportunity to offer argument or evidence'.

time (assigned the number '1' for purposes of calculating weighted averages), 1 to 29 per cent of the time ('2' for weighted averages), 30 to 59 per cent of the time ('3' for weighted averages), 60 to 99 per cent of the time ('4' for weighted averages), and 100 per cent of the time ('5' for weighted averages)—and was structured similarly to an analogous question involving independent legal research to allow comparisons across the legal–evidentiary divide.[159]

Table 2.24 Frequency of discussions regarding factual research methodology with parties (weighted averages followed by standard deviation in parenthesis and sample (N) size)

	Full pop.	Current judges	Current arbitrators	J-A t-stat	Domestic disputes	Int'l disputes	J-A t-stat	Comm. law	Civil law	J-A t-stat
Weighted averages	2.07 (1.54) 164	2.00 (1.41) 2	1.99 (1.51) 127	−.01	1.87 (1.45) 109	2.44 (1.64) 54	2.26*	2.08 (1.56) 120	1.94 (1.41) 32	−.46

As Table 2.24 shows, only one of the comparative pairings reflected a statistically significant difference ($p<.05$) in frequency ratings, with the weighted average of domestic disputes (1.87 out of 5.00) suggesting that most respondents in those matters did not discuss their factual research methodology at all, while the weighted average for respondents in international disputes (2.44) suggested that those individuals discussed their methodology 1 to 29 per cent of the time. Furthermore, of the six cohorts, respondents in international disputes had the highest weighted average, suggesting that judges and arbitrators in international adopt significantly different practices with respect to discussions about independent factual research.

Although it is impossible to conduct a statistical analysis across different tables, Table 2.9 involving discussions regarding legal research methodology can be compared to Table 2.24 to provide at least some preliminary data about judicial and arbitral practices across the legal–evidentiary divide. Notably, all the cohorts but one generated higher numbers in Table 2.24 than in Table 2.9, suggesting that respondents might be more likely to discuss their research methodology in matters involving facts than in matters involving the law. The one exception to that rule was current judges, whose weighted averages were identical in the two tables.

Another important observation involves the relatively low rate at which discussions about the methodology behind independent legal and factual research are taking place. While those numbers can be explained to some extent by the fact that many judges and arbitrators do not conduct independent research of any type, the fact that approximately 20 per cent of respondents to this survey do engage in some form of independent factual research suggests the need for all judges and arbitrators to identify their practices so as to ensure transparency, consistency and predictability in the dispute resolution process.[160]

[159] Table 2.9.

[160] Table 2.20; see also Table 2.7 (discussing the types of additional legal research conducted by respondents, apart from reading the parties' submissions).

The next question in this series asked when discussions about factual research methodology took place, if at all. The question was identical to an earlier query about when respondents discussed their legal research methodology with the parties, which allowed for comparisons across the legal–evidentiary divide.[161]

As Table 2.25 shows, the number of judges who answered this question was not sufficient to generate a statistical analysis with the arbitrator pool, and the majority (56 per cent) of arbitrators indicated that they did not discuss their factual research methodology with the parties. A comparison to Table 2.10 involving the time that respondents discussed their legal research methodology showed considerable similarities in terms of percentages for individual entries for arbitrators (the largest difference was only four percentage points) as well as an identical hierarchy of preferred times. In both cases, those who spoke with the parties about their research methodology were most likely to raise the issue during the hearing, followed by the first procedural meeting or at some other point prior to the hearing.

Comparisons of domestic and international disputes did not generate anywhere near the same degree of consistency. As Table 2.25 shows, the hierarchy of preferences between the two cohorts diverged immediately, with the exception of the most frequently chosen alternative, which indicated that the respondent did not discuss their factual research methodology with the parties. Even this entry showed a deviation between the two cohorts, with 64 per cent of respondents in the domestic group indicating that they did not discuss their factual research methodology with the parties as compared to only 34 per cent of the respondents in the international group, a difference that was statistically significant ($p<.01$). A second statistically significant difference ($p<.001$) involved the option indicating the discussion took place at the first procedural meeting, which was the domestic group's fifth most popular alternative and the international group's second most popular alternative.

Although the two groups differed in their approach to discussions of factual research methodology, their factual research practices were analogous to the way they handled discussions involving legal research methodology, as reflected in Table 2.10. A comparison of Table 2.10 and Table 2.25 shows an identical hierarchy of preferences for the domestic cohort, although the intensity of choices varied slightly, and the international cohort reflected a similar hierarchy of preferences, although the existence of various ties threw the numbers off slightly and the number of adherents to the top two ranking alternatives diverged, with a larger number of respondents indicating that they did not discuss their research methodology in legal matters than in factual matters (45 per cent as compared to 34 per cent, respectively). This phenomenon led to a reversal in relative intensity for the next most popular choice involving discussions at the first procedural meeting, which won 17 per cent of the votes in cases involving legal research but 32 per cent in cases involving factual research. While it is impossible to conduct statistical studies across the two tables, this data suggests a potentially important difference in practice across the domestic–international divide.

[161] Table 2.10.

Table 2.25 Time when respondents discussed factual research methodology with the parties (number of respondents followed by proportion in parenthesis and ranking within the cohort)

	Full pop.	Current judges	Current arbitrators	J-A z-stat	Domestic disputes	Int'l disputes	D-I z-stat	Comm. law	Civil law	C-C z-stat
At the first procedural meeting	20 (.14)	0 (.00) Rank: 2 (tied)	14 (.13) Rank: 3	–	6 (.06) Rank: 5	14 (.32) Rank: 2	–4.01***	9 (.09) Rank: 3 (tied)	7 (.27) Rank: 2	–2.58*
Prior to the hearing	11 (.08)	0 (.00) Rank: 2 (tied)	9 (.08) Rank: 4	–	7 (.07) Rank: 3 (tied)	3 (.07) Rank: 4 (tied)	.10	9 (.09) Rank: 3 (tied)	2 (.08) Rank: 3 (tied)	.14
During the hearing	21 (.15)	0 (.00) Rank: 2 (tied)	18 (.16) Rank: 2	–	14 (.15) Rank: 2	7 (.16) Rank: 3	–.20	18 (.17) Rank: 2	2 (.08) Rank: 3 (tied)	1.20
After the hearing but before the drafting of the award or decision	10 (.07)	0 (.00) Rank: 2 (tied)	5 (.05) Rank: 5	–	7 (.07) Rank: 3 (tied)	3 (.07) Rank: 4 (tied)	.10	9 (.09) Rank: 3 (tied)	1 (.04) Rank: 5 (tied)	.81
During the drafting of the award or decision	3 (.02)	0 (.00) Rank: 2 (tied)	2 (.02) Rank: 6	–	1 (.01) Rank: 6	2 (.05) Rank: 6	–1.33	2 (.02) Rank: 6	1 (.04) Rank: 5 (tied)	–.60
Not applicable – I do not discuss my factual research methodology with the parties	76 (.54)	1 (1.0) Rank: 1	62 (.56) Rank: 1	–	61 (.64) Rank: 1	15 (.34) Rank: 1	3.25**	58 (.55) Rank: 1	13 (.50) Rank: 1	.48
Total	141	1	119		96	44		106	26	

The final comparative pairing involved respondents from common law and civil law countries. The two groups showed a slight divergence in hierarchical preferences in Table 2.25, although only one option (discussions at the first procedural meeting) demonstrated a statistically significant difference in terms of intensity ($p<.05$), with only 9 per cent of common law respondents choosing that alternative as opposed to 27 per cent of civil law respondents. Comparisons to Table 2.10 suggest that the two cohorts adopt relatively similar approaches to discussions involving legal research, although it is difficult to undertake any comparisons of relative hierarchies due to various ties.

One difference that stands out involves the intensity mark for civil law respondents who indicated that they discussed their methodologies during the hearing. According to the two tables, 8 per cent of civil law respondents chose that option in factual matters, as compared to 19 per cent in legal matters. That distinction might warrant further research.

The next question in the series asked respondents to identify the rationale(s) that best described their position regarding discussions with the parties concerning factual research methodology. Because the survey design anticipated that some respondents would be in favour of discussing their factual research methodology with the parties while others would not, the pre-established prompts included three options that explained why respondents shared their methodology with the parties and three options that explained why respondents did not. The question also allowed respondents to provide additional rationales in their own words. Respondents were asked to check all categories that applied, which meant that percentages do not add up to 100. The question was identical in structure to an earlier question involving legal research methodology so as to allow comparisons across the legal–evidentiary divide.[162]

As Table 2.26 shows, none of the individuals who were currently sitting as judges answered this question, which made statistical comparison of responses from judges and arbitrators impossible. However, the data from the arbitrators was interesting in several ways. First, the choice of 'other' as the most popular option might suggest that the six pre-established options were in some way deficient. However, as discussed below, most of the additional comments did not generate new rationales. Second, arbitrators chose three different options in almost equal measure: 'other' (30 per cent); 'I do not discuss my factual research methodology with the parties because my approach is implicit in the task of acting as a judge or arbitrator' (28 per cent); and 'I discuss my factual research methodology with the parties because they need to be able to respond to anything I discover as a matter of procedural justice' (27 per cent). The latter two choices are particularly revealing, in that they not only suggest that the arbitral community is somewhat evenly split about whether to discuss factual research methodology with the parties (a result that is also reflected in Table 2.25) but also identify the most popular contenders within both the pro- and contra-discussion rationales.

162 Table 2.11.

Table 2.26 Rationales for discussing factual research methodology with the parties (number of respondents followed by proportion in parenthesis and ranking within the cohort)

	Full pop.	Current judges	Current arbitrators	J-A z-stat	Domestic disputes	Int'l Disputes	D-I z-stat	Comm. law	Civil law	C-C z-stat
Pro-discussion rationales										
I discuss my factual research methodology with the parties because they need to be able to respond to anything I discover as a matter of procedural justice	45 (.31)	NA	31 (.27) Rank: 3	–	20 (.21) Rank: 3	25 (.49) Rank: 1	−2.62**	30 (.28) Rank: 2	10 (.32) Rank: 2	−.46
I discuss my factual research methodology with the parties to ensure that what I have found is accurate	30 (.20)	NA	21 (.18) Rank: 4	–	18 (.19) Rank: 4	12 (.24) Rank: 2 (tied)	−.68	24 (.22) Rank: 4	3 (.10) Rank: 4 (tied)	1.58
I discuss my factual research methodology with the parties to increase their confidence in the process	24 (.16)	NA	17 (.15) Rank: 5	–	14 (.15) Rank: 5	10 (.20) Rank: 4	−.78	18 (.17) Rank: 5	3 (.10) Rank: 4 (tied)	.98
Contra-discussion rationales				–						
I do not discuss my factual research methodology with the parties because I am confident that what I have found is accurate	3 (.02)	NA	2 (.02) Rank: 7	–	1 (.01) Rank: 7	2 (.04) Rank: 7	−1.18	1 (.01) Rank: 7	2 (.06) Rank: 6 (tied)	−1.85
I do not discuss my factual research methodology with the parties because my approach is implicit in the task of acting as a judge or arbitrator	43 (.29)	NA	33 (.28) Rank: 2	–	31 (.32) Rank: 1 (tied)	12 (.24) Rank: 2 (tied)	1.11	27 (.25) Rank: 3	14 (.45) Rank: 1	−2.14*
I do not discuss my factual research methodology with the parties because that would decrease their confidence in the process	17 (.12)	NA	15 (.13) Rank: 6	–	11 (.11) Rank: 6	6 (.12) Rank: 6	−.06	11 (.10) Rank: 6	4 (.13) Rank: 3	−.41
Other (please describe)	40 (.27)	NA	35 (.30) Rank: 1	–	31 (.32) Rank: 1 (tied)	9 (.18) Rank: 5	1.90	38 (.36) Rank: 1	2 (.06) Rank: 6 (tied)	3.14*
Total	147		116		96	51		107	31	

It is also possible to compare Table 2.26 regarding rationales supporting or rejecting discussions about factual research methodology with Table 2.11, which presented similar data regarding legal research methodology. Interestingly, Table 2.11 shows higher support among arbitrators for the contra-discussion rationale involving the implicit duties of a judge or arbitrator, reporting a 47 per cent adherence rate as opposed to a 28 per cent adherence rate in Table 2.26. Support for the pro-discussion rationale involving procedural justice is approximately even across the two tables (28 per cent in Table 2.11 and 27 per cent in Table 2.26). While it is impossible to conduct statistical studies across tables, these results are of interest.

Table 2.26 also yielded interesting information regarding comparisons across the domestic–international divide. Considerable disparities existed in the hierarchical rankings, and one item—the rationale involving procedural justice—generated a statistically significant difference in intensity ($p<.01$), with those involved in international matters showing a higher level of support than those involved in domestic matters (49 per cent to 21 per cent respectively). The procedural justice entry also showed a statistically significant difference in Table 2.11 involving independent legal research, with specialists in international disputes demonstrating higher levels of concern about procedural justice than specialists in domestic disputes (39 per cent to 24 per cent, respectively). This suggests that judges and arbitrators involved in international commercial dispute resolution are more concerned about procedural justice in both legal and factual matters.

The third comparative axis considers issues along the common law–civil law divide. Although Table 2.26 reflects a number of similarities between the two groups in terms of hierarchical rankings, that consistency only appeared later in the list and did not extend to the most popular alternatives, which involved 'other' for common law respondents (cited by 36 per cent of that cohort, as opposed to 6 per cent of civil law respondents, who put that option in a tie for last place in the civil law group) and 'I do not discuss my factual research methodology with the parties because my approach is implicit in the task of acting as a judge or arbitrator', which was the top option for civil law respondents (cited by 45 per cent of that group, as opposed to 25 per cent of common law respondents, who put that option in third place in the common law cohort). Notably, these two entries both reflected statistically significant differences ($p<.05$) in terms of intensity, which underscores the credibility of the hierarchical data.

These differences are also important to consider given the high degree of consistency reflected in the results reported in Table 2.11 involving independent legal research with the parties. Interestingly, the two tables showed both cohorts (common law and civil law) ranking concerns about procedural justice in the second position, suggesting a certain level of philosophical cohesion across both the common law–civil law and legal–evidentiary divides.

As with other questions, parties were allowed to supplement the pre-existing options relating to the decision to discuss factual research methodology with the parties by marking 'other' and providing additional motivations in their own words. Although this option was the most popular option for several cohorts, the comments often did not reflect new rationales. Instead, individuals used the opportunity to provide additional nuances about the pre-determined choices. For example, several people focused on issues relating to procedural fairness, indicating that they were motivated by the desire to promote 'full transparency' or were concerned that 'it would be unethical for me to conduct independent factual research'. Other respondents described discussing their methodology with the parties to increase the parties' confidence in the process, stating 'when I discuss it with them, it is because I want to know if their response suggests that other avenues should be considered and to enhance the credibility of the process and my rulings and/or awards'.

A significant number of respondents used the text box to reiterate the fact that the individual in question did not conduct independent factual research, although relatively few went on to explain the motivation underlying their practice and instead simply stated that they did not conduct independent factual research. Those who did suggest motivations often did so in general terms, such as 'I consider that improper', which could be read to refer to behaviours implicit in the task of being a judge or arbitrator.

Several respondents used the text box to identify the boundaries of the research that they considered appropriate, rather than why they adopted their particular practice. Comments in this category appeared to be more responsive to matters considered in Table 2.21 about the type of independent factual research respondents conducted. As was the case with that earlier question, several individuals focused on site visits,[163] although those were not the only practices discussed. Other respondents noted that they 'only [conducted] conflict research; discuss only if a potential conflict arises'; 'I rarely if ever do independent factual research except to check population or other public records'; and 'I do not do factual research, unless it is a matter that is within the scope of taking judicial notice'.

Two respondents focused on the nature of their interactions with the parties. For example, one indicated that 'I only ask parties for documents or witness testimony so they know it immediately' while another said, 'I do not discuss the factual research method, but I do discuss the results'.

3. Incorporating evidentiary analyses into reasoned decisions and awards

The next series of questions involving evidentiary considerations focused on how judges and arbitrators incorporate factual reasoning into their written decisions and awards. The series began by asking respondents to indicate the percentage of the factual authorities (evidence) that have been read or reviewed, in whole or in part, that are subsequently mentioned in the written decision or award. The question used the same frequency breakdowns reflected in earlier questions—0 per cent of the factual authorities read or reviewed (assigned the number '1' for purposes of calculating weighted averages), 1 to 29 per cent of the factual authorities read or reviewed ('2' for

[163] Comments in this category included the following: 'site visits in construction cases are normal, and with everyone present, they allow the parties to show me anything they believe that I should see'; 'only applicable to site visits, so self-evident'; '[I] do not do independent factual research other than maybe a site visit'.

weighted averages), 30 to 59 per cent of the factual authorities read or reviewed ('3' for weighted averages), 60 to 99 per cent of the factual authorities read or reviewed ('4' for weighted averages), and 100 per cent of the factual authorities read or reviewed ('5' for weighted averages)—and adopted a structure similar to that of an earlier question involving the incorporation of legal authorities into written decisions and awards, thereby allowing comparisons across the legal–evidentiary divide.[164]

Table 2.27 Percentage of factual authorities that have been read or reviewed and that are reflected in the written decision or award (weighted averages followed by standard deviation in parenthesis and sample (N) size)

	Full pop.	Current judges	Current arbitrators	J-A t-stat	Domestic disputes	Int'l disputes	D-I t-stat	Comm. law	Civil law	C-C t-stat
Weighted average	2.92 (1.02) 226	4.00 (.00) 2	2.90 (1.02) 185	−1.52	2.84 (1.08) 150	3.07 (.86) 75	1.61	2.90 (.99) 173	3.16 (.95) 38	1.48

As Table 2.27 shows, there were no statistically significant differences across any of the three comparative pairings, although the frequency of references did vary somewhat, ranging from a low of 1 to 29 per cent to a high of 60 to 99 per cent. Interestingly, the data reflected in Table 2.27 was very similar to that found in Table 2.14 concerning the incorporation of legal authorities into written decisions and awards, although the numbers in Table 2.27 are slightly higher than in Table 2.14, which suggests that judges and arbitrators may include more references to factual authorities than to legal authorities. That hypothesis was proven true by the coding exercise conducted as part of the larger research study, where all reasoned rulings with the exception of domestic awards included more factual citations than legal citations.[165]

The final survey question on factual authorities asked respondents to identify the factors that they take into account when deciding whether to mention a particular piece of evidence in their written decisions or awards. Respondents were asked to indicate how often they took each of 17 different items, including an option marked 'other', into account, using the standard frequency breakdowns: 0 per cent of the time (assigned the number '1' for purposes of calculating weighted averages), 1 to 29 per cent of the time ('2' for weighted averages), 30 to 59 per cent of the time ('3' for weighted averages), 60 to 99 per cent of the time ('4' for weighted averages), and 100 per cent of the time ('5' for weighted averages). The structure of the question was similar to that of an earlier question involving factors considered when determining whether to include legal authorities in a written decision or award, which allowed for comparisons across the legal–evidentiary divide.[166]

Table 2.28 provides a number of useful insights across the three comparative axes, beginning with the judicial–arbitral analysis. Although the comparison of judicial and

[164] Table 2.14.
[165] Table 4.16.
[166] Table 2.15.

Table 2.28 Factors considered when determining whether to include factual authorities (evidence) in the written decision or award (weighted averages followed by standard deviation in parenthesis, sample (N) size, and ranking within the cohort)

	Full pop.	Current judges	Current arbitrators	J-A t-stat	Domestic disputes	Int'l disputes	D-I t-stat	Comm. law	Civil law	C-C t-stat
A desire to make sure the losing party feels heard	3.59 (1.27) 272	4.67 (.58) 3 Rank: 1 (tied)	3.56 (1.25) 220 Rank: 4	−1.53	3.53 (1.34) 187 Rank: 4	3.70 (1.12) 84 Rank: 4	1.01	3.62 (1.27) 218 Rank: 4	3.40 (1.28) 40 Rank: 4	−1.01
A desire to make sure the winning party feels heard	3.00 (1.35) 268	3.00 (1.00) 3 Rank: 9 (tied)	2.97 (1.33) 216 Rank: 8	−.04	3.01 (1.36) 184 Rank: 9	2.98 (1.33) 83 Rank: 8	−.17	3.03 (1.36) 214 Rank: 9	2.88 (1.30) 40 Rank: 9	−.65
Concern about subsequent procedural review of the decision or award	2.77 (1.40) 272	3.33 (.58) 3 Rank: 7 (tied)	2.77 (1.38) 222 Rank: 11	−.70	2.73 (1.42) 185 Rank: 12	2.84 (1.33) 86 Rank: 10	.61	2.72 (1.42) 216 Rank: 12	2.90 (1.23) 42 Rank: 8	.77
Concern about subsequent review of the decision or award on the merits	2.77 (1.39) 275	3.67 (1.15) 3 Rank: 4 (tied)	2.75 (1.39) 223 Rank: 12	−1.14	2.74 (1.40) 188 Rank: 11	2.86 (1.38) 86 Rank: 9	.66	2.81 (1.39) 219 Rank: 11	2.51 (1.31) 41 Rank: 14	−1.28
Credibility of counsel	1.92 (1.08) 270	1.33 (.58) 3 Rank: 15 (tied)	1.86 (1.06) 218 Rank: 17	.86	1.93 (1.11) 186 Rank: 17	1.88 (1.02) 83 Rank: 16	−.35	1.97 (1.12) 217 Rank: 17	1.70 (.85) 40 Rank: 16	−1.45
Credibility of the parties	2.53 (1.26) 268	3.33 (.58) 3 Rank: 7 (tied)	2.49 (1.28) 216 Rank: 14	−1.13	2.68 (1.28) 183 Rank: 14	2.17 (1.15) 84 Rank: 15	−3.12**	2.70 (1.26) 214 Rank: 13	1.82 (.98) 40 Rank: 15	−4.18***
Credibility of the witnesses	2.99 (1.24) 262	3.00 (1.00) 3 Rank: 9 (tied)	2.94 (1.24) 211 Rank: 9	−.08	3.06 (1.27) 181 Rank: 8	2.82 (1.18) 80 Rank: 11	−1.44	3.08 (1.21) 208 Rank: 8	2.68 (1.35) 40 Rank: 11	−1.88
Importance of the evidence to the disposition of the controversy	4.45 (.84) 272	4.00 (1.00) 3 Rank: 3	4.50 (.79) 222 Rank: 1	1.09	4.47 (.81) 186 Rank: 1	4.40 (.89) 85 Rank: 1	−.64	4.49 (.78) 217 Rank: 1	4.41 (.95) 41 Rank: 1	−.58

Perceived likelihood that the losing party will seek to challenge the decision or award	2.39 (1.28) 266	1.33 (.58) 3 Rank: 15 (tied)	2.41 (1.29) 216 Rank: 15	1.45	2.24 (1.24) 181 Rank: 15	2.70 (1.32) 84 Rank: 12	2.76**	2.33 (1.28) 215 Rank: 15	2.60 (1.22) 40 Rank: 12	1.23
Standard practice (i.e. you follow the same practice in all cases, regardless of other factors)	2.84 (1.51) 271	4.67 (.58) 3 Rank: 1 (tied)	2.84 (1.53) 219 Rank: 10	−2.07*	2.98 (1.52) 185 Rank: 10	2.53 (1.45) 85 Rank: 13	−2.29*	2.84 (1.54) 216 Rank: 10	2.85 (1.48) 40 Rank: 10	.04
Type of evidence (party-drafted document, testimony, expert report, transactional document, etc.)	3.12 (1.29) 269	3.00 (1.00) 3 Rank: 9 (tied)	3.12 (1.29) 218 Rank: 7	.16	3.13 (1.34) 186 Rank: 7	3.06 (1.17) 82 Rank: 7	−.41	3.11 (1.30) 214 Rank: 7	3.12 (1.27) 41 Rank: 7	.05
Type of legal dispute (contractual, regulatory, etc.)	2.64 (1.46) 266	2.00 (1.73) 3 Rank: 14	2.60 (1.45) 216 Rank: 13	.71	2.71 (1.47) 183 Rank: 13	2.45 (1.42) 82 Rank: 14	−1.35	2.66 (1.44) 213 Rank: 14	2.56 (1.54) 39 Rank: 13	−.39
Whether parties dispute the credibility of the evidence in question	3.92 (1.02) 265	3.67 (1.53) 3 Rank: 4 (tied)	3.97 (.99) 215 Rank: 3	.52	3.89 (1.04) 180 Rank: 3	3.96 (.97) 84 Rank: 3	.52	3.93 (1.01) 211 Rank: 3	4.05 (1.02) 41 Rank: 3	.70
Whether parties dispute the interpretation or application of the evidence in question	3.95 (1.01) 270	3.67 (1.53) 3 Rank: 4 (tied)	4.01 (.96) 221 Rank: 2	.61	3.92 (1.02) 185 Rank: 2	4.00 (.99) 84 Rank: 2	.60	3.95 (1.00) 216 Rank: 2	4.09 (1.02) 41 Rank: 2	.82
Whether the parties referred to the document during the hearing	3.44 (1.07) 264	3.00 (1.00) 3 Rank: 9 (tied)	3.44 (1.09) 216 Rank: 6	.70	3.42 (1.10) 181 Rank: 6	3.48 (1.03) 82 Rank: 5	.42	3.48 (1.05) 212 Rank: 6	3.35 (1.19) 40 Rank: 5 (tied)	−.70
Whether the parties referred to the document in their written submissions	3.47 (1.05) 270	3.00 (1.00) 3 Rank: 9 (tied)	3.46 (1.07) 218 Rank: 5	.74	3.51 (1.08) 184 Rank: 5	3.41 (1.00) 85 Rank: 6	−.72	3.51 (1.03) 216 Rank: 5	3.35 (1.19) 40 Rank: 5 (tied)	−.88
Other (please describe below)	2.03 (1.61) 29	.00 NA 0 Rank: 17	2.17 (1.70) 23 Rank: 16	NA	2.09 (1.69) 22 Rank: 16	1.86 (1.46) 7 Rank: 17	−.32	2.13 (1.63) 23 Rank: 16	1.00 (.00) 4 Rank: 17	−1.36

arbitral practices is hindered somewhat by numerous ties, the two tables show numerous discrepancies in their internal hierarchies. Perhaps the most important of these involve the top-ranked options.

Judges indicated that they were most motivated by the desire to make sure the losing party felt heard and to follow their standard practice (meaning a technique used in all cases, regardless of other factors), which were tied for first position among judges. Judges' third most popular choice involved the importance of the evidence to the disposition of the controversy. However, these factors came in fourth, tenth and first, respectively, for arbitrators. The second most popular choice for arbitrators was whether the parties disputed the credibility of the evidence in question and whether the parties disputed the interpretation or application of the evidence in question, which tied for fourth among judges.

Despite these and other disparities in rank order, the intensity marks only reflected a single statistically significant difference ($p<.05$). Interestingly, that discrepancy involved the option involving standard practice, which tied for first position among judges and tenth position among arbitrators. While more research would be beneficial to determine precisely what the two groups consider standard practice, the result suggests that judges may be more mechanistic in their approach to incorporating factual authorities in written outcomes than arbitrators are.

The second comparison involved domestic and international disputes, which showed a high degree of consistency in their internal rankings, particularly at the top end of the scale. The first seven choices were the same across both groups, including the top three choices: the importance of the evidence to the disposition of the controversy, whether the parties dispute the interpretation or application of the evidence in question and whether the parties dispute the credibility of the evidence in question. However, this comparison also generated three statistically significant differences in intensity. Those differences involved the credibility of the parties and the perceived likelihood that the losing party will seek to challenge the decision or award (both coming in at $p<.01$) as well as standard practice ($p<.05$). However, these options all ranked relatively low on the spectrum (between tenth and fifteenth out of 17) and therefore do not cause a great deal of concern.

The third comparative axis looked at practices along the common law–civil law divide. The two cohorts showed a high degree of consistency in their internal rankings, particularly at the top end of the scale. Indeed, the first four choices were the same across both groups and were the same as the top four choices for the domestic and international groups. Only one item—credibility of the parties—generated a statistically significant difference ($p<.001$), with civil law lawyers being far less likely than common law lawyers to consider the parties' credibility as a factor when determining whether to include factual authorities in the written decision or award (1.82 out of 5.00 as compared to 2.70, respectively). While this finding is not critical, given the relatively low placement of this factor in the two groups' internal hierarchies (eleventh and eighth out of 17, respectively), it likely reflects civil law lawyers' longstanding scepticism about the value of evidence from party witnesses.[167]

Although Table 2.28 included a number of items that were relevant only to evidentiary determinations, a majority of the pre-established options in Table 2.28 were also included in Table 2.15, which discussed factors considered by the respondents when determining whether to include legal authorities in the written decision or award. This feature allows a limited comparison of judicial and arbitral practices across the legal–evidentiary divide.[168]

The first observation in this regard involves the nearly universal agreement among comparative cohorts that the importance of the legal or factual authority to the dispute is central to the decision whether to mention that item in the written decision or award. Indeed, entries describing this concept were given first or second rank in both Table 2.15 and Table 2.28.[169] However, judges appear to differ from other cohorts with respect to both legal and factual determinations, as reflected by the fact that judges reversed the relative rankings of the two 'importance' entries in Table 2.15 as compared to all other cohorts and placed the 'importance' entry in Table 2.28 third as opposed to first, as was the case with all other cohorts. While these differences were not statistically significant in the individual analyses, this phenomenon warrants further research.

Another item that bears mention involves relative intensity markings, which appear higher in factual determinations than in legal determinations, at least with respect to the top-ranking choices. For example, the two 'importance' entries in Table 2.15 (importance of the legal authority and the importance of the underlying legal principle to the resolution of the controversy) received an average intensity mark of 4.18 for the full population, whereas the 'importance' entry in Table 2.28 (importance of the evidence to the disposition of the controversy) received a 4.45 for the full population. The next highest ranked entries can be described as involving the level of contentiousness relating to a particular item, with the two entries in Table 2.15 (whether the parties dispute the interpretation or application of the particular legal authority and whether the parties dispute the interpretation or application of the underlying rule or principle) receiving an average intensity mark of 3.87, while the analogous entries in Table 2.28 (whether the parties dispute the credibility of the evidence in question and whether the parties dispute the interpretation or application of the evidence in question) received an average intensity mark of 3.94. The third most highly ranked item in Table 2.15 involved a desire to make sure the losing party felt heard and received a mark of 3.41 for the full population, whereas the same item in Table 2.28 received a mark of 3.59 for the full population.[170]

[167] Ch. 1.III.C.

[168] Given the nature of the data, it is impossible to conduct a statistical study across the two tables. A comparison of weighted averages across the two tables will also not be undertaken here, since the analysis could be thrown off by the larger number of pre-determined options in Table 2.28.

[169] Notably, there were two entries concerning this principle in Table 2.15, as opposed to only one in Table 2.28.

[170] The tables also included entries relating to the desire to make sure the wining party felt heard, but that item had low levels of intensity and low relative rankings, which meant it did not make sense to combine this item with the entry relating to the desire to make sure the losing party felt heard.

The higher intensity scores given to determinations involving factual authorities in this context is consistent with other comparisons across the factual-level divide.[171] It is also consistent with information generated through the coding exercise finding that decisions and awards typically contained more factual citations than legal citations.[172]

As with other questions, respondents were given the opportunity to supplement the pre-determined options by describing, in their own words, other factors relevant to the inquiry in issue. This item was the least or second-least favoured option among all cohorts, which suggests that the pre-determined alternatives sufficiently covered the items that were most important to respondents. This conclusion is further supported by the fact that many respondents did not use the opportunity to identify new options but to instead expand upon or reiterate alternatives that were already included on the existing list. Comments in this category included items such as 'in general, I cite to evidence that is relevant and material to the outcome of the arbitration', 'it really depends on how integral the particular evidence is to the claim/defence/decision' and 'the extent to which interpretation of the document is relevant to my decisional analysis'.

Other respondents summarized their typical practice without indicating the motivation behind their behaviour. These types of comments included 'some evidence is obviously more persuasive and essential to the decision than other evidence; it just emerges from the process'; 'I have always recited some basic background facts in introduction, to help explain the reasoning of the award'; 'I try to at least mention key pieces of evidence'; 'I try to provide a logical set of reasons for the decision and express whether I believe certain witnesses or not'; and 'my decisions are evidence and law driven'.

Some individuals underscored the difficulty associated with discussing citation issues in the abstract. For example, one respondent noted that it was 'impossible to give a general answer. Each case is different', while another indicated that the question of 'which documents and evidence to reference is the result of a complex consideration of all of the above. There is never just one factor' at issue.

One respondent appeared to hearken back to issues discussed in previous questions, noting that s/he thought it was 'not appropriate to rely on facts not invoked by the parties, unless addressed through questions (and therefore, part of the debates)'. While useful, that statement appears more responsive to concerns about procedural fairness and whether parties should be allowed to respond to independent factual research by the judge or arbitrator, which were both considered in Table 2.26.

Of the various comments generated by this question, only one appeared to provide a new factor relevant to the determination of whether to include certain factual authorities in written decisions or awards. That respondent noted that s/he considered the 'quantity of exhibits, and extent of testimonial evidence', an item that should be included as a possible option in any future research in this field. When doing so, researchers should seek to determine whether judges and arbitrators are affected by the

[171] Cf Tables 2.8 and 3.19; 3.9 and 3.22; 3.10 and 3.25; 3.11 and 3.26; 3.12 and 3.24; 3.13 and 3.23; 3.14 and 3.27; 3.15 and 3.28.

[172] Table 4.16 (showing higher number of factual citations than legal citations in virtually all types of reasoned rulings).

number of factual authorities overall (one interpretation of the term 'quantity') or by the number of factual authorities supporting a particular fact issue (another interpretation of 'quantity'). The later definition, in particular, might help parties understand whether and to what extent it is necessary or useful to submit evidence that could be considered cumulative or duplicative.

4. Interim conclusions regarding the use of evidentiary materials

For the most part, survey questions into the use and nature of legal authorities sought to confirm or reject longstanding theoretical assumptions about whether and to what extent differences in practice arose across the judicial–arbitral, domestic–international and common law–civil law divides. Inquiries into the use and nature of factual (evidentiary) materials were somewhat different because of the relative paucity of theoretical, practical and empirical scholarship into factual aspects of the reasoning process. As a result, survey findings generated a great deal of novel information at both the micro- and macro-levels.

One key finding involved the many instances where no statistically significant difference appeared between judicial and arbitral practices relating to the use and consideration of factual authorities. This phenomenon is of course highly pertinent to discussions about the purported difference in the quality and nature of judicial and arbitral decision making.[173] Analyses across the domestic–international and common law–civil law divide were much more likely to generate statistically significant differences.

Another key conclusion involves comparisons between legal authorities and factual authorities. Although the nature of the materials differed, respondents tended to enter higher intensity ratings with respect to factual authorities and practices than with respect to legal authorities and practices. These findings are particularly intriguing because no known study has ever compared judicial and arbitral practices across the legal–evidentiary divide. While more research is necessary to develop a full and nuanced appreciation for this phenomenon, the data reflected herein provides an important first step.

Analyses regarding the relative importance of different types of evidentiary materials and the factors affecting whether and to what extent neutrals will review or rely on those materials are important not only to scholars but also to practitioners. The increasing ease with which evidence, particularly documentary evidence, can be generated has led a rising number of practitioners to engage in 'data dumps' that require judges and arbitrators to sift through reams of information that is only tangentially relevant to the dispute at hand.[174] If counsel had a better understanding of what evidence is persuasive, they might be less likely to introduce extraneous material into the proceedings.

The subsection on independent factual research provided a number of novel revelations based on questions that had never before been empirically considered. Not only did these questions consider whether and to what extent different comparative

[173] Ch.1.III.A.
[174] Ch. 2.IV.B.1; see also Ch. 3.III.C.2.b (presenting interviewee views on the introduction of evidence).

cohorts gathered factual information independently of the parties' submissions, they also identified what type of information was gathered, whether the results or the research methodologies were discussed with the parties, and what the motivating factors were for these matters. While a number of these inquiries would benefit from additional follow-up research, the information presented here provides a useful foundation for further analysis. For example, several of the tables suggested that respondents specializing in international disputes enunciate more of a concern for procedural justice as compared to respondents specializing in domestic disputes, an issue that deserves additional scholarly attention.

Perhaps the most intriguing and innovative aspect of the discussion on independent factual research involved comparisons to similar discussions involving independent legal research. No known studies compare judicial and arbitral behaviour across the legal–evidentiary divide, even though many judges and arbitrators consider factual considerations to be more important than legal considerations in commercial disputes.[175] While the information presented herein may not have been conclusive in all regards, it nevertheless provides an excellent baseline for future research and scholarly analysis.

The one shortcoming in the section on independent factual research involves the lack of data on judicial practices. While current judges answered some of the questions in this section, other questions were skipped, likely because the respondents believed those questions were inapplicable given an early indication that the respondents did not engage in independent factual research.[176] The omission may also have been the result of a belief that divulging the information would constitute an improper imposition into the deliberation process or the view that factual determinations in their jurisdictions are made by another actor in the civil justice system such as a jury. Without more information, it is impossible to know which of these alternatives is true.

Whatever the reason, the absence of data made statistical studies across the judicial–arbitral divide impossible in many cases. Further research on these issues would be beneficial, since anecdotal evidence suggests that some judges do indeed engage in independent factual research, albeit rarely.[177] However, it may be difficult to obtain access to a sufficiently large number of judges who engage in independent factual research to support statistical analyses.[178]

The subsection concerning the incorporation of factual authorities into written decisions or awards also generated some interesting conclusions. First, no statistically significant differences appeared to arise across any of the three comparative pairings with respect to the frequency with which respondents cited factual authorities in written decisions or awards. Second, no statistically significant differences arose with respect to the factors respondents considered most important to the determination of whether to refer to particular pieces of evidence in written decisions or awards. However, when the

[175] Ch. 3.III.C (discussing interviewees' views on the role that fact issues play in commercial disputes).
[176] Table 2.20.
[177] Ch. 1.III.A.
[178] Scholars often find it particularly difficult to obtain access to sitting judges. Chs. 1.II, 2.II.A.

internal hierarchies were considered, judges appeared to be somewhat out of step with other cohorts. Furthermore, the intensity of marks regarding the relative importance of various factors appeared to be higher in matters involving factual authorities than in matters regarding legal authorities.[179]

C. The Reasoning Process

When discussing legal reasoning, it is critical to appreciate the role played by both legal and factual authorities, since those elements are the building blocks of the reasoning process. However, the analysis cannot stop there. Instead, it is necessary to study how judges and arbitrators engage with these elements and incorporate other important considerations, such as those relating to equity and public policy, before coming to a final determination on the merits of the dispute.

Although the legal literature is rife with theoretical and jurisprudential analyses of how judges and arbitrators balance competing factors during the reasoning process, empirical scholarship in this field is relatively rare.[180] This survey therefore sought to study the reasoning process itself, as distinguished from the drafting process, which was addressed separately.[181] Questions fell into several broad categories, including the factors influencing the reasoning process, changes in the reasoning process over time and differences between judicial and arbitral reasoning. Each of these matters is discussed separately below.

1. Factors influencing the reasoning process

Academics working in the area of legal reasoning routinely suggest that judges and arbitrators are influenced by non-legal considerations like equity and public policy.[182] However, the majority of those studies are not empirical in nature, raising questions about the veracity of the underlying claims.[183] This survey sought to test conventional wisdom regarding the reasoning process by asking respondents to indicate how important each of five different factors—binding legal norms, equity or fairness, facts, persuasive or 'soft' legal norms, and public policy—were to their decision-making process. Respondents were instructed to rank these criteria from most important (1) to

179 This information can be compared to analogous analyses in the coding exercise. Tables 4.8–4.17.

180 Ch. 1.III.A.

181 Ch. 2.IV.D.

182 Ch. 1.III.A.

183 Some scholars attempt to measure factors influencing the reasoning process by conducting linguistic or similar studies of reasoned decisions and awards, but it is difficult, if not impossible to identify motivations from the end product. As a result, this study not only conducts quantitative analysis of the end product of the legal reasoning process (i.e. reasoned decisions and awards), it also conducts qualitative analysis of the process through semi-structured interviews and an anonymous survey. While it is possible that respondents to the survey could provide unreliable information (either lying to the survey or lying to themselves), the use of an anonymous instrument helps minimize that risk. Furthermore, the survey was structured in such a way as to diminish the likelihood that respondents would do so. For example, placing the questions on the reasoning process near the end of the survey allows the respondents to gain a certain amount of trust in the objective nature of the study, since earlier questions were neutral and non-threatening.

least important (5), and those choices were then collated to identify the percentage of respondents who chose each option at each rank level for each cohort. Those choices were then statistically analysed across the various comparative pairings.

While it would have been possible to conduct a statistical analysis of different combinations of options (for example, how many respondents ranked the various options in an A, B, C, D, E order as opposed to A, C, E, B, D), that approach was not adopted because it obscured, at least to some extent, the intensity markings for various choices. Those intensity markings were considered important, since a very high intensity mark for a first ranked option compared to an intermediate intensity mark for second place would suggest one approach to legal reasoning, while an intensity mark for a first ranked option that was only slightly above the second ranked option would suggest another.

The question also allowed respondents to indicate that a particular option was not applicable. Although the 'not applicable' data is intriguing,[184] it was not reported here in detail, since it essentially duplicated the lower-ranked options,[185] and it seemed more useful to focus on what respondents did value rather than what they did not value.

As Table 2.29 shows, this question generated only one statistically significant difference ($p<.05$). According to the data, a higher percentage of common law respondents (22 per cent) placed policy in the fourth position than civil law respondents (8 per cent). However, this discrepancy likely does not have a discernible effect on the reasoning process overall, since the item was relatively low in the relative rankings.

The virtual absence of statistically significant differences between the various cohorts suggests that decision makers tend to approach the reasoning process similarly, regardless of their status as judge or arbitrator, the nature of the dispute as domestic or international, or their training in common law or civil law jurisdictions. This alone is a very useful finding, but the data in Table 2.29 also supports other inferences.

First, the relative sub-rankings (i.e. those comparing intensity marks for each cohort within each general ranking) and the data involving the full population of respondents both suggest that the most important factor relevant to the reasoning process are binding legal norms, followed by facts. However, when the percentages for first and second place rankings are considered together, binding legal norms and facts appear to be equally important, with binding legal norms earning 60 per cent and facts earning 61 per cent of the first and second place rankings of the full population.[186]

Furthermore, these two options together comprise 67 per cent of the first-place and 54 per cent of the second-place rankings, suggesting that binding legal norms and facts

[184] The percentages of the full population that chose 'not applicable' for the different options are as follows: binding legal norms (3 per cent); equity or fairness (13 per cent); facts (3 per cent); persuasive or 'soft' legal norms (29 per cent); policy (53 per cent).

[185] For example, one potentially interesting analysis might have been whether any statistical difference arose between the number of judges who marked policy 'not applicable' and the number of arbitrators who did the same. However, only two judges answered this question, and both marked policy as the fifth most important option. Although this result precluded analysis of the 'not applicable' selection, it did permit statistical analysis along the judicial–arbitral divide for the fifth ranked option.

[186] It is impossible to conduct a statistical analysis of this difference.

Table 2.29 Factors relevant to the reasoning process (ranked, with internal rankings per cohort)

	Full pop.	Current judges	Current arbitrators	J-A z-stat	Domestic disputes	Int'l disputes	D-I z-stat	Comm. law	Civil law	C-C z-stat
First ranked option										
Binding legal norms	90 (.39)	1 (.50) Rank: 1 (tied)	72 (.38) Rank: 1	.34	63 (.39) Rank: 1	27 (.39) Rank: 1	.08	73 (.39) Rank: 1	14 (.39) Rank: 1	.06
Equity or fairness	13 (.06)	0 (.00) Rank: 2 (tied)	13 (.07) Rank: 5	−.38	8 (.05) Rank: 5	5 (.07) Rank: 5	−.66	9 (.05) Rank: 5	2 (.06) Rank: 5	−.17
Facts	65 (.28)	1 (.50) Rank: 1 (tied)	54 (.29) Rank: 2	.67	50 (.31) Rank: 2	14 (.20) Rank: 3	1.73	55 (.30) Rank: 2	8 (.22) Rank: 2	.91
Persuasive or 'soft' legal norms	19 (.08)	0 (.00) Rank: 2 (tied)	14 (.07) Rank: 4	−.40	11 (.07) Rank: 4	8 (.11) Rank: 4	−1.17	13 (.07) Rank: 4	5 (.14) Rank: 4	−1.38
Policy	45 (.19)	0 (.00) Rank: 2 (tied)	36 (.19) Rank: 3	−.69	29 (.18) Rank: 3	16 (.23) Rank: 2	−.85	35 (.19) Rank: 3	7 (.19) Rank: 3	−.07
Total	232	2	189		161	70		185	36	
Second ranked option										
Binding legal norms	49 (.21)	1 (.33) Rank: 1 (tied)	45 (.23) Rank: 2	.42	37 (.23) Rank: 2	12 (.17) Rank: 3	1.03	40 (.21) Rank: 2	8 (.21) Rank: 3	.06
Equity or fairness	33 (.14)	0 (.00) Rank: 2 (tied)	27 (.14) Rank: 4	−.69	20 (.12) Rank: 5	13 (.18) Rank: 2	−1.20	28 (.15) Rank: 5	4 (.10) Rank: 5	.72
Facts	78 (.33)	1 (.33) Rank: 1 (tied)	62 (.32) Rank: 1	.06	53 (.32) Rank: 1	25 (.35) Rank: 1	−.36	64 (.34) Rank: 1	11 (.28) Rank: 1	.64

(Continued)

Table 2.29 Continued

	Full pop.	Current judges	Current arbitrators	J-A z-stat	Domestic disputes	Int'l disputes	D-I z-stat	Comm. law	Civil law	C-C z-stat
Persuasive or 'soft' legal norms	41 (.17)	1 (.33) Rank: 1 (tied)	35 (.18) Rank: 3	.69	30 (.18) Rank: 3	11 (.15) Rank: 4 (tied)	.56	30 (.16) Rank: 3	10 (.26) Rank: 2	−1.49
Policy	35 (.15)	0 (.00) Rank: 2 (tied)	26 (.13) Rank: 5	−.68	24 (.15) Rank: 4	11 (.15) Rank: 4 (tied)	−.13	29 (.15) Rank: 4	6 (.15) Rank: 4	−.03
Total	236	3	195		164	72		191	39	
Third ranked option										
Binding legal norms	25 (.10)	0 (.00) Rank: 2 (tied)	17 (.08) Rank: 4	−.42	19 (.10) Rank: 4	6 (.08) Rank: 4	.54	21 (.10) Rank: 4	2 (.05) Rank: 4	.94
Equity or fairness	110 (.43)	2 (1.00) Rank: 1	90 (.43) Rank: 1	1.62	77 (.42) Rank: 1	33 (.45) Rank: 1	−.42	88 (.42) Rank: 1	20 (.53) Rank: 1	−1.18
Facts	16 (.06)	0 (.00) Rank: 2 (tied)	14 (.07) Rank: 5	−.38	11 (.06) Rank: 5	5 (.07) Rank: 5	−.24	14 (.07) Rank: 5	2 (.05) Rank: 4 (tied)	.34
Persuasive or 'soft' legal norms	64 (.25)	0 (.00) Rank: 2 (tied)	52 (.25) Rank: 2	−.81	46 (.25) Rank: 2	18 (.25) Rank: 2	.10	54 (.26) Rank: 2	7 (.18) Rank: 2 (tied)	.99
Policy	41 (.16)	0 (.00) Rank: 2 (tied)	37 (.18) Rank: 3	−.65	29 (.16) Rank: 3	11 (.15) Rank: 3	.87	31 (.15) Rank: 3	7 (.18) Rank: 3 (tied)	−.55
Total	256	2	210		182	73		208	38	
Fourth ranked option										
Binding legal norms	25 (.10)	0 (.00) Rank: 3 (tied)	21 (.10) Rank: 5	−.58	17 (.10) Rank: 5	8 (.11) Rank: 5	−.21	21 (.11) Rank: 5	4 (.11) Rank: 5	.02

Equity or fairness	56 (.23)	1 (.33) Rank: 2	46 (.22) Rank: 2	.45	39 (.23) Rank: 2	17 (.23) Rank: 2	−.03	43 (.22) Rank: 3	11 (.29) Rank: 1 (tied)	−.96
Facts	36 (.15)	0 (.00) Rank: 3 (tied)	33 (.16) Rank: 4	−.76	22 (.13) Rank: 4	14 (.19) Rank: 3	−1.23	25 (.13) Rank: 4	9 (.24) Rank: 3	−1.76
Persuasive or 'soft' legal norms	81 (.33)	2 (.67) Rank: 1	68 (.33) Rank: 1	1.22	56 (.33) Rank: 1	25 (.34) Rank: 1	−.16	64 (.32) Rank: 1	11 (.29) Rank: 1 (tied)	.43
Policy	47 (.19)	0 (.00) Rank: 3 (tied)	37 (.18) Rank: 3	−.81	37 (.22) Rank: 3	10 (.14) Rank: 4	1.48	44 (.22) Rank: 2	3 (.08) Rank: 5	2.40*
Total	245	3	205		171	74		197	38	
Fifth ranked option										
Binding legal norms	26 (.11)	0 (.00) Rank: 2 (tied)	24 (.16) Rank: 3	−.55	15 (.09) Rank: 4	11 (.17) Rank: 3	−1.67	19 (.10) Rank: 4	6 (.20) Rank: 3	−1.57
Equity or fairness	14 (.06)	0 (.00) Rank: 2 (tied)	9 (.06) Rank: 5	−.32	11 (.07) Rank: 5	3 (.05) Rank: 5	.60	13 (.07) Rank: 5	1 (.03) Rank: 5	.75
Facts	79 (.34)	0 (.00) Rank: 2 (tied)	65 (.42) Rank: 1	−1.04	56 (.34) Rank: 2	23 (.35) Rank: 1	−.18	62 (.33) Rank: 2	12 (.40) Rank: 1	−.73
Persuasive or 'soft' legal norms	31 (.14)	0 (.00) Rank: 2 (tied)	23 (.15) Rank: 4	−.53	24 (.15) Rank: 3	7 (.11) Rank: 4	−.77	27 (.14) Rank: 3	3 (.10) Rank: 4	.65
Policy	79 (.34)	2 (1.00) Rank: 1	63 (.21) Rank: 2	1.94	58 (.35) Rank: 1	21 (.32) Rank: 2	.44	66 (.35) Rank: 1	8 (.27) Rank: 2	.93
Total	229	2	184		164	65		187	30	

are the two most important elements to the legal reasoning process in commercial disputes by a considerable margin. Although this conclusion is in many ways expected, it is helpful to have empirical confirmation.

Discerning the third most important factor is more difficult. Policy was the third most highly ranked first place option, whereas persuasive or 'soft' legal norms was the third most highly ranked second place option and equity or fairness was the most highly ranked third place option (binding legal norms and facts were the least popular options from the third ranked position onwards, which is understandable given the very high first and second place showings). Perhaps the best way to identify the third most important factor would be to combine the marks for first, second and third place rankings for the three options other than law and facts. Using the numbers from the full population, equity came in with a combined percentage of 63 while persuasive norms and policy both came in at 50. While it cannot be ascertained whether this result is statistically significant, it nevertheless appears that equity is the third most important factor in the reasoning process, a conclusion that is somewhat surprising given scholarship suggesting that judges and arbitrators are driven, at least to some extent, by policy considerations.[187]

The survey software did not allow inclusion of an open text box in a ranking question, so the next question invited respondents to provide additional comments about factors that are important to the legal reasoning process. Although only a few of the resulting statements were directly responsive to the question, the statements were nevertheless illuminating.

Many respondents focused on the connection between the law and the facts, which is unsurprising given the high rating of those two elements in Table 2.29. In addition to various general comments on this point,[188] one respondent indicated that 'legal reasoning must be correct in law and correctly apply the facts of the case to the legal principles'. Some dispute arose as to whether 'facts are as important as legal precedent'[189] or whether the law was the most important aspect of the reasoning process.[190] For example, one respondent noted that legal reasoning was 'based on facts and law, but subject to credibility of the witnesses' while another suggested that it was 'very important to appraise the real-world importance of the facts in terms of business practice and common sense'.

Some comments focused on particular types of analyses, with one person noting that 'contractual interpretation is often of central importance' to the legal reasoning process

[187] Some questions may arise as to whether the relatively high ranking of equity in the full population numbers was affected by the large number of arbitrators as compared to judges. While this may be to some extent true, it should be noted that the judicial cohort split as to the relative importance of law and facts, placing those two items in a tie for first, but agreed as to the relative importance of equity, jointly ranking it as the third most important factor. Similar concerns could be raised with respect to the somewhat larger number of common law respondents as compared to civil law respondents, but those two cohorts ranked the top three factors identically as a hierarchical matter, and no statistically significant differences arose with respect to intensity markings.

[188] Statements included 'application of law to facts' and 'I do my best to apply the law to the facts'.

[189] Another individual similarly stated that 'binding legal norms and facts are both at the same level of importance'.

[190] Comments in this category included 'always apply the law. Everything else is secondary'.

while another indicated that 'the parties' agreement/contract may (or may not) supersede any of the five factors' listed in Table 2.29. Other statements sought to clarify what might be considered 'law'. For example, one individual highlighted 'industry customs and practices' while another indicated a 'high reliance upon trade practice and usage of the particular trade or industry as to contractual language and/or contractual language because of the importance of enforcing objectively reasonable expectations of parties to a commercial transaction'.

Some comments raised the possibility that process-oriented concerns can affect legal reasoning. For example, one individual indicated that 'the clarity (or lack thereof) of counsel's arguments re the application of "the law" to "the facts" and whether evidence has in fact been introduced establishing the referenced "fact"' can have a significant effect on legal decision makers. Another person said,

> In most cases, there is little dispute about the law, but much dispute about how the law should be applied to the evidence. But in a substantial minority of cases, there is serious disagreement about the proper interpretation of controlling authority or persuasive authority. More reading and interaction with counsel is necessary in those cases.

Some comments anticipated questions that were asked later in the survey. For example, some individuals addressed issues that were covered in Table 2.30 on how the respondent began the reasoning process[191] while others discussed matters covered in Table 2.37 regarding the drafting process.[192]

Some respondents focused on factors that arose as a matter of degree rather than of kind. For example, several respondents cited relevance and materiality as important to their reasoning process. Comments in this category noted that 'relevance is paramount', since 'central issues that are intensely disputed merit full examination and explanation'. Other individuals noted that 'relevance and the weight to be given to evidence are the two dominant controlling factors' in legal reasoning, although 'reliability of sources' is also important.

One individual created a hierarchy of norms, indicating that for him/her,

> Facts and binding legal authority are actually co-equal. Policy is really a subset of the binding legal norms category—often a way to determine what the binding legal norm is—rather than a separate factor. The importance of a soft legal norm varies significantly depending on the circumstances. Knowing that [multiple appellate courts] have

[191] Comments in this category included the following: 'I primarily attempt to resolve issues by applying binding and soft legal standards to the case facts, then consider whether the result derived in that fashion gives rise to additional policy issues or issues of substantive fairness'; 'my process is to first try to master the facts, then master the law, and then apply the law to those facts. It is an iterative process. Focus on disputed items of law or fact.'

[192] Comments in this category included the following: 'when drafting the award, I take all factors into consideration, contract interpretation, facts, evidence in order to make sure that the outcome will be fair to both parties and that no decision will be harsh to one of the parties'; 'legal reasoning should be logical, rational and easily understood in the award' and should reflect a 'proper balancing of legal authority, fairness and facts is necessary for proper resolution'.

come out a certain way on an issue, with none contra, may be very important when dealing with a case of first impression governed by the law of another circuit.

Another respondent provided another way of looking at the legal reasoning process. S/he indicated that

> paradigms are important to my decision-making process, which is why the parties' stories, narratives, opening statements and theories of the case are so important. There's nothing as practical as a good theory. However, I test the theory against the evidence to develop a tentative or preliminary 'rough sense of justice' for the matter, which I modify or abandon as the evidence unfolds. I then cross-check this 'rough sense of justice' against the law to see if the relief that it would afford is lawful or not. If not, I discard it in favour of the constraints of the law, but if the facts could go either way, and I have a rough sense of justice about what the result should be, then I let the evidence support this sense of justice.

This type of overarching perspective was not uncommon. For example, one individual noted the need for 'coherence—legal theory must work properly on different facts' while another noted the importance of 'predictability of result. The rules allow the parties to easily conform their future behaviour to the rules'. Another important consideration was whether 'the arbitration [is] being used for a purpose for which it is not intended or well-suited'.

Some respondents were influenced by what could be characterized as general or external factors. Some of the general considerations involved 'logic', which was mentioned by several respondents, as well as 'the common good' and 'history, culture, logic, sceptical inquiry, impact on individuals'. One individual noted the importance of 'legal culture which varies in different countries and legal systems as well (common law, civil law, Chinese law, Islamic law, dual-law, etc.)'. External considerations included the 'effect on the law, the parties, the community, and policy' as well as the possibility of challenge or review.[193]

Finally, several individuals focused on factors specific to the individual dispute, such as the 'sophistication of the parties'. For example, one individual noted that 'it is important to address all issues raised by parties' and give effect to the 'underlying objectives of the parties'. Another person believed it was important to consider 'the parties' relationship and attitudes towards each other … [and] give indiscriminate respect to all and avoid making negative comments about another person's character or morality'. One person similarly thought that the legal reasoning process was or should be affected by 'whether the parties themselves—not their legal counsel—could or should have understood the legal norm prior to the emergence of the dispute'. Yet another mentioned the

[193] For example, one respondent noted that 'the most important aspect of arbitration is to do everything possible to ensure that the award is enforceable and "bullet proof"'.

importance of 'discussions with counsel before, during, and at the close of the hearing; study of their written submissions', while another emphasized the role that 'lawyers' arguments' play in the reasoning process.

The survey design anticipated that the responses reflected in Table 2.29 and the comments generated in response to the follow-up question would be consistent with the views reflected in legal literature regarding the relative importance of different factors to legal reasoning, as turned out to be the case.[194] However, simply knowing how judges and arbitrators rank different factors does not provide the whole story. The process of reasoning through a legal dispute can involve a number of different techniques, including those that may be outcome-determinative.[195] Furthermore, the process of legal reasoning may vary across jurisdictional lines.[196] As a result, it is important to determine the various steps involved in the reasoning process.

The next question in this series therefore sought to determine which factors respondents relied on when beginning the legal reasoning process and which factors became relevant later. The question asked respondents to identify how they began the legal reasoning process and provided six pre-established options with different scenarios involving law, facts, outcome, and policy.[197] The question also allowed respondents to choose a seventh option marked 'other' and to provide additional modes of reasoning in case the pre-existing alternatives did not adequately capture respondents' standard technique.

This question generated some very intriguing results, not because of the differences between the various comparative cohorts but because of the similarities. As Table 2.30 shows, the most popular technique for all of the groups in the study involved beginning with the facts and then looking for law relevant to those facts. The second most popular technique for all groups except judges involved a blended or iterative approach that simultaneously considered both facts and law. However, no statistically significant difference arose between judges and arbitrators with respect to their intensity of support for this option. Together, these two items won the support of 79 per cent of the full survey population.

Notably, two options that had been expected to rank highly among at least some respondents—i.e. starting with the law and looking for facts relevant to that legal

[194] Ch. 1.III.A.

[195] For example, some scholars have suggested that some judges and arbitrators identify an outcome and then work backwards to justify that result. John M Walker, 'Politics and the Confirmation Process: The Importance of Congressional Restraint in Safeguarding Judicial Independence', (2004) 55 Syracuse L Rev 1, 8. Others suggest different approaches. Jack Knight, 'Are Empiricists Asking the Right Questions About Judicial Decisionmaking?' (2009) 58 Duke LJ 1531, 1541–42 (discussing work of Richard Posner); Richard Posner, *How Judges Think* (Harvard University Press 2008) 84.

[196] For example, scholars have suggested that common law reasoning is inductive while civil law reasoning is deductive. Ch. 1.III.D. The coding analysis conducted as part of this larger study also suggested that various differences arise across jurisdictional lines. Ch. 4.IV.

[197] During the survey design phase, it was anticipated that Table 2.29 would show law, facts, and policy to be the three most important elements of the legal reasoning process, which is why those factors were mentioned in the question associated with Table 2.30. In the future, questions such as that associated with Table 2.30 may want to incorporate equity into the analysis, given that Table 2.29 showed equity to be more important than policy to both judges and arbitrators.

Table 2.30 How the reasoning process begins (number of respondents followed by proportion in parenthesis and ranking within the cohort)

	Full pop.	Current judges	Current arbitrators	J-A z-stat	Domestic disputes	Int'l disputes	D-I z-stat	Comm. law	Civil law	C-C z-stat
I start with the facts and look for law relevant to those facts	131 (.45)	2 (.67) Rank: 1	104 (.43) Rank: 1	.81	84 (.41) Rank: 1	46 (.53) Rank: 1	−1.96	97 (.42) Rank: 1	23 (.54) Rank: 1	−1.44
I start with the law and look for facts relevant to that legal standard	23 (.08)	1 (.33) Rank: 2	17 (.07) Rank: 4	1.73	18 (.09) Rank: 4	5 (.06) Rank: 4	.86	19 (.08) Rank: 4	3 (.07) Rank: 4	.26
I start with the outcome and look for facts and law to support that outcome	2 (.01)	0 (.00) Rank: 3 (tied)	2 (.01) Rank: 6	−.16	2 (.01) Rank: 6	0 (.00) Rank: 6 (tied)	.92	2 (.01) Rank: 6	0 (.00) Rank: 5 (tied)	.61
I start with the policy and look for facts and law to support that policy	0 (.00)	0 (.00) Rank: 3 (tied)	0 (.00) Rank: 7	NaN	0 (.00) Rank: 7	0 (.00) Rank: 6 (tied)	NaN	0 (.00) Rank: 7	0 (.00) Rank: 5 (tied)	NaN
I apply a blended or iterative approach that simultaneously considers facts and law	99 (.34)	0 (.00) Rank: 3 (tied)	87 (.36) Rank: 2	−1.30	73 (.36) Rank: 2	26 (.30) Rank: 2	.88	85 (.36) Rank: 2	13 (.30) Rank: 2	.79
I apply a blended or iterative approach that simultaneously considers facts, law and policy	28 (.10)	0 (.00) Rank: 3 (tied)	21 (.09) Rank: 3	−.54	21 (.10) Rank: 3	7 (.08) Rank: 3	.56	23 (.10) Rank: 3	4 (.09) Rank: 3	.12
Other (please explain)	9 (.03)	0 (.00) Rank: 3 (tied)	9 (.04) Rank: 5	−.34	7 (.03) Rank: 5	2 (.02) Rank: 5	.49	7 (.03) Rank: 5	0 (.00) Rank: 5 (tied)	1.15
Total	292	3	240		205	86		233	43	

standard, on the one hand, and starting with the outcome and looking for facts and law to support that outcome, on the other—were not among the top contenders, with the exception of judges, who indicated that they started with the law and looked for the facts relevant to that legal standard as often as they started with the facts and looked for law relevant to those facts. However, this option did not generate any statistically significant difference between the intensity markings of judges and the intensity markings of arbitrators. Indeed, Table 2.30 shows no statistically significant differences with respect to any of the responses.

Because it was not clear during the survey design phase whether the pre-existing options would address all possible reasoning techniques, respondents were given the opportunity to describe, in their own words, how they began the legal reasoning process.[198] Several individuals indicated that their approach might depend on the case presented to them, making comments such as 'it depends on the facts and the issues'. A number of respondents provided a useful amount of detail about how different situations affected their legal reasoning. For example, one person indicated that his/her reasoning process 'depends on whether there are dispositive cases in clearly analogous factual circumstances. If so, I let the law direct what is relevant, and apply law or facts, syllogistically. If not, the approach is more blended and interactive, sometimes law and facts, sometimes fact, law, and policy.' Another individual noted that it 'depends. Some cases have clear facts, and the challenge is understanding and applying the law. Others are the reverse, the facts are unclear and disputed, while the law is plain.' Interestingly, this latter statement not only reiterates techniques described by participants in the semi-structured interviews, it also echoes observations made by former US Supreme Court Justice Benjamin Cardozo about how the underlying nature of a dispute can affect legal reasoning and drafting.[199]

Other comments discussed analytical techniques that were already reflected in the pre-existing options, albeit with additional detail. For example, one respondent indicated that s/he began by 'examin[ing] the evidence from those with no interest in the outcome and apply[ing] the law to those facts'.

The final group of write-in comments identified novel methodologies that were not reflected in the pre-existing options. For example, one individual said, 'I start with the relief requested by the parties, and apply a blended or iterative approach that simultaneously considers facts and law', while another person said, 'I start to think about how to solve the problem in a best way for all'. Another respondent indicated s/he began by 'identify[ing] issues, then facts, then law'.

2. Changes in reasoning techniques

The legal literature concerning international commercial arbitration suggests that parties are strongly motivated to appoint experienced arbitrators, apparently as a result

[198] For example, the pre-existing options in Table 2.30 did not mention equitable considerations, even though Table 2.29 demonstrated that equity and fairness were very important to respondents.

[199] Benjamin N Cardozo, *The Nature of the Judicial Process* (Yale University Press 1949) 164–65 (discussing three types of judicial writings); Chs. 3.III.A.3, 3.III.B.1, 3.III.C.2.b.

of the assumption that experience correlates to quality of legal decision making.[200] While this study does not attempt to distinguish between practices adopted by judges and arbitrators based on their relative levels of seniority,[201] the survey did seek to address this concern by asking respondents whether their approach to legal reasoning had changed over the course of the individual's career as a judge or arbitrator.

Table 2.31 Whether respondent's approach to legal reasoning changed over time (number of respondents followed by proportion in parenthesis)

	Full pop.	Current judges	Current arbitrators	J-A z-stat	Domestic disputes	Int'l disputes	D-I z-stat	Comm. law	Civil law	C-C z-stat
No	237 (.81)	2 (.67)	193 (.80)	−.59	168 (.82)	68 (.78)	.75	193 (.83)	33 (.75)	1.23
Yes	56 (.19)	1 (.33)	47 (.20)	.59	37 (.18)	19 (.22)	−.75	40 (.17)	11 (.25)	−1.23
Total	293	3	240		205	87		233	44	

As noted in Table 2.13, a resounding majority of respondents (81 per cent of the full population) indicated that their approach had not changed over time, which suggests that conventional wisdom about the improvement of reasoning skills or techniques over time is incorrect. Furthermore, no statistically significant differences arose between any of the comparative pairings, which suggests that neutrals adopt the same approach over time regardless of where they fall along the judicial–arbitral, domestic–international and common law–civil law divides.

Because this issue has never been empirically studied before, it was impossible to anticipate how many respondents would indicate that their reasoning techniques had changed. However, the next question sought to determine how those respondents who had indicated that they had changed their approach to legal reasoning over time had done so. Structurally, the question asked respondents who had answered 'yes' to the previous question to indicate which of five factors—equity, facts, law, outcome, and policy—they came to focus on more and which of those same factors they came to rely on less. Although the question focused on general trends and did not attempt to capture links between individual respondents' initial and current practices, some information about individual preferences can be gleaned from comments provided through an open text box in a follow-up question.

Table 2.32 provides some interesting information that can provide a useful baseline for future studies. For example, nearly half (48 per cent) of respondents who had changed their reasoning techniques during the course of their careers indicated that they came to focus more on facts over time, as compared to only 2 per cent who came to focus less on facts. Much of the shift in favour of facts seems to have come at the expense of a reliance on law and/or outcome, which saw the two biggest losses over time (33 per cent and 31 per cent, respectively). Relatively few respondents increased their

[200] Ch. 1.III.D.
[201] Future works will address that issue. Strong, Experience (n 3).

Table 2.32 How respondent's approach to legal reasoning changed over time (percentages)

	Equity	Facts	Law	Outcome	Policy
Full pop.					
I now focus more on	31%	48%	17%	2%	2%
than on	16%	2%	33%	31%	18%
Current judges					
I now focus more on	0%	100%	0%	0%	0%
than on	0%	0%	0%	0%	100%
Current arbitrators					
I now focus more on	29%	54%	12%	2%	2%
than on	13%	2%	38%	31%	16%
Domestic disputes					
I now focus more on	33%	38%	26%	3%	0%
than on	14%	3%	30%	30%	24%
Int'l disputes					
I now focus more on	26%	68%	0%	0%	5%
than on	22%	0%	39%	33%	6%
Comm. law					
I now focus more on	32%	44%	22%	2%	0%
than on	15%	3%	33%	28%	21%
Civil law					
I now focus more on	27%	64%	0%	0%	9%
than on	10%	0%	40%	40%	10%

reliance on outcome or on policy, with only 2 per cent of the full population indicating that they adopted either approach.

Although the data was not amenable to statistical analysis across comparative cohorts, some trends can be identified with respect to the individual populations. For example, 100 per cent of the judges who responded to this question moved away from policy determinations to fact determinations, suggesting that commentary describing policy-oriented decision making by judges may not be occurring in practice.[202] Similarly, the arbitrator cohort saw the biggest shifts involving increased reliance on facts and decreased reliance on law and outcome. The data on international disputes was remarkable for the fact that zero per cent of the respondents indicated that they increased their reliance on the law or outcome. Zero per cent of that group also indicated that they decreased their reliance on facts, as opposed to the 68 per cent that increased their reliance on that factor.

Perhaps the most intriguing and counterintuitive data comes from a comparison of the data generated by the common law and civil law cohorts. For example, respondents from the common law tradition reported a zero per cent increase in their reliance on

[202] Ch. 1.III.A.

policy, as opposed to a 9 per cent increase from civil law lawyers, an outcome that appeared contrary to conventional wisdom about common law reliance on policy in legal decision making.[203] Information indicating that civil law lawyers not only do not rely more on law over time but actually decrease their reliance on that factor seems similarly suspect, given longstanding views about the deductive nature of civil law reasoning.[204] While further research is necessary to confirm the inferences drawn from this data, these results are intriguing.

Those individuals who had indicated that they had changed their approach to legal reasoning were also offered the opportunity to describe, in their own words, both how and why those changes took place. With respect to the first issue, several comments focused on the role that equity played in the reasoning process, with various respondents indicating that they now relied more on the concept of fairness than they had previously. For example, one individual stated that 'I now allow equity to be a factor, whereas earlier I simply applied the law to the facts', while another person noted that 'I focus more on equity than I did 25 years ago, but not more than I do on facts and law'. However, consistent with survey data that suggested a considerable proportion of respondents decreased their emphasis on equitable considerations over time,[205] several comments described the shift away from purely equitable considerations. For example, one person noted that 'when I served [as a judge] in small claims [court], I placed somewhat more emphasis on "equity" '.

Not all of the comments focused on how or why the respondent's approach to legal reasoning evolved over time. Instead, a number of individuals simply appeared to outline their current methodology, without describing any changes that had taken place. Thus, one individual noted that 'ideally, I would focus on equity and policy, or equitable policies, derived from and tested against the purpose of the law', while another noted that 'facts can cause different conclusions in similar scenarios, e.g. alleged fraud or misrepresentation'.

Many respondents who had changed their reasoning techniques over time described why they were motivated to alter their standard approach. At the most general level, a number of individuals cited 'maturity', 'experience' and an 'evolution of understanding' the duties of a judge or arbitrator, including the 'evolution of a more holistic view of cases', as a way of explaining why their methodologies had changed over time.[206]

At a more detailed level, several respondents noted the increased role that factual determinations played in their reasoning process, which is consistent with quantitative data reflected in Table 2.32. For example, one individual described an 'increased perception of importance of fact determinations and their impact on the outcome' while

[203] Ch. 1.II.

[204] Ch. 1.III.D.

[205] For example, as Table 2.32 shows, 31 per cent of the full population of respondents indicated that they focused more on equity over time while 16 per cent indicated that they focused on equity less.

[206] Comments in this category include the following: 'I hope that I have a better understanding of my responsibilities after 26 years'; 'I have come to recognize the uniqueness of each case coupled with the non-precedent nature of my award'. Another person indicated that the change had come about 'because of two factors—I've mellowed with age and discussions with other arbitrators about their decision-making process'.

another indicated that 'I tend to focus more intensely on the facts and law which applies those facts'.[207] Yet another respondent said that 'I found, over the years, that 80 per cent of arbitration cases really centre on the assessment of facts', while another person said, 'I still consider the law to be the number one consideration, but I find I am involved in fewer cases where the law is determinative and find that the facts are increasingly more important. It may be the cases rather than my approach changing'. This latter notion is intriguing, given recent suggestions in the legal literature that the nature of commercial disputes may be evolving.[208]

While most judges and arbitrators described why they had increased their reliance on factual determinations, other respondents focused why they had switched to more legalistic analyses. For example, one individual noted that 'I find the law guides me to the outcome the parties bargained for, a fair resolution. Disregarding the law to serve an outcome left me dissatisfied'. Another person said that 'I have learned to restrict my consideration of a case to the law and facts', while another respondent indicated that s/he thought the 'exam[ination] of basic principles of law are now much more important than equity'. Some respondents disagreed with that approach, with one individual writing that 'legal principles do not occur in a vacuum. The facts and equities of a case should determine the result, if the law can support it. Sometimes the law requires an unpleasant result'. However, another person sagely noted that 'I feel that "equity" is like "beauty"—it's in the eye of the beholder, and subject to subjective whim. Law is more objective, and consistent with the reasonable expectations of the parties'.

This is not to say that all of the respondents favoured an increased emphasis on either facts or law. For example, one individual noted that 'I care as much about achieving a just result as about analytical precision', while another indicated it was important to 'do substantive justice'. Other comments suggested that 'results need to be equitable if possible'. Interestingly, one individual appeared to rely solely on equity to the exclusion of law, an approach that has largely been discredited in both national and international circles.[209] The contemporary approach was reflected in the comments of the respondent who had come to 'realize[] that parties expect arbitrators to follow the law so that there is predictability in how an outcome will be determined'.

Some answers anticipated later questions, such as those discussed in Tables 2.35 and 2.36, that sought to determine whether and to what extent the act of drafting a reasoned

[207] Other comments in this category include the following: 'I have learned over time to focus on facts and credibility to reach correct conclusions when applying the law'; 'I have learned that the law is usually not in dispute. Facts and credibility drive the decision making process'.

[208] SI Strong, 'Beyond International Commercial Arbitration? The Promise of International Commercial Mediation', (2014) 45 Wash U J L & Pol'y 11, 18–22; SI Strong, 'Increasing Legalism in International Commercial Arbitration: A New Theory of Causes, A New Approach to Cures', (2013) 7 World Arb & Med Rev 117.

[209] The statement in question indicated that 'because arbitration is private, I think it is important to achieve a result that is fair between the parties, when possible, without regard to outside precedent'. This approach, which was frequently seen in the mid-twentieth century in domestic disputes in some countries, most notably the United States, and in international disputes under the concept of *et aequo et bono*, is now curtailed under many arbitral rule sets and is only available with the express consent of the parties. SI Strong, 'Navigating the Borders Between International Commercial Arbitration and U.S. Federal Courts: A Jurisprudential GPS', 2012 J Disp Res 119, 132–33; see also Ch. 1.III.A.

decision or award affects the reasoning process.[210] Comments in this category ranged from the somewhat cryptic statement, 'better award writing', to the more expansive recognition that 'the experience of writing decisions requires you to focus your efforts. That experience over time has resulted in a shift in my approach'.

3. Judicial reasoning versus arbitral reasoning

Another longstanding assumption in the world of commercial dispute resolution suggests that judges adopt a fundamentally different approach to legal reasoning than arbitrators.[211] One way the survey tested this hypothesis was indirectly, by filtering responses across the judicial–arbitral divide and conducting various types of statistical analyses on the resulting data. However, the final subsection in the survey on legal reasoning also sought to address this issue directly by asking respondents who had served as both judges and arbitrators to discuss whether and to what extent their reasoning process differed depending on their status as a judge or arbitrator.

The first question in this series simply sought to establish a baseline for subsequent analysis by asking those respondents who had acted in both judicial and arbitral capacities whether their approach to legal reasoning changed, depending on whether they were acting as a judge or arbitrator. The options included yes, no and 'not applicable' to exclude those who had not acted in a dual capacity.

Table 2.33 Whether the approach to legal reasoning approach varied depending on the role of the decision maker (number of respondents followed by proportion in parenthesis)

	Full pop.	Current judges	Current arbitrators	J-A z-stat	Domestic disputes	Int'l disputes	D-I z-stat	Comm. law	Civil law	C-C z-stat
No	32 (.14)	0 (.00)	22 (.12)	−.52	21 (.13)	11 (.16)	−.63	25 (.14)	5 (.16)	−.26
Yes	9 (.04)	0 (.00)	6 (.03)	−.26	7 (.04)	2 (.03)	.50	7 (.04)	1 (.03)	.21
Not applicable	185 (.82)	2 (1.0)	157 (.85)	.60	131 (.82)	54 (.81)	.32	148 (.82)	26 (.81)	.13
Total	226	2	185		159	67		180	32	

As Table 2.33 shows, a significant majority of individuals who had served as both judges and arbitrators did not change their approach to legal reasoning based on their status as either a judge or arbitrator. This conclusion is even clearer if individuals who marked 'not applicable' are excluded from the calculations. Doing so shows that 78 per cent of the full population of respondents who had served as both judges and arbitrators at some time during their careers did not change their approach to legal reasoning depending on whether they were acting as a judge or arbitrator, with only 22 per cent indicating that they did change their reasoning techniques.

[210] According to the legal literature, providing reasoned decisions and awards often results in better-reasoned outcomes. Ch. 1.II.

[211] Ch. 1.III.A. This assumption can be seen not only in scholarly commentary suggesting that arbitration constitutes a lesser or 'second class' form of justice but also in the relatively high proportion of former judges hired as arbitrators in commercial matters.

Another important finding generated by Table 2.33 involved the absence of any statistically significant differences across any of the three comparative axes at issue in this study.[212] Together, these two findings strongly suggest that the allegation that arbitral justice is somehow different or less than judicial justice is incorrect.

During the survey design phase, it was anticipated that a certain proportion of the population who had served as both a judge and an arbitrator would have changed their approach to reasoning based on their status as a judge or arbitrator. The next question was directed to this group of individuals and sought to determine the nature of the changes. Structurally, the question asked the relevant sub-population to indicate which of five pre-determined options—equity, facts, law, outcome, and policy—they relied on more when acting as a judge as opposed to when they were acting as an arbitrator. Respondents were instructed to check all that applied, so percentages do not add up to 100.

Table 2.34 Factors relied on by respondents more when acting as a judge rather than an arbitrator (number of respondents followed by proportion in parenthesis and ranking within the cohort)

	Full pop.	Current judges	Current arbitrators	J-A z-stat	Domestic disputes	Int'l disputes	D-I z-stat	Comm. law	Civil law	C-C z-stat
Equity	4 (.33)	NA	3 (.33)	-	3 (.33)	1 (.33)	.00	2 (.22)	1 (1.0)	-
Facts	6 (.50)	NA	4 (.44)	-	3 (.33)	3 (1.0)	−2.00*	4 (.44)	0 (.00)	-
Law	9 (.75)	NA	7 (.78)	-	6 (.67)	3 (1.0)	−1.15	7 (.78)	0 (.00)	-
Outcome	1 (.08)	NA	1 (.11)	-	1 (.11)	0 (.00)	.60	1 (.11)	0 (.00)	-
Policy	3 (.25)	NA	2 (.22)	-	2 (.22)	1 (.33)	−.38	3 (.33)	0 (.00)	-
Total	12		9		9	3		9	1	

As Table 2.34 shows, the relatively small sample size made statistical analysis impossible in two of the three comparative pairings. First, none of the judges answered this question because none of the individuals who were currently sitting as judges had answered 'yes' to the preceding question asking about potential changes to reasoning style depending on the respondent's status as a judge or arbitrator. Second, only one member of the civil law group answered the question, even though several members of that group provided written comments in response to a follow-up question asking why the respondents' approaches had changed. As a result, the only statistical test that could be run involved domestic and international disputes. Interestingly, this comparison generated one statistically significant difference ($p<.05$) that suggested that respondents

[212] Although Table 2.33 suggested that none of the individuals currently sitting as judges had ever acted as an arbitrator, one individual who characterized him/herself as a current judge indicated in response to another question that s/he also acted as an arbitrator. However, that individual chose not to respond to this question for unknown reasons.

specializing in international disputes were more likely to rely on facts when acting as a judge than when acting as an arbitrator. This data is intriguing and suggests that those who believe that international arbitration is a second-class form of justice that is only interested in facts (as opposed to law) are incorrect.[213]

The inability to conduct statistical analyses across two of the three comparative axes does not diminish the importance of Table 2.34. For example, data derived from the full population suggests that 75 per cent of judges who also act as arbitrators generally rely more on law when acting as judges than as arbitrators, and 50 per cent rely more on facts. These two entries were chosen considerably more frequently than the other three options, an outcome that is consistent with previous data underscoring the importance of law and facts to commercial dispute resolution.

The next question asked respondents who had said that their reasoning style varied according to their status as a judge or arbitrator to indicate why they adopted different approaches, using their own words. Some answers were relatively circular, indicating simply that 'the job is different' or 'the role of a judge differs from that of an arbitrator'. Other responses cited 'experience' or 'experience, understanding, and age', which may have involved the fact that most individuals come to their arbitral careers after their judicial careers.[214]

Other comments were slightly more on point, although they were also relatively general. For example, individual responses ranged from 'courts are more strictly bound by law, not equity' and 'as a trial judge, I am constrained in my approach by the jurisprudence' to 'arbitration allows more of an equitable approach'. It was interesting that these comments focused primarily on law and equity rather than reflecting on the role that facts, outcome, and policy play on judicial and arbitral determinations, since the survey was structured so as to be neutral regarding the relative importance of different elements of the decision-making process.

One way of explaining the various comparisons between law and equity is to recognize that scholarly commentary from the mid- and late twentieth century often framed judicial determinations as inherently legal and arbitral determinations as inherently equitable.[215] While that distinction may no longer exist in commercial matters, respondents may have sought to address that issue to the exclusion of other relevant considerations because they assumed that those considerations were particularly important to survey designers.[216] As a result, information generated by this final question must be weighed against data generated from other sources.[217]

[213] Chs. 1.III.A, 1.III.B.

[214] Tables 2.1, 2.2.

[215] Ch. 1.III.A.

[216] Social science research can run into difficulties when respondents seek to 'read into' a study and provide answers that they think the examiners believe are 'correct' rather than answers that are in fact true, a phenomenon known as 'social desirability bias'. Paul J Lavrakas, 'Social Desirability', in *Encyclopedia of Survey Research Methods* (Sage Publications 2008).

[217] Specialists in commercial dispute resolution have long argued that the distinction between legal and equitable decision-making is no longer applicable, and the empirical data generated in the current study appears to support that conclusion. Chs. 1.III.A, 3.III.B.1, 3.III.D.3.

4. Interim conclusions regarding legal reasoning

In many ways, the subsection on the reasoning process formed the core of the survey analysis, providing intriguing insights into matters that have not been adequately studied as an empirical matter. For example, the analysis of factors relevant to the reasoning process reinforced data previously adduced in the subsection on factual authorities regarding the critical role that fact determinations and issues play in the resolution of commercial disputes. Not only did Table 2.29 suggest that law and facts were essentially indistinguishable in terms of their relative importance to judges and arbitrators, butTable 2.30 indicated that most respondents began the reasoning process by beginning with the facts and subsequently searching for law relevant to those facts.

This subsection also sought to test longstanding assumptions that judges and arbitrators change their decision-making capabilities over time, leading more senior neutrals to render 'better' decisions. However, this belief appears to be unsupported by empirical data, since the vast majority of respondents indicated that their approach to legal reasoning did not change over time. Within the minority of respondents who did alter their techniques, the overwhelming majority—which included both judges and arbitrators from common law and civil law jurisdictions deciding both domestic and international disputes—increased their reliance on facts, an outcome that was not anticipated by the legal literature.[218]

The final subsection on legal reasoning focused on comparisons between judicial and arbitral reasoning. Although statistical studies conducted throughout the survey provided important information on this issue, this subsection sought to address the issue more directly.

As it turned out, a significant majority (78 per cent) of individuals who had served as both a judge and an arbitrator indicated that they did not alter their approach to legal reasoning depending on whether they sat in a judicial or arbitral capacity. While a number of follow-up questions were posed to respondents who said that they did change their method of reasoning depending on their status as a judge or arbitrator, the small sample size made qualitative and quantitative analysis difficult. As a result, more research is needed to determine how and why a minority of individuals who act as both a judge and an arbitrator use different reasoning techniques, depending on the forum in which they are sitting.

D. Drafting Reasoned Decisions and Awards

The next issue covered by the survey involved drafting a reasoned decision or award. Although some individuals might equate the two processes, the survey distinguished the two because the act of reasoning involves deciding which party will prevail and why and the act of drafting involves communicating some or all of the legal reasoning

[218] Ch. 1.III.

in writing, which is a very different task. Questions fell into several broad categories, including drafting a reasoned decision or award and defining a well-written reasoned decision or award.

1. Drafting considerations

One of the first issues that a judge or arbitrator must consider when drafting a reasoned decision or award is how detailed the document should be.[219] Therefore, the first question in this series sought to establish how important certain factors were to the level of detail reflected in a reasoned decision or award. Respondents were asked to rate nine different pre-established options describing the motivation for reasoned decisions or awards,[220] where 1 was to be considered 'not important at all' and 5 was to be considered 'very important'. The survey also allowed respondents to supplement their answers by marking a tenth option, 'other', and indicating additional authorities in a text box. For purposes of this question, respondents were told to exclude any obligations imposed by contract or any applicable rules.

Table 2.35 shows a considerable amount of agreement between the comparative cohorts about the relative importance of the various factors, particularly at the top end of the rankings. Indeed, all of the different groups ranked the first three items identically, subject to a few ties.

The item in the number-one position involved 'the difficulty, complexity or novelty of the dispute as a matter of fact', which was consistent with findings elsewhere in this study suggesting that fact issues are among the most pressing aspects of commercial disputes.[221] However, the weighted averages associated with the second-most important item—'the difficulty, complexity, or novelty of the dispute as a matter of law'—were so close to those involving fact determinations that it is impossible to conclude that one factor outweighed the other. However, the joint importance of these two factors, as compared to the other factors, is telling.

The third highest placement involved the notion that the act of writing helps decision makers 'think through the analytical process and increases the likelihood of reaching the right outcome'. This principle is discussed with some frequency in the legal literature, along with the fourth-placed factor (for all but judges, who ranked it sixth) involving the desire to make sure the losing party felt heard.[222] Notably, the intensity mark for the third-placed option was relatively close to those generated for the first- and second-placed alternatives, although a substantial gap arose between the third and fourth-placed options.

The high degree of similarity involving the way in which the various cohorts ranked the individual options accompanied an absence of any statistically significant

[219] Commercial decisions and awards can be anywhere from several pages to several dozen pages in length, with some stretching to over 100 pages. Ch. 1.III.C.

[220] These options had been culled from the legal literature. Ch. 1.II.

[221] Ch. 5.II.A; see also William NR Lucy, 'Criticizing and Constructing Accounts of Legal Reasoning', (1994) 14 OJLS 303, 306.

[222] Ch. 1.II.

Table 2.35 Factors important to the determination of how detailed a reasoned decision or award should be (weighted averages followed by standard deviation in parenthesis, sample (N) size, and ranking within the cohort)

	Full pop.	Current judges	Current arbitrators	J-A t-stat	Domestic disputes	Int'l disputes	D-I t-stat	Comm. law	Civil law	C-C t-stat
I believe the difficulty, complexity or novelty of the dispute as a matter of fact requires an in-depth explanation of my reasoning	4.28 (.91) 286	5.00 (.00) 3 Rank: 1	4.27 (.91) 235 Rank: 1	−1.39	4.22 (.95) 199 Rank: 1 (tied)	4.42 (.79) 86 Rank: 1	1.71	4.32 (.88) 227 Rank: 1	4.26 (.90) 43 Rank: 1	−.41
I believe the difficulty, complexity or novelty of the dispute as a matter of law requires an in-depth explanation of my reasoning	4.25 (.98) 285	4.67 (.58) 3 Rank: 2	4.24 (.99) 234 Rank: 2	−.75	4.22 (1.00) 198 Rank: 1 (tied)	4.30 (.92) 86 Rank: 2	.63	4.31 (.91) 227 Rank: 2	4.17 (1.03) 42 Rank: 2	−.90
I believe the nature of the legal dispute (i.e. the type of substantive claims at issue) requires an in-depth explanation of my reasoning	3.65 (1.16) 284	3.67 (1.53) 3 Rank: 7	3.60 (1.17) 233 Rank: 6	−.10	3.68 (1.16) 197 Rank: 6	3.58 (1.17) 86 Rank: 6	−.67	3.68 (1.15) 226 Rank: 6	3.57 (1.13) 42 Rank: 6	−.57
I find the act of writing a reasoned decision or award helps me think through the analytical process and increases the likelihood of reaching the right outcome	4.17 (1.09) 283	4.33 (1.15) 3 Rank: 3 (tied)	4.15 (1.12) 232 Rank: 3	−.28	4.11 (1.17) 196 Rank: 3	4.29 (.89) 86 Rank: 3	1.27	4.21 (1.08) 225 Rank: 3	3.90 (1.12) 42 Rank: 3	−1.70
I want to increase the perceived legitimacy of this particular decision or award	3.86 (1.12) 282	4.33 (.58) 3 Rank: 3 (tied)	3.85 (1.09) 231 Rank: 5	−.76	3.86 (1.15) 195 Rank: 4 (tied)	3.86 (1.04) 86 Rank: 5	.00	3.92 (1.10) 224 Rank: 5	3.67 (1.16) 42 Rank: 5	−1.34
I want to increase the perceived legitimacy of this type of dispute resolution process (i.e. litigation or arbitration)	3.28 (1.32) 284	4.33 (.58) 3 Rank: 3 (tied)	3.24 (1.27) 233 Rank: 8	−1.48	3.42 (1.32) 197 Rank: 7	2.97 (1.28) 86 Rank: 9	−2.66**	3.34 (1.32) 226 Rank: 7	2.90 (1.23) 42 Rank: 9	−2.00*

(continued)

Table 2.35 Continued

	Full pop.	Current judges	Current arbitrators	J-A t-stat	Domestic disputes	Int'l disputes	D-I t-stat	Comm. law	Civil law	C-C t-stat
I want to make sure the losing party feels heard	3.92 (1.07) 283	4.00 (1.00) 3 Rank: 6	3.87 (1.10) 233 Rank: 4	−.20	3.86 (1.12) 197 Rank: 4 (tied)	4.04 (.93) 85 Rank: 4	1.30	3.93 (1.04) 226 Rank: 4	3.76 (1.07) 41 Rank: 4	−.96
I want to make sure the winning party feels heard	3.30 (1.24) 283	2.33 (.58) 3 Rank: 8 (tied)	3.26 (1.24) 233 Rank: 7	1.30	3.35 (1.27) 196 Rank: 8	3.20 (1.78) 86 Rank: 8	−.80	3.32 (1.24) 225 Rank: 8	3.07 (1.13) 42 Rank: 8	−1.22
I want to minimize the likelihood the losing party will seek to challenge the decision or award	3.14 (1.40) 283	2.33 (.58) 3 Rank: 8 (tied)	3.17 (1.37) 232 Rank: 9	1.06	2.97 (1.41) 196 Rank: 9	3.51 (1.29) 86 Rank: 7	3.04**	3.03 (1.39) 225 Rank: 9	3.60 (1.27) 42 Rank: 7	2.47*
Other (please explain below)	2.75 (1.84) 36	.00 NA 0 Rank: 10	2.87 (1.85) 30 Rank: 10	NA	2.75 (1.86) 28 Rank: 10	2.75 (1.91) 8 Rank: 10	.00	2.65 (1.87) 26 Rank: 10	2.86 (1.86) 7 Rank: 10	.26

differences between judges and arbitrators. The other two comparative pairings revealed two statistically significant differences each, with the domestic–international pairings showing an intermediate level of confidence ($p<.01$) and the common law–civil law pairings showing a lower degree of confidence ($p<.05$). Both cases involved, on the one hand, the desire to 'increase the perceived legitimacy of this type of dispute resolution process' (ranked seventh by the domestic and common law groups and ninth by the international and civil law groups), and, on the other hand, the desire to 'minimize the likelihood the losing party will seek to challenge the decision or award' (ranked ninth by the domestic and common law groups and seventh by the international and civil law groups). While the relatively low ranking of these factors within the individual cohorts' internal hierarchies suggests that these variations do not play a major role in judges' and arbitrators' determinations about how detailed a reasoned decision or award should be, further research may be warranted to see whether and to what extent these differences affect other aspects of commercial dispute resolution.

Although respondents were allowed to explain other factors that were relevant to the decision about how much detail to put into a reasoned decision or award, that option showed the lowest intensity mark for all of the individual cohorts. Furthermore, many of the comments did not provide useful additional information, but instead echoed pre-existing options. For example, pre-determined alternatives describing the desire to 'increase the perceived legitimacy of this particular decision or award' or 'this type of dispute resolution process' would likely cover comments like 'I want to establish integrity in the process' and 'I believe commercial parties need to know detailed reasons for an award and that it was not based on the perceived "right" outcome, but the right outcome based on the law and facts as found by me as arbitrator'. Similarly, pre-existing options involving whether the winning or losing party felt heard would likely encompass comments like 'I want to explain to the parties what the key facts or legal rulings were'.

The comments were also less than helpful to the extent they focused on obligations contained in the contract or applicable rules, factors that respondents were explicitly instructed to ignore.[223] However, some individuals did expand slightly on this theme, such as the person who indicated that 'I may do a reasoned award for myself but the provision of a reasoned award turns on what the parties have agreed to'.

Despite these difficulties, many of the comments were both novel and insightful. For example, several respondents focused on monetary considerations, which was also an issue that came up during the interviews.[224] This factor was expressed in a variety of ways, including 'what resources the parties have to pay for the process' and 'the amount in controversy'.

[223] Multiple respondents referred to 'the type of award that the parties have requested' or what was required by the arbitration agreement. Comments in this category include the following: 'It all depends on what the parties agreed to. Even in a complex case I sometimes am compelled to issue a standard (non-reasoned) award with no findings of fact or conclusions of law'; 'I feel the parties in my AAA cases are all entitled to receive a reasoned award. However, in FINRA arbitrations where the "norm" is either no awards (NB panel members often include non-lawyers), I would normally give either just an "explained" decision or no explanation at all'.

[224] Ch. 3.III.E.1.

One individual suggested that his/her 'awards are not driven so much by "detail" but by need for clarity, simplicity, and tight reasoning', a principle that was also evident in a statement focusing on 'the extent and scope of the parties' submissions on any particular issue'. Some respondents focused on larger concerns, as illustrated by the person who noted that 'I hope the decision will aid permanent resolution of the dispute', although that sentiment was not universally shared. Indeed, one respondent appeared to favour less rather than more detail, noting that 'I believe that, generally, explanations can only cause problems. The "whats" matter; the "whys" not so much.' Other comments involving external concerns involve questions of enforceability[225] as well as more personal motivations, such as the statement indicating, somewhat candidly, that writing a detailed award was 'good for my reputation as an arbitrator'.

Another way to approach the process of writing a reasoned decision or award is to contemplate the person(s) for whom the document is written. The legal literature puts a considerable emphasis on knowing who the 'audience' for a decision or award is,[226] so the next question asked respondents explicitly whom they considered their audience to be. The question offered nine different options and asked respondents to rank their top three choices, from most important (1) to least important (3), with the remaining options to be marked 'not applicable'. The data from the top three ranks was then collated to identify the percentage of respondents who chose each option for each cohort, and the information was statistically analysed across the various comparative pairings.[227]

As Table 2.36 shows, the data generated by this question provided results that were both expected and unexpected. Perhaps the most predictable response involved the concept of the losing party as the primary audience for a reasoned decision or award. This option was the most popular first-place ranking among all cohorts, earning the votes of 49 per cent of the full population, and was the second most popular choice for the second-place ranking, winning 17 per cent of the full population, and comprising 78 per cent of the full population's support over the top three rankings.[228]

Determining the second and third most popular choices was more difficult, with counsel and the winning party both earning considerable support. For example, counsel was the second most popular option overall in the first-place position, but achieved only 50 per cent of the votes of the full population when the top three ranks were combined. The wining party was tied for sixth position among first place rankings, but came in at the top position for the second-place rankings and earned 56 per cent of the full population's votes when the figures from the top three rankings

[225] Comments in this category included the following: 'I try to write the award in a way to ensure that the award will be confirmed'; 'I want the award to be enforceable'.

[226] Ch. 1.II. This issue was also addressed in the interviews. Ch. 2.III.A.2.

[227] While it would have been possible to conduct a statistical analysis of different combinations of options (for example, how many respondents ranked the various options in an A, B, C, D, E order as opposed to A, C, E, B, D), that approach was not adopted because it obscured, at least to some extent, the intensity markings for various choices. See also Table 2.29 (describing a similar methodology).

[228] Internal rankings from the individual cohorts varied between second and fourth in the second-place rank position.

Table 2.36 Who the audience is for a reasoned decision or award (ranked with internal rankings per cohort)

	Full pop.	Current judges	Current arbitrators	J-A z-stat	Domestic disputes	Int'l disputes	D-I z-stat	Comm. law	Civil law	C-C z-stat
First ranked option										
A court or tribunal that may review the dispute for procedural error	23 (.09)	1 (.33) Rank: 2	18 (.08) Rank: 4	1.54	16 (.09) Rank: 3	7 (.09) Rank: 4	−.01	18 (.08) Rank: 4	5 (.13) Rank: 3	−.91
A court or tribunal that may review the dispute on the merits	24 (.09)	0 (.00) Rank: 3 (tied)	21 (.10) Rank: 3	−.57	13 (.07) Rank: 4	11 (.14) Rank: 3	−1.73	19 (.09) Rank: 3	3 (.08) Rank: 4	.22
A case administrator or arbitral institution (arbitration only)	4 (.01)	0 (.00) Rank: 3 (tied)	3 (.01) Rank: 9	−.20	4 (.02) Rank: 8	0 (.00) Rank: 9	1.33	3 (.01) Rank: 9	1 (.03) Rank: 7 (tied)	−.55
Counsel	44 (.16)	0 (.00) Rank: 3 (tied)	39 (.18) Rank: 2	−.81	31 (.17) Rank: 2	13 (.16) Rank: 2	.13	34 (.16) Rank: 2	7 (.18) Rank: 2	−.36
Myself	13 (.05)	0 (.00) Rank: 3 (tied)	9 (.04) Rank: 6	−.36	11 (.06) Rank: 5	2 (.02) Rank: 8	1.20	11 (.05) Rank: 5	1 (.03) Rank: 7 (tied)	.68
The losing party	130 (.49)	2 (.67) Rank: 1	105 (.48) Rank: 1	.64	94 (.51) Rank: 1	35 (.43) Rank: 1	1.10	111 (.51) Rank: 1	16 (.41) Rank: 1	1.16
The public	8 (.03)	0 (.00) Rank: 3 (tied)	7 (.03) Rank: 7	−.32	2 (.01) Rank: 9	6 (.07) Rank: 5	−2.79**	4 (.02) Rank: 8	4 (.10) Rank: 5	−2.78*
The winning party	11 (.04)	0 (.00) Rank: 3 (tied)	6 (.03) Rank: 8	−.29	7 (.04) Rank: 7	4 (.05) Rank: 6	−.44	8 (.04) Rank: 7	2 (.05) Rank: 6	−.43

(continued)

Table 2.36 Continued

	Full pop.	Current judges	Current arbitrators	J-A z-stat	Domestic disputes	Int'l disputes	D-I z-stat	Comm. law	Civil law	C-C z-stat
Third parties with an interest in this particular dispute (such as insurers or third-party litigation funders)	11 (.04)	0 (.00) Rank: 3 (tied)	10 (.05) Rank: 5	−.38	8 (.04) Rank: 6	3 (.04) Rank: 7	.23	9 (.04) Rank: 6	0 (.00) Rank: 9	1.30
Total	268	3	218		186	81		217	39	
Second ranked option										
A court or tribunal that may review the dispute for procedural error	32 (.13)	1 (.33) Rank: 1 (tied)	27 (.13) Rank: 4	1.03	13 (.07) Rank: 5	19 (.25) Rank: 3	−3.82***	22 (.11) Rank: 5	10 (.26) Rank: 2	−2.62**
A court or tribunal that may review the dispute on the merits	37 (.15)	1 (.33) Rank: 1 (tied)	31 (.15) Rank: 3	.88	28 (.16) Rank: 3	9 (.12) Rank: 4	.87	34 (.17) Rank: 2 (tied)	3 (.08) Rank: 4 (tied)	1.36
A case administrator or arbitral institution (arbitration only)	8 (.03)	0 (.00) Rank: 4 (tied)	8 (.04) Rank: 6	−.35	6 (.03) Rank: 6	2 (.03) Rank: 7	.34	5 (.02) Rank: 6	1 (.03) Rank: 7 (tied)	−.07
Counsel	27 (.11)	0 (.00) Rank: 4 (tied)	21 (.10) Rank: 5	−.58	22 (.13) Rank: 4	4 (.05) Rank: 5	1.76	24 (.12) Rank: 4	3 (.08) Rank: 4 (tied)	.68
Myself	2 (.01)	0 (.00) Rank: 4 (tied)	2 (.01) Rank: 9	−.17	1 (.01) Rank: 9	1 (.01) Rank: 8	−.61	1 (.00) Rank: 9	1 (.03) Rank: 7 (tied)	−1.35
The losing party	42 (.17)	0 (.00) Rank: 4 (tied)	35 (.17) Rank: 2	−.78	30 (.17) Rank: 2	12 (.16) Rank: 2	.28	34 (.17) Rank: 2 (tied)	7 (.18) Rank: 3	−.29
The public	5 (.02)	1 (.33) Rank: 1 (tied)	3 (.01) Rank: 7 (tied)	4.01***	2 (.01) Rank: 8	3 (.04) Rank: 6	−1.45	3 (.01) Rank: 7 (tied)	2 (.05) Rank: 6	−1.52
The winning party	94 (.37)	0 (.00) Rank: 4 (tied)	77 (.37) Rank: 1	−1.33	68 (.39) Rank: 1	26 (.34) Rank: 1	.73	80 (.39) Rank: 1	11 (.29) Rank: 1	1.16

Third parties with an interest in this particular dispute (such as insurers or third-party litigation funders)	4 (.02)	0 (.00) Rank: 4 (tied)	3 (.01) Rank: 7 (tied)	−.21	4 (.02) Rank: 7	0 (.00) Rank: 9	1.33	3 (.01) Rank: 7 (tied)	0 (.00) Rank: 9	.75
Total	251	3	207		174	76		206	38	
Third ranked option										
A court or tribunal that may review the dispute for procedural error	40 (.15)	0 (.00) Rank: 3 (tied)	38 (.18) Rank: 3	−.81	26 (.15) Rank: 4	13 (.16) Rank: 2	−.34	31 (.15) Rank: 4	8 (.21) Rank: 1	−.92
A court or tribunal that may review the dispute on the merits	47 (.18)	2 (.67) Rank: 1	40 (.19) Rank: 2	2.07*	38 (.21) Rank: 2	9 (.11) Rank: 6	1.94	40 (.19) Rank: 2	6 (.15) Rank: 2	.53
A case administrator or arbitral institution (arbitration only)	17 (.07)	0 (.00) Rank: 3 (tied)	13 (.06) Rank: 6	−.44	6 (.03) Rank: 6 (tied)	11 (.14) Rank: 3	−3.11**	11 (.05) Rank: 6	5 (.13) Rank: 3 (tied)	−1.78
Counsel	59 (.23)	1 (.33) Rank: 2	42 (.20) Rank: 1	.58	44 (.25) Rank: 1	15 (.19) Rank: 1	1.06	52 (.25) Rank: 1	5 (.13) Rank: 3 (tied)	1.62
Myself	6 (.02)	0 (.00) Rank: 3 (tied)	6 (.03) Rank: 8	−.30	3 (.02) Rank: 8 (tied)	3 (.04) Rank: 9	−1.02	4 (.02) Rank: 8 (tied)	2 (.05) Rank: 8 (tied)	−1.21
The losing party	32 (.12)	0 (.00) Rank: 3 (tied)	25 (.12) Rank: 5	−.63	22 (.12) Rank: 5	10 (.12) Rank: 4 (tied)	−.03	28 (13) Rank: 5	3 (.08) Rank: 6 (tied)	.97
The public	7 (.03)	0 (.00) Rank: 3 (tied)	5 (.02) Rank: 9	−.27	3 (.02) Rank: 8 (tied)	4 (.05) Rank: 8	−1.52	4 (.02) Rank: 8 (tied)	2 (.05) Rank: 8 (tied)	−1.21
The winning party	40 (.15)	0 (.00) Rank: 3 (tied)	33 (.16) Rank: 4	−.74	30 (.17) Rank: 3	10 (.12) Rank: 4 (tied)	.89	33 (.16) Rank: 3	5 (.13) Rank: 3 (tied)	.45
Third parties with an interest in this particular dispute (such as insurers or third-party litigation funders)	11 (.04)	0 (.00) Rank: 3 (tied)	10 (.05) Rank: 7	−.39	6 (.03) Rank: 6 (tied)	5 (.06) Rank: 7	−1.06	8 (.04) Rank: 7	3 (.08) Rank: 6 (tied)	−1.09
Total	259	3	212		178	80		211	39	

were combined. The winning party's claim to the second most popular option is further strengthened if the full population figures are weighted to reflect first, second and third place rankings.[229]

Of the remaining four options, the two stand-outs were 'a court or tribunal that may review the dispute on the merits', which won 42 per cent of the votes of the full population among the top three rankings, and 'a court of tribunal that may review the dispute for procedural error', which won 37 per cent of the votes of the full population among the top three rankings. Notably, these two options were split because of the different way that subsequent reviews occur in litigation and arbitration, with litigation involving a review on the merits and arbitration involving a review for procedural errors. If these two options were combined into a general option involving subsequent review, they would attract 79 per cent of the full population over the three rankings, which would be one percentage point higher than the responses for the losing party. However, the option involving the losing party would still receive a higher proportion of the first rank votes (49 per cent compared to 18 per cent for the combined 'review' option), suggesting that the losing party should be considered the most important audience for reasoned decisions and awards.

The final four options were grouped relatively closely. When the full population was considered, 'a case administrator or arbitral institution' earned 11 per cent of the votes over the top three rankings, 'third parties with an interest in this particular dispute' earned 10 per cent, and 'myself' and 'the public' each earned 8 per cent.

The individual responses were robust enough to support statistical analyses across the three comparative axes. Two statistically significant differences arose in the first ranked option, where respondents discussing domestic and international matters differed as to the treatment of the public as a potential audience member ($p<.01$) and common law and civil law respondents differed as to the same element ($p<.05$). Judges and arbitrators also differed ($p<.001$) with respect to their treatment of the public in the third rank. Given the relatively low degree of support for the public as an audience member overall, this latter discrepancy does not appear critical from an analytical perspective.[230]

Statistically significant differences involving substantive or procedural review could reflect important distinctions between groups. For example, two such differences arose in the second rank (across the domestic–international divide ($p<.001$) and across the common law–civil law divide ($p<.01$) in matters involving procedural reviews) and one in the third rank across the judicial–arbitral divide ($p<.05$) in matters involving substantive reviews. While this information provides an insufficient basis for far-reaching conclusions, it does suggest where and how more research might be conducted using a more targeted methodology.

[229] In that calculation, the winning party earns 101 points and counsel earns only 61 points, where each percentage point for first rank is given three points, each percentage point for second rank is given two points and each percentage point for third rank is given one point.

[230] A statistically significant difference ($p<.01$) in the second rank position involving respondents discussing domestic and international matters also appeared relatively unimportant.

The survey design phase anticipated a certain amount of confusion among the respondents with respect to the question regarding the audience for reasoned decisions and awards, since commentary on these matters is somewhat specialized and many judges and arbitrators may never have contemplated the issue.[231] As a result, a follow-up question invited respondents to use an open text box to provide any additional comments they might like to offer about the concept of the audience for reasoned decisions and awards.

A number of the submissions simply elaborated on pre-established alternatives such as the arbitral institution[232] and the author him/herself.[233] Several respondents took issue with the survey design, either criticizing the way the question limited the options to three choices[234] or challenging the way in which the question separated certain pre-established options, particularly with respect to the concept of the parties.[235] Respondents in the latter category, for example, noted that they 'wouldn't rank winner or loser. The parties are equally entitled to know my reasoning', or words to that effect. Another individual stated that 'I don't really separate out parties from counsel. The audience I usually have primarily in mind is, frankly, counsel for the losing party.'

Several people provided additional insights into how they characterized the concept of third parties. For example, one respondent noted that 'if one of the parties is a government or an organization or institution then I write for their understanding too'. Another individual highlighted how the procedural posture of the matter can affect the nature and number of third parties who can be considered audience members, stating 'I also write for any of the others listed who may legitimately view the decision substantively, but that depends on the nature of the dispute'. Another contributor distinguished between primary and secondary audience members, writing that 'while an arbitrator should always have some concern about a possible court review of the award, the process is principally for and about the parties. Pragmatically, there are often insurance coverage issues that exist and an award should be drafted bearing those in mind.'

Several respondents sought to describe the relationship between different types of audience members.[236] For example, one person stated,

> There certainly is some concern for interested third parties, the public and review tribunals, but the principal audience I try to keep in mind is the counsel. They may

[231] Ch. 1.III.A.

[232] Comments in this category included the following: 'the case manager reviews award in draft form before they are issued'; 'administrative secretary'.

[233] Comments in this category included the following: 'to respect your decision and process undertaken you must always satisfy yourself before anyone else'; 'the award needs to include reasoning that convinces me it fairly considers all sides of the argument and explains the conclusion'.

[234] Comments in this category included the following: 'the other choices are also important'; 'I consider a potential audience beyond the top three above, including the risk of any leaks in the future'; 'there are many audiences. They include the parties, counsel and the arbitration authority (for me FINRA or AAA), but also I want to get the decision correct in case of an appeal.'

[235] Comments in this category included the following: 'the award is addressed to the parties which are entitled to receive a fair and reasoned decision. Other types of audience are much less important to me'.

[236] For example, one individual indicated his/her audience encompassed 'both parties, followed by a reviewing court on law'.

> not like the award, but they need to know its why and wherefore as clearly as possible. Counsel can then explain it to the parties, and lead them through the award. It's their case.

Another similarly noted that 'I believe it's important for the parties to have an understanding of the result and reasons for it and that counsel have an idea what "worked" and what "didn't work" in presenting their case'. Going somewhat farther, one individual indicated,

> The losing party must understand why it lost. A court reviewing the case (e.g. for enforcement or annulment purposes) must easily understand how the proceedings were conducted (especially as usually there is no full review); the award must meet the criteria put forward by the law and by the arbitral institution (as institutions are—rightfully—increasingly concerned that awards rendered under their auspices will reflect good/bad on the services they offer).

Some respondents focused less on the audience and more on the purpose of the decision or award, particularly with respect to the arbitral concept of protecting the award.[237] This issue, which was encompassed within pre-established options involving substantive and procedural review, was referred to by one respondent as 'paramount', while another individual stated that 'I write the award primarily so that the parties, counsel and reviewing courts can understand the reasons (legal and factual) for the result and the analytical process employed in reaching the conclusion'. This concept was similarly reflected in a comment indicating that

> the first purpose of the award is to be enforceable i.e. eliminate risk of annulment, and part of this is also to make the award acceptable to the parties, hence the importance of reasons especially for the losing party (in fact most of the time both parties since they might not prevail on all claims).

Several respondents noted the aspiration towards excellence in drafting. For example, one person said that 'there is an unwritten standard of what is expected in a reasoned award, and I want to meet or exceed it'. Another individual indicated that 'I believe that my duty as an arbitrator is to provide the parties with the right result to the best of my judgment, not to reward the party with the best lawyers'. This notion was reiterated by a respondent who stated,

> In some ways I don't think about an audience per se. I think about the creation of a document that lays out the analysis fully and correctly. It matters that the parties and counsel understand it and understand it to have been done fairly. But I understand myself to be

[237] Commentary on arbitration often discusses the need to protect the award from subsequent review or annulment. Ch. 1.III.A.

> writing a piece of legal reasoning that stands up 'objectively', regardless of audience—because that's the right thing to do. (And I know that last part may sound self-righteous, but it's true and this is anonymous.)

Other comments in this category include the statement that 'I want anyone who may read the award to know that I worked hard and conscientiously' as well as the notion that 'I want to make sure the losing party knows I have considered his arguments' One individual sought to explain why s/he adopted this particular approach, noting that 'arbitration has a serious "legitimacy" and perception problem. It is essential that anyone reading my awards be able to see and understand my reasoning and know that everyone was heard and treated fairly.'

Some respondents provided novel alternatives to the pre-established options. For example, several individuals indicated that 'the other arbitrators are the most important' audience members, or words to that effect. Others indicated that they would rank the options differently depending on whether they were acting as a judge or arbitrator.[238]

2. Definitional concerns

Those who are engaged in drafting reasoned decisions or awards come to the process with a view as to what such a document should achieve as a matter of both form and content.[239] As a result, the survey asked respondents to identify those factors that they believed characterized a well-written reasoned decision or award.[240] The survey offered ten different options culled from the legal literature and asked the respondents to rank their top five choices, from most important (1) to least important (5), with the remaining options to be marked 'not applicable.' The data from the top three ranks was then collated to identify the percentage of respondents who chose each option for each cohort, and the information was statistically analysed across the various comparative pairings.[241]

As Table 2.37 shows, the data diverged somewhat significantly, which has a number of repercussions for the legal community. Not only can the variations in viewpoints regarding the nature of a well-written decision or award lead to difficulties relating to the perception of the propriety of a particular document (as might occur when proponents of one dispute resolution process challenge the legitimacy of another dispute resolution process, as is often the case with litigation and arbitration, or when lawyers trained in one

[238] This person indicated that 'since the awards are private, I rank this question differently than I do a judicial decision.'

[239] E.g. SI Strong, 'Reasoned Awards in International Commercial Arbitration: Embracing and Exceeding the Common Law-Civil Law Dichotomy', (2015) 37 Mich J Intl L 1, 15–20 (identifying both structural and process-oriented rationales for reasoned awards); SI Strong, 'Writing Reasoned Decisions and Opinions: A Guide for Novice, Experienced and Foreign Judges', 2015 J Disp Res 93, 101–05 (identifying both structural and process-oriented rationales for reasoned decisions); Ch. 1.III.A.

[240] This issue was also considered in the interviews. Ch. 3.III.A.3. In this context, a 'well-written' decision or award is not synonymous with an outcome that is 'correct' as a matter of law. Instead, the concept of a well-written decision or award encompasses a number of subjective and objective elements relating to the structure, tone, style, content and effect of the decision or award.

[241] While it would have been possible to conduct a statistical analysis of different combinations of options (for example, how many respondents ranked the various options in an A, B, C, D, E order as opposed to A, C, E, B, D), that approach was not adopted because it obscured, at least to some extent, the intensity markings for various choices. See also Table 2.29 (describing a similar methodology).

Table 2.37 Factors characterizing a well-written reasoned decision or award (ranked with internal rankings per cohort)

	Full pop.	Current judges	Current arbitrators	J-A z-stat	Domestic disputes	Int'l disputes	D-I z-stat	Comm. law	Civil law	C-C z-stat
First ranked option										
Clearly states the applicable legal standard and how the facts in this case do or do not meet that standard	145 (.58)	3 (1.00) Rank: 1	117 (.58) Rank: 1	1.48	101 (.58) Rank: 1	43 (.58) Rank: 1	−.01	115 (.57) Rank: 1	27 (.71) Rank: 1	−1.62
Identifies a clear legal standard that can be followed in the future by parties	1 (.00)	0 (.00) Rank: 2 (tied)	1 (.00) Rank: 8 (tied)	−.12	1 (.00) Rank: 8	0 (.00) Rank: 9 (tied)	.65	1 (.00) Rank: 8 (tied)	0 (.00) Rank: 7 (tied)	.43
Identifies a clear legal standard that can be followed in the future by third parties	2 (.01)	0 (.00) Rank: 2 (tied)	0 (.00) Rank: 10	NaN	0 (.00) Rank: 9 (tied)	2 (.03) Rank: 5 (tied)	−2.18*	1 (.00) Rank: 8 (tied)	1 (.03) Rank: 5 (tied)	−1.33
Identifies a clear policy principle that explains the rationale for the decision	8 (.03)	0 (.00) Rank: 2 (tied)	5 (.02) Rank: 5 (tied)	−.28	6 (.03) Rank: 4 (tied)	2 (.03) Rank: 5 (tied)	.30	8 (.04) Rank: 4	0 (.00) Rank: 7 (tied)	1.25
Is as short as possible, given the nature of the dispute	4 (.02)	0 (.00) Rank: 2 (tied)	4 (.02) Rank: 4	−.25	3 (.02) Rank: 6 (tied)	1 (.01) Rank: 8	.21	4 (.02) Rank: 6 (tied)	0 (.00) Rank: 7 (tied	.87
Is logical	13 (.05)	0 (.00) Rank: 2 (tied)	12 (.06) Rank: 3 (tied)	−.43	6 (.03) Rank: 4 (tied)	7 (.09) Rank: 3	−1.94	6 (.03) Rank: 5	5 (.13) Rank: 2	−2.75**
Is understandable by lay readers, including the parties	14 (.05)	0 (.00) Rank: 2 (tied)	12 (.06) Rank: 3 (tied)	−.43	14 (.08) Rank: 3	0 (.00) Rank: 9 (tied)	2.51*	13 (.06) Rank: 3	0 (.00) Rank: 7 (tied)	1.61
Reaches the right outcome as a matter of law	54 (.22)	0 (.00) Rank: 2 (tied)	46 (.23) Rank: 2	−.94	40 (.23) Rank: 2	14 (.19) Rank: 2	.71	50 (.25) Rank: 2	2 (.05) Rank: 3 (tied)	2.68**
Reaches the right outcome as a matter of equity	6 (.02)	0 (.00) Rank: 2 (tied)	5 (.02) Rank: 5 (tied)	−.28	3 (.02) Rank: 6 (tied)	3 (.04) Rank: 4	−1.09	4 (.02) Rank: 6 (tied)	2 (.05) Rank: 3 (tied)	−1.19

Tells a compelling story or provides an emotionally satisfying rationale	2 (.01)	0 (.00) Rank: 2 (tied)	1 (.00) Rank: 8 (tied)	−.12	0 (.00) Rank: 9 (tied)	2 (.03) Rank: 5 (tied)	−2.18*	0 (.00) Rank: 10	1 (.03) Rank: 5 (tied)	−2.31*
Total	249	3	203		174	74		202	38	
Second ranked option										
Clearly states the applicable legal standard and how the facts in this case do or do not meet that standard	38 (.15)	0 (.00) Rank: 4 (tied)	34 (.17) Rank: 3	−.78	31 (.18) Rank: 3	7 (.10) Rank: 4	1.64	34 (.17) Rank: 3	3 (.08) Rank: 5 (tied)	1.40
Identifies a clear legal standard that can be followed in the future by parties	15 (.06)	1 (.33) Rank: 1 (tied)	11 (.05) Rank: 7	2.05*	12 (.07) Rank: 6	3 (.04) Rank: 8	.84	11 (.05) Rank: 7	3 (.08) Rank: 5 (tied)	−.59
Identifies a clear legal standard that can be followed in the future by third parties	2 (.01)	0 (.00) Rank: 4 (tied)	1 (.00) Rank: 10	−.12	0 (.00) Rank: 10	2 (.03) Rank: 9	−2.19*	1 (.00) Rank: 10	1 (.03) Rank: 8 (tied)	−1.33
Identifies a clear policy principle that explains the rationale for the decision	19 (.08)	0 (.00) Rank: 4 (tied)	13 (.06) Rank: 5	−.45	14 (.08) Rank: 5	5 (.07) Rank: 6	.32	14 (.07) Rank: 5	5 (.13) Rank: 4	−1.30
Is as short as possible, given the nature of the dispute	8 (.03)	1 (.33) Rank: 1 (tied)	8 (.04) Rank: 8	2.47*	4 (.02) Rank: 8	4 (.05) Rank: 7	−1.29	4 (.02) Rank: 8 (tied)	3 (.08) Rank: 5 (tied)	−1.99*
Is logical	47 (.19)	1 (.33) Rank: 1 (tied)	40 (.20) Rank: 2	.59	36 (.21) Rank: 2	10 (.14) Rank: 3	1.29	37 (.18) Rank: 2	9 (.24) Rank: 1	−.77
Is understandable by lay readers, including the parties	36 (.15)	0 (.00) Rank: 4 (tied)	28 (.14) Rank: 4	−.70	19 (.11) Rank: 4	17 (.23) Rank: 2	−2.51*	28 (.14) Rank: 4	6 (.16) Rank: 3	−.31
Reaches the right outcome as a matter of law	65 (.26)	0 (.00) Rank: 4 (tied)	52 (.26) Rank: 1	−1.01	47 (.27) Rank: 1	18 (.25) Rank: 1	.38	57 (.28) Rank: 1	7 (.18) Rank: 2	1.25

(continued)

Table 2.37 Continued

	Full pop.	Current judges	Current arbitrators	J-A z-stat	Domestic disputes	Int'l disputes	D-I z-stat	Comm. law	Civil law	C-C z-stat
Reaches the right outcome as a matter of equity	14 (.06)	0 (.00) Rank: 4 (tied)	12 (.06) Rank: 6	-.43	8 (.05) Rank: 7	6 (.08) Rank: 5	-1.12	12 (.06) Rank: 6	1 (.03) Rank: 8 (tied)	.83
Tells a compelling story or provides an emotionally satisfying rationale	4 (.02)	0 (.00) Rank: 4 (tied)	4 (.02) Rank: 9	-.25	3 (.02) Rank: 9	1 (.01) Rank: 10	.20	4 (.02) Rank: 8 (tied)	0 (.00) Rank: 10	.87
Total	248	3	203		174	73		202	38	
Third ranked option										
Clearly states the applicable legal standard and how the facts in this case do or do not meet that standard	23 (.09)	0 (.00) Rank: 4 (tied)	19 (.09) Rank: 5	-.56	17 (.10) Rank: 5	6 (.08) Rank: 5	.54	18 (.09) Rank: 5	3 (.08) Rank: 5	.26
Identifies a clear legal standard that can be followed in the future by parties	12 (.05)	0 (.00) Rank: 4 (tied)	10 (.05) Rank: 7	-.39	8 (.05) Rank: 7	4 (.05) Rank: 6	-.18	11 (.06) Rank: 7	1 (.03) Rank: 8 (tied)	.77
Identifies a clear legal standard that can be followed in the future by third parties	6 (.02)	1 (.33) Rank: 1 (tied)	4 (.02) Rank: 9	3.50***	3 (.02) Rank: 9	3 (.04) Rank: 7 (tied)	-1.02	4 (.02) Rank: 9	2 (.05) Rank: 6 (tied)	-1.14
Identifies a clear policy principle that explains the rationale for the decision	17 (.07)	0 (.00) Rank: 4 (tied)	16 (.08) Rank: 6	-.51	14 (.08) Rank: 6	3 (.04) Rank: 7 (tied)	1.24	14 (.07) Rank: 6	2 (.05) Rank: 6 (tied)	.43
Is as short as possible, given the nature of the dispute	9 (.04)	0 (.00) Rank: 4 (tied)	7 (.04) Rank: 8	-.33	6 (.04) Rank: 8	3 (.04) Rank: 7 (tied)	-.15	7 (.04) Rank: 8	1 (.03) Rank: 8 (tied)	.30
Is logical	60 (.24)	0 (.00) Rank: 4 (tied)	50 (.25) Rank: 1	-.99	38 (.22) Rank: 2	22 (.29) Rank: 1	-1.08	51 (.26) Rank: 1	8 (.21) Rank: 2	.66

Is understandable by lay readers, including the parties	50 (.20)	1 (.33) Rank: 1 (tied)	39 (.19) Rank: 2	.61	39 (.23) Rank: 1	10 (.13) Rank: 4	1.80	42 (.21) Rank: 2	6 (.15) Rank: 3	.80
Reaches the right outcome as a matter of law	36 (.14)	1 (.33) Rank: 1 (tied)	31 (.15) Rank: 3	.86	22 (.13) Rank: 4	14 (.18) Rank: 2	−1.10	23 (.12) Rank: 4	12 (.31) Rank: 1	−3.11**
Reaches the right outcome as a matter of equity	35 (.14)	0 (.00) Rank: 4 (tied)	27 (.13) Rank: 4	−.68	24 (.14) Rank: 3	11 (.14) Rank: 3	−.05	29 (.14) Rank: 3	4 (.10) Rank: 4	.70
Tells a compelling story or provides an emotionally satisfying rationale	1 (.00)	0 (.00) Rank: 4 (tied)	0 (.00) Rank: 10	NaN	0 (.00) Rank: 10	1 (.01) Rank: 10	−1.49	1 (.00) Rank: 10	0 (.00) Rank: 10	.44
Total	249	3	203		171	77		200	39	

legal tradition criticize the usefulness of decisions and awards drafted by lawyers from other legal traditions, as can occur across the common law–civil law divide), they can also lead to practical problems with mutual enforcement of foreign decisions and awards.[242]

While the broad range of options offered in Table 2.37 can make the data difficult to interpret, two items stand out immediately. The most popular choice, winning 58 per cent of the first-place rankings for the full population and 82 per cent of the full population's votes when the top three choices were combined, is the entry for 'clearly states the applicable legal standard and how the facts in this case do or do not meet that standard'. The second most popular choice was 'reaches the right outcome as a matter of law', which won 22 per cent of the first-place rankings for the full population and 62 per cent of the full population's vote when the top three choices were combined. These results are consistent with views expressed elsewhere about the importance of both law and facts, although the strength of the preference for the more process-oriented (as opposed to outcome-oriented) option was unexpected. More research is warranted to discover why judges and arbitrators chose as they did.

The next band of options involves the choice marked 'is logical', which earned 48 per cent of the full population's vote when the three top choices were combined, and 'is understandable by lay readers', which earned 40 per cent of the full population's vote when the top three choices were combined. These items tied for third place among the first-ranked options.

Within the remaining options, the only item that bears mention involves the choice marked 'reaches the right outcome as a matter of equity'.[243] Earlier in the survey, various respondents discussed the role that equity played in the decision-making process,[244] but that emphasis on equity is not reflected as a hallmark of a well-written award. Indeed, this item won only 2 per cent of the full population's votes for the first-ranked option and only earned 22 per cent of the full population's votes when the top three choices were combined. This phenomenon suggests that equitable concerns are of only ancillary importance, at least to most judges and arbitrators.

The responses were robust enough to permit statistical analyses, and a number of statistically significant differences arose across the comparative pairings. Most of the differences involved options at the lower end of the hierarchical scale and were therefore of less relevance to this discussion. However, the common law and civil law groups differed significantly ($p<.01$) with respect to their support for 'reaches the right

[242] The international legal community has sought to remedy this issue in the international realm through international treaties, but difficulties still arise. E.g. Convention of 2 July 2019 on the Recognition and Enforcement of Foreign Judgments in Civil or Commercial Matters (Hague Judgments Convention), <https://www.hcch.net/en/instruments/conventions/full-text/?cid=137> accessed 11 April 2020; United Nations Convention on the Recognition and Enforcement of Foreign Arbitral Awards, 10 June 1958, 330 UNTS 3 (New York Convention); see also UN Commission on International Trade Law, Report of the UN Commission on International Trade Law, Fifty-first session, UN Doc A/73/17 (2018) at Annex I (Singapore Convention on Mediation).

[243] The remaining entries' percentages of the full population, combined over the top three rankings, were as follows: identifies a clear policy principle that explains the rationale for the decision (18 per cent); identifies a clear legal standard that can be followed in the future by parties (11 per cent); is as short as possible, given the nature of the dispute (9 per cent); identifies a clear legal standard that can be followed in the future by third parties (4 per cent); tells a compelling story or provides an emotionally satisfying rationale (3 per cent).

[244] Tables 2.29, 2.32, 2.34.

outcome as a matter of law' in the both the first and third ranked options, suggesting an important distinction in how reasoned decisions and awards are formulated across the common law–civil law divide. Further research on this issue is warranted.

Notably, no statistical differences arose across any of the comparative pairings with respect to the option involving equitable concerns. This information is particularly useful to the analysis of judicial and arbitral practices, given the longstanding assumption that judges make determinations on the basis of law and arbitrators make determinations on the basis of equity.[245]

During the survey design phase, it was anticipated that some individuals might find the preceding question challenging for one reason or another, so the next question offered respondents the opportunity to provide additional comments about the factors that characterize a well-written reasoned decision or award. As it turned out, a number of individuals did in fact find it difficult to rank the ten pre-established options, as reflected in comments indicating that 'I would rank the noted factors as having equal importance', that it was 'not meaningful to rank these' or that 'I was frustrated with having to make so many "not applicable" choices in the preceding question'. One person expanded on this idea, saying that 'it is hard to rank these factors in general for all cases. They vary by the case. Likewise, five were ranked and five were N/A, but sometimes the N/A factors float to the top in a given case.'[246]

Some comments focused on structural issues, providing information that was interesting, albeit somewhat outside the scope of the question. For example, one individual said, 'the narrative part of the award should not be exceedingly long. Arbitrators are not paid by the page', while another indicated that a well-written decision or award 'fairly recites the material facts'. It was also suggested that 'each issue in the case should be addressed with a reason for the award on each issue'. One respondent noted there must be 'adequate citation to the relevant facts in the record and legal authorities' while another said that 'I wage a constant war against legalese'.

Respondents also focused on more conceptual aspects of drafting. For example, one respondent suggested that a well-written decision or award 'connects the outcome(s) to the relief requested by the parties', while another said such documents should be 'well organized; structured in accordance with the circumstances in which the dispute arose, and then in accordance with each of those disputes, usually in chronological sequence'. Another detail identified by a different individual was that 'where evidence is irreconcilable, let parties know finding of credibility of evidence/testimony'.

Several people discussed the communicative aspects of a decision or award. For example, one individual noted that it was 'important that the parties understand that I heard and understood them and why I decided what I decided'. Related comments suggested that the decision or award should be 'objectively understandable by the parties and counsel' and should 'clarify the bases of resolving the dispute so that the

245 Ch. 1.III.A.

246 As noted above, the survey asked respondents to rank their top five choices, but only the top three are reported in Table 2.37 and discussed herein for reasons of space and relevance.

parties will follow my comments so they avoid the need for further arbitrations in future'. One person noted that 'in some cases (e.g. where the parties are in a continuing relationship) a reasoned award may help the parties' ongoing relationship'.

Finally, a number of respondents focused on what might be called overarching issues. For example, one individual said that a well-reasoned decision or award 'demonstrates respect for all parties and witnesses regardless of how they come across or how they perceive each other'. Another similarly noted that 'the arbitrator should have a distinct advantage over the parties and their representatives and witnesses in not being possibly emotionally attached to the dispute and its resolution'. A somewhat related comment indicated that 'every award must demonstrate that the parties received a fair, legitimate hearing, were heard and the disputes determined according to the law and facts'. One individual succinctly noted the importance of 'timeliness'.

3. Interim conclusions regarding drafting reasoned decisions and awards

Although the survey section on drafting was relatively short compared to other sections, the discussion generated some useful insights. For example, the level of detail reflected in a reasoned decision or award is highly influenced by the difficulty, complexity, and novelty of the dispute as a matter of fact and of law. Judges and arbitrators also found the act of writing a reasoned decision or award to be useful in helping them think through the issues in the case, although that process did not mean respondents considered themselves to be an 'audience' for their decisions or awards.

Instead, respondents tended to focus on the losing party as the primary audience member, although courts or tribunals undertaking subsequent reviews ranked equally highly, if two categories of review (substantive and procedural) were combined. Otherwise, respondents tended to view counsel and the winning party as the next most important audience members.

The survey also sought to pinpoint the hallmarks of a well-written decision or award. Interestingly, the respondents clearly elevated process-oriented considerations (i.e. those relating to the clear statement of the relevant legal standard and how the facts do or do not meet the standard identified) over outcome-oriented concerns (i.e. that the dispute was resolved correctly as a matter of law).[247] Furthermore, those two factors (process and outcome) were significantly more important than other alternatives by a significant order of magnitude. While the data was not conclusive about the relevant importance of several of the lower-ranked features, the results from this question provide a useful baseline for future empirical and theoretical research.

E. Judicial and Arbitral Education Relating to Legal Reasoning

Although law students are taught about legal reasoning from the first day of their legal education, those principles are typically introduced in a vacuum, divorced from factual

[247] Table 2.37.

considerations. Furthermore, arguing a dispute is very different than deciding a dispute.[248] As a result, it was anticipated that judges and arbitrators would likely benefit from specialized professional education on how to reflect legal reasoning in decisions and awards.

This study therefore sought to determine whether and to what extent judges and arbitrators are receiving adequate educational support regarding legal reasoning in commercial disputes.[249] Questions in this series sought to establish the nature of existing programs of judicial and arbitral education, the extent to which respondents had relied on those programs in the past and the type of programming that would be optimal going forward.

1. Content and form considerations

The first question in this series sought to set a baseline for further analysis by asking respondents to indicate how they learned to write reasoned decisions or awards. The question offered six pre-established options and asked respondents to check all that applied, which meant that percentages do not add up to 100.

As Table 2.38 shows, the most common response was that the individual 'learned by doing', which was chosen by 83 per cent of the full population and ranked first across all comparative cohorts except for civil law respondents, who ranked that option second.[250] Although this result was expected, based on the legal literature,[251] questions exist about the effectiveness of such an approach. For example, experts in andragogy (adult learning) have touted the effectiveness of experiential learning, but only if the individual in question is given sufficient instruction in best practices and feedback on actual or simulated performance.[252] When it comes to legal reasoning, it is unclear whether that feedback exists, since the standard mechanisms of formal review—substantive review in the case of litigation and procedural review in the case of arbitration—typically focus only on outcomes and do not provide feedback to the drafters on how to improve their reasoning techniques.[253] The one exception might be the International Chamber of Commerce (ICC) Court of Arbitration, which scrutinises ICC awards for technical and format-related concerns prior to releasing the award to the parties.[254] The ICC Court does not address issues relating to outcome but does provide arbitrators with individualized feedback (and occasionally requires revision of the award consistent with that feedback) in order to promote consistency and enforceability of ICC awards.

[248] Emily Kadens, 'The Puzzle of Judicial Education: The Case of Chief Justice William de Grey', (2009) 75 Brooklyn L Rev 143, 143.

[249] Ch. 1.II.

[250] This concept was also mentioned by some interviewees. Ch. 3.III.F.1.

[251] Ch. 1.II.

[252] Malcolm S Knowles, *The Modern Practice of Adult Education: From Pedagogy to Andragogy* (Cambridge Book Co 1980) 45–49 (distinguishing andragogy, the teaching of adults, from pedagogy, the teaching of children).

[253] While it could be argued that successful appeals on the merits and successful challenges on procedural matters indicate errors in judges' and arbitrators' legal reasoning, those mechanisms are content-based rather than process-based and therefore ignore a significant portion of what may be called legal reasoning.

[254] ICC International Court of Arbitration, <https://iccwbo.org/dispute-resolution-services/icc-international-court-arbitration/> accessed 11 April 2020.

Table 2.38 How judges and arbitrators learn to write reasoned decisions or awards (number of respondents followed by proportion in parenthesis and ranking within the cohort)

	Full pop.	Current judges	Current arbitrators	J-A z-stat	Domestic disputes	Int'l disputes	D-I z-stat	Comm. law	Civil law	C-C z-stat
I attended a seminar or symposium on writing reasoned decisions or awards	135 (.52)	1 (.33) Rank: 4	110 (.52) Rank: 3	−.63	106 (.58) Rank: 3	28 (.36) Rank: 4	3.26*	120 (.57) Rank: 3	7 (.19) Rank: 4	4.26***
I completed a university degree program that included coursework specifically focused on writing reasoned decisions or awards	26 (.10)	0 (.00) Rank: 5 (tied)	14 (.07) Rank: 6	−.46	18 (.10) Rank: 6	8 (.10) Rank: 6	−.10	18 (.09) Rank: 6	3 (.08) Rank: 6	.09
I learned by doing	218 (.83)	3 (1.0) Rank: 1	185 (.87) Rank: 1	.67	149 (.81) Rank: 1	68 (.87) Rank: 1	−1.14	178 (.84) Rank: 1	29 (.78) Rank: 2	.90
I learned by reading other reasoned decisions or awards	187 (.71)	2 (.67) Rank: 2 (tied)	155 (.73) Rank: 2	−.24	127 (.69) Rank: 2	60 (.77) Rank: 2	−1.23	150 (.71) Rank: 2	30 (.81) Rank: 1	−1.26
I learned by speaking with more experienced colleagues	98 (.37)	2 (.67) Rank: 2 (tied)	81 (.38) Rank: 4	1.01	66 (.36) Rank: 4	31 (.40) Rank: 3	−.56	81 (.38) Rank: 4	12 (.32) Rank: 3	.69
I read a book or article on writing reasoned decisions or awards	77 (.29)	0 (.00) Rank: 5 (tied)	62 (.29) Rank: 5	−1.11	54 (.30) Rank: 5	22 (.28) Rank: 5	.21	67 (.32) Rank: 5	5 (.14) Rank: 5	2.25*
Total	262	3	213		183	78		211	37	

The second most popular option in Table 2.38 involved learning by reading other decisions or awards. This practice is ranked second with all cohorts except civil law respondents, who ranked it first within their internal hierarchy, and was chosen by 71 per cent of the full population. This result was again expected, based on the legal literature, but is problematic as a matter of best practices in andragogy, since it is an entirely passive form of learning.[255]

The third most popular option, based on marks from the full population (52 per cent), involved attendance at a seminar or symposium on writing reasoned decisions or awards. However, this alternative reflected statistically significant differences along both the domestic–international divide ($p<.01$) and the common law–civil law divide ($p<.001$), with domestic and common law respondents being far more likely to engage in this type of educational offering than their international and civil law counterparts. The domestic–international and common law–civil law cohorts also reflected discrepancies in internal rankings, similar to those that arose across the judicial–arbitral divide, although the differences between judges and arbitrators were not statistically significant.

While seminars and symposia are often considered a 'best practice' in the area of judicial and arbitral education, that perspective may be the result of an unconscious bias in favour of law school-style education.[256] In fact, many seminars and symposia involve a great deal of passive education (i.e. lectures and presentations from faculty), which experts in andragogy note is not as beneficial as more engaged learning (i.e. simulations and practice-based exercises).[257]

The legal literature on judicial and arbitral education frequently discusses the role that acculturation (also known as 'socialization') plays in developing skills among new entrants to the field,[258] and those techniques are still apparently in use, albeit among a minority (37 per cent) of the full population of respondents. Another mechanism that is relatively popular with various professional education organizations—providing written materials involving particular judicial or arbitral skills[259]—received some support in Table 2.38, with 29 per cent of the full population indicating that they had learned how to write reasoned decisions or awards by reading a book or article. Interestingly, a statistically significant difference ($p<.05$) arose on this point between common law and civil law respondents, with common law lawyers being more likely to have engaged in such practices. However, the two groups ranked the item similarly in

[255] Knowles (n 252) 45–49 (noting passive learning is the least effective means of promoting student understanding and retention of information).

[256] SI Strong, 'Richard A. Posner, *Divergent Paths: The Academy and the Judiciary* - How Legal Academics Can Participate in Judicial Education: A How-To Guide by Richard Posner', (2017) 66 J L Ed 421, 430–31 (Strong, Posner) (noting Judge Richard Posner's experience with student bias regarding experiential learning).

[257] Knowles (n 252) 45–49; see generally Livingston Armytage, *Educating Judges: Towards Improving Justice* (Brill 2015); Ch. 1.II.

[258] Kadens (n 248) 146–47; Strong, Judicial Education (n 35) 4; SI Strong, 'Judicial Education and International Courts: A Proposal Whose Time Has Come?', in Freya Baetens (ed), *Identity and Diversity on the International Bench* (Oxford University Press, forthcoming 2020); Ch. 1.II.

[259] E.g. Publications, Federal Judicial Center <https://www.fjc.gov/publications> accessed 11 April 2020 (containing numerous guides, including those relating to the drafting of judicial opinions, for judges and other members of judicial staff).

their internal hierarchies, which may suggest the statistical test should not be given that much weight.

Acculturation and publication are of course useful and potentially effective means of conveying information to the relevant audiences. However, these two mechanisms have little in the way of quality control and can lead to the perpetuation of problematic practices rather than best practices.

The survey also offered respondents the opportunity to describe other ways that they learned how to write reasoned decisions and awards, although the question did not tally the percentage of responses falling under the category of 'other'. Many of the comments confirmed the propriety of the pre-established options, with one person indicating 'all of the above, and still learning'. Other responses in this category included statements that respondents learned through 'mentoring by experienced arbitrators' or by 'working with other arbitrators on a three-arbitrator panel'. Other types of mentorship included learning through clerkships with judges, which was mentioned by several respondents, or in one case, through work as 'an extern at a state appellate court and draft[ing] decisions'.

A large number of respondents indicated that they learned how to write reasoned decisions and awards by drawing analogies from previous practical experience. The highest proportion of comments in this category, and indeed a high proportion of comments overall, involved respondents relying on their experience as an advocate.[260] For example, one individual said,

> I learned also from my practice as counsel: when doing so my purpose was to write my briefs for the arbitrator with a view to find in the award my own reasoning. As an arbitrator the reasoning must convince the parties and their counsels (who will be key as regards a possible challenge) and leave no loophole as regards due process in writing a reasoned award.

Other individuals noted they had learned to write reasoned decisions and awards as a result of their experience as tribunal secretary or through their work as legal scholars, including 'editing cases for teaching materials, and writing law review articles that analysed case decisions'. As one individual said, 'I have been a business/commercial author for decades, so extrapolating that persuasive/explanatory bent to arbitral decisions was easy'.

Some respondents indicated that they relied on skills learned earlier in their careers. For example, one individual noted that 'in Germany, writing judicial decisions is part of the traineeship preceding the second state exam', a factor that may explain why civil law respondents were less likely than common law respondents to engage in most types of educational activities outlined in Table 2.38. Another individual stated that 'I attended a

[260] Comments in this category included the following: 'I learned as an outgrowth of experience as an advocate'; 'as a litigator, I received decisions'; 'I have read thousands of judicial decisions' '50 years as counsel. Many cases, many arbitrations.'

good law school. Exams often required considering facts, researching law (or reviewing applicable law) and writing a judicial-style opinion.'[261] One person went even further back and said that s/he relied on the 'application of principles included in freshman composition in college', a technique that was also mentioned by several participants in the semi-structured interviews.[262]

While these approaches cannot be denied from an empirical perspective, questions arise as to whether learning by analogy should be considered sufficient going forward. Indeed, US Supreme Court Justice Hugo Black—renowned by many for his judicial writing—once said that 'the most difficult thing about coming on to the Court was learning how to write'.[263]

Several respondents took the opportunity offered in this question to identify particular courses that they had taken to learn how to write reasoned decisions and awards. Among the judicial respondents, one individual noted that 'I passed the training for judges and the judge's exam' while another indicated that s/he was 'pursuing a masters in judicial studies at the University of Nevada and [had] successfully completed a course in judicial writing'. Notably, this latter course appears to have been voluntary in nature, since US federal judges and many US state judges are not required to engage in any form of judicial education before or after elevation to the bench.[264] However, another respondent noted that in his/her jurisdiction, 'judges have mandatory continuing judicial education where this is a regular topic'.

Among the arbitral respondents, one individual noted that 'I took the CIArb [Chartered Institute of Arbitration] courses, including the ARF [Accelerated Route to Fellowship], which included such topics, but I had already written a number of awards'. Another person indicated that s/he had taken courses in both judicial and arbitral settings, noting that 'the National Judicial College for judges has a very good program' in addition to various 'arbitration studies'. One respondent said 'I teach writing reasoned decisions and awards', although s/he did not indicate what courses s/he had taken.

The survey then moved on to the next subject, namely whether judges and arbitrators would benefit from educational programming on writing reasoned decisions or awards. The question offered four different pre-determined options that broke down the affirmative answer into three separate categories to distinguish between different levels of seniority among judges and arbitrators. Because the legal literature has identified some concerns about whether and to what extent educational programming affects judicial and arbitral independence,[265] the question explicitly stated that the respondent should assume that any programming would sufficiently safeguard judicial and arbitral independence.

[261] US Circuit Judge Richard Posner has promoted the notion that US law students should learn how to write judicial decisions while in law school. Strong, Posner (n 256) 429.

[262] Ch. 3.III.F.1.

[263] William Domnarski, *In the Opinion of the Court* (University of Illinois Press 1997) 36 (citation omitted).

[264] Strong, Judicial Education (n 35) 10–11 (noting voluntary, as opposed to mandatory, judicial education is often the norm in common law countries); see also Ch. 1.III.A.

[265] Strong, Judicial Education (n 35) 10–11 (noting voluntary, as opposed to mandatory, judicial education is often the norm in common law countries); see also Ch. 1.III.A.

Table 2.39 Whether judges and arbitrators would benefit from educational programming on writing reasoned decisions and awards (number of respondents followed by proportion in parenthesis and ranking within the cohort)

	Full pop.	Current judges	Current arbitrators	J-A z-stat	Domestic disputes	Int'l disputes	D-I z-stat	Comm. law	Civil law	C-C z-stat
No	19 (.07)	0 (.00) Rank: 2 (tied)	14 (.06) Rank: 3	−.45	12 (.06) Rank: 3	7 (.09) Rank: 3	−.64	12 (.06) Rank: 3	5 (.12) Rank: 3	−1.55
Yes, for both new and experienced judges or arbitrators	207 (.76)	3 (1.0) Rank: 1	167 (.76) Rank: 1	.98	145 (.77) Rank: 1	61 (.74) Rank: 1	.49	169 (.79) Rank: 1	28 (.68) Rank: 1	1.49
Yes, for experienced judges or arbitrators only	0 (.00)	0 (.00) Rank: 2 (tied)	0 (.00) Rank: 4	NaN	0 (.00) Rank: 4	0 (.00) Rank: 4	NaN	0 (.00) Rank: 4	0 (.00) Rank: 4	NaN
Yes, for new judges or arbitrators only	45 (.17)	0 (.00) Rank: 2 (tied)	40 (.18) Rank: 2	−.81	31 (.16) Rank: 2	14 (.17) Rank: 2	−.12	33 (.15) Rank: 2	8 (.20) Rank: 2	−.65
Total	271	3	221		188	82		214	41	

As Table 2.39 shows, only a small minority of the full population (7 per cent) believed that new and experienced judges and arbitrators would not benefit from educational programming on writing reasoned decisions or awards. This result is quite different from that generated by the semi-structured interviews, where numerous individuals claimed that judges and arbitrators do not need additional education.[266] While more research is warranted on this point, one explanation for this discrepancy is that interviewees might have interpreted the question as reflecting on them personally, even though it was posed in the abstract, and did not believe that they themselves needed additional training. However, social science research regarding the bias blind spot suggests that people are often incapable of seeing areas in which they themselves are deficient, even though they are capable of seeing similar shortcomings in others.[267] This phenomenon demonstrates why it is useful to engage in several types of empirical research to triangulate results.[268]

When comparing the individual cohorts, it is clear that all groups resoundingly believe that new and experienced judges and arbitrators would both benefit from educational programming on writing reasoned decisions and awards. This option won 76 per cent of the votes from the full population and was ranked in the first position for all six groups, with no statistically significant differences in intensity marks. The second-place option, across all groups, involved educational programming for new judges and arbitrators only (17 per cent of the full population). While it was anticipated that few, if any, respondents would believe that experienced judges or arbitrators would be the only ones to benefit from educational opportunities (indeed, none of the survey participants chose that option), experts in andragogy suggest that some forms of professional education are only really effective after the participants have some level of experience, a factor that those involved in developing educational programming should take into consideration.[269]

Respondents were asked to explain their answers by providing individual comments in an open text box. Numerous individuals recognized the need for continuing education in this area of practice,[270] with one person indicating that 'it's an important subject. The quality of reasoned awards does much to strengthen or undermine public confidence in the alternate dispute resolution process.' Another respondent noted, 'We can always learn and pick up new insights and techniques. Just going to a conference with other arbitrators and judges, or a CLE put on by judges and/or arbitrators, always provides new and better ideas on drafting decisions.'

266 Ch. 3.III.F.3.

267 Lawrence M Solan, 'Four Reasons to Teach Psychology to Legal Writing Students', (2013) 22 J L & Pol'y 7, 10 (defining the bias blind spot as an unconscious tendency 'which prevents us from taking our own biases as seriously as we do the biases of others').

268 Ch. 1.II (discussing triangulation methods).

269 Knowles (n 252) 45–49.

270 Comments in this category included the following: 'we all need to improve'; 'everyone can learn to be better'; 'writing reasoned awards is a skill that improves with training'; 'you can always learn from others no matter the stage of your career and experience'; 'we can all benefit from other's perspectives.'

Some respondents sought to identify the cohort of individuals who would benefit most from educational initiatives. Some distinctions focused on experience. For example, one respondent noted that the 'need may be larger for new arbitrators. But even experienced and well-respected colleagues sometimes fail to draft a coherent, legally sound, properly structured award.' Indeed, one individual indicated that 'I've read some real stinkers from both new and experienced judges and arbitrators', while another person said that 'an appalling number of attorneys and a somewhat less frightening number of judges and arbitrators write (and think?) very poorly'.

A number of respondents discussed the perceived distinctions between senior and junior judges and arbitrators. For example, one individual noted that 'new practitioners need to learn how to write reasoned decisions, and experienced practitioners need to re-examine the quality of their work from time to time', while another indicated that 'none of us is omniscient or perfect. Everyone should be able to learn. Good dedicated judges and arbitrators should have the life-long desire to continue to ensure that they do the best possible job.' Another one person said, 'new judges/arbitrators would benefit the most. Experienced judges/arbitrators can learn new factors that might improve their writing. Older most-experienced judges/arbitrators ... well, maybe not so much.' This latter sentiment was echoed in comments from other respondents who said that it is 'hard to teach older arbitrators' and that 'it's likely "too late" to teach old dogs new tricks'.

Other comments focused on the nature of the judge or arbitrator's experience. For example, one individual noted that 'some judges (continental Europe) might not have understood how important it is to detail the reasons and the facts of the case when they sit as arbitrator. As regards practitioners, when they act as arbitrators some educational programming might ensure better quality.' However, other comments focused on personal attributes, saying 'it depends on the judge/arbitrator's experience and ability. Some may benefit. It comes naturally to others.'

Concerns were also expressed about the possibility of blind spot bias. For example, one individual sagely noted that 'people think they write well, but they often don't', while another indicated that 'not all qualified judges and arbitrators understand how to write good awards'.

A number of respondents focused on the content of educational initiatives. Some comments discussed overarching concerns, such as the one noting 'it is always helpful to find out what the parties want, how you can improve, and how well you are achieving your objectives in the writing of an award'. Another individual thought that educational programs 'would help [judges and arbitrators] understand the process of preparing an opinion'. One person explained that

> experience is good, but a good program would help unlearn certain practices one may have developed that, on examination, are not serving their purpose. A good program would also elevate the overall discipline and quality of preparing an award. It would provide a systematic process formed from a consensus of experienced arbitrators.

Other respondents focused on the details of writing a reasoned decision or award. For example, one person noted that, 'unfortunately, too many lawyers write like lawyers. Plain English is rarely in evidence, and it should be.' Another believed that 'there's a lot of lousy opinions out there. In lots of ways, but mainly in failing to find the right balance between (1) concision and (2) persuasively full explanation', while a third who was likely focusing on international commercial arbitration[271] wrote that,

> in my view, there has developed an unfortunate practice of writing awards of more than 100+ pages, where the vast majority of the award is recitation and the core legal and factual reasoning suffers and can be very limited. This substantially increases costs and delay, and result in the core decision not being adequately explained. An open discussion among new and experienced arbitrators and others would be valuable.

Some respondents expressed some concerns about content format, since 'there are inconsistencies among institutions as to what is a satisfactory award' and 'there are so many cultural differences'. Another individual suggested that 'the logic of arbitration and its distinction from processes at law is poorly understood by lawyers and laymen alike. Refresher courses are valuable, especially as award writing becomes rarer as more cases settle.' Similar sentiments were expressed by the person who wrote that

> everybody can always learn from more training, etc., but training in this area is particularly problematic in that it often sounds prescriptive and fails to take circumstances into account. What is needed of a published award may be very different from the usual private award; what is needed in a context in which parties are from different countries/cultures/legal systems may be different than when the participants are homogenous. An education program, to be any good, would have to [take such nuances into account] rigorously.

Some comments focused on the type of programming that would prove useful. For example, one individual noted that 'there is certainly an art to drafting decisions or awards, including structure, tone, content and reasoning that benefit from basic instruction'. However, as another person noted, 'there is a wide spectrum of needs, so no one approach is right', a view that was echoed by the individual who noted that 'everyone has his own approach. What works for one person may not work for someone else. Perhaps it would help some, but there is nothing like doing it.' Thus, the perspective of the person who indicated that 'I took an online course from the American Arbitration Association. I thought that was a good way to learn' was as valid as the individual who thought 'the emphasis lies on learning by doing'.

[271] International commercial awards are generally much longer than domestic awards, as demonstrated by the coding exercise. Table 4.8; see also Ch. 1.III.C.

Program content may vary depending on the experience of the individual judge or arbitrator.[272] For example, one person said that

> when beginning to write awards it is useful to draw on the experience and expertise of others, and the new arbitrator is most likely to appreciate that fact. After gaining experience an arbitrator will develop his or her own practices and be less susceptible to change. At that point, it would be best to have sessions among respected colleagues sharing experiences and thoughts/conclusions on best practices, rather than a 'training session'.

Not every comment was in favour of continuing education initiatives. Although Table 2.39 showed a significant majority of respondents supported more educational programming on writing reasoned decisions and awards, one individual indicated that 'I do not believe much in educational programs as to how to write a well-reasoned award', while another said that 'I believe more decisions are flawed based on a lack of understanding of the law than are flawed because of lack of understanding of how to write an award'. However, this latter concern could in fact be remedied through educational programming, as noted by the respondent who noted specifically that adopting a more rigorous approach to judicial and arbitral education would likely 'improve the actual decision-making process' as well as 'improve arbitrators' confidence in the outcome of their efforts'.

The next question asked those respondents who had answered yes to the previous question to identify the type of programming that would be most beneficial to judges or arbitrators. This question focused on educational formats as opposed to substantive topics and offered 12 different pre-established options. Respondents were asked to rank their top five choices, from most important (1) to least important (5), with the remaining options to be marked 'not applicable'. The data from the top three ranks was then collated to identify the percentage of respondents who chose each option for each cohort, and the information was statistically analysed across the various comparative pairings.[273] Respondents were told that they should assume the programming would sufficiently safeguard judicial and arbitral independence.

As Table 2.40 shows, the question generated no clear data near the top of the rankings and only a few general trends, suggesting a lack of consensus within the relevant communities. One contender for the most popular option was 'in-person seminar or symposium—mixed format' (meaning a mixture of lecture, discussion and experiential (hands on) elements), which earned the highest percentage of the full population

[272] Indeed, the Federal Judicial Center, one of the premier judicial education institutions in the world, breaks its orientation sessions into several blocks so as to take the needs and experience levels of the recipients into account. Jeremy Fogel and SI Strong, 'Judicial Education, Dispute Resolution and the Life of a Judge: A Conversation with Judge Jeremy Fogel, Director of the Federal Judicial Center', 2016 J Disp Res 259, 268 (discussing two rounds of orientation sessions for new US federal judges plus a mid-career seminar for more established judges).

[273] While it would have been possible to conduct a statistical analysis of different combinations of options (for example, how many respondents ranked the various options in an A, B, C, D, E order as opposed to A, C, E, B, D), that approach was not adopted because it obscured, at least to some extent, the intensity markings for various choices. See also Table 2.29 (describing a similar methodology).

Table 2.40 Methods of delivering judicial or arbitral education (ranked)

	Full pop.	Current judges	Current arbitrators	J-A z-stat	Domestic disputes	Int'l disputes	D-I z-stat	Comm. law	Civil law	C-C z-stat
First ranked option										
Distance (video or audio) seminar or symposium – lecture format	25 (.11)	0 (.00) Rank: 4 (tied)	22 (.12) Rank: 5	–.63	23 (.14) Rank: 2	2 (.03) Rank: 9 (tied)	2.38*	23 (.12) Rank: 3	1 (.03) Rank: 8 (tied)	1.56
Distance (video or audio) seminar or symposium – discussion format	10 (.04)	0 (.00) Rank: 4 (tied)	7 (.04) Rank: 9	–.34	7 (.04) Rank: 9	3 (.05) Rank: 8	–.13	8 (.04) Rank: 9 (tied)	1 (.03) Rank: 8	.32
Distance (video or audio) seminar or symposium – experiential (hands-on) format	5 (.02)	0 (.00) Rank: 4 (tied)	4 (.02) Rank: 12	–.26	5 (.03) Rank: 11 (tied)	0 (.00) Rank: 11 (tied)	1.42	5 (.03) Rank: 11	0 (.00) Rank: 11 (tied)	.94
Distance (video or audio) seminar or symposium – mixed format	19 (.08)	1 (.33) Rank: 1 (tied)	16 (.09) Rank: 6	1.49	14 (.09) Rank: 6	5 (.08) Rank: 6 (tied)	.19	14 (.08) Rank: 6	3 (.09) Rank: 5	–.34
Formal or informal mentor program	15 (.07)	1 (.33) Rank: 1 (tied)	12 (.06) Rank: 7	1.83	9 (.05) Rank: 7	6 (.09) Rank: 5	–1.05	9 (.05) Rank: 8	5 (.16) Rank: 2 (tied)	–2.28*
Identification of reasoned decisions or awards that exemplify best practices (i.e. 'model' or 'ideal' decisions or awards	29 (.13)	0 (.00) Rank: 4 (tied)	23 (.12) Rank: 4	–.65	18 (.11) Rank: 5	11 (.17) Rank: 2	–1.25	22 (.12) Rank: 4	5 (.16) Rank: 2 (tied)	–.58
In-person seminar or symposium – lecture format	10 (.04)	0 (.00) Rank: 4 (tied)	6 (.03) Rank: 10	–.32	8 (.05) Rank: 8	2 (.03) Rank: 9 (tied)	.59	10 (.05) Rank: 7	0 (.00) Rank: 11 (tied)	1.35

(continued)

Table 2.40 Continued

	Full pop.	Current judges	Current arbitrators	J-A z-stat	Domestic disputes	Int'l disputes	D-I z-stat	Comm. law	Civil law	C-C z-stat
In-person seminar or symposium – discussion format	28 (.12)	0 (.00) Rank: 4 (tied)	25 (.13) Rank: 3	–.68	19 (.12) Rank: 4	8 (.12) Rank: 4	–.18	20 (.11) Rank: 5	7 (.22) Rank: 1	–1.74
In-person seminar or symposium – experiential (hands-on) format	32 (.14)	0 (.00) Rank: 4 (tied)	27 (.15) Rank: 2	–.71	22 (.13) Rank: 3	10 (.16) Rank: 3	–.41	27 (.15) Rank: 2	5 (.16) Rank: 2 (tied)	–.14
In-person seminar or symposium – mixed format	39 (.17)	0 (.00) Rank: 4 (tied)	31 (.17) Rank: 1	–.77	27 (.17) Rank: 1	12 (.19) Rank: 1	–.39	35 (.19) Rank: 1	2 (.06) Rank: 6 (tied)	1.77
Mechanisms to facilitate confidential discussion of issues and concern with peers	5 (.02)	0 (.00) Rank: 4 (tied)	5 (.03) Rank: 11	–.29	5 (.03) Rank: 11 (tied)	0 (.00) Rank: 11 (tied)	1.42	3 (.02) Rank: 12	1 (.03) Rank: 8 (tied)	–.58
Written materials	11 (.05)	1 (.33) Rank: 1 (tied)	8 (.04) Rank: 8	2.34*	6 (.04) Rank: 10	5 (.08) Rank: 6 (tied)	–1.30	8 (.04) Rank: 9 (tied)	2 (.06) Rank: 6 (tied)	–.47
Total	228	3	186		163	64		184	32	
Second ranked option										
Distance (video or audio) seminar or symposium – lecture format	7 (.03)	0 (.00) Rank: 3 (tied)	4 (.02) Rank: 12	–.21	7 (.04) Rank: 10 (tied)	0 (.00) Rank: 12	1.69	6 (.03) Rank: 12	0 (.00) Rank: 12	1.04
Distance (video or audio) seminar or symposium – discussion format	13 (.06)	1 (.50) Rank: 1 (tied)	12 (.06) Rank: 7 (tied)	2.41*	12 (.08) Rank: 6	1 (.02) Rank: 11	1.70	12 (.07) Rank: 7 (tied)	1 (.03) Rank: 8 (tied)	.76
Distance (video or audio) seminar or symposium – experiential (hands-on) format	11 (.05)	0 (.00) Rank: 3 (tied)	8 (.04) Rank: 10	–.30	6 (.04) Rank: 12	5 (.08) Rank: 7 (tied)	–1.30	7 (.04) Rank: 9 (tied)	3 (.09) Rank: 4 (tied)	–1.36

Distance (video or audio) seminar or symposium – mixed format	20 (.09)	0 (.00) Rank: 3 (tied)	15 (.08) Rank: 5	–.42	13 (.08) Rank: 5	7 (.11) Rank: 3 (tied)	–.70	18 (.10) Rank: 4 (tied)	1 (.03) Rank: 8 (tied)	1.25
Formal or informal mentor program	16 (.07)	0 (.00) Rank: 3 (tied)	12 (.06) Rank: 7 (tied)	–.37	11 (.07) Rank: 7	5 (.08) Rank: 7 (tied)	–.28	12 (.07) Rank: 7 (tied)	3 (.09) Rank: 4 (tied)	–.56
Identification of reasoned decisions or awards that exemplify best practices (i.e. 'model' or 'ideal' decisions or awards	30 (.13)	1 (.50) Rank: 1 (tied)	25 (.14) Rank: 3	1.48	24 (.15) Rank: 2	6 (.10) Rank: 6	1.08	25 (.14) Rank: 2	4 (.12) Rank: 2 (tied)	.20
In-person seminar or symposium – lecture format	16 (.07)	0 (.00) Rank: 3 (tied)	13 (.07) Rank: 6	–.39	9 (.06) Rank: 8	7 (.11) Rank: 3 (tied)	–1.43	13 (.07) Rank: 6	3 (.09) Rank: 4 (tied)	–.43
In-person seminar or symposium – discussion format	32 (.14)	0 (.00) Rank: 3 (tied)	27 (.15) Rank: 2	–.58	25 (.16) Rank: 1	7 (.11) Rank: 3	.87	31 (.17) Rank: 1	1 (.03) Rank: 8 (tied)	2.04*
In-person seminar or symposium – experiential (hands-on) format	28 (.12)	0 (.00) Rank: 3 (tied)	24 (.13) Rank: 4	–.54	16 (.10) Rank: 4	11 (.17) Rank: 1	–1.54	18 (.10) Rank: 4 (tied)	9 (.28) Rank: 1	–2.85**
In-person seminar or symposium – mixed format	31 (.14)	0 (.00) Rank: 3 (tied)	28 (.15) Rank: 1	–.60	22 (.14) Rank: 3	9 (.14) Rank: 2	–.10	24 (.13) Rank: 3	4 (.12) Rank: 2 (tied)	.12
Mechanisms to facilitate confidential discussion of issues and concern with peers	10 (.04)	0 (.00) Rank: 3 (tied)	10 (.05) Rank: 9	–.34	7 (.04) Rank: 10 (tied)	3 (.05) Rank: 9	–.13	7 (.04) Rank: 9 (tied)	2 (.06) Rank: 7	–.62
Written materials	10 (.04)	0 (.00) Rank: 3 (tied)	7 (.04) Rank: 11	–.28	8 (.05) Rank: 9	2 (.03) Rank: 10	.59	8 (.04) Rank: 9 (tied)	1 (.03) Rank: 8 (tied)	.34
Total	224	2	185		160	63		181	32	

(continued)

Table 2.40 Continued

	Full pop.	Current judges	Current arbitrators	J-A z-stat	Domestic disputes	Int'l disputes	D-I z-stat	Comm. law	Civil law	C-C z-stat
Third ranked option										
Distance (video or audio) seminar or symposium – lecture format	13 (.06)	0 (.00) Rank: 4 (tied)	10 (.05) Rank: 9 (tied)	−.42	10 (.06) Rank: 8	3 (.05) Rank: 9	.41	11 (.06) Rank: 9	1 (.03) Rank: 8 (tied)	.61
Distance (video or audio) seminar or symposium – discussion format	9 (.04)	0 (.00) Rank: 4 (tied)	5 (.03) Rank: 12	−.29	7 (.04) Rank: 11	2 (.03) Rank: 10	.40	7 (.04) Rank: 10 (tied)	1 (.03) Rank: 8 (tied)	.15
Distance (video or audio) seminar or symposium – experiential (hands-on) format	16 (.07)	1 (.33) Rank: 1 (tied)	15 (.08) Rank: 5 (tied)	1.54	12 (.08) Rank: 6 (tied)	4 (.06) Rank: 6 (tied)	.28	14 (.08) Rank: 7	2 (.07) Rank: 7	.21
Distance (video or audio) seminar or symposium – mixed format	13 (.06)	0 (.00) Rank: 4 (tied)	13 (.07) Rank: 7 (tied)	−.48	9 (.06) Rank: 9	4 (.06) Rank: 6 (tied)	−.22	12 (.07) Rank: 8	1 (.03) Rank: 8 (tied)	.70
Formal or informal mentor program	8 (.04)	0 (.00) Rank: 4 (tied)	7 (.04) Rank: 11	−.35	8 (.05) Rank: 10	0 (.00) Rank: 11 (tied)	1.80	7 (.04) Rank: 10 (tied)	0 (.00) Rank: 12	1.10
Identification of reasoned decisions or awards that exemplify best practices (i.e. 'model' or 'ideal' decisions or awards	42 (.19)	0 (.00) Rank: 4 (tied)	33 (.18) Rank: 1	−.81	33 (.21) Rank: 1	8 (.13) Rank: 4	1.35	34 (.19) Rank: 1	4 (.13) Rank: 3 (tied)	.73
In-person seminar or symposium – lecture format	16 (.07)	1 (.33) Rank: 1 (tied)	13 (.07) Rank: 7 (tied)	1.71	16 (.10) Rank: 3 (tied)	0 (.00) Rank: 11 (tied)	2.59**	15 (.08) Rank: 5 (tied)	1 (.03) Rank: 8 (tied)	.96

In-person seminar or symposium – discussion format	24 (.11)	1 (.33) Rank: 1 (tied)	20 (.11) Rank: 3	1.22	14 (.09) Rank: 5	10 (.16) Rank: 2 (tied)	−1.57	17 (.09) Rank: 3	5 (.17) Rank: 1 (tied)	−1.20
In-person seminar or symposium – experiential (hands-on) format	29 (.13)	0 (.00) Rank: 4 (tied)	25 (.14) Rank: 2	−.69	18 (.11) Rank: 2	11 (.18) Rank: 1	−1.27	25 (.14) Rank: 2	3 (.10) Rank: 5 (tied)	.58
In-person seminar or symposium – mixed format	20 (.09)	0 (.00) Rank: 4 (tied)	15 (.08) Rank: 5 (tied)	−.52	16 (.10) Rank: 3 (tied)	4 (.06) Rank: 6 (tied)	.84	16 (.09) Rank: 4	4 (.13) Rank: 3 (tied)	−.77
Mechanisms to facilitate confidential discussion of issues and concern with peers	10 (.05)	0 (.00) Rank: 4 (tied)	10 (.05) Rank: 9 (tied)	−.42	4 (.03) Rank: 12	6 (.10) Rank: 5	−2.30*	7 (.04) Rank: 10 (tied)	3 (.10) Rank: 5 (tied)	−1.45
Written materials	22 (.10)	0 (.00) Rank: 4 (tied)	17 (.09) Rank: 4	−.55	12 (.08) Rank: 6 (tied)	10 (.16) Rank: 2 (tied)	−1.91	15 (.08) Rank: 5 (tied)	5 (.17) Rank: 1 (tied)	−1.44
Total	222	3	133		159	62		180	30	

(17 per cent) in the first ranked position and a combined percentage of 40 per cent over the top three ranked positions. However, this option was challenged for the top position by 'identification of reasoned decisions or awards that exemplify best practices'. Although this option only won 13 per cent of the full population in the first ranked position, placing it in the third highest position within the first ranked group, the combination of percentages of the full population over the top three ranked percentages came in at 45 per cent. Neither these two options showed any statistically significant differences across any of the comparative pairings, which underscores the universal appeal of these two formats. Notably, these two methodologies are not mutually exclusive, which means they can be combined to beneficial effect.

Another possible contender, 'in-person seminar or symposium—experiential (hands-on) format', won the support of 14 per cent of the full population in the first ranked position and 39 per cent of the full population over the top three ranked positions. However, this option showed a statistically significant difference ($p<.01$) between common law and civil law respondents in the second ranked position, which calls its universality into question. A fourth option that might be considered among the top alternatives is 'in-person seminar or symposium—discussion format', which won 12 per cent of the full population's support in the first ranked position and 37 per cent of the full population over the top three ranked positions. This alternative had one statistically significant difference ($p<.05$) in the second ranked position (between the common law–civil law respondents), although its relatively low position in the first-place rankings (only civil law respondents ranked it first) and overall percentage for all three ranks suggest it should not be given the top position.

Although none of the remaining options appear to have garnered enough support to vie for the top positions, it is useful to note their rank order, since providers of judicial and arbitral educational programming can use that information when developing new curricula for particular audiences. The most popular options for the full population were, in descending percentage order spread over the top three rankings:

- 'distance seminar or symposium—mixed format' (23 per cent, no statistical differences between comparative cohorts);
- 'written materials' (19 per cent, a difference between judges and arbitrators in the first ranking, $p<.05$);
- 'mentor program' (18 per cent, a difference between common law and civil law respondents in the first ranking, $p<.05$);
- 'in-person seminar or symposium—lecture format' (18 per cent, a difference between domestic and international disputes in the third ranking, $p<.01$);
- 'distance seminar or symposium—discussion format' (14 per cent, a difference between judges and arbitrators in the second ranking, $p<.05$);
- 'distance seminar or symposium—experiential format' (14 per cent, no statistical differences between comparative cohorts);
- 'mechanisms to facilitate confidential discussion' (11 per cent, a difference between domestic and international disputes in the third ranking, $p<.05$); and

- 'distance seminar or symposium—lecture format' (2 per cent, a difference between domestic and international disputes in the first ranking, $p<.05$).

After considering format-based suggestions on judicial and arbitral education, the survey turned to content-based considerations. The final question in this series asked respondents to identify the types of issues that should be addressed in educational programming on reasoned decisions and awards and provided 11 different pre-established options based on the types of issues discussed earlier in the survey.[274] Respondents were told that 1 reflected an issue that need not be addressed and 5 reflected an issue that must be addressed and were allowed to supplement their answers by marking a twelfth option, 'other', and providing additional topics in a text box. Respondents were also told that they should assume that the programming would sufficiently safeguard judicial and arbitral independence.

As Table 2.41 shows, this question generated an extremely high number of statistically significant differences across two of the three comparative pairings, with 6 of the 12 options demonstrating relevant differences across the common law–civil law divide and 4 of the 12 options indicating notable differences across the domestic–international divide. All of these statistically significant differences also reflected a difference in internal hierarchies, with the exception of the first-ranked item. Only the judicial–arbitral comparison yielded no statistically significant differences, although the two groups' internal hierarchies differed for all but the lowest three entries.

Given these discrepancies, it is impossible to generalize about the results without making reference to the full population data. Under this analysis, the highest ranked option was 'how to structure a reasoned decision or award (4.32 out of 5.00). While this issue appears relatively simple in the abstract, it can prove quite challenging in practice, as many of the participants in the semi-structured interviews indicated.[275]

The second and third most important items involved factual considerations, which is consistent with numerous findings throughout the survey discussing the importance of factual issues in commercial disputes. For example, the second highest mark from the full population involved 'how to apply the facts to the relevant legal standard', while the third involved 'how to approach substantive citation of factual materials' (3.86 and 3.60 out of 5.00, respectively).

The fourth most important item—'how other judges or arbitrators approach reasoned decisions or awards' (3.54 out of 5.00 among the full population)—underscores the importance of acculturation and mentorship in the judicial and arbitral communities,[276] while the fifth and sixth highest-ranking options among the full population—'how to identify the governing legal standard' and 'how to approach substantive citation of legal materials', which earned a 3.49 and 3.44 out of 5.00, respectively—focused on

[274] Notably, educational programming for judges and arbitrators can and should address a wide variety of issues, although many of those topics are beyond the scope of the current analysis. Ch. 1.II (discussing coursework on 'judge craft').

[275] Ch. 3.III.F.4.

[276] Tables 2.38, 2.40.

Table 2.41 Issues to be included in educational programming on reasoned decisions and awards (weighted averages followed by standard deviation in parenthesis, sample (N) size, and ranking within the cohort)

	Full pop.	Current judges	Current arbitrators	J-A t-stat	Domestic disputes	Int'l disputes	D-I t-stat	Comm. law	Civil law	C-C t-stat
How long and how detailed each section of a reasoned decision or award needs to be	2.98 (1.34) 245	2.67 (1.15) 3 Rank: 10	3.06 (1.33) 196 Rank: 10	.51	2.94 (1.35) 174 Rank: 10	3.03 (1.33) 70 Rank: 10	.47	2.87 (1.33) 196 Rank: 10	3.53 (1.25) 36 Rank: 9	2.76**
How long it takes judges or arbitrators to write a reasoned decision or award	2.42 (1.22) 248	2.33 (1.15) 3 Rank: 11	2.41 (1.23) 198 Rank: 11	.11	2.38 (1.22) 176 Rank: 11	2.48 (1.22) 71 Rank: 11	.58	2.37 (1.22) 199 Rank: 11	2.64 (1.25) 36 Rank: 12	1.22
How other judges or arbitrators approach reasoned decisions or awards	3.54 (1.14) 251	4.33 (.58) 3 Rank: 4	3.55 (1.11) 201 Rank: 4	−1.21	3.61 (1.11) 177 Rank: 3	3.37 (1.20) 73 Rank: 9	−1.52	3.58 (1.10) 202 Rank: 3	3.47 (1.18) 36 Rank: 11	−.55
How to apply the facts to the governing legal standard	3.86 (1.18) 250	5.00 (.00) 3 Rank: 1	3.85 (1.14) 200 Rank: 2	−1.74	3.83 (1.19) 175 Rank: 2	3.92 (1.14) 74 Rank: 2	.55	3.83 (1.17) 200 Rank: 2	4.00 (1.15) 36 Rank: 4	.81
How to approach substantive citation of legal materials (i.e. when to refer to legal authorities and how to analyse them in a reasoned decision or award, not what citation format to use)	3.44 (1.20) 250	4.33 (.58) 3 Rank: 5	3.39 (1.19) 200 Rank: 6	−1.36	3.35 (1.25) 175 Rank: 6	3.64 (1.05) 74 Rank: 7	1.75	3.38 (1.22) 200 Rank: 6	3.69 (.98) 36 Rank: 8	1.44
How to approach substantive citation of factual materials (i.e. when to refer to evidence and how to analyse evidence in a reasoned decision or award, not what citation format to use)	3.60 (1.16) 250	4.67 (.58) 3 Rank: 2 (tied)	3.58 (1.15) 200 Rank: 3	−1.64	3.53 (1.22) 175 Rank: 4	3.77 (1.00) 74 Rank: 3	1.49	3.54 (1.18) 200 Rank: 4	3.94 (.98) 36 Rank: 5	1.92

How to distinguish material facts from immaterial facts	3.25 (1.33) 248	3.50 (.71) 2 Rank: 8	3.24 (1.32) 201 Rank: 9	−.28	3.10 (1.35) 175 Rank: 9	3.60 (1.19) 72 Rank: 8	2.74**	3.12 (1.33) 200 Rank: 9	3.77 (1.17) 35 Rank: 7	2.71**
How to identify the governing legal standard	3.49 (1.33) 249	3.67 (1.53) 3 Rank: 6 (tied)	3.48 (1.32) 200 Rank: 5	−.25	3.39 (1.36) 175 Rank: 5	3.74 (1.24) 73 Rank: 4	1.89	3.39 (1.34) 200 Rank: 5	4.03 (1.16) 36 Rank: 3	2.69**
How to structure reasoned decisions or awards	4.32 (.88) 250	4.67 (.58) 3 Rank: 2 (tied)	4.35 (.84) 201 Rank: 1	−.66	4.24 (.92) 177 Rank: 1	4.50 (.75) 72 Rank: 1	2.13*	4.25 (.92) 200 Rank: 1	4.64 (.64) 36 Rank: 1	2.44*
How to weigh different pieces of evidence	3.34 (1.25) 245	3.00 (.00) 2 Rank: 9	3.33 (1.26) 196 Rank: 7	.45	3.17 (1.25) 173 Rank: 7	3.73 (1.18) 71 Rank: 5	3.23**	3.20 (1.26) 196 Rank: 7	4.08 (1.02) 36 Rank: 2	3.96***
How to weigh different legal authorities	3.29 (1.25) 245	3.67 (1.53) 3 Rank: 6 (tied)	3.27 (1.25) 196 Rank: 8	−.55	3.13 (1.26) 174 Rank: 8	3.70 (1.13) 70 Rank: 6	3.29**	3.17 (1.26) 196 Rank: 8	3.86 (1.05) 36 Rank: 6	3.09**
Other (please describe below)	2.50 (1.73) 26	.00 NA 0 Rank: 12	2.60 (1.73) 20 Rank: 12	NA	2.16 (1.61) 19 Rank: 12	3.43 (1.81) 7 Rank: 12	1.73	2.20 (1.58) 20 Rank: 12	3.50 (1.97) 6 Rank: 10	1.67

legal considerations.[277] While the relatively low ranking of these two items could be interpreted as meaning such matters were not important to judges and arbitrators, it is at least equally likely that the respondents felt competent in these areas and therefore believed that they did not need additional coursework on these topics.

Although the option marked 'other' was the second-least popular option among the full population, the comments generated through the open text box nevertheless provide some useful insights into the future of judicial and arbitral education. One individual provided a laundry list of topics that might provide useful to those seeking to design educational programming:

> Principles of clear, authoritative writing; analysis of adequacy of reasoning in light of the simplicity/complexity of the case; how to approach comments on counsel/party behaviours if indicated; vacation/appeal proofing an award; balance of equity and law, especially where contract is silent on applicable law or need to follow it.

As useful as this comment is, it did not focus exclusively on legal reasoning or drafting of reasoned decisions or awards, a phenomenon that was evident in many of the other statements generated in response to this question.[278] For example, several respondents mentioned assessment of witness credibility, while another individual highlighted the need to address 'content requirements; standards applicable to review'. Interpersonal skills such as 'how to convey respect to the parties' were also featured along with basic writing skills, thus showing the importance of 'judge-craft'.[279]

Some respondents focused on the shape that the programming should take. For example, one individual suggested that 'for new arbitrators, samples of reasoned decisions should be provided and discussed', while another recommended that courses 'should be more about tools and examples. Some of the above may differ considerably between cases and/or applicable law.' One respondent similarly recognized that 'some of these vary so much case to case it is difficult to "teach" it', while another individual noted that

> the challenge of coming up with a curriculum for this sort of program is to avoid being too basic. I am always most interested in learning how colleagues in the field handle

[277] The rank order of the remaining items, as reflected by the full population, were as follows: 'how to weight different pieces of evidence'; 'how to weigh different legal authorities'; 'how to distinguish material facts from immaterial facts'; how long and how detailed each section of a reasoned decision or award needs to be'; 'other'; 'how long it takes judges or arbitrators to write a reasoned decision or award'.

[278] Only one respondent focused on substantive issues, stating s/he would recommend coursework involving 'requirements of rules or tribunals for reasoned awards, differences between domestic and international'. This emphasis on doctrinal matters is consistent with the 'law school' model of judicial and arbitral education, whereas the more modern trend is to focus on various professional skills (judge craft) rather than exclusively emphasizing substantive law. Ch. 1.II.

[279] Ch. 1.II (discussing the importance of courses on 'judge craft'). Comments in this category include the following: 'how to write clear, simple sentences'; 'how to ensure clarity'; 'using less legalese'; improving 'grammar, logic and good, structured writing'; 'getting to the point, avoiding rambling or flaunting of knowledge, do it quickly'; "organizing your thoughts' ... too many decisions skip around. Another important topic would be protecting yourself from being overly swayed by very good (or very poor) writing in party briefs'.

similar situations. Thus, a 'discussion' or 'hands on' format that focuses on scenarios or problems is the most useful and the most enjoyable.

2. Interim conclusions regarding judicial and arbitral education

As intriguing as the findings from the individual questions are, the benefits of the data are increased by comparing the results of the difference questions. For example, Table 2.39 showed that most respondents (93 per cent of the full population) considered professional education beneficial for at least a portion of the judicial and arbitral communities, yet Table 2.38, which addressed how respondents themselves had learned how to write decisions and award, showed that the two most-cited forms of judicial and arbitral education—learning by doing (83 per cent of the full population) and reading other decisions and awards (71 per cent of the full population)—did not involve any coursework at all. Furthermore, although 52 per cent of the full population indicated in Table 2.38 that they had attended a seminar or symposium on writing reasoned decisions or awards, it is unclear how rigorous or frequent those sessions were, since a single hour-long seminar over the course of a decades-long career is very different than annual or intermittent intensive training on different aspects of decision- and award-writing.

Another interesting dynamic involved the relatively robust response in Table 2.38 for 'speaking with more experienced colleagues' (37 per cent of the full population). While the legal literature and various comments made in the open text box associated with Table 2.38 suggest that many individuals consider collaborative relationships and discussions to be useful, mentorship and mechanisms to facilitate confidential discussions about issues of interest ranked quite low in the hierarchy of preferred educational formats in Table 2.40 (18 per cent and 11 per cent respectively). A somewhat similar discrepancy can be seen between the number of respondents who said that they had read a book or article on writing reasoned decisions or awards in Table 2.38 (29 per cent) and the number of respondents who believed written materials were a good way of providing judicial and arbitral education in Table 2.40 (19 per cent, with a statistically significant difference between judges and arbitrators ($p<.05$) in the first-place ranking).

While results concerning the future shape and content of judicial and arbitral education were not entirely conclusive, the data does provide educational providers with some general ideas about how to proceed going forward, particularly with respect to course format and subject matter concerns that are not of interest to judges and arbitrators. Furthermore, the empirical information on legal reasoning generated elsewhere in this text should provide useful in terms of developing appropriate content.

F. Additional Issues

The survey closed with an open-ended question that allowed respondents to provide general comments about the survey or any matter discussed herein. A number of useful statements arose in this section, including the recognition that 'there is always a tug of war between a thorough, reasoned decision that hits all of the points, and the cost to the parties. In small cases, I write shorter, more perfunctory decisions, but in the larger cases I devote more time and tend to write longer decisions.' Another individual noted that 'for several questions, I doubt that I have a general answer applicable to all cases and all issues: honestly it depends!'

A number of comments highlighted issues that could be addressed in future research. For example, one individual said that 'having responses segregated for cases involving pro se parties would add granularity—although the survey is already lengthy'. Another indicated that 'the process of decision making in the case of three member tribunals is also an important topic. The role of the party appointed arbitrator is also worthy of candid discussion, particularly when compared to a panel where the arbitrators do not know who appointed them.' Another individual echoed a sentiment that also arose in the interviews,[280] stating, 'I feel one of the biggest obstacles to effective dispute resolution and its explanation in an award or judicial decision is time. Too often, the arbitrator or judge does not or cannot give the matter the time it warrants.'

V. Conclusion

Although the highly detailed and individualized nature of the survey data can make it difficult to identify generalities, several themes appear. First, many of the presumed differences between the way judges and arbitrators approach legal reasoning are not supported by empirical research. To the contrary, judicial and arbitral practices appear largely consistent, thereby contradicting the longstanding assumption by many theorists that arbitration constitutes a different, often lesser, form of justice in commercial matters.[281]

Second, legal reasoning is much more strongly affected by factual issues than theorists appreciate. The elevation of legal analysis over factual analysis can perhaps be attributed to the longstanding academic bias in favour of 'legal science' over more practical matters,[282] but that distinction cannot continue. Instead, scholars and practitioners need to work together to improve and expand theoretical and practical analyses of the role that facts and evidence play in commercial dispute resolution so as to benefit individual parties and the legal community as a whole.

Third, a number of longstanding presumptions about the differences between common law and civil law approaches to legal reasoning appear to be empirically supported, although those differences may not be as deep or as broad as many people

[280] Ch. 3.III.G.
[281] Ch. 1.III.A.
[282] Fogel and Strong (n 272) 272–73; see also Richard A Posner, *Divergent Paths: The Academy and the Judiciary* (Harvard University Press 2016) 10–11 (noting that elite law schools in the United States often 'deride' applicants with practical experience or interest in practical scholarship).

believe. More research is needed to confirm the findings reflected here[283] and determine the full extent of the differences between these two groups, but the results generated by this study provides a useful starting point for analysis.

Fourth, comparisons of practices involving domestic disputes to those involving international disputes generated a number of statistically significant differences, although more research is needed to determine how intense those differences are. Furthermore, the combination of so many different jurisdictions into the domestic category may obscure certain important variations both between different domestic regimes and between domestic and international practice.[284] However, the data presented here provides a helpful foundation for further inquiries.

[283] Some of the data may have been affected by the fact that all of the civil law respondents were fluent in English, which means their legal philosophy may be affected to some unknown extent by rationales and practices found in common law countries, which are primarily English-speaking.

[284] These differences became apparent in the coding exercise. Ch. 4.IV.

3

Semi-Structured Interviews on Legal Reasoning

I. Introduction

The second of the three empirical elements to consider involves a series of semi-structured interviews of judges and arbitrators. The interviews covered the same types of issues addressed by the survey and were meant to identify not only what judges and arbitrators do, but why they adopt that particular practice. A copy of the interview protocol is provided in Appendix II.[1]

The chapter is organized as follows. The discussion begins with methodological and definitional information before moving to the substantive information gleaned from the interviews. The presentation of the interview findings includes subsections concerning the use of legal authorities, the use of factual authorities (evidence), the reasoning process, and the drafting process before concluding with several questions on judicial and arbitral education. The final section of the chapter provides a number of overarching conclusions. The text contains a variety of cross-references to the survey and coding exercise, with additional overarching conclusions appearing in Chapter 5.

II. Methodology

A. Design Criteria

Consistent with best practices in the social sciences, all of the interviews followed a standard script, although some variations were built into protocol to allow for differences in background and variations in interviewee responses. In all, 20 participants answered 27 questions (not including sub-parts and scripted follow-ups) in sessions that lasted approximately one hour. Questions followed the same organizational structure as the survey, beginning with general demographic information about the participants, followed by questions about legal authorities, factual and evidentiary issues, legal reasoning, drafting reasoned decisions or awards, and judicial and arbitral education. Interviews were conducted between January 2018 and July 2018.

Interviewees included judges and arbitrators with expertise in domestic commercial disputes, international commercial disputes, or both. The selection of participants was

[1] Providing copies of research instruments is considered a best practice in empirical research. Susan D Franck, 'Empiricism and International Law: Insights for Investment Treaty Dispute Resolution', (2008) 48 Va J Intl L 767, 787–88.

not random, since it was necessary to ensure that the respondents had at least a minimal amount of expertise in the area of legal reasoning. However, efforts were made to identify representative participants with a diverse range of demographic attributes.[2] As a result, the population included men and women of varying levels of seniority based in countries in Europe, Asia, and the Americas.

When identifying potential interviewees, the focus for judges was on those who acted at the trial rather than appellate level, since first-instance proceedings are more akin to arbitrations.[3] Although it was difficult to obtain access to those who were currently sitting as national or international judges,[4] contacts were made through introductions from colleagues and the author's existing professional network.

Arbitrators were identified through published lists of the most sought-after arbitrators in domestic and international commercial disputes and from professional groups of experienced arbitrators, such as the College of Commercial Arbitrators. A number of former judges who were currently acting as arbitrators were also identified through these means.

Some interviews, including those of both judges and arbitrators, were generated 'snowball' fashion, based on recommendations from other interviewees or generated as a result of a general invitation found at the end of the electronic survey discussed in Chapter 2.[5] Those individuals who volunteered to be interviewed for this study were included so long as they met the study criteria (i.e. had experience as a judge or arbitrator involved in resolving commercial disputes). This approach helped offset any unconscious biases that might have existed during the initial solicitation of study participants.

Although the study was designed to maximize the validity of the results, some methodological concerns nevertheless exist. For example, questions might arise as to the reliability of self-reported data, since some individuals might exaggerate the nature and quality of their legal decision-making processes in order to portray themselves in a favourable light.[6] After considering the issue, it was determined that self-reports would be acceptable in this context given that (1) the veracity of the interview data could be compared to anonymous survey data and objective studies of actual arbitral awards and judicial decisions and (2) the interviews addressed conceptual and motivational issues that have no objectively correct position. While interviewees could nevertheless have sought to emphasize compliance with what they perceived as best practices, that possibility seemed unlikely, given that the questions presumed compliance with established

[2] Lee Epstein and Gary King, 'The Rules of Inference', (2002) 69 U Chi L Rev 1, 113 (discussing how to generate a representative sample in small-n studies).

[3] All of the judicial decisions reviewed in the coding exercise in Chapter 4 were first-instance. Ch. 4.II.A.

[4] Judges are often hesitant to participate in scholarly studies without an introduction from a colleague or a reputable judicial organization. Ch. 1.II (noting difficulties with access to judges).

[5] The electronic survey discussed previously included an invitation to contact the author if the respondent wanted to be interviewed or knew of someone who might want to be interviewed. Appx. I.

[6] Lauren B Edelman, Howard S Erlanger, and John Lande, 'Internal Dispute Resolution: The Transformation of Civil Rights in the Workplace', (1993) 27 L & Soc'y Rev 497, 509–10 (discussing self-reporting and social desirability bias in the context of semi-structured interviews); Paul J Lavrakas, 'Social Desirability', in *Encyclopedia of Survey Research Methods* (Sage Publications 2008) (discussing social desirability bias).

standards of behaviour associated with legal reasoning and focused on what legal reasoning meant to the respondent and how the necessary standards were achieved.[7]

Another potential concern involves the relatively small size of the sample population, combined with a lack of random selection. While this phenomenon could affect the extent to which the material presented herein can be said to reflect a general pattern of legal decision making in commercial disputes, the interviews nevertheless provide important insights into the decision-making process. Indeed, the interviews were never meant to stand independently but instead were intended to supplement findings generated by other parts of the research initiative (i.e. the survey and the coding exercise).

Finally, some criticisms may focus on the limited nature of this research, which is targeted exclusively on legal reasoning in commercial disputes. While it is unclear whether and to what extent the processes used in commercial matters are equally applicable to other kinds of legal disputes, a narrow concentration was believed appropriate to provide the best information possible on commercial decision making. Furthermore, the methodology adopted herein can be used by researchers wishing to undertake similar studies in other fields.

All of the interviews were conducted by the author and were conducted either in-person or by telephone. Although a number of interviewees agreed to have their comments attributed to them personally, the material is presented herein on an anonymous basis to avoid giving undue weight to some comments. However, each of the interviewees was given a unique number (1–20) to allow comparisons of answers across the survey instrument. The text also identifies each interviewee along the three key axes under investigation in this book (judicial–arbitral, domestic–international, and common law–civil law) so as to help contextualize individual statements.

When analysing the interview responses, the goal was to identify common themes and practices to determine: (1) what attributes are most important to legal decision makers; (2) why those attributes are considered important; and (3) whether legal decision making differs across various demographic lines, including the judicial–arbitral, domestic–international, and common law–civil law divides. While the sample size was too small to allow for any causal inferences to be made, information from the interviews helps round out interpretation of the survey material in Chapter 2 and the results of the coding exercise in Chapter 4.

When conducting the interviews, no attempt was made to link the interviewees to either the survey or to the coded decisions or awards. Indeed, the anonymity of the survey made it impossible to know whether an interviewee even completed the survey, although they were made aware of the existence of the survey at the end of the interview in case they wanted to participate in that aspect of the research project. While it might have been possible to seek out published decisions and awards from interviewees in order to compare their interview responses and their actual practices, no effort was made to do so in order to protect the confidentiality of interviewees and to encourage candour during the interview.

[7] This approach has been adopted by other social scientists. Edelman, Erlanger, and Lande (n 6) 510.

B. Definitional Issues

Before beginning the interview, participants were provided with a number of definitions to ensure standard answers. These definitions mirrored those used in both the survey and the coding exercise so as to ensure consistency across the different segments of the study. Thus, interviewees were told that the term 'reasoned decisions or awards', as used in the interview, included but was not limited to judicial decisions and arbitral awards with findings of fact and conclusions of law. Participants were also told to limit their responses to disputes that were commercial in nature, meaning business-to-business or commercial state entity-to-business disputes. Interviewees were told that this definition specifically excluded investor-state arbitration.

The term 'international' was perhaps the most important item to clarify, given the study's focus on comparing domestic and international practices. Interviewees were therefore told that an international dispute was one in which at least two parties came from different countries, where the property in dispute was located in a country different than the disputants or where performance or enforcement was anticipated in a country different than that of the disputants.[8] All other disputes were to be considered domestic. Respondents who had experience in both domestic and international disputes were asked to indicate which category of cases they were discussing and to identify any differences in practice, where relevant.

Interviewees were told to focus on their general practice. However, they were also advised that it might be easiest for them to think about their last commercial dispute when answering the questions, unless they believed that matter was atypical in some manner.

During the preliminary phase of the interviews, participants were asked to indicate whether they had served as a judge, an arbitrator, or both. Participants who had acted in a judicial capacity were also asked to describe the type of court with which they had been involved (i.e. an international court or tribunal, a national or federal court or tribunal, or a sub-national, state or local court). Interviewees were also asked to identify what percentage of the commercial disputes that they had heard on the merits were national versus international in nature.

Based on the responses given, participants were then given the following descriptions, which are used in the analysis below. Interviewees who indicated that they worked in domestic capacities are also described as coming from the common law or civil law tradition, using the same breakdown of legal families used in Chapter 4.[9]

- Domestic judges, meaning those with exclusive experience as a domestic judge. None of the interviewees self-identified as working exclusively as an international judge.

[8] This definition was based on section 202 of the US Federal Arbitration Act. 9 USC s 202.

[9] Appx. III, question 6.

- Domestic arbitrators, meaning those with experience primarily as a domestic arbitrator. Some of these individuals might also occasionally act as international arbitrators, but the interviewees did not consider their international workload to be significant.
- Domestic judge–arbitrators, meaning those with experience as both a judge and an arbitrator in domestic matters.
- International judge–arbitrators, meaning those with experience as both a judge and an arbitrator in international matters.
- International arbitrators, meaning those with experience primarily as an international arbitrator. Some of these individuals might also occasionally act as domestic arbitrators, but the interviewees did not consider their domestic workload to be significant. Some of these individuals might also act as arbitrators in investment (investor-state) disputes, but they were asked to discuss their commercial practice rather than their investment practice.
- Mixed international–domestic arbitrators or judge–arbitrators. These individuals indicated that they had handled a significant amount of both domestic and international work over the course of their careers. Some of these individuals might also act as arbitrators in investment (investor-state) disputes, but they were asked to discuss their commercial practice rather than their investment practice.

III. Substantive Findings

A. General Issues

The survey began with a number of general questions meant to explore the basic assumptions of legal decision makers. Although these questions could be viewed as 'warm ups' for the more detailed and innovative inquiries that came later in the interview, the questions also helped confirm the extent to which judges and arbitrators differed (if at all) with respect to how they viewed the purpose, use, and nature of legal reasoning.

1. Purpose of reasoned decisions and awards

The first question in this series was very general and simply asked the respondent to identify the purpose of a reasoned decision or award. Scholarly and professional literature aimed at judges and, to a lesser extent, arbitrators, have identified a number of structural and non-structural reasons why legal decision makers do or should write reasoned decisions or awards.[10] Although one might expect these

[10] SI Strong, 'Reasoned Awards in International Commercial Arbitration: Embracing and Exceeding the Common Law-Civil Law Dichotomy', (2015) 37 Mich J Intl L 1, 15–20 (Strong, Reasoned Awards); SI Strong, 'Writing Reasoned Decisions and Opinions: A Guide for Novice, Experienced and Foreign Judges', 2015 J Disp Res 93, 101–05 (Strong, Reasoned Decisions) (providing literature survey); see also Ch. 1.II.

rationales to be conveyed to judges and arbitrators through professional training initiatives, educational programs for legal decision makers are not standardized.[11] Furthermore, an unknown proportion of judges and arbitrators have completed little or no coursework in writing decisions or awards, which precludes the direct transmission of information about the purposes of reasoned decisions or awards.[12] Instead, many professionals learn basic behavioural norms, including those relating to the purpose of reasoned decisions and awards, through the process of acculturation.[13]

Despite these difficulties, the interview data nevertheless suggested a relatively strong consensus relating to the purpose of reasoned decisions or awards. First, virtually all of the interviewees—regardless of where they fell along the judicial–arbitral, domestic–international, and common law–civil law divides—indicated that 'it is important for parties to know the basis of the arbitral decision',[14] to use the words of Interviewee 3, an international arbitrator with a civil law background.

Some respondents elaborated on why the parties needed to understand the nature of the decision. For example, Interviewee 10, a common law domestic arbitrator, recognized 'an emotional need for a party to know the content of my decision', while Interviewee 7, an international arbitrator, noted that parties 'will feel better about the intellectual integrity of the process if they see how the arbitrators go forward with their reasoning'. Interviewee 8, an international judge–arbitrator, similarly indicated that a reasoned decision or award 'ensures the parties are informed as to how the tribunal came to its conclusion and sets the basis for the extent to which the parties (or one party) will accept the decision and make its decision as to whether it will seek to set the award aside or have it confirmed'.[15]

Some respondents distinguished between the winning and the losing party.[16] For example, Interviewee 17, an international judge–arbitrator from the civil law tradition,

[11] In fact, judicial and arbitral education is a highly problematic process in many jurisdictions, both in terms of content and quality. SI Strong, 'Judicial Education and International Courts: A Proposal Whose Time Has Come?', in Freya Baetens (ed), *Identity on the International Bench: Geography and Legal Culture* (Oxford University Press forthcoming 2020); SI Strong, 'Judicial Education and Regulatory Capture: Does the Current System of Educating Judges Promote a Well-Functioning Judiciary and Adequately Serve the Public Interest?' 2015 J Disp Res 1, 4–5 (Strong, Judicial Education); Strong, Reasoned Awards (n 10) 5–7.

[12] Judges and arbitrators are not always required to undergo professional education before or after their appointment, and even when such courses are taken (voluntarily or mandatorily), they do not always focus on how to write a reasoned decision or award. Strong, Reasoned Awards (n 10) 5–7; Strong, Judicial Education (n 11) 4–5.

[13] Ch. 1.II; see also Ch. 2.IV.E.1 (discussing survey respondents who 'learned by doing').

[14] Similar responses were provided by Interviewee 2, an international arbitrator ('To provide parties with an understanding of the basis of the tribunal's decision.'); Interviewee 4, a mixed international–domestic arbitrator ('The parties are entitled to some description of the process.'); Interviewee 5, a common law domestic judge–arbitrator ('To inform parties of the basis of the decision on each issue involved in the case.'); Interviewee 6, a mixed international–domestic arbitrator ('To tell parties why they won or lost.'); Interviewee 11, a common law domestic judge–arbitrator ('The purpose is to let the parties know why you are ruling the way you do.'); Interviewee 12, a common law domestic judge–arbitrator ('To let the parties know the underlying reasoning for making the decision.'); Interviewee 14, an international judge–arbitrator ('To fulfil the mandate given, decide the issues and let parties know why we decided as we did.'); Interviewee 15, a common law domestic judge–arbitrator (noting that reasoned decisions and awards were both for the parties); and Interviewee 16, an international judge–arbitrator ('To faithfully and correctly decide parties' dispute and give reasons for the award.').

[15] Interviewee 19, an international arbitrator, noted that reasoned decisions and awards 'maximize the chance [the parties] will understand the process and abide by the outcome'.

[16] Cf Table 2.36 (discussing the audience for a reasoned decision or award).

suggested that the purpose of a reasoned decision or award is 'to explain to parties, especially losing parties, the reason for the award'.[17] Interviewee 20, a mixed international–domestic arbitrator from the civil law tradition, went even further and noted that the purpose of a reasoned decision or award is

> to provide parties with considerations why the tribunal decided one way or another—the parties have pled their case and need to have a clear explanation of why the way they put their case is not the outcome. Both parties must understand the way the arbitrator decides; the losing party needs to understand clearly why that particular position prevails.

One respondent (Interviewee 6, a mixed international–domestic arbitrator) went so far as to say that a reasoned decision or award 'may help the parties if they have ongoing relations because the dispute will come up again—[it] could improve their relationship'.

Other individuals emphasized the connection between the parties and the decision maker. For example, Interviewee 1, a mixed international–domestic arbitrator, stated that reasoned decisions and awards were necessary 'to communicate to parties the basis of the arbitrator's conclusion in a way that shows a proper understanding of the dispute'. Interviewee 13, a common law domestic judge–arbitrator speaking primarily as an arbitrator, went slightly further, stating that the reason s/he 'bring[s] in precedents' and offers 'my take on credibility of witnesses and what theories of fact and law on which [the decision or award] is based' is 'to allow the parties to understand why I've decided in a certain way'. Interestingly, one common law domestic judge–arbitrator (Interviewee 12) stated that the purpose of reasoned decisions and awards was 'to allow [the parties] the opportunity to challenge, meaning if you give a simple answer—and that is rare now—it is less likely for people to challenge your ruling; there is less basis for a challenge'.[18]

Although responses focused heavily on the need to provide parties with an understanding of the outcome of the dispute, interviewees also provided a number of other rationales for reasoned decisions and awards. The second most popular response involved the role that reasoned decisions and awards play in appellate or review processes. For example, Interviewee 2, an international arbitrator, said that reasoned decisions and awards 'provide a record of reasoning to enable a

[17] Interviewee 17, an international judge–arbitrator from the civil law tradition, similarly noted that reasoned decisions and awards were necessary 'to explain to parties, especially losing parties, the reason for the award'. Interviewee 18, another international judge–arbitrator with civilian training, also stated that reasoned decisions and awards were 'first to explain why the winning party has won, and second and more importantly, to explain to the party that has lost why he has lost'.

[18] This view is somewhat contrary to those who believe that reasoned decisions or awards are less likely to generate challenges, either because the losing party understands the decision maker's rationale or because fully reasoned decisions or awards demonstrate the absence of a reason to challenge. Strong, Reasoned Awards (n 10) 20; Strong, Reasoned Decisions (n 10) 107. Commentary on arbitration often discusses the need to protect the award from subsequent review or annulment. Ch. 1.III.A; see also Table. 2.36.

reviewing court (if any) to understand arbitral reasoning, essentially protecting the award'.[19]

Not surprisingly, those who came from an arbitration background tended to focus on procedural concerns, since review of arbitral awards is limited to procedural errors in most jurisdictions. Thus, Interviewee 1, a mixed international–domestic arbitrator, noted the need 'to demonstrate to reviewing court (if any) that the arbitrator has treated the parties equally and given them a fair opportunity to present'.[20] Those with judicial experience similarly noted that reasoned decisions and awards were useful 'to some extent . . . to give comfort to courts who hear annulment proceedings to show that the proceeding was correct' (Interviewee 17, an international judge–arbitrator).

As predicted by the legal literature,[21] several respondents indicated that reasoned decisions and awards provided an opportunity for the author to check his or her own decision-making process. Thus, Interviewee 4, a mixed international–domestic arbitrator, stated that writing a reasoned award was 'a way of forcing me to improve the quality of my decision making, to see if it reads as well as it is in my head'. Interviewee 7, an international arbitrator, stated that a 'very important reason' for reasoned decisions and awards

> is because it causes arbitrators to think rigorously. I have had many deliberations in which the panel thinks they've figured it out, and when I write the decision, I find the law is not precisely as we assumed. I have had at least one case where the panel decided the text of the law would not permit the outcome we had contemplated.

Interviewee 19, an international arbitrator, similarly indicated that the purpose of reasoned decisions and awards was 'to make sure the decision maker pays attention to what they're doing—that they're not just flipping a coin. Reasoned awards provide discipline for the decision maker and understanding to the parties.'

Rather than focusing on individual needs, some respondents emphasized systemic needs. For example, Interviewee 1, a mixed international–domestic arbitrator, noted that reasoned decisions and awards 'demonstrate to third party reviewers of the award the legitimacy of the dispute resolution process in arbitration'. Interviewee 9, a common law domestic judge, stated,

> It's a justice system and everyone is entitled to their day in court and a well-reasoned decision explaining the judge's thoughts. Just as criminal law says I must give reasons—commercial law is the same. Our democracy needs a reasoned award—it's part of our justice system. For example, even if we don't agree, we can understand the reasoning.

[19] A similar response came from Interviewee 18, an international judge–arbitrator from a civil law background, who said a reasoned award was necessary 'to clarify to a judge who has to do something with the award and show that the arbitrators did things properly'.

[20] Interviewee 4, a mixed international–domestic arbitrator, similarly noted that 'there have been occasions, more procedural than substantive in recent years (when I started, the scope of review was broader), where I have written for "a reviewer", be it court or otherwise'.

[21] Ch. 1.II.

Interestingly, Interviewee 15, another common law domestic judge–arbitrator with extensive judicial experience, noted a significant difference in the nature of reasoned decisions in his/her jurisdiction, depending on the type of court. As s/he said, 'I've seen [state/local] court decisions with one-line decisions and orders drafted by the parties and the judge simply stamps [the document] 'so ordered'. In [national/federal] court, every decision was reasoned'.

Another systemic rationale involves the creation of hard and soft precedent by both judicial decisions and arbitral awards.[22] For example, one former common law domestic judge (Interviewee 15) noted that the purpose of reasoned judicial decisions was to 'set precedent for future disputes that raise the same issues'. A similar rationale was enunciated by Interviewee 8, an international judge–arbitrator, who stated that a decision or award that was made public could serve 'potentially as a resource/precedent, as it were, or a decision of interest for other tribunals before which similar issues may be raised'.

Respondents also identified a number of rationales that were not commonly discussed in the legal literature. For example, Interviewee 6, a mixed international–domestic arbitrator, noted that a reasoned decision or award 'can help counsel understand whether they hit the mark—how they did—almost like a report card' and 'give[s] feedback if [counsel] were credible'. Interviewee 10, a common law domestic arbitrator, also noted that reasoned decisions and awards may be helpful if there are 'third party participants who need to know the content of the arbitration'.[23]

2. Audience for reasoned decisions and awards

The second question in this series asked who the respondents considered to be the audience for reasoned decisions or awards.[24] This question offered an indirect means of confirming the responses to the previous question, since the purpose of a reasoned decision or award often implies the existence of an audience.

As expected, most of the respondents listed the parties as their primary audience members, with four individuals—Interviewees 3, 5, 13, and 19—indicating that the parties were their exclusive audience. Interviewee 18, an international judge–arbitrator, specified his/her audience as 'the losing party—though both parties can be considered the losing party in some cases because they may not get all they ask for'. The emphasis on the parties was consistent with data derived from the survey.[25]

Several respondents defined 'parties' to include counsel or specified counsel along with the parties.[26] Thus, Interviewee 17, an international judge–arbitrator, stated that his/her audience was 'the parties, including counsel, and more so the losing party, since

[22] Although arbitral awards do not create precedent with respect to substantive concerns, they can act as a type of persuasive authority, particularly with respect to questions of arbitral procedure. SI Strong, *International Commercial Arbitration: A Guide for US Judges* (Federal Judicial Center 2012) 22, <https://www.fjc.gov/publications> accessed 11 April 2020.

[23] Interesting, respondents to the survey did not indicate a high degree of concern for third parties. Ch. 2.IV.D.1.

[24] This issue was also addressed in the survey. Table 2.36.

[25] Ch. 2.IV.D.1.

[26] Interviewee 11, a common law domestic judge–arbitrator ('Counsel and parties.').

they need to know what they did wrong'. That sentiment was echoed by Interviewee 12, a common law domestic judge–arbitrator who said that 'attorneys are parties. I write with the party that would consider themselves the losing party in mind. I tend to write for all to read/understand but so losing party can understand'.

A number of individuals indicated that they wrote for courts that might be asked to review an award.[27] In some cases, the respondent made a judgment call regarding the likelihood of review. For example, Interviewee 1, a mixed international–domestic arbitrator, stated that it 'depends on whether I believe the award is likely to be reviewed by a court. If not, the parties and fellow arbitrators. If review is likely, then I'd include the reviewing court'. Interviewee 2, an international arbitrator, similarly focused 'mostly [on] the parties', but indicated that 'I also bear in mind that the award has to be comprehensible to anyone called on to review it, meaning courts, not the public'. That sentiment was shared by Interviewee 4, a mixed international–domestic arbitrator who said his/her audience was 'the parties' and, 'to a lesser extent, a reviewer that is built into the rules or by the nature of the dispute, where there should be some review'.

Not everyone focused primarily on the parties. For example, Interviewee 9, a common law domestic judge, said,

> The [appellate court] is my first audience—I want to be affirmed. Then, lawyers, to show that I have heard their arguments and did my legal research. Finally, the parties—they put their faith in our courts and a decision gives them the full measure of justice. Both sides are entitled to know why the outcome came out as it did.

Interviewee 14, an international judge–arbitrator, believed that 'the primary audience is the parties', but 'beyond that, we are always mindful of how someone who doesn't know the case would understand our reasoning. The ultimate reader is the curial court.'

Several respondents raised systemic concerns. For example, Interviewee 15, a common law domestic judge–arbitrator, said that his/her audience was the court, as well as 'all people who read legal decisions. Lawyers will look for precedent. Sometimes the audience is the public, if [the issue involves] ... systemic change (outside the common law context).' Interviewee 16, an international judge–arbitrator, noted that s/he had 'had discussions with [a quasi-public arbitral institution] where they say we're writing for the file to develop [a particular body of] law', although Interviewee 16 continued to write 'for the parties and only secondarily for the greater development of law'.

Other respondents focused on external audience members. For example, Interviewee 8, an international judge–arbitrator, indicated that although the parties were his/her first audience, 'to the extent the award is made public, [the audience includes] lawyers operating in the field and their clients, and arbitrators in the field'. Conversely,

[27] Interviewee 6 ('Having been in-house, the first audience is the client (actual party). Also counsel. Also district court.').

Interviewee 10, a common law domestic arbitrator, indicated the most 'significant' audience was 'third parties who are participating in payment of award', with the parties constituting a 'less significant' audience.

3. Hallmarks of a well-written reasoned decision or award

The final question in this series asked respondents to identify the hallmarks of a well-written reasoned decision or award.[28] This is not an issue that has been considered in detail by either scholars or courts,[29] which may have contributed to the diversity of the responses provided by interviewees.

Interviewee 19, an international arbitrator from the common law tradition, described the views of several respondents[30] when s/he said that a well-written reasoned decision or award contains

> a recitation of facts that are relevant to the outcome; a full but succinct outline of parties' positions on dispositive issues and a decision that clearly connects the relevant facts, applies the law to the relevant facts, leading to a decision affecting the outcome, without dicta and without deciding issues not central to the dispositive issue. The most important part is the 'knitting' portion—knitting the facts to the law to the outcome.

Although this description is reminiscent of standard common law thinking, the technique is not limited to those from a common law background. For example, Interviewee 20, a mixed international–domestic arbitrator from the civil law tradition, said,

> First, one has to make the parties clear that you understood their arguments ... so you put in the award the argument of the parties to show you understood the parties. Second, show you understand the facts of the case. Third, show you applied the law to the facts of the case and why you applied the law as you did.

Another frequent response involved matters relating to structure. For example, Interviewee 4, a mixed international–domestic arbitrator, indicated that 'clarity of the syllogistic process, applying facts to principles of law or procedure is the most significant—this includes being complete. The most significant goal is having a very clear presentation of legal principles and facts applied to those principles.' Interviewee 6, a mixed international–domestic arbitrator, noted that a well-written reasoned decision or award was 'efficient, detailed, well-organized, applying law to facts so the basis for the outcome is clear' and providing an 'adequate explanation of outcome and basis for the outcome'.

[28] This issue was also addressed in the survey. Table 2.37.

[29] Ch. 1.III.A.

[30] Interviewee 5, a common law domestic judge–arbitrator ('Each issue is dealt with and the reasoning of the award explained; legal authorities cited; factual issues explained so parties understand how I dealt with individual issues ruled on.'); Interviewee 11, a common law domestic judge–arbitrator ('State facts, apply law to facts and then give award.').

The interview responses were unclear as to whether judicial decisions did or should differ structurally from arbitral awards. On the one hand, Interviewee 14, an international judge–arbitrator, indicated that a reasoned award

> is structured so that people know where to find what they're looking for, which makes writing the award different than a judgment. Judges have artistic license to write as they want to get a certain point. In arbitration, structure is more formalistic, in that you usually follow a particular order. After that, clarity of reasoning is important.

Differences between judicial and arbitral writing were also mentioned by Interviewee 15, a former common law domestic judge now working as an arbitrator. S/he stated that 'clarity' was a critical component of a reasoned decision or award, meaning that 'you need to state what the findings are and what the conclusion is'. Indeed, Interviewee 15 went on to note that 'today I'm struggling with a difficult arbitration case where I'm parsing state court decisions and they're badly written—the state court judge maybe didn't understand the issues'.

Although some judges took a somewhat lax view to structure, other judges did not. For example, Interviewee 9, a common law domestic judge, indicated that s/he adopted a very rigorous approach to structuring reasoned decisions, stating,

> Every order is the same—it's IRAC [Issue-Rule-Application-Conclusion].[31] What's background, what's controlling law—you need to explain that you're not just reciting [the relevant rules of civil procedure]. You need to thoughtfully lay out facts and discuss those in important part. Usually there's no dispute about the law, especially if it's contract law.
>
> I want citations to the record for the [appellate court] and the parties. The facts come out of someone's brief.
>
> We put citations in orders we do because we make parties put citations in the briefs. All of those follow the IRAC analysis.

Arbitrators also discussed questions of structure. For example, Interviewee 3, a civil law international arbitrator, noted that 'the International Law Association has a new study on precisely the reasoning of awards. I think this is a good topic because there are lots of mistakes on reasoning.' S/he went on to note that, 'for reasoning, you take claims and then reason your decision on the claims, on the basis of the argument from parties, though you do not need to address all the arguments parties present. You justify your decision on the claims.' Interviewee 2, an international arbitrator, also noted the need for 'completeness, not meaning every last point raised but needing to address each claim and the primary arguments at issue so there's no complaint that the tribunal failed to respond to issues'.

[31] 'IRAC' is a method of organizing legal analysis often used by lawyers in common law jurisdictions. SI Strong, *How to Write Law Exams: IRAC Perfected* (2d edn, West Publications 2021 forthcoming) (Strong, *IRAC Perfected*) (published in the US only); SI Strong, *How to Write Law Essays and Exams* (5th edn, Oxford University Press 2018) (Strong, *How to Write*) (published the UK and Commonwealth).

Some respondents emphasized issues of style when discussing the hallmarks of a well-written decision or award. For example, Interviewee 18, an international judge–arbitrator from the civil law tradition, said that a well-written reasoned decision or award should be

> clear, concise, not too academic, analysing facts (not ignoring them) and combining facts with legal rules and some reference to law. I'm not a fan of too many academic footnotes. Parties are not interested in academic awards—you have to solve a problem; you're not establishing a *Grundtest* (that's more an investment arbitration issue anyway). Arbitrators should not be cavalier, but should focus on a beaten track.

Interviewee 16, another international judge–arbitrator, indicated that the most important elements for him/her were,

> not in order of importance: one, well-organized and crafted on a purely logical layout. Two, coherent exposition and application of law, facts, and contract. Three, well-written stylistically and otherwise, to the extent this gives the award authority—it is not better because it has literary pretentions, but it needs to be persuasive.

Interviewee 2, an international arbitrator, also focused on the concept of good writing and defined that as 'not meaning stylish per se, but inspiring confidence in the parties as to the quality of the reasoning and skills of the arbitrator. I've seen ungrammatical and sloppy writing in other awards, and that suggests sloppy legal reasoning.'[32]

Interviewee 7, an international arbitrator, indicated that a well-written reasoned decision or award

> sets forth the factual and procedural background of the matter, including references to legal authorities (statutes and cases), and focusing on key issues—do not get bogged down in trivia.
>
> It has good, clear writing like you see in a law review article or a legal opinion.
>
> It walks the see-saw/tightrope between being too technical and not technical enough; it's written so your elderly aunt or uncle could understand it but includes the technical elements. That's why I think footnotes are important; they help avoid interruptions to the flow.

The concept of 'readability' was mentioned by several respondents. For example, Interviewee 8, an international judge–arbitrator, stated that a well-written reasoned decision or award 'is written in an integrated way and is readable—dealing with the facts and law in the case.' Interviewee 1, a mixed international–domestic arbitrator, also mentioned 'readability' in addition to 'defensible logic' and a 'principled application of legal standards as determined by the arbitrator to the facts as determined by the arbitrator.'

[32] Interviewee 2 also noted the need for 'clarity' and 'organization—helping readers to understand each section.'

Critically, both judges and arbitrators emphasized the need to address the law, thereby rejecting the longstanding assumption that arbitrators do not apply the law.[33] Thus, in addition to the references to the controlling law noted above, Interviewee 9, a common law domestic judge, emphasized that a well-written reasoned decision or award 'applies whatever the applicable law is', while Interviewee 12, a common law domestic judge–arbitrator, identified the critical elements as 'recitation of facts, identification of any points of contention, prior arbitral awards or case law that would impact my reasoning, mixing that in with facts and reasoning of case—that's also how I write. The hallmark means those aspects of the award.'

Finally, several respondents focused on the effect of a well-written reasoned decision or award. For example, Interviewee 10, a common law domestic arbitrator, stated that a well-written reasoned decision or award 'doesn't result in questions'. Interviewee 17, a civil law international judge–arbitrator, noted that such a decision or award 'should advise about all important points so that when the parties read them, the decision makes sense. The award must look fair.'

4. Structure of a reasoned decision or award

The final question in this series asked how the respondent usually structured a reasoned decision or award. Some individuals, such as Interviewee 9, the common law domestic judge who relied on IRAC, had already discussed issues relating to structure.[34] However, this question provided other interviewees with the opportunity to address structural considerations.

The responses indicated no real difference between judges and arbitrators[35] and between national and international decision makers in terms of the substance of the decision or award. However, some variations appeared to exist with respect to the discussion of procedural issues.[36] Arbitrators—particularly international arbitrators—seemed more likely to include a section on procedural history.[37] For example, Interviewee 4, a mixed international–domestic arbitrator, specifically noted that his/her writing style

> depends on the international institution or whether the case is international versus domestic. In domestic cases, especially AAA [American Arbitration Association] cases, they typically do not require lots of procedural history, but that is expected in

[33] Ch. 1.III.A; see also SI Strong, 'Truth in a Post-Truth Society: How Sticky Defaults, Status Quo Bias and the Sovereign Prerogative Influence the Perceived Legitimacy of International Arbitration', 2018 U Ill L Rev 533, 537–39 (2018) (noting reasons for pervasive misunderstanding of the nature of arbitration).

[34] Ch. 3.II.B.3. Some respondents, including Interviewee 9, a common law domestic judge, Interviewee 11, a common law domestic judge–arbitrator, and Interviewee 12, a common law domestic judge–arbitrator, answered this question by referring back to their responses to the previous question. Interviewee 12 also noted, 'I do an outline and then broaden the outline. When I start writing, I don't always know the answer.'

[35] The similarities in approach to structural issues existed not only between those who worked exclusively as judges or arbitrators, but also in instances where individuals worked as both judges and arbitrators. Indeed, Interviewee 11, a common law domestic judge–arbitrator, specifically stated that s/he did not adopt a different structural approach to decisions rendered as a judge and awards rendered as an arbitrator. Ch. 3.III.B.2.b.

[36] The survey also distinguished between treatment of substantive and procedural issues. Ch. 2.IV.A.1.

[37] The survey also suggested that international arbitrators were more concerned with procedural justice than other types of respondents. Ch. 2.IV.B.2; Table 2.23.

> international rules, and the ICDR [International Centre for Dispute Resolution] is (or people at the ICDR are) beginning to favour that, so I put the procedural history and status of the dispute in the beginning.

Those who acted a judicial capacity—particularly in a domestic setting—seemed less likely to include procedural histories. The reason behind this difference probably related to the fact that the judges in the study were first-instance rather than appellate judges, and procedural histories are often considered less necessary at the trial level.[38] However, some former common law domestic judges, such as Interviewee 15, did mention the need to start with 'jurisdiction and procedural history' before moving to facts, followed by conclusions of law.

The interview protocol did not seek to establish the motivation for international arbitral practice per se, but the various differences that arose could be attributed to standardized education on best practices in international arbitration (such as that offered by the Chartered Institute of Arbitrators (CIArb) or by arbitral institutions such as the AAA);[39] standardized award-review mechanisms imposed by arbitral organizations such as the International Chamber of Commerce (ICC);[40] informal socialization (acculturation) among arbitrators through international conferences or through years of experience of reading arbitral awards while acting as an advocate;[41] and/or the influence of decisions from international courts such as the International Court of Justice (ICJ).[42] Indeed, Interviewee 13, a common law domestic judge–arbitrator, specifically noted that

> with the AAA, [I] follow the format—intro of case, identity of parties, witnesses, who is at table. State facts in complaint and answer, then go into presentation by claim on facts, rebutted by respondent and then how I view facts, then relationship with conclusions of law I draw to extent they're relevant, then decision that brings together the rationale from findings of fact. The last point is boilerplate where you assign the amount due and who pays and that you're functus officio.

Interviewee 14, an international judge–arbitrator, similarly noted that,

> in a sense, we're beaten into shape by the ICC because the ICC scrutinizes the award and you get guidance notes you must follow. The order is dictated to you. You pay a lot of attention to procedural history, which is not seen in a judgment, but you have to record that here. Here, one has to take the procedural history into account because

[38] Strong, Reasoned Awards (n 10) 29, 42 (discussing arbitrators' need for procedural histories and chronologies); Strong, Reasoned Decisions (n 10) 109 (discussing appellate courts' need for procedural histories).

[39] Ch. 3.III.F.

[40] For example, Interviewee 3, a civil law international arbitrator, noted in response to the question about the hallmarks of a well-written reasoned decision in award that 'when the ICC scrutinizes an award that says "on the basis of the text above, the tribunal concludes this", the ICC asks for [an additional] reason'.

[41] Ch. 1.II (regarding acculturation); Table 2.38 (regarding experience reading awards as an advocate).

[42] Experts in international commercial arbitration are also often experts in international investment arbitration and/or public international law and thus are familiar with the work of international courts and tribunals. James Crawford, 'The Ideal Arbitrator: Does One Size Fit All?', (2017) 32 Am U Intl L Review 1003, 1014.

> the award may be read in more than one enforcing country and you must take those traditions into account and must know the differences that are required.

Another area where differences appeared involved the likelihood of including a separate section on the parties' contentions. Interviewee 4, a mixed international–domestic arbitrator, noted that 'I find it clunky to follow a rigid obligation to state the parties' position on each issue, but some institutions think it's important. I try to comply with the organization's rules because the parties chose those rules for a reason.'

Several respondents indicated that they had a general pattern that they followed in most cases. For example, Interviewee 1, a mixed international–domestic arbitrator, used a specific template—'(1) paragraph with short conclusion; (2) summarize parties' positions; (3) procedural history; (4) history of dispute; (5) contentions of the parties; (6) applicable legal standard; (7) apply standards to facts; (8) reach conclusion'—that was very similar in substance to the IRAC model used by Interviewee 9, a common law domestic judge.[43]

Interviewee 2, an international arbitrator, indicated that the 'sequence may vary, case to case', but usually included

> who the parties are, including counsel. Procedural history—not a comprehensive history, but the major steps. The text of the arbitration agreement, the governing law, the seat, any applicable rules. I don't necessarily have a standalone statement of facts—sometimes I put the facts in the legal analysis, since a long fact section in the abstract can be off-putting to some parties. Instead, I may just do an overview of cases with undisputed factual elements. Legal sections—each claim or material legal issue is separate. I summarize the parties' arguments then address the relevant legal or contractual provisions and facts that lead to my decision. In complex cases, I put the facts relevant to each claim near the legal analysis. *Dispositif*—decision/ conclusion section with relief provided. If jurisdiction is contested, I do that section by itself.

Other respondents adopted a similar approach,[44] although the length of each section often depended on the specifics of the case itself,[45] as suggested by the coding

[43] Ch. 3.III.A.3; Strong, *How to Write* (n 31) ch. 1; Strong, *IRAC Perfected* (n 31) ch. 1.

[44] Interviewee 5, a common law domestic judge–arbitrator ('First, procedural summary of case, then brief factual/substantive summary, then findings of the arbitrator or panel discussing individual issues in light of procedural and substantive law.'); Interviewee 6, a mixed international–domestic arbitrator ('Intro; talk about procedures leading up to the hearing so all the different aspects of the case, including the orders I've issued; overview of hearing (witnesses, how many documents in evidence); set forth the issues; if there's an important law, give legal framework; summarize key facts; provide clear reasoning and order clearly. I will discuss in summary the parties' arguments.'); Interviewee 8, an international judge–arbitrator ('Generally speaking, I will recite facts and contentious of the parties that are the basis on which the award or decision is rendered and then give the tribunal's analysis of the case and then the decision.'); Interviewee 16, an international judge–arbitrator ('It can vary in unusual cases. Usually, it will be the classic introduction, factual background, procedural background in actual procedure, then key threshold issues if there are any (or if the case depends on illegality, etc., decide those up front), then to individual claims and counterclaims and then cost and administrative matters, and then award (*dispositif*).').

[45] Interviewee 17, an international judge–arbitrator from the civil law tradition ('First list parties and tribunal, then procedural history, sometimes a short fact statement (depends on the case), shorter or longer description of

exercise.[46] Interestingly, no distinction as to structure appeared to arise with respect to common law versus civil law experts.[47]

Not all respondents adopted a standardized approach. For example, Interviewee 3, an international arbitrator, indicated that s/he had 'no real standard structure' but instead proceeded on a case-by-case basis.

Some discrepancies arose as to whether to break the substantive discussion down issue-by-issue or claim-by-claim, rather than including all of the facts or all of the law at once. For example, Interviewee 19, an international arbitrator, stated that

> I start with an introduction—very short but gives the outcome, since I hate to flip to the back. It's usually something like, 'this case concerns a share purchase agreement, the parties have claimed X, and the claimant prevails for the reasons set forth below'. Then I set out the relevant facts, then the applicable law and relevant contracts. Then I provide the parties' positions and discuss the issues.
>
> The big question is always whether to go issue by issue or to set out the parties' positions in whole. For me, it depends on whether you need to decide everything or whether one item will be dispositive. For example, if I am going to dismiss on jurisdictional grounds, I will give all the parties' positions at once but be somewhat more succinct on the merits because I'm not going to reach those. If I must address the claims on the merits, then I will likely go issue by issue, giving the outcome on each.

The concept of breaking down the analysis issue-by-issue or claim-by-claim as best suits the dispute is in accordance with suggestions made in academic works discussing the structure of legal analysis.[48] This seems to be the approach adopted by Interviewee 18, an international judge–arbitrator, who noted that s/he would normally 'take the position of the parties and then try to sketch their positions topic by topic, then give the view of the tribunal. I prefer to do it topic by topic, not all at once.' Interviewee 16, another international judge–arbitrator, also indicated that s/he organized decisions and awards by 'individual claims and counterclaims and then cost and administrative matters'.

As useful as this approach can be, there are times when it can cause difficulties. For example, although Interviewee 4, a mixed international–domestic arbitrator, normally used an issue-by-issue approach, s/he admitted 'this can be clunky if the parties give me 25 issues and only one or two are dispositive. There are times I say, "if an issue is not

parties' position then analysis. If it's a preliminary matter like jurisdiction or burden of proof, then probably I'd structure it according to claims, but it depends on the subject matter.').

[46] The coding exercise calculated the length of certain sections of reasoned decisions and awards, and many of these analyses showed very large standard deviations. Ch. 4.IV.A.

[47] For example, the approach adopted by Interviewee 13, a common law domestic judge–arbitrator, appears quite similar to the approach adopted by Interviewee 20, a mixed international–domestic arbitrator from a civil law background, who referred back to the response relating to the hallmarks of a well-written reasoned decision or award, and stated, 'As above—put in/summarize in the best possible fashion the positions of the parties. First have the facts of the case that parties agreed to, then facts found by the tribunal, then parties' argument, then how the tribunal applies the law.'

[48] Strong, *IRAC Perfected* (n 31) ch. 3 (discussing the need to discuss different causes of action separately); Strong, *How to Write* (n 31) ch. 3 (same).

addressed here, I have rejected it" because I just can't make myself go through all the issues.' Interviewee 4 similarly noted that an arbitrator must include 'a very, very clear conclusion with relief granted'.

B. Legal Authorities

The next section of the interview focused on the use and interpretation of legal authorities. Questions focused on matters such as the relative importance of legal authorities, methods of reviewing legal authorities, the time involved in reviewing legal authorities, independent legal research, citation of legal authorities, and advice from judges and arbitrators to counsel regarding legal authorities. These issues were considered in both the survey[49] and the coding exercise.[50]

1. Relative importance of legal authorities

The series began by asking about the type of legal authorities (statutes, cases, scholarly works, etc.) that the respondent considered most important when s/he was drafting a reasoned decision or award.[51] As noted earlier in this chapter, respondents of all types—both judges and arbitrators, including those specializing in national and international disputes—described the centrality of law to a well-reasoned decision or award.[52] No differences appeared to arise along the various axis of inquiry (judicial–arbitral, domestic–international, and common law–civil law), although variations did appear between individual respondents, suggesting that most discrepancies arise as a result of individual temperament and decision-making philosophies, not as a result of particular functions or legal backgrounds.

The first question sought to determine how respondents defined a 'legal authority' and how they prioritized various types of authorities, two issues that were also considered in the survey and coding exercise.[53] Although the legal literature traditionally claimed that common law and civil law lawyers diverge in how they view legal authority, that hypothesis was not borne out in the interviews, suggesting that the two legal traditions are in fact converging, as suggested by more recent commentary.[54] However, some discrepancies did arise, albeit in some unexpected ways.

For example, some differences in the use of legal authorities could arise as a result of the arguments posed by counsel rather than by the training and experience of the neutral. Indeed, Interviewee 2, an international arbitrator from a common law background, noted that

> mostly I rely on what the parties have cited. Typically, I do not do my own research. Common law lawyers tend to give me cases, civil law lawyers give me scholars.

[49] Ch. 2.IV.A.
[50] Ch. 4.IV.
[51] This issue was addressed in the survey. Tables 2.5–2.6.
[52] Chs. 3.III.A.3, 3.III.A.4.
[53] Chs. 2. IV.A.1, 4.IV.
[54] Ch. 1.III.C.

> I read as a corrective to make sure that the award reflects the framework of the governing law (civil or common) and reflects the mandatory law and procedural rules. The balance of authorities depends on the jurisdiction in question.

Interviewee 2 noted that some variations may arise as a result of the controlling law, a point that was also made by Interviewee 3, an international arbitrator from the civil law tradition. S/he said that the relative importance of different types of legal authorities 'depends on the applicable law', noting that

> articles of civil or commercial codes will be more important and mostly addressed by the parties in civil law cases. Case law is more important in cases controlled by the common law.
>
> It depends on the hierarchy of norms under the applicable law. For example, in England, you do not rely on doctrinal authorities [scholarly writings], but in civil law matters, you do.

Interviewee 8, an international judge–arbitrator, similarly stated that the most important legal authority was, 'first and foremost, the applicable law. Beyond that, there may be pertinent academic authorities or decisions of other tribunals that tend to support or confirm the findings of the tribunal in the application of the law.' Interviewee 4, a mixed international–domestic arbitrator, indicated that 'I don't have a single rule. I am guided by the issues and law at stake.' However, s/he also stated that s/he was guided,

> first and foremost, [by] the rules of arbitration. These do not deal with the merits, but they are important.
>
> On the merits, first are those authorities dictated by the party's contract—if they choose a law, that dictates the importance of the authorities. In the US, cases matter according to the federal/state hierarchy. The parties' choice of substantive law determines if I find secondary authority helpful. I don't always quote it, but I find secondary authority helpful.
>
> If it's a [statutory] question, the code that's most applicable is the one from the state. If international treaty issues are involved, then treaties are the primary law and international law will instruct on other applicable authorities.

Some respondents believed that the relative importance of particular legal authorities changed according to the type of dispute.[55] For example, Interviewee 6, a mixed international–domestic arbitrator, said the relative importance of different authorities 'depends on the case. Often it is case law for commercial cases, but even in commercial cases (for example, in intellectual property matters), statutes and regulations can be important.' Interviewee 19, an international arbitrator, stated that 'in commercial matters,

[55] Interviewee 12, a common law domestic judge–arbitrator ('Depends on the type of subject matter—normally case law.'); Interviewee 13, a common law domestic judge–arbitrator ('Depends on the type of case and the arbitration agreement.').

usually the contract and major decisions in the relevant national law [are the most important]. If there are international law issues, then so-called "international precedent". If it's a jurisdictional issue regarding timing, then sometimes statutes will be relevant.' However, Interviewee 19 also noted that 'most cases turn on the facts', not on the law, an issue that is discussed further below and that is reinforced in other aspects of the study.[56]

Interviewee 7, an international arbitrator, said,

> A lot depends on the case. Some turn on a statute. Often, when the matter is governed by US law, cases become very important because the statute will allow one or two inferences and case law will tell which is right. For example, I had an insurance dispute about whether a policyholder should recover, but the law often sets forth the definition of a 'reasonable settlement' in cases, not statutes.
>
> Scholarly works, in most commercial disputes, are not important for substantial matters, but they are important for procedural matters, such as the extent of document production.

Interviewee 7's view about the importance of scholarly works as a general proposition appears to be borne out by the survey and coding exercise, including the suggestion that scholarly works are used differently depending on whether the dispute is substantive or procedural.[57] When pressed on whether any differences existed based on whether the matter was governed by the common law or civil law, Interviewee 7 stated that

> in practice, there's no real difference. When one decides a case under common law (English or US) law, one cites cases, but in the civil law (I have handled matters under French, German, Swiss, Italian, and Spanish law), one cites statutes. The common law also has statutes, but you do get into cases in a way you don't with civil law.
>
> Regarding scholarly opinion—under civil law, there is the concept of *jurisprudence constante*—a continual line of case law. Often you get a professor to say the *jurisprudence constante* provides X as the right answer, so a scholarly opinion does come in more often because case law comes in via the opinion of the professor. You would not cite the cases directly; you'd cite the professor.

The concept of the highest form of authority in the controlling jurisdiction was emphasized by Interviewee 15, a common law domestic judge–arbitrator. When asked which type of legal authority was most important, s/he said, 'binding authority is the most important. The Supreme Court or my circuit is governing law as interpreted by a higher court. When I have a statute, I'm bound by the terms if you understand its terms. Scholarly commentary is not binding.' Interviewee 20, a mixed international–domestic

[56] Ch. 3.III.B.5.5; see also Table 2.11.
[57] Tables 2.5, 2.6, 4.12, 4.13.

arbitrator from a civil law background, also noted that the decision about which law is most important

> depends heavily on the system of law that you're applying. If it's a civil system, then the key sources are the contract, codes, and statutes, and then jurisprudence and third-party doctrine/authors. In most civil law systems, there is no system of precedent, so jurisprudence [case law] is auxiliary. In common law systems, the main source of authority is precedent, statutes and legal authorities. The order changes depending on the type of law and the legal system.

Interviewee 16, an international judge–arbitrator, also recognized that the analysis 'depends on applicable law and depends on case' but noted that it was 'trite' to claim that 'that relevant authorities are the most relevant'. For Interviewee 16, the first, most important authority was 'the best substantive law if it is the substantive law. Second, I like precedents even under other substantive law. I even find other awards persuasive. Sometimes you have an expert on law—especially "exotic" law. If I can't read the law myself, I like an expert.'

The distinction between common law and civil law authorities was also recognized by Interviewee 17, an international judge–arbitrator from the civil law tradition. On the one hand, s/he noted that that the relative importance of a particular authority 'depends which law I'm under—I apply a lot of different law. It may depend on whether I apply common law—then there's a lot more emphasis on decisions. If I apply civil law, I would quote decisions but put equal emphasis on doctrinal law.' However, Interviewee 17 also noted that

> I generally have a section in my first order that says the parties are to put forward legal authorities in support of their points but the tribunal has the power but not the obligation to do its own research. If it does its own research but reaches a conclusion not in response to the parties' briefings or that would surprise the parties, it will allow a response from the parties.
>
> I think, unlike other arbitrators, that I can reach the law that attorneys do not research. They may miss points, then I look stupid if I didn't research.

The notion of independent legal research is an important one and is discussed more fully below[58] and in the survey.[59]

Perhaps the most notable feature of the various responses was that virtually all interviewees indicated that statutes were of primary importance, regardless of the respondent's status as a judge or arbitrator or their affiliation with the common or civil law.[60] For example,

[58] Ch. 3.III.B.4.

[59] Ch. 2.IV.A.2.

[60] This conclusion may appear at odds with citation count data generated in the coding exercise, but that material reflected the type of authorities cited in a decision or award and the frequency of citations, not how important individual authorities were in the minds of the judges and arbitrators. Tables 4.12–4.14.

Interviewee 11, a common law domestic judge–arbitrator, simply indicated 'statutes' in response to this question. Interviewee 9, a common law domestic judge, said, 'We start with the statute, then [appellate court] and Supreme Court precedents, then go outside for anything that's not been addressed. I have yet to find an issue that another circuit hasn't addressed if the [appellate court] hasn't, so it's very unusual to cite to scholarly work.' Interviewee 5, a common law domestic judge–arbitrator, similarly indicated that s/he found 'statutes and cases' the most important type of legal authority.

No difference in approach arose along the domestic–international axis, either. For example, Interviewee 1, a mixed international–domestic arbitrator from the common law tradition, said that the most important legal authorities to him/her were, 'where applicable, statute or rule first, then jurisprudence, meaning cases (national law), ICJ (if it is relevant) and arbitral rulings. The ICJ cases would be persuasive.' Interviewee 18, an international judge–arbitrator from the civil law tradition, similarly said that s/he would 'start with statutes, and if there's well-established court precedents, then rely on those. If there are no precedents, then it's more delicate.'

Interviewee 10, a common law domestic arbitrator, indicated that for him/her,

> case law of the jurisdiction in question is probably the greatest [influence]. I do not pay much attention to scholarly works because if I'm at the cutting edge, it's my cutting edge, not someone else's. If I'm not at the cutting edge, then I have case law. I do not use case law from outside the jurisdiction because it's not usually relevant unless I'm at the cutting edge.

Interviewee 14, an international judge–arbitrator, made an important observation about the role that acculturation plays in judicial and arbitral drafting and decision making. According to him/her,

> There's a difference between what authorities are important to me and the authorities that are important to the ICC—they have a more rigorous scrutiny process, and they can be difficult when you make a proposition of law that is so plain it brooks no argument, but if it has not been specifically conceded, you must put in a cite, and if it is a cite the parties haven't noted, you must go back to the parties and ask their permission. Once you're used to the ICC, you do it that way even if it's not required.
>
> Subjectively, what an arbitrator looks for—if the proposition of law is well accepted, you only need to cite a major textbook or a major case. Counsel may cite multiple cases, but that's not really necessary for the tribunal unless a case is disputed by the other side. If the law is developed in a series of cases, you may need to cite sources of cases.

Those respondents whose rationales were not clear from their previous answers were then asked why they responded as they did. Sometimes the decision maker's practice arose as a function of the nature of the legal authority. For example, as Interviewee 11, a common law domestic judge–arbitrator, noted, 'Because [statutory law] is the primary law, case law merely interprets the statutes.' Interviewee 1, a mixed international–domestic arbitrator, similarly stated that s/he relied on 'statutes and rules, if dispositive, then jurisprudence, because jurisprudence will not add to non-ambiguous matters. [I rely on] jurisprudence because most statutes and rules are ambiguous, and jurisprudence is helpful to understanding the matter and is occasionally binding.'

Other respondents focused on their function as a decision maker. Thus, for example, Interviewee 9, a common law domestic judge, indicated that

> I think it's my job—I'm a trial court judge—I'm not an appeals court judge or Supreme Court Justice. I'm not making policy or procedure. I'm just applying it. If [the legislature] opined on it, they win. If it's ambiguous, an appellate court will see [it]. I leave policy decisions to someone else unless it's a matter of first impression.

Interviewee 5, a common law domestic judge–arbitrator, raised the tricky notion of equity.[61] S/he said,

> This is an issue of interest to me—the law versus equity in arbitration. It's different in international matters because of [the role of] *amiable compositeurs*, but in the United States, arbitrators should follow the law and statutes and cases in common law (US) jurisdictions because they are the bases for law. They are the most important things. I also examine journals and scholarly works if parties cite them, and maybe I do some independent research.

Interviewee 6, a mixed international–domestic arbitrator, did not differentiate between judicial and arbitral functions. Instead, s/he simply noted that the reason behind the relative importance of legal authorities was 'to give legal guidance, the relevant guidance for issues'. Interviewee 12, a common law domestic judge–arbitrator, noted that 'I'm usually following a rule of law in arbitration because the proceeding is an alternative to litigation, so I rely on case law, sometimes statutory law'.

A number of individuals, particularly those with experience as arbitrators, focused on the principle of party autonomy. Thus, Interviewee 4, a mixed international–domestic arbitrator, said, 'Inherent in what I'm saying is that the parties have the right by contract to choose the law that applies, and I respect the parties' right and try my best to follow their choice'. Interviewee 10, a common law domestic arbitrator, similarly stated that 'when parties enter into a contract with an arbitration clause, I believe it's their general understanding or their conscious or unconscious expectation that the [legal] environment affects their business expectations'.

2. Method of reviewing legal authorities

Some authorities have criticized the role that third parties (such as law clerks in judicial proceedings and tribunal secretaries in some arbitral settings) play in the

[61] Equity was discussed at various times in the survey. Chs. 2.IV.A.1, 2.IV.C.1, 2.IV.C.2; Tables 2.29, 2.34, 2.37.

decision-making process, claiming alternatively that reliance on such individuals either constitutes an improper delegation of authority or breaches the principle of confidentiality.[62] While most of the debate focuses on the third party's role in drafting the reasoned decision or award, similar concerns can also be raised with respect to the third party's role in researching and reviewing legal authorities.[63] Therefore, the interview protocol asked several questions about the involvement of law clerks or assistants in the review of legal authorities before moving on to actions undertaken by the respondent him/herself.

a. Law clerks and assistants

The first question in this series asked whether the respondent had a law clerk or assistant who read the legal authorities that the parties referred to in their submissions. Eleven of the 20 interviewees indicated that they did use or had at one time used a law clerk or assistant in some capacity. Three of the 11 individuals had never worked as judges, suggesting that the use of clerks or assistants is not exclusively tied to the judicial function. This latter conclusion is reinforced by the fact that, of the nine interviewees who indicated that they never used a law clerk or assistant to review legal authorities, four had experience as judges. Notably, two judge–arbitrators—Interviewee 11 and Interviewee 15—indicated that they used a law clerk or assistant when they were working as a judge, but not (or at least, in the case of Interviewee 15, 'not often') when they were working as an arbitrator.

Some interviewees interpreted the term or function of 'law clerk or assistant' relatively narrowly. For example, Interviewee 7, an international arbitrator, indicated that s/he did not have an assistant

> in the sense of a US law clerk. Often, if I have a research assistant, I will ask them what they think and we will debate, but I do not have a law clerk like other arbitrators do (i.e. those in France or Switzerland). It's more of a dialogue, because for me, the best way of understanding the law is if I have a debate. After that, I will have 100 per cent more understanding at the end.

Interview 4, a mixed international–domestic arbitrator, also said that s/he did not have a law clerk or assistant per se, but 'have sometimes had students/interns to help me. However, they don't read legal authorities to the exclusion of my doing it.' Interviewee 16, an international judge–arbitrator, also noted that s/he did 'not usually' have a law clerk or assistant, although 'I have had trainees and lawyers' assist at times.

Interviewee 5, a common law domestic judge–arbitrator, explained his/her rationale, stating,

> Only a few people use assistants, and most are former judges. I seldom/never do. I had a case where the clause allowed it, but that that's the only time I used a clerk/assistant.

[62] Ch. 1.III.A.
[63] Ch. 1.III.A.

> I don't use a clerk because that's the reason we're hired—our expertise. Also, that other individual has not done a conflicts check, which could taint the award. Third, unless it's disclosed in advance, the parties expect the arbitrator to read [materials] and decide the award. Finally, the parties' authority is the basis for my award, so I can ask them to brief an issue if I have to. My authorities are based on those authorities the parties give to me.

Interviewee 18, an international judge–arbitrator, had a similar reason for not using a law clerk or assistant, stating,

> The decision is my decision—you can't delegate the analysis to a clerk. You need to read the authorities to get the full flavour of the case. You do not need to read 100 per cent of cases; parties (typically in investment matters) quote too many cases to confirm the obvious. You don't need that. In commercial matters, the parties are not elaborating much on unimportant things. I have a case where three authors are discussing a matter, and I must analyse it carefully—these legal arguments are very important.[64]

A number of respondents indicated that they did use law clerks or assistants. For example, Interviewee 17, an international judge–arbitrator from the civil law tradition, stated that

> I always have someone. It depends on my instructions. In my procedural order/letter, I set forth the tasks of the legal secretary because I think it's fair that the parties know what I am going to do. This applies to both commercial and investment proceedings. My clerk reads the authorities, and I read the important ones, too.
>
> My overall view on delegation as arbitrator, especially as chair (because I usually chair) is that there should be no secret about it. I consider that I do not do a good job in large cases without help. I have armies of attorneys appearing in front of me, with voluminous and complex files. You can't pretend you can do it all—you need help.
>
> How you do it: it differs between arbitrators, but I should have intellectual control over proceedings and decisions. I do not need to write every procedural order or every part of the award, but I need to recognize the end item as my work product. In the international world, there's a big debate about what secretaries can do. I saw these challenges coming and decided I need to be clear about where I do delegate—that's how I drew up my standard letter. They agree or I withdraw.

[64] Although the interview protocol indicated that focus was on commercial practices, Interviewee 18, an international judge–arbitrator from the civil law tradition, did distinguish between commercial and investment arbitration, as did Interviewee 2, an international arbitrator from the common law tradition. As Interviewee 2 said, 'I read everything except in treaty cases (PCA [Permanent Court of Arbitration] and ICSID [International Centre for Settlement of Investment Disputes]) where there's an institutional tribunal secretary—they do not read cases but may draft the procedural history. I do not have an assistant in commercial cases because they're not provided to me.'

As Interviewee 17 noted, judges and arbitrators use their law clerks and assistants in different ways. For example, Interviewee 8, an international judge–arbitrator, indicated that he has his/her law clerk read the authorities 'to the extent my law clerks are not already familiar with the law'. Interviewee 20, a mixed international–domestic arbitrator from the civil law tradition, said that his/her law clerk or assistant 'reviews authorities and explores if all the authorities have been identified'.

Those respondents who indicated that they did use a law clerk or assistant were then asked to estimate the percentage of the legal authorities the clerk or assistant read in whole or in part, and how the determination was made for the clerk or assistant to read the authorities in full or in part. Two individuals—Interviewee 8, an international judge–arbitrator, and Interviewee 11, a common law domestic judge–arbitrator—stated that their law clerks or assistants read all of the legal authorities, although Interviewee 11 noted that s/he only used a clerk or assistant when acting in a judicial capacity.

Somewhat worryingly, several respondents indicated that they did not know how many authorities their law clerks or assistants read or how the determination on what to read was made. For example, Interviewee 15, a common law domestic judge–arbitrator, stated 'I don't know. They did the work, I didn't. If a brief had a hundred cases, I don't know if they read all of them; lawyers cite the cases for standards we know or include unnecessary string cites.' Interviewee 3, an international arbitrator from a civil law background, simply said 'I don't know.'

Other respondents did not know the precise number of authorities read by the clerk or assistant, but had a standard review methodology in place. For example, Interviewee 14, an international judge–arbitrator from the common law tradition, stated that 'I don't do an audit', but also indicated that

> we usually read at the same time—I skim to get an impression while s/he reads in parallel. I will then have a discussion with my associates; to save time, I'll say 'I know X & Y cases, so don't read those cases, focus on P & Q instead'. That can focus the associates.

Interviewee 20, a mixed international–domestic arbitrator from a civil law background, stated,

> When the debate is about a key law under which all the other debate stems, they need to read that authority in its entirety—that is the starting point. For the other sources, [law clerks or assistants read] 30 to 50 per cent of the text. Normally, only 3 or 4 (10 per cent) of the total legal authorities are critical to read.

Interviewee 9, a common law domestic judge, said,

> We get briefs, and there may be a hundred cites. Once we've gone through the response and reply, we find there's two to three issues. If it's a reasoned decision, I have a career

> clerk reading one to three key cases, a term clerk who's reading them and I am reading them. If the [appellate court] has three cases, I need to figure out which of the three cases is key—other circuits are not at issue.

The next question involved the means by which a law clerk or assistant communicated with the judge or arbitrator regarding the content of the legal authorities s/he had read. The responses here were relatively idiosyncratic, which was consistent with the statement from Interviewee 15, a common law domestic judge–arbitrator, who indicated that 'different people communicate in different ways. Usually [my clerks would communicate] through the draft opinion itself with parentheticals. If I questioned something, I'd look at that case—I couldn't read all of them because I was in the court room.' Interviewee 14, an international judge–arbitrator, said that s/he communicated with clerks through

> a bench memo—it can be quite short. We have preliminary discussions before doing the bench memo. It depends in a way on how counsel refers to or relies on authority. Many times, they don't discuss cases unless it's a major point where the law is developing or is in controversy, but usually they footnote it and you see where the argument makes sense based on the way they explain the law in our situation. If you see a new perspective or question raised, then you focus on those points or cases.
>
> It's not realistic for a clerk to read all the cases. Counsel has a different role—they cite to a lot of authorities to give weight to their submissions and don't know what I know [which means they need to include additional material to cover their bases]. Clerks make sure the cases are accurate for the proposition cited.
>
> You read briefs in tandem—you read both sides' briefs and see how much law is in dispute between the authorities. If there's nothing in dispute, there's no need to read the case.

Other respondents offered other insights. For example, Interviewee 3, an international arbitrator from the civil law tradition, said s/he communicated 'either through a written memorandum or face to face', as did Interviewee 11, a common law domestic judge–arbitrator (at least when acting as a judge, which is the only time s/he used clerks). Interviewee 8, an international judge–arbitrator, said s/he communicated 'generally orally' with clerks and assistants, while Interviewee 9, a common law domestic judge, communicated by 'highlighting cases, sticky notes'.

b. *Judges and arbitrators*

The next question in this series asked whether the respondent personally read all of the legal authorities, in their entirety, that the parties referred to in their submissions. Only two respondents—Interviewee 9, a common law domestic judge, and Interviewee 20, a mixed international–domestic arbitrator from a civil law background—said unequivocally that they read all the authorities in their entirety.

The remainder of the responses showed varying degrees of personal attention to the legal authorities.[65]

Some individuals did not know their general practice or indicated that it varied from case to case,[66] while others found it difficult to enunciate the how and why of their general practice. For example, Interviewee 11, a common law domestic judge–arbitrator, simply justified his/her method of dealing with legal authorities by saying 'because it's the correct approach'. Although more details were eventually provided through follow-up questions, the interchange with Interviewee 11 was somewhat tense, which could suggest that s/he was somewhat uneasy about detailed scrutiny of the decision-making process.[67] Indeed, several other individuals commented at various parts of the exchange that they had never thought about some of the issues raised by the interview protocol.

Typically, respondents—including both judges and arbitrators—focused on items that they considered central to the dispute. For example, Interviewee 3, an international arbitrator from the civil law tradition, said that 'I personally read only those materials that are relevant to the case and only refer to the passages that are most relevant. For example, if the parties refer a 350-page award to me as authority, I will only read the portion referred to, not the full award.'[68] Interviewee 2, an international arbitrator from the common law tradition, similarly stated that

> I read the material legal submissions, not all. For example, if there are string cites on basic issues, I don't need to read all those or on matters that are uncontested.
>
> For material, contested issues, I will read all items cited to me because it's important to understand the relevant law. I also go beyond just reading quotes, since I was counsel for many years and I know it's all about spin. Quoted materials do not give a full understanding of the cases. You would be a naïve arbitrator to believe only what's quoted to you.

Other respondents took a different view regarding reliance on quoted material. For example, Interviewee 16, an international judge–arbitrator, said, 'I look at all the authorities. Usually they're submitted for a few quotes and I can't read them all in their entirety, but I'll usually read to check quotes.'

[65] A number of respondents simply answered this question in the negative, without further explanation. Interviewee 1, a mixed international–domestic arbitrator ('No.'); Interviewee 19, an international arbitrator ('Never.'). Others simply provided percentages. Interviewee 5, a common law domestic judge–arbitrator ('Peruse 100 per cent, read 70 per cent.'); Interviewee 19, international arbitrator ('10 to 50 per cent. It depends.').

[66] Interviewee 1, a mixed international–domestic arbitrator ('Unknown in full; unknown in part. Varies from case to case.'); Interviewee 4, a mixed international–domestic arbitrator ('The percentage—I have no idea. Would vary depending on advocates. Some very fine advocates, especially those who come from a US appellate background, believe string cites are important to show credibility.').

[67] Those who have served as judges are often not used to being challenged. Ch. 2.IV.A.2 (discussing judicial hubris). This was not the only instance in which a former judge adopted a somewhat hostile tone in response to questions, though only a minority of judges or judge–arbitrators exhibited such behaviour.

[68] The survey considered whether and to what extent judges and arbitrators reviewed arbitral awards as part of the substantive and procedural analysis. Ch. 2.IV.A.1.

Several respondents focused on the concept of relevancy. For example, Interviewee 13, a common law domestic judge–arbitrator, said that s/he did not read all of the authorities, but that it 'depends on the case. If [the parties] introduce authorities that have nothing to do with the case, I don't read them. I read if relevant.' Interviewee 6, a mixed international–domestic arbitrator, also read the legal authorities 'to a varying degree'. For him/her, the most important criterion was also relevance to issues. For example, s/he said,

> If it's a contract case, with contract law, I may read the whole case because the reasoning there may help me with reasoning for my award.
>
> When reading a brief, if a legal precept stands out, I'll read that right away; it helps me to understand how to decide. If there are lots of cases, I peruse the headnotes to see how much more I should read. I will call it triage.

Other respondents used a similar type of 'triage' method. For example, Interviewee 5, a common law domestic judge–arbitrator, stated that s/he did not read all the legal authorities but focused on 'the seminal/most important cases. I often read, print and [check the subsequent treatment of] the main cases. I will read the headnotes of the others if I think they're tangential.' Interviewee 10, a common law domestic arbitrator, indicated that s/he read all the legal authorities 'for the most part', although 'if I'm doubtful of content, I will read the abstract or legal summary to get an idea of the content. Otherwise I read them top to bottom.'

A number of respondents provided reasons why they did not read all of the legal authorities presented to them by counsel, either as part of their initial answer or in response to a follow-up question. Some of these rationales—such as relevancy or materiality—appear in the preceding paragraphs.[69] However, other explanations also arose.

One factor that was mentioned by several respondents involved a pre-existing familiarity with the law in question. Interviewee 12, a common law domestic judge–arbitrator, was among those who took this approach, stating s/he did 'not always' read all the legal authorities, although 'I do sometimes, depending on if I know the law. If I know the law, I will not read the law.' Interviewee 8, an international judge–arbitrator, similarly stated 'I'm usually familiar with them already. I can't say I read from first word to last word of all authorities cited to me.' Interviewee 11, another common law domestic judge–arbitrator, indicated that 'as judge—yes, [I read the cases in full] unless they were boilerplate cases (like standard of review for motion to dismiss) or where I was particularly familiar with the principle. If the case was new, I read it in its entirety. As arbitrator—same.' While this approach is in many ways alarming, since important nuances could exist in the unread materials, it is consistent

[69] For example, Interviewee 1, a mixed international–domestic arbitrator, indicated in response to the follow-up question that s/he did not read all the legal authorities 'because most legal authorities do not refer to issues in controversy'. Similarly, Interviewee 3, an international arbitrator, indicated, 'I do not read more because it's not essential. I only read what's important.'

with empirical research regarding overconfidence and egocentrism among judges and arbitrators.[70]

Interviewee 16, an international judge–arbitrator, initially appeared to fall in this same category of respondents when s/he noted that 'I don't read all of the documents because it's not necessary because usually I don't need to read the case or doctrine to understand it'. However, Interviewee 16 also raised another important and potentially problematic reason why judges and arbitrators may limit their review of the materials, indicating that 'sometimes, even if I read a second language, it's hard to read the authorities in its entirety—I won't spend all the time if I understand the basic holding'. Although Interviewee 16 was the only respondent who mentioned concerns about foreign languages, one would expect similar issues to arise with other judges and arbitrators operating in cross-border settings.

Linguistic fluency is not the only problem facing legal decision makers; time is another significant constraint. For example, Interviewee 5, a common law domestic judge–arbitrator, said that 'there's no time to read every case cited, and I bring lots of experience as a litigator, so I only want to update my knowledge. If it's a new issue, I will read. Most are principles I'm familiar with already.' Interviewee 12, a common law domestic judge–arbitrator, similarly stated that

> I feel very comfortable in some areas that I know the law and the cases. I rely sometimes on parties' extrapolations, but not always—if I have a question I go to the authorities.
>
> Time is a factor. I do not write lengthy or scholarly awards—I am 'medium'—I don't believe the reasons people go to arbitration require 30, 40, 50 pages.[71]

Another rationale related to scheduling involved concerns about the sheer volume of submissions. For example, Interviewee 7, an international arbitrator, noted that s/he did not read the legal authorities in their entirety 'because it's impossible. I read in entirety the submissions that are relevant to deciding the issues. String citations—if the case is never discussed or questioned, I won't read it. I will read those cases in dispute.' Interviewee 4, a mixed international–domestic arbitrator, similarly stated that

> I wish I could [read everything]. I try to read as much as I can, but sometimes the volume is too great. I try to look at cited authority, and I will see if it matches the general principle of law that is asserted. If there's a statute that's integral to the decisive issue, I'll always read those completely. With string cites, I glance at them.

[70] Susan D Franck and others, 'Inside the Arbitrator's Mind', (2017) 66 Emory LJ 1115, 1163 (discussing empirical research on egocentrism, also known as self-serving bias, in both judges and arbitrators); Ch. 2.IV.A.2 (discussing judicial hubris).

[71] In this comment, Interviewee 12 used scholarliness as a pejorative, a perspective that was echoed in other interviews. Ch. 3.IV.G (discussing 'professorial types'). Although it is outside the scope of the current research, it might be helpful to obtain a better understanding of what respondents mean by a 'scholarly' or 'academic' decision or award and why such items are framed in such a negative light.

String citations, meaning a series of judicial decisions or arbitral awards that all stand for the same proposition of law, were mentioned by several other respondents, typically in a negative light. For example, Interviewee 19, an international arbitrator, said, 'Too many [legal authorities] are string cited and irrelevant.' Interviewee 5, a common law domestic judge–arbitrator, said, 'Sixty per cent [of the legal authorities] I read in their entirety, 40 per cent I skim. Lawyers should give me the main case. String cites I will probably not read in whole.' Interestingly, the coding exercise suggests that some decision makers, most notably US judges, may also use string citations in their writing.[72]

Another reason why some judges and arbitrators might not read the legal authorities in their entirety involved the nature of the dispute in question and in particular whether the dispute was likely to turn on the facts versus the law.[73] For example, Interviewee 14, an international judge–arbitrator, stated that s/he 'can't give a percentage' of the legal authorities read in full, although

> I tend not to read authorities in full. In commercial arbitration, you get few cases with meaty questions of law, unlike when I was a judge. I also know a lot more now [since I'm more senior]—now I know when something sounds right. Unless the case is really major—if there are seven Supreme Court cases, I'm not going to read all of them.
>
> Once you get into the civil law authorities, those are shorter and you need to read those in full. The way they lay out argument is different than in the common law. In the common law, you look for the decisive points. If it is an important case, counsel will point you to the part to read.[74]
>
> Sometimes you read outside sources—I did that a lot as a judge, or got a clerk to do. If I do that as an arbitrator, I send back the case for review. As a judge, I used to play games with counsel—show the amount of learning [outside research] I had. Now, I'm very influenced by the ICC—I can't let anything external influence my view without getting the parties' opinions on those external authorities.

One individual—Interviewee 8, an international judge–arbitrator—indicated that 'to some extent, I depend on my law clerks to do research and to have familiarity with the cases. My law clerks are usually devoted to this field with considerable experience. That is why I have law clerks.' This response of course raises questions about the appropriate delegation of authority, as previously discussed.[75]

[72] Table 4.12; see also Ch. 4.II.B, 4.IV.B.1.

[73] This distinction is consistent with the three types of disputes identified by US Supreme Court Justice Benjamin Cardozo. Benjamin N Cardozo, *The Nature of the Judicial Process* (Yale University Press 1949) 164–65 (noting different types of analysis and decisions are required by disputes that turn on facts, disputes that turn on the law, and disputes that turn on both the facts and the law); Strong, Reasoned Awards (n 10) 33–36 (discussing similar issues in the arbitral context).

[74] This distinction between how common law and civil law authorities must be read is intriguing, but does not appear to be borne out by survey data. Table 2.7 (suggesting fewer judges and arbitrators from the civil law tradition read judicial decisions in full than judges and arbitrators from the common law). However, the survey did not distinguish between the type of judicial decisions in question, a point that may benefit from further research.

[75] Ch. 3.III.B.2.a.

Some respondents said that they preferred to read authorities themselves, regardless of the time and difficulty involved. For example, Interviewee 10, a common law domestic arbitrator who noted that s/he read most of the legal authorities him/herself, stated that 'I wish to be thorough and consider the issues the parties raise as relevant. I understand that there are times when the parties flail and don't quite know what they are saying. Then I will scan abstracts to get an idea of the content.'

Finally, some respondents indicated a scepticism regarding the reliability of legal authorities presented to them. For example, Interviewee 11, a common law domestic judge–arbitrator, indicated that s/he 'read to know—I can't trust what people write. I've often found citations that were misleading or incomplete. The parties were inappropriately creative with cases.'

3. Time of reviewing legal authorities

The next question in this series focused on when the judge, arbitrator, or law/clerk assistant read legal authorities. This issue is important not only because concerns are occasionally raised about the extent to which individual judges and arbitrators are prepared for hearings, but also because the legal literature suggests that there are significant differences in practice across national and international lines as well as the common law–civil law divide. For example, advocates in international arbitration and civil law disputes are generally understood to provide neutrals with a great deal of written material prior to the hearing, whereas advocates in domestic common law do not.[76]

To reach this issue, interviewees were asked when they read legal authorities: before, during, or after the hearing. No pattern was discerned relating to differences between judges and arbitrators or between the internationality of the dispute or the decision maker's home legal tradition, except to the extent the respondents indicated whether they were likely to receive pre-hearing submissions on the law.

Several respondents indicated that they read the legal authorities at all three times, for slightly different purposes. For example, Interviewee 4, a mixed international–domestic arbitrator, said that s/he read the materials before, during, and after the hearing.

> When precisely depends on the nature of the issue or my personal familiarity with the law. If the controlling law is [the law of my home jurisdiction], I may not read the authorities if I know the body of law well. There's no pattern to my approach to reading legal authorities, though I try to be familiar with the legal principles. I'm often chosen as arbitrator because of my expertise in a particular body of law, so I feel the parties know what they're getting.

Interviewee 19, an international arbitrator, also noted that 'I can read different authorities in all three phases.' S/he read legal authorities prior to the hearing 'to be

[76] Ch. 1.III.C.

ready to ask questions', during the hearing to 'get context' and after the hearing 'because I'm writing the award'. Interviewee 19 further noted that, 'in international commercial arbitration, when you read the memorials, there are a handful of cases that both parties cite in the body of their submissions, and I read those in full. Those cases that are just cited in the footnotes are typically extra, and I don't read those.' Most of the respondents who indicated that they read the legal authorities before, during, and after the hearing did so for reasons similar to Interviewees 4 and 19, although most individuals indicated an emphasis on reading the materials after the hearing, during the drafting of the reasoned decision or award.[77]

Another group of respondents said that they read the materials exclusively before or after the hearing, but not during the hearing.[78] However, most appeared to read legal authorities both before and after the hearing, although the rationale varied somewhat.[79] For example, Interviewee 2, an international arbitrator, indicated that his/her approach

> is case-specific. If the hearing is primarily to hear witnesses, then the cases are not critical in advance; instead, I make sure to read the exhibits in advance.
>
> If the hearing is primarily to question counsel during open and close—in other words, if I think the issues in the dispute will be legal, not factual—then I'll read the cases in advance. However, if my sense of the memorials is that it's a fact case, then I'll double check the legal authorities when writing the award, but if counsel doesn't disagree about the law, then I won't waste time during the hearing to ask about the law. I aim to make hearings efficient.

In some cases, the decision depends on how the proceeding is structured, particularly with respect to whether and when the legal authorities are required to be submitted. For example, Interviewee 12, a common law domestic judge–arbitrator, said that s/he tended to review materials 'after the hearing' because 'often I don't receive legal authority briefings in advance of a hearing—I don't require them. We cover if parties want to, but often they elect not to brief.' However, Interviewee 5, another common law domestic judge–arbitrator, noted that

[77] Interviewee 7, an international arbitrator ('All three. Mostly after because that's when I'm writing up the award.'); Interviewee 8, an international judge–arbitrator ('All three, depending on the case and the degree to which a particular authority is critical to the decision in the case.'); Interviewee 13, a common law domestic judge–arbitrator ('All three. Sometimes legal authorities are presented early on scope of depositions, arbitrability, etc. I read when the position briefs are sent pre-hearing.'); Interviewee 15, a common law domestic judge–arbitrator ('All three. Depending on case—if you're having oral arguments, you read the items before. Definitely after—we'll read the key cases when writing the award.'); Interviewee 16, an international judge–arbitrator ('All three. Not always, but I will refer to authorities when studying the files and definitely read the authorities afterwards. I don't read all the authorities before the hearing.'); Interviewee 17, an international judge–arbitrator ('Generally before, but also during the hearing things will come up—issues that did not look relevant but do become relevant. You will then go back and read those items.').

[78] Interviewee 6, a mixed international–domestic arbitrator ('Many of them before.'); Interviewee 9, a common law domestic judge, possibly speaking about issues on motion rather than the dispute on the merits ('Before the hearing on a dispositive action, we set up oral arguments and we give ourselves some leeway—that's possible because our district is caught up, so I have time to read. Sometimes we have an order drafted and I ask what the issue is and we have a big memo prepared in advance.').

[79] Interviewee 3, an international arbitrator from a civil law background ('We read the authorities before and after the hearing.'); Interviewee 11, a common law domestic judge–arbitrator ('Before and after.').

> if a brief is filed before, I'll read the main cases before so that I can get context for the facts. Mostly I read after. Seventy-five per cent of cases have post-hearing briefs (the cases are of the size to need them), and 50 per cent of those have closing arguments and post-hearing briefs.
>
> I do most of my research after the hearing. I deliberate with the panel immediately following and split up the legal issues and who should do what on each issue regarding research. After the briefs are filed, we meet again to see if we need to revise our research.

Interviewee 14, an international judge–arbitrator, similarly stated that s/he

> probably [doesn't] read authorities themselves before the hearing because it depends when the opening submissions are received. If I get them a month before, I will ask a clerk to do a preliminary review. If I get them a week before, then we're racing to get our impression of the law on the facts.
>
> In commercial cases, there are not that many burning questions of law. Most counsel focus on the facts, not the law—these are contract cases involving what the contract means and what happened and whether that was a breach. That needs knowledge of the whole framework. Everyone is scrambling to know the factual background and where the dispute lies. Once you know the facts, you can look at the law.
>
> Some legal teams break up cases into facts and law—the first chair deals with the facts and a junior person deals with the law.

This concept of legal research and preparation versus factual research and preparation is discussed further below.[80]

Those respondents who focused on reading the materials prior to the hearing typically did so in order to contextualize the hearing. For example, Interviewee 20, a mixed international–domestic arbitrator, indicated that s/he read 'normally, before, so I can go to the hearing knowing what you're talking about, to understand the framework of the law'. Interviewee 10, a common law domestic arbitrator, stated that s/he 'never' read the authorities during a hearing but instead read them 'mostly before—I might come back to them after. I do not generally accept matters that have not been raised in advance. If something comes up in a hearing, I may go back and see it, but I will have already read the materials.'

Conversely, Interviewee 1, a mixed international–domestic arbitrator, noted that s/he read the authorities 'most often, after [the hearing]; occasionally before. If a legal issue is in controversy and seems dispositive, I will read before' the hearing. Interviewee 18, an international judge–arbitrator, similarly stated that 'when it's obvious that certain legal authorities are crucial, then I read them before so that I can ask directed questions at the hearing. When the authorities are not obvious, then I read them after the hearing.'

[80] Ch. 3.III.C.3.

4. Independent legal research

One issue that is not well-covered in the legal literature involves the propriety of independent legal research by judges and arbitrators, including how such research is conducted.[81] However, the concept of independent legal research—defined for purposes of both the interviews and the survey as anything other than reading the parties' legal submissions—touches on a number of important jurisprudential debates.[82]

First, the question of independent legal research is related to debates about whether legal disputes should be considered public or private in nature. While the legal literature at one time confidently characterized litigation as a public dispute resolution mechanism and arbitration as 'merely' private (a characterization that often leads arbitration to be downgraded as less important),[83] the line between the two has begun to blur. Not only can arbitration be framed as reflecting a variety of 'public' qualities, both within the area of treaty-based (investment) proceedings and within commercial proceedings, which increasingly touch on matters of regulatory concern,[84] but questions have arisen as whether and to what extent litigation belongs to the parties as opposed to society as a whole.[85]

Another issue involves whether and to what extent independent legal research by judges and arbitrators affects procedural justice. These concerns are often framed in individual terms (i.e. the parties must be allowed to respond to any legal allegations relevant to the decision-making process) and thus resonate most clearly with those who view the resolution of a legal dispute as a private matter that is or should be controlled by the parties.[86] However, some differences may appear across common law–civil law divide, both as a jurisprudential matter (i.e. questions relating to who 'owns' the dispute) and as a practical matter (i.e. structural opportunities for parties to respond to judicial activities).[87]

a. Approach to independent legal research

This series began with a question about the kind of independent legal research interviewees conducted. Although the question triggered a variety of individual responses, no trend was discovered along any of the axes of inquiry (judicial–arbitral,

[81] Strong, Reasoned Awards (n 10) 25–27; Strong, Reasoned Decisions (n 10) 126; Ch. 1.III.A.

[82] The survey identified a number of possible types of actions and sought to identify the frequency with which each type was undertaken. Table 2.7.

[83] Judith Resnik, 'Diffusing Disputes: The Public in the Private of Arbitration, the Private in Courts, and the Erasure of Rights', (2015) 124 Yale LJ 2804, 2806–07; Ch. 1.I.

[84] Gary B Born, *International Commercial Arbitration* (Wolters Kluwer 2014) 1039–40.

[85] SI Strong, 'Limits of Procedural Choice of Law', (2014) 39 Brooklyn J Intl L 1027, 1060–63 (Strong, Procedural Choice). This issue has been discussed, to some extent, in the context of class actions in the United States, where questions arise as to whether settling or not settling with the lead plaintiff in a class suit either moots the class action or destroys the possibility of class certification. *Campbell-Ewald Co v Gomez*, 136 S Ct 663, 672 (2016) (holding refusal of settlement by lead plaintiff did not moot class claim); *Franco v Allied Interstate LLC*, No 13-cv-4053 (KBF), 2018 WL 3410009, *6 (SDNY 13 July 2018) (denying certification on grounds that lead plaintiff who declined offer of settlement was not an adequate representative of the class.).

[86] Resnik (n 83) 2806–07; Strong, Procedural Choice (n 85) 1060–63; Ch. 1.I.

[87] Civil law trials are often multi-phased, as opposed to common law trials, which usually involve one major hearing. Ch. 1.III.C.

domestic–international and common law–civil law). Instead, differences appeared to be generated as a result of different individual views about the role of a neutral.

To some extent, issues relating to independent legal research should not be exaggerated, since the amount of independent legal research that is being undertaken appears to be relatively minor, at least in most cases.[88] For example, Interviewee 5, a common law domestic judge–arbitrator, stated that the amount of independent legal research s/he conducted was

> frankly, not much. Normally, I count on the parties to give me the authorities. I may [check for subsequent treatment] and see if the cited cases lead to anything and may read those. It's appropriate for arbitrators to rely on the parties to identify the issues and have the parties give the authorities. If I think there's something else, I ask for briefs.

Interviewee 7, an international arbitrator, said that s/he undertook

> generally, no [research] other than a dialogue with my colleagues. I don't think it's fair to do independent legal research. I had one case where our co-arbitrator said, 'I'm troubled because both sides missed a key issue' and gave the legal authority. It seemed he was right; the lawyers had ignored a key issue. We asked the parties the next day for further briefing.
>
> That's an exception to the general rule. A good arbitrator sticks with what the parties have provided. If you don't, you should get the parties' view. You should never write an opinion that's not been fully mooted by the parties.

This is not to say that judges and arbitrators do not conduct independent legal research. Indeed, some respondents indicated a fairly robust approach. For example, Interviewee 9, a common law domestic judge, stated that

> we do independent research on everything, [then] my career clerk, term clerk and I argue [about our findings]. My career clerk was a defence lawyer, I was a plaintiff's lawyer, so we come from different perspectives. I have enormous respect for her—sometimes I do legal research to prove her wrong and vice versa. We do it to convince each other.

However, Interviewee 9 noted that his/her approach was unusual because 'I have the luxury of time', unlike many domestic judges in his/her home jurisdiction.

Interestingly, although arbitrators are often said to have more time (or at least more flexibility) than judges,[89] one respondent indicated that many arbitrators actually

[88] Interviewee 6, a mixed international–domestic arbitrator ('Rare I do any.').

[89] Alysia l A Cuilwik, 'The Potential Arbitrability of Lender Liability Claims Arising From International Lending Agreements', (1990) 8 Boston U Intl LJ 85, 119; cf Chris Guthrie, Jeffrey J Rachlinski, and Andrew J Wistrich,

operate under time constraints that are at least as pressing as those facing judges.[90] While the arbitral community has been working to combat the problems associated with over-scheduled arbitrators, it would appear that more work needs to be done in this regard.[91]

As suggested, it appears that most differences in approach arise because of differences in how the judge or arbitrator perceives his/her function. For example, Interviewee 11, a common law domestic judge–arbitrator, stated that his/her research methodology 'in court [was] whatever we thought was relevant or had bearing on the case. In arbitration, [I do] nothing unless I think there should be something else, then I bring the issue to the parties and ask them to comment.' Interviewee 15, another common law domestic judge–arbitrator, stated that s/he did no independent legal research as a judge because the court from which s/he came 'is rich in law clerks (3 to 5 law clerks per judge). I don't know what they did. I know my instructions were that they were not bound by the cases in the brief—they *should* find additional cases and should look for wide authority.'

Several respondents indicated that their approach to independent legal research depended on the quality of the submissions from the parties. For example, Interviewee 2, an international arbitrator, said,

> If the parties are experienced counsel, then I do not look for more. If the papers suggest sloppiness or a mandatory issue that's not fully briefed, then I may do some research on my own. However, if I find anything that would make a difference in the outcome, I bring it to the attention of counsel and ask for a comment. I've done that once or twice. It is rare but it can be done.

Interviewee 10, a common law domestic arbitrator, similarly indicated that

> I do as little as possible. I generally explain to the parties (not necessarily the attorneys) that it's their attorney's job to present authorities that are reliable. There may be a reason why the attorney does not present something. It's not my job to be the advocate.
>
> Sometimes when I've smelled an issue that needs to be investigated—especially if there's an imbalance of power—the less sophisticated party may not know to mention

'Blinking on the Bench', (2007) 93 Cornell L Rev 1, 35 (footnotes omitted) (discussing time constraints on the bench and noting that "[j]udges facing cognitive overload due to heavy dockets or other on-the-job constraints are more likely to make intuitive rather than deliberative decisions because the former are speedier and easier"); Letter from Alex Kozinski, US Circuit Judge, 9th Circuit, to Samuel A Alito, Jr, US Circuit Judge, 3rd Circuit (16 January 2004) 5 (noting that time constraints mean that appellate judges in the United States spend 5–10 minutes reviewing unpublished opinions that have been drafted entirely by law clerks or staff attorneys), <http://www.nonpublication.com/kozinskiletter.pdf> accessed 11 April 2020.

[90] Ch. 3.III.G (Interviewee 2 (discussing the 'what do you do it you don't have time—the "oh my god" realities' of arbitral practice). This concept has also been raised in the scholarly literature. E.g. Nikolaus Pitkowitz and Alice Fremuth-Wolf, 'The Vienna Repositioning Propositions', 2018 Austrian YB Intl Arb 209, 238; Anne-Véronique Schlaepfer and Marily Paralika, 'Striking the Right Balance: The Roles of Arbitral Institutions, Parties and Tribunals in Achieving Efficiency in International Arbitration', (2015) 2 BCDR Intl Arb Rev 329, 336, 339–40.

[91] Pitkowitz and Fremuth-Wolf (n 90) 209; Schlaepfer and Paralika (n 90) 329.

> something and the other party may try to keep me from noting. In those cases, I notice. It's like a pro se defendant in court.

Interviewee 16, an international judge–arbitrator, adopted a similar technique, saying,

> I adhere to the concept *jura novit curia*, so I will do research if I'm not satisfied by what the parties present or if I'm curious about something or don't think the lawyers are very good. Quite often, I do legal research personally. Sometimes I have a younger lawyer do it, though it's mostly me.

Although Interviewees 2, 10, and 16 all came from common law backgrounds, this approach was not limited to common law lawyers. For example, Interviewee 17, an international judge–arbitrator from the civil law tradition, noted that it

> could be that I find parties have not well-covered a legal issue, then I ask an assistant to do research (or I do it myself). I do it because I'm not entirely confident in what parties put forward.
>
> [However,] I rely mainly on parties' reasoning. If I depart significantly from the parties' position, then I allow a response. I follow the [US] Federal Rules of Civil Procedure regarding the determination of foreign law (Rule 44.1)—that inspires me.

Interviewee 3, an international arbitrator trained in the civil law, similarly stated,

> Sometimes I ask my clerk to do specific research on specific issues. For the most part, parties submit so many materials that it is not necessary to go beyond that, but sometimes parties will argue something, like fraud, and I want to know about the issue in broader context so that I can understand the issues, even if I don't discuss the research in my award.

The notion of what is discussed in the decision or award is covered later in this chapter.[92]

In some cases, independent legal research is not triggered by the quality of the parties' submissions but by particular issues reflected therein. For example, Interviewee 8, an international judge–arbitrator, indicated,

> Something I read may remind me of another case that was not cited that I need to re-read to make sure my recollection is correct. I may read any time before or after a hearing. For example, it may appear after a hearing that a decision of another tribunal is more critical or relevant to the decision and I may need to read it more closely.

[92] Chs. 3.III.B.5, 3.III.E.2.

Interviewee 4, a mixed international–domestic arbitrator, similarly noted that, 'as a normal matter, I don't do independent research', but 'occasionally after arguments, the legal research will lead to another case. If it's significant, I give the parties a chance to comment. That's happened only a few times in 25 to 30 years of sitting as an arbitrator.'

Interviewee 13, a common law domestic judge–arbitrator, indicated that s/he conducts 'legal research that arises because of parties' briefs. For example, if I want to find out if the assertion in the briefing is correct, I don't rely solely on parties' submissions—they lead me to the core issues.' However, 'when doing research, I limit myself to the [home jurisdiction and] scope of arbitration.'

Interviewee 14, an international judge–arbitrator, indicated that s/he believed it appropriate to research

> anything that hits you when you read the submissions. Maybe you're reading and seeing an issue that's not addressed. You do research any time you have an itch you need to scratch. You look into whether this claim gives rise to the relief they're asking for—how do you get from point A (facts) to point B (relief).

A number of respondents indicated that they limited the scope of their research to background issues. For example, Interviewee 12, a common law domestic judge–arbitrator, indicated that 'I will occasionally go to law journals, not cases, if I'm not in an area that I'm familiar with. I do not research outside what the parties have briefed.' Interviewee 1, a mixed international–domestic arbitrator, similarly stated that, although the approach 'varies from case to case', typically, 'if dipositive of the legal controversy, I may look at parties' authorities but also authorities cited in those authorities. Maybe also a treatise if it will be helpful.'

Interviewee 19, an international arbitrator from the common law tradition, said,

> I go look at treatises for general coverage of the issue. I do not 'out-research' counsel, though—I do not do my own research to see if they caught all the cases. However, in a recent case, one of my co-arbitrators happened to know of a case that was on point that the parties hadn't cited, and in that case, we asked the parties to brief the issue involving that case.

Interviewee 20, a mixed international–domestic arbitrator from the civil law tradition, indicated that in commercial proceedings,

> normally the parties submit everything, but sometimes parties cite local law that might have a conflict of laws issue. Then we would ask the parties to give the tribunal their views under the conflict of laws rules.
>
> Normally we frame the issue and give them page limits. They file simultaneous submissions and then allow a reply.

Interviewee 18, an international judge–arbitrator, stated,

> When it is clear that a delicate legal problem will arise and is crucial to the dispute, I insist the parties submit their conclusions, and I invite specific analysis on certain issues from the parties. After the hearing, arbitrators should not do legal research because you have to submit the issue to the parties and re-open the hearing, since the parties need to respond. Arbitrators must ask parties to both address new points.

As these excerpts make clear, most arbitrators, particularly those in the international realm, believe that parties should be allowed the opportunity to respond to independent legal research as a matter of procedural justice, a conclusion that was borne out by the survey data.[93] Judges do not necessarily follow the same approach, which may suggest an important difference between litigation and arbitration.

Those interviewees who did not indicate their rationale in their initial response were asked to explain their approach in a follow-up question. The responses again split primarily along philosophical lines rather than in accordance with the respondent's function or training. Thus, a number of individuals characterized legal disputes as 'belonging' to the parties.[94] As Interviewee 5, a common law domestic judge–arbitrator, said,

> It's the parties' case—they've raised and vetted the issues before the hearing. Weak issues have been dismissed or I say they won't fly. I don't want to come out of left field on anything. If I come up with something, I ask the parties to brief the issue further.
>
> I like to say my arbitrations are 'cooperative'. I think it's important that the parties get involved in the process; they need to see the language in the procedural order in advance, they have to have input into discovery, etc. The benefit of arbitration is its flexibility, and the parties need to be part of that process so the outcome has their input and their buy-in into the process.

Interviewee 4, a mixed international–domestic arbitrator who said s/he did relatively little independent research, adopted that methodology because 'I admire and appreciate good advocacy. I enjoy hearing and reading argument that incorporates legal principles. I'm often brought in because I'm familiar with the principles of law, and most of the principles are not new, though I enjoy things that are new'. Interviewee 6, a mixed international–domestic arbitrator who also rarely did any independent legal research, justified his/her actions on the grounds that 'I don't want to bring in theories or arguments not introduced by parties or even be influenced by those'.

Other respondents recognized the centrality of the parties to the dispute-resolution process, although they specifically noted that they did not entirely abandon their independent judgment. For example, Interviewee 12, a common law domestic judge–arbitrator, stated, 'I believe you allow the parties to put on the case

[93] Tables 2.11, 2.13, 2.23, 2.26.

[94] This is in accordance with the legal literature on arbitration and, to a lesser extent, litigation. Ch. 1.I.

in litigation and arbitration. In general, unless an injustice will be done, you allow parties to conduct their cases'. Interviewee 19, an international arbitrator, justified his/her approach on similar grounds, indicating that 'it's an adversarial process—counsel argues their case and we consider what they think is important. However, if I know of something or find something else that's relevant, I bring it to the attention of the parties.'

Other respondents justified independent legal research by pointing to the need to decide the outcome properly as a matter of law.[95] Often these individuals exhibited a certain amount of scepticism about the quality or motivation of counsel. For example, Interviewee 15, a common law domestic judge–arbitrator, indicated that 'the parties are advocates and only cite helpful authorities. The court should look beyond those authorities.'[96] Interviewee 13, also a common law domestic judge–arbitrator, said that s/he conducts independent legal research 'because arguments in parties' submissions are self-serving, and I want to find out if the argument—not just cases—is correct'. In particular, Interviewee 13 wanted to know 'if there is a black letter, new approach to cases [affecting] the theory of the case'. Interviewee 16, an international judge–arbitrator, similarly stated that s/he conducted independent legal research 'because I want to be sure that I have the right law, and sometimes one or both parties do not give me the right authorities'.

Two of the responses demonstrated the power of acculturation and of institutional control over judicial and arbitral practice.[97] On the one hand, Interviewee 9, a common law domestic judge, indicated that the approach s/he used 'was taught to me when I was clerking'. Legal clerkships provide a powerful and enduring means of conveying professional norms and conventions, as discussed later in this chapter.[98] Conversely, Interviewee 11, a common law domestic judge–arbitrator, stated that s/he adopted a hands-off policy in arbitration

> because the AAA wants me to do that. I disagree, but I do it. I think that is unnecessary because, as in a court case, counsel has the burden to tell (identify) what's relevant. If the court/arbitrator does their job for counsel, you should be able to rely on what you find.

This statement suggests that judicial and arbitral institutions can do a great deal to shape the behaviour of neutrals, for good or for ill, a point that reinforces the importance of judicial and arbitral education. Both the interview and survey instruments considered matters relating to professional education, even though the subject is seldom discussed in the scholarly literature.[99]

[95] For example, Interviewee 1, a common law domestic arbitrator, said s/he conducted independent legal research 'because I focus on the legal issues in controversy'.
[96] Interviewee 15 appeared to be speaking about judicial practice at this point, not arbitral practice.
[97] Ch. 1.II (discussing acculturation in the development of judges and arbitrators).
[98] Ch. 3.III.B.2.a (discussing clerkships); see also Ch. 1.II (discussing acculturation).
[99] Chs. I.III.A, 2.IV.E, 3.III.F.

b. Response to independent legal research

The next question in this series asked whether the interviewee provided the parties with an opportunity to respond to the results of any independent legal research conducted by individual in question. This question was also included in the survey.[100]

Several individuals responded with an unqualified 'no'[101] while other individuals provided a categorical 'yes',[102] reflecting a similar division in the survey data.[103] Several people indicated that they sometimes allowed a response. For example, Interviewee 8, an international judge–arbitrator, said,

> It depends. If it is before or during the hearing, I'm likely to ask parties about it. If it's after the hearing and we're in deliberations, the answer is no (and it happens if parties do not refer to relevant decisions). Sometimes other cases are decided after the case we've heard, and the tribunal will allow parties to make written submissions on the other cases.

Interviewee 9, a common law domestic judge, said,

> Rarely, but we have. If we have questions, we email the parties, which is odd for a judge. [In a recent] non-commercial case, I said, 'I found this, can you tell me the parties' positions'. We have a faster discussion [via email]—I ask for a 24-hour turnaround. This isn't easy—we're trying to do what's right.
>
> Rarely do I give an opportunity to respond because rarely do the lawyers miss anything. Good lawyers usually pinpoint the key issue—it's not like they miss the key case—so rarely do we come up with something new. If we do come up with something new, they're wonderful litigators, and I feel we should continue the conversation with them.

Respondents were subsequently asked why they adopted their particular approach. The rationales varied significantly, with some—such as that enunciated by Interviewee 12, a common law domestic judge–arbitrator who said 'to make sure I haven't missed anything'—demonstrating a laudable humility. Other responses—such as that enunciated by Interviewee 15, also a common law domestic judge–arbitrator, who said, 'I'm not in the habit of testing my opinions through counsel'—suggested a high degree of confidence in their own abilities, a phenomenon that is often discussed with concern in the legal literature.[104]

[100] Ch. 2.IV.A.2.

[101] Interviewee 1, a mixed international–domestic arbitrator from the common law tradition; Interviewee 3, an international arbitrator from the civil law tradition; Interviewee 13, a common law domestic judge–arbitrator; Interviewee 15, a common law domestic judge–arbitrator.

[102] Interviewee 5, a common law domestic judge–arbitrator; Interviewee 6, a mixed international–domestic arbitrator; Interviewee 19, an international arbitrator.

[103] Table 2.12.

[104] Chs. 1.II, 2.IV.A.2 (discussing overconfidence among judges).

Other individuals indicated that they do not allow parties to respond to independent legal research 'because I stay within the confines of what the parties have cited or within what they've cited, so they're on notice', as Interviewee 1, a mixed international–domestic arbitrator stated. Interviewee 16, an international judge–arbitrator who typically does not allow the parties to respond, noted that 'I'm mindful of the limits to *jura novit curia*. Usually my research is in areas already raised by the parties—I'm just getting additional authorities.' However, Interviewee 16 also noted that s/he adopted this approach, at least in part, because of timing considerations, since the issue typically arose 'fairly late in the process.'. Interviewee 10, a common law domestic arbitrator, also mentioned concerns about timing, stating that 'I don't recall if I've had to because it's a rare thing, and usually it's something I've picked up late, when the hearings may be closed. It's rare that this happens.'

Those who allowed parties to respond to independent legal research primarily did so to comply with procedural justice, a rationale that was also popular in the survey.[105] For example, Interviewee 8, an international judge–arbitrator, indicated that s/he permitted party input 'to ensure fairness to parties—due process'.[106] Interviewee 6, a mixed international–domestic arbitrator, said, 'I think it's fair—it's the parties' proceeding. [Furthermore,] colleagues in practice say they hate awards [that include] something the parties didn't raise.'

Notably, this practice crossed over the common law–civil law divide. While Interviewees 6 and 8 were trained in the common law, Interviewee 3, an international arbitrator from the civil law tradition, adopted a similar approach

> because you should never base the reasoning of the award on arguments that the parties have not argued (i.e. a new theory)—that would be a breach of due process. You always base your decision on the parties' arguments, and if they don't have a good point, you handle it at the hearing. There's no need to raise the issue afterwards if you handle it during the hearing. If you think there's a more appropriate theory (and it depends on the legal culture in question), then you raise it at the hearing. The Swiss do it necessarily; I do not usually do it. Instead, I usually rely on what the parties argue.

5. Citation of legal authorities

The next series of questions focused on the purpose and practice of citing legal authorities in reasoned decisions or awards, an issue that is often ignored in scholarly commentary.[107] The survey also included questions about citation of legal authorities,[108] but it was hoped that the interview responses would provide additional illumination on these important issues.

[105] Table 2.11.

[106] Interviewee 19, an international arbitrator, also indicated 'Due process'.

[107] Commentators writing in this field tend to focus on superficial issues such as whether citations should be in the body of the text or in footnotes.

[108] Ch. 2.IV.A.3.

a. Reason for legal citations

The first question in this series asked interviewees why they cited legal authority in a reasoned decision or award. Several respondents—both judges and arbitrators operating in a variety of legal settings—indicated that legal citation was necessary to demonstrate that the outcome of the dispute was not purely arbitrary. For example, Interviewee 17, an international judge–arbitrator from the civil law tradition, said s/he used legal citations 'to substantiate my decision, to show it's based on the law and not a whimsical idea of mine.' Interviewee 3, an international arbitrator also from the civil law tradition, similarly stated,

> You must apply the law, so you must cite the law that the parties have invoked. You must base your decision on the law and you must meet the arguments of the parties.
>
> For example, both parties may invoke a legal decision and give different interpretations. You must enter into this debate. It is an important decision regarding the application of the law to the issue, and you must address that controversy and reach a conclusion on the issue.

Although Interviewees 3 and 17 were both trained in the civil law, their approach was very similar to that adopted by respondents from common law countries.[109] For example, Interviewee 15, a domestic judge–arbitrator with common law training, noted that s/he used legal citations 'to show that the decision respects and abides by the law. You need to show that you haven't made up the law out of whole cloth but are establishing legal principles.' Interviewee 13, a common law domestic judge–arbitrator, said s/he used legal citations 'mainly to show parties what my thinking is based on—[that the decision or award is] not just my personal theory on how to work out' the dispute.

Other respondents provided multiple reasons for the use of legal citations. Interviewee 2, an international arbitrator, noted,

> It goes back to [the first question of the interview]. One, to assure parties that my decision was not knee-jerk sympathy but a true assessment of applicable law, you need to 'show your work.' Two, there's a possibility that the award may be reviewed, and mandatory law may be relevant.

[109] Interviewee 4, a mixed international–domestic arbitrator from the common law tradition ('I don't do it massively. I think probably legal authority is a major premise of the syllogism—if there's any question about that premise, I like to tell parties the principle and the authority. It's reflective of my thought process—I'm not always critical of legal authority but completing the syllogistic process is usually pretty easy because I have consulted legal authority.'); Interviewee 5, a domestic judge–arbitrator from the common law tradition ('In my view, as a judge or as an arbitrator, our job is to apply the law to the facts. Arbitrators can do that with more equity than judges. [However,] it's important parties know my reasoning is based on the authorities cited and its application to the facts.'); Interviewee 20, a mixed international–domestic arbitrator from the civil law tradition ('I cite legal authority to give the parties additional reasoning why the tribunal has to reach that conclusion—it is not something the tribunal has created out of the blue—there are authorities that go along with that decision. Sometimes there's little legal authority or you do not agree with courts. Then you give your reasoning without giving anything other than general rules of interpretation but no legal authorities.').

Interviewee 8, an international judge–arbitrator, also identified two key factors, although in his/her case, they were 'to reinforce the authority of our decision and therewith its potential acceptance by the parties'.

Some respondents focused on process considerations. For example, Interviewee 14, an international judge–arbitrator, said that s/he cited legal authority

> because usually a legal conclusion requires a number of steps—you climb them in order. You must advance a proposition and if it's not needed or self-indulgent, you must show that this is the proposition and these are the authorities—no need to explain them in depth unless one side doesn't accept the case or proposition.

Interviewee 16, an international judge–arbitrator, indicated that legal citations were necessary 'both to sustain legal points/analyses I'm making and to provide a further framework for the decision. It seems perfectly normal in judicial and quasi-judicial decisions. I think the arbitral role is quasi-judicial, even if it is private.' Interviewee 6, a mixed international–domestic arbitrator, also noted this concept of a framework, and provided three reasons for legal citations:

> One, if it's been cited to me as a framework they want me to follow.
>
> Two, if it's a helpful framework, it helps me analyse facts in light of law.
>
> Three, I view my responsibility to protect the award—I do not want to give either party a way to overturn the award.

Not everyone took the view that legal citations were necessary or wise. For example, Interviewee 11, a domestic judge–arbitrator from the common law tradition, said,

> I will do [include legal citations] if the conclusion needs more weight, but I avoid doing it excessively because there's then the argument that you're not following legal authority. Arbitrators need not do conclusions of law unless that's specified by the parties, so I use citations as little as possible. Most commercial cases are breach of contract, which is not usually a very convoluted road map.

Interviewee 19, an international arbitrator, was also influenced by the nature of commercial disputes and identified 'three possible reasons' for including legal citations:

> First, the parties have cited something in a compelling manner—there are a handful of cases that are compelling. Second, citations add weight to the outcome if the outcome turns on law. Third, I think about the reviewing court—the court will expect to see case law when reviewing the award.
>
> I have issued several awards with no authority because the dispute turned on the facts. I see no reason to cite a case to say, 'the contract has been breached'.

Interviewee 12, a domestic judge–arbitrator, also adopted this technique, noting that 'sometimes precedent can be determinative of an issue, and in those cases, if I've had to interpret a case, they need to understand my interpretation, but my awards are not laden with citation. Usually I'm more focused on the facts.' Questions about fact citation and analysis (i.e. evidentiary matters) are discussed later in this chapter.[110]

A few respondents suggested that the decision whether to include legal citations in a reasoned decision or award turned on the parties' expectations or how the parties have argued the case. For example, Interviewee 1, a mixed international–domestic arbitrator, indicated that s/he cited legal authority 'because my audience expects me to cite' those materials. Interviewee 10, a common law domestic arbitrator, similarly noted that s/he used legal citations 'only in matters in which the parties have made the background circumstances important [or] when I'm distinguishing a case or saying, "I'm not guided by" something'. Interviewee 18, an international judge–arbitrator, similarly limited the number of legal citations s/he used, noting that

> I don't cite too much—only when it's crucial, meaning when there is no other way to solve an issue. If I have one party saying a point is black and the other party saying it is white, then I have to issue a decision that decides the opposing positions.

Only one respondent, Interviewee 9, a common law domestic judge, referred to structural rationales, stating that 'the foundation of the judiciary is that there's precedent. I want businesses to know that if you play by the rules, you win. Citing precedent that controls behaviour reaffirms the lesson to play by the rules.' One respondent—Interviewee 7, an international arbitrator—focused on more individual concerns, noting that s/he cited legal authority 'to be sure I've gotten the correct answer—to check myself', although s/he also used legal citations 'to give the parties some assurance that the award complies with applicable norms; that the arbitrators are not merely deciding according to their gut'.

b. Frequency of legal citations

Some of the answers to the preceding question indicated how frequently individual respondents cited legal authorities. However, the next question in this series dug deeper on that issue, asking interviewees to identify how often they discussed a legal authority or legal principle in depth in a reasoned decision or award as opposed to merely in passing. This issue, which was also raised in the survey[111] and was objectively evaluated in the coding exercise,[112] did not generate any clear differences among interviewees along any of the three axes of comparison.

[110] Ch. 3.III.C.5.
[111] Ch. 2.IV.A.3.
[112] Chs. 4.IV.A, 4.VI.B.1.

Although a few respondents attempted to describe their citation practice in terms of a percentage,[113] several indicated that they could not provide specific numbers.[114] However, most respondents indicated that they rarely or infrequently went into depth when citing legal authorities, although exceptions were made in appropriate circumstances.[115] Respondents demonstrated a particular dislike of string citations, both in submissions from advocates and in reasoned decisions and awards.[116]

Individual answers provided useful insights into judicial and arbitral practices. For example, Interviewee 12, a common law domestic judge–arbitrator, said s/he cited legal authorities 'in depth infrequently, only [undertaking a detailed analysis] if it's a major focus of contention between the parties.' Interviewee 2, an international arbitrator trained in the common law, indicated that 'there's no need for string cites or to refer to all cases, but certainly if there's a statutory element or I'm answering questions of law, I show my work.'

Interviewee 13, a common law domestic judge–arbitrator, provided another reason for going into depth with a particular analysis, indicating,

> If the legal opinion was out of line with the parties' position, I explain why. If it's not, I simply say Jones v Smith and give a footnote. I think each case is unique, so it's difficult to give a one-size-fits-all answer. It depends on the case/witness and how much the case relies on legal authorities versus credibility of witnesses and exhibits.

Interviewee 20, a mixed international–domestic arbitrator, showed how formalistic considerations about the placement of citations (in footnotes or in the body of the text) dovetailed with substantive concerns. S/he indicated that the approach

> depends [on the nature of the dispute]. In some cases, the key point depends on a debate between the legal authorities—then you must discuss those decisions in detail. Normally, unless you need that, I quote certain parties of decisions and in the footnotes send the parties to the rest of the decision.

Interviewee 17, an international judge–arbitrator, also discussed how the varying nature of the dispute can affect the citation process, saying his/her approach

> depends on the case and legal issues. It can happen that part of the case turns on the application of some legal authorities—then I go into depth.

[113] Interviewee 5, a common law domestic judge–arbitrator ('About one-third of the time.'); Interviewee 19, an international arbitrator from the common law tradition ('25 per cent of the time I cite in depth.').

[114] E.g. Interviewee 11, a common law domestic judge–arbitrator ('There's a middle ground—don't know how to answer.').

[115] Interviewee 1, a common law international arbitrator ('Rarely in depth.'); Interviewee 10, a common law domestic arbitrator ('Rarely in depth.'); Interviewee 16, an international judge–arbitrator ('Not very much detail.').

[116] String citations were criticized in other contexts as well. Ch. 3.III.B.6.

> How often? Hard to say. It happens more in investment than commercial [arbitration] because the state of development of investment cases. Investment law is less developed than national commercial law. So, 25 to 30 per cent of the cases, maybe, maybe more.

Interviewee 4, a mixed international–domestic arbitrator from the common law tradition, indicated a connection between the frequency and depth of legal citations to the frequency of 'unique principles of law. I probably do this in less than half my cases because most cases don't turn on matters of law; most cases turn on determining what the facts are and how to apply them.' Interviewee 15, a common law domestic judge–arbitrator, was one of the few that said s/he cited legal authorities 'often in great depth', although s/he recognized that 'every claim is different. Your discussion may require great depth and distinguishing because the parties relied on the wrong principle. Neutrals often need to be attuned to facts more because the legal authority is applicable. I also often distinguish because of facts.'

The need to vary one's approach was echoed by Interviewee 18, an international judge–arbitrator, who stated, 'In depth only when it's necessary. If you have a case from a higher court and your facts are a little different, you indicate what the court said and confirm that in our case, the same would apply.' Interviewee 8, another international judge–arbitrator, similarly noted that the frequency and depth of legal citation 'depends on the degree of relevance of the cited decision to the decision the tribunal is making. It could be choosing between conflicting decisions of other tribunals which makes it more important to deal with such a decision.' Interviewee 7, an international arbitrator, adopted an analogous approach, indicating that 'there have been some instances where the parties debate an issue and then I discuss it in depth if parties disagree on the meaning of the case. In other cases, it doesn't matter.'

Interviewee 6, a mixed international–domestic arbitrator, also indicated that the frequency of citation 'depends on how pivotal the legal authority is'. However, s/he went on to say that, 'unlike with judicial opinions, I don't routinely discuss cases in depth. Why? Because an award is not precedential, others will not read' it.

This emphasis on structural issues was echoed by Interviewee 9, a common law domestic judge, who said,

> In a real reasoned decision, we do it every time. If there's that level of dispute, there's something that needs to be discussed. I seldom see time wasted on [irrelevancies]—it's too expensive. If they've put their faith in our judiciary, the least I can do is explain my position about those conflicting cases.

Some might read these two statements as reflecting the superior nature of judicial decisions. However, not all judicial decisions are fully reasoned, as Interviewee 9 noted. Instead, many judges deal with disputes that turn only on the facts or on the application of existing law, both matters that generate no precedents, even in common law jurisdictions, and the interview protocol indicated the focus of this study was exclusively on reasoned decisions.[117] Furthermore, only a proportion of judicial decisions are reported, and of those that are reported, the vast majority are appellate in nature.[118] First-instance matters that are reported tend to be decided on motion rather than on the merits.[119]

Those respondents who did not discuss the rationales behind their individual approaches as part of the preceding question were asked in a follow-up to describe what drives their decisions about whether to discuss a particular legal authority, either in passing or in detail. The answers here largely tracked those in the preceding paragraphs. For example, as Interviewee 2, an international arbitrator, said,

> If the threshold on arbitrability is hotly contested, it would not do to use a *deus ex machina* approach—you need to unpack the arguments, look at all decisions and say why a certain line of cases is persuasive. If there's a material impact on the outcome, then you discuss the law. [However,] applying uncontroversial legal principles is simple—then you cite cases in passing, although you may need to go into depth on facts.

Interviewee 19, an international arbitrator, echoed a view held by several respondents,[120] noting that 'I discuss something in depth because I have to describe and explain why an authority affects the outcome, or I have to distinguish that authority'. Interviewee 5, a common law domestic judge–arbitrator, said that 'I try to evaluate which issue is dispositive, then cite legal authorities relating to the most important issues. Therefore, I cite in more detail the authorities applying to those most important issues.' Interviewee 1, a mixed international–domestic arbitrator, similarly indicated that 'I normally ... use authority to identify the principle I'm applying. I do not parse the underlying facts or authorities in the authority in my award.'

6. Advice from judges and arbitrators to counsel regarding legal authorities

The final question in this series asked respondents to describe what they wished parties and counsel knew about how judges and arbitrators approach legal authority. Although some individuals had no particular advice, most did. For example, Interviewee 8, an international judge–arbitrator, said, 'I wish they'd understand why we do what we do with such authority.' However, Interviewee 9, a common law domestic judge, made an important point when s/he said, 'We judges all do it differently. No one is right or wrong—we're humans and knowing your judge is really important. We want to be affirmed—we all want to do what's legally correct.' Interviewee 6,

[117] Cardozo (n 73) 164–65; Strong, Reasoned Decisions (n 10) 114; Ch. 3.II.B.

[118] It is unclear what proportion of judicial decisions are reported in any particular jurisdiction, let alone overall. Ch. 4.II.A.

[119] Ch. 4.II.A.

[120] Interviewee 6, a mixed international–domestic arbitrator ('How pivotal it is.'); Interviewee 10, a common law domestic arbitrator ('If it influences my thinking.'); Interviewee 16, an international judge–arbitrator ('Because I think it's helpful and sustains the legal analysis.').

a mixed international–domestic arbitrator, made the same point from the arbitral perspective, stating, 'There are variances between arbitrators in terms of how they approach matters. When choosing an arbitrator, look into these issues as part of due diligence.'[121]

One of the most common responses involved excessive citation by parties to legal authorities that were not central to the case.[122] Interviewee 7, an international arbitrator, said that counsel 'should focus on key legal authorities. It's counterproductive to say, "here are 16 cases to consider" because the panel will not have a good discussion of all 16. It's better to focus on two.' Interviewee 2, another international arbitrator, similarly stated that 'where issues are not contested, you do not need to run down every last authority. I often see the first ten pages discussing uncontroversial issues. You need to focus on what's in dispute and make that comprehensible.'

Interviewee 1, a mixed international–domestic arbitrator from a common law background, had two related suggestions, saying, 'One: arguments about fly specking differences in terminology in different awards and cases is not terribly helpful. Two: giving me lots of reading about items not in controversy is a waste of time and money—your money'. This advice crossed the common law–civil law divide, as noted by the response from Interviewee 20, a mixed international–domestic arbitrator from a civil law background, who indicated,

> It would be good if parties identified legal authorities that are truly relevant. There's a tendency to cite everything that's remotely relevant. You need to focus on the relevant points.
>
> In the past, I have asked parties to argue the first round, then, before the second round of submissions, we have a preliminary case hearing where the tribunal will discuss what will be the scope of the second round and what legal issues they want to hear more about. If you guide the parties like this, it will be more focused on legal issues, not throwing out every case of the last 20 years.

This is not to say that judges and arbitrators did not want in-depth discussion of appropriate authorities. For example, Interviewee 4, a mixed international–domestic arbitrator, said,

> Where the legal principle is clear, present it as clearly as it is—do not take well-established principles and fight over them. However, where the principles are in conflict, I'd like parties to address the issue and say why a particular principle is more significant. If there's doubt on the principle at issue, then the parties also need to address that. [Some disputes] need good, clear legal advocacy based on a complicated area of law that is in flux.

[121] Chapter 5 suggests creation of a questionnaire to help with this issue. Ch. 5.IV.

[122] Interviewee 19, an international arbitrator ('They should focus more on the main authority and leave out "Christmas tree" material [things to make the award look fancy].').

How one refers to authority is also important as a matter of both form and function. For example, Interviewee 7, an international arbitrator, noted that 'when [counsel] discuss cases, they should look at the facts. It's most disconcerting when parties cite a case with a couple words and don't look at the context. Words have significance only in context. I had a professor who said, "You get the facts or the facts get you."' Interviewee 5, a common law domestic judge–arbitrator, noted the need to be even-handed in presenting materials, stating that 'in [national] court, you need to present contrary authorities as party of your ethical duties, and I wish parties in arbitration knew that and did that'.

Interviewee 2, an international arbitrator, focused on the form of legal citations, noting,

> If you cite something, include a quote or jump cite. If you just say a case stands for proposition X, I can't be sure. A quote or jump cite makes it easier to confirm.
>
> Counsel submissions are only useful if they're persuasive, and as counsel you write to make the arbitrator's life easy. To be assured that you're correctly interpreting law, provide information for the arbitrators to check. Don't assume arbitrators take your spin at face value.

Several other individuals made similar statements. For example, Interviewee 12, a common law domestic judge–arbitrator, noted that it was important for counsel to know 'that we do check the propositions for which they're being cited, so they shouldn't try to misguide the court or the arbitrator'. Interviewee 10, a common law domestic arbitrator, said the most important tip was 'don't baffle me with BS [bullshit]. Tell me why something is relevant. I like highlighting to show me the relevance, but don't try to trick me. Don't make me work for it unnecessarily.'

Interviewee 15, a common law domestic judge–arbitrator, wanted counsel to know 'that they can't hide. So many cites are not on point and are distinguishable—the lawyers think we'll miss it.' Furthermore, as Interviewee 5, a common law domestic judge–arbitrator, noted,

> I bring my experience from the bench [and bar]. I was an arbitrator at the same time I was a litigator, and I bring the practical experience from that. I wish parties knew I could see through mis-citations and overstatements. More candour from the parties would be good because I can read through BS.

Interviewee 16, an international judge–arbitrator, provided additional insights on these issues. His/her suggestions were:

> First, to make things user-friendly to the arbitrator. String cites without explaining why you've introduced things is not user-friendly.
>
> Second, to realize that the arbitrator is trying to solve a problem. This goes to both arguments and citations of authorities. If the authorities don't help solve the dispute,

they don't help the arbitrator. A brief with lots of citations is elegant but doesn't necessarily help the arbitrator.

Respondents identified a number of different reasons why counsel had problems with legal citation. For example, Interviewee 11, a common law domestic judge–arbitrator, believed that 'inexperienced or new lawyers get overbroad when applying the law to the facts or don't know the difference between a holding and dicta'. Interviewee 14, an international judge–arbitrator, thought that it can be 'tough because counsel can't assume that all three members of the panel are equally familiar with the law, especially if they are not all from the same jurisdiction. [As a result, counsel] must aim [their legal analysis] at the lowest common denominator.'

C. Factual Authorities (Evidence)

Most academic and practical analysis of judicial and arbitral decision making focuses on legal authorities, providing little insight into the role that factual authorities (evidence) play in legal determinations.[123] However, as seen from the preceding paragraphs, judges and arbitrators routinely emphasize the central importance of facts to the commercial decision-making process.[124] Therefore, the interview protocol asked a series of questions about evidentiary matters, intentionally paralleling the inquiries made regarding legal authorities to allow for comparisons across the legal-evidentiary divide. Many of these matters were also addressed in the survey.[125]

1. Relative importance of evidence

The first question in this series asked respondents to identify the types of evidence (party-generated documents, third-party generated documents, testimony, etc.) they found most persuasive. Although this question tracked a similar question relating to legal authorities, the situation was slightly different because most jurisdictions do not have a formal hierarchy relating to the persuasiveness of evidence and issues relating to the comparative persuasiveness of evidence are seldom discussed in the legal literature or in legal education.[126] The situation is exacerbated by the fact that many civil law jurisdictions do not have formal rules of evidence, let alone hierarchies of persuasiveness.[127]

These factors suggest that the concept of priority and persuasiveness in evidentiary matters would be much more open to individual interpretation than priority and

[123] Ch. 1.III.A.

[124] Ch. 3.B.

[125] Ch. 2.IV.B.

[126] While many common law jurisdictions offer law students coursework covering the formal rules of evidence, those classes tend to focus on admissibility rather than persuasiveness.

[127] Frederick Schauer, 'On the Supposed Jury-Dependence of Evidence Law', (2006) 155 U Penn L Rev 165, 174. Arbitration also does not typically require adherence to formal rules of evidence, even in common law jurisdictions.

persuasiveness in legal matters. However, as the following paragraphs suggest, variation between interviewees, particularly between those acting as judges and those acting as arbitrators, is not as significant as one might expect.

For example, when asked to identify the type of evidence that they found most persuasive, several respondents immediately pointed to the governing contract. Interviewee 15, a common law domestic judge–arbitrator, said that 'in a contract dispute, the contract is controlling. Written documents are more important than parole evidence. If the contract is not ambiguous, that's the end of the matter. Only if the contract is ambiguous do I need to look at collateral documents.' Interviewee 9, a common law domestic judge, similarly stated that it 'depends on the case. If it's a contract dispute, their contract will mean the world—we'll have almost no case law in dispute. It all depends on the commercial context.'

Once the discussion moves past the importance of the governing contract, the standard assumption, based on scholarly commentary, is that common law lawyers will be more persuaded by oral testimony, while civil law lawyers are expected to be more persuaded by documents.[128] Lawyers involved in international commercial arbitration are said to exist somewhere in the middle of the two traditions as a result of the purposive blending of common law and civil law procedures in international arbitration.[129]

As it turns out, there is a distinction between those who prefer testamentary evidence and those who prefer documentary evidence, but the split does not appear to occur over the common law–civil law divide. Instead, the issue appears to be much more a matter of personal preference.

While this phenomenon could be affected by the fact that the civil law representatives in this study tended to be internationalists rather than pure domestic experts, conclusions about the individualized nature of evidentiary hierarchies are supported by the fact that several respondents from the common law tradition indicated that they relied more on documents rather than testimony,[130] particularly when the documents were created at the time the dispute arose.[131] Thus, Interviewee 1, a mixed international–domestic arbitrator from the common law tradition, said that, 'where applicable, documents are more persuasive than oral testimony to prove something. Oral testimony is helpful if it is an admission against interest. No view [distinction] between party and third-party documents—varies by situation.'

Interviewee 5, a common law domestic judge–arbitrator, adopted an analogous approach, stating,

[128] Ch. 1.III.C.

[129] Ch. 1.III.C.

[130] Interviewee 10, a domestic common law arbitrator ('Documents.'); Interviewee 11, a common law domestic judge–arbitrator ('Documents and testimony.'); Interviewee 12, a common law domestic judge–arbitrator ('Documents that are critical elements of their proof, whether they be documents in writing [or] occasionally demonstrative or photographic. Voluminous documents where the arbitrator's attention has been focused on the relevant portion.').

[131] Interviewee 14, an international judge–arbitrator from the common law tradition ('We are taught the most reliable evidence are contemporaneous documents rather than ex post facto evidence.'); Interviewee 19, an international arbitrator from the common law tradition ('Contemporaneous documents.').

> I guess the core contract documents of course are persuasive or important. I also have found more and more evidence (a large percentage) are emails because those are contemporaneous and are therefore persuasive.
>
> I listen to testimony from a credibility standpoint, but witnesses are well-prepared before hearings. Letters, emails, texts are all contemporaneous and therefore important.

Interviewee 2, an international arbitrator from the common law tradition, offered a similar view, stating,

> It all depends on the case. Contemporaneous evidence is more compelling than after-the-fact evidence created with an eye toward litigation. Of course, there are cases where the spin is going on in contemporaneous documents as well.
>
> Sometimes you have no documents on an issue—then witness recollection is key.
>
> I have problems with over-lawyered witness statements.[132] When the witness is on the stand, there's a great deal of variation, so witness examination is an important part of any case if the case turns on witness recollection. As a result, I'm troubled by excusing of witnesses on cross-examination, since it does a disservice to the tribunal, who can't decide credibility issues. I therefore like live testimony, although not necessarily live direct.

Interviewee 8, an international judge–arbitrator with a common law background, stated that

> it's always true that actual documentation which is contemporaneous with events that are at the core of the dispute are the most persuasive. This includes contemporaneous notes, because what people do and say at the time something happens is most persuasive.
>
> Beyond that, live testimony tested by cross-examination of witnesses in the hearing so that you can develop your own impression of their credibility (meaning fact not expert witnesses).
>
> I do not subscribe to the civil law view that any individual who participated in the events in issue (for example, an employee or a director) are to be given no credence whatsoever. I have had civil law-trained lawyers say more than once that 'I don't believe witnesses because they're lying'. I asked a colleague why he rejected testimony, and he said that we'd never ask a person to choose between the truth and his/her employer.

Contrary to Interviewee 8's experience, some civil law-trained respondents did not reflect a preference for documentary evidence. For example, Interviewee 18, an

[132] In international commercial arbitration, it is increasingly common for individuals to provide their affirmative testimony through a written witness statement. The witness is then subject to live cross-examination. International Bar Association, IBA Rules on the Taking of Evidence in International Arbitration (2010) art 4, <https://www.ibanet.org/Publications/publications_IBA_guides_and_free_materials.aspx> accessed 11 April 2020.

international judge–arbitrator with a civilian background, indicated that 'it's hard to identify a distinct hierarchy. Witnesses can be useful because they give flavour of the time frame that's important. Correspondence can be useful, though, because it can show how a dispute has arisen.'

Other respondents from the civil law tradition indicated a respect for documentary evidence, but not to the exclusion of testamentary evidence. For example, Interviewee 3, an international arbitrator with a civil law background, said the persuasiveness of evidence

> depends on the case. Some cases can be decided only on the documents. In most cases, documents are most persuasive, since they are drafted in non-suspect circumstances. Normally documents are the best evidence.
>
> For testimony—it depends on the witness. There are different types of witnesses. Some are very open and very good. Others are reticent and don't want to answer, and then you have the witnesses who lie. Witness statements are very important, especially if all parties agree or there is a statement by a witness against their own interest.

Interviewee 17, an international judge–arbitrator from the civil law tradition, similarly said that

> I am persuaded more by fact-contemporaneous documents that can be entered by parties or third parties. Testimony maybe less. However, I find oral and written testimony (especially oral) often very helpful because it gives colour to what was until then grey. I often understand much better what has happened by listening to witnesses. I don't always understand the underlying issues, and oral testimony allows that.

Interviewee 20, a mixed international–domestic arbitrator with civil law training, described the rationales underlying his/her approach, noting a preference

> normally [for] contemporary documents—they best speak to what happened at the time. Then witnesses could be second, but the problem there is that lots of study on the psychology of witnesses shows that their recollection is often not correct (false memories, etc.), which is why contemporaneous documents are better.

Interviewee 13, a common law domestic judge–arbitrator, also indicated that

> credibility is key. One tip I've learned is that I have developed a sixth sense on what a witness is really testifying to.[133] For example, a case where every time a witness was asked about an event, he said, 'Can you repeat that?'—that happened ten times. That's

[133] Notably, individuals often overestimate the extent to which they can tell whether another person is lying. Eitan Elaad, 'Effects of Feedback on the Overestimated Capacity to Detect Lies and the Underestimated Capacity to Tell Lies', (2003) 17 Applied Cognitive Psych 349.

> an example of less credibility than someone who answered easily—this was someone who wanted to gain time.

Some respondents were unable to provide a general rule of practice.[134] For example, Interviewee 4, a mixed international–domestic arbitrator, said,

> I don't know if there's any single type. I am relatively open to all sorts of evidence, but I am a common law-trained trial lawyer with many years working under the rules of evidence, so if there is documentary evidence that has not had a foundation established and if it contains multiple layers of hearsay that has not been corroborated or authenticated elsewhere, it is often less significant for me.
>
> I believe in the value of cross examination, so I find live testimony very valuable in all ways. However, I believe I do not overweigh any type of evidence, including expert testimony. I think I'm reasonably open and reasonably cynical about different types of evidence.

Interviewee 6, a mixed international–domestic arbitrator from a common law background, followed a similar hierarchy, preferring 'testimony first—usually fact testimony; documents follow; expert testimony (I have a lot of those) third most important'. Interviewee 7, an international arbitrator, said it

> depends on context. I have had cases where testimony decided the matter—for example, a witness contradicted himself and showed that one side's case was hopeless. I've had other cases where a letter has been produced and showed one side was acting not in good faith. An expert sometimes will be helpful, but mostly on damages.

Those individuals who did not explain their methodology in their initial answers were asked to explain the motivation for their particular approach in a follow-up question. The responses were consistent with those indicated above. For example, numerous respondents were concerned about fabrication of testimony after the dispute arose. Interviewee 1, a mixed international–domestic arbitrator, indicated that 'contemporaneous documents are often not generated with litigation in mind (although they sometimes are). Oral testimony is always litigation-oriented and has a point of view. Often it has material omissions.' Interviewee 10, a common law domestic arbitrator, drew an analogy between judicial and arbitral procedure, saying, 'The documents I'm seeing are usually generated in the ordinary course of business—the parties are not in CYA [cover your ass] mode. Just as those items have more power in litigation, they have more power here.'

Those with judicial experience enunciated similar views. For example, Interviewee 5, a common law domestic judge–arbitrator, said contemporaneous documents were

[134] Interviewee 16, an international judge–arbitrator ('In one case, it may be a letter; in another case, you need 10 witness statements. It depends on the case.').

persuasive 'because those documents reflect the thinking of the person at the time they were written, not six months or a year later'. Interviewee 8, an international judge–arbitrator, believed 'documents created at the time of events, when generally speaking the dispute has not yet crystallized and we are not in litigation, are more persuasive'.

Some respondents prioritized testimony over documents. For example, Interviewee 6, a mixed international–domestic arbitrator, said that 'the percipient witness and their credibility is important to relevant facts. Documents don't always speak for themselves. They're secondary because they're only helpful with testimony, [which] can put documents in context.' Interviewee 6 indicated that s/he did not give much value to expert testimony in particular because 'people don't know how to use [experts] in arbitration. They're usually there as third attorneys, not to answer questions.'

Interviewee 12, a common law domestic judge–arbitrator, had an interesting response, saying that s/he was 'quite broad in what I allow in. For example, I say I'll admit a phone book if they want to submit it so that no one feels I haven't taken it in and considered it, even if I don't think it's worth considering.'

2. Method of reviewing evidence

The next series of questions focused on how judges and arbitrators reviewed the evidence submitted to them. These questions were in many ways similar to those relating to legal authorities and to questions included in the survey.[135]

a. Law clerks and assistants

Although earlier questions revealed that very few respondents actually used a law clerk or assistant,[136] the interview protocol (which was established prior to the first interview and standardized so as to comply with best practices in social science research) included a question asking the interviewee to indicate what percentage of the evidentiary documents submitted by the parties were read by the respondent's law clerk or assistant in whole or in part. Of the 20 interviewees, four indicated that they used law clerks or assistants to review evidentiary materials.

Interestingly, these four interviewees relied significantly, if not exclusively, on the evidentiary reviews conducted by their law clerks or assistants. For example, Interviewee 11, a common law domestic judge–arbitrator, indicated that, 'as a judge—my clerk read. I didn't read very many' documents, while Interviewee 15, a common law domestic judge–arbitrator, said that, 'as a judge, [I read] only key documents'. Similar techniques were used by Interviewee 8, an international judge–arbitrator from the common law tradition, who said, 'My clerk reads everything that comes in,' and Interviewee 17, an international judge–arbitrator from the civil law tradition, who indicated that '[t]he assistant looks at everything. What I look at depends on the case.'

Interestingly, all four respondents worked as judges, either in common law or civil law jurisdictions, which could suggest that arbitrators are more 'hands-on'

[135] Chs. 2.IV.B, 3.III.B.2.

[136] Ch. 3.III.B.2.a.

than judges with respect to evidence in commercial disputes. While one of the four respondents—Interviewee 15—justified having his/her clerk read the bulk of the evidentiary documents because 'I was inundated with documents', it appears unlikely that Interviewee 15 received more documents than some arbitrators, particularly those involved in international matters, who routinely receive thousands, if not tens of thousands, of pages of documents from the parties.[137]

Those respondents who used a law clerk or assistant were then asked how they communicated with those individuals. This issue was also addressed in connection with independent legal research.[138]

Interviewee 8, an international judge–arbitrator, indicated that his/her law clerk or assistant prepared 'a bench memo [that] is comprehensive in laying out the issues and evidence supporting each contention on the law and facts and gives me the complete picture'. Interviewee 8 went on to say that s/he nevertheless ended up reading a number of evidentiary documents: 'which ones will be clear from the bench memo, which will identify which are the most critical ones. I'll read those before the hearing.' While this technique does ensure that the judge–arbitrator eventually reads the evidence submitted by the parties, it gives a great deal of power to the law clerk or assistant.

b. Judges and arbitrators

The next series of questions asked interviewees to estimate how many of the documents submitted by the parties the respondent personally read in whole or in part. This issue was also addressed in the survey.[139]

Very few respondents indicated that they read all of the documents in their entirety,[140] and those that did usually worked in areas where relatively few materials were submitted to the decision maker. For example, Interviewee 10, a common law domestic arbitrator, said that s/he read all of the evidentiary submissions in whole, but noted that s/he 'rarely see more than 500 pages in my disputes'. Interviewee 13, a common law domestic judge–arbitrator, also reported reading all the evidentiary submissions, which would range 'for insurance cases, 25 from each party. Franchise cases—25 to 30 from the franchisor, less than 20 from the franchisee. Construction—I'm deluged—no less than 50 exhibits, many blueprints.'

Other respondents described very different evidentiary norms and practices. For example, Interviewee 18, an international judge–arbitrator, noted that

> I just received today some dozen of binders, and I doubt there will be many relevant documents. There are approximately 200 to 300 pages per binder, and I doubt that the parties expect me to read 12,000 pages—it would be far too costly to do that. The

[137] Ch. 3.III.C.2.b (noting thousands of pages of documents submitted to arbitrators).
[138] Ch. 3.III.B.4.
[139] Table 2.19.
[140] Interviewee 15, a common law domestic judge–arbitrator ('Do not know—expect not 100 per cent.'); Interviewee 19, an international arbitrator ('I read 50 to 100 per cent.').

> parties submit too many documents—that's a general problem in arbitration. Parties don't take the risk to limit themselves to the relevant documents.

Some respondents used different techniques, depending on the nature of the dispute. For example, Interviewee 1, a mixed international–domestic arbitrator, said his/her approach 'varies from case to case. When I have 200 or fewer documents, I will review most at least in part. When I have hundreds and hundreds, I'm less likely to read in part or in whole.'

Interviewee 4, a mixed international–domestic arbitrator, also noted that his/her approach

> varies massively. In some cases, parties agree to present bundles and bundles and bundles of documents,[141] and it's a disservice to the parties if I take the time to read them all. Other parties are far more directed in their presentation, and when I see that, I'm more likely to read all the documents. It's also not just quantity—there's also discretion in choosing which documents to review.

Interviewee 7, an international arbitrator, had a similar response, noting that s/he 'can't say there's an absolute rule'. For example,

> some matters have a small number of documents where I read everything. However, I had one case where the insured wanted [certain] costs to be paid by the insurer. The insurer made the shocking argument that as part of the costs, the workers had been given too much in lunch reimbursements, so they submitted thousands of lunch receipts. This was evidence, and we should read it, but we're not going through thousands of lunch receipts. Instead, the tribunal appointed an expert to give a report on the amount of lunch that was ordered and the amount that was appropriate.

Interviewee 11, a common law domestic judge–arbitrator who had his/her law clerk or assistant read the bulk of the documents when acting as a judge, said that when s/he was working as an arbitrator,

> I read the core documents. About 15 per cent. Notably, juries do the same thing—when you send in documents, there are a couple of documents that you can tell have been read (crumpled, etc.) and others have not. The reason lawyers introduce all documents is to establish a record. They know no one will read them—it's so they can argue that it's part of the record. That's technically true even if the documents are not considered.

[141] In some domestic litigations and in international arbitration, the term 'bundle' refers to the documentary submissions. In some cases, parties will submit a smaller selection of key documents known as the 'trial bundle' (occasionally referred to as the 'core bundle') that is to be used during the hearing.

Interviewee 17, an international judge–arbitrator, similarly noted,

> Expert attachments are sometimes huge, and there's just one sentence that's helpful, so it's hard to answer. Parties file a lot of documents to be there, but no one expects you to read them all. In my procedural order, parties must refer expressly to documents in written pleadings—they must say the exhibits on which they rely and those I should read.

Other respondents noted that their practice depended on the strategy adopted by counsel, particularly whether and to what extent the document is discussed bwa the parties.[142] For example, Interviewee 2, an international arbitrator, indicated,

> It is hard to say. It depends if [the attorneys] give all the documents to the tribunal or only those relating to materially contested issues. I will read in full the materials on contested issues. That's why a narrow fact section in the award only relating to contested issues is helpful, because it focuses your reading.
>
> It's ultimately a judgment call. If it's key, you read it in full. You have to triage the documents.

Interviewee 12, a common law domestic judge–arbitrator, similarly said that it 'depends on length. If the phone book comes in, I don't read it all. If it's a 50-page document and parties only cite one page, I read the page they've cited and I don't read the rest.' Interviewee 14, an international judge–arbitrator, similarly noted that s/he followed the lead of counsel, stating that

> we don't read all the documents in the trial bundle. If there's a core bundle, we might read all, but we will read all that the parties refer to. Counsel introduce a wide range of documents for safety, and there's no rule on how to enter documents. If there's a contract, you must give the entire document, not single pages. The Court of Appeal [in one nation] admits just single pages now.[143]
>
> In [another national court], before trial they give me (the judge) a reading list and counsel tells the judge how much time to spend reading. Counsel must also give a draft order; before you get the draft, there's lots of waffling.

Interviewee 9, a common law domestic judge, adopted a similar approach, noting that s/he read

> a very small percentage [of materials] because you may get a 100-page document, but only one to two pages are really in dispute. A great lawyer makes it so that I don't have

142 Interviewee 16, an international judge–arbitrator ('I look at 100 per cent of the documents, but read about 60 per cent in whole. For example, a corporate report, I may look at numbers but won't read the report in whole unless the parties call it to my attention.').

143 Common law jurisdictions typically embrace what is called the 'rule of completeness', which means that if a single page of a document is entered into evidence, the other side is entitled to call for the entire document to be entered into evidence so that the record is complete. The court that Interviewee 14 is referring to has obviously adapted that rule to minimize the number of pages of submitted to judges.

> to read the entire document—he or she gives me the pages. If you make me read the whole document, you're not being an effective advocate.

Interviewee 20, a mixed international–domestic arbitrator from the civil law tradition, also adopted this methodology, saying,

> The parties normally submit thousands of documents, but in the pleadings, they identify a percentage of key documents. I read all of those because it's necessary to read documents that parties invoke in other documents.
>
> As for percentages, it depends on the pleadings—maybe 30 per cent. It's impossible to read every single paper. If you get a hearing bundle, that's very helpful. It's very rare that I've been surprised by documents in the hearing that I've not seen before.

Other civil law international arbitrators took a similar approach. Thus, Interviewee 3, an international arbitrator with civilian training, noted that 'sometimes, I receive 250 binders of documents, and not all are important. The hearing bundle may be two binders of documents—you read what is most important.' Interviewee 3 went on to indicate that 'I do all of the review—my clerk does not. I [also] read all the witness statements.'

Several respondents emphasized how their own individual methodology affected their approach to evidence. For example, Interviewee 5, a common law domestic judge–arbitrator, said,

> I read 100 per cent [of the documents] in whole or in part. I try to hone in on key documents. Often, I have three to four volumes of exhibits. Those that are referred to and admitted are the most important. If the document is not dealt with or referred to, then I may not look at it in detail.
>
> I'm old school—I require hard copies so that I can write on those documents at the time of testimony. Hearings are more efficient if they're digitalized, but I like hard copies.

Interviewee 6, a mixed international–domestic arbitrator, said, 'First, I keep track of exhibits in the hearing and will re-read the important ones. I will not read every document parties want to put in evidence.'

Perhaps the most important issue relating to evidence involves how judges and arbitrators identify which documents they should read. As the preceding paragraphs suggest, many respondents focused on materials that had been discussed by counsel in written submissions or during the hearing or that were contained in trial bundles. This approach was confirmed through a follow-up question to those respondents who had not outlined a specific methodology when discussing the percentage of evidentiary documents they read.

In response to this follow-up question, Interviewee 6, a mixed international–domestic arbitrator, said that s/he decides to read a particular document because 'either counsel calls attention to it in briefing or uses it with a witness. But sometimes I look at the documents surrounding the document to flesh out/further contextualize' the analysis.

The notion of reading related documents was also mentioned by Interviewee 1, a mixed international–domestic arbitrator. S/he had 'no formula—I'll often just start going through [the documents] to see what's there', but 'often, I read documents appended to expert reports. Those are often valuable for more than what the expert says, since they're not culled for a specific purpose.' Interviewee 1 also said s/he 'will look at exhibits to which parties direct my attention' and 'will look at contemporaneous documents, so I ask parties to give documents in chronological order.'

Not all respondents thought it appropriate or necessary to look beyond the materials focused on by the parties. For example, Interviewee 12, a common law domestic judge–arbitrator, noted that 'I'm guided by the parties. It's not a question of which [documents] I read. I read for the reason it's submitted and won't go further if the opposing party doesn't take me further.' Interviewee 11, a common law domestic judge–arbitrator similarly indicated that 'I read the contract between the parties, documents supporting testimony and documents supporting the theory of the case.'

Nevertheless, many respondents used the parties' positions as a starting point.[144] For example, Interviewee 7, an international arbitrator, indicated that s/he always reads the documents 'that the parties focus on, for example, if there's a lot of cross-examination.' Interviewee 19, another international arbitrator, noted that

> I always read documents mentioned in the main text of the memorials. If they're in the footnotes or not mentioned at all, I usually don't, although I may read them after the hearing.
>
> In a recent case, I had 40 volumes (three-ring binders) of mostly invoices and purchase slips for a retail business. I'm not going to read all of those. I'm guided by the parties' relevance on those.

Other respondents relied on their experience in similar matters when deciding what to read. For example, Interviewee 16, an international judge–arbitrator, said that 'parties call attention to certain things or I know items are important through experience/understanding the case. Sometimes I have seen that type of document before.'

Those respondents who had not already identified a comprehensive methodology were then asked whether their decision to read a particular item was triggered by the type of document, the type of substantive dispute, the actions of parties or counsel, or something else. Interviewee 1, a mixed international–domestic arbitrator, said,

[144] Interviewee 4, a mixed international–domestic arbitrator ('The advocates' written submissions have a huge impact [on what I read] because I admire and recognize good advocacy, and when I'm presented with it (and I've seen a lot), I want to follow it. That's also true at hearings, whether oral presentations by argument or written submissions.'); Interviewee 9, a common law domestic judge ('Relevancy and advocacy.').

> All of these things are valid. I have no formula. Unusually, I look at financing associated with underlying transaction; I often look at those documents because they have information that litigation counsel often doesn't think about.
>
> I'll also read offering documents because litigation counsel often won't read or know about those. As a transactional lawyer, I will see things they don't. This may be idiosyncratic to me as a transactional lawyer.

Interviewee 6, a mixed international–domestic arbitrator, and Interviewee 11, a common law domestic judge–arbitrator, indicated that all of the elements listed in the question were important, while Interviewee 3, an international arbitrator, indicated that there was no difference between the different categories listed in the question. Interviewee 8, an international judge–arbitrator, indicated that his/her approach was 'the result of years of experience. Instinctively and by training I understand what are the principal documents.'

3. Time of reviewing evidence

The next question in this series involved the time at which the interviewees reviewed evidentiary materials: before, during, or after the hearing. This issue was also raised with respect to legal authorities.[145]

Responses varied, albeit with no apparent pattern relating to the interviewees' role as a judge or arbitrator, the type of dispute (domestic or international) or the individual's legal training (common law or civil law). For example, one group of respondents indicated that they reviewed the evidence before, during, and after the hearing, although the purpose or scope of review differed according to the stage of the proceedings.[146] Interviewee 2, an international arbitrator, said,

> I read at all three times—before, during, and after. I read most material items before the hearing so I can ask follow-up questions of witnesses. Of course, you won't know exactly what will be relevant. I read during the hearing if it becomes relevant, then re-read at the drafting stage.
>
> Previously I used hard copies of everything, tabbed. Now I'm trying to do it with electronic copies, but it's hard.

Interviewee 11, a common law domestic judge–arbitrator, noted that s/he read at all three times

> because you don't have all the documents before—you may have some based on the filings (claim, counterclaim, etc.). I read during when I'm presented with testimony

[145] Ch. 3.III.B.3.

[146] Interviewee 4, a mixed international–domestic arbitrator ('Yes to all three. There's no significant pattern. It depends on the case and the nature of advocacy. I may do all three in some cases.'); Interviewee 5, a common law domestic judge–arbitrator ('All three.'); Interviewee 7, an international arbitrator ('All three.'); Interviewee 9, a common law domestic judge ('All three.'); Interviewee 15, a common law domestic judge–arbitrator ('All of the above.'). Other respondents were a little less rigid in their approach, as exemplified by Interviewee 1, a mixed international–domestic arbitrator, who reviewed evidentiary materials 'before or during [the hearing]. I refer back in award drafting.'

and mark it to be read. Afterwards—the documents always have most meaning at this point because now you know what's been presented.

Interviewee 16, an international judge-arbitrator, adopted a similar approach, noting that 'during the hearing I look at the documents that are shown to the witness, but I leaf through the documents before and certainly after'. Interviewee 19, another international arbitrator, indicated that s/he reviewed the evidence not only before the hearing, but also during the hearing, although the latter review was not limited to 'the documents the parties use in the hearing. I am often prompted to go look at other documents. After [the hearing], I always re-read [a document] if the reference is going into the award.' Interviewee 10, a common law domestic arbitrator, followed the same pattern, noting that s/he read the documents 'before—always. During—because part of oral testimony. After—only if I need to take another look.' Interviewee 17, an international judge-arbitrator, indicated that s/he reviewed the evidence

before [the hearing and] sometimes during because I didn't realize a document was important (meaning I read it at night or during the hearing). You also re-read during the drafting of an award, but you shouldn't discover the document then, otherwise you don't ask the right questions.

Other respondents focused their review on the time before and after the hearing. For example, Interviewee 3, an international arbitrator, said that before the hearing, s/he 'read all the witness statements and all the documents I think are important. If there are one hundred documents, I read them all. If there are three thousand documents, I read the most important. After [the hearing], I read additional documents that I now know are important.' Interviewee 14, an international judge-arbitrator, said that 'we read what the lawyers tell us to read in two phases—the opening submissions and post-hearing briefs'. Interviewee 13, a common law domestic judge-arbitrator, similarly indicated s/he read 'the ones submitted before—before. The hearing and post-submission documents and transcript—after'.

Interviewee 18, an international judge-arbitrator, explained his/her process in slightly more detail, indicating,

Before, I read submissions, and when I need clarification, I go to the fact documents, but I don't read them all beforehand—I only verify. Afterwards is the same—I only look at fact documents if they're really relevant.

One respondent—Interviewee 8, an international judge-arbitrator—discussed timing issues involving his/her law clerks or assistants, stating 'they read everything before the hearing, when they're doing the long bench memo, that I then study sufficiently early to have the best appreciation of the alleged facts'.

Only two respondents indicated that they did not begin their review until the hearing,[147] although this approach appeared somewhat out of step with general consensus. Indeed, as noted by Interviewee 20, a mixed international–domestic arbitrator who reviewed evidence 'always before' the hearing, 'there's nothing more irritating to the parties that an unprepared arbitrator'.

4. Weight of evidence

One of the least-discussed matters in the legal literature involves the weight judges and arbitrators give to different types of evidence, so the next question in this series specifically asked respondents to describe how they weighed evidence. Not surprisingly, a number of responses were similar to those generated in response to questions about the relative importance of different types of evidence.[148] For example, several individuals indicated that contemporaneous documents were the most compelling form of evidence. Interviewee 8, an international judge–arbitrator, stated,

> Contemporaneous documents/communications are the most persuasive, so I give them a good deal of deference, but it depends on how well-stated they are. Some are confusing or ambiguous or defy their own internal logic. Once people are in litigation, they might approach things with a different perspective. If the written witness statement or oral testimony seems strained vis-à-vis the contemporaneous documents, the witness will be cross-examined and, depending on how that goes, may be subjected to questions from me.

Interviewee 15, a common law domestic judge–arbitrator, indicated s/he gave 'greatest weight to the governing document', such as a contract. After that, the

> only question is ambiguity—then you must give weight to contemporaneous documents. Witnesses have an interest in the outcome. They're usually aligned with the parties, so I give them less weight. The same is true of experts—they're usually hired guns aligned with their client. Some experts are neutral, however. So, most weight to documents, then expert witnesses, then fact witnesses.

Another frequent response involved the concept of corroborating evidence. Interviewee 16, an international judge–arbitrator from the common law tradition, stated that in his/her approach,

> where evidence is concordant with something else in the file, it gets more weight. For example, if a witness statement is consistent with letters, that gives both the statement and the letters more weight.

[147] Interviewee 6, a mixed international–domestic arbitrator ('During and after.'); Interviewee 12, a common law domestic judge–arbitrator ('During the hearing.').

[148] Ch. 3.III.C.1.

> Testimony is more subjective. If it is live, we can have impressions of witness conduct and knowledge, but the same basic rule applies—is the live testimony consistent with witness statements and documents.

Interviewee 17, an international judge–arbitrator from the civil law tradition, similarly noted,

> There are witnesses whose testimony are corroborated by documents/testimony, [just as there are] also documents that are corroborated by other evidence. You look at the fuller picture. Some things don't fall into place—usually you place less emphasis on those. You rely on those [items] that give a consistent picture by looking at all the evidence.

Other respondents identified a more complex strategy. For example, Interviewee 6, a mixed international–domestic arbitrator, stated,

> For testimony of fact witnesses, it depends on how knowledgeable they are about what they're testifying about, how credible they are, whether the testimony is corroborated by contemporary documents.
>
> Regarding documents—I give weight depending on whether there is a witness corroborating.
>
> Regarding experts—[it depends on] how well acquainted they are with the facts of the case and with what needs to be proven, and how they answer questions. They're there to help me/the panel, so if they're dodging questions or not knowledgeable, I don't give them much weight.

Several individuals indicated that decisions relating to the weight of a particular piece of evidence was linked to the proposition the evidence was meant to support. Interviewee 13, a common law domestic judge–arbitrator, said,

> The weight is a function of the reason the item was submitted. If it is peripheral issue or an issue I don't think is definitive, I give it less weight. If an objection is made to an exhibit, I admit it for what it's worth, which means I'm giving it little weight. Rather than not admit it, I let it in and give it little weight.

Interviewee 5, another common law domestic judge–arbitrator, was slightly less rigorous in his/her methodology and said s/he assigned weight to different pieces of evidence

> partially based on the testimony, partially based on the type of dispute and whether it is a key or tangential document. I assign weight based on what I hear at the hearing. It also depends on the type of claims. If it's a contract case, that makes the contract more important.

Interviewee 12, a common law domestic judge–arbitrator, was unable to describe a particular practice, but identified a number of relevant features, including 'relevancy to the issue; whether it's cumulative or not; clarity of the point the document substantiates; certainty of authenticity. Some is based on how it's referred to/presented by the parties.'

A significant number of respondents struggled to answer the question, with some indicating an inability to provide an answer in the abstract.[149] Other individuals provided relatively simplistic or circular rationales.[150]

Other respondents merely referred to knowledge gained from experience. For example, Interviewee 4, a mixed international–domestic arbitrator, said,

> I don't know. I think it's the judgment of being a good lawyer and decision maker. It's like the chicken and the egg—you need a lot of years to be exposed to a lot of things to be able to bring that judgment to bear on a dispute. I have no formula and am trying to remain surprised in every case.

Interviewee 10, a common law domestic arbitrator, said,

> I think we have a natural filter based on our understanding of the inherent reliability of evidence. I monitor body language, fidgeting, etc. When you've been around the block, you get a read on people. I do leave room to adjust my expectations.

Interviewee 19, an international arbitrator, said,

> You just know. Contracts are the most important. Contemporaneous exchanges of documents, emails, notes by principle actors and witnesses are my greatest interest.

The difficulties faced by these respondents in enunciating their approach to evidence underscores the lack of standardization relating how evidence can or should be weighed. While some observers may take the view that such flexibility is a necessary part of the adjudicative process, social scientists have found that the absence

[149] Interviewee 1, a mixed international–domestic arbitrator ('I can't generalize.'); Interviewee 7, an international arbitrator ('Depends on what the conflict is. I had a case where the person said, "I can remember what the engineer told me because we were on a hill and he said X." On cross examination, he gave more details about the day, and later a letter showed the conversation was in February in Montana. No one would be on a hill in Montana in February. Normally I believe the witness, but if they're contradicted by a letter, then I believe the letter.'); Interviewee 18, an international judge–arbitrator ('Cannot say in the abstract. It depends. Some documents are so crucial and so glaring that you must pay attention to them. For example, I had an antitrust case—one email was so clearly showing the antitrust breach, you give great importance to the document.'); Interviewee 20, a mixed international–domestic arbitrator ('It's a case by case issue. Some documents are definitive. Some documents you must evaluate all together to provide strong evidence. It depends on the type, amount of documents and whether one or two documents will give the answer or if you need a group of documents that are persuasive. Sometimes one document makes the difference, but that's rare.').

[150] Interviewee 2, an international arbitrator from a common law background ('To be persuasive, evidence needs to be prepared by someone with knowledge.'); Interviewee 3, an international arbitrator from a civil law background ('Depends on the case. I base my decision on the evidence that is most convincing. Sometimes it's letters, sometimes cross-examination, sometimes witness statements, sometimes a mix.'); Interviewee 11, a common law domestic judge–arbitrator ('The practical answer—you give it [weight] to the evidence that supports or disputes the claim.').

of a formal methodology or objective criteria can create an environment where unconscious biases can flourish, which is of course problematic for both litigation and arbitration.[151]

5. Citation of evidence

The next inquiry in this series addressed citation of evidence, focusing not on formalistic considerations but instead on the substantive question of how judges and arbitrators decide which factual issues or evidence to discuss in a reasoned decision or award. A similar question was asked on the survey[152] and an analogous question was asked in the section involving legal authorities so as to allow comparisons across the legal-evidentiary divide.[153]

Not surprisingly, most respondents simply indicated that they discussed those factual issues that were raised by the parties. For example, Interviewee 2, an international arbitrator from a common law background, indicated that s/he included 'the ones that parties say I need to decide', while Interviewee 3, a civil law-trained international arbitrator, stated that 'I often ask parties to agree on a list of issues. If they can't, then they separately identify issues, and I compile a list and submit it to the parties.'

This is not to say that respondents surrendered all responsibility for identifying the relevant factual issues. To the contrary, a number of individuals indicated that their opinions, combined with the views of the parties, were the deciding factor.[154]

For example, Interviewee 10, a common law domestic arbitrator, said that 'I usually don't decide that. The parties decide that, though it's affected by how I shepherd parties early on.' Interviewee 20, a mixed international–domestic arbitrator with a civil law background, indicated that 'you get a list of parties' positions including what facts are relevant to the parties and then see if those are relevant to you. Then you see if those facts are proven and how.' Interviewee 8, an international judge–arbitrator, stated that 'that decision is essentially made for one by the state of the record. It's a question in part of on what facts the decision turns and what evidence you accept or reject.'

Some disparity arose with respect to the amount of respect given to the parties' formulation of the issues and evidence. For example, Interviewee 7, an international arbitrator, emphasized that 'one must discuss them [parties' contentions] in their entirety. You give more emphasis to issues the parties argue, but you can't leave anything out'. On the other hand, Interviewee 15, a common law domestic judge–arbitrator, indicated that 'I have to decide which of many issues really need to be decided. Not all issues raised by the parties matter. They may talk for days, but that doesn't really affect the

[151] Guthrie, Rachlinski, and Wistrick (n 89) 40–41, 43 (noting usefulness of checklists and multifactor tests in overcoming unconscious biases).

[152] Ch. 2.IV.B.3.

[153] Ch. 3.III.B.5.

[154] Interviewee 6, a mixed international–domestic arbitrator ('Whether it's been raised by the parties; whether I believe it's important to the determination of the matter.').

outcome.' Interviewee 17, an international judge–arbitrator from the civil law tradition, took a slightly different view, stating,

> It's a function of the legal analysis: what are legal questions that must be answered to get to the result. It's also a function of the parties' submissions. If they present a lot, I will address more material even if I don't think it is important. I discuss it to make them feel that they've been heard, especially the losing party.[155]

Interviewee 12, a common law domestic judge–arbitrator, also addressed the role that parties' argument plays, noting that

> I usually start with the elements/burden of proof and usually am guided by the parties, although I am not confined by the parties. If I see something placed in evidence, if it might impact on the award, I may go outside the argument made if it's clear on the evidence that this is a point that might be determinative.

Other respondents also focused on the elements of the legal claims to be proven.[156] For example, Interviewee 1, a mixed international–domestic arbitrator, indicated that his/her decision on which facts or evidence to discuss turned on 'understanding the cause of action and deciding which facts are necessary to decide those elements.' Interviewee 4, another mixed international–domestic arbitrator, similarly stated,

> The answer flows from the syllogistic process, starting with the legal principle that I conclude is applicable on the authorities and the advocacy that is dispositive. Sometimes the evidence is relevant to one or two different issues, and sometimes it applies to several issues. Determining the relevant evidence is not a simple process, but it flows from the legal principles most likely to properly resolve the dispute.
>
> There are times when I thought a certain legal principle was determinative and I've been convinced by my colleagues on the panel that other legal principles were more important and I changed my mind. Just because I start with one principle and look at the facts relevant to that principle doesn't mean I won't go back and revisit the legal principle. I have more than once backed up to review and re-do my legal analysis. Sometimes I come to different conclusions about issues and sometimes I come to a different conclusion about the winner of the dispute, especially when I'm in a panel.

[155] The notion of making sure that the parties, especially the losing party, feel heard was addressed in the survey. Tables 2.15, 2.23, 2.28.

[156] Interviewee 5, a common law domestic judge–arbitrator ('It's based on the type of case. I base my analysis on the testimony of the witness and the issues in the case.'); Interviewee 9, a common law domestic judge ('Usually it is in the moving parties' brief. Goes back to IRAC—we deal with issues people bring to us. If the parties have three issues, then we'll have three issues in the rule of law section [and thus must deal with those issues in the factual analysis].'); Interviewee 11, a common law domestic judge–arbitrator ('Ones that particularly support the claims or disputes the claim.'); Interviewee 13, a common law domestic judge–arbitrator ('What is the issue? I look at the central issue of the case—the facts (documents or testimony) that bear on that core issue, then I include it.').

Interviewee 14, an international judge–arbitrator, also discussed how panel deliberation affects the review and citation of factual material, stating,

> In a three-person tribunal, very often this is the subject of internal discussions. Everyone pitches in and thinks about what are the most important issues. You have a decision tree and think, 'here's where we are, there's where we want to go—what evidence do you need to build to the end'.

Some respondents focused on the concept of relevancy. For example, Interviewee 16, an international judge–arbitrator, said that s/he cited to 'the items that are most telling and revelatory and that give the best and most reasonable explanation of the events'. Interviewee 18, another international judge–arbitrator, indicated that s/he included particular pieces of evidence 'when they are relevant. For example, the parties could seek to create an atmosphere by depicting their previous history, but this has nothing to do with the dispute, so I don't mention that.'

Several responses suggested that the evidence that is the most relevant is the material that has been discussed the most. Thus, Interviewee 19, an international arbitrator, said the factual materials that are discussed in the reasoned decision or award

> identify themselves to me—they emerge from the pack as being the most important. Gerry Aksen used to say, 'I want you to give me the notebook you have that you put under your pillow at night—the key documents, not just the trial bundle', and I've yet to see a case that has more than one binder of key evidence.
>
> Recently, I have started asking counsel to try not to create different witness documents but to give us the same documents in a single bundle so that I have one copy of the contract, one copy of the famous letter of X and the response of Y. I then use colour stickers, a different colour for the claimant and respondent, and tag the documents every time they're used. At the end, I can see which documents have been discussed. Some never have been.

Those respondents who did not discuss the rationales motivating their citation practice were then asked a follow-up question focusing on why they include those particular references in their reasoned decisions or awards. Several individuals adopted what might be called a structural approach, claiming that factual analysis was a necessary element of the legal reasoning process.[157] As Interviewee 5, a common law domestic judge–arbitrator, said, 'It's necessary to apply the law to the facts, and if you don't mention the facts and your interpretation of the law to the facts, you've not described your thinking to the parties'. Interviewee 13, another common law domestic judge–arbitrator,

[157] Interviewee 8, an international judge–arbitrator ('They're required for a reasoned award.'); Interviewee 10, a common law domestic arbitrator ('I can't conceive of a way you do not do that.'); Interviewee 11, a common law domestic arbitrator ('Because they're the basis for your award.'). This rationale was discussed in the survey. Table 2.28.

similarly indicated that 'the facts drive the award. It depends on the theory of the case but depends greatly on testimony.'

Similar views were expressed by respondents from the civil law tradition. For example, Interviewee 3, an international arbitrator with civilian training, noted that evidence was vital to a reasoned decision or award 'because you must reason your decision on the facts'. Interviewee 20, a mixed international–domestic arbitrator with a civil law background, indicated that s/he included citations to the evidence 'because parties need to understand what the tribunal thought was relevant and proven or not proven'.

Other respondents hearkened back to the need for parties to understand the reasons driving the outcome. Thus, Interviewee 12, a common law domestic judge–arbitrator, noted that 'fact citations anchor the logic of my award. I seek for parties to understand my reasoning, and when you anchor [your discussion] to evidence, they see the award is based on evidence they've provided.' Interviewee 16, an international judge–arbitrator, said that

> I think it gives more weight to the award and explains how I came to my conclusion. In contrast, in sports [arbitration] cases, they don't want that—I had too many references to exhibits. They said to never refer to evidentiary documents (unlike legal authority, which they like).
>
> I think my way is the right way and shows the rigor of your analysis. If you're basing your decision on that document or testimony, you should say so.

Finally, some individuals included factual citations as a means of checking their own reasoning processes. For example, Interviewee 19, an international arbitrator, noted that 'for a while, I stopped using references, I just said "the December 10 letter" not "Exhibit X", but now I do because it's a discipline to me to re-read the documents, and parties know that I meant that particular letter'.

6. Advice from judges and arbitrators to counsel regarding evidence

The last question in this series asked respondents to identify what they wished parties and counsel knew about how judges and arbitrators approach evidentiary issues. While Interviewee 3, an international arbitrator, believed that 'they know—the work of an arbitrator is no different than the work of counsel—they know what's important in terms of law, evidence, etc.', most respondents had one or more suggestions to make. Indeed, Interviewee 8, an international judge–arbitrator, specifically stated that 'for their own benefit or the benefit of their clients, lawyers should really know on some basis about how arbitrators approach issues'.

Interviewee 1, a mixed international–domestic arbitrator, identified three issues that were echoed by other respondents, stating, 'One—they [parties and counsel] should focus only on material disputes of facts. Two—repetitive evidence loses its value. Three—hyperbole and exaggeration undercut what counsel is trying to do. Note these three items also apply to oral arguments.' Interviewee 13, a common law domestic judge–arbitrator, similarly noted that 'I wish they knew it's important, and an incredible witness demeans the argument of the party and it's better that person not be called—it does irreparable harm. Same with incredible documents.'

Other respondents underscored the problem of excessive materials.[158] For example, Interviewee 2, an international arbitrator, noted that counsel and advocates should

> recognize reality. An arbitrator cannot read and remember 20,000 documents; triage is necessary. Responsible arbitrators will want to reassure themselves [that] the documents say what counsel says they say. So, make those two tasks easier; give a core bundle or a post-hearing brief. Tell the arbitrators what to focus on. There will be disagreement, but it helps the arbitrators. Tell them what to read and organize the materials in a user-friendly fashion.

Interviewee 15, a common law domestic judge–arbitrator, similarly remarked that

> I wish they would not put in the amounts of documents that they do. Throwing the kitchen sink in just makes it harder to get the right outcome. Cluttering the record is disturbing. If they knew what we do, maybe they'd do things differently.
>
> In arbitration, counsel often know [what decision makers do] because they also sit as arbitrators. Lawyers in court have never been judges.

Interviewee 17, an international judge–arbitrator, noted that

> sometimes I feel I'm flooded with lots of facts and there's no proper articulation of relevant material. It's all on the same level, and there are facts that I can disregard to apply the relevant rule of law. Parties should be more selective and more courageous in selecting and presenting materials. Sometimes I have to go look for facts because they're not presented. So be selective—don't present too many things.

Although most respondents focused on problems associated with presenting too much information, Interviewee 6, a mixed international–domestic arbitrator, noted that s/he 'wish[ed] [counsel] knew that simply checking a box (for example, saying this witness will testify to this) may not be enough. How good someone's memory is, how much detail they have, how credible they are—that's more important' when considering evidentiary issues.

Other respondents recognized the paradox involved in presenting evidence. As Interviewee 7, an international arbitrator, noted,

> It would be helpful if parties knew that although I will look at all issues, I will focus on the main issues. But they can't know what those main issues are, of course. For

[158] Interviewee 19, an international arbitrator ('I would like parties to ID [identify] the most important documents separately even if they include the rest.').

> example, they may argue point two as an alternative in case I don't decide for them on point one, but I can't tell them to stop arguing point two because I have decided point one in their favour.

Not everyone takes that type of hands-off approach. For example, Interviewee 18, an international judge–arbitrator, indicated that 'if a party insists on discussing things that aren't relevant, I will tell them not to waste their time'. Interestingly, the different approaches identified by Interviewee 7 (a common law lawyer) and Interviewee 18 (a civil law lawyer) appear to mirror standard assumptions about the nature of common law litigation (where the parties are in control of the process), as compared to civil law litigation (where the judge takes a leading role in developing the case).[159] However, this distinction did not appear to be borne out by other interviewees responding to this question and may merely reflect individual preferences. Indeed, later in the interview process, Interviewee 7 indicated that s/he adopted certain techniques that are often considered more typical of the civil law tradition than the common law tradition.[160]

This is not to say that differences between common law and civil law judges and arbitrators do not exist. For example, Interviewee 4, a mixed international–domestic arbitrator, was of the view that

> different arbitrators definitely approach fact issues *very* differently. For example, many common law lawyers are not capable or interested in taking any approach to the hearing of evidence other than through live testimony. Some civil law lawyers take the opposite approach. Oral testimony is wasted on them. However, there are many arbitrators who try to use the best of both worlds. I've not sat on an exclusively civil law panel since I am a common law lawyer, but I have sat as the sole common law lawyer on a panel.
>
> My domestic experience involved exclusively common law panels. During those years, the skills were not that different in terms of how to present to a judge/jury versus an arbitrator. Even if the evidentiary rules didn't technically apply, the advocates still needed to ask good questions to get good testimony and use prior documents and testimony to challenge various witnesses.
>
> I now hear complaints about US lawyers trying cases as if to a jury. I think that jurors are human, as are arbitrators, so I don't have a problem with that. Hopefully, the advocates use clear, simple language and ask good questions and use documents to support their evidence. Those should be transferable skills.

However, Interviewee 4 him/herself adopted certain civil law methodologies in appropriate cases, demonstrating the flexibility associated with internationally minded arbitrators.[161] Interviewee 5, a common law domestic judge–arbitrator, also indicated in

[159] Javier H Rubinstein, 'International Commercial Arbitration: Reflections at the Crossroads of the Common Law and Civil Law Traditions', (2004) 5 Chi J Intl L 303, 308; Ch. 1.III.C.

[160] Ch. 3.III.D.

[161] Ch. 3.III.D (noting that s/he asked questions of counsel in construction cases).

response to a later question that s/he adopted what might be called civil law techniques in domestic arbitration, suggesting that the common law–civil law distinction is perhaps not as robust as it once was.[162]

Notably, not every common law respondent supported the incorporation of common law trial techniques in arbitration. For example, Interviewee 14, an international judge–arbitrator from a common law background, noted,

> For me, I do not think there's much value in cross-examination. People ask too many questions that don't get them anywhere. Commercial arbitration is different than litigation. Cross-examination has less of a role in international commercial arbitration because most matters are decided on the papers. Most matters of the size we have leave a paper trail, and testimony adds little. Lots of people waste time. The documents say what they say. It's the exceptional case where you can deny your own words.

Interviewee 10, a common law domestic arbitrator, suggested that counsel might adopt trial techniques because

> attorneys are largely uncomfortable with not having the certainty of court rules. If they're insecure, they make their parties insecure, so I get levels of anxiety from witnesses that I would not expect to see in court. They think they know how to act in court but not in arbitration, and attorneys don't help. We need a 'Law and Order—Arbitration'.

Several respondents provided tangible tips to counsel. For example, Interviewee 11, a common law domestic judge–arbitrator, indicated that 'I wish they'd put down the elements and the evidence in a document, not for us but for themselves. A lot of testimony and documents are not relevant. Sometimes the client wants it in, so they say it for emotional reasons.' Interviewee 20, a mixed international–domestic arbitrator, said,

> Normally, arbitrators are influenced by how parties frame the issues. I'd like parties to know the more concrete the facts are, the better. If they can provide a timeline, that's also very helpful.
>
> Often, I see loopholes or gaps in the pleadings. The parties should know that if they give a narrative with the timeline, that helps.

Another useful tip came from Interviewee 9, a common law domestic judge, who noted that arbitrators and 'judges want to get it right. We don't believe any personal animosity will make it right. Insulting the opposing lawyer is bad advocacy. When you're being uncivil, I believe you're telling me the law and facts are not on your side and that's all you

[162] Ch. 3.III.D.

have—incivility'. Similarly, Interviewee 12, a common law domestic judge–arbitrator, said that counsel should know 'that we approach them with fairness, neutrality and without bias and seek their guidance as to relevancy and weight that should be given to evidence'. Finally, Interviewee 16, an international judge–arbitrator, noted that counsel should remember 'that we're not stupid. Just lay the evidence out clearly, including the awkward stuff'.

D. The Reasoning Process

Although legal and evidentiary issues are part of the legal reasoning process, the next set of questions focused specifically on judicial and arbitral reasoning per se. Notably, the interview protocol made a clear distinction between the reasoning process and writing the decision or award, which was covered later in the interview.[163] Questions about the reasoning process focused not only on the respondent's standard practices but also on differences that might arise as a result of different functions that the respondent might carry out. Many of the issues analysed here were also considered in the survey.[164]

1. The basic process

The first question in the series focused on how the respondent went about reasoning through a decision or award. Some individuals had no pre-established methodology that they routinely followed,[165] whereas other individuals took a relatively structured approach to the reasoning process. For example, Interviewee 2, an international arbitrator, said, 'You make your own outline of issues you need to decide—a decision-tree analysis—what are the core issues and what are the documents for those issues' and then go from there.

Other respondents varied their approach according to the nature of the dispute. For example, Interviewee 3, another international arbitrator, indicated that it

> depends on the complexity of the case. Some cases, even if they are big, are less complex, and after reading [the submissions] you have a feeling about the case. Then, at the hearing, you test your feelings against the arguments and you ask questions to test your feelings.
>
> In some complex cases, you may not have a global feeling. You work through the issues, and only at the end do you reach a conclusion.
>
> The best scenario is that you have a feeling and test that by asking questions during the hearing.

[163] Ch. 3.III.E.

[164] Ch. 2.IV.C.

[165] Interviewee 16, an international judge–arbitrator ('I don't have a set pattern that I'm aware of. I turn everything over in my mind, especially the issues that trouble me. Usually there are one to two major issues, and I go back to the documents and do some soul-searching. I have no checklist—it's a more ontological process.').

The concept of a 'gut feeling' was also enunciated by Interviewee 8, an international judge–arbitrator, who indicated that

> sometimes—probably a lot—by the time the hearing comes, by which time you're quite familiar with the case from written submissions, one has a sense of who legally is on the right side and should win. Sometimes you don't. Sometimes the legal issues are so novel that coming out of the hearing, you're in some degree of uncertainty. Then the deliberations among the tribunal will bring things into more focus, where your colleagues stand.
>
> Sometimes we have to ask parties for further submissions or bifurcate proceedings if liability is found but the evidence on damages is insufficient.

Interviewee 3 noted above that s/he began the reasoning process by testing certain assumptions during the hearing. Other respondents indicated that they adopted a similar process. For example, Interviewee 4, a mixed international–domestic arbitrator, said that

> I will often, when I have good quality advocates, assertively lay out the problems I have with their positions when we get to closing so that they can hear my thoughts and address them. That's not done by a lot of arbitrators, but it helps me greatly when I think I've put myself in an intellectual corner and a good advocate can bring me out.

Interviewee 5, a common law domestic judge–arbitrator, similarly stated,

> If I'm a sole arbitrator, I have read the authorities before the hearing, and I may not have any briefs yet but I have done some of my own research, I've forced the parties to hone the issues and exclude unsupported arguments. We go into the hearing focusing on what I want addressed. I'm an activist arbitrator and ask a lot of questions without taking over cross-examination. I will tell the parties what I want addressed in closing arguments or briefs. I prepare a draft of the award as soon after getting the legal authorities as possible (i.e. after closing or post-hearing briefs).

Interviewee 17, an international judge–arbitrator, also started the reasoning process early, noting,

> At the time when I'm preparing and during the hearing, I think about this. When I prepare to deliberate, I do a list of issues and look at what are the relevant elements (facts and law) that I need to understand to have my roadmap of my decision. I then do a roadmap of my decision that I share with my co-arbitrators.

Other respondents indicated that they begin the reasoning process from an evidentiary perspective by considering their hearing notes in tandem with the parties' submissions.[166] Thus, Interviewee 20, a mixed international–domestic arbitrator, said,

> I start with the facts. If my co-arbitrators and I have some understanding of the facts, then applying the law is easier. If you don't agree on the facts, it's harder.
>
> Then you go to the evidence—what are the consequences of this particular fact. Then you move to the legal reasoning—what are the consequences of that fact.

Other respondents indicated that their reasoning process begins during or before the hearing. For example, Interviewee 12, a common law domestic judge–arbitrator, said that

> I take copious notes, have notes with stars and signals—different coloured pens to highlight different things—and almost always ask for briefing from parties. [Then I] take my notes apart and make piles of different issues and place different testimony together in those piles. So, if there are two to three issues to be determined, I have piles then begin an outline of thoughts on different piles. I do this on paper, not on a computer. Then I form opinions on issues and see how they fit with burdens of proof.
>
> The majority of the time I have a good feeling on how it falls into place. Occasionally I change my mind because briefing affects how I see an issue or evidence. Not until I put pen to paper do I lock into what the award will do. I rely heavily on notes but sometimes briefing changes my mind.

Interviewee 13, a common law domestic judge–arbitrator, similarly stated that

> I make notes during the testimony of a witness and make margin notes determining what that testimony has to do with the issue at hand. Then I weigh the credibility of the witness. When I get the transcript, I measure it against my notes to consider if I decided correctly while in the hearing.

Other respondents focused on the law as the starting point of their analysis. For example, Interviewee 9, a common law domestic judge, said, 'We read briefs and try to make sure we know controlling law. We hope to narrow that down in oral argument, then write our opinion.'

Interviewee 14, an international judge–arbitrator, adopted a mixed approach, stating,

> I break down each side's core reasoning as to why they think the facts and law lead to their conclusion, then reduce that to skeleton proportions and see which is the most important. If A + B = C, do we believe all the elements of the arguments, or is it X + Y = Z?

[166] Interviewee 6, a mixed international–domestic arbitrator ('I start with arguments of parties and the legal framework if I've been given it, arguments of parties and facts—I look at all of that.'); Interviewee 11, a common law domestic judge–arbitrator ('Elements and facts/evidence that support those elements.').

2. Changes over time

Although parties in litigation have no opportunity to choose their judge, many in the commercial realm believe that experience is perhaps the single most important quality that an arbitrator should have, an attribute that has made it increasingly difficult for young arbitrators to obtain appointments.[167] However, this preference for experienced decision makers only makes sense if the performance of judges and arbitrators change and improve over time. In order to get to that issue, the next question in this series asked whether the respondent's approach to legal reasoning had changed over the course of that person's career.[168]

As it turned out, several individuals were not sure whether and to what extent their legal reasoning process had changed over time.[169] A significant number of respondents indicated that they believed their approach to legal reasoning had not changed during the course of their careers,[170] thereby suggesting that concerns about appointing more junior individuals as arbitrators may be misplaced. Those who indicated that their process had indeed evolved suggested that the changes were relatively minor. Indeed, most respondents who indicated a change in their approach to legal reasoning said that they had primarily become more confident. For example, Interviewee 17, an international judge–arbitrator, said, 'I have become more confident in my own assessment, which doesn't detract from vigorous legal analysis. [It's just that now] I trust my legal intuition.' Interviewee 19, an international arbitrator, said that 'I've gotten older and wiser now—I'm much more confident in zeroing in on key legal issues without needing to recite everything else. I'm more confident in finding my way through the maze.' Interviewee 10, a common law domestic arbitrator, said that 'I suppose it has, maybe because I am more willing to trust my mental landscape than at first, 20 years ago'.

Other changes were also relatively minor. For example, Interviewee 2, an international arbitrator, said that his/her approach to legal reasoning had 'not really' changed over the course of his/her career; although 'I have become more efficient, the fundamentals are no different'. Interviewee 7, another international arbitrator, similarly said, 'I wouldn't say it's changed but it has become more finely tuned. I've seen how complicated issues are. I often say what I do is sit not as an expert but as a specialist. Doing this for a living makes for a sharper point on the pencil.'

Some respondents noted that changes had occurred not so much in their approach to legal reasoning but in the legal environment in which they worked. Thus, Interviewee 3, an international arbitrator, said that his/her typical practice had 'unfortunately' changed. 'I say unfortunately because lawyers cannot make things simple any more.

[167] Ch. 1.III.D.

[168] This issue was also addressed in the survey. Tables 2.31, 2.32.

[169] Interviewee 4, a mixed international–domestic arbitrator ('I assume so, but I don't know for sure. I hope it has and will continue to do so, though I don't know how I'd want it to change.'); Interviewee 16, an international judge–arbitrator ('Hard for me to know. Yes, a little bit.').

[170] Interviewee 6, a mixed international–domestic arbitrator ('No.); Interviewee 8, an international judge–arbitrator ('Not that I'm aware.'); Interviewee 9, a common law domestic judge ('No.'); Interviewee 11, a common law domestic judge–arbitrator ('No.'); Interviewee 12, a common law domestic judge arbitrator ('No.'); Interviewee 13, a common law domestic judge–arbitrator ('No, not really.').

The shorter, the better, when it comes to case presentations, but often parties write hundreds of pages and you must address all those issues. Arbitration has become more complex than before.'[171]

Interviewee 4, a mixed international–domestic arbitrator, identified another external pressure that can affect legal reasoning, citing 'information technology [as something] that's had a big impact on my processes and probably on others as well'. Interviewee 20, a mixed international–domestic arbitrator, indicated that s/he had changed as a result of exposure to other legal traditions, stating that, 'as a civil law trained lawyer, I tended to give the law first, then the rest, but international arbitration does not function in that way, and no common law or civil law lawyers in international arbitration work that way'.

Interviewee 14, an international judge–arbitrator, was one of the few respondents who identified a significant change in the way s/he approached the reasoning process, noting that

> I [now] have a technique [relating to how I] listen to evidence. One forms a strong view after reading the submissions (the standard of submissions is much higher [in international arbitration] than in domestic), then you must go through the evidence. As I listen, I don't record anything because that's in the transcript. [Instead,] I write down my impressions—'silver bullets' I call them—key points that are questions to be answered or debunked by the other side.
>
> I may end up with 25 to 40 silver bullets that capture my imagination as we go through the points. These are different than the impressions you get on first reading; your understanding may change. When all these flashes of insight come, I write them down—they may not be logical but they are mini-Eureka moments. If you don't answer these questions, the outcome must go a certain way.

Interviewee 18, an international judge–arbitrator, was also able to enunciate how his/her reasoning had changed, noting,

> It's more clear-cut now. Less book, more practical. As a person, you're inclined to decide because a court/tribunal has decided something. The more you grow up, you see those people can make mistakes and you have your own views.
>
> I've also become more aware of commercial/economic realities. You still base your decision in the law, but you also root it in the business world. Also, you ask why the parties have a dispute and whether I should focus on the triggering incident.

Finally, Interviewee 5, a common law domestic judge–arbitrator, indicated that 'I've come to feel that arbitration has little chance of appeal, and I need to give the parties

[171] The increasingly complexity of international commercial arbitration has been discussed in the legal literature. SI Strong, 'Increasing Legalism in International Commercial Arbitration: A New Theory of Causes, A New Approach to Cures,' (2013) 7 World Arb & Med Rev 117, 118–27 (2013); Ch. 1.III.A.

all the opportunity [possible] to provide all the evidence so that they can get the fairest outcome on the law that applies to the case'.

3. Changes due to function—judges versus arbitrators

Conventional wisdom has long held that the nature and quality of judicial reasoning differs from that of arbitral reasoning, with arbitral reasoning often considered to reflect 'second class' justice even in those fields—such as international commercial arbitration—that involve exceptionally complex issues of law and fact and highly sophisticated procedures.[172] The next question in this series therefore asked those respondents who had served as both a judge and an arbitrator whether their reasoning process changed depending on the capacity in which they were acting.[173]

Most of the 11 interviewees who had served or were serving as judges indicated that their reasoning processes did not change according to whether they were acting in a judicial or arbitral capacity. Indeed, three answered the question with a categorical 'no',[174] while another—Interviewee 14, an international judge–arbitrator—indicated that my 'reasoning does not, though I may express myself differently in writing. As an arbitrator, I write in the third person, whereas as a judge, I write in the first person—it's much more personal. I have a [personal] attachment to decisions but not awards.'

Of the respondents who did distinguish between their work as judges and as arbitrators, two focused on the role of equity in their determinations, although both took pains to emphasize that equity did not replace the law. For example, Interviewee 16, an international judge–arbitrator, said, 'It's hard to answer, [but] I'm even more susceptible now [as an arbitrator] to equitable type arguments and a little less patient with purely technical arguments, though I'll pay attention to that'. Interviewee 5, a common law domestic judge–arbitrator, indicated that,

> as a judge, I feel I must consider the rules of evidence/procedure and must consider law technically. When I was [a judge], I had to apply the law technically even if the outcome was not fair.
>
> As an arbitrator, I do not disregard the law, but I can bring in fairness more than a judge. The parties do or should consider this factor when choosing arbitration. [For example, arbitrators are] not bound by the rules of evidence or procedure. I tell the parties ahead of time that if the document is not admissible in court, I will take it anyway [in arbitration] unless it's privileged, and I give it the credibility it deserves.

172 Indeed, some commentators have claimed that international commercial arbitration provides 'Rolls-Royce justice'. Russell J Weintraub, *International Litigation and Arbitration: Practice and Planning* (Carolina Academic Publishers 1994) 455.

173 This issue was also addressed in the survey. Tables 2.33, 2.34.

174 Interviewee 8, an international judge–arbitrator ('No.'); Interviewee 11, a common law domestic judge–arbitrator ('No.'); Interviewee 13, a common law domestic judge–arbitrator ('Not my reasoning, no.').

Interviewee 15, a common law domestic judge–arbitrator, identified a separate issue when contemplating 'the biggest distinction between a judge and an arbitrator', noting that

> I'm struck by the fact that you're more personally responsible as an arbitrator because you don't have a law clerk. Judges can sometimes pass off the responsibility to read cases/documents [to their clerks], and a judge simply reviews drafts and makes sure they're convinced it's right. The arbitrator must do things personally in a way that I didn't as a judge.
>
> Also, arbitrators are under time pressures. Judges rule when s/he rules—there are no deadlines. Arbitrators have 30 days to rule. That can be an impossible task. You may have to ask for an extension, but then you get a bad reputation. Otherwise the award may suffer.

Interestingly, several of the issues described by Interviewee 15 were also identified by other individuals in response to earlier questions.[175]

4. Changes due to dispute—domestic versus international

One of the major themes in this study involves potential differences in legal reasoning across the domestic–international divide, so the next question in this series asked interviewees who had experience in both domestic and cross-border disputes whether and to what extent their reasoning process changed, depending on the nature of the dispute. While a number of individuals had already touched on these matters earlier in the interview process, this question generated a number of interesting responses among those who routinely handled both types of disputes.[176]

Two respondents indicated a clear difference in how they handled domestic and international matters. For example, Interviewee 20, a mixed international–domestic arbitrator from a civil law country, said there was 'definitely' a difference, noting,

> We say '[domestic] arbitration in [my nation] is a judicial process with the right to receive good coffee'. We draft the award like a judicial decision with all the formalities, the nitty-gritty, long descriptions of the procedural steps, long description of legal conflicts. That's one reason I don't do national disputes any more.

Interviewee 6, a mixed international–domestic arbitrator from a common law country, also saw a difference between domestic and international decision making, but described the distinction as arising as a result of institutional influences, stating,

> For example, in ICDR and AAA matters, there's no different in reasoning, but if I do an ICC case, I have the terms of reference, issues set in stone, and may get feedback from

[175] Ch. 3.III.B.2, 3.III.C.2.

[176] Interviewees 3 and 12 indicated that they did not accept enough matters outside their standard area of expertise to answer this question. Interviewee 5, a common law domestic judge–arbitrator who handled a small percentage of international cases, indicated that s/he did not change his/her approach to legal reasoning depending on the nature of the dispute.

the ICA Court. [There also] may be international legal precepts that force you to provide a framework that is different than what you use domestically.

However, Interviewee 4, another mixed international–domestic arbitrator with common law training, said that s/he did 'not intentionally' change his/her methodology, although s/he was 'sure it does'. For example,

> In international matters, I try to be sensitive to decision making processes of non-common-law trained lawyers. I can't say what I do specifically, but the most apparent issue involves the 'swearing contest', which reflects different legal approaches. Most civil law lawyers view [questionable oral testimony] as the natural state of affairs and don't listen to the witness. Common law lawyers are of course more comfortable with testimony.
>
> Beyond that, the International Bar Association has done a terrific job of melding common law and civil law approaches.

5. Changes due to role—panels versus single decision makers

During the design of the interview protocol, it was anticipated that some participants would identify potential differences in legal reasoning, depending on whether the individual was acting alone or as part of a panel.[177] The next question therefore asked interviewees that precise question.[178] No differences were anticipated or identified between judges and arbitrators, since judges at first instance typically work alone, and no differences arose depending on the type of dispute (domestic or international) or the interviewee's legal background (common law versus civil law).

Five individuals suggested that their reasoning process might differ depending on whether they were sitting alone or as part of a panel, although those statements were made with varying degrees of confidence. For example, Interviewee 12, a common law domestic judge–arbitrator, was clear that

> the process changes. I prefer/enjoy panels. Depending on the chair, the process can change dramatically. For example, even before the briefing, panels may have a post-hearing discussion of general thoughts on outcome, so that's different. Sometimes chairs take control and want to take the lead in drafting—that's the prerogative of the chair. I like a more collaborative approach.

Interviewee 4, a mixed international–domestic arbitrator, believed that

> when I'm acting as a sole arbitrator, I'm just not as good as when I'm on a panel. No matter how hard I try, I'm not as good as when I'm with two other people who have

[177] Although first-instance judges typically work alone, arbitrators often work in panels. Some research exists on how arbitrators are affected by others in a panel. Edna Sussman, 'The Arbitrator Survey – Practices, Preferences and Changes on the Horizon', (2015) 26 Am Rev Intl Arb 517, 529.

[178] Some survey respondents indicated that this would be a fruitful area of research, although the issue was not included in the survey itself for reasons of space. Ch. 2.IV.F.

seen and heard the evidence and who have their own approaches. I find, with rare exceptions, my reasoning improves by hearing the reasoning of others and attempting to present my own reasoning.

This statement can be misunderstood, but there's an intellectual competition during deliberations to improve the process. I love it when co-panellists approach the process differently and we argue strongly. It's the internal adversary process in deliberations.

If I'm on my own, I do the best I can to try to avoid single-brain thinking.

Interviewee 19, an international arbitrator, was a little more tentative, saying that his/her legal reasoning 'could' change, explaining that 'when you're alone, you don't have anyone to toss ideas around with. I can see how things could change if you had others to bounce ideas off of. The process changes because in a panel, you do discuss things and the reasoning is richer as a result.' Interviewee 14, an international judge–arbitrator, similarly stated that changes could arise 'because you get input from the other two panellists'. Interviewee 16, another international judge–arbitrator, was also somewhat hesitant, noting that 'it can do if I hear something from the other arbitrators, especially if they know more on certain subjects. So yes, but not radically. I'm open to influence.'

The majority of respondents believed that the legal reasoning process did not change depending on whether they sat alone or on a panel. Four individuals, including two from the common law and two from the civil law, provided categorical statements regarding their practices,[179] while other responses were slightly more nuanced. For example, Interviewee 11, a common law domestic judge–arbitrator, indicated that 'the only thing is that you may have to discuss your reasoning but it doesn't mean your reasoning changes'. Interviewee 10, a common law domestic arbitrator, similarly noted that 'what changes is that I have to articulate my mental landscape with a panel, and I can just work it when I'm solo'.

Interviewee 17, an international judge–arbitrator, had an interesting perspective, noting that 'I rarely act alone, though when I have two co-arbitrators, if they're inclined to their own [appointing] parties, you kind of act alone. You must integrate different viewpoints and that may have some bearing on the outcome. Is the reasoning process different? I don't think so, no. Not conceptually.'

Other respondents saw no difference with respect to the method of reasoning, although they thought being part of a panel might necessitate some minor changes to accommodate multiple viewpoints. For example, Interviewee 2, an international arbitrator, said, 'Deliberation may differ. As a solo, you may say X issue is key, so you start with that. In a three-party deliberation, you might need a different order.' Interviewee 8, an international judge–arbitrator, also believed that his/her reasoning did not change, although

[179] Interviewee 3, an international arbitrator from a civil law background ('No change when acting on a panel.'); Interviewee 6, a mixed international–domestic arbitrator from a common law background ('Don't think so'); Interviewee 13, a common law domestic judge–arbitrator ('No.'); Interviewee 20, a mixed international–domestic arbitrator from a civil law background ('No.').

> if I'm sitting with two other people, we may influence each other's thinking. I remember a case with two people where I was insistent that there was jurisdiction on one claim and submitted my dissenting opinion and was eventually asked to rewrite that as a unanimous decision (which they had opposed before).

Other respondents had similar views about the benefits of being on a panel. For example, Interviewee 18, an international judge–arbitrator, said being in a panel is 'more comfortable because when you're a sole arbitrator, you can maybe be one-sided or do not benefit from the input of colleagues, so the reasoning is less complete. Interaction of the panel is key for me.'

A number of respondents focused on how panel deliberations were conducted, particularly when the respondent was chair. For example, Interviewee 5, a common law domestic judge–arbitrator, said.

> If I'm the chair, even if I'm writing the award, we get together after the hearing and give our preliminary thoughts and break up the issues. If I'm the chair, I talk through the matter with the wings so I can incorporate any dissents or conflicting views in the award. I do as much analysis as I can then so that the draft is as close to the final award as possible.

Interviewee 18, an international judge–arbitrator, indicated that s/he acted primarily as chair and adopted the following procedure:

> Before the hearing, I make a provisional list of issues/questions and ask colleagues how/why they feel about it. This is part of forming one's decision. You have an opinion in discussion with colleagues, then it depends on the reaction of your colleagues and yourself. You ask why you believe your position is correct, and slowly your opinion and others' opinions are formed. It is an interaction with two colleagues. Eventually it becomes clear why you have that opinion and something you thought was important at first becomes less important (and vice versa).

Interviewee 19, an international arbitrator, adopted a similar approach, noting,

> When I'm chair, I do an outline of issues to be resolved and discuss them one by one, or, if we jump around, I save the hardest (meaning the toughest to deliberate) until the last, because that's when tempers can flare. The outline is very important to sort out the plan for the award. It shows where you don't agree.

Interviewee 14, an international judge–arbitrator, reinforced the importance of the chair, indicating,

> If I'm not the chair, I would pay particular attention to the chair. The chair usually spends more time, is the first to come up with a preliminary view and tries to give guidance. It's helpful when the chair gives you a steer as to what to look out for.

Finally, some differences also appeared to arise depending on the nature of the dispute. For example, Interviewee 18, an international judge–arbitrator, said,

> My reasoning on the [international court] is triggered by the arguments of the parties but the real work is done by [the panel] and the reasoning is the interaction of [the panel] who discuss the case *ad nauseum* and in great detail.
>
> The concern about what parties have argued in commercial cases is not as critical as in the [international court]. In commercial arbitration, you are trying to get an understandable award for the losing party (which can be both [meaning both parties could lose on certain issues]) and be satisfied by a court. At the [international court], there is no annulment procedure; you just need to address all the issues or the [international court] loses credibility.

6. Advice from judges and arbitrators to counsel regarding the reasoning process

The final question in this series asked respondents to indicate what they wished parties and counsel knew about how judges and arbitrators approach legal reasoning. A number of individuals referred to their previous answers,[180] but most respondents offered additional advice. Notably, two respondents—Interviewee 8, an international judge–arbitrator, and Interviewee 20, a mixed international–domestic arbitrator—both said explicitly that they wished counsel knew how judges and arbitrators conducted legal reasoning. As Interviewee 20 said, 'I wish parties knew how we reason—what are the facts, what is the evidence to support those facts, then what are the legal ramifications. Parties are starting to understand that more. That helps.'

Several arbitrators noted that counsel should do a better job in focusing their arguments. For example, Interviewee 17, an international judge–arbitrator, said counsel should understand 'that minor issues, side issues, skirmishes in the end are unuseful and unhelpful'. Interviewee 19, an international arbitrator, similarly noted that 'they should know to put most attention on the main legal arguments so it is perfectly clear to the judges that that's the main issue instead of trying to give everything equal weight. You shouldn't be afraid to say what is the main argument.'

Interviewee 5, a common law domestic judge–arbitrator, said that

> I wish counsel would recognize judges and arbitrators are lawyers themselves and will approach cases from a reasonableness/fairness perspective. They can see through the BS.
>
> Those who are belligerent are directly opposite to the cooperative process I use. So, I say quickly that I'll not put up with that. The scorched-earth approach is not appropriate in litigation or arbitration.

[180] Interviewee 2, an international arbitrator ('Same as before.'); Interviewee 7, an international arbitrator ('Same as above. Focus on main issues.'); Interviewee 8, an international judge–arbitrator ('Same as before. Wish they knew how we do it.'); Interviewee 16, an international judge–arbitrator ('Already answered—try to make it user-friendly. Don't dumb it down, but "this is why this argument makes sense". It's not an abstract exercise. Not all lawyers are good at this.').

Interviewee 12, a common law domestic judge–arbitrator, wanted counsel to know that

> generally, we anchor ourselves to legal rules of law in deciding and writing an award, so they should focus on testimony and documents and exhibits that support the legal decisions and not be concerned with emotional appeals. Don't try a case in arbitration like you would a jury trial.

Interviewee 9, a common law domestic judge, similarly stated that, 'for me, I believe every judge wants to follow the [governing law]. It is not a game. We want to follow case law. When you dress it up in other ways, you lose what I try to do, which is correctly apply [governing] law.'

Other respondents wanted counsel to appreciate how judges and arbitrators think. For example, Interviewee 10, a common law domestic arbitrator, said, 'We think in outlines. If you present in outline form, we will grasp what you want to convey more quickly.' Interviewee 11, a common law domestic judge–arbitrator, wanted counsel to know 'I'm a linear thinker', but s/he recognized that 'not everyone is like that'. Interviewee 11 also noted that 'we are or should look at elements and evidence supporting those elements. It's like putting square pegs in square holes and round pegs in round holes. If that's difficult, you're on the wrong thing [making a bad argument].'

Interviewee 11 made another, somewhat startling, observation, saying, 'So many judges don't like to make decisions but you must do it. I tell young judges the parties don't know what do to if you don't do it [make a decision]. You can't always be right. Just pull the trigger.' Other respondents—including those with no judicial experience—noted that they were very comfortable making judgment calls,[181] so the ability to make decisions easily is something that appears to be more a matter of personality than function.

E. Writing a Reasoned Decision or Award

Although the legal reasoning process is closely linked to the writing of a reasoned decision or award, the interview protocol differentiated between the two so as to allow more detailed analysis. The next series of questions therefore focused on exclusively on issues relating to the drafting process. A similar set of inquiries were posed in the survey.[182]

1. Deciding whether to write a reasoned decision or award

Although the issue is not often discussed in the legal literature, judges and arbitrators do not write fully reasoned decisions and awards in all circumstances.[183] Instead,

[181] Interviewee 10, a common law domestic arbitrator ('I love being judgmental, so there's never been an issue' with respect to writing reasoned awards).

[182] Ch. 2.IV.D.

[183] Ch. 1.III.A; see also Strong, Reasoned Awards (n 10) 33–36 (providing a taxonomy of arbitral awards); Strong, Reasoned Decisions (n 10) 113–14 (discussing three types of judicial decisions).

judges frequently write unreasoned judicial memoranda or orders in addition to entering oral decisions from the bench, while arbitrators issue procedural orders and 'standard' awards that typically reflect very little in the way of reasoning.[184] Even those rulings that are fully reasoned are not always published, either in judicial or arbitral reporters.[185]

Given the lack of information about which disputes merit fully reasoned rulings, it was considered useful to ask about the factors that influence the determination to write a fully reasoned decision or award. Most of the answers focused on standard features of litigation and arbitration, including those relating to the creation of precedent in litigation and the role that party agreement plays in arbitration. For example, Interviewee 9, a common law domestic judge, reflected what might be called the purely judicial perspective, saying, 'We are not writing a reasoned decision unless it's dispositive (bench trial, summary judgment, etc.). All else can be resolved in one page. I can't give a well-reasoned decision on motion for extension of time and get everything else done.'

Interviewee 15, a common law domestic judge–arbitrator, reinforced these principles, stating,

> As a judge, if you think it's important to set precedent, you're always going to write. Some matters are just minor, and you're not doing to write [a full opinion], for example, for discovery matters. You [write reasoned opinions] on those items you think need to be in the record or if you think there will be an appeal. Some judges forget that and rule from the bench. The court of appeals doesn't like oral decisions.

Conversely, nearly all of the respondents with arbitral experience indicated that they provided reasoned awards because of obligations placed on the arbitrator by the parties, either expressly in the arbitration agreement or implicitly through arbitral rules adopted by the parties.[186] One respondent—Interviewee 16, an international

[184] Cardozo (n 73) 164–65; Strong, Reasoned Awards (n 10) 2, 33–36 (providing a taxonomy of arbitral awards); Strong, Reasoned Decisions (n 10) 113–14 (discussing three types of judicial decisions).

[185] Determinations about the publication of judicial decisions often lies with the court, although procedures vary from jurisdiction to jurisdiction. Ch. 4.II.A. Determinations about the publication of arbitral awards typically lies with the administering arbitral institution, although publication can also arise if and when a party seeks to enforce an award in court. SI Strong, 'Research in International Commercial Arbitration: Special Skills, Special Sources', (2009) 20 Am Rev Intl Arb 119, 143 (noting arbitral awards published by arbitral institutions are often denatured (anonymized)).

[186] Interviewee 1, a mixed international–domestic arbitrator ('Almost all contracts require reasoned awards.'); Interviewee 5, a common law domestic judge–arbitrator ('The arbitration agreement controls'); Interviewee 6, a mixed international–domestic arbitrator ('Did the parties ask for it; do the rules/arbitral clause require it.'); Interviewee 7, an international arbitrator ('Rules of most major institutions and ad hoc rules require reasoned awards, so no issue about that.'); Interviewee 8, an international judge–arbitrator ('Never have been in a case that did not require a reasoned award.'); Interviewee 13, a common law domestic judge–arbitrator ('In AAA, unless the agreement provides for a reasoned award, there is none. A AAA reasoned award is a function of what parties have requested, and they give the detail they want (standard, reasoned, etc.).'); Interviewee 15, a common law domestic judge–arbitrator ('The parties in arbitration want a reasoned award.'); Interviewee 17, an international judge–arbitrator ('I have never issued a decision that was not reasoned.'): Interviewee 18, an international judge–arbitrator ('All are reasoned awards for me.'); Interviewee 19, an international arbitrator ('International commercial arbitration is always reasoned.').

judge-arbitrator—also noted that jurisdictional requirements could be relevant, stating that

> you always have to do a reasoned award in Switzerland and most European countries. How long? Depends on the complexity of the case (although it can be complex and short), depends on the nature of the case. For example, construction cases need to be longer, with longer facts. The degree of formality required or not [varies] by arbitral institution—they have their [individual] obsessions.

2. Deciding how much detail to include in a reasoned decision or award

The interview protocol was not limited to questions about whether to write a reasoned decision or award. Instead, respondents were asked to and most did provide additional information about how they determined the amount of detail that went into those rulings.

Several respondents focused on issues relating to the possibility of appeal or review.[187] For example, Interviewee 7, an international arbitrator, said that

> I can count on one hand the times I did not have a reasoned award, and in those circumstances, the parties said they explicitly did not want a reasoned award.
>
> I go into enough detail to make sure parties know you understand the case so the award withstands a challenge. In the old days, the AAA discouraged reasoned awards because it gave the loser a hook for the challenge. The alternative is now true—if you have a decision that is not well reasoned, the parties can say the arbitrator did not understand or intentionally disregarded the law. When you're writing, one always thinks about judicial review.

Interviewee 1, a mixed international–domestic arbitrator, reflected this approach, indicating that 'the more likely the award is to be reviewed, the more details I will include'. However, Interviewee 10, a common law domestic arbitrator, still followed the older technique, noting that,

> to me, a reasoned award has internal breakdowns. It doesn't just give the total outcomes. I do that when I'm asked to or [when there's] obviously a third-party player who needs to know [the outcome of the dispute]. For example, an insurance carrier may be involved and will only cover some issues. I need to be clear so the insurer knows what's covered.
>
> I use 'full reasoning' rarely. I didn't become a judge because as an arbitrator I don't need to explain myself. If you explain yourself in the current legal environment, you're more likely to be challenged. I'll do a legally reasoned award in unusual circumstances, *only* when cutting-edge issues are involved.

[187] These concerns were also considered in the survey. Tables 2.15, 2.28, 2.36.

Other differences arose across the judicial–arbitral divide. For example, Interviewee 11, a common law domestic judge–arbitrator, noted that,

> as a judge, you're subject to appeal, so you maybe write more detailed judgments and orders, and you may cite more law because the court of appeal will be looking at that more closely.
>
> As an arbitrator, there is no appeal, so you have to be just as careful, but you don't need every detail tied down like a trial court. Also, the parties often tell you if they want a short, reasoned opinion—they don't want to pay for a scholarly opinion. On a $400 million case, I wrote a 72-page opinion—that was the exception.

When discussing the amount of detail they used, most respondents focused on the complexity of the dispute and the need to keep the award in proportion to the cost and size of the dispute. For example, Interviewee 2, an international arbitrator, said,

> Whether this is 15 pages or 200 pages depends on how many issues need to be decided (sometimes there's only one) and how much law or fact needs to be unpacked (maybe a statute of limitations analysis can decide everything). Length is driven by what needs to be decided.
>
> I'm doing the parties a disservice if I give 200 pages on a single issue. A short award for a complex issue is equally problematic, since it will be conclusory.
>
> I'm also influenced by the timetable and amount in dispute. I would never let amount in dispute generate a sloppy or unenforceable award, but I think about what the parties expect. If they have 800-page memorials, they don't want a ten-page award and vice versa.

Interviewee 8, an international judge–arbitrator, similarly stated that,

> regarding detail—that's determined by the complexity of the case and the volume of evidence and the extent to which the evidence conflicts. Also, the difficulty, if any, in applying the law to the facts as the tribunal determines them. All depends on what we've heard—whether it's a simple case with one to two issues or a more complex matter.

This approach was not limited to those handling international matters. Interviewee 15, a common law domestic judge–arbitrator, said that, 'regarding length, as a judge—the complexity of the case matters. The more you need to decide, the longer the decision will be. In [my home jurisdiction], you don't want to do two hundred to five hundred-page decisions very often.' Interviewee 17, an international judge–arbitrator, also indicated that

> the detail depends on several factors. I can do a summary or more extensive award. It depends on how parties plead the case. If they do a lot, they probably expect the

> same detail from the arbitrators. It also depends on the stakes. The amount in dispute or issues that are raised on principle or that are relevant to other international arbitrations, such as public [treaty-based] arbitrations. Some issues are more complex. Some outcomes are more or less obvious. If they're not obvious, you explain more.

Interviewee 4, a mixed international–domestic arbitrator, had similar views, noting that

> other than a few settings like high-volume consumer settings with the AAA, I can't remember where I didn't put some reasoning into the award. Seldom do parties want me to simply provide a dollar amount alone. I don't remember the last time I didn't provide some reasoning.
>
> The next most significant factor is that the size and length and degree of analysis in the written award has to bear some proportion to the amount in dispute. It's less of an issue for me now that so few of my cases are small (less than several hundreds of thousands of dollars). However, it's critical that all parts of the process consider accessibility of the disputants to the process. I will not write one hundred pages for a $100,000 dispute (overstating the matter somewhat, but you get the idea).
>
> Other than that, I do my best to make the award short and communicate my reasoning about what the parties need to know.

Other respondents focused on the need to write succinctly. For example, Interviewee 5, a common law domestic judge–arbitrator, said,

> The AAA says reasoned awards do not include findings of fact or conclusions of law—you just need to explain the findings in your award. Unless required by the arbitration agreement, findings of fact and conclusions of law are not necessary as a general rule. The award should be as succinct as possible.

Interviewee 6, a mixed international–domestic arbitrator, similarly said,

> If the rules or clause don't [mandate a reasoned award] and parties did not ask for it, then I think [the deciding factor is] whether it would be helpful or not to the parties, whether the cost of award would justify writing it versus what is at stake. If the clause provides for it, [the amount of detail] depends on what the parties' arguments are, the complexities of the matter, how much is at stake.

Interviewee 19, an international arbitrator, echoed these sentiments, noting that 'regarding detail, it depends on the case. I try to keep my awards as short as possible.'

Other responses included a statement from Interviewee 3, an international arbitrator, who said, 'It's a matter of experience. I know what to do to include reasoning. I'm very careful about it. I make sure that I have reasoned the decision on all claims and addressed claims of parties directly or indirectly.' Interviewee 18, an international judge–arbitrator, took the view that 'a reasoned award should be consistent, concise, clear and deal with all relevant issues—not too complicated, because that would mean the reasoning is weak'.

3. Deciding how to draft a reasoned decision or award

Once a judge or arbitrator decides to draft a reasoned decision or award and determines the requisite amount of detail, s/he must determine how to structure the analysis. The next question in this series therefore asked respondents to discuss how they went about drafting reasoned decisions or awards. No discernible difference arose along any of the comparative axes (judicial–arbitral, domestic–international, and common law–civil law). Instead, interviewees appeared to follow their own individual preferences.

Several respondents indicated that they had a standardized routine that they used when drafting a decision or award.[188] For example, Interviewee 13, a common law domestic judge–arbitrator, said that

> post-hearing, I get the brief and transcript. Often, I'm constrained by time because the agreement has a time deadline [for issuing the award]. I follow my format: background details, then position statement by each party, combination of facts and arguments, then I set out my findings of fact and make comments, then I reach conclusions of law, then I go into my rationale, where I take two sets of facts, my findings of facts and work them into a discussion with the law, then I list my award—who gets money. It's a form in the sense of headings but the guts are different for each case.

Interviewee 2, an international arbitrator, noted that

> I don't have a template but create an outline/table of contents and start filling it in. I do the procedural history first—that forces you to remember development of the case. You lose that if the tribunal secretary does the procedural history.
>
> Then I turn to the analysis and also do a summary of party contentions to help remind me of key cases and exhibits. I'll take notes during the hearing on [the anticipated] outcome but won't write that section until after [I've done] others because your gut may be wrong.

Interviewee 19, an international arbitrator, adopted a similar approach, saying,

> I try to draft the preliminary sections ahead of time—who are the parties, what are their positions, etc.—so that after the hearing I can focus on resolution of the legal issues. I also go back in and fill in section on the oral testimony and the rest of the parties' submissions.

[188] Interviewee 10, a common law domestic arbitrator ('I coach elementary school forensics. I tell them to make an outline to force categorization, structure, groupings. I use the same approach in awards. Doing things in outline form helps me focus my thinking and that matches well with my mental landscape.'); Interviewee 11, a common law domestic judge–arbitrator ('Start by summarizing the facts and what was presented after the hearing, then tie to conclusions of law, then tie to damages and make the award.').

> I have a section that I call the parking lot at the end of the draft—these are items that I am not sure about. I throw them into the parking lot, and when I'm done with the award, I'll review the parking lot and often find treasures there.
>
> I also bracket material a lot. If I'm the chair and I'm not sure if we want to include something as a group, and if I have three options, I'll put them all in to help with deliberations.

Other individuals approached the drafting process from what might be called a substantive perspective.[189] For example, Interviewee 9, a common law domestic judge, characterized his/her writing process as 'IRAC-heavy. I identify the issues the moving party (or whoever has the burden) has raised and address each of those in decision serially.'[190] Interviewee 3, an international arbitrator from the civil law tradition, adopted a somewhat similar approach, indicating that

> usually I draft issue by issue. If there are lots of legal issues, I start with a chapter on legal issues so that my ideas are clear on the law, then I go issue by issue or chapter by chapter. However, it depends on the type of case. For example, I have had construction cases with two hundred issues.

Interviewee 1, a mixed international–domestic arbitrator, said,

> In commercial dispute, only rarely is there a disputed legal standard because most of the body of law is contract law; regulatory issues may be different. [If the dispute turns on the] application of the contract, not much is in legal controversy, so I will focus more on facts then. The process is iterative in those cases. I use the record to flesh out what parties are saying. Sometimes as I write the story of the facts, I get a clearer view.

Other respondents sought the parties' assistance in the drafting process. Interviewee 4, a mixed international–domestic arbitrator, used that approach, noting,

> If it's a significant case and I'm dealing with lawyers who understand the process, I will ask them for findings of fact and conclusions of law. However, I won't do that if they use it as an additional opportunity for advocacy or if my colleagues on the panel dislike that method. Many arbitrators do not do this.
>
> I request all written submissions to be in Word (not pdfs) so that I can get citations, etc. in digital form. I don't pull out the arguments of the parties but if they have a

[189] Interviewee 12, a common law domestic judge–arbitrator ('Outline, then broaden by referencing the support for how I come down on issues that must be decided to get an award. Separate factors and write about each factor. In commercial matters, take it topic by topic and don't just state "here's what claimant said and here's their evidence"').

[190] IRAC stands for 'Issue-Rule-Application-Conclusion', a standard common law analytical technique. Strong, *IRAC Perfected* (n 31) ch. 1; Strong, *How to Write* (n 31) ch. 1; Ch. 3.III.A.3.

concise quotable legal authority, I'll start there by constructing the legal principle as a freestanding matter.

Sometimes, depending on the arbitral rules and what the institutions require, I may construct 'shell' portions of the award regarding the parties' positions that are pulled from the submissions.

To me, I never know whether I'll start with the outcome following a series of recitations or whether I'll go issue by issue. It depends on the case or if I'm on a panel.

Interviewee 7, an international arbitrator, also relied heavily on party submissions, stating,

I'm a big fan of post-hearing briefs. You have to read more, but the briefs tell you what the parties think is important. Then I sketch the key issues, give the parties' arguments and then my conclusion. I feel strongly that post-hearing briefs are excellent. Not all arbitrators think that, but in most complicated cases, they have multiple twists, and post-hearing briefs give the parties the chance to connect the dots for the arbitrator.

Finally, some respondents used a combination of approaches. For example, Interviewee 6, a mixed international–domestic arbitrator, said,

I break it down—start with the introduction and background (what happened), background facts, law that's important—and do that first. Sometimes I outline before I start writing, so I have a path to follow. Sometimes I delve into it from the briefs and arguments. In significant cases, where I have arguments after post-hearing briefing, the argument is excellent—they really help (along with my questions), and the panel is prepared to listen carefully and have questions in mind.

Interviewee 16, an international judge–arbitrator, similarly stated,

After mulling it around a lot and depending on my soul-searching, I start making notes to myself—there may be lines I want to use. I will outline (for me) where I think I'm going. Sometimes I put [down] all the headings (like an outline) and these may change—what are the questions in dispute (for example, was the option exercised, was the exercise properly done, etc.)—then I fill in sections trying to go from beginning to end. For me, it is hard to go back to fill in sections that I skipped, so I proceed in a linear fashion.

It depends also on if this is a 10-page sports award or an 80-page decision with lots of facts.

Some respondents incorporated an iterative element into the drafting process. For example, Interviewee 15, a common law domestic judge–arbitrator, said that

ninety-nine per cent of [a first-instance judicial decision] is drafted first by the clerk. This is a little more true of appellate courts as well, sadly—sad because they have nothing else to do other than write opinions. [Judge Richard] Posner was famous for writing his first drafts.

Interviewee 8, an international judge–arbitrator, made a similar comment, indicating,

> There's a difference between [an international court] and arbitration. In arbitration, there's difference between whether you're acting as the chair or not.
>
> If I'm the chair and my colleagues anticipate a draft from me, my clerk will be familiar with deliberations because he or she has sat in on them (this happens infrequently) or I've given an oral or written readout of the outcome of the deliberations [to my clerk]. Then I sit down with my clerk and outline what's to be in the award and how it's to be written. The clerk then does a draft, and I make a mess of it with a blue pencil—partly because it needs to sound like me, and every arbitrator has his or her own style. Once I have a draft, I circulate it to colleagues, they make comments, and I finalize.
>
> If I'm party-appointed, then after deliberations we see an award and comment on it.
>
> On a multi-person court, there are deliberations and the president of the tribunal has the responsibility of preparing the award, which is circulated in draft to the other judges.

Interviewees 8 and 15 both came from the common law tradition. However, their drafting techniques were not that different from those discussed by respondents from civil law backgrounds. For example, Interviewee 17, an international judge–arbitrator, said that s/he

> starts with [panel] deliberations. I take notes of deliberations and have pre-deliberation notes. Generally, I have uncontroversial points (all except the discussion or part of the discussion) drafted before deliberations. Then I draft parts myself or give instructions to my assistant to do a first draft on the basis of the deliberations and my summary of the deliberations. I work a lot on the framework, but I could tell an assistant to do things. It's a long process, and I go to my co-arbitrators who may have issues or comments.

Interviewee 18, another international judge–arbitrator, indicated that, in his/her experience,

> normally the chair writes [the reasoned decision or award]. You get the feeling of your colleagues at the hearing or stay half a day afterwards to go over the questions to be solved. You get your gut feelings. Sometimes, if you get along very well and they [your colleagues] are reasonable, then you may be able to divide the drafting work. The drafting is done by the chair, who submits the draft to colleagues, and then you go over the submissions of the parties to make sure that you've covered everything.

4. Changing the outcome during the drafting process

According to the legal literature, the process of writing a reasoned decision or award helps assure a 'better', meaning more accurate, outcome.[191] This theory suggests that judges and arbitrators can and sometimes do change their minds during the process of drafting a reasoned decision or award.[192] The next series of questions tested this hypothesis by asking respondents whether they had ever changed their mind about the outcome of a dispute when writing a reasoned decision or award, how frequently such changes occurred and why such changes arose.

a. Whether and to what extent changes occur

Most respondents indicated that changes in the outcome could possibly occur or did occur, although Interviewee 18, an international judge–arbitrator, sagely noted, 'Do we call it changing minds or seeing the light?'[193] Interviewee 4, a mixed international–domestic arbitrator, was the only one who changed his/her mind frequently, saying, 'It happens very often, either to a small extent or to the extent of changing the outcome'. Interviewee 4 also noted that s/he was often influenced by the thinking of co-arbitrators.

Those individuals who indicated that they made changes as a result of the reasoning process typically noted that the changes were relatively minor. For example, Interviewee 2, an international arbitrator, said, 'I have not changed about who wins, though it could happen. However, I have changed my mind about weight to give to individual factors.' Interviewee 16, an international judge–arbitrator, indicated that 'I can remember changing my mind on parts, but I can't remember changing my mind 100 per cent. As sole arbitrator, I cannot recall changing my mind 180 degrees while writing. Maybe 90 degrees, since I usually have more than one issue or claim.' Interviewee 8, another international judge–arbitrator, noted that

> I've certainly changed my mind in the process of deliberations or the award being drafted. Sometimes it can be not clear in my mind which way to go and I can be persuaded. This can happen anywhere along the way—hearing to deliberation to awards. If we have differences on the tribunal and I'm alone in my thinking, I've been persuaded by my colleagues.

The responses of Interviewees 8 and 16 suggest that the process of deliberation among a multi-person panel can affect the outcome, thereby supporting the preference of some practitioners and commentators for arbitral tribunals over sole decision makers.[194] However, this phenomenon does not support the suggestion by some that

[191] Ch. 1.II.

[192] Sussman (n 177) 525, 533 (studying frequency of changes in anticipated outcome and when such changes occur).

[193] Interviewee 1, a mixed international–domestic arbitrator ('Yes.'); Interviewee 13, a common law domestic judge–arbitrator ('Yes.'); Interviewee 19, an international arbitrator ('Yes.').

[194] Wendy Miles, 'Practical Issues for Appointment of Arbitrators', (2003) 20 J Intl Arb 219, 227; Yu-Jin Tay, 'Reflections on the Selection of Arbitrators', in Albert Jan van den Berg (ed), *International Council of Commercial Arbitrators Congress Series No. 17: International Commercial Arbitration: The Coming of a New Age?* (2003) 112, 114–15.

arbitrators are less capable than judges or less reliant on the law,[195] particularly since at least one respondent who changed his/her mind as a result of input from others was a domestic judge.[196] Instead, these reports reinforce research from the social sciences about the difference between solitary and group decision-making processes.[197]

The vast majority of respondents indicated that they changed their minds extremely rarely.[198] For example, Interviewee 5, a common law domestic judge–arbitrator, noted that 'I can remember changing my mind about an issue, and I had a few panels where we disagreed. Generally, after the hearing I know where I am headed. I keep an open mind but I rarely change my mind about the outcome after the hearing concludes.' Interviewee 12, a common law domestic judge–arbitrator, and Interviewee 19, an international arbitrator, both indicated that they changed their minds in around 10 per cent of their cases, while Interviewee 13, a common law domestic judge–arbitrator, estimated his/her change rate at less than 20 per cent.

Interviewee 9, a common law domestic judge who conferred frequently with his/her law clerks, appeared to change his/her mind most frequently, indicating that such changes happened 'about two times a month'.[199] Not only does this statement suggest that judges are as susceptible of change as arbitrators, it also generates questions about potential differences between judges and arbitrators due to the well-established preference among parties for arbitrators who are strong-minded and less likely to be swayed by colleagues.[200]

b. *Why do changes occur*

The next question focused on why judges and arbitrators changed their minds when drafting reasoned decisions and awards. Although some individuals found it difficult to enunciate their motivations,[201] others provided useful insights into the judicial and arbitral reasoning process.

[195] Ch. 1.III.A. Indeed, first-instance judges typically work alone and are thus liable to make the same types of errors as arbitrators working alone, although the opportunity for an appeal on the merits provides a safeguard against judicial errors.

[196] Interviewee 9, a common law domestic judge ('Yes. When we get down to the tough ones, we have an area in the library and sit and talk (me and my three [law clerks]).').

[197] E.g. Attila Ambrus, Ben Greiner, and Parag Pathak, 'Group Versus Individual Decision-Making: Is There a Shift?' Economics Working Papers 0019, Institute for Advanced Study, School of Social Science (2009) 1.

[198] Interviewee 1, a mixed international–domestic arbitrator ('Rarely—though not so rare that it never happens.'); Interviewee 3, an international arbitrator ('Probably yes, but in most cases not.'); Interviewee 6, a mixed international–domestic arbitrator ('It's happened. Not often.'); Interviewee 7, an international arbitrator ('I do. Not that often, but it has happened.'); Interviewee 8, an international judge–arbitrator ('Not too often.'); Interviewee 17, an international judge–arbitrator ('Yes. Not that often—it's happened maybe two, three, four times.'); Interviewee 10, a common law domestic arbitrator ('Rarely.'); Interviewee 11, a common law domestic judge–arbitrator ('Sometimes—very few times.').

[199] Notably, Interviewee 9 indicated earlier in the interview that his/her approach to legal reasoning differed from other judges in his/her jurisdiction, both with respect to the amount of time (see Ch. 3.III.B.4.a relating to the 'luxury of time') and with respect to staffing arrangements ('I have brilliant inquisitive folks on my team, and I made a decision not to have a judicial assistant because I'd rather have lawyers [i.e. additional staff attorneys] to help me.'). Interviewee 9 also noted that those changes s/he made are 'rarely about what the controlling law should do', which challenges a longstanding assumption that arbitrators focus on the facts while judges focus on the law. Ch. 1.III.A.

[200] Parties have traditionally considered strength of character and conviction when appointing arbitrators, along with the ability of their arbitrator to persuade others. Douglas Pilawa, 'Sifting Through the Arbitrators for the Woman, the Minority, the Newcomer', 2019 51 Case Western Reserve J Intl L 408–11.

[201] Interviewee 18, an international judge–arbitrator ('Hard to say.').

Interviewee 6, a mixed international–domestic arbitrator, enunciated the rationale of several individuals when s/he said that 'when I put pen to paper, the argument may not hold together'. Interviewee 15, a common law domestic judge–arbitrator, similarly indicated that 'it's like writing an essay—sometimes (rarely) it just doesn't write. As you write, you find it hard to support your argument. If it's too hard, you can't go there, so you may need to go the other way.' Interviewee 18, an international judge–arbitrator, also believed that 'the proof is in the pudding. When you write down the award, you may change your mind.'

Interviewee 19, an international arbitrator, recognized the connection between writing and reasoning, noting that changes occur 'because something sounds right from all you've been listening to, but as you write the award, you ask yourself, did I read that right, did I give enough credence to the defence, etc. and see how it all writes'. Interviewee 3, a civil law international arbitrator, experienced the same phenomenon, noting that,

> in a number of cases, it is in writing the award that you know how to reason it. For example, when you're on a panel, you may think the issue is X, but when you write and review the documents, you see whether you have the evidence to support that outcome.

Interviewee 2, an international arbitrator, reinforced this concept, saying,

> You may think a document is helpful, but as you write, you remember other items that are important, too, so the emphasis may shift, or on re-reading cases, I may see [one decision is] just parroting another case that is distinguishable.
>
> Writing has a testing function. It has never caused me to change my mind, but it has confirmed my analysis.

Some individuals, such as Interviewee 1, a mixed international–domestic arbitrator, indicated that they 'learn the facts better' during the writing process. Interviewee 13, a common law domestic judge–arbitrator, similarly noted that 'I've gone in with certain preconceptions that evidence at hearing overcomes'. Others, such as Interviewee 10, a common law domestic arbitrator, change their minds because they notice during the writing process that they have double-counted certain elements.[202]

Some respondents focused on legal issues. For example, Interviewee 12, a common law domestic judge–arbitrator, changed his/her mind as a result of

> perspectives I didn't recognize during the hearing, usually because I didn't understand the law. I don't get oral argument at the end in commercial cases. Occasionally I say to

[202] Interviewee 10, a common law domestic arbitrator ('Because when I'm in the process of writing, I decide I had the same issue in a couple of categories in my mental landscape and assessed the same penalty twice. That can change my outcome.').

counsel, in front of clients, 'These are the issues I need briefed.' I do that 10 to 15 per cent of the time. I pose questions both ways so that they won't read into my questions.

As Interviewee 11, a common law domestic judge–arbitrator, noted, 'If you're writing, you track the issues as you go. As a judge, several times I gave an order from the bench, and twice as I was giving the ruling orally, I talked myself out of it and had to reverse course. This happened twice in 15 years.'

Other respondents focused on the dynamics associated with group deliberations. For example, Interviewee 17, an international judge–arbitrator, said that if a difference of opinion existed after deliberations, 'and I was clear on my side, then it [the analysis] just does not work during the drafting process. In those cases, I go back to my co-arbitrators, and I go home to look at the materials and then make my decision.'

F. Judicial and Arbitral Education Relating to Legal Reasoning

According to the legal literature, many judges and arbitrators do not undertake specialized educational programming relating to reasoning and drafting decisions and awards.[203] The final topic of discussion in the interviews therefore focused the process of learning to write a reasoned decision or award, not only to increase the legal community's understanding of how information about the nature of reasoned decisions and awards is conveyed within the judicial and arbitral communities, but also to determine how judicial and arbitral education on this subject might be improved. Many of the issues discussed in the interviews were also raised in the survey so as to allow cross-study comparisons.[204]

1. How respondents learned to draft reasoned decisions and awards

The first question in this series focused on how interviewees learned to write a reasoned decision or award, a question that was also asked on the survey.[205] This inquiry sought to determine whether judges and arbitrators learn primarily through formal, standardized methods of education or whether more informal processes such as those involving socialization or acculturation predominate.[206] Notably, the interview protocol focused exclusively on interviewees' beliefs about how they learned to write reasoned decisions and awards and did not seek to test the effectiveness of any particular mechanism.

According to the responses, most judges and arbitrators did not learn to write reasoned decisions and awards through formal means. Indeed, a number of individuals indicated that they had never taken any coursework on this subject,[207] with Interviewee 15, a

[203] Ch. 1.III.A.
[204] Ch. 2.IV.E.
[205] Table 2.38.
[206] Ch. 1.II (discussing socialization or acculturation).
[207] Interviewee 3, an international arbitrator ('No classes.'); Interviewee 6, a mixed international–domestic arbitrator ('Not a course—maybe a AAA CLE program.'); Interviewee 8, an international judge–arbitrator ('No classes.'); Interviewee 11, a common law domestic judge–arbitrator ('No classes.'); Interviewee 13, a

common law domestic judge–arbitrator, dismissing the need or value of such coursework, claiming, 'Either you're good or you're not. Some judges never learned to write.' Interviewee 3, an international arbitrator, similarly said that said s/he learned to write reasoned awards 'by experience. I never had a problem with it. I have had no awards overturned.'

Some individuals who had taken such coursework indicated that they found it useful. For example, Interviewee 12, a common law domestic judge–arbitrator, said that s/he had taken

> multiple AAA courses in my early time as an arbitrator. Used to be in person—usually went every one to two years. Over time, I went to ABA arbitration training courses. The last ten years, I took lots of CLEs on how to write.

Interviewee 14, an international judge–arbitrator, had a similar experience, noting,

> I did not go to judge school (I was a judge first). I went through the CIArb Fellowship course—heavy emphasis on award writing, and you must take a test at the end. I took that course right at the beginning of my career. There I learned the difference between an award and a decision.

Other people indicated that they took some form of coursework but did not find it helpful.[208] Many of these individuals indicated that their learning came by watching more experienced arbitrators and/or by reading decisions or awards. Thus, Interviewee 1, a mixed international–domestic arbitrator, indicated s/he had learned 'first, by watching others and reading judicial decisions. Later, by applying advocacy skills to writing—the skills apply equally to writing.' Interviewee 19, an international arbitrator, said, 'I taught myself. I saved the good awards that were delivered in cases of mine when I was counsel. I didn't take any courses.' Interviewee 2, another international arbitrator, said that s/he learned

> by reading [awards] as counsel. I have [also] flipped through guidance documents—arbitral checklists from ICCA [International Council for Commercial Arbitration],[209] IBA Arb40 [International Bar Association Arbitration Committee for Under-40s],[210] etc. I do not follow a template; I just develop my style independently.

Many judges appeared to have the used the same approach. For example, Interviewee 11, a common law domestic judge–arbitrator, said that s/he learned through 'practice,

common law domestic judge–arbitrator ('No classes.'); Interviewee 17, an international judge–arbitrator ('Nobody—on the job.'); Interviewee 18, an international judge–arbitrator ('No. I taught one once.').

[208] Interviewee 2, an international arbitrator ('Maybe a mandatory AAA course, but that's not where I learned my skills.'); Interviewee 16, an international judge–arbitrator ('I'm an auto-didact. I have been counsel in many cases, so I have seen a lot. I may have gone to courses, but that's not how I learned. Being in the arbitral world and reading so many awards has been most important.').

[209] International Council for Commercial Arbitration, Drafting Sourcebook for Logistical Matters in Procedural Orders, <https://www.arbitration-icca.org/projects/Protocols.html> accessed 11 April 2020.

[210] International Bar Association, Arbitration Committee Toolkit for Award Writing, <https://www.ibanet.org/LPD/Dispute_Resolution_Section/Arbitration/Default.aspx> accessed 11 April 2020.

practice, practice. You read appellate cases as a lawyer and as a judge, see how they do it. That's the model, especially as a judge.' However, other judges, such as Interviewee 9, a common law domestic judge, indicated that s/he had taken several courses on writing reasoned decisions through formal judicial education programs.[211] This difference may have arisen because Interviewee 9 and Interviewee 11 worked as judges in different legal systems, but it may also be due to the fact that many common law judges are not required to take any judicial education courses before or after their elevation to the bench.[212] Even those individuals, such as Interviewee 15, who work in judicial systems that strongly encourage participation in judicial orientation training do not always take advantage of the opportunities presented to them, a phenomenon that may be explained by what is referred to as 'judicial hubris'.[213]

Some of the individuals who had engaged in professional education programs suggested that training techniques have changed over the course of time. For example, Interviewee 4, a mixed international–domestic arbitrator, said s/he learned to write reasoned awards in a

> couple ways. In the early years of my arbitral career, I was introduced to arbitration via construction arbitration, which had only a handful of arbitrators. I sat with some excellent arbitrators during that time. Back then, there were those in the field who discouraged giving reasons in awards (this was 30 years ago), but I sat with some excellent arbitrators who did give reasons, and I learned how to do that by observing good legal writers.
>
> Then the time came when domestic institutions began to offer programs on award writing, and I took some of them 20 years ago.
>
> In the international realm, I saw the different sets of rules and the different approach. I took the CIArb three- to four-day Fellowship program that included crafting an award as a part of a proctored exam. The CIArb training discussed the different sections of an award and is a well-structured approach to international awards. I was then exposed to award-writing in different settings—ICSID [International Centre for Settlement of Investment Disputes], ICC, etc. Each has its own approach, and I've learned from fabulous arbitrators and institutions over the year. I keep learning.

Interviewee 5, a common law domestic judge–arbitrator, had a similar experience, noting s/he learned through

> experience: serving on three-person panels with more experienced people and seeing how they did it. The AAA has had training sessions that have been valuable over the

[211] Many countries have national institutions for judicial education and training. Strong, Reasoned Decisions (n 10) 95.

[212] Ibid.

[213] Ch. 2.IV.A.2. For example, Interviewee 15, a common law domestic judge–arbitrator who came from the same legal system as Interviewee 9, indicated that s/he had not taken certain orientation courses that virtually all judges in that jurisdiction attend upon elevation to the bench.

> years. Other arbitration seminars have helped. However, I developed my own style from the beginning and stuck with that. My first classes with the AAA were in the mid-1980s.

Although many judges and arbitrators learned to write reasoned decisions and awards as a result of their experience as counsel and/or as a judge or arbitrator, several respondents mentioned another form of experience—that of acting as a law clerk—as being useful. Interviewee 6, a mixed international–domestic arbitrator, said that, 'very simply', his/her education had begun by 'working for a judge. I clerked for a brilliant judge. I also was a staff attorney at court, and we drafted sometimes for the judges. My boss was a great writer. I learned from him.' Interviewee 9, a common law domestic judge, similarly stated that s/he had learned during his/her clerkship from both the judge and the senior clerk, noting that the senior clerk 'told me the form. It's not any different than what's taught in law school or seen in [appellate] case law. Follow IRAC, don't write a law review article.'

Interestingly, when answering this question, a number of individuals failed to distinguish between good writing skills as a general proposition and writing reasoned decisions and awards,[214] a phenomenon that was also seen in certain responses to the survey.[215] For example, although Interviewee 7, an international arbitrator, did say that s/he learned 'by practice [and] time—sitting down and doing it over and over', s/he also noted that

> I am forever grateful for a freshman counsellor in undergraduate college who helped my writing, and I go back to those principles. When I was a young [professional], a more senior person said 'your [writing] goes in circles'. That hurt my feelings, but he was right, and I tried to make my discussions have a beginning, middle and end. Criticism has taught me.

Interviewee 18, an international judge–arbitrator, offered a similar response, stating,

> My basic academic writing started at [university]—doing first, second, third drafts—something I continue to do. Everything has three drafts.
>
> I draft by hand, not computer, since I think computer screens look too neat and you lose your self-criticism. If you write by hand, you feel the pain and can change the text more easily.

As a follow-up question, those respondents who had taken a course on writing reasoned decisions or awards were asked why they did so. Most indicated that the courses

[214] Interviewee 8, an international judge–arbitrator ('Going back to [the beginning of my career]—I had strictly domestic commercial arbitration. I had to sit down and write, and it came naturally. I had to tell what the dispute was about, the contentions, then give the law and facts.'); Interviewee 10, a common law domestic arbitrator ('I have been writing since I was seven—my mom was a teacher, my dad a rhetorician.').

[215] Ch. 2.IV.E.1.

were mandatory if the individual in question was to remain a judge or arbitrator or if the individual wished to obtain certain professional credentials. Thus, Interviewee 1, a mixed international–domestic arbitrator, indicated that s/he took the CIArb course 'because it was mandatory for Fellowship' and possibly certain AAA training 'because it was mandatory for staying on the roster'. Interviewee 2, an international arbitrator, similarly indicated that s/he took 'maybe a mandatory AAA course to get on the roster ten years ago to fulfil a requirement, but that's not where I learned my skills. CIArb—I have taught the course for Fellows but never took it. Teaching classes is useful.' Interviewee 9, a common law domestic judge, indicated that s/he had received training as part of a strongly recommended orientation course for new judges in his/her legal system, although Interviewee 15, a common law domestic judge–arbitrator from the same jurisdiction, had opted not to take that course.

2. Advice regarding the drafting process

The next question in the series asked respondents to identify what they wished they had known when they first started writing reasoned decisions or awards. Several individuals could not think of anything in response to this question,[216] and a few indicated that they already knew everything they needed to know as a judge or arbitrator as a result of their earlier experiences.[217] However, several individuals did provide substantive suggestions.

First, several individuals mentioned that they wished they had known more about gauging the appropriate length of a reasoned decision or award. Interviewee 9, a common law domestic judge, cited the old adage, 'If I had more time, I'd have written a shorter document,' and noted that, in his court,

> we have that time, so we aim to get quickly to the decision. Winning or losing is important, but how you get there is also important. I don't have to explain everything, but I need to say why I arrived here—I need to strike a balance. That's the justice system.

Interviewee 13, a common law domestic judge–arbitrator, said s/he wished s/he had been aware of the 'mantra "the more you write the less sure you are"'. As a result, Interviewee 13, like Interviewee 9, now 'aim[ed] for brevity'.

Interviewee 17, an international judge–arbitrator, also found him/herself 'struggling to keep the award short and simple when cases are complicated or over-lawyered'. However, Interviewee 17 was not sure whether s/he was writing longer decisions and awards because the disputes were becoming more complex or because 'I've become more critical'.

[216] Interviewee 4, a mixed international–domestic arbitrator ('I don't know. It's been a long time.'); Interviewee 8, an international judge–arbitrator ('Can't think of anything.').

[217] Interviewee 3, a civil law international arbitrator ('Nothing. I didn't need anything. I knew.'); Interviewee 6, a mixed international–domestic arbitrator ('Nothing, because I was in the hot seat as a law clerk. A good judge will ask you to justify what's on the page.'); Interviewee 15, a common law domestic judge–arbitrator ('Nothing—we're trained in law school by reading other courts' opinions. You've been reading good writing for a long time by the time you get to the bench.').

These statements about length are intriguing, given that arbitral awards have long been criticized on the grounds that they are both shorter and less analytically rigorous than judicial decisions,[218] although the coding exercise that was conducted as part of this study suggested that decisions and awards do not differ significantly with respect to length when the dispute is of a commercial nature.[219]

Another series of comments focused on process considerations. For example, Interviewee 19, an international arbitrator, said,

> I wish I'd followed a colleague's advice to do the vanilla parts of an award [the procedural history, parties, etc.] first. When I don't do that beforehand, I regret it. If you have done the facts first and actually laid out the key parts, you're more prepared for the hearing. That takes a long time to do. After the hearing, it's more important to get into the second part of the award (the legal analysis).

Interviewee 18, an international judge–arbitrator, similarly noted that when s/he began working as an adjudicator, 'I was naïve. What I now know is that it takes more time than you think' to produce a reasoned decision or award.

Other respondents focused on cooperation with the parties. For example, Interviewee 5, a common law domestic judge–arbitrator, said that 'I wish I had thought about involving the parties in addressing the issues as I do now. Early on, I decided the parties should do research that leads up to reasoning in the final award.' Interviewee 12, a common law domestic judge–arbitrator, indicated that s/he wished s/he had known 'not to reach a conclusion until you're pretty much through the process. [Also,] don't be afraid to ask for views post-hearing as long as you include both parties in the discussion.'

Interviewee 1, a mixed international–domestic arbitrator, indicated that s/he wished s/he had known 'who the audience was [and the] importance of due process in court/annulment committees in reviewing the award'. Interviewee 11, a common law domestic judge–arbitrator, wished that s/he had known 'maybe [to] include more facts', while Interviewee 16, an international judge–arbitrator, said that s/he wished s/he had known

> first, how important it is to have an overview of where the evidence is—not just the general facts, but what the documents say. It helps with the hearing and with writing the award. Second, I wish I'd known how stressful it is—some cases are easy, but some are not.

3. Need for educational programming

The next question in this series asked respondents whether they thought judges and arbitrators would benefit from educational programming on reasoned decisions or

[218] Ch. 1.III.A.
[219] Ch. 4.IV.

awards, assuming judicial and arbitral independence were respected in the design of the program. This question was also included in the survey.[220]

While one individual categorically denied the need for educational programming,[221] most people were in favour of additional training relating to reasoned decisions or awards.[222] For example, Interviewee 4, a mixed international–domestic arbitrator, said that 'of course' there was a need, since s/he had 'seen some judges trying to make the transition [to arbitration] and do an awful job', which suggested that 'they would benefit greatly' from additional instruction. Interviewee 4 also said that 'I still enjoy programs that have brand-new content and formats, especially if they have a drafting component, since that helps refresh my understanding of issues involving drafting'.

Although many respondents were in favour of additional coursework, Interviewee 16, an international judge–arbitrator, put his/her finger on the crux of the issue, stating, 'Yes—we all have something to learn. Whether I'd attend, I don't know. I flatter myself that I think I know how to do it.' This statement shows an admirable understanding of the 'bias blind spot', meaning the ability to see faults or biases in others but not in oneself.[223]

Interviewee 2, an international arbitrator, also identified problems with his/her colleagues, noting that it was 'hard to say "no" [to the need for more education] because some arbitrators write sloppy awards and are overturned'. However, Interviewee 2 believed that 'for many experienced arbitrators, the coursework is less important than taking care and taking time'. In particular, Interviewee 2 noted that 'arbitrators need not to have too much on their docket [since] that creates errors'.

Concerns about time pressures also came up with Interviewee 1, a mixed international–domestic arbitrator who was also in favour of educational programming. Interviewee 1 believed that 'many awards and decisions are poorly written', largely because

> too many lawyers are taught to write by law professors. Generally, law professors don't have practical experience, so they write in a way that is not as helpful as it could be. Law review writing is like building a house: very structured, with the roof put on last.
>
> Practical writing [is different.] Time pressures mean you get the roof up first and deal with the most important points even if it is not in logical order, then go back and fill in gaps. [You] write the important bits first in case you run out of time and space.

220 Ch. 2. IV.E.

221 Interviewee 18, an international judge–arbitrator ('No.').

222 Interviewee 5, a common law domestic judge–arbitrator ('Yes.'); Interviewee 9, a common law domestic judge ('I think we'd all benefit—we all can learn.'); Interviewee 10, a common law domestic arbitrator ('I do, especially if judges have not been appellate judges.'); Interviewee 11, a common law domestic judge–arbitrator ('Sure.'); Interviewee 12, a common law domestic judge–arbitrator ('Yes.'); Interviewee 13, a common law domestic judge–arbitrator ('Yes.'); Interviewee 19, an international arbitrator ('Yes, for some that I've worked with.').

223 Ch. 1.II. The bias blind spot can lead to problems in both judicial and arbitral settings and can be linked to problems of judicial or arbitral 'hubris'. Ch. 2.IV.A.2

Interviewee 17, an international judge–arbitrator who was in favour of additional coursework, had a slightly different perspective on the question of judicial and arbitral education. S/he said,

> To me, what is probably the most difficult is not to write but to conduct the process—you want to get a unanimous award, so you need to think about what concessions you can make and should make. Sometimes I make concessions and regret it. Writing is easy alone in my study.

Although many respondents supported increasing judicial and arbitral education, others noted certain difficulties that might arise with implementing such a plan. For example, Interviewee 3, an international arbitrator, believed that judges and arbitrators would 'probably' benefit from additional coursework, although

> the reasoning of awards does not have an international standard, and it is not the same in all jurisdictions. So, any program on this would have to be aimed at different countries or groups of countries (for example, civil law versus common law countries), but not the whole world.

Other problems might arise as a matter of individual personalities. For example, Interviewee 6, a mixed international–domestic arbitrator, noted that s/he had attended a particular 'program on drafting [and] got something from it, but lots of other arbitrators were arguing back against the suggestions. Overall, I'd say "sure", if you self-select—it shouldn't be mandatory. Should be voluntary.'

Other respondents also cast doubt on the usefulness of educational programming as a general proposition. For example, Interviewee 8, an international judge–arbitrator, said that 'I suppose there are some who could benefit, but I tend to think it's pretty simple, and most judges who have come to the bench with considerable experience at the bar should know how to do it'. Interviewee 15, a common law domestic judge–arbitrator, was equally sceptical, noting,

> I don't think judges need training. Most [national] judges are prominent, experienced lawyers who are presumed to know this type of thing, but the vast number of [local or regional] court judges who are selected in other ways probably could use some coursework.
>
> For arbitrators—I don't know enough. They often don't have [decades of] experience on the bench, but they're probably good and prominent lawyers.
>
> When I [was acting as a judge and] chose a special master—they were good lawyers but had never written a judicial decision. They put too much of their thinking into the decision, and I told them to go straight to the decision.

Those who did not explain their motivation in their initial response were asked in a follow-up question why they did or did not support educational programming regarding legal reasoning. Responses varied, with some individuals focusing on systemic considerations. Interviewee 11, a common law domestic judge–arbitrator, was in favour of additional programming because 'writing good decisions is an important thing—that's how you communicate and gives integrity to the justice system, be it court or arbitration'. Interviewee 5, a common law domestic judge–arbitrator, was of a similar mind, saying,

> It helps to have some conformity in how awards are written, both with respect to format and how the reasons are applied. Some institutions (AAA and JAMS) will look at draft awards and make suggestions on format or on how issues are addressed, but the more you know ahead of time, the better.

Other people focused on more individual concerns. For example, Interviewee 12, a common law domestic judge–arbitrator, believed that 'those with training will generally do better and gain more respect in the arbitral community'. Interviewee 10, a common law domestic arbitrator, said,

> First-level judges often do not have reasoning skills—I'm sorry but it's true—and what I see is that they have taken the party briefs and used that as their order even if it doesn't match up with the outcome. I don't think they know what they're doing. I don't see that with appellate judges.

4. Type of educational programming

The last question in this series asked what kind of programming respondents believed would be most beneficial for judges and arbitrators seeking to learn more about writing reasoned decisions and awards. The survey asked a similar question to allow for cross-study comparison.[224]

A number of individuals focused on the need to identify best practices in legal reasoning and drafting, such as through the provision of exemplars. Thus, Interviewee 19, an international arbitrator, suggested 'being given models of what experts believe to be good awards in different categories of cases, as well as examples of bad awards. The ICC process of scrutiny goes a long way towards educating arbitrators on what are best practices. That's why ICC and SIAC are valuable institutions.' Interviewee 16, an international judge–arbitrator, similarly suggested that judges and arbitrators 'study well-written and not-well-written awards and identify the problems'. Interviewee 2, an international arbitrator, also supported 'courses that present best practices and warnings'.

Other respondents focused on the need for hands-on, experiential learning.[225] As Interviewee 4, a mixed international–domestic arbitrator noted, 'The most difficult programs are those that are hands-on, but they are an important component of any

[224] Ch. 2.IV.E.

[225] Experts in andragogy (adult education) suggest that experiential learning is optimal for experienced individuals. Malcolm S Knowles, *The Modern Practice of Adult Education: From Pedagogy to Andragogy* (Cambridge Book Co 1980) 45–49.

training process. Examples of things that can go wrong are also useful, but you learn the most from making the error yourself.' Interviewee 5, a common law domestic judge–arbitrator, similarly stated that 'interactive/experiential is good. Writing up your own draft awards and discussing those drafts with participants is valuable.'

Interviewee 10, a common law domestic arbitrator, provided some more tangible suggestions in this regard, indicating that the best courses involved 'writing exercises: 15-minute fact vignettes followed by 30 minutes in which to do outlines. If you did six of those in a day, maybe with group or private critique, you could make forward progress.' Interviewee 1, a mixed international–domestic arbitrator, 'found the CIArb [drafting] course extremely valuable' for precisely this reason, since 'it goes through issues, makes you write, then critique' your writing.

Other respondents focused on the substantive issues that they thought should be covered in judicial or arbitral education. For example, Interviewee 14, an international judge–arbitrator, said courses

> need to be oriented to [actual] practice. I'm just back from [a developing nation], where I was a trainer for the High Court bench. They just adopted [certain international instruments and model laws, and] they needed the judges to be trained on how to interpret those documents. I spent a day talking about the difference between litigation and arbitration at the interlocutory and final level.

Interviewee 11, a common law domestic judge–arbitrator, said that instructors should focus on teaching judges and arbitrators 'how to put the square peg in the square hole. Don't ramble. Keep focused. I've seen people give the whole history of contract law. No one wants to pay for that or read it. It makes you look like a fool.' Interviewee 2, an international arbitrator, said that it 'depends on who you're targeting. If new arbitrators, then focus on: one, required elements for enforceability; two, overturned cases—what mistakes are made. Scare tactics lodge deeply in their minds.'

G. Forward-Looking Proposals

The final question in the interview protocol asked whether there were any topics relating to reasoned decisions or awards that had not been covered but that should be addressed. While many respondents said that there were no additional items to discuss,[226] other individuals provided useful suggestions for academics, advocates, and policy makers.

Several people focused on areas that could benefit from additional scholarly research. For example, Interviewee 18, an international judge–arbitrator, suggested

[226] Interviewee 4, a mixed international–domestic arbitrator ('No.'); Interviewee 5, a common law domestic judge–arbitrator ('No.'); Interviewee 6, a mixed international–domestic arbitrator ('Don't think so.'); Interviewee 11, a common law domestic judge–arbitrator ('No.'); Interviewee 13, a common law domestic judge–arbitrator ('No.'); Interviewee 14, an international judge–arbitrator ('No.'); Interviewee 15, a common law domestic judge–arbitrator ('No.'); Interviewee 17, an international judge–arbitrator ('No.').

'maybe something about the role of tribunal secretaries in drafting'. Interviewee 1, a mixed international–domestic arbitrator, suggested inquiries into the 'impact of oral advocacy on arbitration', based in part on his/her view (echoed by numerous others)[227] that 'hyperbole and exaggeration of points is not helpful'. Interviewee 1 also noted that 'written documents are more useful to me because oral advocacy simplifies the issues, and it's hard [for counsel] to direct me to items in the record', since 'oral advocacy summarizes facts and is not as well connected to the record as written advocacy'.

Interviewee 2, an international arbitrator, noted that 'some mistakes made in this area [legal reasoning] are not because arbitrators don't know any better, it's because they're overworked. It would be interesting in future to explore [the impact of] arbitral dockets [on the nature and quality of reasoned awards] and length of awards' as well as any effect that scheduling concerns have on 'successful challenges.'[228] Interviewee 2 also noted that the conventional wisdom that 'a short award could be "more" enforceable' may in fact be 'a plea for more careful awards'. Indeed, Interviewee 2 was of the view that

> the quality of awards must reflect not only questions about the ideal but also whether the ideal can be done in reality. How much time does it take, what do you do it you don't have time—the 'oh my god' realities. Most arbitrators don't sacrifice quality, but it would be interesting to know what people do.

Interviewee 12, a common law domestic judge–arbitrator, said,

> You should ask whether arbitrators always feel constrained by the law or whether they believe they have latitude to do justice. I'm not sure every arbitrator thinks the same way on that. They probably think they follow the rule of law but they don't. For me, I try to follow the rule of law and not deviate. I don't know if that's right or not, but I suspect that if you polled occasional arbitrators (meaning those with only one or two [proceedings] a year), they're not as concerned about that.

Notably, the survey specifically addressed a number of these issues.[229]

Several people provided practical advice to adjudicators and advocates. For example, Interviewee 7, an international arbitrator, indicated that

> I find [drafting reasoned awards] more difficult because I see wrinkles in cases I wouldn't have seen if I were younger. I'd say to counsel: you will get more points if you realize these issues are difficult. Simply telling me this is an open and shut case is not persuasive because there are lots of different elements. Many lawyers are trained to make that type of argument, but they're not persuasive.

[227] See also Ch. 3.III.C.6 (indicating over-zealous advocacy can backfire).

[228] Such a study might resemble recent research in the judicial realm. Brian Sheppard, 'Judging Under Pressure: A Behavioral Examination of the Relationship Between Legal Decisionmaking and Time', (2012) 39 Florida St U L Rev 931; see also Jeffrey J Rachlinski and Andrew J Wistrich, 'Judging the Judiciary by the Numbers: Empirical Research on Judges', (2017) 13 Ann Rev L & Soc Sci 203, 223 (noting judges perform worse under time pressure).

[229] Ch. 2.IV.F.

Interviewee 19, an international arbitrator, provided slightly different advice, noting,

> If I have the time and discipline to write non-deliberative parts [of an award] before a hearing, I know the material and conduct the hearing better. Front loading is always better with reasoned awards. That's what parties deserve to know. They should help make arbitration better, do whatever you can to help the arbitrator prepare in advance. Don't give them one hundred volumes of documents without saying which are the most important, for example, since that doesn't help them prepare.

Interviewee 19 also said that 'I also don't see any reason in international commercial arbitration why we don't have parties drafting findings of fact and conclusions of law for arbitrators to consider. I think that'd be fantastic.' However, that particular proposition met with mixed reviews from other respondents.[230]

Two comments focused on the type of individuals who are involved in adjudicatory activities. Interviewee 8, an international judge–arbitrator, said,

> For people who argue cases, who have experience as sitting as arbitrators, even though there are objections to double-hatting, there are huge benefits to counsel. It was a huge benefit to me when I was returning to [private practice] after [having served as a judge–arbitrator]. If you have experience with both, you are better at each.

Interviewee 16, an international judge–arbitrator, similarly noted 'how important it is for arbitrators to have lots of experience as counsel—that may affect how they address the proceedings, especially proof-taking'. However, Interviewee 16 reflected something of a bias,[231] expressing concerns about

> professorial types that rose to prominence in arbitration but have never been counsel, so they don't know what's involved in prepping cross-examination, etc. It may be because of my background as counsel, but I think it's critical that arbitrators have experience. That has to affect how they write their decision because it affects how they perceive proof, especially at the hearing.

Finally, Interviewee 10, a common law domestic arbitrator, identified several systemic concerns, stating,

> I believe clauses permitting arbitrators to allocate party fees and costs is a powerful tool in controlling frivolous and harassing arbitration. Those clauses should be embraced because they bring about justice. For example, I had a case where I did not have that

[230] Chs. 2.IV.A.2, 3.III.E.3 (discussing giving draft portions of a reasoned decision or award to the parties or obtaining the parties' assistance in drafting).

[231] Ch. 3.III.C.2.b (noting bias against 'scholarly' work or training).

power, and the outcome, though appropriate, did not give full justice because the winning party had spent about the amount of the award to get the outcome. My award could never reflect true justice.

IV. Conclusion

Although the highly detailed and individualized nature of interview data can make it difficult to identify broad themes, the current study does allow for some wide generalizations. First, the vast majority of interviewees mentioned the importance of facts and factual analyses at some point during the discussion. While this may not surprise practitioners, judges, and arbitrators, academics have seldom considered how questions of fact affect legal reasoning. As this study has shown, factual considerations are both central to the reasoning process and capable of scholarly study. Hopefully, this research will generate new lines of inquiry in the coming years, including work of both a theoretical and empirical nature.

Second, the data suggested that judges and arbitrators have widely divergent opinions and practices relating to legal reasoning in commercial disputes, although those differences do not reflect a clear divide between judicial and arbitral norms. To the contrary, the interviews conducted in this study strongly suggest that different approaches to legal decision making are inherent among both judges and arbitrators. As a result, this study appears to disprove conventional wisdom suggesting that the nature and quality of judicial decision making is both different than and superior to arbitral decision making.

Normally, when faced with a range of behaviours, lawyers try to characterize one set of practices as 'right' and the other as 'wrong'. However, that type of binary thinking is not appropriate here, since many if not all of the practices discussed herein can be justified by reference to values considered legitimate as a matter of legal theory. For example, those interviewees who undertook independent legal or factual research could and often did justify those practices as necessary to get to the truth of the matter, a goal that is undeniably part of the dispute resolution process, while those who refused to undertake such research could and often did explain their actions by claiming that the dispute was 'owned' by the parties (a particularly important principle in common law countries) or by reference to concerns about the equality of arms between the parties (a value that is respected in both common law and civil law countries).

Scholars have long recognized that well-functioning legal systems simultaneously embrace a number of motivating 'stories', a concept that might be described as a reasonable pluralism of dispute system design and practice.[232] That understanding allows individual judges and arbitrators to prioritize different behaviours based on different

[232] Kathryn Abrams, 'Hearing the Call of Stories', (1991) 79 Cal L Rev 971, 1043; Daniel A Farber and Suzanna Sherry, 'The 200,000 Cards of Dmitri Yurasov: Further Reflections on Scholarship and Truth', (1949) 46 Stan L Rev 647, 648; see also Hiro N Aragaki, 'Deliberative Democracy as Dispute Resolution? Conflict, Interests, and Reasons', (2009) 24 Ohio St. J Disp Res 407, 416–18.

value judgments about what is most important about legal decision making. So long as the various motivating factors can be linked to legitimate norms within the system, the method used by the neutral is appropriate. As a result, all or virtually all of the actions taken by the interviewees could be said to be legitimate within their own motivating framework.

While the study did not identify any key differences along the three axes of comparison (judicial–arbitral, domestic–international or common law–civil law), such distinctions were not anticipated, given the small sample size. Instead, the primary purpose of the interviews was to supplement and in some cases complement the survey by generating more in-depth and detailed responses to questions than were possible in the survey. As it turned out, the material gathered from the interviews was largely consistent with that produced by the survey, thereby validating the results from both studies.

4

Quantitative Analysis of Reasoned Decisions and Awards

I. Introduction

The third and final of the three empirical elements to consider involves a quantitative analysis of judicial decisions and arbitral awards. This portion of the study sought not only to generate its own independent data but also to assess the validity of at least some of the results generated by the international survey and semi-structured interviews.[1] The breadth and diversity of data produced during this phase of the study provided rich fodder for independent and comparative analysis, although the research generated so much information that it was impossible to discuss all possible permutations in exhaustive detail in this text. However, a number of issues will be addressed in future analyses.[2] A copy of the coding book is reproduced in Appendix III.[3]

The chapter is organized as follows. The discussion begins by describing the methodology used to create the data set and coding criteria, followed by a section providing demographic and background information to help set the substantive analysis in context. Next, the chapter provides the substantive findings from the coding exercise, including information generated by a novel paragraph-counting technique and by a citation count analysis of both legal and factual authorities. The exercise was designed to track a number of issues addressed in the survey and semi-structured interviews, thereby allowing triangulation of data, and the chapter contains a number of cross-references to the survey and interviews discussed earlier in this text. Additional overarching conclusions appear in Chapter 5.

[1] Chs. 1.I, 1.III.A; see also Ch. 1.II (discussing triangulation of empirical research).

[2] E.g. SI Strong, 'Does Experience Matter? An Empirical Analysis of Seniority and Number of Disputes Heard on Legal Reasoning in Commercial Dispute Resolution' (forthcoming) (Strong, Experience); SI Strong, 'Does Gender Affect Legal Reasoning in Commercial Dispute Resolution? An Empirical Analysis' (forthcoming) (Strong, Gender); SI Strong, 'How Does Investment Arbitration Compare to Other Adjudicative Processes? An Empirical Analysis' (forthcoming) (Strong, Investment Arbitration); SI Strong, 'Proceedings in the English Commercial Court and Proceedings in International Arbitration: A Distinction Without An Empirical Difference?' (forthcoming) (Strong, English Commercial Court); SI Strong, 'The Effect of Motion Practice on the Nature of Dispute Resolution and the Creation of Precedent: An Empirical Analysis' (forthcoming) (Strong, Motion Practice).

[3] Providing copies of research instruments is considered a best practice in empirical research. Susan D Franck, 'Empiricism and International Law: Insights for Investment Treaty Dispute Resolution', (2008) 48 Va J Intl L 767, 787–88.

II. Methodology

The validity of any empirical research study turns on the quality of the methodology and the degree to which the study addresses the underlying research question.[4] The purpose of the coding exercise was to obtain objective data on actual judicial and arbitral practices, both to corroborate (if possible) information obtained from the survey and semi-structured interviews and to generate independent data that would prove useful to the legal community.[5]

During the study design process, several methodological issues had to be considered, including identification of a suitable group of decisions and awards to form the basis of the study; creation of an analytical framework that would test for characteristics analogous to those studied in the survey and semi-structured interviews; and generation of quantitative data that could be compared across the judicial–arbitral, domestic–international and common law–civil law divides.

A. Generating the Data Set

The first methodological task involved identification of judicial decisions and arbitral awards that would be suitable for quantitative study. As a matter of best practices in empirical research, it is necessary to describe the sampling methodology to expose and explain any actual or potential biases that might affect study results.[6]

As a matter of research design, the goal was to identify representative samples of judicial decisions and arbitral awards, using selection criteria that were not related to the variables under investigation.[7] Initially, it was anticipated that most of the difficulties would involve finding a suitable number of arbitral awards in their original (unredacted) form. Requests for assistance were issued to domestic and international arbitral institutions, but those organizations were either unable or unwilling to provide access to their original arbitral awards, even under conditions of confidentiality.[8] While it would have been useful to have access to these materials, the failure of this approach had its benefits, in that the study was not limited to a single institutional provider.

[4] Ch. 1.II (discussing the research questions for the current study); see also Ch. 2.II.

[5] Anselm Strauss and Juliet Corbin, *Basics of Qualitative Research: Techniques and Procedures for Developing Grounded Theory* (Sage Publishing 1998) 41 (discussing the need for precisely formulated research questions).

[6] Franck (n 3) 787.

[7] Lee Epstein and Gary King, 'The Rules of Inference', (2002) 51 U Chi L Rev 1, 113 (promoting this approach in small-n studies). Notably, the samples used in this study were not randomly selected, both because the datasets from which the decisions and awards were pulled were not random (e.g. the decisions were published, which in many cases involved an unknown selection process, and the awards were brought to US courts for enforcement or vacatur) and because the study reviewed all decisions and awards meeting particular criteria. Ibid 108 (describing how random selection operates in practice). However, the absence of random selection is not necessarily problematic, particularly in small-size studies. Ibid 113.

[8] One institution was willing to provide access to its database but would have placed limitations on the use of the data (such as prior approval of any analysis of the awards) that were inconsistent with independent scholarly research. This approach is of course highly problematic. SI Strong, 'The Fallacy of Transparency: How to Address Arbitral and Judicial (Non)Cooperation With Independent Scholarship' (forthcoming) (Strong, Transparency).

The search for original commercial awards next turned to public sources, most notably the judicial dockets of US federal courts. The Bloomberg legal database allows detailed searches of materials found on the US federal courts' Public Access to Court Electronic Records (PACER) system, which includes the entire docket of all of the parties' submissions to the court as well as all court rulings.[9] By searching in Bloomberg for cases involving enforcement, confirmation, or annulment of arbitral awards, it was possible to obtain original arbitral awards filed in support of the various requests for judicial relief. Differences in the relevant legal terminology required slightly different search parameters for domestic[10] and international awards,[11] but the searches were expected to yield similar types of results. Searches were limited to two different time periods—2003–2005 and 2015–2017—that matched similar time period restrictions for the judicial decisions.[12]

Several hundred cases were identified through this process, although not all of the arbitral awards were in English.[13] The results were then reviewed to eliminate default awards, interim or partial final awards, clause construction awards in class suits, and final awards incorporating elements found in interim or partial final awards, since those types of awards did not address the full panoply of legal and factual issues existing between the parties and were therefore not sufficiently similar to the types of judicial decisions that were analysed in the study.[14] The initial review also eliminated any awards that were not commercial in nature.[15] Ultimately, 70 commercial awards were fully coded, with 34 of those awards being characterized as domestic and 36 being characterized as international, using the same definition for 'international' used elsewhere in the study.[16] Each group was further divided into reasoned awards (22 domestic and 32 international) and standard (unreasoned) awards (12 domestic and 4

[9] US Courts, Public Access to Court Electronic Records, <https://www.pacer.gov/login.html> last accessed 11 April 2020.

[10] Domestic awards were identified using the search sequence 'confirm! or vacat! /s award and "commercial arbitration rules"' in addition to the relevant date parameters.

[11] International awards were identified using the search sequence 'award /s enforc! and "New York Convention" or "Convention on the Recognition or Enforcement" or "Panama Convention"' in addition to the relevant date parameters.

[12] The 2003–2005 time range reflected the earliest dates for which trial court dockets were available on Bloomberg, while the 2015–2017 time range reflected the latest calendar years for which dockets were available, given the start of the study in 2018. Initially the thought was to compare potential differences between the two time periods, but the sample sizes turned out to be too small to support such studies.

[13] As discussed in more detail below, the decision was made to limit the review to English language results. See also Ch. 2.II.A.

[14] Awards rendered in a documents-only proceeding were retained, since arbitrators in those matters were required to consider party submissions on both law and facts.

[15] The Bloomberg search produced a number of awards that were more properly characterized as involving consumer, employment or investment disputes. The investment awards were particularly interesting, since most arise out of arbitration agreements found in contracts between an investor and a state entity rather than out of a treaty. While the non-commercial awards were eliminated from the current study, a comparison of the investment awards to commercial decisions and awards will be conducted in the future. Strong, Investment Arbitration (n 2).

[16] International awards were defined as disputes in which at least two parties came from different countries, where the property in dispute was located in a country different than the disputants, or where performance or enforcement was anticipated in a country different than that of the disputants. This definition, which was also used in the survey and the semi-structured interviews, was based on section 202 of the US Federal Arbitration Act. 9 USC s 202; Chs. 2.II.A, 3.II.B.

international).[17] This information is itself illuminating, since it suggests that reasoned awards are the norm in commercial arbitration, which is not the case in other types of arbitration.[18]

While standard awards may initially appear irrelevant to the current analysis, many of the negative conceptions of arbitration appear to be associated with these types of awards.[19] Therefore, it is useful to present data about the nature and depth of legal and factual analysis in standard commercial awards to allow comparisons to reasoned commercial awards and judicial decisions. This approach is particularly appropriate given that arbitrators are not the only ones who issue unreasoned rulings. To the contrary, many judicial decisions are also unreasoned.[20] While the current study does not present information on unreasoned judicial rulings, future studies of litigation and arbitration would do well to compare the number and nature of unreasoned judicial rulings to the number and nature of standard awards.[21]

Although the arbitral search methodology sought to comply with best practices in empirical research, some concerns nevertheless arose. For example, the search focused exclusively on awards that were brought to US courts for enforcement, confirmation, or annulment. Not only does this phenomenon raise questions about a possible bias toward US-style arbitration,[22] it also raises questions about whether the awards in the study are sufficiently similar in terms of quality as compared to the judicial decisions, since the awards could be considered 'problematic' (to the extent they triggered enforcement, confirmation, or annulment actions) while the judicial decisions reflect the 'best' form of judicial writings (since they have been chosen for publication).[23]

Future studies may be able to eliminate these sorts of concerns by obtaining arbitral awards from a wider geographic region or that have not been made subject to enforcement proceedings. The research methodology might also be improved by obtaining

[17] Standard awards are typically only a page or two in length and provide the outcome of the arbitration with little or no evidentiary or legal support. David C Singer and Christina G Hanson, 'Making It Final: The Elements of a Tribunal's Award', (2019) 37 Alternatives to the High Cost of Litigation 117, 117.

[18] For example, consumer, employment and securities arbitration typically generate standard awards. W Mark C Weidemaier, 'Judging-Lite: How Arbitrators Create and Use Precedent', (2012) 90 N Carolina L Rev 1091, 1100 n 36.

[19] Ch. 1.III.A. Standard awards are most prevalent in consumer and employment arbitration in the United States, although such awards are occasionally used in commercial matters, as this research shows.

[20] Benjamin N Cardozo, *The Nature of the Judicial Process* (Yale University Press 1949) 164–65 (discussing three types of judicial writings); SI Strong, 'Writing Reasoned Decisions and Opinions: A Guide for Novice, Experienced and Foreign Judges', 2015 J Disp Res 93, 113–15; see also Chs. 3.III.A.1 (noting times when a judge did not issue a reasoned decision), 3.III.E.1 (same).

[21] Unreasoned judicial rulings are beyond the scope of the current research and are somewhat difficult to find, since they are often not published in standard legal reporters. However, unreasoned judicial rulings are public documents in some jurisdictions (such as the United States) and thus could be made the subject of academic research. In the United States, those documents might be located through the Bloomberg legal database, which provides searchable access to federal dockets.

[22] All of the domestic arbitrations were based in the United States and thus only involve US parties. International awards either involved award creditors with assets in the United States or US-based arbitral proceedings.

[23] While it is unclear why certain decisions are chosen for publication, some scholars have suggested that 'published decisions tend to be policy judgments with greater political consequences than their unpublished counterparts', which, if true, could skew the type of legal reasoning reflected in the decision. CK Rowland and Robert A Carp, *Politics and Judgment in Federal District Courts* (University Press of Kansas 1996) 14.

judicial decisions that are unpublished. However, the materials generated in this study provide a sufficient starting point for analysis.

As challenging as it was to find arbitral awards that were appropriate for study, the task of identifying analogous judicial decisions proved even more difficult. As a conceptual matter, the judicial decisions needed to come from first-instance courts, since trials, like arbitrations, decide questions of both law and fact. The judicial decisions also had to be decided on the merits, rather than on motion, so as to parallel arbitral determinations.[24] Finally, the judicial decisions had to focus on the same type of commercial disputes that arise in national and international arbitrations.

The first jurisdiction that was chosen to study was the United States. As a theoretical matter, US decisions were anticipated to be highly analogous to many of the arbitral awards, particularly those that were domestic in nature, and as a practical matter, US decisions were expected to be relatively easy to locate due to search functions available via the Westlaw-US subscription database, which not only provides access to first-instance decisions in both US state and federal courts but which also allows use of the West key number system as a means of identifying relevant subject matter.[25] After reviewing the available options, the decision was made to use West key numbers 95 (contracts), 289 (partnership) and 308 (principal and agent), since those topics would generate judicial decisions that would be most analogous with commercial arbitral awards.[26]

Initially, the target date range was identical to that used for awards (i.e. 2003–2005 and 2015–2017). However, the initial search generated a shockingly small number of first-instance decisions.[27] Ultimately, only seven trial-level state and federal cases were decided on the merits during the relevant time period (five in the 2003–2005 period and two in the 2015–2017 period), as compared to 115 state and federal trial-level decisions that were decided on motion between 2003 and 2005, with an additional 182 state and federal decisions decided on motion between 2015 and 2017.[28]

Given the size of the United States, it seemed strange that only 120 first-instance decisions dealing with contract, partnership, or principal/agent matters should be reported nationwide during the 2003–2005 time frame, with only 184 such decisions

[24] While arbitral matters are occasionally decided on motion or made subject to interim or partial awards, this study focused on solely on final awards and excluded any partial or interim awards that were generated through the Bloomberg search.

[25] Over 100 years ago, West Publishing developed a system of indexing US legal decisions based on various questions of substantive and procedural law. Maggie Keefe, 'Using the West Key Number System', ThomsonReuters.com, <https://legal.thomsonreuters.com/en/insights/articles/using-the-west-key-numbers-system> accessed 11 April 2020. Although some concerns exist about relying on the West key number system to generate target populations in empirical legal research, scholars have concluded that the benefits of using a system designed and generated by expert editors outweigh the costs. Joshua M Silverstein, 'Using the West Key Number System as a Data Collection and Coding Device for Empirical Legal Scholarship: Demonstrating the Method Via a Study of Contract Interpretation', (2016) 34 J L & Commerce 203, 227–28.

[26] Silverstein (n 25) 207 (noting '[c]ontract interpretation is one of the most important topics in commercial law'). Although Westlaw-US does not have a general key number for commercial law, commentators have approved of the use the Westlaw-US key number system in empirical legal scholarship. Ibid 216–20 (noting examples).

[27] The initial review also eliminated non-commercial cases and decisions rendered on default.

[28] This phenomenon will be further analysed and discussed in an upcoming article. Strong, Motion Practice (n 2). Notably, these numbers omit matters decided on default and non-commercial disputes.

between 2015–2017.[29] The dearth of materials could be explained by several factors, such as the tendency in the United States to publish appellate opinions rather than trial court decisions,[30] the relatively well-settled nature of contract law,[31] or the 'vanishing trial' syndrome that has been said to exist in the United States in the wake of the 1976 Pound Conference on the Causes of Popular Dissatisfaction With the Administration of Justice (Pound Conference).[32]

Although the Pound Conference was convened by US Supreme Court Chief Justice Warren Burger and thus had the initial support of the judiciary, judges, scholars, and policy makers have subsequently (and continually) debated the wisdom of reducing litigation in courts through the use of so-called alternative dispute resolution (i.e. negotiated and mediated settlements as well as arbitration).[33] To some extent, criticism of the 'ADR movement' of the 1980s and 1990s is most appropriately directed at consumer, employment, and labour disputes, since those fields not only saw a significant rise in arbitration following the Pound Conference but also involve a number of questionable practices ranging from a high percentage of standard (unreasoned) awards to the use of 'mandatory' arbitration agreements (meaning agreements imposed by the stronger party on the weaker party in a contract of adhesion).[34] Commercial disputes, on the other hand, have long been subject to arbitration in the United States, even predating the 1926 Federal Arbitration Act, and typically involve reasoned awards and arise as a result of arbitration agreements that have been individually negotiated by commercial actors of relatively equal power and sophistication.[35] Nevertheless, as a matter of study design it was important to consider whether any differences existed between the number and nature of commercial litigations arising before and after the 1976 Pound Conference. Therefore, searches were run for first-instance decisions from all US state and federal courts between 1973 and 1976, applying the same search criteria that was used for the 2003–2005 and 2015–2017 time periods. As it turned out,

[29] Other research based on the West key number system have generated far larger datasets involving thousands of cases. Silverstein (n 25) 226. However, those studies do not appear to have been limited to first-instance courts with decisions on the merits, but instead included decisions on motion and appellate opinions.

[30] Ibid 230. The dearth of trial-level decisions on the merits is not limited to contract cases. Michael Heise, 'The Past, Present and Future of Empirical Legal Scholarship: Judicial Decision Making and the New Empiricism', 2002 U Ill L Rev 819, 838 n 97, 844 (noting approximately 4 per cent of tort cases filed reach a judge or jury for final disposition).

[31] Silverstein (n 25) 207–08 (discussing resurgence of interest in contract interpretation after 'decades of neglect'); see also Chs. 3.III.B.3, 3.III.C.2.b, 3.III.E.3 (reflecting comments by interviewees concerning the settled nature of contract law).

[32] American Bar Association, 'Report of the Pound Conference Follow-Up Task Force', (1976) 74 FRD 159; William H Erickson, 'The Pound Conference Recommendations: A Blueprint for the Justice System in the Twenty-first Century', (1977) 76 FRD 277; Marc Galanter, 'The Hundred-Year Decline of Trials and the Thirty Years War', (2005) 57 Stan L Rev 1255, 1256 (discussing the 'vanishing trial' and noting a steep drop in absolute numbers of trials in the US since 1985); Lisa Traum and Brian Farkas, 'The History and Legacy of the Pound Conferences', (2017) 18 Cardozo J Conflict Res 677.

[33] For example, some observers suggest that mediation and arbitration inappropriately 'rob' society of the benefit of binding precedent on various legal issues. Owen Fiss, 'Against Settlement', (1984) 93 Yale LJ 1073; Myriam Gilles, 'The Day Doctrine Died: Private Arbitration and the End of Law', 2016 U Ill L Rev 371, 409–10.

[34] E.g. Jean R Sternlight, 'Creeping Mandatory Arbitration: Is It Just?', (2005) 57 Stan L Rev 1631, 1632–33.

[35] Richard Chernick, 'Imposed-Arbitration Reforms Threaten to Stifle Strengths of Commercial Arbitration', (2002) 9 Disp Res Magazine 16, 16; Sternlight (n 34) 1635.

the results were again very low, with only 20 state and federal decisions arising on the merits between 1973 and 1975, in comparison to 31 cases decided on motion.

Looking at the three time periods in tandem could lead to the conclusion that contract disputes are litigated relatively infrequently in the United States or, alternatively, that such disputes are seldom published in official reporters, either because the law of contract is relatively well-settled or because the disputes turn primarily on individual facts.[36] However, the relatively high proportion of disputes decided on motion during all three periods also raised questions about whether the low number of commercial disputes that were decided on the merits might be the result of innovations introduced by the Federal Rules of Civil Procedure in 1938 and subsequently adopted by various state courts as a means of reducing litigation in the United States.[37] In order to test this hypothesis, a search was run on first-instance decisions from US state and federal courts between 1935 and 1937, applying the same search criteria that were used for the other three time periods. Interestingly, only 10 trial-court decisions were rendered on the merits between 1935 and 1937, with 14 cases decided on motion during the same time period.

According to the above figures, the number of reported first-instance decisions in the relevant fields has risen over time (24 cases between 1935 and 1937, 51 cases between 1973 and 1975, 120 cases between 2003 and 2005, and 184 cases between 2015 and 2017), which is consistent with the general increase in litigation in the United States in the last century.[38] However, the percentage of trial-level decisions in those fields that were reported and decided on the merits has decreased.[39] Between 1935 and 1937, 42 per cent of the relevant first-instance disputes were decided on the merits, as compared to 39 per cent between 1973 and 75, 4 per cent between 2003 and 2005 and 1 per cent between 2015 and 2017.[40] While some of the decline appears to be attributable to the rise of ADR, including both arbitration and mediation, in the post-Pound Conference era, it is also possible that the increased use and sophistication of motion practice in US state and federal courts affected these numbers.[41]

As intriguing as this data may be, more research would be needed before any firm conclusions could be drawn about the cause of the decline in decisions on the merits

[36] Rowland and Carp (n 23) 14.

[37] Judith Resnik, 'Failing Faith: Adjudicatory Procedure in Decline', (1986) 53 U Chi L Rev 494, 511–12 (discussing the high percentage of cases decided on motion in the United States).

[38] Galanter (n 32) 1259 (noting growing caseloads have resulted in increasing numbers of cases filed, even though the number of trials on the merits has dropped, both in percentage and absolute terms).

[39] Ibid 1256–59 (citing past studies).

[40] These figures are different than those cited in other studies as a result of differences in geographic and subject matter scope. For example, one longitudinal study conducted on cases handed down from 1820 to 1970 from the Circuit Court of St Louis, Missouri, indicated that although the percentage of cases decided on the merits remained relatively steady during the first 100 years of the study, coming in at around 25 to 30 per cent, after 1925 the percentage dropped to around 15 per cent. Wayne McIntosh, *The Appeal of Civil Law: A Political-Economic Analysis of Litigation* (University of Illinois Press 1990) 124, as quoted in Galanter (n 32) 1257–58. However, that study was based on docket data rather than on published decisions, as the current study is. Stephen Daniels, '"You Can't Interview the Dead": McIntosh's *The Appeal of Civil Law* and the Debate Over Longitudinal Studies of Courts', (1992) 17 L & Soc Inquiry 291, 292.

[41] Galanter (n 32) 1256, 1262–63 (considering variety of reasons for decline in trial rates); Resnik (n 37) 511–12; Strong, Motion Practice (n 2).

over the last century.[42] As a result, the decision was made not to include data from the 1935–1937 and 1973–1975 time periods in the current analysis, particularly given the absence of arbitral awards from comparable periods. However, that material may provide a basis for future scholarship.[43]

The original study design contemplated inclusion of judicial decisions from more than one country, an approach that was made all the more necessary as a result of the small number of decisions from US courts. Within the common law world, the best jurisdiction appeared to be England, since the study could focus on decisions rendered by the English Commercial Court, a first-instance court that hears national and international commercial disputes akin to those addressed in the US judicial decisions and arbitral awards that had been selected.[44] The search was conducted on Westlaw-UK and used the search term 'co(commercial) and contract' in order to increase the likelihood that the dispute involved contract-related disputes.[45] The time period was restricted to a single time span (2015–2017) because of the high number of anticipated responses.

After excluding anomalous data,[46] the search identified a relatively high number of decisions (92) on the merits, although an even higher number of matters (298) were decided on motion.[47] According to these numbers, 24 per cent of the contract-related disputes heard by the English Commercial Court between 2015 and 2017 were decided on the merits. While this proportion is significantly higher than that reflected in the United States, the English judicial system has been steadily increasing efforts to reduce litigation in recent years, and it remains to be seen whether these efforts affect the percentage of cases that are decided on motion in the English Commercial Court.[48]

[42] Franck (n 3) 786–87 (noting the need to be cognizant of the limitations of data produced in any study).

[43] Strong, Motion Practice (n 2).

[44] Some commentators have suggested that the English Commercial Court operates as a viable alternative to international commercial arbitration. SI Strong, 'International Commercial Courts and the United States: An Outlier by Choice and by Constitutional Design?' in Xandra Kramer and John Sorabji (eds), *International Business Courts – A European and Global Perspective* (Eleven International Publishing, 2019) 255, 256 (Strong, International Commercial Courts). However, that hypothesis needs to be further tested. Strong, English Commercial Court (n 2).

[45] Westlaw-UK does not adopt the West key number system, so an electronic query had to be devised that would generate results similar those associated with the US search protocol.

[46] For example, matters dealing with the Commercial Circuit Court (formerly the Mercantile Court) and the Commercial Court of Northern Ireland were eliminated from the search results, since those are not the same entities as the English Commercial Court. Matters that were heard on default or that addressed only part of an overall claim (such as costs) were also excluded.

[47] Motions in the English system are similar but not identical to motions in the US system. Strong, Motion Practice (n 2).

[48] England and Wales have adopted various mechanisms to encourage settlement before cases are even filed in court. Civil Procedure Rules (England and Wales), Practice Direction—Pre-Action Conduct and Protocols, para. 6 (discussing the requirement of a 'letter before action' to trigger settlement discussions); SI Strong, 'Defining the Litigation Default', (2018) 37 Civil Justice Q 463, 465 (discussing how the Woolf Reforms sought to decrease litigation in English courts by amending the Civil Procedure Rules to encourage settlement). This differs from US practice, where attempts to settle a case have traditionally arisen only after litigation is initiated. Linda Nussbaum, 'Mediation as Regulation: Expanding State Governance Over Private Disputes', 2016 Utah L Rev 361, 362 (noting a shift in some fields to require mediation prior to filing). In arbitration, parties are increasingly using multi-tiered (step) clauses that require parties to attempt to mediate a dispute prior to filing for arbitration. SI Strong, 'Realizing Rationality: An Empirical Assessment of International Commercial Mediation', (2016) 73 Wash & Lee L Rev 1973, 2026 (citing empirical study showing international commercial mediation was most likely to arise as a result of a pre-dispute contractual provision).

Together, the US and English cases provided a suitably diverse perspective on how common law courts consider commercial disputes. However, it was necessary to consider whether the civil law perspective could also be integrated into the study.

The first difficulty was linguistic. Because civil law legal systems often descend from either the French or German legal systems, it initially appeared as if any civil law analysis would have to be conducted in a language other than English. However, bilingual research was problematic not only from a resource perspective[49] but also from a methodological perspective, since the survey and interviews were conducted in English and all of the awards that were analysed were in English.[50] Introducing research materials in another language in only one portion of the study would not only run the risk of translation errors, it would also affect the linguistic balance created by the use of English elsewhere in the study.

Questions then arose whether the Canadian province of Quebec could be used as a civil law comparator. Although Canada is typically considered a common law country, Quebec has strong historical ties to France, not only culturally and linguistically but also legally, which has led some commentators to characterize Quebec as a mixed legal system. However, Quebec is often deemed to act as a civil law system with respect to private law concerns despite its overall character as a mixed legal system.[51] Upon closer review, it was found that decisions from Quebec courts are drafted in the civilian style, which would offer a useful comparison to common law decisions from the United States and England. Furthermore, decisions from the Quebec courts are published in both English and French, thereby eliminating the need to engage in bilingual legal analysis. For these reasons, the decision was made to include Quebec in the project.

Once Quebec became part of the study, it was necessary to construct a protocol that would identify first-instance judicial decisions that were analogous to the US and English decisions and arbitral awards. The search was conducted in Westlaw-Canada, with a restriction on cases from Quebec and including the word 'contract'.[52] The search was limited to one year (2017) because of the large number of decisions that had to be reviewed and excluded for various reasons. For example, not only did the coders have to exclude decisions that were decided on motion rather than on the merits, they also had to exclude French-language decisions (which were identical to English-language decisions), decisions that were not commercial in nature, and decisions that were not

[49] Coders would have to be not only conversationally fluent in a second language but also legally fluent, which is much more difficult to find in a prospective research assistant. SI Strong, Katia Fach Gómez, and Laura Carballo Piñeiro, *Comparative Law for Spanish-English Speaking Lawyers: Legal Cultures, Legal Terms and Legal Practices / Derecho comparado para abogados anglo- e hispanoparlantes: Culturas jurídicas, términos jurídicos y prácticas jurídicas* (Edward Elgar Publishing 2016) ch. 1 (discussing differences between conversational and legal fluency).

[50] The few awards that were generated through the Bloomberg search that were not in English were excluded from this study.

[51] William Tetley, 'Mixed Jurisdictions: Common Law v Civil Law (Codified and Uncodified)', (2000) 60 Louisiana L Rev 677, 684, 695 (discussing how principles of English and commercial law were combined with principles of French law in the Civil Code of Lower Canada of 1866, which was in place when Quebec became part of the Dominion of Canada). However, some scholars question whether legal reasoning in Quebec is as civil law-oriented in practice as it is said to be as a formal matter. Catherine Valcke, 'Quebec Civil Law and Canadian Federalism', (1996) 21 Yale J Intl L 67, 114.

[52] Westlaw-Canada does not use the West key number system.

from one of the various courts of first instance (the Court of Québec, the Superior Court, the Federal Court, and the Human Rights Tribunal).[53]

Ultimately, 28 first-instance, commercial decisions were found that were decided on the merits, with an additional 71 matters that were decided on motion. These numbers suggest that 28 per cent of commercial contract-related disputes in Quebec are decided on the merits, which is the highest percentage of the jurisdictions included in this study and statistically significant when compared to the percentage of US decisions decided on the merits.[54]

Although the methodology used to identify judicial decisions in all three jurisdictions sought to generate a representative sample, a number of concerns nevertheless exist. Perhaps the most important of these involves the fact that the West legal databases rely primarily on published judicial rulings, which are only a small subset of judicial writings.[55] Because it is unknown what percentage of reasoned rulings are published[56] and what the precise criteria for publication are,[57] analysis of published decisions may be flawed for lack of a sufficiently representative dataset.[58] Future studies could overcome this issue by studying both published and unpublished judicial decisions on the merits, although this might require the cooperation of one or more judicial research institutes.[59]

Another issue involves the relative quality of the decisions and awards. As noted previously, only the most important judicial decisions are published, whereas only the most dubious arbitral awards are brought to court for confirmation, enforcement, or annulment, which could create some analytical distinctions across the judicial–arbitral divide. Future studies could overcome this issue by including awards that were not in any way challenged, although this would require the cooperation of one or more arbitral institutions.[60]

[53] The Quebec Judicial System, <https://www.educaloi.qc.ca/en/capsules/quebec-judicial-system> accessed 11 April 2020.

[54] The discrepancies between the different cohorts are statistically significant, using a two-tailed z-test. Chs. 2.II.A (discussing methods of statistical analysis used in this text, including two-tailed z-tests), 4.II.B (same). Although no difference arose between the Quebec courts and the English Commercial Court, both courts showed marked differences when compared to US courts. For example, the Quebec courts differed from US courts from 2015–2017 (p<.001), US courts from 2003–2005 (p<.001), and US courts from 1935–1937 (p<.05). The English Commercial Court differed from US courts from 2015–2017 (p<.001), US courts from 2003–2005 (p<.001), and US courts from 1973–1975 (p<.05). Differences also arose within the US decisions. For example, US courts from 2015–2017 differed from US decisions from 1973–1975 (p<.001) and US decisions from 1935–1937 (p<.001), while US courts from 2003–2005 differed from US decisions from 1973–1975 (p<.001) and US decisions from 1935–1937 (p<.001). This data is discussed further in Strong, Motion Practice (n 2).

[55] Silverstein (n 25) 230.

[56] Some data exists with respect to appellate decisions in the US federal system, but the percentages are likely much lower for first-instance courts. Letter from Alex Kozinski, US Circuit Judge, 9th Circuit, to Samuel A Alito, Jr, US Circuit Judge, 3rd Circuit (16 January 2004) 10 (noting 9th Circuit Court of Appeals only publishes 15 per cent of cases), <http://www.nonpublication.com/kozinskiletter.pdf> accessed 11 April 2020.

[57] In Australia, those determinations are made by the publishers of individual court reporting systems. Robin Creyke and others, *Laying Down the Law* (10th edn, LexisNexis Butterworths 2018) 172–74 (noting the editor of each reporting series decides which cases should be reported, although unreported appellate decisions are often freely available on the internet). In the United States, those determinations are generally made by individual courts. Deborah Jones Merritt and James J Brudney, 'Stalking Secret Law: What Predicts Publication in the United States Courts of Appeals', (2001) 54 Vanderbilt L Rev 71. However, many reporting systems focus primarily on appellate rather than first-instance decisions. Silverstein (n 25) 230.

[58] Rowland and Carp (n 23) 14.

[59] Such cooperation has traditionally been difficult to obtain. Ch. 2.II.A; Strong, Transparency (n 8).

[60] Such cooperation has traditionally been difficult to obtain. Ch. 2.II.A; Strong, Transparency (n 8).

Potential problems also exist with respect to the nature of the underlying disputes. While every effort was made to ensure subject matter consistency between different jurisdictions and between litigation and arbitration, some discrepancies can be found. For example, matters filed with the English Commercial Court are often quite complex, involving both national and international disputes, whereas matters filed in the Quebec courts tend to be smaller and more local in nature, with cases heard in US state and federal courts falling somewhere in the middle.[61] While these differences are in some ways unavoidable, they make comparisons about legal reasoning per se difficult, particularly if statistical studies are to be run.[62] This study sought to overcome some of these concerns by providing and analysing medians in addition to averages in cases where the standard deviation suggested particularly wide variation in reported results. Future studies could overcome this issue by controlling for the size and complexity of the dispute,[63] although that would likely require extending the relevant time periods and expanding subject matters under investigation so as to ensure a dataset that was big enough to support statistical analyses, a process that could cause difficulties of its own.

B. Generating the Coding Criteria

The second methodological task involved creation of a 'code book' that specified the information to be pulled by the coders from the individual decisions and awards.[64] Coders were given extensive training on the use and interpretation of the code book and were required to coordinate with each other and with the principal researcher throughout the coding process to ensure intercoder reliability. After the completion of the coding process, the principal researcher reviewed the data to confirm consistency across the data set.

The code book required coders to consider 76 different datapoints. Judicial decisions and arbitral awards were treated identically, although some information (such as demographic information about second and third decision makers) did not need to be completed in judicial matters, since judges at first instance sit alone, and arbitral matters involve a sole arbitrator. The first 41 items in the code book involved information necessary to identify and describe the dispute (i.e. case name, caption, number of parties, quantum of the dispute, etc.) as well as information about the parties and counsel (i.e. name, location, type of legal system).[65] The study also sought detailed

[61] Tables 4.1, 4.2.

[62] As noted in the paragraphs and tables below, many categories of analysis included very large standard deviations, which doubtless affected the outcome of the various statistical tests.

[63] One technique might involve limiting analysis only to certain types of disputes (i.e. bilateral matters), certain sizes of disputes (i.e. amounts in dispute), and/or certain sizes of decisions or awards (i.e. number of pages or paragraphs). However, those techniques are themselves problematic to the extent they eliminate some of the natural diversity inherent in commercial legal disputes.

[64] The coders were all graduate-level law students (JDs and LLMs) from universities in the United States.

[65] Future studies may consider connections between parties and counsel and between counsel and the dispute (for example, whether they always come from the same jurisdiction or legal tradition), but those concerns are not directly relevant to legal reasoning and therefore are not discussed herein.

information about the decision makers themselves (i.e. name, age, gender, place of legal qualification (if any), type of legal system where legally qualified, etc.). Much of this information is reported here for context but is not independently analysed for reasons of space and relevance.[66]

The remaining 35 data points provided material for two substantive inquiries. One aspect of the study built off empirical work previously conducted in this field involving citation counts of legal authorities in decisions and awards.[67] However, the current inquiry differed from previous studies in two ways. First, unlike earlier analyses, the research conducted herein distinguished between different types of legal authorities and identified how many citations were to unique sources as opposed to previously-mentioned sources. This approach not only demonstrated the diversity of source material but also the depth of analysis of individual authorities. Both of these issues are of interest to the current project, since they shed light on longstanding assumptions about presumed differences in reasoning across both the judicial–arbitral and common law–civil law divides.

The citation count analysis also differed from earlier studies by including factual authorities (i.e. evidence). Again, coders were asked to both quantify several different types of factual authorities and distinguish between initial and subsequent citations to those materials so as to determine the depth of discussion regarding particular sources of information. This is the first time this type of inquiry has been conducted in the commercial realm, thereby providing unique insights into judicial and arbitral reasoning.[68]

As useful as citation counts may be, they do not tell the whole story. For example, a judge or arbitrator may spend a significant amount of time discussing a particular authority without including any or many formal citations. Conversely, some decision makers may make frequent use of 'string citations' (multiple citations for the same proposition without any real analysis), thereby making a written ruling appear more legalistic than it actually is. Furthermore, citation counts do not quantify the amount of time judges and arbitrators spend discussing the relationship between the facts and the law, which many decision makers, including participants in the international survey and semi-structured interviews conducted as part of this study, find to be the most challenging and important aspect of legal reasoning.[69]

The second substantive element of the coding exercise sought to address these concerns by counting the number of paragraphs that each decision and award spent on different types of analyses. As explained in more detail below, coders were asked to count the number of paragraphs associated with procedural issues, parties' arguments, pure factual concerns, pure legal concerns, mixed issues of fact and law (i.e. discussions in which the law was applied to the facts), and the final disposition of the case. Because the length of a decision or award often varies depending on the nature of the dispute and the personal preferences of the decision maker, the study did not focus on the absolute

[66] Some of the data will be analysed in subsequent articles. Strong, Experience (n 2); Strong, Gender (n 2).
[67] Ch. 1.II.
[68] Ch. 1.II (noting lack of empirical research into use of factual authorities (evidence) in any context).
[69] Chs. 2.IV.E, 3.III.A.3.

numbers associated with each type of paragraph but instead calculated the percentage of the total decision or award that was associated with each type of paragraph.

Initially, it was anticipated that the data generated from both the citation count and the paragraph count would be statistically analysed across the judicial–arbitral, domestic–international and common law–civil law divides. However, widespread statistical analysis proved problematic, given the relatively small sample sizes in some categories of cases.[70] Therefore, this chapter does not undertake statistical comparisons across the three axes of comparison.

Furthermore, some of the most interesting data—such as several apparent distinctions between judicial practices in England and the United States—are technically outside the scope of the current research project, since they involve differences within the common law as opposed to differences between the common and civil law. Rather than lose that detail, this chapter reports the information generated from different jurisdictions separately and does not attempt to combine data sets unnaturally simply to create cohorts that are large enough to support statistical analysis.

For the most part, the discussion also does not conduct statistical studies of standard (unreasoned) awards, since those awards are by definition outside the scope of the current study. However, the information is reported for context and to assist other scholars working in this field.

Despite these difficulties, a number of statistical analyses were run on the coded material. Two of the tests used in this chapter (t-tests and two-tailed z-tests) were also used in the survey.[71] However, this chapter also used a two-tailed Mann-Whitney U test to double-check t-test calculations in situations where it appeared that large standard deviations might have thrown off results from the t-test.[72] This approach was considered appropriate because the Mann-Whitney U test compares the medians of two independent populations (μ_1 and μ_2) along a single variable, whereas the t-test compares the averages (means) of two independent populations in order to determine whether any difference exists other than that attributable to chance.[73] It was believed that comparing medians might be more accurate than comparing averages (means) in cases involving large standard deviations.

In all cases, the null hypothesis (H_0) anticipated that the comparative cohorts were the same (H_0: $\mu_1 - \mu_2 = 0$ or, equivalently, $\mu_1 = \mu_2$), while the alternate hypothesis (H_1)

[70] For example, the study was designed to distinguish between domestic and international decisions, thereby allowing a comparison to domestic and international awards, but the small sample size of the three types of judicial decisions made that analysis impossible.

[71] Ch. 2.II.A. T-statistical tests compare the averages (means) of two independent populations (μ_1 and μ_2) along a single variable to determine whether any difference exists other than that attributable to chance, while two-tailed z-statistical tests compare the proportional responses of two independent populations (μ_1 and μ_2) along a single variable to determine whether any difference exists other than that attributable to chance. T-test statistics were run on Tables 4.2, 4.3, 4.8, 4.12, 4.14, and 4.16 and calculated via Medcalc. Medcalc <https://www.medcalc.org/calc/comparison_of_means.php> accessed 11 April 2020. Z-test statistics were run on Tables 4.1, 4.4, 4.6, 4.9–4.11, 4.13, 4.15, and 4.17 and calculated via Social Science Statistics. Social Science Statistics <https://www.socscistatistics.com/tests/ztest/default2.aspx> accessed 11 April 2020.

[72] The Mann-Whitney U test was used on Tables 4.2, 4.3, 4.8, 4.12, 4.14, and 4.16 in addition to the t-test.

[73] Mann-Whitney U tests were calculated via Social Science Statistics. Social Science Statistics <https://www.socscistatistics.com/tests/mannwhitney/default2.aspx> accessed 11 April 2020. In this research, all Mann-Whitney U tests were two-tailed.

was that the comparative cohorts were not the same ($H_1: \mu_1 \neq \mu_2$). As was true with the survey analysis, statistical significance was deemed to exist in cases with an alpha (*a1*) level of $p<.05$ or lower.[74] The study reports *a1* levels of $p<.05$, $p<.01$ and $p<.001$, which are the same levels of significance used in the survey.[75] However, this chapter does not use asterisks to indicate the various significance levels in individual figures but instead refers to significance levels in the narrative.

III. Demographic and Background Information

Before addressing the substantive findings, it is useful to provide some demographic and background information about the disputes as well as about the parties, counsel, and decision makers. This section not only sets the larger analysis in context, it also offers material that has independent significance for those who study or engage in commercial litigation and arbitration.

As mentioned previously, all of the disputes in this study were commercial in nature. However, the study identified a number of other important attributes.

The first characteristic to be charted involved the location of the dispute. All of the judicial proceedings took place in the situs of the court (England, Quebec, and the United States). Furthermore, as was to be expected given the search methodology, all of the domestic arbitrations appeared to be based in the United States, although drafting conventions in domestic US arbitration made it impossible to confirm that supposition.[76] The US decisions and awards with an identifiable seat were further distinguished on the basis of location, using federal circuit numbers to identify the relevant region,[77]

[74] Ch. 2.II.A. Statistical significance refers to 'the likelihood, or probability, that a statistic derived from a sample represents some genuine phenomenon in the population'. Timothy C Urdan, *Statistics in Plain English* (Routledge 2005) 50 (discussing statistical analysis in empirical legal research); see also Epstein and King (n 7) 60; Weidemaier (n 18) 1091.

[75] Ch. 2.II.A. A *p* value of .05 means there is a 5 per cent likelihood (or less) that the difference between the two populations is attributable to chance, while a *p* level of .01 means there is a 1 per cent likelihood that the difference between the two populations is attributable to chance. *P* levels of .001 are even more robust, meaning that there is a .1 per cent likelihood that the difference between the two populations is random. Robert W Frick, 'The Appropriate Use of Null Hypothesis Testing', (1996) 1 Psych Methods 379–90 (discussing the appropriate *p* value associated with null hypothesis testing).

[76] Unlike international arbitral practice, which requires the tribunal to indicate the seat of the proceedings, domestic arbitral practice in the United States does not require the tribunal to indicate where the proceedings were seated. As a result, it was impossible to identify the seat of arbitration for 10 (45 per cent) of the 22 domestic awards that were reasoned. Of the 12 standard (unreasoned) domestic awards, seven (58 per cent) did not clearly indicate their seat.

[77] The US federal circuit courts of appeal include the First Circuit (Maine, Massachusetts, New Hampshire, Rhode Island); the Second Circuit (Connecticut, New York, Vermont); the Third Circuit (Delaware, New Jersey, Pennsylvania); the Fourth Circuit (Maryland, North Carolina, South Carolina, Virginia, West Virginia); the Fifth Circuit (Louisiana, Mississippi, Texas); the Sixth Circuit (Kentucky, Michigan, Ohio, Tennessee); the Seventh Circuit (Illinois, Indiana, Wisconsin); the Eighth Circuit (Arkansas, Iowa, Minnesota, Missouri, Nebraska, North Dakota, South Dakota); the Ninth Circuit (Alaska, Arizona, California, Hawai'i, Idaho, Montana, Nevada, Oregon, Washington); the Tenth Circuit (Colorado, Kansas, New Mexico, Oklahoma, Utah, Wyoming); and the Eleventh Circuit (Alabama, Florida, Georgia). The coding process also considered whether decisions or awards came from the District of Columbia or any of the US territories or dependencies (American Samoa, Guam, Northern Mariana Islands, Puerto Rico, US Virgin Islands).

regardless of whether the ruling was from a state or federal court[78] or reflected a reasoned[79] or standard (unreasoned) arbitration award.[80] One initial goal of the study was to determine whether any differences in reasoning arose between commercial awards rendered in different regions within the United States, but the small sample size made that inquiry impossible.

Although the study was not designed to investigate differences in legal reasoning based on judicial or arbitral rules of procedure, it bears mention that all but one of the domestic awards were decided under the Commercial Arbitration Rules of the American Arbitration Association (AAA).[81] The remaining reasoned award went forward on an ad hoc basis.

The international awards were much more diverse in terms of their arbitral seats. Of the 32 reasoned awards, 21 (65 per cent) came from proceedings seated in the United States.[82] This data is intriguing, since it appears to confirm anecdotal information about the relative importance of New York (which is within the Second Circuit) and Florida (which is within the Fourth Circuit) as the centres of influence for international arbitration in the United States. Of the remaining 11 awards, two (6 per cent) came from proceedings seated in Switzerland, four (14 per cent) came from proceedings seated in the United Kingdom, one (3 per cent) came from Italy, one (3 per cent) came from Ukraine, one (3 per cent) came from China, one (3 per cent) came from Japan, and one (3 per cent) came from Brazil. Notably, all four of the standard awards involving international disputes came from the United States.[83]

The international awards were equally diverse in terms of their governing procedural rules. Of the 32 reasoned awards, 14 were decided pursuant to the rules of the

[78] Of the seven decisions in this study, two (29 per cent) came from locations within the Second Circuit, one (14 per cent) came from a location within the Third Circuit, one (14 per cent) came from a location within the Fourth Circuit, two (29 per cent) came from locations within the Fifth Circuit, and one (14 per cent) came from a location within the Seventh Circuit.

[79] The location for 12 of the 22 reasoned domestic awards could be determined. The numbers were as follows: three awards (14 per cent) came from locations within the Second Circuit, one (5 per cent) came from a location within the Third Circuit, two (9 per cent) came from locations within the Fifth Circuit, three (14 per cent) came from locations within the Sixth Circuit, one (5 per cent) came from a location within the Tenth Circuit, and two (9 per cent) came from locations within the Eleventh Circuit. Notably, the absence of commercial awards from the remaining jurisdictions does not mean that commercial arbitration is not used in these locales; it simply means that no cases seeking to confirm or vacate a commercial arbitral award and attaching an original arbitral award were found during the relevant time periods.

[80] The location for five of the 12 standard domestic awards could be determined. The numbers were as follows: two (17 per cent) came from locations within the Third Circuit, two (17 per cent) came from locations within the Fifth Circuit, and one (8 per cent) came from a location within the Tenth Circuit.

[81] All of the standard domestic awards were decided pursuant to the AAA Commercial Arbitration Rules, as were 21 of the 22 reasoned awards.

[82] Of the 16 international proceedings in the United States, one (3 per cent) came from a location within the First Circuit, nine (28 per cent) came from locations within the Second Circuit, one (3 per cent) came from a location within the Third Circuit, one (3 per cent) came from a location within the Fifth Circuit, one (3 per cent) came from a location within the Seventh Circuit, two (6 per cent) came from locations in the Ninth Circuit, five (16 per cent) came from locations in the Eleventh Circuit, and one (3 per cent) came from the District of Columbia. Notably, the absence of international awards from the remaining jurisdictions does not mean that international commercial arbitration is not used in these locales; it simply means that no cases seeking to confirm or vacate an international award and attaching an original arbitral award were found during the relevant time periods.

[83] One award (25 per cent) came from a location in the First Circuit, one (25 per cent) came from a location in the Second Circuit, one (25 percent) came from a location in the Fourth Circuit, and one (25 per cent) came from a location in the Ninth Circuit.

International Center for Dispute Resolution (ICDR), eight were decided pursuant to the rules of the International Chamber of Commerce (ICC), and two were decided on an ad hoc basis without any governing rule set. One award was also decided under the rules of each of the following arbitral institutions: the Arbitration Court of Rome, the Center of Industries of São Paulo/Federation of Industries of São Paulo (CIESP/FIESP), the London Court of International Arbitration (LCIA), JAMS International, the Japan Commercial Arbitration Association, the Shanghai International Arbitration Centre, and the Ukrainian Chamber of Commerce. One award was also rendered pursuant to the United Nations Commission on International Trade Law (UNCITRAL) Arbitration Rules.[84] Of the four standard awards dealing with international disputes, three were decided pursuant to the ICDR Arbitration Rules and one was decided under the Financial Industry Regulatory Authority (FINRA) Arbitration Rules.

Another important demographic detail involves the nature of the dispute as domestic or international in scope. While the study was originally designed to allow the data to be filtered to support a comparative analysis of judicial reasoning across the domestic–international divide, such an inquiry proved impossible given the small number of judicial decisions in some jurisdictions. However, the data provided important contextual information.

Table 4.1 Type of decision or award (actual numbers followed by proportion in parenthesis)

	Domestic	International	Total
Judicial decisions – England	21 (.23)	71 (.77)	92
Judicial decisions – Quebec	25 (.89)	3 (.11)	28
Judicial decisions – US	4 (.57)	3 (.43)	7
Awards – domestic reasoned	22 (1.00)	0 (.00)	22
Awards – international reasoned	0 (.00)	32 (1.00)	32
Awards – domestic standard	12 (1.00)	0 (.00)	12
Awards – international standard	0 (.00)	4 (1.00)	4

As Table 4.1 shows, a substantial proportion of English decisions were international in nature. This phenomenon is consistent with the English Commercial Court's longstanding reputation for excellence in complex commercial disputes and the English

[84] Although UNCITRAL does not administer arbitrations, it has promulgated arbitration rules that can be adopted for use in ad hoc proceedings.

courts' willingness to hear any matter that is governed by English law, even if the parties or the dispute have no other connection to the United Kingdom.[85] Conversely, the vast majority of decisions from Quebec were domestic in nature. Although the courts in Quebec are, like other courts in Canada, considered efficient and competent,[86] Quebec is not known as an international commercial centre, which explains why most disputes were local in nature. The difference between the percentage of domestic disputes in the English Commercial Court and the Quebec courts was statistically significant ($p<.001$) under a two-tailed z-test.

Although the US sample was quite small, the percentage of international disputes fell halfway between that of the English Commercial Court and the Quebec courts. While it is impossible to draw any firm conclusions from this information, the data seems to support anecdotal evidence indicating that US courts, particularly US federal courts in commercial centres like New York and Florida, are considered an acceptable forum for cross-border business disputes, although several features of US civil procedure, including those relating to jurisdiction, make the United States less attractive to international parties than some other countries, including England.[87] The percentage of domestic disputes in US courts was not statistically significant as compared to either the English Commercial Court or the Quebec courts, which may be a feature of the US courts' intermediate stance or the small sample size.

When designing the study, it was anticipated that the amount in dispute would likely be higher in international matters than in domestic matters. While quantum does not always correlate to legal complexity, some interviewees indicated that they wrote their decisions or awards somewhat differently depending on the amount of damages claimed.[88] Thus, it was important to consider the average amount in dispute in the decisions and awards discussed in this chapter.

[85] Pamela K Bookman, 'The Adjudication Business', (2020) 45 Yale J Intl L 227, 235. In 2015, the English High Court released figures indicating that 63 per cent of matters in the English Commercial Court involved international parties, although that number included all matters, not just those involving the search terms used herein. Adam Sanitt, 'The Financial List: Resolving Financial Markets Disputes in London', Norton Rose Fulbright (November 2015), <http://www.nortonrosefulbright.com/knowledge/publications/134005/the-financial-list-resolvingfinancial-markets-disputes-in-london> accessed 11 April 2020.

[86] According to World Bank data for 2020, Canada scored 11 out of 18 in terms of the quality of judicial processes, which is the approximate average for high income economies. Ease of Doing Business in Canada, The World Bank, <https://www.doingbusiness.org/en/data/exploreeconomies/canada#DB_ec> accessed 11 April 2020. Higher scores are correlated with higher quality judicial systems. Doing Business, Methodology, The World Bank, <https://www.doingbusiness.org/en/methodology/enforcing-contracts> accessed 11 April 2020. In comparison, the United Kingdom and the United States both scored 15 out of 18. Ease of Doing Business in the United Kingdom, The World Bank, <https://www.doingbusiness.org/en/data/exploreeconomies/united-kingdom#DB_ec> accessed 11 April 2020; Ease of Doing Business in the United States, The World Bank, <https://www.doingbusiness.org/en/data/exploreeconomies/united-states#DB_ec> accessed 11 April 2020. In terms of comparative worldwide rankings for the enforcement of contracts, the United States was ranked at 17, the United Kingdom was ranked at 34, and Canada was ranked at 100 out of 190 countries. Doing Business, Rankings, The World Bank, <https://www.doingbusiness.org/en/rankings> accessed 11 April 2020.

[87] Samuel P Jordan, 'Reverse Abstention', 92 Boston U L Rev 1771, at 1809–10 (2012); SI Strong, 'Congress and Commercial Trusts: Dealing With Diversity Jurisdiction Post-Americold', (2017) 69 Florida L Rev 1021 1027; Christopher A Whytock, 'The Evolving Forum Shopping System', 96 Cornell L Rev 481, 530 n 215 (2011).

[88] Indeed, one of the interviewees made this point explicitly. Ch. 3.III.E.2.

Table 4.2 Size of damages awards in US dollars (averages rounded to the nearest thousand followed by medians rounded to the nearest thousand in brackets, standard deviation rounded to the nearest thousand in parenthesis and sample (N) size)

Judicial decisions – England	27,914,000 [2,984,500] (60,134,000) 34
Judicial decisions – Quebec	323,000 [48,000] (968,000) 25
Judicial decisions – US	1,280,000 [83,000] (2,646,000) 5
Awards – domestic reasoned	3,139,000 [1,126,000] (4,476,000) 19
Awards – international reasoned	11,646,000 [2,260,000] (21,277,000) 26
Awards – domestic standard	276,000 [138,000] (365,000) 8
Awards – international standard	1,373,000 [737,000] (1,736,000) 4

Table 4.2 reflects both the average and median amount awarded by judges and arbitrators in various proceedings, with damages awarded in foreign currency converted to US dollars as of the date of the decision or award.[89] The table reports only actual damages awards and excludes matters where the claimant/counterclaimant did not prevail or where the only relief was non-monetary in nature.[90] The figures did not include attorneys' fees, arbitrators' fees, administrative fees, or interest so as to provide

[89] Currency conversations were made using the following website: <http://www.xe.com/currencytables/> accessed 11 April 2020. The underlying data also indicated whether injunctive or other forms of non-monetary relief was provided, although that information is not reported here.

[90] Information on the quantum of dispute was included even though damage calculations are often erratic and non-rational as a result of anchoring and other cognitive distortions. Jeffrey J Rachlinski, Andrew J Wistrich, and Chris Guthrie, 'Can Judges Make Reliable Numeric Judgments? Distorted Damages and Skewed Sentences', (2015) 90 Indiana LJ 695, 696–97 (discussing anchoring bias); Jeffrey J Rachlinski and Andrew J Wistrich, 'Gains, Losses, and Judges: Framing and the Judiciary', (2018) 94 Notre Dame L Rev 521, 550 (evaluating judicial responses to a simulated contract dispute).

a more accurate comparison of quantum between proceedings that routinely impose such fees and those that do not. Furthermore, the reported amounts do not incorporate any applicable setoffs but instead combine damages awarded to both claimants and counterclaimants so as to reflect the true amount in dispute.

As Table 4.2 shows, the highest average damages appeared in the English Commercial Court by a considerable magnitude of difference, with awards rendered in international commercial arbitration coming in second. This outcome was somewhat surprising, given conventional wisdom that international commercial arbitration is the mechanism of choice for resolving large, complex disputes.[91] A t-test comparing these two figures showed no statistically significant difference, likely because the standard deviation for both figures was quite large.

One possible way of avoiding problems associated with high standard deviations is to compare median figures. Under this analysis, decisions from the English Commercial Court again showed the highest damages amount, with international commercial arbitration reflecting the second highest amount, which can be read to confirm information gleaned from the comparison of average damages. Although the difference between the English Commercial Court and international commercial arbitration was much smaller, the difference was statistically significant under a Mann-Whitney U test ($p<.05$). Interestingly, the data from the English Commercial Court showed statistically significant differences in relation to all other cohorts, with the exception of domestic reasoned awards and standard awards from international commercial arbitration.[92]

The data regarding the smallest damages awards was somewhat mixed. When comparing averages, the smallest amounts were generated in standard (unreasoned) domestic arbitration followed by litigation in the Quebec courts, a difference that was not statistically significant under a t-test comparison, likely as a result of small sample sizes and large standard deviations. This result is consistent with the local nature of the two types of disputes and with the notion that, given the choice, parties who have relatively small-value claims in arbitration typically do not want to pay for a fully reasoned award.[93] However, when comparing medians, the smallest amounts were generated in Quebec courts, followed by US courts, with standard domestic arbitration coming in third. A Mann-Whitney U test showed a statistically significant difference between decisions in Quebec courts and awards in reasoned domestic arbitration ($p<.001$), but no other statistically significant differences arose between any of the reasoned rulings.[94]

[91] Gary B Born, *International Commercial Arbitration* (2d edn, Wolters Kluwer 2014) 93, 97.

[92] There were too few standard awards from international commercial arbitration to support statistical analysis. The Mann-Whitney U test showed the following differences between the English Commercial Court and other comparative groups: Quebec courts ($p<.001$); US courts ($p<.05$); standard domestic arbitration ($p<.01$).

[93] Arbitrators are paid by the hour under a number of arbitral rule sets, which suggests that parties can achieve significant savings by asking for a standard (unreasoned) award, which takes much less time to write than a fully reasoned award. Henry G Stewart, 'Trials of a Neophyte Neutral: The Transition From Full-Time Advocate', (2003–2004) 58 Disp Res J 39, 39 (noting the amount of time it takes to write an award); SI Strong, 'Reasoned Awards in International Commercial Arbitration: Embracing and Exceeding the Common Law-Civil Law Dichotomy', (2015) 37 Mich J Intl L 1, 34 (Strong, Reasoned Awards).

[94] Damages awards in reasoned forms of domestic arbitration showed a statistically significant difference from standard (unreasoned) forms of domestic arbitration ($p<.05$).

The data presented a number of surprises. For example, it was not anticipated during the study design process that there would be any standard awards rendered in the cross-border context, nor that they would resolve such financially significant disputes if they did exist. Although the figures in the standard international awards was doubtless affected by a very large FINRA award of $3,869,000, both the average damages amount and the median damages amount in standard international arbitration were considerably higher than comparable figures in standard domestic arbitration.

Another surprise involved the fact that damages in reasoned domestic awards exceeded damages in US decisions, both in terms of average and median numbers. While neither a t-test nor a Mann-Whitney U test comparing the average and median figures between the two groups showed a statistically significant difference, this data may suggest that US parties are taking their highest-valued commercial disputes to arbitration, unlike international parties, who are taking their highest-valued commercial disputes to the English Commercial Court. While more research is needed to confirm this hypothesis, the data is intriguing.

Quantum is only one way to evaluate the size and complexity of a commercial dispute. Another way to think about complexity involves the number of parties. Recent years have seen the rise of multiparty disputes in both litigation and arbitration,[95] although no information yet exists as to whether parties to such matters prefer one venue over another.

As Table 4.3 shows, all of the cohorts under investigation show averages above 2.00, confirming that the standard two-party dispute is not the only type of configuration possible in contemporary commercial settings. The highest average unexpectedly came from standard international awards, but that figure can be explained by a small sample size and single outlier with a very large number of parties.[96] The next highest average came from the English Commercial Court, although there again, a high standard deviation suggests that the average is not a reliable number. The median data is likely more useful and suggests that bilateral and small multiparty disputes (i.e. those involving three or four parties) are the norm in the commercial world.

After demonstrating that judicial and arbitral disputes are not exclusively bilateral in nature, the study went on to consider the affiliation of the additional parties. The options included additional plaintiffs/claimants; additional defendants/respondents; additional plaintiff/claimants and additional defendants/respondents; and no additional parties. During the design phase, it was anticipated that this calculation would not only provide useful insights into the nature of multiparty disputes in different proceedings but would also avoid the impact of high standard deviations on calculations of average numbers of parties.

[95] SI Strong, 'Increasing Legalism in International Commercial Arbitration: A New Theory of Causes, A New Approach to Cures', (2013) 7 World Arb & Med Rev 117, 119 (Strong, Increasing Legalism). Notably, class actions and class arbitrations were excluded from the study, since those matters are typically not considered commercial in nature.

[96] One of the standard international awards had 15 parties. Since that data set included only four entries, this single proceeding, which went forward under the FINRA rules, had an inordinate impact on the average. Without this entry, the average for standard international awards would have been 2.33.

Table 4.3 Total number of parties (averages followed by medians in brackets, standard deviation in parenthesis and sample (N) size)

Judicial decisions – England	4.15 [2.00] (10.24) 92
Judicial decisions – Quebec	3.00 [3.00] (2.00) 28
Judicial decisions – US	3.43 [3.00] (1.51) 7
Awards – domestic reasoned	3.32 [2.00] (1.89) 22
Awards – international reasoned	2.72 [2.00] (2.17) 32
Awards – domestic standard	2.33 [2.00] (0.65) 12
Awards – international standard	5.50 [2.50] (6.35) 4

As Table 4.4 shows, multiparty disputes arose in all the comparative cohorts, albeit at different frequencies. Under a two tailed z test of the reasoned rulings, the only statistically significant differences involved 'no additional parties' in international awards, which differed from 'no additional parties' in decisions of the English Commercial Court at the $p<.001$ level, decisions of the Quebec courts at the $p<.05$ level and domestic awards at the $p<.01$ level. This suggests that international commercial arbitration is more likely to be bilateral in nature, as compared to proceedings in these other fora. While decisions from US courts initially appeared to be very different from other rulings with respect to 'no additional parties', the sample size seemed to be too small to generate statistically significant differences. Finally, the fact that the two arbitral procedures had the highest proportion of bilateral disputes was not surprising, given the difficulty associated with adding additional parties in arbitration.[97]

[97] SI Strong, 'Third Party Intervention and Joinder as of Right in International Arbitration: An Infringement of Individual Contract Rights or a Proper Equitable Measure?', (1998) 31 Vanderbilt J Transnatl L 915, 918–20.

Table 4.4 Affiliation of additional parties in commercial disputes (actual numbers followed by proportion in parenthesis)

	Plaintiff/ claimant	Defendant/ respondent	Both plaintiff and defendant	No additional parties	Total
Judicial decisions – England	16 (.17)	17 (.18)	11 (.12)	48 (.52)	92
Judicial decisions – Quebec	2 (.07)	9 (.32)	4 (.14)	13 (.46)	28
Judicial decisions – US	2 (.29)	2 (.29)	1 (.14)	2 (.29)	7
Awards – domestic reasoned	0 (.00)	6 (.27)	4 (.18)	12 (.55)	22
Awards – international reasoned	3 (.09)	5 (.16)	3 (.09)	21 (.66)	32
Awards – domestic standard	0 (.00)	3 (.25)	0 (.00)	9 (.75)	12
Awards – international standard	0 (.00)	2 (.50)	0 (.00)	2 (.50)	4

The final demographic element to consider involves the number and nature of decision makers. The discussion begins by investigating whether the disputes in question were resolved by one or three individuals. This is of course primarily an arbitral issue, since litigation in first-instance courts always involves one judge.[98]

As Table 4.5 shows, the number of arbitrators appeared to be directly correlated to whether the award was reasoned or unreasoned, with sole arbitrators more likely in matters involving standard awards.[99] However, a substantial number of reasoned decisions were rendered by individual arbitrators in both domestic and international disputes. A higher percentage of international arbitrations were heard by tribunals as compared to domestic arbitrations, but that difference was not statistically significant.

One of the most pressing challenges currently facing the arbitral community involves the diversity (or lack thereof) of the arbitral pool. While diversity can include a number of different features ranging from professional training, age, and seniority to nationality, race, and gender, not all of these attributes could be accurately identified based on information contained in the decision or award.[100] However, the data on gender could be and was considered.[101]

[98] Parties in arbitration sometimes prefer to have their disputes heard by tribunals, likely because of concerns about the absence of an appeal on the merits. Wendy Miles, 'Practical Issues for Appointment of Arbitrators', (2003) 20 J Intl Arb 219, 227; Yu-Jin Tay, 'Reflections on the Selection of Arbitrators', in Albert Jan van den Berg (ed), (2003) 17 *ICCA Congressional Series: International Commercial Arbitration: The Coming of a New Age?* 112, 114–15. Arbitrations governed by English law may be subject to an appeal on the merits unless the parties opt out of the relevant provision. Arbitration Act 1996, s 69.

[99] The entry indicated as 'other' involved a 12-person tribunal in large multiparty ICDR arbitration. Only the chairperson and first two listed wing arbitrators were used for purposes of the current analysis.

[100] Some of these attributes are studied in other contexts. Strong, Experience (n 2); Strong, Gender (n 2).

[101] The gender of the various decision makers was confirmed by online biographies. None of the biographies suggested the individual in question identified as gender non-binary.

Table 4.5 Number of decision makers (actual numbers followed by proportion in parenthesis)

	One	Three	Other	Total
Judicial decisions – England	92 (1.00)	0 (.00)	0 (.00)	92
Judicial decisions – Quebec	28 (1.00)	0 (.00)	0 (.00)	28
Judicial decisions – US	7 (1.00)	0 (.00)	0 (.00)	7
Awards – domestic reasoned	13 (.59)	9 (.41)	0 (.00)	22
Awards – international reasoned	11 (.34)	20 (.62)	1 (.03)	32
Awards – domestic standard	11 (.92)	1 (.08)	0 (.00)	12
Awards – international standard	3 (.75)	1 (.25)	0	4

As Table 4.6 shows, the vast majority of judges, sole arbitrators, and arbitral chairs in this study were men. When considering judicial decision makers, a two-tailed z-test analysis showed a statistically significant difference ($p<.001$) between the gender of judges on the English Commercial Court and the gender of judges on the Quebec courts. While this might initially be interpreted to reflect a key difference between common law and civil law jurisdictions, there was no statistically significant difference between the gender of judges on the Quebec courts and the gender

Table 4.6 Gender of judge, sole arbitrator, or arbitral chair (actual numbers followed by proportion in parenthesis)

	Male	Female	Total
Judicial decisions – England	85 (.92)	7 (.08)	92
Judicial decisions – Quebec	18 (.64)	10 (.36)	28
Judicial decisions – US	6 (.86)	1 (.14)	7
Awards – domestic reasoned	20 (.91)	2 (.09)	22
Awards – international reasoned	26 (.81)	6 (.19)	32
Awards – domestic standard	8 (.67)	4 (.33)	12
Awards – international standard	4 (1.00)	0 (.00)	4

of judges on US courts. As a result, the relevant difference appears to extend only to England and Quebec.

In the case of arbitration, no statistically significant differences involving gender arose between the two types of reasoned awards (domestic and international), nor did any statistically significant differences involving gender arise between the two types of domestic awards (reasoned and standard).[102]

Finally, judicial practices were compared to arbitral practices. No statistically significant differences arose when comparing the two cohorts that were most similar in terms of size and number of international disputes (decisions from the English Commercial Court and reasoned international awards), nor did any statistically significant difference exist when comparing the two cohorts that were most similar in terms of national outlook (decisions from US courts and reasoned domestic awards). As a result, the conclusion appears to be that men are more likely, and in some cases considerably more likely, than women to be appointed or selected as a commercial decision maker in litigation or arbitration.

While first-instance courts have only a single decision maker, some arbitrations have two additional decision makers, alternatively referred to as party-appointed or 'wing' arbitrators. As Table 4.7 shows, the same preference for male arbitrators existed even among these individuals.

Table 4.7 Gender of wing arbitrators (actual numbers followed by proportion in parenthesis)

	Male	Female	Total
Awards – domestic reasoned	15 (.83)	3 (.17)	18 arbitrators (9 disputes)
Awards – international reasoned	33 (.82)	7 (.18)	40 arbitrators (20 disputes)
Awards – domestic standard	2 (1.00)	0 (.00)	2 arbitrators (1 dispute)
Awards – international standard	2 (1.00)	0 (.00)	2 arbitrators (1 dispute

One problem with these types of quantitative analyses is that they do not provide any insight into why the reported event occurred.[103] For example, it might be possible to interpret the current data to suggest that the numbers of male and female decision makers are not as disparate as they seem but that female judges simply do not have their decisions published at the same rate as male judges and female arbitrators do not have their awards brought to court for confirmation, enforcement, or annulment at the same rate as male judges. However, the better interpretation would be to view this data

[102] There were too few standard international awards to conduct a reliable statistical comparison.

[103] The disconnect between observed outcome and underlying motivation was one of the reasons why this study undertook a multi-pronged analysis. Ch. 1.I.

as confirming other empirical research demonstrating a bias against the appointment of women as both judges[104] and arbitrators.[105] While various arbitral institutions have sought to improve these numbers (similar initiatives do not appear to exist in many judicial settings),[106] the data generated here suggests that there is a long way to go before reaching parity.

IV. Substantive Findings

As intriguing as the demographic information is, the primary focus of this study is on the substantive inquiries. The following discussion is broken down into two sections, one addressing the paragraph-by-paragraph analysis and one addressing the citation count analysis.

A. Paragraph Analysis

One of the most innovative aspects of the current research involves the comparison of different types of decisions and awards on a paragraph-by-paragraph basis. The coding team was instructed to count the number of paragraphs associated with procedural issues, parties' arguments, purely legal concerns, purely factual concerns, mixed issues of law and fact (i.e. the application of the law to the facts), and the final disposition of the case.[107] Although the raw data generated some useful information, the primary focus was not on absolute numbers but on percentages and other types of analyses that avoided problems associated with varying levels of complexity in the underlying dispute (i.e. the likelihood that complex disputes would require more discussion than simple disputes would).

[104] Judicial Diversity Statistics 2019, Courts and Tribunals Judiciary (UK), <https://www.judiciary.uk/about-the-judiciary/who-are-the-judiciary/diversity/judicial-diversity-statistics-2019/> accessed 11 April 2020; 2019 US State Court Women Judges, National Association of Women Lawyers, <https://www.nawj.org/statistics/2019-us-state-court-women-judges> accessed 11 April 2020; Susan D Franck, 'Introductory Remarks', (2017) 111 Am Soc'y Intl L Proceedings 289, 290–92 (Franck, Introductory Remarks) (citing statistics on the number of women judges and arbitrators in various fora around the world). Women tend to be appointed more frequently as judges at the lower level of the hierarchy and in less prestigious courts, such as family courts.

[105] Markus Altenkirch and Jan Fohloff, 'Gender Diversity in International Arbitration – Statistics', Global Arb News (3 July 2017), <https://globalarbitrationnews.com/gender-diversity-in-international-arbitration-some-statistics/> accessed 11 April 2020; Peter Bert, 'Women Arbitrators in German – DIS Publishes 2016 Gender Balance Statistics', Dispute Resolution Germany (14 July 2017), <http://www.disputeresolutiongermany.com/2017/07/women-arbitrators-in-germany-dis-publishes-2016-gender-balance-statistics/> accessed 11 April 2020; Franck, Introductory Remarks (n 104) 290–92; Joseph D Garrison, 'Perceived Differences in Male and Female Arbitrators and Mediators', (2012) 18 Disp Res Magazine 29, 30–31.

[106] Although the study design initially hoped to be able to compare data across two different time periods (2003–2005 and 2015–2017) to see whether any changes had occurred, the sample size was not large enough to support statistical analysis across the two groups.

[107] Elements that are not discussed fully herein may form the foundation of future research. E.g. Strong, English Commercial Court (n 2); Strong, Experience (n 2); Strong, Gender (n 2); Strong, Investment Arbitration (n 2); Strong, Motion Practice (n 2).

Table 4.8 Paragraph analysis (averages followed by standard deviation in parenthesis and sample (N) size; medians in brackets for total paragraphs only)

	Total paragraphs	Percentage facts	Percentage law	Percentage application
Judicial decisions – England	130.83 [91.5] (99.00) 92	0.35 (0.16) 92	0.17 (0.12) 92	0.19 (0.14) 92
Judicial decisions – Quebec	148.39 [107.50] (122.48) 28	0.37 (0.13) 28	0.10 (0.08) 28	0.20 (0.15) 28
Judicial decisions – US	79.14 [79.00] (42.13) 7	0.45 (0.18) 7	0.17 (0.11) 7	0.15 (0.09) 7
Awards – domestic reasoned	79.68 [63.50] (64.90) 22	0.29 (0.16) 22	0.08 (0.12) 22	0.05 (0.07) 22
Awards – international reasoned	133.28 [129.00] (89.78) 32	0.29 (0.19) 32	0.07 (0.05) 32	0.15 (0.19) 32
Awards – domestic standard	5.33 [5.00] (2.02) 12	0.05 (0.11) 12	0.01 (0.03) 12	0.04 (0.11) 12
Awards – international standard	21.75 [14.00] (19.77) 4	0.38 (0.26) 4	0.05 (0.06) 4	0.05 (0.06) 4

The discussion begins with Table 4.8, which provides the averages and medians for the total number of paragraphs in each comparative cohort as well as the average percentage of paragraphs dedicated to the three elements most closely affiliated with legal reasoning: discussions solely relating to facts, discussions solely relating to law, and discussions applying the facts to the law. While the relatively high standard deviations found in some entries make statistical analysis difficult, the information presented in the table is nevertheless illuminating.[108]

The first feature to be discussed involves the overall length of the various decisions and awards. Somewhat unexpectedly, the highest average length comes from decisions originating in Quebec, even though Tables 4.1 and 4.2 show that Quebec courts typically handle matters that are domestic rather than international and that involve

[108] The study did not compare median percentages of the various types of paragraphs to average percentages of the various types of paragraph because it was decided that the act of calculating percentages and then averaging those percentages sufficiently minimized the effect of any outliers.

relatively low amounts in dispute. Although this data could be interpreted to confirm anecdotal and other evidence suggesting that civil law drafting techniques differ from those used in common law jurisdictions,[109] the total number of paragraphs from Quebec courts did not produce a statistically significant difference from that of any of the other reasoned decisions or awards, using a t-test analysis. Indeed, comparisons of average number of paragraphs showed no statistically significant difference among the reasoned rulings, likely as a result of high standard deviations and, in some cases, small sample size.

The outcome was somewhat different for analyses involving medians. Under the Mann-Whitney U test, reasoned arbitral awards in the domestic realm showed a statistically significant difference when compared to the English Commercial Court ($p<.01$), the Quebec courts ($p<.05$) and reasoned international awards ($p<.06$),[110] while standard (unreasoned) domestic awards showed a statistically significant difference ($p<.001$) when compared to all three types of judicial decisions and to reasoned domestic awards.

The data on medians is quite interesting, in that it supports a statistically significant difference between the length of judicial decisions (regardless of jurisdiction) and domestic arbitral awards (both reasoned and unreasoned), thus suggesting a certain degree of distinctiveness between judicial and arbitral practice, at least in the domestic realm. The material also suggests some differences between domestic and international practice, at least in matters generating reasoned awards. The one type of distinction that does not appear to exist involves common law and civil law practices, at least when the courts of Quebec are used as a stand-in for civil law reasoning.

The next item to consider involves the percentage of paragraphs dealing solely with facts. As column three of Table 4.8 demonstrates, these percentages are relatively consistent among reasoned rulings, which suggests that judges and arbitrators treat fact discussions similarly across the judicial–arbitral, domestic–international and common law–civil law divides. This conclusion is further reinforced by the absence of any statistically significant differences under a t-test calculation. This information is quite interesting, given the importance of factual matters to survey respondents and interviewees.[111]

The situation is slightly different with respect to purely legal analyses. Column four of Table 4.8 shows the percentage of paragraphs in the various reasoned decisions and awards that deal solely with the law. As it turns out, a t-test analysis of the reasoned rulings shows several statistically significant differences.

[109] Ch. 1.III.C. Notably, the total paragraph count simply speaks to the style of drafting legal rulings rather than to legal reasoning per se.

[110] Interestingly, there was no statistically significant difference between reasoned domestic awards and US decisions, which might be explained by the fact that all of the reasoned arbitral awards appeared to come from the United States. However, the only other statistically significant difference involving US decisions and other reasoned rulings was in the comparison with decisions from Quebec, which suggests that the US approach to decision making is not entirely uniform across the judicial–arbitral line.

[111] Chs. 2.IV.B, 3.III.C.

The first such difference ($p<.01$) arises in the judicial context and involves decisions from the English Commercial Court and the courts of Quebec. While this data could be interpreted to confirm longstanding assumptions about the nature of legal reasoning across the common law–civil law divide,[112] no statistically significant differences arose between decisions from Quebec and the United States, which suggests that type of broad inference is inappropriate. However, no statistically significant difference arose between decisions from the United States and the English Commercial Court, which could indicate that the problem lies with the small US sample size.

The next set of statistically significant differences appeared in the context of reasoned international awards. Two distinctions, both at the $p<.001$ level, arose: between reasoned international awards and decisions from the English Commercial Court, and between reasoned international awards and decisions from US courts. The first of these two distinctions is particularly intriguing, given allegations by some commentators, supported by empirical evidence presented in Tables 4.1 and 4.2, that the English Commercial Court is in direct competition with international commercial arbitration for high-value international disputes.[113] While these results appear to suggest that judges on the English Commercial Court are somewhat more legalistic than international arbitrators (an issue that is discussed more in connection with Tables 4.12 and 4.13), this data could be affected by the fact that common law jurisdictions tend to publish only those awards that are most likely to affect the development of law or policy.[114]

No statistically significant difference appeared between the Quebec courts and international arbitration. This phenomenon could be interpreted to mean that civil law litigation is indistinguishable from international commercial arbitration, but that appears to be contrary to practical experience.[115] Furthermore, some questions arise as to whether the type of disputes reflected in the Quebec courts (i.e. primarily local, low-value claims) are sufficiently analogous to the types of disputes heard in international commercial arbitration. The analysis associated with Tables 4.12 and 4.13 may help clarify how to deal with these dichotomies.

T-test comparisons were also made between judicial decisions and domestic awards. Interestingly, no statistical difference arose between judicial decisions from US courts and reasoned domestic awards. This result, combined with the absence of any difference in how US judges and domestic arbitrators approach facts in reasoned rulings, appears to reject the longstanding notion that arbitration in the United States is a more fact-based and less law-based process than litigation.[116] While the traditional viewpoint may be valid

[112] Ch. 1.III.C.

[113] Bookman (n 85) pt. IV; Tables 4.1, 4.2.

[114] Rowland and Carp (n 23) 14.

[115] Strong, Reasoned Awards (n 93) 14 (noting that most international awards are written in a common law style and providing examples). Notably, some efforts have been made to increase the influence of the civil law in international arbitral proceedings, which may extend to the way awards are written. Klaus Peter Berger, 'Common Law vs. Civil Law in International Arbitration: The Beginning or the End?' 36 J Intl Arb 296, 299–300 (2019) (questioning whether the adoption of the Rules on the Efficient Conduct of Proceedings in International Arbitration (Prague Rules) reflects a movement away from the traditional view of international arbitration proceedings as a blend of common law and civil law procedures).

[116] Ch. 1.III.A.

when US decisions are compared to standard (unreasoned) awards,[117] Table 4.1 shows that reasoned awards are more common than standard awards in commercial disputes, with 65 per cent of the domestic awards in this study being reasoned as opposed to standard.[118]

The final issue to discuss with respect to Table 4.8 involves the percentage of paragraphs that included both factual and legal elements and were therefore considered to 'apply' the law to the facts. As the table shows, reasoned rulings were very consistent in this regard, with the only statistically significant difference ($p<.01$) arising between US decisions and domestic awards. It is unclear why the reasoned domestic awards had such a low percentage of 'application' paragraphs, although future research may delve into that point.

Comparisons of the percentage of paragraphs involving certain types of discussions provide one type of insight into legal reasoning. Another technique involves identifying how many decisions and awards have a higher number of paragraphs concerning one analytical element as compared to another. This approach was adopted to help offset the effect of any ambiguities that were expected to and did in fact arise in the initial data as a result of large standard deviations.

Table 4.9 Comparison of percentage of fact paragraphs to law paragraphs (actual numbers followed by proportion in parenthesis)

	Fact percentage higher	Law percentage higher	Two percentages identical	Total
Judicial decisions – England	72 (.78)	19 (.21)	1 (.01)	92
Judicial decisions – Quebec	25 (.89)	3 (.11)	0 (.00)	28
Judicial decisions – US	5 (.71)	2 (.29)	0 (.00)	7
Awards – domestic reasoned	20 (.91)	1 (.05)	1 (.05)	22
Awards – international reasoned	27 (.84)	2 (.06)	3 (.09)	32
Awards – domestic standard	2 (.17)	1 (.08)	9 (.75)	12
Awards – international standard	4 (1.00)	0 (.00)	0 (.00)	4

Table 4.9 begins that analysis by comparing the average percentage of paragraphs involving factual issues to the average percentage of paragraphs involving legal issues

[117] A t-test comparison of US judicial decisions and standard (unreasoned) domestic awards showed a statistically significant difference ($p<.001$) in terms of the percentage of paragraphs devoted to law. No statistically significant difference arose between US judicial decisions and standard international awards, although the sample sizes may have been too small to identify any relevant differences. Furthermore, the averages for the standard international awards may have been affected by one award rendered under the FINRA Arbitration Rules that was much longer than the other awards in that category.

[118] Notably, the parties are the ones who decide whether to obtain a reasoned or standard award. In commercial arbitration, bargaining regarding the nature of arbitration is normally at arm's length between two commercial entities and thus reflects the agreement of the parties more than is the case in consumer, employment, and labour arbitration.

and noting when the fact percentage was higher, when the law percentage was higher, and when the percentages were identical. Though relevant to all three comparative axes considered in this text (judicial–arbitral, domestic–international and common law–civil law), this analysis is particularly important to the debate about the relative nature of litigation and arbitration, which has traditionally claimed that litigation focuses more on law and arbitration focuses more on facts.[119] While this claim likely arises as a result of a lack of understanding regarding either the special nature of published judicial decisions[120] or a failure to distinguish between commercial arbitration (which tends to use reasoned awards) and other forms of arbitration (which tend to use standard (unreasoned) awards), the recursive nature of the allegation suggests it still needs to be addressed.

The first issue to note is that no statistically significant differences arose in Table 4.9 between the different judicial decisions under a two-tailed z-test calculation of the fact percentages, which suggests that no differences exist across the common law–civil law divide. Furthermore, no statistically significant differences relating to the fact percentages arose between any of the judicial decisions and either of the two types of reasoned awards, which rebuts conventional wisdom suggesting that arbitration is more fact-oriented than litigation, at least when the types of rulings are sufficiently analogous (i.e. published judicial decisions and reasoned arbitral awards).

The only statistically significant differences that arose with respect to fact percentages involved standard domestic awards, which differed from all three types of judicial decisions ($p<.001$ for both the English Commercial Court and the Quebec courts and $p<.05$ for US courts). While this outcome was likely affected by the fact that 75 per cent of the standard domestic awards reflected the same percentage of paragraphs involving facts as law, the data is nevertheless telling.

The last comparison focused on reasoned awards. Interestingly, no statistically significant difference in the percentage of fact paragraphs arose between reasoned domestic awards and reasoned international awards, suggesting that domestic and international commercial arbitration are not as different as previously anticipated.[121]

The next analysis involved a comparison of the percentage of paragraphs dedicated solely to factual issues to the percentage of paragraphs reflecting a combination of law and facts (i.e. the application of the law to the facts). No known study has yet considered how these types of 'application' discussions affect legal reasoning across any of the various comparative axes.

As Table 4.10 shows, the percentage of fact paragraphs was higher than the percentage of application paragraphs for all reasoned rulings, in some cases considerably more. This finding confirms data from both the survey and semi-structured interviews, underscoring the importance of factual discussions to legal reasoning in both litigation

[119] Ch. 1.III.A.

[120] Rowland and Carp (n 23) 14.

[121] Ch. 1.III.B. No comparisons were undertaken between reasoned and standard awards, given the number of matters with identical percentages among standard domestic awards and the small sample size for standard international awards.

Table 4.10 Comparison of percentage of fact paragraphs to application paragraphs (actual numbers followed by proportion in parenthesis)

	Fact percentage higher	Application percentage higher	Two percentages identical	Total
Judicial decisions – England	61 (.66)	30 (.33)	1 (.01)	92
Judicial decisions – Quebec	20 (.71)	8 (.29)	0 (.00)	28
Judicial decisions – US	6 (.86)	1 (.14)	0 (.00)	7
Awards – domestic reasoned	18 (.82)	2 (.09)	2 (.09)	22
Awards – international reasoned	24 (.75)	8 (.25)	0 (.00)	32
Awards – domestic standard	2 (.17)	3 (.25)	7 (.58)	12
Awards – international standard	4 (1.00)	0 (.00)	0 (.00)	4

and arbitration.[122] However, a two-tailed z-test yielded no statistically significant differences involving any of the reasoned rulings.[123]

The final paragraph analysis involved a comparison of the average percentage of paragraphs solely addressing the law to the average percentage of paragraphs addressing a combination of law and facts (i.e. applying the law to the facts). Again, no known study has yet considered how these types of 'application' discussions operate across the various comparative axes discussed in this text.

As Table 4.11 shows, the percentage of paragraphs dedicated to the application of law to facts was higher than the percentage of paragraphs dedicated exclusively to the law in matters involving the English Commercial Court, the Quebec courts, and international arbitration. However, those numbers did not always generate statistically significant differences. Indeed, the only statistically significant difference between any of the reasoned rulings arose under a two-tailed z-test calculation involving the Quebec courts, which differed from both US judicial decisions and reasoned domestic awards, both at the $p<.05$ level.[124] While this could be interpreted as signifying a difference between common law and civil law reasoning techniques, the absence of a difference between the Quebec courts and the English Commercial Court suggests that inference is too broad. Instead, the data is better interpreted as indicating a difference between civil law

[122] Ch. 2.IV.B.1 (discussing importance of facts in the survey); Ch. 3.III.C (discussing importance of facts in interviews).

[123] The high percentage of fact paragraphs in standard international awards was expected, given the general lack of analysis in standard awards. Initially the number of standard domestic awards that showed an identical percentage of fact and application paragraphs was surprising, but on closer examination it was found that many standard domestic awards had no paragraphs devoted either to the facts or the application of the law to the facts, which makes sense given the summary nature of standard awards.

[124] Z-tests were not run on data involving standard awards because of the high proportion of disputes with identical percentages.

Table 4.11 Comparison of percentage of law paragraphs to application paragraphs (actual numbers followed by proportion in parenthesis)

	Law percentage higher	Application percentage higher	Two percentages identical	Total
Judicial decisions – England	42 (.46)	49 (.53)	1 (.01)	92
Judicial decisions – Quebec	8 (.29)	19 (.68)	1 (.04)	28
Judicial decisions – US	5 (.71)	2 (.29)	0 (.00)	7
Awards – domestic reasoned	14 (.64)	4 (.18)	4 (.18)	22
Awards – international reasoned	14 (.44)	17 (.53)	1 (.03)	32
Awards – domestic standard	3 (.25)	2 (.17)	7 (.58)	12
Awards – international standard	2 (.50)	0 (.00)	2 (.50)	4

drafting techniques (at least in Quebec) and US-style drafting techniques in both litigation and arbitration.[125]

B. Citation Count Analysis

As intriguing as a paragraph-by-paragraph analysis of commercial decisions and awards may be, it is an untested methodology. As a result, the coding exercise also adopted the more conventional technique of counting citations as a means of gauging decision makers' approach to legal reasoning. However, this study improved on traditional citation count methodologies not only by distinguishing between different types of legal citations and by counting both initial and subsequent citations but also by counting factual authorities (evidence) in addition to legal authorities.

1. Legal authorities

The study began by focusing on legal authorities. While this analysis built off existing empirical research,[126] it added to that knowledge by expanding the range of authorities considered to include international treaties (which included treaties and conventions); statutes or regulations (which included any legislative or administrative enactments);

[125] As indicated previously, all of the domestic awards were decided under the AAA Commercial Arbitration Rules, which suggests they involved US parties and arbitrators. Notably, the absence of any statistically significant difference between decisions rendered by US courts and the English Commercial Court makes interpretation of the data somewhat more problematic, since the direct comparison of the two common law jurisdictions shows no relevant difference.

[126] Ch. 1.III.

arbitral rules (which meant any institutional or non-institutional rule set for arbitration); judicial decisions (which included decisions from any jurisdiction); arbitral awards (which meant arbitral awards involving matters other than the instant dispute); commentary (which included books, articles, and other forms of scholarship); and other legal authorities (which included any materials not included in the previous categories).[127] The coding exercise was also unique in that it differentiated between initial and subsequent citations to the various authorities.[128]

Table 4.12 provides a wealth of information about how judges and arbitrators use legal authority in commercial dispute resolution. Much of the data is self-explanatory

Table 4.12 Average number of legal citations per decision or award (averages followed by medians in brackets, standard deviation in parenthesis and sample (N) size)

	Judicial decisions – England	Judicial decisions – Quebec	Judicial decisions – US	Awards – domestic reasoned	Awards – int'l reasoned	Awards – domestic standard	Awards – int'l standard
Initial treaties	5.24 [4.00] (4.23) 21	1.00 [1.00] – 1	0.00 – – 0	2.50 [2.50] (1.69) 8	1.38 [1.00] (.96) 13	0.00 – – 0	1.00 [1.00] – 1
Subsequent treaties	3.76 [3.00] (3.25) 21	2.00 [2.00] – 1	0.00 – – 0	5.50 [6.00] (2.81) 6	9.00 [13.00] (6.89) 5	0.00 – – 0	0.00 – – 0
Initial statutes or regulations	4.09 [2.50] (3.99) 64	7.62 [6.00] (6.07) 26	7.00 [7.00] (5.45) 7	4.25 [3.50] (3.62) 16	2.70 [2.00] (2.18) 27	1.00 [1.00] – 1	1.00 [1.00] – 1
Subsequent statutes or regulations	5.55 [3.00] (7.37) 56	7.37 [4.00] (6.82) 19	7.00 [7.00] – 1	7.50 [7.00] (4.22) 10	9.64 [4.50] (11.48) 14	0.00 – – 0	0.00 – – 0
Initial arbitral rules	5.25 [1.00] (8.50) 4	0.00 – – 0	0.00 – – 0	4.08 [2.00] (6.42) 13	2.48 [1.00] (2.04) 27	1.00 [1.00] (0.00) 4	2.00 [2.00] – 1
Subsequent arbitral rules	2.25 [2.00] (1.26) 4	0.00 – – 0	0.00 – – 0	7.18 [8.00] (4.51) 11	4.25 [4.00] (2.41) 16	0.00 – – 0	0.00 – – 0
Initial judicial decisions	8.43 [5.00] (11.28) 72	11.56 [7.50] (14.13) 18	39.14 [29.00] (28.43) 7	8.27 [4.00] (8.96) 15	6.50 [3.50] (6.35) 20	0.00 – – 0	0.00 – – 0

Continued

[127] Appx. III. Any reference to the above items was included in the citation count, regardless of whether it was independently cited by the judge or arbitral tribunal or whether it was simply embedded in quoted material.

[128] Subsequent references were calculated regardless of the form of the subsequent citation. In other words, a subsequent citation could include a shortened name of the initial authority or could involve some sort of abbreviation, such as id, ibid, op cit, or loc cit.

Table 4.12 Continued

	Judicial decisions – England	Judicial decisions – Quebec	Judicial decisions – US	Awards – domestic reasoned	Awards – int'l reasoned	Awards – domestic standard	Awards – int'l standard
Subsequent judicial decisions	7.27	7.33	13.86	7.80	5.64	0.00	0.00
	[5.00]	[3.00]	[8.00]	[4.00]	[2.00]	–	–
	(8.98)	(9.74)	(16.95)	(7.76)	(9.09)	–	–
	60	15	7	10	14	0	0
Initial arbitral awards	1.75	1.00	0.00	3.33	4.25	0.00	1.00
	[1.50]	[1.00]	–	[2.00]	[1.50]	–	[1.00]
	(1.04)	–	–	(3.50)	(7.23)	–	–
	8	1	0	9	8	0	1
Subsequent arbitral awards	2.14	3.00	0.00	7.67	6.60	0.00	0.00
	[2.00]	[3.00]	–	[7.00]	[8.00]	–	–
	(1.07)	–	–	(7.47)	(5.32)	–	–
	7	1	0	9	5	0	0
Initial commentary	5.41	3.33	1.00	3.00	4.50	0.00	0.00
	[5.00]	[2.50]	[1.00]	[2.00]	[3.00]	–	–
	(3.67)	(2.50)	0	(2.45)	(3.21)	–	–
	64	12	3	6	8	0	0
Subsequent commentary	8.29	6.60	0.00	6.75	3.00	0.00	0.00
	[5.00]	[3.00]	–	[8.00]	[2.00]	–	–
	(8.08)	(6.35)	–	(3.20)	(2.00)	–	–
	55	5	0	4	4	0	0
Initial other authority	12.00	5.20	4.50	6.71	4.69	0.00	1.00
	[6.00]	[5.00]	[4.50]	[2.00]	[2.00]	–	[1.00]
	(16.66)	(3.71)	(4.95)	(9.34)	(5.17)	–	–
	54	15	2	7	13	0	1
Subsequent other authority	12.29	4.82	2.00	3.67	16.20	0.00	2.00
	[8.00]	[4.00]	[2.00]	[3.00]	[16.00]	–	[2.00]
	(12.63)	(4.26)	–	(2.73)	(11.12)	–	–
	49	11	1	6	5	0	1

and will not be discussed in detail.[129] Instead, the focus will be on three types of authorities—statutes and regulations; judicial decisions; and scholarly commentary—that are central to commercial legal disputes and that are most likely to demonstrate differences across the judicial–arbitral, domestic–international and common law–civil law divides.[130] However, it is hoped that the information contained in Table 4.12 will prove useful in future studies in this area of law.

Before beginning, it should be noted that the sample (N) size used to calculate the data in Table 4.12 reflects the number of decisions that included that particular type of

[129] For example, decisions from the English Commercial Court show a higher incidence of treaty citations than decisions from Quebec or the United States because the English Commercial Court hears a larger number of international disputes. Table 4.1. While some of the data in Table 4.12 initially appeared surprising, it made sense on closer analysis of the underlying materials. For example, treaty references in domestic awards initially seemed odd, but were explained on closer examination by various references to insurance 'treaties'. Similarly, the number of citations to arbitral rules and arbitral awards in the English Commercial Court decisions appeared questionable at first, since the study excluded actions to enforce or annul arbitral awards. However, on closer examination, it was discovered that these citations reflect the fact that the English Commercial Court frequently hears matters that are part of parallel proceedings, and judges frequently refer to past or ongoing arbitral proceedings to establish the scope of the instant dispute.

[130] Ch. 1.III (discussing treatment of legal authorities in different jurisdictions).

authority rather than the total number of decisions or awards in that particular cohort. This approach was considered preferable because the absence of a reference to a particular type of authority might have been due to the type of dispute rather than the personal predilections of the judge or arbitrator. For example, the absence of a reference to a statute might simply reflect the absence of a statutory claim.

The analysis consisted of a t-statistical test conducted on averages involving all reasoned rulings, considering both the initial references (meaning the first citations to unique materials within the relevant categories) and subsequent references (meaning citations to materials that had already been mentioned once in the relevant categories). A Mann-Whitney U test was conducted on similar groups of data, using medians.

The first item to consider involves initial references to statutes or regulations. According to t-test calculations on reported averages, a statistically significant difference arose between the Quebec courts and the English Commercial Court ($p<.01$) and between the Quebec courts and international commercial arbitration ($p<.001$). Since awards in international commercial arbitration are often considered to be written in more of a common law rather than civil law style,[131] this result could be interpreted to support conventional wisdom suggesting that civil law jurisdictions rely on statutes more than common law jurisdictions do. While the absence of a statistically significant difference between the courts of Quebec and the United States could be taken to rebut that notion, some commentators have suggested that the United States has become increasingly reliant on statutory law.[132] Although this data is very interesting, more research is needed before a firm conclusion can be reached.

The only other statistically significant difference relating to the average number of initial citations of statutes and regulations involved US decisions and international awards ($p<.01$). The higher number of statutory references in US decisions was in many ways unexpected, although it is possible that US courts attract a higher number of statutory or regulatory disputes than international arbitration, based on concerns about non-arbitrability of certain types of claims.[133]

Analysis of the median data supported the t-test results. For example, the same degree of statistical certainty arose with respect to differences between the Quebec courts and the English Commercial Court ($p<.01$) and between the Quebec courts and international commercial arbitration ($p<.001$), although a slightly lower degree of certainty arose with respect to statistical differences involving US decisions and international awards ($p<.05$ under the Mann-Whitney U test, as opposed to $p<.01$ under the t-test). Comparison of median data also showed a statistically significant difference ($p<.05$) between the Quebec courts and domestic arbitration that did not appear in the comparison of averaged data, though the relatively low rate of statistical significance suggests this discrepancy can be disregarded.

131 Strong, Reasoned Awards (n 93) 14.

132 Guido Calabresi, *A Common Law for the Age of Statutes* (Harvard University Press 1982) 5–7; Neal Devins and David Klein, 'The Vanishing Common Law Judge?' (2017) 165 U Penn L Rev 595, 597.

133 Born (n 91) 1039–43.

The next item to consider involves the average number of subsequent citations to statutes or regulations, an analysis that identifies whether judges and arbitrators simply refer to an authority in passing or discuss that item in depth. The data does not appear to support the notion that judges in the United States frequently adopt 'string citations', meaning references to materials that are never discussed beyond the initial reference, with respect to statutory materials, since only one US decision contained a subsequent reference to a statute or regulation, even though seven decisions contained an initial reference to such materials.

Arbitrators in international commercial disputes appear to take precisely the opposite approach to statutes and regulations, with a very high average number of subsequent citations. However, a t-test analysis showed no statistically significant difference between any the different cohorts' subsequent citations to statutes or regulations, likely because of relatively small sample sizes and high standard deviations.

These results were again supported by analysis of the medians. Although it was impossible to run a Mann-Whitney U test on the US decisions due to the small sample size, comparisons of all other reasoned rulings failed to show any statistically significant differences, with the exception of the comparison between the English Commercial Court and domestic arbitration ($p<.05$). Although this result might be disregarded as being inconsistent with the t-test data, the results under the Mann-Whitney U test are consistent with what might be expected, given the relative size and complexity of cases in those two fora.

The next item to discuss involves judicial decisions, beginning with the average number of initial citations. In this case, decisions from US courts showed a statistically significant difference with respect to all other cohorts, either at the $p<.001$ level (decisions from English Commercial Court, domestic awards, and international awards) or the $p<.01$ level (decisions from Quebec courts). These outcomes were confirmed by an analysis of medians under the Mann-Whitney U test, with identical data arising in all respects except for the comparison between US courts and domestic arbitration, where the level of certainty was $p<.01$ under the Mann-Whitney U test and $p<.001$ under the t-test.

Given the absence of any other statistically significant differences among the reasoned rulings, this data does not support any relevant distinctions along the standard comparative axes (judicial–arbitral, domestic–international and common law–civil law). However, the results do suggest that US courts are an outlier with respect to the number of citations to judicial decisions. These results may explain why some people within the US legal community characterize arbitration as a 'second-class form of justice',[134] if the concept of a reasoned ruling is gauged solely or primarily by the number of citations to judicial decisions.

The next item to consider involves the average number of subsequent references to judicial decisions. US courts were again unique in that they were the only group that featured the same number of matters with subsequent citations as initial citations (7 each). However, the frequency of subsequent citations in US decisions did not give rise to any statistically

[134] Ch. 1.III.A.

significant differences when compared to other reasoned rulings. Furthermore, none of the other reasoned rulings were statistically different from each other under the t-test, and only one combination—US courts compared to international commercial arbitration—showed a statistically significant difference under the Mann-Whitney U test ($p<.05$).

This information, combined with the results involving initial citation of judicial decisions, suggests that US courts cite case law more frequently than other comparative cohorts, but only at a superficial level. This conclusion suggests that US judges (who often complain about 'string citations' in submissions) are as prone to such practices as advocates are.[135] Alternatively, it may be that US judges are citing judicial decisions not so much for their precedential value, but instead simply to demonstrate 'judicial learning'.[136] In either case, it would be useful for future research to determine why US judges engage in this practice, since it may be one reason why advocates continue to provide string cites.

The third area of comparison involves scholarly commentary. The only statistically significant difference ($p<.05$) that arose with respect to average number of initial citations was between decisions from the English Commercial Court and US courts. No statistically significant differences arose under the t-test between any of the reasoned rulings with respect to subsequent commentary.

It was difficult to corroborate the t-test data with an analysis of medians because the sample sizes were too small to support a Mann-Whitney U test for all comparisons, except for that involving the English Commercial Court and the Quebec courts. In that case, no statistically significant difference arose.

To some extent, the disparity between the US and English averages may be explained by the complexity of the matters heard in the English Commercial Court, which might require citation to scholarly works when a gap exists in established law. However, it is also possible that US judicial practices reflect the view enunciated by a number of US judges that US legal scholarship is impractical.[137] In any event, the data from both the t-tests and the Mann-Whitney U tests did not appear to support the longstanding claim that judges from civil law jurisdictions rely on scholarship more often than judges from common law countries.[138]

During the design phase, it was anticipated that problems with sample sizes and standard deviations could arise, resulting in data that could not support useful statistical analyses. Furthermore, the analysis conducted in Table 4.12 did not take into account how many decisions or awards within each cohort referred to the various types of authority. The next calculation sought to overcome these challenges by analysing the proportion of references to each type of authority within each cohort.[139] While this

[135] Ch. 3.III.B.2.

[136] Dyson Heydon, 'Judicial Activism and the Death of the Rule of Law', (2003) 23 Australia Bar Rev 110, 118–19 (noting many judges cite a large number of cases but fail to follow the reasoning reflected therein and suggesting the citations 'seem more designed to highlight supposed judicial learning than to advance the reasoning in any particular direction relevant to the issues between the parties').

[137] Debra Cassens Weiss, 'Law Prof Responds After Chief Justice Roberts Disses Legal Scholarship', ABA J (7 July 2011), <https://www.abajournal.com/news/article/law_prof_responds_after_chief_justice_roberts_disses_legal_scholarship> accessed 11 April 2020.

[138] Ch. 1.III.C.

[139] This figure was obtained by dividing the number of decisions or awards that referred to each type of authority by the total number of decisions or awards in that particular cohort.

analysis could be affected by the type of dispute at issue (for example, a statute or regulation cannot be cited as authority unless the claim is based on a statute or regulation), the information was nevertheless considered useful as a means of understanding the types of legal materials that are considered persuasive in a particular forum and the likelihood that a judge or arbitrator will discuss an authority in depth, as opposed to merely in passing.

Table 4.13 Proportion of decisions or awards per cohort citing legal authority (actual numbers followed by proportion in parenthesis)

	Judicial decisions – England	Judicial decisions – Quebec	Judicial decisions – US	Awards – domestic reasoned	Awards – int'l reasoned	Awards – domestic standard	Awards – int'l standard
Initial treaties	21 (.23)	1 (.04)	0 (.00)	8 (.36)	13 (.41)	0 (.00)	1 (.25)
Subsequent treaties	21 (.23)	1 (.04)	0 (.00)	6 (.27)	5 (.16)	0 (.00)	0 (.00)
Initial statutes or regulations	64 (.70)	26 (.93)	7 (1.00)	16 (.73)	27 (.84)	1 (.08)	1 (.25)
Subsequent statutes or regulations	56 (.61)	19 (.68)	1 (.14)	10 (.45)	14 (.44)	0 (.00)	0 (.00)
Initial arbitral rules	4 (.04)	0 (.00)	0 (.00)	13 (.59)	27 (.84)	4 (.33)	1 (.25)
Subsequent arbitral rules	4 (.04)	0 (.00)	0 (.00)	11 (.50)	16 (.50)	0 (.00)	0 (.00)
Initial judicial decisions	72 (.78)	18 (.64)	7 (1.00)	15 (.68)	20 (.62)	0 (.00)	0 (.00)
Subsequent judicial decisions	60 (.65)	15 (.54)	7 (1.00)	10 (.45)	14 (.44)	0 (.00)	0 (.00)
Initial arbitral awards	8 (.09)	1 (.04)	0 (.00)	9 (.41)	8 (.25)	0 (.00)	1 (.25)
Subsequent arbitral awards	7 (.08)	1 (.04)	0 (.00)	9 (.41)	5 (.16)	0 (.00)	0 (.00)
Initial commentary	64 (.70)	12 (.43)	3 (.43)	6 (.27)	8 (.25)	0 (.00)	0 (.00)
Subsequent commentary	55 (.60)	5 (.18)	0 (.00)	4 (.18)	4 (.12)	0 (.00)	0 (.00)
Initial other authority	54 (.59)	15 (.54)	2 (.20)	7 (.32)	13 (.41)	0 (.00)	1 (.25)
Subsequent other authority	49 (.53)	11 (.39)	1 (.14)	6 (.27)	5 (.16)	0 (.00)	1 (.25)
Total	92	28	7	22	32	12	4

Table 4.13 provides a very different perspective than Table 4.12 on the use of legal authority in commercial dispute. Although much of the data is self-evident (for example, the absence of any citations to treaties in the Quebec courts is not in any way surprising,

given the largely domestic nature of the disputes heard by those courts),[140] it is useful to discuss several overarching themes.

Perhaps the most striking item involves the lack of diversity in terms of legal authorities in US courts, with only statutes and judicial decisions appearing in a majority of the decisions. Furthermore, 100 per cent of US decisions cited both of those authorities, demonstrating that legislation is becoming a major force in the US legal system. While this data must be considered in light of Table 4.12, which indicates that US courts rely more heavily on judicial decisions than any other dispute resolution method studied herein, it nevertheless suggests that the nature of the US common law system is changing.[141]

Other surprises came as a result of two-tailed z-tests conducted on the same three types of authorities discussed with respect to Table 4.12 (statutes and regulations; judicial decisions; and scholarly commentary). Interestingly, the percentage of decisions from the English Commercial Court that contained an initial reference to statutes and regulations showed a statistically significant difference ($p<.05$) when compared to the percentage of decisions from the Quebec courts citing the same source of authority. Although the US decisions had a higher percentage of references to statutes and regulations (100 per cent), no statistically significant difference arose, perhaps because of the small sample size.

When subsequent citations to statutes and regulations were considered, two statistically significant differences arose. In this case, decisions from the United States were found to be statistically different from decisions from both the English Commercial Court and the Quebec courts (both at the $p<.05$ level), with US courts citing these types of authorities far less frequently than the other courts. This phenomenon suggests that the US emphasis on statutes arises on a relatively superficial level as compared to other courts and suggests that US courts might be engaged in string citations not only of judicial decisions, as Table 4.12 intimated, but also of statutes and regulations.

When the analysis shifted to judicial decisions, no statistically significant differences arose with respect to initial citations. However, differences arose with respect to subsequent citations involving decisions from the English Commercial Court and international awards; decisions from US courts and decisions from Quebec; decisions from US courts and domestic arbitration; and decisions from US courts and international arbitration (all at the $p<.05$ level). Three of these four combinations include decisions from US court, and for a good reason: the data showed that 100 per cent of US courts in the study contained at least one subsequent citation to a judicial decision. This was far higher than most other percentages, including the English Commercial Court, which generated the next-nearest figure (65 per cent). While this result could be interpreted as negating the earlier conclusion about US courts engaging in string citations, that appears incorrect, since Table 4.13 only requires one subsequent citation to a previously mentioned authority. Since US courts cite the highest average number of judicial

[140] Table 4.1.
[141] Calabresi (n 132) 5–7; Devins and Klein (n 132) 597.

decisions of all the various cohorts,[142] it is not surprising that US courts also have the highest subsequent citation rate.

The comparisons involving international arbitration also bear mention. Although practitioners frequently complain that international arbitration is becoming increasingly legalistic,[143] Table 4.13 indicates that international arbitrators do not include as many subsequent citations to judicial decisions as judges in US courts and the English Commercial Court.[144] These results are similar to those generated in Table 4.8, where reasoned international awards were found to generate statistically significant differences, both at the $p<.001$ level, as compared to both the English Commercial Court and US courts. The cross-confirmation of these results improves the likelihood of their validity, although the data does not provide insights into why the variation exists. One possibility is that the results are affected by the fact that common law jurisdictions tend to publish only those awards that are most likely to affect the development of law or policy.[145] Further research, including comparisons between unpublished judicial decisions and arbitral awards, might shed more light on this issue.

It is also noteworthy that Table 4.13 did not show a statistically significant difference between the Quebec courts and the two common law courts. Common law judges have traditionally been said to rely more heavily than civil law judges on previously rendered judicial decisions,[146] which, if true, should lead to a marked difference in both initial and subsequent citations to such authorities. However, the absence of such results suggests that civil law judges rely on judicial decisions with some frequency, as noted by contemporary commentators.[147]

The next type of authority to consider involved scholarly commentary. Again, the results from the coding process challenged conventional wisdom. For example, according to the legal literature, the highest proportion of citations should have been found in civil law jurisdictions.[148] However, Table 4.13 shows the English Commercial Court having the highest percentage of citations to scholarship. Furthermore, the figures for the English Commercial Court reflected a statistically significant difference as compared to the numbers from the Quebec courts ($p<.05$), domestic arbitration ($p<.001$), and international arbitration ($p<.001$). Since the US courts had the same percentage of citations as the Quebec courts, it is likely that difference would also have been statistically significant had there been a larger sample size from the US.

The same trend occurred when considering the number of citations to subsequent commentary, with decisions from the English Commercial Courts providing the only statistically significant differences when compared to other reasoned rulings. The Quebec courts, domestic arbitration, and international arbitration were all distinguishable from the English Commercial Court at the $p<.001$ level, while US courts were distinguishable at the $p<.01$ level.

[142] Table 4.12.
[143] Ch. 1.III.A; see also Strong, Increasing Legalism (n 95) 119.
[144] Ch. 1.III.B.
[145] Rowland and Carp (n 23) 14; see also Ch. 4.II.A.
[146] Ch. 1.III.C.
[147] Ch. 1.III.C (noting possible convergence between common law and civil law practices).
[148] Ch. 1.III.C.

While surprising, these results could be explained by reference to the type of disputes heard in the English Commercial Court. Because the English Commercial Court specializes in complex, high-value, and often international commercial matters,[149] English judges may be faced with cutting-edge legal issues and/or questions of foreign law that benefit particularly from scholarly perspectives. While more research would be needed to confirm this explanation, it makes sense on an intuitive level.

2. Factual authorities (evidence)

The next series of issues involves factual authorities (evidence). Since this was the first known attempt to quantify citation rates for evidentiary matters, care had to be taken when designing the different categories to ensure that they described materials that might be used in all types of commercial disputes, regardless of where the dispute was heard.

Table 4.14 Average number of factual citations per decision or award (averages followed by medians in brackets, standard deviation in parenthesis and sample (N) size)

	Judicial decisions – England	Judicial decisions – Quebec	Judicial decisions – US	Awards – domestic reasoned	Awards-int'l reasoned	Awards – domestic standard	Awards-int'l standard
Initial contract cites	8.20 [4.00] (10.01) 81	5.56 [2.00] (6.81) 25	21.20 [5.00] (25.08) 5	7.27 [2.00] (17.33) 22	7.42 [2.00] (14.62) 31	1.11 [1.00] (0.33) 9	1.50 [1.00] (1.00) 4
Subsequent contract cites	18.39 [11.00] (24.42) 64	11.86 [10.50] (8.66) 22	15.25 [16.5] (11.62) 4	16.50 [18.00] (9.56) 20	18.81 [9.00] (25.80) 27	3.00 [2.00] (1.72) 5	1.00 [1.00] – 1
Initial witness testimony cites	6.54 [4.00] (7.10) 72	3.90 [3.00] (4.15) 21	25.00 [8.00] (39.32) 7	8.75 [3.00] (13.41) 12	10.28 [3.50] (16.24) 18	1.00 [1.00] – 1	1.00 [1.00] – 1
Subsequent witness testimony cites	7.10 [6.00] (6.40) 49	8.41 [7.00] (8.41) 17	25.40 [14.00] (26.00) 7	9.50 [9.50] (6.38) 10	14.50 [7.00] (17.37) 16	0.00 – – 0	2.00 [2.00] – 1
Initial other document cites	8.81 [7.00] (10.26) 70	18.08 [15.00] (16.33) 25	30.00 [25.50] (28.35) 6	6.50 [3.50] (6.31) 10	15.76 [5.00] (24.65) 21	0.00 – – 0	17.00 [17.00] – 1
Subsequent other document cites	7.61 [6.50] (5.10) 46	13.83 [4.00] (18.81) 24	7.25 [7.00] (4.92) 4	10.50 [7.50] (10.04) 8	12.07 [7.00] (13.31) 14	0.00 – – 0	0.00 – – 0

As Table 4.14 shows, the factual analysis included three different categories of evidentiary materials, broken into initial and subsequent citations, using the same

[149] Table 4.1.

technique that was reflected in Table 4.12.[150] Since many commercial disputes are contractual in nature, it was considered useful to begin the analysis with a separate category identifying the contract(s) at issue in the dispute in order to provide a more accurate picture of what judges and arbitrators were actually doing. However, even this technique was not enough to avoid some very large entries and high standard deviations, suggesting that some of the disputes either involved multiple contracts between multiple parties or multiple contracts between two parties.[151] Both of these features are consistent with commentary and anecdotal evidence suggesting that commercial disputes are moving away from a single-contract, bilateral model toward more multiparty, multicontract disputes.[152] While Table 4.14 provides a useful starting point for analysis, future studies may want to focus on particular types of disputes (either bilateral or multilateral, single contract or multiple contract) so as to minimize the standard deviations.

The second category of authorities involved witness testimony, which included written and oral testimony taken either before or during the hearing so as to overcome procedural differences between the different cohorts.[153] While it may be useful in the future to distinguish between testimony given by parties, third parties, and experts,[154] it was unknown at the time the study was designed whether the data would support that level of nuance. Having set the foundation with this research, future work in this field can delve further into these issues.

The final category of evidence involved 'other documents', meaning any document other than the contract(s) at issue in the instant dispute. These documents might be mentioned independently by the judge or arbitral tribunal or might be cited in a passage quoted from other sources.

As was the case with Table 4.12, the sample (N) size used in Table 4.14 reflects the number of decisions that included that particular type of evidence rather than the total number of decisions or awards in that particular cohort. This approach was considered preferable because the absence of a reference to a particular type of authority might have been due to the type of procedure rather than the personal predilections of the judge or arbitrator. For example, some arbitrations might proceed on a documents-only basis, even though many courts seldom if ever use that technique.

[150] Again, the initial citation refers to the first mention of a unique authority, regardless of whether it was independently named by the judge or arbitral tribunal or whether it appeared in a block quote. Subsequent references were calculated regardless of the form of the subsequent citation. In other words, a subsequent citation could include a shortened name of the initial authority or could involve some sort of abbreviation, such as id, ibid, op cit, or loc cit.

[151] Table 4.3 (noting incidence of multiparty disputes in individual cohorts).

[152] Strong, Increasing Legalism (n 95) 119.

[153] For example, unlike other courts and many international arbitrations, US courts allow parties to take deposition (pre-trial testimony taken under oath) and admit that testimony into evidence in certain circumstances. Conversely, international arbitrators frequently consider written witness statements outlining the individual's affirmative testimony, a practice that is not routinely used in many courts or in domestic arbitration.

[154] Conventional wisdom suggests that common law and civil law lawyers have differing views about the propriety of party testimony. Ch. 1.III.C.

Despite these efforts, the data reflected relatively high standard deviations in most categories, as well as a few instances of small sample sizes, both of which could affect statistical analyses between the various cohorts. As a result, a Mann-Whitney U test was run in addition to a t-statistical analysis to try to cross-verify the results. When conducting statistical tests, the focus was on reasoned rulings, even though Table 4.14 included data from standard (unreasoned) awards for context.

The inquiry began with the contract citations. In this case, the only statistically significant difference under a t-test analysis was between initial references in decisions from Quebec and the United States ($p<.01$). No other combinations showed significant differences, either in initial or subsequent citations, which was somewhat predictable given that all of the disputes involved commercial disputes.

The Mann-Whitney U test generated different results, at least with respect to initial contract citations. That test showed no difference between the Quebec and US courts, thereby contradicting the t-test analysis of reported averages. However, the Mann-Whitney U test of median data showed a statistically significant difference between the English Commercial Court and Quebec courts ($p<.05$), domestic arbitration ($p<.001$), and international arbitration ($p<.01$). The discrepancy of outcomes between the two statistical tests suggests further research is needed to confirm which results are correct. Notably, the Mann-Whitney U test showed no statistically significant differences with respect to subsequent contract citations, which is consistent with the t-test data.

The next item to consider involved witness testimony. Here, US courts stood as an outlier as compared to other judicial systems, with t-test reflecting statistically significant differences for initial citation rates when compared to the English Commercial Court ($p<.001$) and the courts in Quebec ($p<.05$). T-tests also showed a statistically significant difference between US courts and the English Commercial Court ($p<.001$) and the courts in Quebec ($p<.01$) with respect to subsequent testimony. In both cases, US judges cited testimony far more frequently than judges from other jurisdictions, suggesting that the best way to enter evidence in US courts is through testimony. Interestingly, no statistically significant differences arose between US courts and either domestic or international arbitration with respect to initial or subsequent testimony, suggesting that use of witness testimony is also very important in arbitral settings.

The only statistically significant difference involving arbitration was between international arbitration and the English Commercial Court ($p<.05$) in cases involving subsequent testimony. This finding suggests that arbitrators in international disputes do not initially cite witness testimony more frequently than judges in the English Commercial Court but do discuss that testimony in more depth. This information is intriguing, given the competition between the English Commercial Court and international arbitration for large, high-value disputes.[155]

As with the contract citation analysis, Mann-Whitney U tests of medians showed a number of differences as compared to t-tests of averages. When median figures were

[155] Strong, International Commercial Courts (n 44); Table 4.1.

analysed, the only statistically significant differences with respect to initial testimony arose between the English Commercial Court and the Quebec courts ($p<.05$), and the only statistically significant difference in subsequent testimony arose between the English Commercial Court and the US courts ($p<.05$). The discrepancy in outcomes under the t-test and Mann-Whitney U test suggests that further research is needed, although it appears more likely that the Mann-Whitney U test is the more accurate of the two tests, given the large standard deviations in most entries.

The final item to consider involves evidentiary materials other than the contract(s) at issue. In terms of average numbers of initial citations, US courts showed a statistically significant difference to the English Commercial Court ($p<.001$) and to domestic arbitration ($p<.05$), although no differences arose with respect to subsequent citations. However, the English Commercial Court showed a statistically significant difference when compared to the courts of Quebec with respect to both initial citations ($p<.01$) and subsequent citations ($p<.05$). While this might be interpreted to reflect a difference between common law and civil law analysis, the absence of a statistically significant difference between US courts and the courts of Quebec preclude such an interpretation.

The results were relatively similar for analysis of medians, although the level of certainty was slightly different. For example, with respect to initial citations to other evidentiary materials, the Mann-Whitney U test showed differences between the same cohorts as under the t-test (the English Commercial Court and the Quebec courts, the English Commercial Court and US courts, and US courts and domestic arbitration), but all at the same level of certainty ($p<.05$) rather than different levels of certainty as was the case with the t-test. With respect to subsequent citations, the Mann-Whitney U test showed no statistically significant differences, not even between the English Commercial Court and the Quebec courts, as was the case under the t-test.[156]

While the information generated by Table 4.14 is interesting, it does not provide widespread support for the longstanding assumption that common law jurisdictions are universally more interested in witness testimony than civil law jurisdictions under either of the two statistical tests. The data also fails to validate the opposite proposition, namely that civil law jurisdictions are always more reliant on documentary evidence than common law jurisdictions. Instead, the results seem to suggest that judicial practices are for the most part relatively consistent with one another and with arbitral practices. The sole exception appears to be US courts, which differ starkly from other courts under t-test analyses of initial witness testimony, and the English Commercial Court, which tends to differ from other courts and arbitration with respect to median numbers of citations of initial contract citations. More research is needed to confirm these findings, since the results under the two statistical analyses differ in some regards and may have been affected by the relatively small sample sizes and/or large standard deviations.

[156] The sample involving subsequent citations by US courts was too small to support an analysis under the Mann-Whitney U test.

During the design phase, it was anticipated that problems with sample sizes and standard deviations could arise, resulting in data that could not support useful statistical analyses. Furthermore, the analysis conducted in Table 4.14 did not take into account how many decisions or awards within the total population referred to various types of evidence. Therefore, the next calculation considered the proportion of references to each type of factual authority within each cohort so as to better understand the types of factual authorities that are considered persuasive in a particular place or procedure and the likelihood that a judge or arbitrator will discuss an authority in depth, as opposed to merely in passing.[157]

Table 4.15 Proportion of decisions or awards per cohort citing factual authority (actual numbers followed by proportion in parenthesis)

	Judicial decisions – England	Judicial decisions – Quebec	Judicial decisions – US	Awards – domestic reasoned	Awards- int'l reasoned	Awards – domestic standard	Awards- int'l standard
Initial contract cites	81 (.88)	25 (.89)	5 (.71)	22 (1.00)	31 (.97)	9 (.75)	4 (1.00)
Subsequent contract cites	64 (.70)	22 (.79)	4 (.57)	20 (.91)	27 (.84)	5 (.42)	1 (.25)
Initial witness testimony cites	72 (.78)	21 (.75)	7 (1.00)	12 (.55)	18 (.56)	1 (.08)	1 (.25)
Subsequent witness testimony cites	49 (.53)	17 (.61)	5 (.71)	19 (.86)	16 (.50)	0 (.00)	1 (.25)
Initial other document cites	70 (.76)	25 (.89)	6 (.86)	19 (.86)	21 (.66)	0 (.00)	0 (.00)
Subsequent other document cites	46 (.50)	24 (.86)	4 (.57)	8 (.36)	14 (.44)	0 (.00)	1 (.25)
Total	92	28	7	22	32	12	4

Table 4.15 provides a somewhat different perspective than Table 4.14 on the use of factual authorities in commercial disputes. Indeed, on first glance, the data suggests much more consistency across the various lines of inquiry than was the case with Table 4.14. However, a two-tailed z-test analysis identified a number of important distinctions.

For example, when considering initial contract citations, statistically significant differences arose between US decisions and domestic awards ($p<.01$) and between US decisions and international awards ($p<.05$). With respect to subsequent contract citations, the only statistically significant difference arose between US decisions and domestic awards ($p<.01$). None of these results were seen in Table 4.14.

[157] This figure was obtained by dividing the number of decisions or awards that referred to each type of authority by the total number of decisions or awards in that particular cohort.

When the analysis turned to witness testimony, more differences arose. As was the case with Table 4.14, citation rates for initial testimony showed statistically significant differences between US courts and the English Commercial Court ($p<.001$), the Quebec courts ($p<.01$), domestic arbitration ($p<.001$), and international arbitration ($p<.001$). When these results are compared to Table 4.14, the strong inference is that US judges' approach to witness testimony is different than that of other judges and arbitrators. Notably, the data does not indicate whether US judges adopt this approach because they find witness testimony more persuasive than other forms of evidence or because lawyers present witness testimony more frequently than other forms of evidence, but further research may be able to answer that question.

Other statistically significant differences relating to initial testimony involved comparisons between the English Commercial Court and domestic arbitration ($p<.05$) and the English Commercial Court and international arbitration ($p<.05$). When subsequent testimony was considered, domestic arbitration became the outlier, showing statistically significant differences as compared to the English Commercial Court ($p<.001$), the Quebec courts ($p<.05$), and international arbitration ($p<.01$). Together with the results regarding US courts, this information suggests highly individualized approaches to witness testimony, with no clear trends across the three axes of comparison (judicial–arbitral, domestic–international and common law–civil law). However, US litigation and domestic (US) arbitration appear to favour testimony much more than other dispute resolution processes.

The final analysis involves citations to documents other than the contract(s) at issue. Here, the only statistically significant differences were between decisions of the Quebec courts and international awards ($p<.05$) for initial citations, and between the Quebec courts and the English Commercial Court, domestic arbitration and international arbitration for subsequent citations (all at the $p<.001$ level). This data is consistent with findings from Table 4.14 between the Quebec courts and the English Commercial Court with respect to subsequent citations, but not any of the other findings. However, differences of intensity (as measured in Table 4.14) do not always have to correlate to differences of frequency (as measured in Table 4.15).

Thus far, the citation count analysis has focused solely on legal authorities and factual authorities. The next two calculations make comparisons across the legal–factual divide.

The inquiry begins by looking at the total number of legal and factual citations in each comparative cohort and comparing both the average and median figures. This analysis provides an understanding of the relative importance of legal authorities as compared to factual authorities in each comparative cohort.

As Table 4.16 shows, both the average and median number of factual citations was higher than the analogous number of legal citations in all reasoned and standard (unreasoned) rulings, with the exception of domestic awards.[158] This result was unexpected,

[158] Most types of decisions and awards had at least one legal citation and one factual citation, meaning that the N number was the same as the total number of entries in the cohort. However, reasoned domestic awards and standard domestic awards had some awards with no legal or factual citations. Notably, the four reasoned domestic awards that did not include a legal citation included detailed factual analysis, including those involving the interpretation of contracts, which were classified as fact documents rather than legal documents.

Table 4.16 Comparison of total legal and factual citations (averages followed by medians in brackets, standard deviation in parenthesis, and sample (N) size)

	Total legal citations	Total factual citations	Ratio: legal to factual citations
Judicial decisions – England	38.74 [32.00] (34.11) 92	39.00 [33.50] (25.80) 92	.99 [.96]
Judicial decisions – Quebec	30.96 [20.50] (36.43) 28	48.18 [35.00] (39.87) 28	.64 [.59]
Judicial decisions – US	62.43 [41.00] (49.19) 7	95.14 [55.00] (109.68) 7	.66 [.75]
Awards – domestic reasoned	41.28 [40.50] (27.53) 18	38.14 [33.00] (28.82) 22	1.08 [1.23]
Awards – international reasoned	27.03 [16.50] (27.87) 32	56.16 [27.00] (62.21) 32	.48 [.61]
Awards – domestic standard	1.00 [1.00] (0.00) 5	2.89 [3.00] (2.32) 9	.35 [.33]
Awards – international standard	1.75 [1.50] (0.96) 4	6.75 [4.00] (7.63) 4	.26 [.38]

since it contradicts conventional wisdom suggesting that arbitration is more fact-oriented than litigation. Instead, the data suggests that in the domestic commercial context, arbitrators not only are more reliant on law than on facts but are also more reliant on law than judges in any of the countries under consideration.

A t-statistical test was run across columns two and three of Table 4.16 to compare the incidence of legal citations and factual citations within an individual cohort. Here, the only statistically significant difference arose in international awards ($p<.05$), where factual citations were considerably more prevalent than legal citations. This result was not expected, given claims that international arbitration is becoming too legalistic.[159]

Next, the study compared data horizontally within the second and third columns. First, a t-test was run on the averages involving total legal citations. Statistically significant differences were found between the English Commercial Court and US courts

[159] Ch. 1.III.B.

($p<.05$), the English Commercial Court and international arbitration ($p<.05$), and US courts and international arbitration ($p<.05$). This data was largely reinforced by a Mann-Whitney U test run on the median data, which showed statistically significant differences between the English Commercial Court and international arbitration ($p<.05$) and US courts and international arbitration ($p<.05$). Together, this information strongly suggests that international awards include fewer citations to legal authorities than decisions from the English Commercial Court or US courts.

Next, a t-test was run on the averages involving total factual citations. Statistically significant differences were found between the English Commercial Court and US courts ($p<.001$), the English Commercial Court and international arbitration ($p<.05$), and US courts and domestic arbitration ($p<.05$). While these results were similar to those generated with respect to legal citations, they were not reinforced by the Mann-Whitney U test, which showed no statistically significant differences between any of these cohorts. While this discrepancy suggests the need to conduct more research, the most likely interpretation of the data is that no differences exist with respect to factual citation norms as per the Mann-Whitney U test, since the large standard deviations may have affected the averages and thus the results under the t-test.

The last and perhaps the most interesting aspect of Table 4.16 involves the fourth column, which indicates the ratio of legal citations to factual citations in each comparative cohort, using both averages and medians.[160] Although it is not possible to run a statistical analysis of this data, the figures are useful in identifying the relative importance of law to the facts in each type of proceeding. As the table shows, several natural pairings can be found, namely between the English Commercial Court (.99/.96) and domestic arbitration (1.08/1.23); decisions from Quebec (.64/.59) and decisions from the United States (.66/.75); and standard (unreasoned) domestic awards (.35/.33) and standard (unreasoned) international awards (.26/.38).[161]

While the last of these three comparisons was to be expected, the other two pairings were not. For example, US courts would have been expected to resemble the English Commercial Court more than Quebec courts, given that the United States and England are both common law jurisdictions. Similarly, it would have seemed more likely that the English Commercial Court would resemble international arbitration rather than domestic arbitration, given that the English Commercial Court and international arbitration resolve matters of relatively similar size and complexity.[162]

While more research is needed to confirm and expand upon these results, some preliminary conclusions can be drawn. First, the results suggest that the longstanding notion that domestic arbitration is a 'second class' form of justice because it does not rely on legal authorities is incorrect, since that was the only mechanism that had more legal

[160] This figure was obtained by dividing the average number of legal citations in each cohort by the average number of factual citations in the same group.

[161] The first number in each parenthetical refers to the ratio of total legal citations to total factual citations using averages, while the second number in each parenthetical refers to the ratio of total legal citations to total factual citations using medians.

[162] Tables 4.1, 4.2.

citations on average than factual citations.[163] Second, the data may be interpreted as showing that international arbitration, which is frequently criticized as being too 'legalistic', has actually retained a more pragmatic approach, since it had the lowest law-to-fact ratio of all the reasoned rulings when considering average citation rates.[164]

The final analysis in this study considered how many decisions or awards in each cohort had a higher number of legal citations as compared to factual citations, using an analytical technique that was methodologically akin to that used in Table 4.9. While this technique can eliminate some useful nuances in the data, it does help minimize the effect of wide standard deviations by considering only whether the total number of legal citations was higher than the total number of factual citations within each individual decision or award. Though pertinent to all three comparative axes considered in this text, this inquiry is particularly relevant to the debate about the relative nature of litigation and arbitration, which has traditionally suggested that litigation focuses more on law while arbitration focuses more on facts.[165]

Table 4.17 Comparison of legal and factual citations (actual numbers followed by proportion in parenthesis)

	Law citations higher	Fact citations higher	Two citations identical	Total
Judicial decisions – England	45 (.49)	41 (.45)	6 (.07)	92
Judicial decisions – Quebec	7 (.25)	18 (.64)	3 (.11)	28
Judicial decisions – US	3 (.43)	4 (.57)	0 (.00)	7
Awards – domestic reasoned	10 (.45)	13 (.59)	1 (.03)	22
Awards – international reasoned	8 (.25)	24 (.75)	0 (.00)	32
Awards – domestic standard	1 (.08)	8 (.67)	3 (.25)	12
Awards – international standard	0 (.00)	3 (.75)	1 (.25)	4

As anticipated, Table 4.17 tells a slightly different story than Table 4.16 about the relative importance of law and facts. Only one entry—decisions from the English Commercial Court—reflects a higher number of legal citations as compared to factual citations. While this information suggests that most judges and arbitrators (other than judges in the English Commercial Court) tend to rely more heavily on factual authorities than on legal authorities when supporting their reasoned decisions, a

[163] Ch. 1.III.A.

[164] Ch. 1.III.B. The lowest ratio for median data came from Quebec, but the difference between the Quebec ratio and the international arbitration ratio was not as large as with ratios involving averages, and thus is likely not as significant.

[165] Ch. 1.III.A.

two-tailed z-test analysis showed that the results from the English Commercial Court are only statistically significant when compared to the Quebec courts ($p<.05$) and international arbitration ($p<.05$). Although it is impossible to make broad inferences from this data, the distinction between the English Commercial Court and international arbitration is particularly intriguing, given the way that the two fora compete for large-sum international disputes.[166]

V. Conclusion

Despite the challenges associated with problematic data sources, small sample sizes, and large standard deviations, the quantitative analysis of judicial decisions and arbitral awards yielded some very interesting information. Some of the surprises arose as part of the demographic and background analysis. For example, longstanding assumptions about parties preferring to have their high-value, cross-border business disputes resolved in international commercial arbitration were called into question, given information about the nature of cases heard in the English Commercial Court.[167] Similarly, conventional wisdom suggesting that domestic arbitration is a 'second class' form of justice focusing primarily on low-value claims was challenged by data suggesting that the damages asserted in commercial arbitration exceed those in many national courts.[168] Other revelations involved the complexity of the various proceedings[169] and the number and nature of decision makers.[170]

However, the study's usefulness extended beyond demographic considerations. Instead, the research both confirmed and challenged conventional wisdom about the nature of legal reasoning in commercial disputes along all three comparative axes at issue in this text.

The first area of comparison involved legal reasoning across the judicial–arbitral divide. The research certainly showed a number of statistically significant differences between litigation in particular courts and arbitration, although they did not always arise as anticipated. For example, during the design phase it was expected that most of the differences would arise between US courts and domestic arbitration, particularly once it was discovered that most if not all of the domestic arbitration awards in the study came from the United States.[171] That expectation was certainly met with respect to standard (unreasoned) awards, which were categorized separately from reasoned rulings. However, the distinctions between US decisions and reasoned domestic awards were not as pronounced as critics often claim. Furthermore, in many cases the

166 Table 4.1.
167 Tables 4.1, 4.2.
168 Table 4.2.
169 Tables 4.3, 4.4.
170 Tables 4.5–4.7.
171 Ch. 4.III.1.

differences involved matters on which US courts differed even as compared to other judicial processes.[172]

The recent rise of international business courts has triggered questions about whether and to what extent courts such as the English Commercial Court can be considered to compete with international commercial arbitration for 'litigation business'.[173] This study identified a number of areas where the English Commercial Court showed a statistically significant difference from international arbitration.[174] Further research is need to clarify these distinctions, since the 'litigation market' can only operate properly if consumers of the relevant services (i.e. litigants) are aware of the relevant differences and can make an informed choice as to where and how they wish to proceed, but the data generated by this research provides an important foundation for future inquiries.[175]

The second comparative axis to consider involves domestic and international disputes. Although the sample sizes were too small to allow comparisons of domestic and international disputes in national courts, as was initially hoped, it was possible to compare reasoned awards generated in domestic and international arbitration.[176] Interestingly, only one statistically significant difference arose between the two procedures, suggesting that domestic arbitration, at least in the US commercial context, is as legalistic as international commercial arbitration.[177]

The third area of comparison involves common law and civil law legal traditions. While this analysis was particularly challenging as a matter of methodology,[178] some inferences could nevertheless be made. Interestingly, the results did not for the most part confirm various longstanding assumptions about the nature of common law and civil law reasoning. Instead, the data suggested that differences in legal reasoning typically arise on a jurisdiction-by-jurisdiction basis rather than across legal families. This conclusion is based on the fact that statistically significant differences often arose between Quebec and one of the two common law jurisdictions but very seldom between Quebec and both of the common law jurisdictions.

Of course, interpretation of empirical data can be challenging, and other explanations may be possible. For example, in a number of cases, US courts were seen to be an outlier,

[172] Tables 4.8 (regarding percentage of application paragraphs); 4.12 (regarding initial judicial decisions); 4.13 (regarding subsequent judicial decisions); 4.14 (regarding initial citations to other documents); 4.15 (regarding initial and subsequent citations to contracts and initial citations to witness testimony).

[173] Bookman (n 85); Strong, International Commercial Courts (n 44); SI Strong, 'The Future of International Commercial Courts in English-Speaking Jurisdictions: The US and Australia Compared', (forthcoming 2021) 115 AJIL Unbound.

[174] Tables 4.8 (regarding percentage of law paragraphs); 4.13 (regarding subsequent citations to judicial decisions and to initial and subsequent commentary); 4.14 (regarding subsequent testimony); 4.15 (regarding initial citations to witness testimony); 4.16; 4.17.

[175] Law and economics scholars have discussed the benefits associated with competitive differences, although consumers of the relevant services (in this case, dispute resolution services) have to be aware of the differences if the relevant market is to operate properly. Peter B Rutledge, 'Convergence and Divergence in International Dispute Resolution', 2012 J Disp Res 49, 50.

[176] Data was presented on standard (unreasoned) awards generated in both domestic and international arbitration but was not routinely subjected to statistical analysis, both because of relatively small sample sizes and because unreasoned awards were not the focus of this study.

[177] Fig. 4.14 (involving factual citation rates).

[178] Ch. 4.II.A.

differing not only from the Quebec courts but also from the English Commercial Court and arbitration.[179] In other cases, no such distinctions arose. Thus, it may be that the Quebec courts (or courts from other civil law jurisdictions) may show a sharper distinction when compared to decisions from common law countries other than the US or England. More research will be needed before a firm conclusion can be drawn.

One of the more innovative aspects of this project has involved efforts to determine how judges and arbitrators handle factual issues and authorities as compared to legal issues and authorities. Not only did the coding exercise generate detailed data about how judges and arbitrators use particular types of legal and factual authorities,[180] it also provided insights into whether judges and arbitrators relied more on legal or factual authorities.[181] This information not only offers scholars intriguing new areas of study, it also provides practitioners with useful information on how judges and arbitrators support their reasoning process. While the current data does not support any inferences about why judges and arbitrators adopted the approaches they did,[182] the material presented here provides a useful starting point for future research.

The final item to mention involves data involving the application of law to facts. This aspect of legal reasoning has not been studied before and was only analysed in this study through a paragraph-by-paragraph analysis. According to one test, the percentage of paragraphs devoted to application analyses showed a statistically significant difference between US judicial decisions and domestic awards, with judges taking more time to discuss the connection between the law and the facts.[183] However, none of the comparative cohorts showed any significant differences in the number of paragraphs devoted to application analyses as compared to facts, although the Quebec courts differed from both US courts and domestic arbitration when the number of application paragraphs was compared to the number of law-oriented paragraphs.[184] While these findings do not show overall trends, they suggest more research involving application analyses might be useful.

[179] This disparity was particularly marked with respect to citations to judicial decisions and witness testimony. Tables 4.12–4.14.

[180] Tables 4.12–4.15.

[181] Tables 4.9, 4.16–4.17.

[182] For example, decision makers could cite certain factual authorities more frequently because they value those authorities more or because the advocates presented more of those authorities. Advocates can have their own range of reasons for introducing certain types of evidence, ranging from a belief in what the decision maker will find most persuasive to issues involving availability of such materials or the nature of the dispute.

[183] Table 4.8.

[184] Table 4.10.

5
Conclusion

I. Introduction

As the preceding pages have shown, legal reasoning is a complex and often highly individualistic endeavour. While it is possible to identify a number of overarching trends, the devil is, as always, in the details. As a result, this chapter does not seek to provide a single, pithy summary of the findings presented herein but instead relies on the extensive cross-referencing in the substantive discussions to guide analysis of particular issues across the three research streams.

The goal in this chapter is to put the research into a larger practical and scholarly context, and the discussion is organized as follows. The chapter begins by considering how the empirical data presented in this text measures up to theoretical studies in this area of law, pulling together select elements from the three research strands (i.e. the international survey, semi-structured interviews and coding exercise)[1] and focusing on particular issues of interest across the three major areas of comparison (i.e. the judicial–arbitral, domestic–international and common law–civil law divides). While this analysis is by no means comprehensive, it nevertheless provides a high-level overview of general research outcomes. Next, the chapter discusses certain unanticipated data that was generated during the course of the study and seeks to situate that information within the academic understanding of legal reasoning. Finally, the focus turns to the various ways that studies in legal reasoning might develop in the future as a result of the research reflected herein.

II. Testing Theoretical Assumptions Through Empirical Analysis

Chapter 1 provided theoretical and historical context for the current analysis by reviewing the scholarly literature on legal reasoning.[2] Now that the empirical data has been presented, it is time to determine whether and to what extent those theoretical assumptions hold true.[3]

[1] Comparisons are not possible across all aspects of the three research strands owing to limitations of the individual methodologies. For example, the survey and interviews were both capable of considering questions of motivation, whereas the coding exercise focused exclusively on actual practices. Ch. 1.II. However, the study was designed to maximize the ability to triangulate data across all three research streams. Ch. 1.II.

[2] Ch. 1.III.

[3] The study also shed light on a number of demographic and background considerations involving judges and arbitrators, although those items are not discussed herein. Chs. 2.III, 4.III.

A. Judicial Versus Arbitral Practice

The primary goal of this book was to test the validity of the longstanding assumption that arbitration constitutes a 'second class' form of justice as compared to litigation.[4] In so doing, the project considered the building blocks of legal reasoning (i.e. legal authority and factual authority (evidence)) as well as the reasoning process itself.

While some differences arose on individual data points, the study did not find widespread disparities between judicial and arbitral practices. To the contrary, all three research strands consistently suggested that judges and arbitrators approach commercial dispute resolution in a very similar manner.[5]

This point can be illustrated in a number of ways, although the simplest may involve the use of legal authorities. According to some commentators, the elevation of litigation over arbitration is justified because arbitrators are believed to rely on legal authority less frequently than judges and on facts and/or equitable arguments more frequently than judges.[6] However, data from both the survey and the interviews suggested that judges and arbitrators are largely consistent when it comes to how they view and use legal authorities.[7] The coding exercise reinforced this conclusion by identifying numerous instances where no statistically significant differences arose between the use of legal authorities in judicial decisions and in reasoned awards.[8]

This is not to say that individual disparities did not exist. Perhaps the most interesting of these arose in the coding exercise, which identified a number of statistically significant differences between international commercial arbitration and the English Commercial Court.[9] This phenomenon was intriguing for two reasons. First, as a theoretical matter, the data seemed to refute the claim by some commentators that international commercial arbitration is as legalistic as complex commercial litigation.[10] Second, as a practical matter, the English Commercial Court has frequently been characterized as a direct competitor of international commercial arbitration, and these distinctions may prove important to consumers of litigation and arbitration services.[11]

[4] Ch. 1.III.A.

[5] In social scientific terms, the study failed to reject the null hypothesis that no differences exist between legal reasoning in commercial litigation and legal reasoning in commercial arbitration, at least on an overarching basis. Ch. 1.I.

[6] Ch. 1.III.A.

[7] Tables 2.5–2.6; Ch. 3.III.B.1.

[8] Ch. 4.IV.

[9] Tables 4.8 (regarding percentage of law paragraphs); 4.13 (regarding subsequent citations to judicial decisions and to initial and subsequent commentary); 4.14 (regarding subsequent testimony); 4.15 (regarding initial citations to witness testimony); 4.16; 4.17.

[10] Gary B Born, *International Commercial Arbitration* (Wolters Kluwer 2014) 2129; Russell J Weintraub, *International Litigation and Arbitration: Practice and Planning* (Carolina Academic Publishers 1994) 455 (discussing 'Rolls Royce justice'); Ch. 1.III.A.

[11] Pamela K Bookman, 'The Adjudication Business', (2020) 45 Yale J Intl L 227; SI Strong, 'International Commercial Courts and the United States: An Outlier by Choice and by Constitutional Design?' in Xandra E Kramer and John Sorabji (eds), *International Business Courts: A European and Global Perspective* (Eleven International Publishing 2019) 255.

Though more research is necessary to confirm and elaborate on these findings, the data is nevertheless pertinent to both scholars and practitioners.

Another useful illustration involves the various motivations enunciated by judges and arbitrators for particular procedural practices. These issues were tested extensively by the survey and interviews, and both studies suggested that judges and arbitrators approach the dispute resolution process relatively similarly and with relatively similar goals.[12] However, the research did challenge certain longstanding assumptions about why judges and arbitrators act as they do, suggesting that neutrals of both types are primarily motivated by practical rather than philosophical considerations.[13] Again, these results will be useful to both practitioners and scholars as they consider how to present their arguments in actual disputes as well as how to revise theoretical models about legal reasoning.

One of the most innovative aspects of this study involved the integration of factual (evidentiary) matters into the legal reasoning analysis. While factual considerations are typically ignored by scholars and theoreticians,[14] the current study showed that judges and arbitrators both believe that factual issues are central to the resolution of commercial disputes.[15] Furthermore, the research strongly suggests that judges and arbitrators approach factual authorities and issues in a very similar manner.[16] When taken as a whole, these findings appear to reject longstanding claims in the scholarly literature that judges focus on the law while arbitrators focus on the facts.[17]

Although the study placed considerable emphasis on evaluating longstanding assumptions about purported differences between judges and arbitrators, the research also sought to illuminate a number of ancillary points regarding arbitral and judicial practice.[18] One such inquiry sought to understand what factors, if any, led judges and arbitrators to alter their approach to legal reasoning. Numerous interviewees remarked on how little their decision-making process changed as a result of the passage of time, changes in status (i.e. whether the individual was acting as a judge or arbitrator), changes in the type of dispute (i.e. whether the matters was domestic or international in nature), and the neutral's role within a panel.[19] The survey reinforced a number of these findings,[20] thereby casting additional doubt on the notion that legal reasoning improves with age, seniority, and/or status as a judge or arbitrator.[21]

[12] Tables 2.7–2.13; Ch. 3.III.2.

[13] Ch. 2.IV.A.4. Additional insights were provided by interviewees. Ch. 3.III.B.5.

[14] Ch. I.III.A.

[15] Chs. 2.IV.B.4, 3.III.C. For example, survey data suggested that law and facts were essentially indistinguishable in terms of their relative importance to judges and arbitrators and that most judges and arbitrators begin the reasoning process by considering the facts and subsequently searching for law relevant to those facts. Tables 2.29–2.30.

[16] Tables 4.8, 4.10, 4.16, 4.17; Chs. 2.IV.B.4, 3.III.C.

[17] Ch. 1.III.A.

[18] Chs. 2.III, 4.III.

[19] Chs. 3.III.D.2–3.III.D.5

[20] For example, a significant majority (78 per cent) of surveyed individuals who had served as both judges and arbitrators indicated that they did not alter their approach to legal reasoning depending on whether they were acting in a judicial or arbitral capacity. Ch. 2.IV.C.4.

[21] Chs. 1.III.A, 4.III.1.

Another innovative aspect of the study involved its emphasis on judicial and arbitral education, which has been largely ignored in the legal literature.[22] Both the survey and the interviews focused heavily on drafting and learning to draft reasoned rulings, since many neutrals find that task particularly challenging.[23] Interestingly, both research strands found that judges and arbitrators were equally influenced by the difficulty, complexity, and novelty of the dispute as a matter of fact and of law when deciding how detailed to make their decisions and awards, further reinforcing the notion that litigation and arbitration are very similar processes.[24] The study also generated some useful but unanticipated results, such as the finding that judges and arbitrators both elevate process-oriented concerns (i.e. those relating to the clear statement of the relevant legal standard and how the facts do or do not meet the standard identified) over outcome-oriented concerns (i.e. those indicating that the dispute was resolved correctly as a matter of law) when drafting reasoned rulings.[25]

Questions on judicial and arbitral education extended beyond the drafting process and included educational concerns more broadly. In many ways, the responses reflected the ambiguous nature of the field of judicial and arbitral education as a whole. For example, the vast majority of survey respondents considered professional education beneficial for at least some members of the judicial and arbitral communities, yet the two most-cited forms of judicial and arbitral education—learning by doing and reading other decisions and awards—do not involve any coursework.[26] Furthermore, survey respondents indicated that 'speaking with more experienced colleagues' was an important means of learning how to act as a judge or arbitrator even though they ranked mentorship and mechanisms to facilitate confidential discussions about issues of interest quite low in the hierarchy of preferred educational formats.[27]

Rather than clarifying the survey data, the interviews added to the confusion, with interviewees expressing less enthusiasm than survey respondents about the need for judicial and arbitral education.[28] The reason for this phenomenon is unclear, although it could be the result of conscious or unconscious concerns about looking bad to the interviewer.[29]

[22] Ch. 1.II.

[23] Ch. 2.IV.E.1; see also William Domnarski, *In the Opinion of the Court* (University of Illinois Press 1997) 36 (quoting US Supreme Court Justice Hugo Black as saying said that 'the most difficult thing about coming on to the Court was learning how to write').

[24] Chs. 2.IV.D.4, 3.III.E.

[25] Chs. 2.IV.D.3, 3.III.A.1, 3.III.B.5.A. Notably, the top two factors were significantly more important to survey respondents than other alternatives by a significant order of magnitude. Table 2.37.

[26] Tables 2.38–2.39.

[27] Tables 2.38–2.40.

[28] Ch. 3.III.F.3.

[29] Susan D Franck and others, 'Inside the Arbitrator's Mind', (2017) 66 Emory L J 1115, 1163 (discussing empirical research on self-serving bias in both judges and arbitrators).

B. Domestic Versus International Practice

The second goal of this book was to compare legal reasoning across the domestic–international divide. Difficulties in data collection limited the usefulness of the coding exercise on this topic, except perhaps with respect to comparisons between international commercial arbitration and the English Commercial Court, although the latter is perhaps best characterized as a mixed domestic–international forum.[30] However, the survey and interviews were able to provide some useful insights.

The interviews identified few, if any, distinctions between domestic and international practice, suggesting that the null hypothesis that no differences exist between legal reasoning in domestic and international commercial matters was not disproven.[31] Survey results reinforced this conclusion, although some exceptions did arise. For example, the survey identified a number of differences in how legal and factual authorities were viewed in domestic versus international disputes[32] and suggested that specialists in international dispute resolution might have a heightened regard for procedural justice as compared to those specializing in domestic disputes.[33] While additional research on these questions would be welcome, the overall trend showed consistency across the domestic–international divide.

C. Common Law Versus Civil Law Practice

The third goal of this book was to compare common law and civil law practice. For decades, the two legal traditions have been perceived as distinct in a number of key regards, although recent academic work has suggested a potential convergence.[34] While the research in this text supported the notion of convergence in some regards, there were some instances where conventional common law–civil law distinctions regarding the use of different legal authorities remained.[35] As a result, it seems that the process of convergence is neither fully complete nor all-encompassing.[36]

Difficulties in data collection limited the usefulness of the coding exercise in comparing common law and civil law practices.[37] However, the problems associated with the coding exercise actually turned out to be beneficial in that they produced some unique insights that could trigger new forms of comparative legal research, as discussed in the next section.

[30] Ch. 4.V.
[31] Chs. 1.I, 3.IV.
[32] Ch. 2.IV.B.4, Tables 2.5–2.6.
[33] Ch. 2.IV.B.4.
[34] Ch. 1.III.C.
[35] Chs. 2.IV.A.4, 3.III.B.
[36] In social scientific terms, it can be said that the null hypothesis that no differences exist between legal reasoning in common law and civil law legal systems, at least in the commercial context, was neither fully proven nor disproven. Ch. 1.I.
[37] Ch. 4.II.A.

III. Unanticipated Results

Although empirical research is bound to generate a number of unexpected results, some findings are entirely outside the anticipated scope of inquiry. Such was the case with this study, which generated a number of substantive and procedural insights that merit special mention as well as follow-up research.

The first item to discuss arose during the course of the coding exercise and involved various differences between the common law jurisdictions under investigation.[38] While scholars have long debated the differences associated with civil law legal reasoning in the French and German traditions, little, if any, research has been conducted with respect to differences in common law reasoning, likely because common law countries are all derived from the same historical source.[39] Nevertheless, the coding exercise identified a number of statistically significant disparities between reasoning conducted by the English Commercial Court and US courts.[40] These issues deserve more practical and scholarly consideration, particularly since some of the differences could be outcome-determinative.

The second item to discuss involves the importance of factual (evidentiary) considerations in the legal reasoning process. While many interviewees mentioned the central role that facts play in the determination of commercial disputes,[41] the survey drove that point home in an entirely new way by showing that respondents generated higher intensity ratings when discussing the persuasiveness of factual authorities than when discussing legal authorities.[42] Although more research is needed to understand this phenomenon, no known study has ever considered differences across the legal–factual divide, and these findings provide an important first step in what may be a new area of practical and scholarly inquiry.

The preceding two items involved substantive surprises, but this project also generated several unexpected procedural results. One such revelation involved the difficulties associated with obtaining judicial decisions for the coding exercise.[43] While this phenomenon might initially appear to be nothing more than a research design issue, it actually suggests a number of misapprehensions about the nature of public justice. For example, the lack of transparency in some countries about the criteria governing

[38] Logistical and linguistic issues precluded comparisons within the civil law tradition in the current study, although additional research along these lines would be very useful. Ch. 4.II.A.

[39] SI Strong, Katia Fach Gómez, and Laura Carballo Piñeiro, *Comparative Law for Spanish-English Speaking Lawyers: Legal Cultures, Legal Terms and Legal Practices / Derecho comparado para abogados anglo- e hispanoparlantes: Culturas jurídicas, términos jurídicos y prácticas jurídicas* (Edward Elgar Publishing Ltd 2016) chs. 3–6 (comparing legal reasoning across common law–civil law divide and also within different common law systems).

[40] Ch. 4.IV.

[41] Ch. 3.III.C.

[42] Ch. 2.IV.B.4.

[43] Ch. 4.II.A; see also SI Strong, 'The Effect of Motion Practice on the Nature of Dispute Resolution and the Creation of Precedent: An Empirical Analysis' (forthcoming). Difficulties in obtaining arbitral awards were anticipated but were nevertheless problematic. Ch. 4.II.A; see also SI Strong, 'The Fallacy of Transparency: How to Address Arbitral and Judicial (Non)Cooperation With Independent Scholarship' (forthcoming) (discussing also problems associated with interviewing sitting judges).

publication of judicial decisions[44] and the challenges associated with obtaining and analysing unpublished decisions[45] suggest that judicial processes and determinations are not as 'public' as some scholars contest. Furthermore, these difficulties make it impossible to conduct a rigorous and comprehensive evaluation of the true nature of judicial reasoning, let alone compare those processes to arbitral reasoning. If litigation and arbitration are to be compared critically, then the comparison should include both published and unpublished judicial decisions.

The final item to mention is in many ways the most important. Throughout this study it has become apparent that there is a significant amount of variation in how individual judges and arbitrators approach legal reasoning. This phenomenon is contrary to conventional wisdom that suggests that judges—as a group—decide matters in one way and arbitrators—as a group—decide matters in another.[46] Instead, the data suggests that choices about legal reasoning are very personal and cut across the judicial–arbitral divide. These differences have traditionally been both praised and protected under the rubric of judicial and arbitral independence, but the number and nature of disparities make it difficult for parties to predict how their disputes will be decided and how they should shape their factual and legal submissions.[47] The problem is further exacerbated by the fact that some differences can be outcome-determinative, creating concerns about the quality of justice at the systemic level. More research and policy analysis are needed to determine how to minimize problematic differences in the reasoning process while retaining positive aspects of individualized decision making.

IV. Future Developments in Studies of Legal Reasoning

As the preceding section suggests, good empirical research generates as many questions as it answers. It therefore may be helpful to conclude this discussion with some suggestions on how the study of legal reasoning might develop in the future as a result of the findings outlined in this text.

The first proposal is to increase the amount and type of empirical research being conducted in the area of legal reasoning. This project has embraced a number of different methodologies that might be adopted or adapted for use by others. For example, researchers might use the instruments used herein to study legal reasoning in other fields (such as consumer law or securities law) or in other populations (such as those outside the English-speaking world) to see whether and to what extent the current findings resemble norms and practices found elsewhere.[48] In so doing, scholars could

[44] While some countries publish all judicial decisions, others—such as the United States—publish only a small percentage. Ch. 4.II.A.

[45] Some legal databases (such as Westlaw-US) provide access to unpublished decisions but it is unclear what criteria are used to determine which unpublished materials are included on computerized databases.

[46] Jeremy Fogel and SI Strong, 'Judicial Education, Dispute Resolution and the Life of a Judge: A Conversation with Judge Jeremy Fogel, Director of the Federal Judicial Center', 2016 J Disp Res 259.

[47] Parties in arbitration have always been aware of this issue, at least to some extent, which is why so much weight is put on the decision of who should serve as arbitrator. Ch. 4.III.1.

[48] Appx. I–III (reproducing the survey instrument, interview script, and coding book used herein).

improve on the techniques used herein, perhaps by limiting quantitative investigations to rulings that are more consistent with respect to length or complexity so as to eliminate the analytical ambiguities associated with large standard deviations.[49] Alternatively, researchers might decide to pursue some of the unexpected results that were generated during the course of this project.[50]

Another way that the field of legal reasoning might develop comes from the realization that judges and arbitrators each have their own individual approaches to legal reasoning, based not on their status as judges or arbitrators but instead on their own individual adjudicative philosophies. Rather than attempt to minimize these differences, the legal community might instead seek to make the process more transparent so that parties are better prepared to provide individual judges and arbitrators with the type of information that they most value. Indeed, several individuals mentioned during the interviews that they wished parties and counsel better understood how the reasoning process worked.[51] This technique has already been adopted to some degree in the world of international commercial arbitration, where organizations like Arbitrator Intelligence seek to de-mystify the arbitral process by providing information about how individual arbitrators approach certain procedural and substantive issues.[52] Similar initiatives might be usefully adopted in domestic arbitration and in litigation. Future research projects might not only seek to identify the types of issues on which individual decision makers differ but also how judicial and arbitral preferences can and should be properly conveyed to the parties.[53] Policy makers might also wish to support this type of project, since improving the legal community's understanding of the reasoning philosophy adopted by a particular decision maker not only increases the quality of justice but also helps improve the efficiency of the dispute resolution process by ensuring that party submissions meet the needs of the judge or arbitrator in question.

The fourth and final way that the field of legal reasoning might change in the future involves improved access to research materials. Although conventional wisdom suggests that judicial reasoning is entirely public, scholars often find it difficult to obtain access to unpublished judicial decisions.[54] Additional difficulties arise when academics want to engage with judges on scholarly initiatives. While some judges are willing to participate in independent scholarly studies, most invitations are turned down unless they come from people who are previously known to the judge (such as former clerks) or who win the approval of a 'gatekeeper' individual or institution.[55] These types of

[49] Ch. 4.II.A.

[50] Ch. 5.III.

[51] Chs. 3.III.B.6, 3.III.C.6, 3.III.D.6.

[52] Arbitrator Intelligence, <https://arbitratorintelligence.com/about-1> last accessed 11 April 2020 (providing information about 'timing and duration, case management and procedural orders, document disclosure, rulings on jurisdiction and interim relief, damages analysis, and legal methodologies' of individual arbitrators).

[53] For example, it would be unfair if one party had access to detailed information about how a judge or arbitrator approached legal reasoning but the other party did not.

[54] For example, some of these decisions may be available, but only by going physically to the court to obtain the rulings. Furthermore, there may be no way to search decisions by subject matter. A related issue involves the failure to identify how decisions to publish judicial opinions are made. Ch. 4.II.A.

[55] Gatekeepers might exist at judicial research institutions (such as the Federal Judicial Center in the United States or the European Judicial Training Network) or at professional organizations for judges (such as the Standing International Forum of Commercial Courts or the United Kingdom Association of Women Judges).

screening mechanisms can result in scholarly biases, where the only perspectives that are heard are those that generate positive views of the judiciary.

Similar problems exist in the arbitral realm. Although a few arbitral institutions will allow academics to review original awards lodged with the institution, some organizations may impose conditions that are inconsistent with scholarly independence,[56] resulting in the same type of biased analyses that can occur in judicial settings. While it may be easier for scholars to gain access to arbitrators than to judges, there are increasing concerns about survey or interview fatigue as requests for participation grow more frequent.

While there is no easy answer to the question of access, various options exist. For example, judicial research organizations and arbitral institutions might set up systems by which a limited number of scholars could obtain access to neutrals and materials each year, thereby reducing the burdens on individuals and institutions. Requests for access could be reviewed by an independent body to ensure a diversity of viewpoints among researchers. The key in both cases would be to minimize the potential for bias while maximizing practical and scholarly understanding of legal reasoning in litigation and arbitration.

Of course, there are many other ways in which the field of legal reasoning might develop in the coming years, both as a practical and theoretical matter. Hopefully, the research reflected in this text has provided a useful contribution to this burgeoning field of study and to the ongoing debate about judicial and arbitral decision making in domestic and international commercial disputes.

[56] Ch. 4.II.A.

APPENDIX I

Instrument: Electronic Survey

Following is the survey instrument used to generate the data discussed in Chapter 2. Although the full text of the instrument included 73 questions, each participant only saw 50–60 questions due to the use of skip logic, which eliminated certain questions based on an individual's previous responses.

The survey was designed to allow the data to be filtered in a variety of ways to facilitate detailed analysis. While several such filters have been used to generate the information discussed in this book, other inquires have been curtailed due to space restrictions. However, these issues will be considered in follow-up articles.[1]

Introduction and Consent Form

I would like to invite you to complete a survey that will form part of a research project that I am conducting in conjunction with the Center for the Study of Dispute Resolution at the University of Missouri School of Law, where I am a senior faculty member. The project seeks to improve our understanding of how judges and arbitrators resolve complex commercial disputes in both national and international settings. If you have acted as a judge or as an arbitrator in either a domestic or cross-border commercial dispute, I am interested in your thoughts.

The research focuses on legal reasoning and how judges and arbitrators write reasoned decisions and awards. The data generated by this project will help parties make more informed choices about whether to have their commercial disputes resolved in litigation or arbitration and will help identify how providers of judicial and arbitral education can better meet the needs of judges and arbitrators.

The survey includes questions on the following issues:

- general, non-identifying information about respondents (demographics);
- use of legal authorities;
- consideration of factual and evidentiary issues;
- approach to legal reasoning;
- drafting reasoned decisions or awards; and
- judicial and arbitral education involving legal reasoning.

The sensitive nature of this topic may cause some concerns about confidentiality. Please be assured that this survey is entirely anonymous, and there is no way that I can identify you unless you make your identity known through specific comments. In order to further ensure the confidentiality of the process, I will also ask you not to mention your or anyone else's name in any written comments. In any publications or presentations based on this research, I will not disclose any personally identifying information that may be provided.

The survey is comprised of 73 of questions, although not all participants will answer all questions. You can expect to answer approximately 50–60 questions out of the total of 73, including a number of questions concerning demographics. It should take you approximately 30 minutes to complete the survey. Your participation in this survey is completely voluntary, and you may stop at any time. If you cannot complete the survey in one sitting, you may return to the survey at a later date/time. However, you must hit 'next' at the bottom of the page to save the material on that page and you must log in at the same computer to access your saved material. The survey will remain open until 11:59 p.m. Central Daylight Time (CDT) on Monday, 7 May 2018.

[1] E.g. SI Strong, 'Does Experience Matter? An Empirical Analysis of Seniority and Number of Disputes Heard on Legal Reasoning in Commercial Dispute Resolution' (forthcoming); SI Strong, 'Does Gender Affect Legal Reasoning in Commercial Dispute Resolution? An Empirical Analysis' (forthcoming).

The study is funded in part by the American Arbitration Association-International Centre for Dispute Resolution (AAA-ICDR) Foundation, a 501(c)(3) not-for-profit organization that is separate from both the AAA and the ICDR. Although the AAA-ICDR Foundation provided funding for certain aspects of this research, the Foundation is in no way involved in the design, content, or analysis of the survey.

If you have any questions about this project, you can contact me at +1-573-882-2465 or strongsi@missouri.edu. If you have any questions about your rights as a research subject, you can contact the University of Missouri Campus Institutional Review Board at +1-573-882-9585 or umcresearchirb@missouri.edu.

Please feel free to forward the link to this survey [link provided] to colleagues who have acted as judges or arbitrators in commercial matters at either the national or international level.

Thank you in advance for your insights into these important issues.

Kind regards,

Prof. S.I. Strong, J.D., Ph.D.
Manley O. Hudson Professor of Law
University of Missouri School of Law
Columbia, MO 65211 USA
Telephone: +1-573-882-2465
Email: strongsi@missouri.edu
Bio: http://law.missouri.edu/about/people/strong/

Campus IRB Approved Date: January 16, 2018
Project Number: 2010449C

Definitions of 'Commercial', 'International', and 'Reasoned Decision or Award'

This survey focuses exclusively on commercial disputes, which is defined herein as business-to-business or commercial state entity-to-business disputes. Although you may act as a judge or arbitrator in other types of matters, your responses here should focus solely on your experience as a judge or arbitrator of commercial disputes. Thus, for example, you should not discuss your experience with investor-state arbitration or consumer arbitration here.

Some questions distinguish between international and domestic proceedings. This survey takes a broad view of internationality and defines an international dispute as a dispute where at least two parties come from different countries; where the property in dispute is located in a country different than the disputants; or where performance or enforcement is anticipated in a country different than that of the disputants.

Finally, for purposes of this survey, a reasoned decision or award is defined as including but not limited to decisions or awards with findings of fact and conclusions of law.

Demographic Information

1. The next two questions ask you to describe your current role as a judge or arbitrator. If you currently act simultaneously as both a judge and an arbitrator, please describe both roles.
   Please describe your current role as a judge.
   I do not currently act as a judge.
   I am a member of an international (supranational) court or tribunal
   I am a member of a national (federal) court or tribunal
   I am a member of a local or state (sub-federal) court or tribunal
2. Please describe your role as an arbitrator.
   I do not currently act as an arbitrator

I act only as a domestic commercial arbitrator
I act only as an international commercial arbitrator
I act as both a domestic and international commercial arbitrator

Role as International Commercial Arbitrator

3. Please describe your role as an international commercial arbitrator.
   I act only as an international commercial arbitrator
   I act only as an investment (investor-state) arbitrator[2]
   I act as both an international commercial and investment (investor-state) arbitrator

Demographic Information, cont.

4. Please state the number of years that you have been qualified as practising lawyer, or, if your jurisdiction contemplates judicial employment directly after the completion of legal education rather than after a period of legal practice, the number of years that you have been qualified as a judge. If you are not qualified as a lawyer or judge, indicate the number of years since completing your first university degree.
   0-5 years
   6-15 years
   16-25 years
   26-35 years
   36-45 years
   More than 46 years
5. Please state the number of years that you have acted as a judge and/or arbitrator, either full- or part-time.
   0–5 years
   6–15 years
   16–25 years
   26–35 years
   36–45 years
   More than 46 years
6. Please state whether you have worked as both a judge and an arbitrator, either at the same time or at different points in your career.
   No
   Yes

Worked as Both Judge and Arbitrator

7. If you worked first as a judge, please answer the following. If you did not, please skip this question.
   I worked first as a judge for [drop down box 0-50] years
   and have now worked as an arbitrator for [drop down box 0-50] years
8. If you worked first as an arbitrator, please answer the following. If you did not, please skip this question.
   I worked first as an arbitrator for [drop down box 0-50] years
   and have now worked as a judge for [drop down box 0-50] years
9. I have worked simultaneously as a judge and arbitrator for [drop down box 0-50] years

[2] The survey was designed so that anyone who marked 'yes' to this question was sent to the final page and eliminated from the survey. As it turned out, no one marked this response.

10. Please describe the type of court or arbitration that you worked in prior to your current employment. Check all that apply.
    international/supranational court
    national (federal) court
    state/local (sub-federal) court
    domestic arbitration
    international arbitration
    mixed domestic/international arbitration

Demographic Information, cont.

11. Of all the commercial disputes that you have handled as a judge or arbitrator in the last three years, what percentage of those matters were international in scope?
    0%
    1–20%
    21–40%
    41–60%
    61–80%
    81–100%
12. Please state the jurisdiction in which you are primarily based.
    [drop down box offering countries of the world]
13. If you chose Canada as the jurisdiction in which you are primarily based, please choose one of the following:
    [drop down box offering the provinces and territories of Canada]
14. If you chose United Kingdom as the jurisdiction in which you were primarily based, please choose one of the following:
    [drop down box offering legal jurisdictions within the United Kingdom]
15. If you chose the United States as the jurisdiction in which you were primarily based, please choose one of the following:
    [drop down box offering the states and territories of the United States]
16. Please state the primary jurisdiction in which you are qualified to practise law or act as a judge. If you are not qualified as a lawyer or judge, please check NA.
    [drop down box offering countries of the world plus NA]
17. If you chose Canada as the primary jurisdiction in which you are qualified to practise law or act as a judge, please choose one of the following:
    [drop down box offering the provinces and territories of Canada]
18. If you chose United Kingdom as the primary jurisdiction in which you are qualified to practise law or act as a judge, please choose one of the following:
    [drop down box offering legal jurisdictions within the United Kingdom]
19. If you chose the United States as the primary jurisdiction in which you are qualified to practise law or act as a judge, please choose one of the following:
    [drop down box offering the states and territories of the United States]
20. Please state the secondary jurisdiction in which you are qualified to practise law or act as a judge. If you are not qualified as a lawyer or judge in a secondary jurisdiction, please check NA.
    [drop down box offering countries of the world plus NA]
21. If you chose Canada as the secondary jurisdiction in which you are qualified to practise law or act as a judge, please choose one of the following:
    [drop down box offering the provinces and territories of Canada]
22. If you chose United Kingdom as the secondary jurisdiction in which you are qualified to practise law or act as a judge, please choose one of the following:
    [drop down box offering legal jurisdictions within the United Kingdom]

23. If you chose the United States as the secondary jurisdiction in which you are qualified to practise law or act as a judge, please choose one of the following:
    [drop down box offering the states and territories of the United States]
24. Many respondents have experience with commercial disputes in both domestic and international settings. The following questions are general in nature, so your responses should encompass your general practice. However, you must focus your responses on either domestic or international cases (not both), and you must be consistent throughout the survey as to the type of matters you are addressing. It may be useful to answer questions based on what you did in the last case you heard, assuming that it was typical of your normal practice.
    Please indicate which type of disputes you will be discussing in this survey.
    Domestic commercial disputes
    International commercial disputes
25. If you chose domestic commercial disputes in the previous question, please indicate the jurisdiction of the disputes you will be discussing.
    [drop down box offering countries of the world]
26. If you chose Canada as he jurisdiction of disputes you will be discussing, please choose one of the following:
    [drop down box offering the provinces and territories of Canada]
27. If you chose United Kingdom as the jurisdiction of disputes you will be discussing, please choose one of the following:
    [drop down box offering legal jurisdictions within the United Kingdom]
28. If you chose the United States as the jurisdiction of disputes you will be discussing, please choose one of the following:
    [drop down box offering the states and territories of the United States]
29. Please state the number of arbitrations and/or litigations in which you have acted as arbitrator or judge in the last five years.
    1–5
    6–15
    16–25
    26–35
    36–45
    46–55
    56–65
    66–75
    More than 76
30. Please state the gender with which you identify.
    Female
    Male
    Prefer not to say

Questions Involving Legal Authorities

31. Please indicate how important each of the following legal authorities are to you when deciding substantive (rather than procedural) aspects of commercial disputes, where 1 is not important at all and 5 is very important.
    Arbitral awards involving the parties to this dispute
    Arbitral awards involving parties other than those involved in this dispute
    Domestic regulations, statutes, or administrative rules
    International treaties
    Judicial decisions from the jurisdiction whose law controls the matter
    Judicial decisions from jurisdictions other than the jurisdiction whose law controls the matter
    Legislative history of domestic regulations, statutes, or administrative rules

Legislative history of international treaties (travaux préparatoires)
Scholarly works (articles, books, treatises)
Soft law (i.e. non-binding but persuasive guidelines, declarations, or codes of conduct)
Other (please describe below)

32. Please indicate how important the following legal authorities are to you when deciding procedural (rather than substantive) aspects of commercial disputes, where 1 is not important at all and 5 is very important.
    Arbitral awards involving the parties to this dispute
    Arbitral awards involving parties other than those involved in this dispute
    Domestic regulations, statutes, or administrative rules
    International treaties
    Judicial decisions from the jurisdiction whose law controls the matter
    Judicial decisions from jurisdictions other than the jurisdiction whose law controls the matter
    Legislative history of domestic regulations, statutes, or administrative rules
    Legislative history of international treaties (travaux préparatoires)
    Scholarly works (articles, books, treatises)
    Soft law (i.e. non-binding but persuasive guidelines, declarations, or codes of conduct)
    Other (please describe below)
33. What type(s) of additional legal research do you or your legal clerk/assistant conduct, if any, apart from reading the submissions of the parties? Please identify how often you conduct such research. (0% of the time, 1–29% of the time, 30–59% of the time, 60–99% of the time, 100% of the time)
    Check for subsequent negative treatment or overruling of an arbitral award cited by the parties
    Check for subsequent negative treatment or overruling of a judicial decision cited by the parties
    Check for subsequent negative treatment or overruling of regulations, statutes, or treaties identified by the parties
    Check for subsequent negative treatment or overruling of scholarly commentary, soft law, or persuasive authority identified by the parties
    Conduct independent research into arbitral awards
    Conduct independent research into judicial decisions
    Conduct independent research into regulations, statutes, or treaties
    Conduct independent research into scholarly commentary, soft law, or persuasive authorities
    Read, in full, arbitral awards identified by the parties
    Read, in full, judicial decisions identified by the parties
    Read, in full, regulations, statutes, or treaties identified by the parties
    Read, in full, scholarly commentary, soft law, or persuasive authorities identified by the parties
    Read, in part, arbitral awards identified by the parties
    Read, in part, judicial decisions identified by the parties
    Read, in part, regulations, statutes, or treaties identified by the parties
    Read, in part, scholarly commentary, soft law, or persuasive authorities identified by the parties
    Other (please describe below)
34. What factors affect your decision whether to read a legal authority in full or in part? Please identify how often each factor affects your decision whether to read a legal authority in full or in part. (0% of the time, 1–29% of the time, 30–59% of the time, 60–99% of the time, 100% of the time)
    Credibility of the parties or counsel
    Extent of your pre-existing knowledge of the legal rule or principle in question
    Importance of the legal principle to disposition of the controversy
    Novelty of the legal authority (i.e. how recently the authority was adopted or enacted)
    Novelty of the underlying legal principle (i.e. how frequently the issue has been addressed in practice)
    Perceived likelihood that the losing party will seek to challenge the decision or award

Standard practice (i.e. you follow the same practice in all cases, regardless of other factors)
Type of legal authority (treaty, statute, judicial decision, etc.)
Type of legal dispute (contractual, regulatory, etc.)
Whether the parties dispute the interpretation or application of the particular legal authority
Whether the parties dispute the interpretation or application of the underlying rule or principle
Other (please describe below)

35. How often do you discuss your legal research methodology with the parties?
0% of the time
1–29% of the time
30–59% of the time
60–99% of the time
100% of the time

36. If you discuss your legal research methodology with the parties, when does that discussion usually take place?
At the first procedural meeting
Prior to the hearing
During the hearing
After the hearing but before the drafting of the award or decision
During the drafting of the award or decision
Not applicable—I do not discuss my legal research methodology with the parties

37. What rationale(s) best describe(s) your position regarding discussions concerning your legal research methodology? Please check all that apply.
I discuss my legal research methodology with the parties because they need to be able to respond to anything I discover as a matter of procedural justice
I discuss my legal research methodology with the parties to ensure that what I have found is accurate
I discuss my legal research methodology with the parties to increase their confidence in the process
I do not discuss my legal research methodology with the parties because I am confident that what I have found is accurate
I do not discuss my legal research methodology with the parties because my approach is implicit in the task of acting as a judge or arbitrator
I do not discuss my legal research methodology with the parties because that would decrease their confidence in the process
Other (please describe)

38. If you conduct independent legal research, how often do you allow the parties an opportunity to provide written or oral responses to that research?
0% of the time
1–29% of the time
30–59% of the time
60–99% of the time
100% of the time

39. What rationale(s) best describe(s) your position regarding allowing parties to respond to your independent legal research? Please check all that apply.
I discuss the results of my independent legal research with the parties because they need to be able to respond to anything I discover as a matter of procedural justice
I discuss the results of my independent legal research with the parties to ensure that what I have found is accurate
I discuss the results of my independent legal research with the parties to increase their confidence in the process
I do not discuss the results of my independent legal research with the parties because I am confident that what I have found is accurate
I do not discuss the results of my independent legal research with the parties because my approach is implicit in the task of acting as a judge or arbitrator

I do not discuss the results of my independent legal research with the parties because that would decrease their confidence in the process
Other (please describe)

40. What percentage of the legal authorities that you have read or reviewed, in whole or in part, do you subsequently mention in your written decision or award?
0% of the authorities I read or review are mentioned in my written decision or award
1–29% of the authorities I read or review are mentioned in my written decision or award
30–59% of the authorities I read or review are mentioned in my written decision or award
60–99% of the authorities I read or review are mentioned in my written decision or award
100% of the authorities I read or review are mentioned in my written decision or award

41. What factors do you take into account when deciding whether to mention a legal authority in a written decision or award? Please identify how often you take each factor into account. (0% of the time, 1–29% of the time, 30–59% of the time, 60–99% of the time, 100% of the time)
A desire to make sure the losing party feels heard
A desire to make sure the winning party feels heard
Concern about subsequent procedural review of the decision or award
Concern about subsequent review of the decision or award on the merits
Importance of the legal authority to resolution of the controversy
Importance of the underlying legal principle to resolution of the controversy
Novelty of the legal authority (i.e. how recently the authority was adopted or enacted)
Novelty of the underlying legal principle (i.e. how frequently the issue has been addressed in practice)
Perceived likelihood that the losing party will seek to challenge the decision or award
Type of legal authority (treaty, statute, judicial decision, etc.)
Type of legal dispute (contractual, regulatory, etc.)
Whether the parties dispute the interpretation or application of the particular legal authority
Whether the parties dispute the interpretation or application of the underlying rule or principle
Other (please describe below)

Questions Involving Factual Issues

42. Please indicate how important the following types of evidence are to you when determining factual issues, where 1 is not important at all and 5 is very important.
Documents written by an expert witness
Documents written by a party (other than any relevant contracts or transactional documents)
Documents written by a third party
Oral testimony from an expert witness at the hearing
Oral testimony from a party witness at the hearing
Oral testimony from a non-party witness at the hearing
Pre-hearing testimony of an expert witness (written witness statement or deposition testimony)
Pre-hearing testimony of a party witness (written witness statement or deposition testimony)
Pre-hearing testimony of a third-party witness (written witness statement or deposition testimony)
Relevant contract(s) or transactional document(s)
Other (please describe type of evidence)

43. What percentage of the documents submitted to you by the parties do you read in their entirety? Do not include documents read during the hearing itself.
0% of the documents submitted
1–29% of the documents submitted
30–59% of the documents submitted
60–99% of the documents submitted
100% of the documents submitted

44. What percentage of the documents submitted to you by the parties do you read in part? Do not include documents read during the hearing itself.
    0% of the documents submitted
    1–29% of the documents submitted
    30–59% of the documents submitted
    60–99% of the documents submitted
    100% of the documents submitted
45. Please indicate how important the following factors are to your decision whether to read, in whole or in part, documents submitted to you by the parties, where 1 is not important at all and 5 is very important.
    Credibility of counsel
    Credibility of the parties
    Credibility of the witnesses
    Extent of your understanding of the document during the hearing
    Extent of your recollection of the document from the hearing
    Extent of your understanding of the facts generally during the hearing
    Extent of your recollection of the facts generally from the hearing
    Importance of the document to the disposition of the controversy
    Standard practice (i.e. you follow the same practice in all cases, regardless of other factors)
    Type of document (party-drafted document, expert report, transactional document, etc.)
    Type of legal dispute (contractual, regulatory, etc.)
    Whether the parties dispute the credibility or content of the document in question
    Whether the parties dispute the interpretation or application of the document in question
    Whether the parties referred to the document during the hearing
    Whether the parties referred to the document in their written submissions
    Other (please describe below)
46. Do you or your law clerk/assistant conduct independent factual research? This does not include asking questions of a witness that is already present at a hearing.
    No
    Yes
47. If you answered yes to the previous question, what kind of independent factual research do you or your law clerk/assistant conduct? Please check all that apply.
    Ask for appointment of an expert that the parties have not proposed, regardless of whether the expert will be appointed by the parties or the panel
    Ask for a particular document to be produced
    Call a witness to testify at a hearing even though a party has not called that person
    Conduct a site visit
    Conduct factual research on the internet
    Other (please explain)
48. If you or your law clerk/assistant conduct independent factual research, how often do you allow the parties an opportunity to provide written or oral responses to the results of your independent research?
    0% of the time
    1–29% of the time
    30–59% of the time
    60–99% of the time
    100% of the time
49. What rationale(s) best describe(s) your position regarding allowing parties to respond to your independent factual research? Please check all that apply.
    I discuss the results of my independent factual research with the parties because they need to be able to respond to anything I discover as a matter of procedural justice
    I discuss the results of my independent factual research with the parties to ensure that what I have found is accurate

I discuss the results of my independent factual research with the parties to increase their confidence in the process
I do not discuss the results of my independent factual research with the parties because I am confident that what I have found is accurate
I do not discuss the results of my independent factual research with the parties because my approach is implicit in the task of acting as a judge or arbitrator
I do not discuss the results of my independent factual research with the parties because that would decrease their confidence in the process
Other (please describe)

50. How often do you discuss your factual research methodology with the parties?
0% of the time
1–29% of the time
30–59% of the time
60–99% of the time
100% of the time

51. If you discuss your factual research methodology with the parties, when does that discussion usually take place?
At the first procedural meeting
Prior to the hearing
During the hearing
After the hearing but before the drafting of the award or decision
During the drafting of the award or decision
Not applicable—I do not discuss my factual research methodology with the parties

52. What rationales best describes your position regarding discussions concerning your factual research methodology? Check all that apply.
I discuss my factual research methodology with the parties because they need to be able to respond to anything I discover as a matter of procedural justice
I discuss my factual research methodology with the parties to ensure that what I have found is accurate
I discuss my factual research methodology with the parties to increase their confidence in the process
I do not discuss my factual research methodology with the parties because I am confident that what I have found is accurate
I do not discuss my factual research methodology with the parties because my approach is implicit in the task of acting as a judge or arbitrator
I do not discuss my factual research methodology with the parties because that would decrease their confidence in the process
Other (please describe)

53. What percentage of the factual authorities (evidence) that you have read, reviewed, or heard do you subsequently mention in your written decision or award?
0% of the authorities I have read, reviewed, or heard are subsequently mentioned
1–29% of the authorities I have read, reviewed, or heard are subsequently mentioned
30–59% of the authorities I have read, reviewed, or heard are subsequently mentioned
60-99% of the authorities I have read, reviewed, or heard are subsequently mentioned
100% of the authorities I have read, reviewed, or heard are subsequently mentioned

54. What factors do you take into account when deciding whether to mention a particular piece of evidence in your written decision or award? Please identify how often you take each factor into account when deciding whether to mention a particular piece of evidence in your written decision or award. (0% of the time, 1–29% of the time, 30–59% of the time, 6099% of the time, 100% of the time)
A desire to make sure the losing party feels heard
A desire to make sure the winning party feels heard
Concern about subsequent procedural review of the decision or award
Concern about subsequent review of the decision or award on the merits
Credibility of counsel

Credibility of the parties
Credibility of the witnesses
Importance of the evidence to disposition of the controversy
Perceived likelihood that the losing party will seek to challenge the decision or award
Standard practice (i.e. you follow the same practice in all cases, regardless of other factors)
Type of evidence (party-drafted document, testimony, expert report, transactional document, etc.)
Type of legal dispute (contractual, regulatory, etc.)
Whether parties dispute the credibility of the evidence in question
Whether parties dispute the interpretation or application of the evidence in question
Whether the parties referred to the document during the hearing
Whether the parties referred to the document in their written submissions
Other (please describe)

Questions Involving Legal Reasoning

55. What factors do you consider important to legal reasoning? Please rank the following factors or indicate NA if you believe that factor is not relevant to legal reasoning.
Binding legal norms
Equity or fairness
Facts
Persuasive or 'soft' legal norms
Policy
56. If you have additional comments about factors that are important to legal reasoning, please state them here.
57. How does your legal reasoning process begin?
I start with the facts and look for law relevant to those facts
I start with the law and look for facts relevant to that legal standard
I start with the outcome and look for facts and law to support that outcome
I start with the policy and look for facts and law to support that policy
I apply a blended or iterative approach that simultaneously considers facts and law
I apply a blended or iterative approach that simultaneously considers facts, law and policy
Other (please explain)
58. Has your approach to legal reasoning changed over the course of your career as a judge or arbitrator?
No
Yes
59. If you answered yes to the previous question, how has your approach to legal reasoning changed?
I now focus more on (equity, facts, law, outcome, policy) than on (equity, facts, law, outcome, policy)
Additional comments
60. If you answered yes to the penultimate question, why has your approach to legal reasoning changed?
61. For those who have acted as both judges and arbitrators, does your approach to legal reasoning change depending on whether you are acting as a judge or arbitrator?
No
Yes
Not applicable
62. If you answered yes to the previous question, how has your approach to legal reasoning changed? Indicate which factors you focus(ed) on more when you were/are a judge than when you act(ed) as an arbitrator. Please check all that apply.
Equity
Facts
Law

Outcome
Policy
Additional comments

63. If you answered yes to the penultimate question, why has your approach to legal reasoning changed?

Questions Involving How Reasoned Decisions or Awards Are Written

64. Please indicate how important the following factors are to your determination of how detailed a reasoned decision or award should be, where 1 is not important at all and 5 is very important. For purposes of this question, you should exclude any obligations imposed by contract or any applicable rules.
    I believe the difficulty, complexity, or novelty of the dispute as a matter of fact requires an in-depth explanation of my reasoning
    I believe the difficulty, complexity, or novelty of the dispute as a matter of law requires an in-depth explanation of my reasoning
    I believe the nature of the legal dispute (i.e. the type of substantive claims at issue) requires an in-depth explanation of my reasoning
    I find the act of writing a reasoned decision or award helps me think through the analytical process and increases the likelihood of reaching the right outcome
    I want to increase the perceived legitimacy of this particular decision or award
    I want to increase the perceived legitimacy of this type of dispute resolution process (i.e. litigation or arbitration)
    I want to make sure the losing party feels heard
    I want to make sure the winning party feels heard
    I want to minimize the likelihood the losing party will seek to challenge the decision or award
    Other (please explain below)
65. Who do you consider your audience when writing a reasoned decision or award? Please rank your top three choices, and mark NA for the remainder.
    A court or tribunal that may review the dispute for procedural error
    A court or tribunal that may review the dispute on the merits
    A case administrator or arbitral institution (arbitration only)
    Counsel
    Myself
    The losing party
    The public
    The winning party
    Third parties with an interest in this particular dispute (such as insurers or third-party litigation funders)
66. If you have additional comments about your audience when writing a reasoned decision or award, please make them here.

Questions Involving Judicial and Arbitral Education Relating to Legal Reasoning

67. What factors characterize a well-written reasoned decision or award? Please rank up to five factors, and mark NA for the remainder.
    Clearly states the applicable legal standard and how the facts in this case do or do not meet that standard
    Identifies a clear legal standard that can be followed in the future by the parties
    Identifies a clear legal standard that can be followed in the future by third parties
    Identifies a clear policy principle that explains the rationale for the decision

Is as short as possible, given the nature of the dispute
Is logical
Is understandable by lay readers, including the parties
Reaches the right outcome as a matter of law
Reaches the right outcome as a matter of equity
Tells a compelling story or provides an emotionally satisfying rationale

68. If you have additional comments about the factors that characterize a well-written reasoned decision or award, please make them here.
69. How did you learn to write reasoned decisions or awards? Please check all that apply.
I attended a seminar or symposium on writing reasoned decisions or awards
I completed a university degree program that included coursework specifically focused on writing reasoned decisions or awards
I learned by doing
I learned by reading other reasoned decisions or awards
I learned by speaking with more experienced colleagues
I read a book or article on writing reasoned decisions or awards
Other (please explain)
70. Do you believe that judges or arbitrators would benefit from educational programming on writing reasoned decisions or awards? Assume for purposes of this question that the programming would sufficiently safeguard judicial and arbitral independence.
No
Yes, for both new and experienced judges or arbitrators
Yes, for experienced judges or arbitrators only
Yes, for new judges or arbitrators only
Please explain your answer.
71. If you answered yes to the previous question, what kind of programming would be most beneficial to judges or arbitrators? Please rank up to five types of programming, and select NA for the remainder.
Distance (video or audio) seminar or symposium—lecture format
Distance (video or audio) seminar or symposium—discussion format
Distance (video or audio) seminar or symposium—experiential (hands on) format
Distance (video or audio) seminar or symposium—mixed (lecture, discussion and experiential) format
Formal or informal mentor program
Identification of reasoned decisions or awards that exemplify best practices (i.e. 'model' or 'ideal' decisions or awards)
In-person seminar or symposium—lecture format
In-person seminar or symposium—discussion format
In-person seminar or symposium—experiential (hands on) format
In-person seminar or symposium—mixed (lecture, discussion, and experiential) format
Mechanisms to facilitate confidential discussion of issues and concerns with peers Written materials
72. Please indicate which issues should be addressed in educational programming on reasoned decisions or awards, where 1 indicates an issue that need not be addressed and 5 indicates an issue that must be addressed. Assume for purposes of this question that the programming would sufficiently safeguard judicial and arbitral independence.
How long and how detailed each section of a reasoned decision or award needs to be
How long it takes judges or arbitrators to write a reasoned decision or award
How other judges or arbitrators approach reasoned decisions or awards
How to apply the facts to the governing legal standard
How to approach substantive citation of legal materials (i.e. when to refer to legal authorities and how to analyse them in a reasoned decision or award, not what citation format to use)
How to approach substantive citation of factual materials (i.e. when to refer to evidence and how to analyse evidence in a reasoned decision or award, not what citation format to use)

How to distinguish material facts from immaterial facts
How to identify the governing legal standard
How to structure reasoned decisions or awards
How to weigh different pieces of evidence
How to weigh different legal authorities
Other (please describe other issue)

73. Do you have any general comments about this survey or any matter discussed herein?

Conclusion

This concludes the survey. Thank you for your insights.

Please feel free to forward the link to this survey [link] to colleagues who have acted as judges or arbitrators in commercial matters at either the national or international level.

If you are interested in being interviewed for a related project on judicial and arbitral reasoning, please contact me at strongsi@missouri.edu or +1-573-882-2465. Interviews can be conducted on either a confidential or attributed basis. Please note that there is no way to tie interview subjects to survey results, since the surveys are completely anonymous.

Prof. S.I. Strong, J.D., Ph.D.
Manley O. Hudson Professor of Law
University of Missouri School of Law
Columbia, MO 65211 USA
Telephone: +1-573-882-2465
Email: strongsi@missouri.edu
Bio: http://law.missouri.edu/about/people/strong/

APPENDIX II

Protocol: Semi-Structured Interviews

Following is the protocol used to generate the data discussed in Chapter 3. Material shown in brackets was adapted according to the background of the interviewee and his/her responses to previous questions.

Thank you very much for agreeing to be interviewed for my research study on legal reasoning. In the course of our conversation, we'll cover a variety of issues, including legal authorities, evidence, legal reasoning, how reasoned decisions and awards are written, and judicial and arbitral education relating to legal reasoning. You are free to decline to answer any individual question or to terminate the interview at any time. I would expect this conversation to last approximately one hour, although we can go longer or shorter, as you wish.

* * *

I'd like to start with a few background questions and definitions to make sure that we're on the same page.

First, how long have you acted as [an arbitrator] [a judge] and about how many disputes have you resolved on the merits during that time? [If you have acted as both a judge and an arbitrator, please distinguish between the two functions.]

Of that number, what percentage of the disputes were commercial in nature, meaning business-to-business or commercial state entity-to-business disputes? [for arbitrators: This definition excludes investor-state proceedings.]

Finally, what percentage of your commercial matters have been international, as opposed to domestic, in nature? For purposes of this interview, I define an international dispute as one where at least two parties come from different countries; where the property in dispute is located in a country different than the disputants; or where performance or enforcement is anticipated in a country different than that of the disputants.

Thanks. Now, going forward, I am interested in your general practice. However, it may be easiest for you to think about your last commercial dispute when answering the following questions. If your last dispute was atypical in some way, just let me know.

During our discussion, I would ask that you please avoid providing any information that could identify any parties or lawyers. Even if you do make such a reference, I will not name that person or party in my research findings.

[Since you have addressed both domestic and international disputes, it would be useful to know which type you're addressing and if your practice differs depending on which type of case it is.]

Finally, just to be clear, the term 'reasoned decisions or awards', as used in this interview, includes but is not limited to decisions or awards with findings of fact and conclusions of law.

* * *

I will now turn to the substantive interview. Do you have any questions before we begin?

1. In your mind, what is the purpose of a reasoned decision or award?
   a. Who do you consider your audience when writing reasoned decisions or awards?
   b. What do you believe are the hallmarks of a well-written reasoned decision or award?
2. How do you usually structure a reasoned decision or award?
3. What type of legal authorities (statutes, cases, scholarly works, etc.) are most important to you when you're drafting a reasoned decision or award?
   a. Why is that?
4. Do you have a law clerk or assistant who reads the legal authorities that the parties refer to in their submissions?
   a. What percentage of the legal authorities does your law clerk or assistant read in their entirety? In part? How is the determination made to read the authorities in full or in part?

   b. How does your law clerk or assistant communicate with you regarding the content of the legal authorities he or she has read?
   c. Do you personally read all of the legal authorities that the parties refer to in their submissions in their entirety?
   d. Why or why not?
   e. [if not100%: What percentage of the legal authorities do you read in full? What percentage of the remaining legal authorities do you read in part?]
5. When do you [or your law clerk or assistant] read legal authorities—before, during, or after the hearing?
6. What kind of legal research do you [or your law clerk or assistant] conduct apart from reading the parties' written submissions?
   a. Why do you use that approach?
   b. Do you provide the parties with an opportunity to respond to the results of any independent legal research that you [or your law clerk or assistant] conduct?
   c. Why or why not?
7. Why do you cite legal authority in a reasoned decision or award?
   a. How often do you discuss a legal authority or legal principle in depth in a reasoned decision or award as opposed to merely in passing?
   b. What drives your decisions about whether to discuss a particular legal authority, either in passing or in detail?
8. What do you wish parties and counsel knew about how judges or arbitrators approach legal authority?

* * *

9. What types of evidence (party-generated documents, third-party generated documents, testimony, etc.) do you find most persuasive?
   a. Why is that?
10. What percentage of the evidentiary documents submitted to you by the parties does your law clerk or assistant read in whole? In part?
    a. How does your law clerk or assistant communicate with you regarding the documents he or she has read in whole or in part?
    b. What percentage of the evidentiary documents submitted to you by the parties do you personally read in whole? In part?
    c. How do you determine which documents you [or your law clerk or assistant] should read?
    d. Is that determination based on the type of documents, the type of substantive dispute, the actions of parties or counsel, or something else?
11. When do you [or your law clerk or assistant] read fact documents—before, during, or after the hearing?
12. How do you decide how much weight to give different types of evidence?
13. How do you decide which factual issues or evidence to discuss in a reasoned award?
    a. Why do you include those references?
14. What do you wish parties and counsel knew about how judges or arbitrators approach factual issues?

* * *

15. How do you go about reasoning through a decision or award? This is different than writing the award, which we will discuss later.
    a. What do you consider first and where do you go to from there?
16. Has your approach to legal reasoning changed over the course of your career?
    a. If so, how and why?
17. [You have acted as both a judge and an arbitrator. Does your reasoning process change depending on the capacity in which you are acting?]
18. Does your reasoning process change depending on whether the dispute is domestic or international in nature? If so, how and why?

19. [for arbitrators: Does your reasoning change depending on whether you are in a panel as opposed to acting alone? If so, how and why?]
20. What do you wish parties and counsel knew about how judges or arbitrators approach legal reasoning?

* * *

21. What factors go into deciding whether to write a reasoned decision or award and how much detail should go into that document?
22. How do you go about drafting a reasoned decision or award?
23. Do you ever change your mind about the outcome of a dispute when writing a reasoned decision or award?
    a. Why does that happen?
    b. How often does that happen?

* * *

24. How did you learn to write a reasoned decision or award?
    a. Have you ever taken a course on writing reasoned decisions or awards?
    b. When and why did you take that course?
25. What do you wish you had known when you first started writing reasoned decisions or awards?
26. Do you think judges or arbitrators would benefit from educational programming on reasoned decisions or awards, assuming judicial and arbitral independence were respected in the design of the program?
    a. Why or why not?
    b. What kind of programming would most beneficial?
    c. Why?
27. Is there anything I've not asked that I should ask?

Thank you very much for taking the time to speak with me today. I very much enjoyed our conversation and hope that you did, too.

I am also conducting an electronic survey that covers a number of similar issues regarding legal reasoning. If you would like to participate in that survey, please let me know and I will send you the link [when it is available]. The electronic survey is entirely anonymous, and there is no way that I would be able to connect your survey responses to your interview responses.

If you have colleagues who you believe would be interested [in being interviewed or] in participating in the electronic survey, just let me know. I can contact them or they can contact me, whichever you think is most appropriate.

APPENDIX III

Coding Book: Quantitative Analysis

Following is the general outline of the coding book used to generate the quantitative data discussed in Chapter 4. Specific instructions to the coding team (such as those involving formatting) are not included. Some of the information identified in the various data points was gleaned from the decisions and awards themselves, while other items (such as the gender and age of the judge or arbitrator) required research into publicly available materials. Some entries (such as the percentage of paragraphs devoted to a particular type of discussion) involved mathematical calculations using information derived from the decisions and awards. Responses to the individual questions were entered into an excel spreadsheet to facilitate statistical analysis. Data entry was an iterative process with various checks to ensure consistency.

This book does not discuss all of the information generated by the coding exercise for reasons of space. However, omitted material will be considered in several follow-up articles.[1]

Background/Demographic Questions

1. Caption of award or decision
2. Location/citation of award or decision
3. Date of award or decision
4. Size of award or decision, rounded to the nearest thousand [sums subsequently converted into US dollars to facilitate analysis]
   a. Combine claims and counterclaims to identify total amount in dispute; do not offset claims and counterclaims but add them together
   b. Use 'ID' if the award does not include a monetary award but instead only offers injunctive or declarative relief, or if the claim is denied
   c. Do not include amounts relating to arbitrator fees, administrative fees, attorneys' fees, or interest
5. Place where award or decision was rendered
   a. Use a numerical code to identify locations around the world [country codes omitted]
   b. If the award does not indicate where it was rendered, use X
6. Type of jurisdiction where award or decision rendered
   a. common law [0] [jurisdictions listed separately]
   b. civil law [1] [jurisdictions listed separately]
   c. other [2]—defined as mixed jurisdictions (i.e. South Africa) and Islamic jurisdictions (i.e. Iran) [jurisdictions listed separately]
   d. Use X if you did not find a seat in the previous question
7. Name of first plaintiff/claimant
8. Home jurisdiction of first plaintiff/claimant
   a. [use codes identified in question 5]
9. Type of jurisdiction of first plaintiff/claimant
   a. [use codes identified in question 6]
   b. common law [0]

[1] E.g. SI Strong, 'Does Experience Matter? An Empirical Analysis of Seniority and Number of Disputes Heard on Legal Reasoning in Commercial Dispute Resolution' (forthcoming); SI Strong, 'Does Gender Affect Legal Reasoning in Commercial Dispute Resolution? An Empirical Analysis' (forthcoming); SI Strong, 'Proceedings in the English Commercial Court and Proceedings in International Arbitration: A Distinction Without An Empirical Difference?' (forthcoming).

   c. civil law [1]
   d. other [2]
   e. Use X if you did not find a jurisdiction in the previous question
10. Name of law firm representing first plaintiff/claimant
    a. Include only the first named law firm if there are several
    b. Use the name of the party if the party acts pro se
    c. If you cannot find a name of a lawyer/law firm, enter NA
11. Jurisdiction of law firm representing first plaintiff/claimant
    a. [use codes identified in question 5]
    b. Use office where lead lawyer located
    c. If no lead lawyer is indicated, use the state/province/country where the arbitration/litigation was seated if the law firm has an office there, using the smallest possible geographic location
    d. If no lead lawyer is indicated and the law firm does not have an office in the state/province/country where the arbitration/litigation was seated, use the law firm's headquarters
    e. If you cannot find a name of a lawyer/law firm or a jurisdiction, enter NA
12. Type of jurisdiction for law firm representing first plaintiff/claimant
    a. [use codes identified in question 6]
    b. common law [0]
    c. civil law [1]
    d. other [2]
    e. Enter NA if you cannot find a name of a lawyer/law firm or a jurisdiction
13. Name of first defendant/respondent
14. Home jurisdiction of first defendant/respondent
    a. [use codes identified in question 5]
15. Type of jurisdiction for first defendant/respondent
    a. [use codes identified in question 6]
    b. common law [0]
    c. civil law [1]
    d. other [2]
    e. Use X if you did not find a jurisdiction in the previous question
16. Name of law firm representing first defendant/respondent
    a. Include only the first named law firm if there are several
    b. Use the name of the party of the party acts pro se
    c. If you cannot find a name of a lawyer/law firm, enter NA
17. Jurisdiction of law firm representing first defendant/respondent
    a. [use codes identified in question 5]
    b. Use office where lead lawyer located
    c. If no lead lawyer is indicated, use the state/province/country where the arbitration/litigation was seated if the law firm has an office there, using the smallest possible geographic location
    d. If no lead lawyer is indicated and the law firm does not have an office in the state/province/country where the arbitration/litigation was seated, use the law firm's headquarters
    e. If you cannot find a name of a lawyer/law firm or a jurisdiction, enter NA
18. Type of jurisdiction for law firm representing first defendant/respondent
    a. [use codes identified in question 6]
    b. common law [0]
    c. civil law [1]
    d. other [2]
    e. Enter NA if you cannot find a name of a lawyer/law firm or a jurisdiction
19. Additional parties
    a. As plaintiff/claimant [0]
    b. As defendant/respondent [1]
    c. As both plaintiff/claimant and defendant/respondent [2]
    d. Use X if there are no additional parties

20. Total number of parties, including all plaintiffs/claimants and all defendants/respondents
    a. Start with 2 for bilateral disputes and increase as necessary
21. Is the award or decision domestic or international
    a. Domestic [enter 0]
    b. International [enter 1]
    c. The dispute is domestic if it is entirely between parties of the same country and lacks some sort of international nexus, such as property located abroad, enforcement abroad or some other relationship with a foreign state, including an award or decision that was rendered in a foreign state
22. Number of decision makers
    a. If one, enter [0]
    b. If three, enter [1]
23. Name of judge/arbitrator/chair of panel (if three arbitrators)
24. Gender of judge/arbitrator/chair of panel (if three arbitrators)
    a. male [0]
    b. female [1]
25. Age of judge/arbitrator/chair of panel (if three arbitrators) at time of decision or award
    a. If under 30 years of age, use [0]
    b. If 31–40 years of age, use [1]
    c. If 41–50 years of age, use [2]
    d. If 51–60 years of age, use [3]
    e. If 61–70 years of age, use [4]
    f. If 71–80 years of age, use [5]
    g. If over 81 years of age, use [6]
    h. If you can only find a graduation date for the individual, estimate the age of receipt of first degree as 22, then calculate appropriate age range for the individual and add * to the numerical value (ex: 5* for estimated 71–80 years of age)
    i. Use NA if you cannot find an age or graduation date
26. Jurisdiction where judge/arbitrator/chair of panel (if three arbitrators) is admitted
    a. [use codes identified in question 5]
    b. For judges—assume they are admitted in the jurisdiction where they sit
    c. For arbitrators—see online bios
    d. Use NA if cannot find a jurisdiction
    e. Use NL if the arbitrator is not a lawyer
    f. Use jurisdiction where award was rendered if the arbitrator is admitted in multiple jurisdictions and the jurisdiction of the award is one of the jurisdictions
    g. Use first listed jurisdiction if the arbitrator is admitted in multiple jurisdictions and the jurisdiction where the award was rendered is <u>not</u> one of the jurisdictions where the arbitrator is admitted
27. Type of jurisdiction where judge/arbitrator/chair of panel (if three arbitrators) is admitted
    a. [use codes identified in question 6]
    b. common law [0]
    c. civil law [1]
    d. other [2]
    e. Use NA if cannot find a jurisdiction
    f. Use NL if the judge/arbitrator/chair of panel (if three arbitrators) is not a lawyer
28. Whether the jurisdiction where judge/arbitrator/chair of panel is admitted is same as jurisdiction where award or decision rendered
    a. yes [0]
    b. no [1]
    c. judge/arbitrator/chair of panel is not a lawyer [2]
29. Name of party-appointed arbitrator no. 1 (if three arbitrators)
    a. Use X if there is no party-appointed arbitrator no. 1 (i.e. if the matter was decided by a judge or by a single arbitrator)

30. Gender of party-appointed arbitrator no. 1
    a. male [0]
    b. female [1]
    c. Use X if there is no party-appointed arbitrator no. 1
31. Age of party-appointed arbitrator no. 1 (if three arbitrators) at time of decision or award
    a. If under 30 years of age, use [0]
    b. If 31–40 years of age, use [1]
    c. If 41–50 years of age, use [2]
    d. If 51–60 years of age, use [3]
    e. If 61–70 years of age, use [4]
    f. If 71–80 years of age, use [5]
    g. If over 81 years of age, use [6]
    h. If you can only find a graduation date for the individual, estimate the age of receipt of first degree as 22, then calculate appropriate age range for the individual and add * to the numerical value (ex: 5* for estimated 71–80 years of age)
    i. Use NA if you cannot find an age or graduation date
32. Jurisdiction where party-appointed arbitrator no. 1 (if three arbitrators) is admitted [use codes identified in question 5]
    a. See online bios
    b. Use NA if cannot find a jurisdiction
    c. Use NL if the arbitrator is not a lawyer
    d. Use jurisdiction where award was rendered if the arbitrator is admitted in multiple jurisdictions and the jurisdiction of the award is one of the jurisdictions
    e. Use first listed jurisdiction if the arbitrator is admitted in multiple jurisdictions and the jurisdiction where the award was rendered is <u>not</u> one of the jurisdictions where the arbitrator is admitted
33. Type of jurisdiction where party-appointed arbitrator no. 1 (if three arbitrators) is admitted
    a. [use codes identified in question 6]
    b. common law [0]
    c. civil law [1]
    d. other [2]
    e. Use X if there is no party-appointed arbitrator no. 1
    f. Use NA if cannot find a jurisdiction
    g. Use NL if party-appointed arbitrator no. 1 is not a lawyer
34. Whether the jurisdiction where party-appointed arbitrator no. 1 (if three arbitrators) is admitted is same as jurisdiction where award or decision rendered
    a. yes [0]
    b. no [1]
    c. party-appointed arbitrator no. 1 is not a lawyer [2]
    d. Use X if there is no party-appointed arbitrator no. 1
    e. Use NA if cannot find jurisdiction
35. Name of party-appointed arbitrator no. 2 (if three arbitrators)
    a. Use X if there is no party-appointed arbitrator no. 2 (i.e. if the matter was decided by a judge or by a single arbitrator)
36. Gender of party-appointed arbitrator no. 2
    a. male [0]
    b. female [1]
    c. Use X if there is no party-appointed arbitrator no. 2
37. Age of party-appointed arbitrator no. 2 (if three arbitrators) at time of decision or award
    a. If under 30 years of age, use [0]
    b. If 31–40 years of age, use [1]
    c. If 41–50 years of age, use [2]
    d. If 51–60 years of age, use [3]
    e. If 61–70 years of age, use [4]

   f. If 71–80 years of age, use [5]
   g. If over 81 years of age, use [6]
   h. If you can only find a graduation date for the individual, estimate the age of receipt of first degree as 22, then calculate appropriate age range for the individual and add * to the numerical value (ex: 5* for estimated 71–80 years of age)
   i. Use NA if you cannot find an age or graduation date
   j. Use X if there is no party-appointed arbitrator no. 2

38. Jurisdiction where party-appointed arbitrator no. 2 (if three arbitrators) is admitted
   a. [use codes identified in question 5]
   b. See online bios
   c. Use NA if cannot find a jurisdiction
   d. Use NL if the arbitrator is not a lawyer
   e. Use jurisdiction where award was rendered if the arbitrator is admitted in multiple jurisdictions and the jurisdiction of the award is one of the jurisdictions
   f. Use first listed jurisdiction if the arbitrator is admitted in multiple jurisdictions and the jurisdiction where the award was rendered is not one of the jurisdictions where the arbitrator is admitted
   g. Use X if there is no party-appointed arbitrator no. 2
39. Type of jurisdiction where party-appointed arbitrator no. 2 (if three arbitrators) is admitted
   a. [use codes identified in question 6]
   b. common law [0]
   c. civil law [1]
   d. other [2]
   e. Use X if there is no party-appointed arbitrator no. 2
   f. Use NA if cannot find a jurisdiction
   g. Use NL if party-appointed arbitrator no. 2 is not a lawyer
40. Whether the jurisdiction where party-appointed arbitrator no. 2 (if three arbitrators) is admitted is same as jurisdiction where award or decision rendered
   a. yes [0]
   b. no [1]
   c. party-pointed arbitrator no. 2 is not a lawyer [2]
   d. Use X if there is no party-appointed arbitrator no. 2
   c. Use NA if cannot find jurisdiction

Substantive Questions

For questions 41 to 45, if there are no paragraphs for that category, enter X.

41. Total number of paragraphs in award/decision relating to procedure
42. Total number of paragraphs in award/decision relating to facts
43. Total number of paragraphs in award/decision relating to arguments of the parties
44. Total number of paragraphs in award/decision relating to applicable legal standard
45. Total number of paragraphs in award/decision relating to mixed issues of law and fact (i.e. application of law to facts)
46. Total number of paragraphs in award/decision relating to conclusion
47. Total number of paragraphs in award/decision
48. Percentage of paragraphs regarding facts out of total number of paragraphs in award/decision
49. Percentage of paragraphs regarding applicable legal standard out of total number of paragraphs in award/decision
50. Comparison of percentage of paragraphs involving facts to percentage of paragraphs involving applicable legal standard
   a. if fact percentage higher than law percentage, enter [0]
   b. if law percentage higher than fact percentage, enter [1]
   c. if two percentages are identical, enter [2]

51. Percentage of paragraphs regarding mixed law/fact (application) out of total number of paragraphs in award/decision
52. Comparison of percentage of paragraphs involving facts to percentage of paragraphs involving mixed law/fact (application)
    a. if fact percentage higher than mixed law/fact percentage, enter [0]
    b. if mixed law/fact percentage higher than fact percentage, enter [1]
    c. if two percentages are identical, enter [2]
53. Comparison of percentage of paragraphs involving applicable legal standard to percentage of paragraphs involving mixed law/fact (application)
    a. if law percentage higher than mixed law/fact percentage, enter [0]
    b. if mixed law/fact percentage higher than law percentage, enter [1]
    c. if two percentages are identical, enter [2]

For questions 54 to 74, if there are no paragraphs for that category, enter X. For all references to legal authorities (items 54 through 68), count any legal authorities included within quoted materials. References to factual authorities (evidence) may reflect a formal reference to a particular document (for example, a line to deposition testimony or a contract marked as an exhibit) or may refer the authority in the narrative ('the witness Joe Jones said' or 'the contract in question said'). Count both for entries 69 through 74.

54. Number of legal authorities cited in the award or decision relating to initial cites of international treaties or conventions
55. Number of legal authorities cited in the award or decision relating to short form citations of international treaties or conventions, including id, ibid, op cit, loc cit
56. Number of legal authorities cited in the award or decision relating to initial cites of statutes or regulations, which includes any legislative or administrative enactments
57. Number of legal authorities cited in the award or decision relating to short form citations of statutes or regulations, including id, ibid, op cit, loc cit
58. Number of legal authorities cited in the award or decision relating to initial cites of arbitral rules, which includes any institutional or non-institutional rule set
59. Number of legal authorities cited in the award or decision relating to short form cites of arbitral rules, including id, ibid, op cit, loc cit
60. Number of legal authorities cited in the award or decision relating to initial cites of judicial decisions, which includes decisions from any jurisdiction
61. Number of legal authorities cited in the award or decision relating to short form cites of judicial decisions, including id, ibid, op cit, loc cit
62. Number of legal authorities cited in the award or decision relating to initial cites of arbitral awards, which includes arbitral awards involving matters other than the instant dispute
63. Number of legal authorities cited in the award or decision relating to short form cites of arbitral awards, including id, ibid, op cit, loc cit
64. Number of legal authorities cited in the award or decision relating to initial cites of commentary, including books, articles, and any other form of scholarship
65. Number of legal authorities cited in the award or decision relating to short form cites of commentary, including id, ibid, op cit, loc cit
66. Number of legal authorities cited in the award or decision relating to initial cites of other legal authority
    a. This category includes references to any type of legal authority not included in the previous categories as well as procedural awards previously rendered in the same proceedings (the law of the case)
67. Number of legal authorities cited in the award or decision relating to short form cites of other legal authority, including id, ibid, op cit, loc cit
68. Total of all types of legal citations, including all initial cites and short cites
69. Number of factual authorities (evidence) cited in the award or decision relating to initial cites of the contract at issue
70. Number of factual authorities (evidence) cited in the award or decision relating to short form cites of the contract at issue, including id, ibid, op cit, loc cit

71. Number of factual authorities (evidence) cited in the award or decision relating to initial cites of witness testimony (written or oral, before or after hearing)
72. Number of factual authorities (evidence) cited in the award or decision relating to short form cites of witness testimony (written or oral, before or after hearing), including id, ibid, op cit, loc cit
73. Number of factual authorities (evidence) cited in the award or decision relating to initial cites to other fact documents
74. Number of factual authorities (evidence) cited in the award or decision relating to short form cites of other fact documents, including id, ibid, op cit, loc cit
75. Total of all types of factual citations, including all initial cites and short cites
76. Compare total number of citations of legal authorities to total number of citations of factual authorities
    a. if total number of legal authorities higher than factual authorities (evidence), enter [0]
    b. if total number of factual authorities (evidence) higher than legal authorities, enter [1]
    c. if total number of actual authorities (evidence) the same as legal authorities, enter [2]

Index

Note: Due to the preponderance of tables in Chapters 2 and 4, an entry in a table is indicated with page number followed by *t*, but the entry may well appear in the text on that page also.

The manufacturer's authorised representative in the EU for product safety is Oxford University Press España S.A. of el Parque Empresarial San Fernando de Henares, Avenida de Castilla, 2 – 28830 Madrid (www.oup.es/en or product.safety@oup.com). OUP España S.A. also acts as importer into Spain of products made by the manufacturer.

www.ingramcontent.com/pod-product-compliance
Lightning Source LLC
LaVergne TN
LVHW062110200926
848484LV00007B/1632